Jews and Muslims in British Colonial America

Jews and Muslims in British Colonial America

A Genealogical History

ELIZABETH CALDWELL HIRSCHMAN *and*
DONALD N. YATES

McFarland & Company, Inc., Publishers
Jefferson, North Carolina, and London

LIBRARY OF CONGRESS CATALOGUING-IN-PUBLICATION DATA

Hirschman, Elizabeth Caldwell, 1949–
Jews and Muslims in British colonial America : a genealogical history /
Elizabeth Caldwell Hirschman and Donald N. Yates.
p.   cm.
Includes bibliographical references and index.

ISBN 978-0-7864-6462-3
softcover : acid free paper ∞

1. Jews — United States — History —17th century.
2. Jews — United States — History —18th century.
3. Muslims — United States —History —17th century.
4. Muslims — United States — History —18th century.
5. United States — History — Colonial period, ca. 1600–1775.
6. United States — Ethnic relations.
I. Yates, Donald Neal.
II. Title.
E184.3512.H57 2012   305.800973 — dc23   2011048960

BRITISH LIBRARY CATALOGUING DATA ARE AVAILABLE

Front cover images © 2012 Shutterstock

Manufactured in the United States of America

*McFarland & Company, Inc., Publishers
Box 611, Jefferson, North Carolina 28640
www.mcfarlandpub.com*

Table of Contents

Preface

For most Americans, the story of their nation's origins seems safe, reliable and comforting. We were taught from elementary school that the United States was created by a group of brave, white Christians drawn largely from England who ventured to these shores in search of religious freedom and the opportunity to fulfill their own destiny. Recent revisions to this idealized and idyllic narrative have never seriously questioned its basic tenets. So although we now recognize some of the contributions made by Africans to America's success and feel perhaps a heightened sense of regret, remorse and even guilt over the destruction of American native cultures, we never have had much reason to doubt the basic premise of the story. Our founding mothers and fathers were white, Christian and British.

In this work, we present a series of Colonial documents, contemporary firsthand accounts, records, portraits, family genealogies and ethnic DNA test results which fundamentally challenge the national storyline depicting America's first settlers as white, British and Christian. We postulate that many of the initial colonists were of Sephardic Jewish and Muslim Moorish ancestry. Usually arriving as crypto–Jews with their religious adherence disguised, and crypto–Muslims, these immigrants served in prominent economic, political, financial and social positions in all of the original colonies.

The evidence in support of this radical new narrative begins with an examination of the British colonial companies organized in England to bring settlers to North America and exploit the natural riches believed to be there.

Of course, both Spain and France had already made forays into North America, founding St. Augustine and exploring parts of the coastline as far north as Newfoundland, though their activities as foreign powers are given short shrift in our Anglo-centric version of the birth of America. What is even less frequently mentioned regarding these Spanish and French settlements and voyages is that many of the colonists and sailors were of Sephardic Jewish and Muslim Moorish descent. Several of those aboard Christopher Columbus's first voyage in 1492 and famously even Columbus (Colon) himself were of Jewish ancestry. They were Jews or crypto–Jews.

One historian of Inquisitional Spain and biographer of Christopher Columbus, Simon Wiesenthal, notes that "throughout the sixteenth century the movement of the Marranos to the New World had continued," and that "after the expulsion of the Jews and flight of the Marrano element, it was the turn of the Moriscos to serve as scapegoats for the ills of society." The same writer estimates that, all told, Spain lost one and one-half million people as a consequence of the "purification" of its population of Jews and Moors. "Many occupations were virtually abandoned," he writes. "Trade, the crafts, and the sciences languished. Moreover, since these branches of endeavor had been the domain of Jews and Moriscos, they had become in themselves suspect. Spaniards had to be extremely careful about entering any of these fields.... Spanish life as a whole was the worse for these injustices.... Spain was swamped with fortune hunters from all parts of Europe ... but they could not revive the Spanish economy. Just as the irrigation canals dug by the Moors in Andalusia were allowed to silt up, so the very channels on which the country's health depended fell into neglect."[1]

We document that Spain's loss was Britain's gain. Beginning with the initial planning, organization and promotion of the first British colonial efforts, Sephardic Jews and Muslim Moors were present as navigators, ship captains, sailors, metallurgists, cartographers, financiers and colonists. Among these we find Joachim Ganz, Simon Ferdinando, Walter Raleigh, John Hawkins, Humphrey Gilbert, Richard Hakluyt Sr. and Jr., Francis Drake, Martin Frobisher and Abraham Ortelius.

The first and second British colonies in North America, Virginia and Massachusetts were provisioned, funded and peopled by persons of Sephardic Jewish and Muslim Moorish descent. Current genetic genealogical studies of the Appalachian descendants of these early colonists demonstrate that they carried DNA haplotypes (male or female lineages) and genes from Sephardic, Ottoman and North African founders. Further, these early North American colonists often bore straightforwardly Jewish and Muslim surnames. Attested are Allee, Aleef, Sarazin, Moises, Bagsell, Haggara, Ocosand and even Saladin. Indeed, given the patently non–Christian backgrounds of so many settlers up and down the Atlantic coastline of the American colonies, it becomes difficult to ignore the significant declarations of religious tolerance inscribed in the U.S. Constitution.

Even (and particularly) New York, founded by the Dutch as New Amsterdam, was heavily peopled by Sephardic Jews and Muslim Moors. The presence of persons from these ethnic affiliations on the governing boards of the Dutch West and East India Companies is no accident. They included Jonathan Coen (Cohen) and Cornelius Speelman (another classic Jewish name). Other New Amsterdam, and later New York, residents were Jacob Abrahamsen and Denys Isacksen. We present contemporaneous testimony suggesting that even the leading Knickerbocker families of the New York colony — the van Cortlandts, Philipses, van Rensselaers, De La Nos and De Lanceys — were of Sephardic ancestry.

This fresh look at Colonial American genealogies and settler lists presents for the first time in one source the Spanish, Hebrew, Arabic and Jewish origins and meaning of more than 5,000 surnames, the vast majority of them widely assumed before to be sturdy British family names of ancient bearing. Many of our name etymologies plainly contradict the standard reference works. The decipherment of surname history is an involved subject, one that can extend over centuries of transformation in several countries and require knowledge of a multitude of languages. For instance, in order to understand the sea change suffered by the ancient Jewish name Phoebus to English Phillips (and Scottish Forbes and Frobisher), with stages along the way as Pharabas and Ferebee and Furby, one must have an appreciation for the synthesizing religions of the Roman Empire, including the Cult of Mithras and naming practices of Greek-speaking congregations of Jews, as well as conversion of Berber populations to Judaism, conquest of Spain by Berber armies in 710 and subsequent development of Judeo-Arab culture, not to mention the medieval French, Norman, Anglo-Saxon and Scottish linguistic, orthographic and social filters the surname passed through until it became enshrined in modern times as "good ole English" Phillips.

In their *Dictionary of English Surnames*, P. H. Reaney and R. M. Wilson derive all variations from the Greek name Philippus. Its true etymology, at least for Jews who adopted the name, was established, like many others, by the Victorian scholar Joseph Jacobs, who made so many far-reaching contributions to Jewish historical studies that he may be said to have redefined the field. The monumental dictionary of Sephardic surnames by Guilherme Faiguenboim, Paulo Valadares and Anna Rosa Campagnano, another indispensable guide much relied upon by us in our investigations, has detailed entries under Febos, Farabo, Pharabas and even Phillips. To those in the know, Phillips was a transparently Jewish surname, a venerable one at that.[2]

The question is often asked why Jews changed their names "so much." Let us answer that in the words of Leon Harris (originally Hirsch), the author of a history of American Jewish families who built great department store chains like Gimbels, Nieman-Marcus and Sears. He begins by acknowledging that Jews who altered their surnames from Nusbaum to Norman, and Rabinovitch to Robinson, have often been made the butt of jokes, and have even been characterized as betrayers of their heritage and tradition. But in fact, Harris writes, because for centuries they only had single names, and only in the past two hundred years were they forced to adopt definitive family names for military conscription and tax collection purposes, "they did not take seriously these names that they had assumed under duress. Many indeed gave no more thought to choosing a surname than a man might today if required to select a social security number." If that was the case for people of open Jewish descent, we can well imagine the ease with which persecuted Jews seeking to disguise their origins adopted serviceable and neutral-sounding new surnames or accommodated Hebrew names like Naphtali to Hirsch (German for "stag") and then to Harris.

Two issues arise from these new perspectives. First, how did refugee Jews and Muslims gain awareness of and access to the British colonization efforts in North America? To answer this, we chronicle the significant efforts by English, Scottish and Irish Freemasons in recruiting and protecting the identities of these non–Christian settlers. Leaders in Freemasonry attempted to create a safe-haven for multi-ethnic peoples regardless of religious creed, much as they commit themselves today to charitable and non-sectarian international causes.

The second perplexing issue is, given an overweening Sephardic Jewish and Muslim presence in the American colonies prior to 1776, why that version of history was not the narrative promulgated to generations of Americans in their textbooks and public records? Our present study does not purport to answer this riddle. Some of it has to do with the declining fortunes of Ottoman civilization during these formative years of national identity, along with a shifting definition of what constituted Jewry, Judaism and Jewishness. Certainly we can speculate that with the passage of the national Racial Exclusionary Act of 1790, which targeted not only persons of African and indigenous descent but also those who were "Jews, Saracens, Turks, Egyptians, and other pagan and Infidel races," American families whose ancestors included persons from these now *non grata* groups decided to quietly cover up their origins, declaring themselves from that point forward to be, publicly at least, ordinary British Christian folk. This choice represents not only a tragic loss of identity for the individual families involved, effectively negating their own history, but it also serves to falsify the true nature of the American colonial experience — a lamentable legacy for all the generations who came after, including our own.

Introduction

America is frequently portrayed as the daughter of Mother England. Its social history is approached as a study in similarities and contrasts. It is interesting, then, to take a look at genealogy, that handmaiden of history, and compare the goals and varieties of ancestry tracing in the two countries. Not surprisingly, there are many shared characteristics as well as distinct differences. In the British Isles hardly any pedigree can be documented farther back than about the middle of the twelfth century. Few American genealogies extend beyond the *Mayflower* or Jamestown. Each time period was a determining moment in the future of a nation. The proudest boast of the Englishman has always been to claim descent from Those Who Came with the Conqueror, which as L.G. Pine points out, is a "strange national trait, to be proud of one's conquerors."[1] A similar tendency can be seen in America, where people, perversely, trace their roots back to some unpleasant religious extremist, Indian fighter or scapegrace younger son of an aristocratic lineage. American genealogies rarely jump the Atlantic, and in Norman pedigrees there seems always to be a disconnect between the invasion of 1066 and sudden appearance of the family's supposed ancestor on, say, the Pipe Rolls from the reign of Henry II or Magna Carta of 1215. In America we sometimes have the ship's passenger list mentioning our ancestor but then a maddening interval of silence before a reliable nexus of birth, marriage and death records can be established. Oral traditions fill in the breach.

In the case of the Normans and of America with its founding fathers (and less frequently evoked founding mothers) we are dealing with a small set of foreigners who came from across the sea, quickly gained control and entirely displaced the native population. It has been said that three-quarters of the families inhabiting the Old South can trace descent from as few as fourteen individuals of just as many surnames who came to the Jamestown colony — Gates, Heard, Sands, Throckmorton, Walker, Wooten and others. On a different level, an interlocking presidential dynasty has been suggested with twelve patrician families at its core — Adams, Bayard, Breckbridge, Harrison, Kennedy, Lee, Livingston, Lodge, Randolph, Roosevelt, Taft and Tucker — most of which we will have recourse to mentioning in the chapters of this book.[2]

Between the Battle of Hastings in which the English king Harold II fell in 1066 and compilation of the Domesday Book in 1085, a period of only two decades, virtually every piece of land and livestock, as well as all titles and inheritances, came to rest in Norman hands, allotted to retainers and relatives as payment for their role in imposing French law and order on England. No Anglo-Saxon pedigrees are believed to have survived, any more than Indian tribal hierarchies in colonial American history. For instance, Hereward the Wake, the last leader of the resistance to the Normans, has been put forward as the ancestor of the baronet Wakes, of the Howards (who became Dukes of Norfolk) and of the Harwards and Hayworths, but the compilers of official aristocratic genealogies like Burke's Peerage firmly dismiss any such connection. The arrival of the Normans was a clean sweep, just as the vanquishing of the native tribes in America and obliteration of their culture created a complete ground zero. Pocahontas occupies a similar position in the American imagination as Hereward the Wake and Robin Hood in the British.

Despite the small nucleus and founder effect, both the Normans and American colonists were extremely diversified in their rank-and-file. The former included Danes, Vikings, Norwegians, Flemings, Picards, Bretons, Frenchmen (many from Toulouse and Aquitaine in the South, the region called Languedoc) and a number of Spanish or French Jews and Muslims. The last-mentioned typically operated the armories, mints and construction industries while supplying most mercantile professions with a strong component as well as all banking personnel and civil servants because of their literacy and fluency in accounting. The Norman capital of Rouen possessed one of the largest Jewish communities in Europe, ranking alongside Toulouse, Rome, Constantinople and such Spanish cities as Toledo and Cadiz. The institutions of the exchequer (originally a chessboard or abacus), Star Chamber (based on the concept of *starr*, Arabic for "note"), sheriffs, marshals and other civil titles came from Mozarabic Spain or the South of France and were not outgrowths of the original machinery of Norse, Norman, Anglo-Saxon or Frankish states. In identical fashion, the emigrants who trickled and then streamed into the Colonies comprehended Scotsmen, Irishmen, Welsh, Channel Islanders, Border Scots, French, Dutch, Flemish, Germans, Poles, Swedes, Swiss and Cornishmen, as well as people from London and the English heptarchy — Kent, Essex, the West Country, the Midlands, Sussex, Northumbria and Yorkshire. Both movements had a transnational character. Although the Normans thought of themselves as Frenchmen, they had not resided long enough in Normandy to become amalgamated with the local population and were still pagan Norsemen at heart. The largest emigration of all occurred with the so-called Huguenots, who, as we shall see, were in many cases second or third generation Spanish and Portuguese Jews who traded their French colors for English, Flemish or some other nationality as they fled religious persecution.

The first president of Nigeria, Nnamdi Azikiwe, once remarked America "is a country built more on people than on territory." He saw Jews as the ingredient that gave Americans their characteristic distinctiveness and diversity, saying they "will come from everywhere: from France, from Russia, from America, from Yemen.... Their faith is their passport." Jews and Muslims form, in a sense, the inner sanctum of both the Norman Invasion and occupation of British North America six hundred years later. Between the two turning points were long centuries of crypto–Judaism and crypto–Islam — phenomena that are more apparent and better understood in genealogy than history.

What are some of the differences? The earlier influx of foreigners created a closely knit, landed aristocracy based on the feudal system of a warrior caste, while the later event left a more democratic — or truth to tell, oligarchic — hegemony in place, one based on commercial and egalitarian values rather than a hierarchical religious or military code. It was a modern expanding scientific worldview that prevailed in America, not a medieval "great chain of being" focused on one's parish and the surrounding countryside. Another major difference was that the Norman Invasion was over and done with in a few years whereas the

Colonies were settled in intermittent waves of shifting and changeable nature and was not concluded until the official closing of the western frontier in 1890. Thus American genealogy divides by state, and we speak of Massachusetts genealogies, Virginia, Carolina and so forth. The marked variety of colonial lifeways of those who formed the vanguard and subsequent body of settlers is reflected in the design of our book, which proceeds from "Virginia: First — and Not So English — Colony" to "Georgia, the Last Colony." Although our purview stops at 1776, and hardly ever goes beyond the fall line of rivers emptying into the Atlantic, the character of each colony can be followed in the latitudinal movement of its inhabitants into the vacated lands of the Ohio and Mississippi rivers. America was settled from east to west. The post-colonial demographics of Kentucky and Tennessee reflected those of Virginia, Maryland and North Carolina.

In addition to Jewish genealogies, we have made an effort to bring to life some of the forgotten women who shaped the Colonial American experience. These include the ancient *Ur* mother of European royalty, the Occitan Jewish Queen Itta, Charlemagne's great-great-great-grandmother; Mary Lago, the Sephardic Jewish mother of the Quakers' founder George Fox; and Malea Cooper, the Jewish mulatto wife of Daniel Boone's guide (whose Hebrew name is the same as one of President Barack Obama's daughters). Some of their stories will surprise readers, running counter to traditional historical accounts. Few people realize that one of the Salem witches mounted a legal defense using the family's professional connections and wealth. Sarah Town(e) Cloyes (or Clayes) fought her accusers and lived to become a founder of the town of Framingham, Massachusetts. The mother of Patrick Henry, according to diarist William Byrd, was "a handsome woman of the Family of Esau" whose first husband in Aberdeen, Scotland, was "of the Family of Saracens." The Cherokee Beloved Woman Nancy Ward bore an Arabic name. One of the subthemes of the present study is the interaction between immigrants and American Indians. Readers will find Cherokee, Creek, Choctaw and other genealogies that reflect intermarriage between Jews or Muslims and America's native inhabitants, believed in the thinking of the day to be Abraham's children.

In America, unlike Britain, it is not true that "only the eminent have anything like a genealogy."[3] Genealogy in this country is the second most popular hobby after gardening. We are assured, and it stands to reason, that every individual no matter how elusive or obscure left some evidence of their existence in public records. More and more, the genealogies compiled and published forsake the manufactured Lives of Great Men to include maternal connections, ordinary folk and minorities. With the emerging tools of the Internet it is possible to be both thorough and accurate and produce detailed genealogies motivated by a desire for gathering facts, for telling the truth and for redressing some of the injustices of traditional, orthodox accounts. The footnotes in this study are intended not only to document origins and surname histories in unequivocal fashion but also to cast a sidelight on celebrated Jewish Americans who can trace back to colonial forebears and their relatives in European Jewry. These range from the Massachusetts Kennedys to the Byrds of Virginia, from actors Johnny Depp and Adrien Brody to actresses Roseanne Barr and Gwyneth Paltrow, from writers Louise Glück and Neil Simon to politicians Barbara Boxer and Bernie Sanders and jurists Stephen Breyer and Elena Kagan. As biased and purpose-made genealogies recede into the background, privileged historical theses with vested interests must also be on the defensive. We hope that the remarkable stories of the men, women and families in this work will serve as a reminder of America's early diversity and stimulus for rewriting some of the inaccurate and injudicious portions in the proud chronicle of her birth and formative years.

CHAPTER ONE

Mapmakers, Privateers and Promoters

The year 1492 saw one door close on Iberian Jews and Muslims and another open an ocean away. That year witnessed three events in Spain that had sweeping implications for the colonization of the New World. The first was the fall of Muslim Granada to the Christian Reconquista. Islamic rule in the Iberian Peninsula came to an abrupt end after nearly eight hundred years. Second, a royal edict of expulsion was issued aimed at Spain's Jewish population. It gave them three months, later extended to six, to convert to Christianity or leave the realm, their property confiscated. Third was the voyage of Cristobal Colon in search of a trans–Atlantic passage to China and the Indies. On the periphery of these events, the same year brought such developments as the death of the founder of the first modern state, Lorenzo the Magnificent, grand-duke of Tuscany; invasion of Italy by the French king Charles VIII, with the consequence that the Renaissance began to spread northward; secularization and decline of the papacy with the ascension of the infamous Borgia Pope Alexander VI; and construction by German mapmaker Martin Behaim of the first globe.

All these occurrences made for a defining moment in European history. It was a turning point that spelled the death throes of the claustrophobic Christian Middle Ages and harbingered the birth of the Modern Era. Expansive horizons now beckoned to all people. Secular forms of government were emerging; new currents of pluralism were afoot. Whether Jews helped cause this groundswell of change or represented merely one contributory factor, they certainly participated in the course of events and benefited from the promising new opportunities. They were at the forefront of discovery, exploration and settlement of the new lands in the West.

Both academic studies and informal family histories attest that many of the Spanish and Portuguese colonists in Central and South America, Mexico and the Caribbean were Conversos and Moriscos.[1] Although they might appear to be good Catholic Christians on the surface, they were in reality crypto–Jews and crypto–Muslims, secret Jews and secret Muslims. They practiced the traditions of Judaism and Islam in the privacy of their own homes, sometimes in small *de facto* communities or intermarried family groups. Both Judaic and Islamic law excused this behavior on grounds that such temporizers were constrained to submit to political pressures to save life and property. The earliest martyrs to the commandment of the Torah requiring Jews to declare themselves as separate and set apart from other people were called Anusim ("forced ones"). The Inquisition rolled out a dragnet complete with tip sheets, rewards and public spectacles, the feared auto-da-fes. Judaizers as well as Moriscos were burned at the stake as heretics. Spain's Muslim population survived longer than its Jews, but the final wave of extradition for them came in 1614.[2] They left in droves for safe havens in the Low Lands, England and Ottoman Empire. The grisly machinery of the Holy Office was not shut down for good until 1822. The Spanish government did not permit Jews to return officially or become citizens until the Franco regime in the 1940s and 1950s.

But proscription of Jewish practices and beliefs had never been perfect. Rules were relaxed from time to time and from place to place. King Manuel of Portugal welcomed thousands of Jewish exiles across the border and tolerated openly Jewish subjects in his realm until 1497. Navarre was long an exception to persecution of Jews. Local enforcement of anti–Semitic laws across Spain and Portugal was shifting and uneven. Officials often colluded in protecting persons of Jewish and Muslim ancestry who were important to the smooth functioning of the state. In truth, the three cardinal events mentioned above are interwoven, for historians have identified five Jews among the 90 sailors in Columbus' expedition. All of them were probably intent not only on finding the riches of the East Indies but also on escaping religious persecution at home. The man we know as Columbus was in all likelihood of Jewish ancestry. He is believed to have been a descendant of Spanish Jews, the Colon family, who had converted and moved to Genoa following the massacre of 1391. The prominent historian Salvador de Madariega wrote an authoritative biography in which he came to this conclusion, and Nazi hunter Simon Wiesenthal's book *Sails of Hope* popularized the idea.[3] Among other clues, Wiesenthal drew attention to Columbus' use of Hebrew ciphers in his private correspondence with his son Diego. In a letter to Diego de Deza, the tutor of Prince Juan, moreover, Columbus wrote, "I am a servant of the same Lord who raised up David"—a curious allusion, according to Wiesenthal.[4]

Historians speculate that the first European to sight land on October 12, 1492, was also Jewish. The sailor Juan Rodriguez Bermejo, called Rodrigo de Triana, left Spain upon Columbus' return and entered the service of the Moors in Morocco. His name and memory are honored today by American Jews for whom the story of the auspicious beginning is a point of immense pride. Hundreds of Jews exiled from Spain and Portugal followed Bermejo and made a name for themselves as the "Jewish pirates of the Caribbean," as author Edward Kritzler calls them, including Moroccan-born Samuel Palache, "the Pirate Rabbi."[5]

The focal point of the present work, however, is not the southern or central portions of the Americas, not the Spanish and Portuguese colonies in the Americas. A case will be made here for a crypto–Jewish and crypto–Muslim presence in British North America. We propose that many of the initial colonists in Virginia, South Carolina, Pennsylvania, Massachusetts and Maryland were of Jewish and Moorish descent — if not of Jewish and Moorish self-identification or public labeling as such. Appendix A presents an abundance of source materials concerning Jewish surnames. The question of any given individual's religious adherence can be bracketed for the time being. At any rate, each claim about religion has to be answered on a case by case basis, and very little research has been completed on the varieties of the Jewish religious experience in colonial America.[6] Appendix B, "Rituals and Practices of the Secret Jews," and Appendix C, "Muslim Rituals and Beliefs," contain a mixture of religious traditions and social customs. What is central to our inquiry is ancestry. We suggest Dutch New Amsterdam, later British New York, and New Jersey harbored and sometimes welcomed people of Jewish ancestral origins and affinities.

Although the historical backdrop to these developments may be familiar, some salient events are worth repeating.[7] Beginning with pogroms in Barcelona in 1391, and increasingly a century later when Inquisition tribunals were established throughout Spain, Sephardic Jews made their way by the thousands to France, the Netherlands, Switzerland, Germany, Austria and Britain. Once denounced or exposed in their homeland, Jews were not allowed to immigrate to Spanish possessions in the New World, although many went there as New Christians or Conversos. Beginning in 1492, the Muslims of Spain and Portugal were likewise forced to accept conversion to Christianity or flee their homes. Unlike their Jewish counterparts, they were not explicitly forbidden to immigrate to New Spain. Their influence in the Americas is largely unstudied, and certainly unappreciated. The death knell for them came in 1609 when several hundred thousand Moriscos remaining in Spain and Portugal were declared undesirable subjects of the crown and also summarily ordered into exile. They left in droves for non–Catholic lands, many settling as merchants in England and Scotland.

Although the bulk of the refugees fled to North Africa and Ottoman or Turkish lands in the Levant, thousands of others sought safety in France and the Low Countries. As Protestantism swept across Western Europe, many of these Jewish Conversos and Moriscos became — often only outwardly — Protestant. Swelling the ranks of the dissenters, some even provided leaders for the Huguenots, Hussites, Anabaptists, Calvinists, German Reformed, Walloons, Mennonites, Dunkards, Quakers, Puritans and Presbyterians. When the British, Dutch and French began establishing colonies on the Atlantic Seaboard, they sent as colonists not subjects of high political and social rank from their respective countries but for the most part recently arrived, patently anti–Catholic, newly-minted Protestants. Many were debtors, prisoners or servants, castoffs of society who were struggling to get onto their own feet in a new country.

England's reliance on Iberian Jews to promote its interests abroad goes back as far as the Tudors. Henry VIII used Spanish Jewish lawyers to justify his divorce from Catherine of Aragon. One of them, an Italian banker tapped for his shrewdness and knowledge of international law, was the ancestor of Oliver Cromwell, Protector of the Commonwealth. In 1594 Rodrigo Lopez was Elizabeth's court physician. He was executed on charges of treason and plotting to poison her. The fledgling colony of Iberian Jews exiled from England found shelter mainly in Holland, where they helped found Amsterdam's significant Marrano community in 1598. They returned to England after a lapse of more than three hundred years in 1664 when Amsterdam rabbi Menasseh Ben Israel lobbied Cromwell to allow Jews again in England. They were provisionally but unofficially readmitted. Elizabeth's successor, James I, brought a Scottish and Stewart predisposition toward Jewish merchants and extended many privileges to Jews and native crypto or former Jews. As historian David Cesarani reminds us, London's Jews were uniquely both court Jews and port Jews, since the capital was the seat of government as well as the center of England's maritime trade.[8] Under Cromwell, London-based merchants such as Antonio Fernandez Carvajal, Manuel Dormido and Simon de Carceres acted as valued counter-intelligence agents against the Spanish. Charles II sojourned among Dutch Jews during his exile in the Netherlands. His marriage to Catherine of Breganza was brokered by the Portuguese-Jewish merchants Duarte da Silva and Fernando Mendes da Costa, and it was Charles who granted religious liberty to Jews in 1673. The influence of these Marranos culminated in the Glorious Revolution, when William III hired the Amsterdam-based firm of Machado and Pereira to provision his expedition to England. William also invited the family of Lopes Suasso to settle in England. He knighted Solomon de Medina, his most important army contractor and banker. In 1697 the number of Jew brokers in the financial district around the Tower quarter in London was so

great they had to be limited by law to twelve. They continued to monopolize the stock exchange and shipping insurance business.

The Muslim presence in England was different. Muslims had a distinct identity and central geographical focus that clearly separated them from Christians. Consequently, few chose to settle in London or Amsterdam. It was the Tudors, in particular Queen Elizabeth, who first welcomed Moors from Spain and the Mediterranean to England and encouraged English merchants to trade with them in North Africa and the Ottoman Empire. Like Jews, they were often pressed into military and intelligence actions. According to Nabil Matar in *Turks, Moors, and Englishmen in the Age of Discovery*,[9]

> From 1575 to 1588, immigrants were repeatedly made to join in national defense, and in 1596, it was reported by the Fugger spy that the English fleet that attacked Cadiz had been accompanied by "five galleys from Barbary" and that the English took with them to Barbary some of the ships they captured there. Evidently the military cooperation between Britons and Moors covered both land and sea operations and was based on what seemed to be (although it was never formalized) a strategic alliance between London and Marrakesh.

Not only did Moors travel to England on business, but some even decided to stay, converting to Anglicanism and marrying English women. In 1625, official records show "3 or 4 Turkes or Moores" in Exeter, thirty in Plymouth, three or four in Bristol and ten with Baronet Seymour (an English Jewish surname).[10] Moorish names documented in England at the time are Hammett (from Mohammed), Mansur (Manser), Mustain (Muston, Musson), Ali (Alye, Allie), Alouf (Aleff), Walid (Wally, Ridge, Whalley), Ballu (Ballou, Bellow, Bellows), Said (Seed, Sead), Ward (Wardiyya, Rose), Sillau (Sally), Halil (Kalil), Dey (Dee), Dinar (Diner, Dinner), Khan, Lucas (Louks), Malek, Malim, Osman (Osmond), Othman, Reys (Rei, Rayes, Ray), Dodo (Dodds, Daudin, Dode, Dodon, Dodier, Dodoret, etc., all from David), Sherife (Sherive, from Shariff, Arabic "leader") and Sidan.[11] In turn, Englishmen like John Ward, James Procter of Southampton and Sir Francis Verney fraternized with the Muslims and converted to Islam. Contemporary pamphlets vilify them. The play by Robert Davorne, *A Christian Turn'd Turk* (1612), specifically targeted Ward, whose name was Arabicized to Wardiyya ("of the rose"), and whose flagship was manned by an Anglo-Turkish crew of 400 pirates.[12] From these facts we can see that the line between Christian and Muslim in England was far from clear-cut when the first American colonies were planted.

Colonial census records, genealogies, marital patterns, ship passenger lists and DNA test results all combine to suggest that a high number of the earliest and historically prominent colonial Americans were of Jewish and Muslim descent. Many of them may have practiced the faiths of their fathers and mothers in secret before relocation to North America and have been Jews in a religious sense. Certainly, some openly returned to Judaism there after centuries of maintaining an underground existence.

How did this happen? We have glanced at some of England's connections with Iberian Jews, but that is only half the story. The rest concerns its own crypto–Jewish families, and the key to understanding them lies in Cornwall and Devon. These are the southwestern coastal sections of England where, since the time of the Minoans and Phoenicians in the Early Bronze Age, tin and copper were smelted and transported to Gaul, ports in North Africa and indeed all over the Mediterranean.[13] Cornwall was the primary source in antiquity for tin oxide ore, mined in a number of alluvial deposits as pebbles and gravel in stream

Opposite: **English navigators and explorers included many West Country gentlemen (Picture Collection, The New York Public Library, Astor, Lenox and Tilden Foundations).**

beds. Stream-tinning gave way in early antiquity to underground mining in the larger granite veins in upland Cornwall and Devon.[14] Recent DNA surveys of Cornwall and Devon populations have established that both male and female Semitic and Mediterranean haplotypes are present in the contemporary population in relatively high frequencies compared to England as a whole — as high as 6 percent for the characteristic North African male lineage known as E3b.[15] Evidently, a colony of Phoenicians, Carthaginians and the like not only settled there in ancient times but also left descendants who still dwell in the region. Topographic names speak for Middle Eastern influences. The main river is the Tamar, Hebrew and Arabic for date palm. Its Latin form is *phoenix*, reflected in the name of the Phoenicians, who used the date palm as an emblem of state on their currency. There are towns named Marazion, Cairo and Menheniot. In fact, an ancient tradition derives the name Britannia, originally called Bretanika by the Greeks, from the Phoenician word Bratanac, or Baratanac (Country of Tin).[16]

By the 1200s CE, Carthage and Phoenicia had long since departed from the world stage, but the association of Middle Eastern people with Cornish tin mining was still strong. In 1290 Edward I decreed that all Jews in England must either exit the country or (and this is the portion of the royal decree glossed over by many historians) accept conversion to Christianity.[17] As the authors and others have argued,[18] this was quite likely the origin of an exodus of Jews to Scotland and an organized crypto–Jewish presence in England, especially in Cornwall and Devon. According to traditional accounts, the next known openly Jewish figure to set foot in the district was a certain Joachim Ganz, "invited by the Company for the Mines Royal to advise [them] on copper extraction." He went first to Keswick to inspect copper mines and produced a report on the treatment of copper ores. Next he spent three years in Cornwall from 1586 to 1589, until he was expelled "for drawing too much unfavorable attention to his religious beliefs."[19] This description of Ganz appears to be not only anti–Semitic but also less than candid, for he continued to be retained by various British government representatives until 1608. He is, in fact, the very same Jewish metallurgist who made multiple trips to North America in the employ of Sir Walter Raleigh and later the Virginia Company. He was present and active both in the Roanoke and Jamestown colonies.

The question arises whom Ganz was working with in Devon and Cornwall and why. The short answer is the West Country gentlemen, as they were called at the Elizabethan court, a remarkable group of landowners and privateers from Cornwall and Devon who changed the course of English, American and world history. That they were of crypto–Jewish origin no one has suggested or suspected among modern-day historians. However, strong circumstantial evidence favors this inference.

Sir Walter Raleigh (1552–1618)

Walter Raleigh's earliest known ancestor is believed to be Simon (Hebrew name) de Ralegh (also a town in Devonshire).[20] He was born 1195 in Devon and was reportedly a merchant. Biographer John William Shirley writes that his father, also named Walter, was from Fardell in Devon, a merchant "who owned at least one ship for his trade."[21] Evidently, like many other families, the Raleighs were Anglo-Norman. Their forebears came over from France with William the Conqueror. In recent generations they married Champernouns (from Cambernon in Normandy), Drakes and the daughter of a Genoese (Italy) merchant family whose name is unknown. Sir Walter's mother was by descent a Champernoun and

Carew (Cornish). By an earlier marriage, she bore three sons, John, Humphrey and Adrian Gilbert (Norman surname). Raleigh's brother-in-law and cousin was Sir Richard Grenville (1542–1591), a cousin also to Drake. These families were not only heavily intermarried, generation to generation, but also multiply implicated in settling colonial America. The Champernouns, Raleighs, Gilberts, Drakes and Carews were ardent Protestants by the late 1500s, but before that, they were, we suggest, in varying degrees, crypto–Jews. They were people of Jewish heritage mutually recognized, who had begun to dissemble their roots and religion since the forced conversion of English Jews under Edward I in 1290. As can be seen in portraits, the Raleighs, Drakes and Gilberts were uniformly dark with prominent noses, high foreheads and narrow faces — not unlike Iberian and Moroccan Jews.

As an aside on Genoese Jews,[22] a Jewish mercantile family from Genoa who had connections both in the Low Countries and royal court in England under the Tudor monarchs were the Anthonys or Anthons. The earliest of these was a goldsmith and wind instrument player brought to London

Sir Humphrey Gilbert (Print Collection, Miriam and Ira D. Wallach Division of Art, Prints and Photographs, The New York Public Library, Astor, Lenox and Tilden Foundations).

by Henry VIII, John Anthony, also known as Antonious Moyses. He was one of twenty Jews who were court musicians. A descendant, Mark Anthony, was sent to school in Italy by his father but ran away, was captured by Algerian pirates, and sold into slavery in Algiers. The captain of a British ship took pity on him, carried him to America, and resold him to pay for his passage in 1698. A farmer in New Kent County, Virginia, bought him for three years. The young man ended up establishing a trading post and marrying Isabella Hart of a leading Jewish trader family in Virginia, while his son Joseph married Elizabeth Clark of another Jewish mercantile company. A granddaughter, Sarah Clark Anthony, married Thomas Cooper, grandson of a crypto–Jewish London merchant and son of an Indian trader. Cooper was a founding figure in American Freemasonry (Chapter Ten). These Coopers are ancestors of both authors.

In the 1570s Walter Raleigh was sent to Munster Province in Ireland where Queen Elizabeth was striving to put down revolts by the Catholic Irish. Here Walter and his cousins — the Gilberts, Grenvilles, St. Legers and Zouches — took part in military operations near Cork. Elizabeth was impressed with not only Raleigh's political acumen but also his dark good looks. She awarded him the royal license as exporter of woolen broadcloth, a lucrative sinecure. He was also appointed Warden of the Stannaries, director of the Cornish tin mines. In later life, he was alternately in and out of royal favor, unpopular for his religious skepticism at the same time that he was celebrated as an advocate of religious

tolerance. These ambiguities are consistent with a crypto–Jewish background. Spanish Jews were naturally tolerant of others' religious practices, the famous tenet of *covivencia* having been one of the pillars of civil society that prevailed for so long under the Arabs. In many cases, Spanish Jews were also adherents of Averroism. This was an Arab school of philosophy that extended far beyond its founder Averroes' arguments about the oneness of reality. Jewish Averroists were attracted by the potential they saw in the school of thought for resolving the conflicts between philosophy and religion. They tended to believe that both philosophy and religion were equally valid metaphysical constructs even when they appeared to produce different answers to the same question.[23] It goes without saying that this way of thinking was fraught with the perils of rationalization and solipsim. Yet a certain vein of intellectual laziness and cynicism suited perfectly the style of living of many crypto–Jews, according to their chief chronicler David Gitlitz in *The Religion of the Crypto-Jews.*

By 1584 Raleigh was exploring the North American coastline with his half-brother Sir Humphrey Gilbert, their goal the establishing of British colonies in parlous territories. Colonizing the New World with English subjects was a core aspect of Elizabeth's political strategy to challenge Spanish hegemony.[24] The cast of characters involved in these often-surreptitious efforts included not only Raleigh, Gilbert, Drake and their several cousins, but also other persons we believe to be of Sephardic Jewish or Morisco extraction. Among these are the two Richard Hakluyts (a probable Moroccan name),[25] uncle and nephew, hired as the West Country gentlemen's London publicists; cartographer and mathematician John Dee (Turkish *dey*, "court member"); astronomers Thomas Harriot[26] and Stephen Parmenius (Italian surname); ship captains Arthur Fassi (Moroccan name),[27] Simon Ferdinando (Sephardic surname),[28] Thomas Cavendish (Devonshire surname and probably from the Mediterranean before that),[29] Philip Amadas (Sephardic surname),[30] Pedro Diaz (Sephardic),[31] Arthur Barlowe ("son of Lowe, Levi")[32] and metallurgist Joachim Ganz, who, as previously mentioned, was an Ashkenazi Jew. Hardly one of the West Country gentlemen's associates was *not* of a surname that can't be documented in the records of the Spanish Inquisition, as compiled by Père Bonnin in *Sangre Judia.*[33] Almost all can be found in Guilherme Faiguenboim and collaborators' *Dictionary of Sephardic Surnames* (second edition, 2004). The names in this essential handbook are cross-referenced to local Sephardic Jewish genealogies for Amsterdam, London, Tunisia, Brazil and other Diaspora communities.

Raleigh's accomplishments won him a knighthood and governorship of Virginia. The company's first efforts at colonization in Roanoke 1586–1591 ended in failure, but as we argue in chapter three, there is evidence from the passenger lists, foodstuffs and occupations of the colonists that they might have been Sephardic refugees. Names such as Ananais Dare (Jewish first name and likely Jewish last name through a Norman family[34]) and Dionys Harvey (Greek first name, Breton and Norman surname formed apparently from Hebrew *har*, "mount"[35]) are clearly not English. Nor are accountants and university professors among those normally enlisted to sail off and subdue the wilderness. Arguably these particular draftees consented to participate in the Roanoke settlement of 1587 because they feared the upcoming Spanish invasion of England in 1588 and trusted the Jewish and Morisco organizers of the settlement to protect them. One of the financial underwriters of the project was Raleigh's father-in-law, William Sanderson,[36] a wealthy London merchant. Although Raleigh's Roanoke colony was never rescued, he did not abandon his efforts to colonize America. In 1595 he launched a new effort, this time directly challenging Spanish power in Central America by planting a British colony in Guiana on the Spanish Main. William Sanderson provided the funding, and Oxford mathematics and navigation professor

Lawrence Keymis (from Hebrew *kheemaee*, "chemist"?)[37] and Sir Robert Crosse[38] were also involved in it.

Sir Francis Drake

Drake was born in Devon around 1540 and was a kinsman of the Hawkins family, which included John Hawkins, one of the great English sailors of the period. Biographer Peter Whitfield comments that "in Drake resentment of Spain became a passion."[39] He learned sailing, as did most of his compatriots, from Sephardic and Morisco navigators like Martin Cortes and Pedro da Medina. In 1595, John Davis[40] translated Medina's navigational writings into *The Seaman's Secrets*. The Cornish ports of Bristol and Plymouth, both known to have crypto–Jewish communities, became breeding grounds for a generation of privateers eager to damage Spain's interests in the Americas.

Drake was perhaps foremost among them. He spent his early years engaged in contraband trade skirmishing with the Spanish in the Canaries and the Azores, both of which harbored large crypto–Jewish communities.[41] Drake captained a ship owned by his kinsman Hawkins named the *Judith* (heroine from Hebrew legend). Within a few years he had fervently committed himself to destroying Spanish holdings in the Americas. As his biographer points out, "Spain and all things Spanish became his prey ... he would dedicate himself to attacking and plundering Spanish possessions."[42]

In May 1572, Drake set sail from Plymouth in a ship named *The Swan and the Pasha* (English royal emblem and Ottoman title). Arriving in Panama, he formed an alliance with a group of French Huguenot privateers. These, we can surmise, included many crypto–Jews if a study of the antecedents of Huguenots among refugees of the Spanish Inquisition can be believed.[43] They succeeded in capturing a Spanish treasure caravan totaling 300 tons of silver. Drake returned to England not only a stupendously wealthy man, but also a national hero catapulted to the highest fame.

Among Drake's other exploits was the first English circumnavigation of the world sailing in the *Golden Hind* (cabalistic title),[44] following Sephardic/Morisco maps drawn by Mercator, Abraham Ortelius (Ortello, Italian) and Fernaõ Vaz[45] Dourado.[46] Perhaps his most revealing initiative, with regard to our thesis, was leading the Great

Nineteenth-century engraving of a portrait of Drake by an unknown artist, circa 1580. The original telltale six-pointed stars in his coat of arms in the upper left were changed to eight-pointed, evidently to obscure his Jewish origins (Print Collection, Miriam and Ira D. Wallach Division of Art, Prints and Photographs, The New York Public Library, Astor, Lenox and Tilden Foundations).

West Indian Raid in 1585, which took a fleet of over 20 ships and 1,000 soldiers on a destructive blitz through the Spanish Caribbean, including the ports of Santo Domingo in Hispaniola and Saint Augustine in Florida. The tour ended with a stop to bring relief to his kinsman Raleigh's floundering Roanoke Colony off the Virginia coast. In each foray into Spanish territories, Drake made a special effort to sack and ruin Catholic churches. At the same time he officiated in Old Testament prayer and psalm reading on board ship. His final stroke against the Spanish came in 1588 when on the aptly named *Revenge* he led the British victory in the fight against the Armada.

We propose that not only was Drake aware that he had Sephardic Jewish antecedents, but the Spanish were as well. His surname Drake is Spanish for dragon.[47] DNA samples from Drake's brother's descendants (Francis had no children) show their Y chromosome to be type R1a1—a common Ashkenazi Levite lineage.

John Hawkins

John Hawkins (1532–1595) was a kinsman of Drake, and his life serves as a critical piece of evidence for our Sephardic-Morisco thesis. His father, William, was the leading merchant in Plymouth during the 1530s and traded in the Caribbean and with Portuguese-held Guiana. The ports of Plymouth and Bristol from which he sailed were notable locations for what have been termed port Jews. From Plymouth and Bristol men sailed in the company of Magellan (1480–1521) and Sebastian Caboto (1476–1557).[48] Among these ambiguous figures was Captain Roger Barlow, who later accompanied Drake to North America.[49]

The Hawkins family history in Cornwall can be traced to the late 1400s, when John Hawkins (Hauquin)[50] of Towistock (i.e., Tawes)[51] married Joan Amydas (compare Amadas, above) of Launceston. All these names appear to be Sephardic Jewish. John and Joan Hawkins had a son, William, who by 1524 was treasurer for the Corporation of Plymouth and tax collector for Devon county. William married Joan Trelawny (Trelauni, Cornish surname), fathering sons William in 1519 and John in 1532. A later Richard Hawkins from this same line, born 1560, would marry Judith Heale of a Bristol family which immigrated to Virginia in 1620, and which is related to one of the authors (Hirschman). The Heale family's name underwent permutation to Hale in the Colonies. They are listed as free persons

Sir John Hawkins. Hawkins' surname was rendered Haquines in Spanish, a common Sephardic surname from the Hebrew for physician (Print Collection, Miriam and Ira D. Wallach Division of Art, Prints and Photographs, The New York Public Library, Astor, Lenox and Tilden Foundations).

of color in Tennessee during the late 1700s and are considered Melungeon, members of a Lower Appalachian ethnic isolate believed to derive from Portuguese Jews and fellow travelers like Moriscos and Scotsmen.[52]

Hawkins' biographer, James Alexander Williamson, states, "The customs ledgers of Henry VIII show William Hawkins exporting cloth and tin to the ports of Western Europe and importing a variety of goods, the salt of Rochelle, wines of Bordeaux, Portugal and Spain, sugar and pepper probably from Portugal, olive oil ... and soap from Spain.... It is very probable that some of the sugar and wines were bought from the Canaries."[53] In all these ports, Jews, crypto–Jews, Moors and crypto–Muslims were often in control of maritime trade. Hawkins also traded with Portuguese Brazil, under the invading Dutch the first land in the West that opened up for free-standing Sephardic settlements. He dealt with other merchants such as Robert Reneger, Thomas Borey and John Phillips.[54] The pattern of trading and origin of these surnames are indicative of Sephardic Jewish ethnicity.

By 1548 the Hawkins family and its associates were trading in Morocco, a haven for both Sephardim and Moriscos. The French ports with which the family traded — Dieppe, Rouen and La Rochelle — were also heavily populated by Protestant Huguenots, many of whose origins were Sephardic and Morisco.[55] These French Protestants by 1560 had undertaken attacks on Spanish interests in Cartagena, Santa Marta, Havana and Santiago. One may speculate that when Rouen, a center of English Jewry exempt from many of the regulations concerning Jews since the time of William the Conqueror or before, passed to the French under Queen Mary in 1553, many Rouennais Jews threw in their lot with the Huguenots to escape the growing anti–Jewish climate. Rouen and Le Havre became popular stopping-off points for Spanish Jews in exile.

At any rate, it was the Sephardic and Morisco population of Spain — fleeing after 1492 to France, the Dutch Republic and England — that was most committed psychologically and militarily to her destruction as a world power. The Protestant regimes in France, Holland, and Britain undoubtedly were aware that several of their most fervently

Admiral Sir Charles Howard, 1st Earl of Nottingham. This portrait exemplifies the physical appearance of several persons in Britain's Navy under the rule of Elizabeth I. Are they of Sephardic or Morisco descent? Indicatively, Howard's flagship was named the *Ark Royale* (Print Collection, Miriam and Ira D. Wallach Division of Art, Prints and Photographs, The New York Public Library, Astor, Lenox and Tilden Foundations).

anti–Spanish and pro–Protestant sailors and soldiers were Sephardic Jews and Moriscos beneath Christian camouflage, but they also were politic enough to let this go in order to obtain their talents and passion as anti–Catholic warriors.

During the 1560s John Hawkins established himself as a trader-merchant in the Canary Islands. Here one of his foremost friends and partners was the Genoese-descended merchant Pedro de Ponte. The Ponte/Ponto family was — and is — a prominent one in the Canaries. It is self-avowedly of Sephardic extraction.[56] In 1559 Hawkins married Katherine Gonson, the daughter of Benjamin Gonson (Scottish/Norwegian surname), treasurer of the navy. The marriage led to his connection to a set of powerful men dominating Britain's naval operations: William Winter, Lionel Ducket and Sir Thomas Lodge. Hawkins' partners included Juan Martinez[57] of Cadiz, Spain, and Lorenzo Barnaldey of Santo Domingo,[58] "a lawyer and a converted Jew."[59] One of the captains sailing often on Hawkins' trading and raiding expeditions, another kinsman, John Lovell, also carries a Sephardic surname.[60] Others include Guillermo de Oclando, Valentine Verd (Green) and Robert Barrett (who reportedly spoke Spanish).[61] Barrett was captured by the Spanish and burned alive by the Inquisition in Seville in 1570. Others of Hawkins' men seized by the Spanish and tortured by the Inquisitional proceedings were William Collins, Paul de Leon ("from Leon"), William Griffin, George Riveley, John Moon (Luna),[62] John Lee, William Brown, Thomas Goodal, John Gilbert, Roger Armar,[63] John Grey, John Martin,[64] George Dee/Day (Diaz) and Miles (Greek Milo) Phillips,[65] natives to the Netherlands, France, Ireland and England. Many of these were not English, but to judge from their surnames, Sephardic or Moorish.

By 1569 the Huguenots and English merchants in the port of Plymouth were working in concert to assail Spanish shipping and the imperial treasure fleet. The French cardinal Chattillon, a Huguenot (likely Sephardic, despite his Catholic office, the name perhaps originally Castillon),[66] was in London on a campaign urging an attack on "all the enemies of God, otherwise called Papists."[67] Drake's kinsmen the Champernowns were deeply involved in this effort, as was a "Cornish-man" named Philip Budocushyde.[68]

Martin Frobisher (about 1535–1594)

Frobisher was a privateer with roots not in Cornwall or Devon but Yorkshire, according to biographer James McDermott.[69] The family had crossed the border from Scotland and bore originally the name Forbusher, a variant of Forbes, related like Phillips to the Jewish names Phoebus, Pharabee and Feraby. Martin Frobisher's mother, Margaret York, was closely related to "Sir John Yorke of London: the notable merchant-tailor, financier and Iberian trader."[70] John Yorke traded in Antwerp and Calais, acted as assay-master at the London Tower Mint in 1544, raised foreign funds for Henry VIII and helped found the Southwick Mint — all typical occupations for Conversos.[71] By 1547 he was sheriff of London. "He acted as one of the King's principal financial agents in the Netherlands ... and most lucratively he received unprecedented terms to supply the Tower Mint with silver bullion from Flanders."[72] From this description of his activities and titles, John Yorke would also appear to be of Sephardic descent.

It was into his uncle John Yorke's home and business that young Martin Frobisher was sent to learn a trade by his mother. Frobisher was posted abroad on trading trips to the Barbary Coast and the Portuguese African slave colony of Guinea by a syndicate of London merchants that included, besides his uncle, Thomas Lok, Edward Castelyn ("Castilian"),

Sir George Barne, Anthony Hickman[73] and Nicholas Lambert. The Loks are described as "fervent Protestants," one of them, John Lok, having made a "personal pilgrimage to Jerusalem" in 1553.[74] The name appears to come either from Hebrew Loach לוה, "number table, tariff, calendar" or the Spanish place-name Logo. Famous bearers of the Louk/Lok surname lived in Morocco, Tangiers, and Spain, as well as modern-day Israel.[75]

The Loks, George Barne,[76] William Toweison, John Castelin and Stephen Borough (Baruch, Hebrew for "blessed") were principals in the Muscovy Company, an English-Russian trading venture established in the 1550s. The company's directors were the Earl of Leicester, William Cecil, 1st Baron Burghley and Sir Francis Walsingham, principal advisor to Elizabeth, a man who was in the eyes of his contemporaries "the most ardent anti-Catholic in England."[77]

Another Lok family member, Michael, was a brilliant cartographer and astronomer, who spoke Spanish, French, Italian, Latin and Arabic, and who had traveled to France,

Martin Frobisher after Cornelis Ketel's portrait in the Bodleian Library (Print Collection, Miriam and Ira D. Wallach Division of Art, Prints and Photographs, The New York Public Library, Astor, Lenox and Tilden Foundations).

Spain, Portugal, Venice, Greece and the Levant. Michael ended his career in Aleppo, Turkey, serving there as the consul of the English Levant Company.[78]

Frobisher accompanied both Drake and Raleigh on their Spanish raids and assisted with the initial push to establish the Roanoke Colony. Dying without issue, he left his estate to nieces and nephews. His will was witnessed by Thomas Colwell, Anthony Lewes (civic name for sacred name Levi), Timothy Perrot and Richard Farrer (Spanish for "blacksmith," a common Jewish trade).[79] His wife, Dorothy, shortly thereafter married Sir John Saville (Jewish form of Samuel),[80] baron of the exchequer, often an office held by Jews.

Robert (Robin) Sidney (Sidoney), Earl of Leicester

The list of family names of likely Sephardic or crypto-Jewish ancestry in Elizabethan England would not be complete without two much more prominent players in the trade and diplomacy of the day. The first is the Sidneys, also spelled Sidoney, as in Sidon, Palestine. One of the leading figures in this line was Robert (Robin) Sidney, earl of Leicester (1563–1626). Robin is a form of Reuben, a name favored by crypto-Jews. Robert Sidney's father, Henry, "was a radical Protestant," according to biographer Hay.[81] In 1579 Robert was placed under the tutelage of Hubert Languet, a scholarly Huguenot émigré. On a tour through the Low Countries, France and Germany, Languet introduced him to the eminent champions of Protestantism in the late 1500s, including the Prince of Orange, François de La Nove (de la No).[82] Robert's older brother, Phillip, also ardently Protestant, was tutored by a Mr.

Savill (medieval Hebrew Zavil). He numbered among his friends and associates such men as John Norryes (Noor, Arabic for light), Walter Raleigh and Joachim Camerasi. In the 1570s Philip Sidney attempted to form a unified European Protestant coalition against the Catholic Church and Spain. In the early 1580s he argued for an assault on Spain itself. He is best remembered for his *Defense of Poesy*, a seminal treatise on literature from the Renaissance period. One of his best friends was the occult humanist Giordano Bruni, who helped introduce the Cabala and Egyptian magic in his native Italy. Sidney's last work, left incomplete at his death, was a verse translation of the Psalms.

Robert married Barbara, the daughter of wealthy John Gamage,[83] in 1584. By 1589 he had been named governor of Flushing in the British-held province of Zealand in the Netherlands, where he instituted free-trade channels with England and required his soldiers to follow strict Calvinist religious practices. He became allied, personally and politically, with the House of Orange, especially with Louise de Coligny's son, Count Maurice (medieval Hebrew form of Moses).

The Sidney family was also intimately involved in New World colonization from the 1580s. The Virginia Company, one of their many investments, is described as embodying "the Radical Protestant element's interest in the New World ... all of the company of Sir Thomas Gates, the first governor of Virginia, had served under Prince Maurice of Nassau."[84]

Robert Devereux

The d'Evreux Family came to England with the Norman Conquest.[85] They take their name from Evreux, a town in lower Normandy near Rouen. By the 1570s they were allied with dyed-in-the-wool Protestants in Elizabethan England, marrying into the Knolly, Perrot and Sidney (Sydoney) families. Note the use of Robin for Robert. In 1573, Walter Devereux, now earl of Essex, was dispatched to Ireland to colonize Ulster for England. His wife, Lettice (Leticia, a Roman Jewish name), was described as dark and beautiful, and was the granddaughter of Mary Boleyn.[86] Their son, Robert, exceedingly handsome and a future favorite of Elizabeth I, began attending college in 1579 at Cambridge at age 10, taking both his bachelor's and master's degrees and becoming fluent in Greek and Hebrew. While at Cambridge he became friends

Robert Devereux after Marcus Gheeraerts the Younger (Print Collection, Miriam and Ira D. Wallach Division of Art, Prints and Photographs, The New York Public Library, Astor, Lenox and Tilden Foundations).

with William Meyrick (probably from Hebrew name Meïr). Among the family retainers was Anthony Bagot (another probable Sephardic name).[87]

When his close friend Sir Philip Sidney was killed fighting the Spanish in the Netherlands, Robert married his widow. As historian Robert Lacey naively describes it: "Robert Devereux paid court to [Sidney's] widow, Frances. It was a chivalrous, charmingly medieval conceit linked to the Old Testament tradition of brothers caring for each other's widows. And what were Sidney and Essex, if not brothers-in-arms? ... There seemed no other good reason for such a match. The lady was not wealthy and her father, Sir Francis Walsingham, was very near his end."[88] In our view such a marriage was sanctioned not because it was a quaint custom or conceit but because of the Jewish ancestry of the three parties involved. It satisfied Levirate law, which required a Jewish male, if free, to marry his brother's widow, based on the Torah (Deut. 25:5–10).[89] Countless examples of this type of marriage can be adduced from the family histories of colonial American Jews, as we shall see in due course.

Dr. John Dee

Without the talents of the Elizabethan academician John Dee, a brilliant polymath who claimed to be a magician, England's entry into the New World would assuredly have been second rate. He was born in London in 1527. His father, Roland, was a textile merchant and his mother was Jane Wild. He grew up near Lombard Street, the banking district named for the Italian and Jewish merchants who settled there in the 1100s.[90]

In 1547 John Dee became a professor of Greek at Cambridge, where one of his students was Sir Phillip Sidney. Notably, Dee signed his name only with · , a Greek Delta. The university was in the process of overhauling its curriculum to include, among other subjects, readings in Greek and Arabic mathematics. Much of Dee's research in astronomy, mathematics and engineering was preserved through the efforts of Elias Ashmole (Hebrew or Arabic name), an antiquarian and Freemason whom we will discuss at length when we turn to Freemasonry in Chapter Ten. Dee's work was grounded in Hermetic ideas then in the ascendancy in the Low Countries, which had recently received a rich intellectual infusion from Iberian Conversos and Moriscos following the expulsions of 1492, 1497, 1540 and 1580. In June 1548 Dee moved to the University of Louvain, near Brussels, where he joined fellow Protestant humanists Roger Ascham (named after the Yorkshire village of Askham), Gemma Frisius (Gemma, usually now a feminine name, is Arabic for the name of a star), and Gerard Mercator (i.e., "merchant," the translation for the Hebrew name Jacob), who were constructing surveying and navigational charts of the known world. Ascham wrote *The Schoolmaster*, regulating English grammar for the first time. Also in this brilliant milieu were Abraham Ortelius, an Italian cartographer believed to be a Converso, Pedro Nunez (a Portuguese Converso navigator),[91] John Cheke (Czeck), William Cecil and the Duke of Northumberland. It was a brilliant coterie of international savants if ever there was one.

Dee was deeply involved in the Duke of Northumberland's attempts to place Lady Jane Grey[92] on England's throne, narrowly escaping the reprisals of Queen Mary. Suffering similar loss of their jobs or banishment were Dee's friends John Day (né Diaz), a prominent printer; John Field, a publisher and astronomer; and Sir Thomas Berger, royal accountant and auditor. All were whispered to be part of a "secret Protestant cell" clustered around Princess Elizabeth.[93] Another of these was a John Philpot, archdeacon of Winchester Cathedral (Norman surname, from Greek Phillipos). Philpot spoke and read Hebrew, had studied at Oxford University and traveled to Venice and Padua, both of which cities had robust Converso and Morisco populations. He refused to conduct Mass as long as Mary was England's queen. Ultimately he was burned at the stake. Foxe's *Book of Martyrs* recounts how Queen Mary's prosecutors cruelly imprisoned, tortured, tried and executed Philpot at Smithfield, near London, December 18, 1555. It was a case that might have been taken out of the pages of the Spanish Inquisition.

Dee barely escaped the same fate but survived until Elizabeth ascended to the throne through the help, among others, of Robert Dudley, John Ashley, and Pedro Nunez, the Portuguese Converso mathematician and cosmographer (1502–1578). Once Elizabeth was queen, Dee began to flaunt his cabalistic knowledge. As Elizabethan historian Woolley, perhaps disingenuously, writes, "Dee had taught himself Hebrew [and] acquired Hebrew texts."[94] John Cheke had also advocated being fluent in both Hebrew and Greek. Dee went much deeper and began investigating gematria, the cabalistic sephirot, cryptology and mathematics. By 1563, he was back in Antwerp involved with a secretive group that invited "all lovers of truth ... of whatever nation and religious power they be" to become part of an intellectual brotherhood.[95]

Dee acted as a consultant to Sir Lionel Duckett, lord mayor of London, and Walter Raleigh, helping them oversee tin mines on Raleigh's property in Devonshire. It was his cartographic expertise that enabled the English Muscovy Trading Company to travel the 1,500 miles distance to reach Moscow and secure trade relations with Russian Tsar Ivan the Terrible in 1550. Twenty years later he was collaborating with Martin Frobisher, Michael Lok, and Stephen Borough in a zealous nationalistic campaign to find a Northwest Passage to China.

In 1577 Dee published a remarkable book outlining a plan for building a worldwide British Empire titled, in brief, *General and Rare Memorials*. Its frontispiece displayed Elizabeth I at the helm of a ship. Above her hung "the sun, the moon, the stars, and a glowing sphere bearing the tetragrammaton" (Hebrew anagram for God's name).[96] All these emblems were symbols charged with cabalistic meanings in vogue from the current writings of metaphysician Giordano Bruno and Platonist Pico della Mirandola in Italy. Dee's household had become a popular meeting place for European intellectuals of probable Sephardic or Morisco descent who dabbled in magic: mapmaker Abraham Ortelius, Alexander Simon, known as the Persian Ninevite, lawyer Richard Hakluyt, Simão Fernandez, the Converso navigator for the Roanoke voyages, Sir Humphrey Gilbert, half-brother to Sir Walter Raleigh, and astronomer Thomas Hariot.

Traveling to Bohemia in 1584, Dee was guest at the home of Thaddeus Hajek (Hayek), astronomer and physician to Holy Roman Emperor Rudolf II. Hajek's father was the alchemist Simon Bakalar, who like Thaddeus bears an Arabic surname. The vice chancellor to Emperor Rudolf was Jakob Kurz, a botanist and astronomer. In our view, these royal courtiers, like Dee and several of his English and Dutch associates, were descendants of Converso and Morisco exiles from Iberia.

Sir Richard Grenville

Grenville represents a transitional figure who will take us from England to North American shores. He was a Cornishman whose antecedents can be reliably traced back no further than 1513 in England. The family's name was originally spelled Grenfield in English and Campo Verde in Spanish, the latter being a Sephardic surname. They married into the Courtenay, Arundell (Aaron with theophoric *el* suffix), Vivian ("life," Chaim in Hebrew), St. Aubyn, Gilbert and Bonville ("good house") families.

Richard's father Roger was married to a cousin, Thomasine Cole, near the Tavy (Tau, a Greek letter) and Tamar rivers in Devonshire.[97] Richard himself married Mary St. Leger, whose family was mentioned earlier. Other St. Legers in the same generation took spouses by the name of Stukeley, Bellew and Tremayne.[98] A generation earlier, we find the Grenvilles, Tremaynes, Champerowns and Gilberts multiply intermarried, including Raleighs, forming a tightly-knit, markedly endogamous community in Cornwall.

By 1585 Walter Raleigh had taken up his late half-brother Humphrey Gilbert's charter to colonize North America for the English crown. The effort was strongly supported by Thomas and Richard Hakluyt, who wrote tracts on its behalf, as well as by Thomas Cavendish,[99] Thomas Harriot and Ralph (Rafe, modeled on the Hebrew name Raphael) Lane. As A. L. Rowse describes the venture,

> The little fleet which Grenville commanded consisted of seven sails: the *Tiger* of 140 tons, a flieboat called the *Roebuck* of the same burden, the *Lion* of 100 tons, the *Elizabeth* of 50 tons, and the *Dorothy*, a small bark, with two pinnaces for speedy service. There were aboard a number of gentlemen, mostly young men, who had volunteered to make trial of the new country. There was Ralph Lane, one of the Queen's equerries, whom Grenville appointed to take charge of the colony on his return. Thomas Cavendish, the brilliant young navigator who repeated Drake's exploit of circumnavigating the globe, was another; he was now twenty-five, and it seems to have been his first introduction to the sea. Equally interesting was the presence of Thomas Harriot, who became the foremost scientist and mathematician in England; he was now about the same age as Cavendish, but unlike him he remained a whole year in the new country under Lane's government, and later wrote the *True Report of Virginia*, a document full of close observation and scientific curiosity. Grenville took with him a considerable west-country contingent: there was Philip Amadas, who remained on under Lane as "Admiral of the country"; John Arundell, Grenville's half-brother; his brother-in-law, John Stukeley, a Kendall, one of the Prideaux of Padstow, a Courtenay, Anthony Rowse, the friend and later executor of Drake's will along with others.[100]

Surely an odder group to assemble for a high-risk colonizing expedition across the Atlantic cannot be imagined — unless there was an overriding purpose to their efforts.

Grenville — like Drake, Sidney and Raleigh — participated in the Protestant colonization of Munster Province in Ireland that proceeded hand in hand with England's drive toward the New World. Prior to joining the Irish campaigns he put his estate in order in Cornwall and named as trustees Walter Raleigh, Sir Arthur Bassett, Sir Frances Godolphin, Henry Killegrew, Richard Bellow (Jewish surname), his brother-in-law John Hele (Heale — a Sephardic Melungeon family mentioned earlier), Christopher Harris (in German, Hirsch, the Biblical emblem of the tribe of Naphtali) and John Facey (Fassey, or Fassi, a Sephardic surname meaning "from Fez, Morocco"), leaving his estate, should he die, to his son Bernard. In 1585 his daughter Mary wed her close cousin Arthur Tremayne — a traditional practice for both Sephardim and Moriscos. Accompanying Grenville to Ireland for colonization were "chiefly members of his own family circle. There was his second son, John, and there was his half-brother, John Arundell, who had accompanied him on the Virginia voyage in 1585. Then there were Christopher Harris of Radford, who later married Grenville's daughter Bridget; Thomas Stukeley who may have been brother of the John who went on the 1585 voyage, and was Grenville's brother-in-law; John Bellew, another brother-in-law; John Facey who signed Grenville's family settlement as a witness in 1586."[101]

Grenville played a significant role in repelling the Spanish Armada three years later. He sailed with captains Fenner and Crosse (Cruz, a common Converso surname, as already mentioned) and a cousin, James Erisey. He purchased supplies for that voyage from Harry, John, Richard and Thomas Juell ("jeweler," a Jewish occupation). Finally, in 1589 he was wounded in battle aboard his ship, the *Revenge*. Captured, he died speaking his final words in Spanish, "Here die I [having] fought for country, Queen, religion and honor." After his death, his son Bernard married Elizabeth Beviel "on the edge of the moor overlooking Camel Valley" in Cornwall.[102] The Grenville family changed its name once again in the 1600s to Granville. This became a popular boy's name among crypto–Jewish Appalachian families.

We close this chapter in the hopes that the reader is now willing at least to entertain the possibility that Conversos and Moriscos were not only present and active but also prominent and even dominant in important affairs in England, France and the Netherlands during the 1500s. Their ranks included some of the most notable scientists, soldiers and adventurers of that period. All eyes were now turned on a religious haven on the other side of the world. Even before the present age, America served as a magnet for those who suffered persecution at home. It was in England, with the assistance and vision and talents of Sephardic Jews and their allies among crypto–Jewish British families, that the greatest aspirations were nurtured toward realization of this destiny.

CHAPTER TWO

Sephardim in the New World

What were the origins of Sephardic Jews? Where and when did they form into a coherent community or, as Portuguese Jews in sixteenth century England and the Netherlands expressed it, "nation"? Most historians believe that a small contingent of Hebrews from ancient Judea made their way to the Iberian Peninsula by the time of the rise of Rome. Others propose the nucleus of Sepharad may have come into being there much earlier around the time of the building of the Second Temple in the sixth century BCE.[1] Jews were often fellow travelers with Phoenicians, who occupied parts of Spain in the mid-eighth century BCE. Certainly, Spanish Jewry was well established by Roman times, when Jews constituted a quarter of the population in the East Mediterranean and a tenth in the empire as a whole. These figures mirror the frequencies of male genetic lineage J, a predictor of the distribution of Jews. Judaic scholar Paul Wexler, however, maintains that the majority of Sephardic Jews was of North African Berber origin and converted to Judaism sometime before the 711 CE Arab invasion of the Iberian Peninsula.[2] The word Sephardi itself has been explained as a form of North African Gothic *svart* ("black, dark"), an etymology with roots in the fifth century CE Vandal and Visigothic invasions.

An alternative (or supplementary) theory is that a large number of Sephardic Jews came into existence with a conversion event in southern France 750–900 CE. A proselytizing movement is believed to have been centered on the establishment of a prominent Talmudic academy in Narbonne. Supporting the conversion of Frankish, Burgundian and Languedoc populations to Judaism is the research of Jane Gerber showing that many Sephardic Jews believed themselves to be descendants of King David of Israel. This belief evidently was fostered by the Davidic-descended Babylonian Jews who founded the Narbonne academy, chief among them Machir and his children and grandchildren, who intermarried with the Carolingian and Aquitanian nobility. It was the master of the Narbonne yeshiva, exilarch Machir ben Habibai, also known as Theodoric, count of Septimania, variously referred to by contemporaries as king of the Jews and prince of Narbonne, reputedly of Davidic descent himself, who introduced the tradition when he arrived from Babylon in 771 CE.[3] Thus when these Romano-Frankish and Visigothic and other local countrymen converted to Judaism, they saw themselves as adoptive heirs of the House of David. In a few generations a mythic lineage was remembered as a hereditary claim founded on blood and genealogy. It was passed forward as truth (see Appendix A on the "good name"). In the nineteenth century, Davis was the second best known Jewish name in England, borne by 1 in 32 of donors to Jewish charitable causes, according to Joseph Jacobs' tally for the *Jewish Encyclopedia*.

In a sense, all Jews are converts. Contemporary Jewish studies generally acknowledge that the monotheistic, endogamous Hebrews portrayed in the Bible are largely mythic constructions used to create cosmological coherence and a nationalistic concept of identity across a very diverse landscape of tribes and ethnic groups in the ancient Middle East.[4] It was the rule rather than exception among various settlements of early Jews to backslide into the worship of local pagan cults and deities, especially Astarte/Ashtoreth, consort of the powerful Canaanite god, Baal. Even at the time of the Roman dispersal from Judea, Jews comprised various classes, royal, aristocratic and common, and exhibited wavering degrees of commitment to monotheism and Mosaic law.[5] Furthermore, many had become Hellenized, taking on Greek names, speaking, reading and writing in koiné Greek rather than Hebrew, even adopting Greek customs such as social bathing, going to the theaters and visiting pagan temples.[6]

Not even the most zealous modern-day genealogical efforts have been able to establish a direct, unbroken link to the earliest Israelite or Palestinian rabbis, high priests of the Temple, or for that matter, Biblical patriarchs in remote antiquity. Thus instead of using a norm of authenticity built around a core of founding fathers and mothers, one is perhaps better advised to approach Judaism as an ever-changing, multi-ethnic religion surviving the cataclysms of history by constantly reinventing and reconstituting itself. If historical Jews have gone through occasional bottlenecks and periodic disintegration, they have also experienced periods of triumphal expansion and efflorescence. In these periods of upswing, conversion to Judaism rather than persecution and apostasy was the rule. The Roman world was one such golden age, and early medieval Spain and Southern France another.

Sephardic Genetic Heritage

Paul Wexler in *The Non-Jewish Origins of the Sephardic Jews* makes a persuasive case that today's Sephardic Jews originated primarily in proselytes from North Africa of Berber ethnicity who merged with later converts in Iberia. (We would append "and the South of France.") He demonstrates that a small number of descendants of Judean or Palestinian Jews in North Africa and on the Iberian Peninsula underwent intermarriage with their more populous neighbors of Romance, Berber, Gothic and Arabic origin. He believes that this process took place in three phases:

(a) First, in North Africa in the seventh and early eighth centuries pursuant to the Arab settlement of North Africa.
(b) Then, in the Iberian Peninsula between 711 and 1492 (the respective dates of the Muslim invasion and the expulsion of the Jews from the Kingdom of Spain by the Christian monarchs).
(c) Finally, again in North Africa after 1391 (where Iberian Jews began to settle in large numbers as a result of the nation-wide pogroms against the Jews in the Iberian Peninsula).

Non-Jews played the dominant role in the first period, while in the last two it was the Judaized descendants of Arab, Berber and Iberian converts who were the formative elements.[7]

In accord with this outline of events, and differing only little from it, new DNA studies show that the bulk of male Sephardic Jews came from European backgrounds, especially haplogroups R1b and I, while North African converts (E3b and T) occupy only a minor role in Sephardic ancestry. Various country studies bear this out. These include DNA samples collected in the Canary Islands, the Azores, Cuba, Puerto Rico, Mexico and New Mexico — all recognized sites of Sephardic Anusim ("forced ones") or Crypto-Jews or Conversos. Since these studies include surnames, they open up important insights concerning the names of known Sephardim in the post–Inquisition diaspora.[8] Sephardic surnames are concentrated in the first colonies that Spain and Portugal planted in the Canary Islands, Azores, Madeira, Cuba, Hispaniola and the others.[9] Let us address them one by one.

Canary Islands

The Canaries lie less than a hundred miles off the coast of Africa on the same latitude as the kingdom of Mali south of Morocco. Historically, they served as an important way station for east-west trade channels across the Atlantic. The North Equatorial Current and winds going along with it sweep past the islands on a clockwise course that carries ships to the Antilles in the Caribbean in a little more than a month. This was the same route Columbus took in 1492 and on all subsequent voyages. In fact, the admiral had connections in the Canaries. He had an affair with the lady of Gomera, Dona Ines de Peraza.[10]

The islands originally were settled by the Guanches, a fair-haired, light-skinned people whose history and culture are largely unknown, but who carried mainly matrilineal DNA type U6, a North African or Afro-Asiatic type, although their particular sub-group, U6b1, branched off from the mainline type in remote antiquity and is no longer found in African Berbers. Despite having been invaded by Arabs under the command of Ben-Farroukh around 1000 CE and visited in 1291 by two Genoese galleys, they seem to have preserved their original stock unmixed to the time of the Spanish conquest, which occurred soon after the 1341 landfall of a large group of Portuguese, Italian and Spanish sailors arriving under Angiolina del Tegghis de Corbizz, a Florentine.[11] Some of the Spanish and Portuguese intermarried with local women, so that Guanche mitochondrial DNA survives in their present-day descendants. Ensuing warfare extinguished the native male lines. The primary settlement took place under Juan de Bethencourt. The king of Castile granted him a charter, with the result that colonists were drawn from France and Spain — Juan de Rouille, Juan de Plessis, Gadifer de la Salle and Maciot de Bethencourt among them. The Canaries started out as a crypto–Jewish refuge, similar to the island of Leghorn in Italy, for the bishop designated to provide spiritual guidance to the venture was Alberto de las Cassas, like Bethencourt a Sephardic patronym. From its inception, the community had strong ties to Marrano and other crypto–Jews in southern France and Britain, especially in Plymouth, Bristol and southwestern Scotland.

By the 1500s the new Canarians were numerous enough to provide settlers for Spain's colonies in the New World. The Canaries served as the proving ground for most of the institutions later introduced to the Americas — the plantation economy, an emphasis on cash crops such as sugar cane, slavery, military conquest and the extermination of native peoples under the pretext of conversion.[12] After prospering in the Canaries, several families moved on to Hispaniola, Cuba, Puerto Rico and Saint Augustine. Over 4,000 Canarians ventured to Louisiana in 1778. They also settled in Venezuela, Guatemala, Nicaragua and Paraguay. Many of these Canary Island descendants now claim Sephardic ancestry.

Y chromosome scores from the Canary Islands DNA project at Family Tree DNA, a commercial genetic genealogy company with public project pages, display a set of lineages consistent with a Moorish-Iberian heritage. The two primary ones are haplogroup R1b (56 percent) and E3b (18 percent), followed distantly by G and I. There is also a small amount of T, which may be Phoenician, as about 10 percent of the ancient Phoenician port of Cadiz belongs to that lineage. Unusual are two O3 East Asian males, surnamed Yan and San, probably recent additions from the days of Spain and Portugal's far-flung world empires. The presence of Sephardic surnames such as Benetez, Diaz, Durant, Gersone, Hernandez, Nunez, Perez, Rodriguez and Torres corroborates a significant measure of Jewish descent.[13] A much larger study confirms a strong Jewish presence on the island based on a disproportionate amount of J lineages.

Canary Island Surnames

Surname	Haplogroup	Surname	Haplogroup
Aquino	R1b	Martinez	E3b
Arbelo	I	Morales	G2
Bellot	R1b	Nunez	R1b, I
Chao	R1b	Pena	R1b
Delgado	E3b, R1b	Perez	R1b, I, G, E3b
Diaz	R1b	Ramirez	T
Durant	R1b	Ramos	R1b
Gershoni	E3b	Rodriguez	R1b
Gomez	G	Roque	R1b
Hernandez	E3b, R1b	Rosales	R1b
Lopez	R1b	Santana	R1b
Lujan	E3b	Socarraz	R1b
		Torres	R1b

Azores

The Azores are situated northwest of the Canary Islands, where the easterly North Atlantic Current turns about and becomes the Canaries Current. They are an ideal return harbor and restocking point for North Atlantic trade vessels. Unlike the Canaries, they were uninhabited when the Portuguese arrived in the 1400s — perhaps owing to the inhospitable, volcanic nature of their creation. They were colonized first in 1439 by people drawn from the Spanish provinces of Algarve and Alentejo.[14] In the following centuries, settlers from other European countries arrived, most notably from Northern France and Flanders. The islands became home to several ecclesiastical seminaries and were placed under the governance of the hereditary counts of Villa Franca, who were descended from Rui Gonçales de Camara (died 1522). Most of the inhabitants made their living as farmers, fishermen and merchants. In the 1700s the economy turned to the production of citrus, especially oranges (sadly, in 1890 these groves were destroyed by parasites). The Azores also had a lucrative cloth-dying trade with Britain during the 1600s.

British factors with whom the Azores traded in colonial times include John Ellis (Hebrew Elias), Richard Langford, Thomas Prevost (a Templar name), William Ray (Reyes, Spanish for king) and Henry Walker. In 1640 the British traders were represented by Matthew Godwin, Philip Palgrave and Christopher Williams, and in 1669 we find the names of John and William Chamberlin together with John Stone — all gentlemen said to be "very

Portuguese [that is, Jewish] in manner, with Portuguese wives."[15] There are also French traders: Christophe and Jean Bressan and Bernard Fartoat (Arabic: Phartouat).[16] Several Huguenot businessmen based in La Rochelle had interests in the Azores, including the Marrano Labat family[17] who helped settle French Canada, Louis de la Ronde, Hermigo Nolette and Antoine Sieuvre. One Abram Vogullar (Vogeler, Vogelier "seller of birds," Ashkenazi[18]) served as combined Swedish, Danish, Dutch, Hamburg and Spanish consul.

The Azores have been documented as having a significant Converso population, although the first phase of Jewish influence is usually glossed over. All but one of the surnames included in the Azores project examined here were judged to be probably Sephardic. Some of the names we can point to with certainty as Sephardic are Borges, Bethencourt, Pereira, Pires, de Melle, de Sousa,[19] Fernandes, Olivera, Magellan, Jacome, Rosa,[20] Silveira da Rosa, Periera da Rosa, Machado, Braz de Costa Loureiro, de Freitas[21] and Tavares. As for DNA, R1b is the primary male haplogroup, as in the Canaries. A larger study without surnames produced a similar genetic profile in which R1b accounts for more than half of male clans. Interestingly, Middle Eastern Semitic type J is the second most common lineage in this study, with more than twice the frequency of mainland Portugal. These findings strengthen the supposition that there was a significant Sephardic-Moorish presence on the islands.

"I am the last Jew in all of the Azores," Jorge Delmar told a travel reporter in 2010. "Thirty years ago, there were sixteen Jewish families on this island," Delmar said. The import-export businessman said the Azores used to have a community of Jews who held "services in the old synagogue and made all the festivities in my grandfather's house." All the others, he said, have died, converted or moved away. He is the only one left. His one-man history of the Jewish Azores starts with the Bensaudes, "who had the trade connections that enabled them to link England, Brazil and Newfoundland with the Azores," and names Luna Benarus, a luxury innkeeper on the island of Faial who maintains her father and grandfather's siddurs, haggadahs and other mementos of a Jewish past in an antique oak cabinet.[22]

We are not aware of any DNA surname data for the Madeiras. These are the closest of all the Atlantic islands to Portugal and were first settled in 1419 before the Spanish and Portuguese Inquisitions and expulsion of Jews from Iberia. According to Mordecai Arbell, author of *The Jewish Nation of the Caribbean*, they figure later as an important haven for Sephardim and serve as a natural stepping stone to the Americas. At first, the new settlers were primarily petty criminals, but under Manuel I, New Christians or Conversos began to pour into the colony. By the end of the sixteenth century, however, after various attacks by the local bishop and rectors of the Jesuit college at Funchal, Jews forsook the islands for Amsterdam and Brazil. The famous rabbi Menasseh Ben Israel was probably born in the Madeira archipelago. It was here that the planting of sugarcane was first perfected, along with sugar refining. When the Jews who pioneered these processes moved on to Brazil at the invitation of the Portuguese governor Duarte Coelho Pereira, their expertise went with them.

Cuba

Columbus arrived in Cuba on his first voyage in 1492 and found three different native peoples dwelling there, Tainos, Ciboneys[23] and Guanajatabeyes. Estimates of the indigenous population at that time range from 50,000 to 300,000. Over the next seven decades most of the original inhabitants died out due to virulent epidemics and the unstinting warfare brought on by the incoming Europeans. The first Spanish settlement was established in 1511 by Diego Velazquez, who served as governor until 1524. Cuba's early population was quite mixed, consisting of 7,000 persons in 1544, of whom 600 were Spanish, 800 were African slaves and the remainder Indians and mulattos.[24] The primary economic activity at first was shipbuilding. By the early 1700s, the focus had shifted to tobacco, with sugarcane plantations and cattle ranches also remaining prominent.

A large-scale population disruption occurred in 1762 when British forces attacked and occupied Havana, one of the major cities of New Spain. The island's governor, Juan de Prado, most of the Spanish administrators and the *peninsulares* fled en masse. After eleven months of British rule, which opened the island to trade with North America and England, Cuba was ceded back to Spain in exchange for Florida. Subsequently the slave population of Cuba increased dramatically, growing to 44,000 by 1774. By 1791 (at which time Florida was again in Spanish hands), the number of slaves had reached 84,000, most of them being employed in sugarcane. That same year, a slave rebellion on Santo Domingo (Haiti, Hispaniola) caused many French sugar planters to flee to Cuba. Among the major sugar magnates at the time were Francisco de Arronga, Conde de Casa Montalvo[25] and José Richardo O-Farrill (an Irishman).

Cuban DNA shows that the classic European component of the population is even higher than in the Canary Islands and Azores, comprising nearly three-quarters of all males, providing additional support for the proposal that the characteristic Sephardic Jewish lineage is R1b, not J. Surnames echo those of the Canaries and Azores. Among those carried by Converso or Morisco families are: Cruz (Cross), Perez, Banos (Jewish and Moorish, depending on the branch), Betancourt, Reyes (Royal), Almora ("the Moor"), Batista (Baptist, John the), Carballo,[26] Carillo, Corea, Diaz, Duarte, Elizondo, Farinas, Ferro (blacksmith, a Jewish-dominated craft), Galvez, Garcia, Gusman,[27] Maria, Martin, Moreira (Moor), Morena, Ortega, Romero, Salvador (Savior), Sanchez (perhaps originally the same as Cohen, "priest, holy man"), Sardinas (from Sardinia), Valdez and Villareal (Royal House).

Cuban Surnames. Family Tree DNA, *www.familytreedna.com.*

Albuerne	Borrego	Diaz	Gonzalez (Etor)	Marin[31]
Almora	Bruno	Duarte[29]	Govantes	Martin
Alvarez	Caballero	Echazabal	Guerra	Maruga
Alvarez-Perez	Cadalso	Echemendia	Guerrero	Masias
Anastoa	Caneras	Elizondo	Gusman	Mihica
Archuela	Caraballo	Esquivel	Hernandez	Montano
Areces	Caraballosa	Estopinao	Herrera	Monzon
Argete	Carballo	Farinas	Ibanez[30]	Moreira
Arteaga	Carballosa	Fernandez	Izquierdo	Morena
Avila[28]	Caullo	Ferrales	Lauzenique	Morgado
Bacallao	Correa	Ferro	Lazo de la Vega	Morillo
Ballerilla	Crepo	Fundora	Leiva/Leyva	Nido
Banio	Cruz	Galas	Lima	Pena
Banos	de la Llata	Galvez	Liz	Pena y de Borbon
Batista	del Pino y Tous	Garcia	Llanes	Perdomo
Bayares	del Pozo	Garcia de Oranos	Lopez	Perez
Betancourt	Desdia	Gasque	Lugo	Perez (Martinez)
Blanco	Deulopeu	Gavira	Marcello	Peroy

Portuondo	Riviera	Salas[32]	Suarez	Vasquez[33]
Prieto	Rodriguez	Salvador	Tascoa	Vejarano
Pruna	Romero	San Jorge	Tellez	Velasco
Pupo	Rotxes	Sanchez	Temprano	Villaria
Ramirez	Rubio	Sanchez-Pereira	Torre	Villareal[34]
Reyes	Ruiz	Sancibrian	Uria(s)	
Ricardo de	Saa	Sardinas	Valdez	
Aldana	Saavedia	Socarraz	Valera	

Puerto Rico

Puerto Rico is located in the Caribbean Sea not far from Cuba, Jamaica and Hispaniola. The island was settled by indigenous peoples of the Archaic culture of the West Indies in the first century CE, or earlier. Around 120 CE, a second group of natives representing the Arawak culture reached the island, perhaps from South America. By 1000 CE, Tainos established themselves on Puerto Rico. They had a well-developed language and civilization, as well as advanced agricultural practices. Europeans came to Puerto Rico in 1493 with the second voyage of Columbus, and in 1508 Juan Ponce de Léon founded the first permanent settlement. Natives were forced into servitude or hunted down and killed, resulting in a devastating collapse of the local population and culture.[35] As in other colonies, it was the native men and their male lineages that bore the brunt of this. DNA samples collected on the island clearly show that Taino ancestry survives through the female line, whereas male lines go the way of the Canaries and other conquered lands. Puerto Rico was a favorite place for the Spanish to send native slaves captured in the Carolinas. Many of these Indians escaped into the hills and their descendants remain there today. The Puerto Rican indigenous haplotype pattern is especially diverse.

Owing to its central location, Puerto Rico was subjected to repeated depredations by French, English and Portuguese privateers. A fort was built by the Spanish settlers from 1530 to 1540 to defend the island. Spanish officials on the island during the late 1500s included the following: Menendez de Valdes, Pedro Suarez, Pedro Tello de Guzman, Pardo de Osorio,[36] Antonio Calderon,[37] Antonio Mosquero and Juan de Haro. These surnames further suggest that the island was a Sephardic (and Moorish) community; Mosquera, for example, is clearly Islamic.[38] Settlers on Puerto Rico were mainly drawn from Castile, with some "Italians, Portuguese and Flemish."[39] Were some of these friends or relatives of Spanish Jews? By the late 1500s Canary Islanders and additional Portuguese settlers had arrived. In 1683, 200 more Canarian families came to Puerto Rico, followed by another three hundred in 1691. These arrivals shifted the overall population of the island toward a Canarian profile, as several of the original Castilian families had moved to colonies on the mainland of the Americas or died from epidemics that periodically swept the island.

Puerto Rico DNA is enlightening in that it includes sixteen instances of male African descent, but again, the most common haplotype is R1b, evidenced in one-half the population. Next come I, J and E3b. The relatively high level of Semitic–North African lineages, coupled with R1b and I, suggests Puerto Rico was made up primarily of a Sephardic and Moorish population, in other words earlier and later converts to Judaism or Islam.

The surnames in the Puerto Rico sample are strongly suggestive of Converso-Morisco backgrounds: Bautista, Benitez, Bernal, Betancourt, Borges, Candelaria,[40] Carrero, Casillas, Castellano, Castello, Colon, Cordova, Correa, Cruz, de Gracia, de Jesus, de la Reyes, Dias,

Espinosa, Febus (Phoebus, Pharabus, Forbes),[41] Ferrer, Flores, Garcia, Guzman, Jimenez, Leon, Lopez, Marrero, Maysonet (French Maisonett), Medina (Arabic), Mendez, Miranda, Muniz,[42] Navarro, Nieves, Oliveras, Olmeda, Ortega, Padilla, Pardo, Perez, Reyes, Robes, Romero, Rossy, Santiago, Santos, Vega, Yanez and Zayas.

Puerto Rico Surnames. Family Tree DNA, *www.familytreedna.com.*

Adorno	Cardona	Espinosa	Montes	Rangel[50]
Agosto	Carrero	Febus	Montesinos[45]	Reyes
Aguiar	Cartagena	Feliciano	Moyi (Irsi)	Robles
Albadalyo	Casillas	Fernandez	Mulero	Roig
Alicia	Castaner	Ferrer	Muniz	Rolon
Alvadalijo	Castello	Flores	Munoz	Romero
Alvarado	Castillieno	Fontan	Muriel	Rosa
Alvarez	Chevires	Fontanes	Narvaez	Rosado
Ambel	Clas	Garcia	Natal	Rosario
Ambert	Cofresi	Gerena	Navarro	Rossy
Aponte	Colberg	Gil[43]	Navedo	Ruiz
Aranda	Collazo	Gines	Negrin	Rus
Arbelo	Colon	Gomez	Negron	Saavedia
Arce	Colon de Bonilla	Gonzalez	Neris	Salazar
Archilla	Colon de Torres	Grana	Nevarez	Saliedo
Arellano	Cordero	Guilarte	Nieves	Saldana
Arroyo	Cordova	Guillen	Ocasio	Salgado
Arvela	Correa	Guzman	Ojeda	Sanchez
Avila	Cortes	Hernandez	Olivares	Santana
Aviles	Crespo	Hidalgo	Oliver	Santiago
Ayala	Cruz	Hinojosa	Oliveras[46]	Santos
Ayes	Cruzado	Huertas	Olmeda (O)	Senano
Badalejo	Cuesta	Irizany	Oquendo	Sepulveda
Balasquisle	Cuevas	Jimenez	Orozco	Sierra
Ballistie	Davila	Lauriano	Ortega	Solis
Batista/Bautista	de Castro	Lebron	Ortiz	Solla
Beltran	de Gracia	Leon	Otero	Soto[51]
Benitez	de Jesus	Longrais	Pabon	Sotomayor
Bermudez	de la Cruz	Lopez	Pacheco[47]	Tirado
Bernal	de la Luz	Lugo	Padilla	Toledo
Betancourt	de la Pena	Maldonado	Padro	Torres
Bonilla	de la Reyes	Marrero	Pantoja (J)[48]	Ubarri
Borges	de la Rios	Martin	Pardo	Valentin
Borrero	de la Rosa	Martinez	Pedrosa	Vallejo
Bragante	de la Torre	Matos	Pena	Vazquez
Brau	del Castillo	Maysonet	Peralta	Vega
Bravo	Delgado	Medina	Peraza	Velasco
Brigantti	de los Santos	Mejias	Perez	Valazquez
Brito	del Rosario	Mendez	Pinero	Valez
Burgos	del Valle	Mendoza	Pinzon	Vera
Burset	De Rio	Menendez	Ponce	Viera
Camacho	De Toro	Mirabal[44]	Quinones	Villafane
Camino	Diaz	Miranda	Quirindoago	von Kupferstein
Camunas	Diclet	Moctezuma	Ramirez[49]	(Ashkenazic)
Candelaria	Dominguez	Montalvo	Ramos	
Caraballo	Esko	Montarez	Ramos Colon	

Mexico

It is customary to speak of Mexico, whose ancient name is Anahuac, as the home of indigenous empires, and with good reason. The Aztec or Mexica who lent their name to the modern country that emerged were only the last of a long succession of civilizations beginning with the Olmec and continuing through the Izapa, Teotihuacan, Maya, Zapotec, Chichimeca, Toltec, Mixtec, Huaxtec and Purepecha. All of these peoples lived a settled existence in urban centers. The conquistador Hernan Cortes and his small force of Spaniards arrived in 1521. Due to plagues and epidemics, as well as warfare, the native population of the Valley of Mexico was reduced from eight million to less than half that number in a few short years. During the 300-year colonial period that followed there emerged a distinctive new *mestizo* (mixed) class of people born of Spanish fathers and Mexican mothers. Thousands of African slaves were imported to work in the mines, ranches and encomiendas. With Mexico City as its capital, this extremely diversified land called New Spain stretched from the Rio Arriba and Rio Abajo of present-day New Mexico to Costa Rica and included all the Spanish Caribbean islands and Florida as well. Spain's South American possessions were called New Granada. They fall outside our scope.

In 1571 King Philip II instituted an Inquisition tribunal for all of New Spain seated in Mexico City. Its purpose was "to free the land which has become contaminated by Jews and heretics, especially the Portuguese nation"— eloquent testimony that Mexico and the surrounding countries were havens for crypto–Jews. The Mexican Genealogy and DNA Project with a large sample size yields results that mirror the haplogroup profile seen in the other studies we have glanced at. Once again, R1b (Atlantic Coast European) was predominant (56 percent), followed by I at 12 percent, E3b (North African) at 12 percent, J2 (Mediterranean) at 9 percent, and J1 (Semitic) at 1.5 percent. Haplogroup G (Central Asian, often also Jewish), was present in Mexico at 5 percent. Also reported in small frequencies were T (believed to come from Phoenicians), R1a1 (East European, common among Ashkenazi Jews) and O (East Asian). Repetition of both the rankings and relative percentages of the major lineages lends support to the proposition that such a profile reflects an ancestral Sephardic Jewish population.

All of the Mexican study participants carry Hispanic surnames. Most of these are Sephardic and we have seen them in the other studies discussed so far: Acosta, Arebalo, Arriola, Ascensio, Campos, Cervantes, Chacon, Correa, Diaz, Elyondo, Flores, Gallegos, Garcia, Herrera, Leal, Leon, Loera, Mares, Mastinez, Miranda, Moreno, Nunez, Olivas, Palacios, Pena, Ramirez, Rivera, Rodriguez, Romero, Salas, Sanchez, Soto, Tarin, Trevino, Vidal, Villareal, Yanez, Ybarra.

Mexico Surnames with Haplogroup Assignments.
Mexico Genealogy and DNA Project.

Aburto	J2a1	Arredondo	E3b	Canales	G	Diaz	Q3
Acosta	R1b	Arrida	E3b	Canales	R1b	Elizondo	Q
Alderete	R1b	Arriola	R1b	Cano	G2	Escalante	R1b
Aquihaga	Q	Ascensio	Q3	Cano	R1b	Felguerez	T
Aquinaga	E3b	Avila	E3b2	Carral	R1a1	Felix	I1c
Mares	R1b	Bejarano	Q3	Cervantes	R1b	Felix	J2
Aranzazu	E3b	Botello	Q	Chacon	E3b2	Fernandez	R1b
Arebalo	I1c	Burquez	O3	Chapa	R1b	Fernandez	G2
Armijo	R1b	Campos	R1b	Correa	I1c	Flores	E3b

Name		Name		Name		Name	
Flores	R1b	Hinojosa	I1b2	Ochoa	R1b	Salinas	I1c
Galarza	I1c	Holguin	R1b	Ochoa	E3b	Salinas	R1b
Gallardo	R1b	Huante	E3a	Olivas	R1b	Sanchez	R1b
Gallegos	R1b	Jimenez	O	Olivas	E3b	Serda	R1b
Garcia	I1b2	Leal	R1b	Ortiz	J2	Serros	R1b1
Garcia	I1c	Leal	G2	Pacheco	R1b	Solis	R1b
Garcia	J1	Leon	R1b	Palacios	Q3	Sotelo	R1b
Garcia	T	Loera	Q3	Pena	I1b2	Soto	G2
Garza	R1b	Lopez	J2	Pinedo	R1b	Suarez	Q
Garza	I1c	Lopez	R1b	Puetes	R1b	Tarin	R1b1
Gomez	J2	Lozano	R1b	Quiroz	E3b	Tarin-Segura	G2
Gomez	R1b1	Madden	E3b2	Ramirez	Q3	Terrazas	R1b
Gonzalez	J2	Martinez	R1b	Ramirez	R1b	Trevino	R1b
Gonzalez	I1b2	Martinez	G2	Ramos	R1b	Trevino	J2
Gonzalez	E3b	Medrano	J2	Rivera	R1b	Valdez	R1b
Gonzalez	E3b2	Miranda	I1b	Rocha	Q3	Venegas	I1c
Guajardo	J2f1	Montes	Q	Rodarte	Q3	Vidal	R1b
Guajardo	J2	Moreno	Q3	Rodriquez	R1b	Villareal	E3b
Guerra	R1b	Moreno	J2	Romero	J2	Villareal	R1b
Hernandez	E3b	Moreno	R1b	Rosales	R1b	Yanez	R1b
Hernandez	Q3	Navarro	R1b	Ruiz	R1b1	Ybarra	R1b
Herrera	R1b	Nunez	R1b	Salas	R1b		

New Mexico

The story of Jews in New Mexico begins with the establishment of the New Kingdom of Léon, a large territory embracing most of present-day Tampico, Chihuahua, Nuevo Léon, Texas, Arizona, California and New Mexico. King Philip II gave the right to colonize this vast area to a New Christian, Don Luis de Carvajal. His ten-year governorship ended when the Mexican Inquisition learned that many of Carvajal's colonizers were crypto–Jews. Among the earliest settlers, first in Tampico, then in Mexico City, were Carvajal's sister, Doña Francisca; her husband, Don Francisco Rodriguez de Matos (purportedly a rabbi); and their numerous children, including Carvajal's namesake and successor, young Luis. Most of the Carvajal and Rodriguez family were prosecuted by the Inquisition, and many were burned at the stake in auto-da-fés. Still, some of the Mexico City Converso community managed to move to New Mexico as soon as settlement there was organized in 1598, reorganized in 1610, and once more after the Pueblo Revolt of 1680. Bernardo Lopez de Mendizaval was governor of New Mexico from 1659 to 1661 before being removed and sent back to Mexico City to answer charges of Judaizing or openly returning to Judaism. One of his soldiers, Francisco Gomez Robledo, was also summoned before the Inquisition.[52]

Many, if not the vast majority, of the families studied in Angelico Chavez' compendium of New Mexico genealogies were originally crypto–Jewish.[53] In fact, it is said that there are only about twelve original families. Their coats of arms are still displayed on the steps of the governor's palace in Santa Fe during Spanish Market. All are intermarried in ways that are the despair of genealogists and real estate lawyers. The names are Baca, Chavez, Cruz, Duran, Garcia, Jimenez, Lopez, Lucero, Luna, Martinez, Trujillo, Sanchez and Vigil.[54]

Presumably the New Mexico DNA project should contain a higher percentage of Jewish ancestry than that of Mexico, since it is believed that more openly Jewish Conversos migrated northward from Mexico to distance themselves from the Inquisition.[55] The DNA evidence for such a supposition is equivocal, however. The R1b (Atlantic Coast haplogroup) proportion remains virtually unchanged at 56 percent. The East Mediterranean or Semitic percentage (J) rises to 18 percent, although not significantly different from the distributions found in Mexico. E3b (North African) declines somewhat, as does also G, effectively counterbalancing the increase in J as far as Semitic/Mediterranean ancestry is concerned. I haplogroups decline also in New Mexico.

New Mexico Surnames with Haplogroup Assignments.
New Mexico DNA Project.

Abeyta	R1b	Gallegos	I	Lujan	E3b	Ramirez	E3b
Anaya	R1b	Galvan	R1b	Luna	R1b	Read	R1b
Apodaca	R1b	Gaona	I	Madrid	J2	Rincon	R1b
Aquilar56	Q	Garcia	Q	Madrid	E3b	Rivera	R1b
Aragon	R1b	Garcia de Jurado	J	Maldonado	R1b	Rivera	J
Archibeque	R1b	Garcia de Noriega	R1b	Maldonado	E3b	Rodriguez	R1b
Archuleta	E3b	Saiz	R1b	Manchego	R1b	Rodriguez	I
Armijo	R1b	Gavitt	E3b	Marcilla	E3b	Romero	R1b
Arrey	J2	Gonazlez	Q	Mares	R1b	Romero	G2
Ayala	R1b	Gonzalez Bernal	J2	Marquez	R1b	Romero	J2
Baca	R1b	Sancez	Q3	Martin Serrano	R1b	Romero	Q3
Baca	I	Griego	G2	Martinez	R1b	Romero	Q
Barreras	R1b	Guajardo	J2f1	Martinez	J2	Romero Robledo	R1b
Bejarano	Q3	Guajardo	J2	Martinez	J1	Ronguillo	O3
Brito	R1b	Guerra	R1b	Mirabal	R1b	Salazar	J
Bustamante	R1b	Gutierrez	I	Mandragon	J2	Sanchez de Inigo	J
Campos	R1b	Gutierrez	J2	Montano	J	Sandoval	R1b
Carrasco	R1b	Guzman	Q	Montoya	R1b	Santistevan	I
Casaus	I	Sena	J	Morga	R1b	Santistevan	Q3
Castillo	R1b	Serna	G2	Murchison	R1b	Sedillo	J2
Cervantes	R1b	Serna	Q	Olivas	E3b	Tafoya	T
Chavez	I	Silva	R1b	Olivas	R1b	Tenorio	J
Chavez	R1b	Hernandez	E3b	Ortega	R1b	Torres	R1b
Cisneros	R1b	Hernandez	R1b	Ortiz	J2	Torres	I1b
Coca	R1b	Herrera	R1b	Ortiz	R1b	Trujillo	J2
Coca	J2	Herrera	C3	Ortiz	E3b	Valdez	R1b
Contreras	Q	Hidalgo	R1b	Otero	R1b	Valdez	E3b
Cordoba	J2	Hill	R1b	Pacheco	R1b	Valencia	R1b
Curtis	R1b	Jardine	R1b	Padilla	R1b	Varela	R1b
Deaguero	J2	Kirker	R1b	Pena	I1b	Velasquez	Q
Delgado	R1b	La Badie	I1b	Peralta	I	Vergara	R1b
Dominguez	R1b	Lara	R1b	Perea	J2	Vigil	R1b
Duran	R1b	Leal	R1b	Pittel	R1b	Villescas	G2
Esquibel	R1b	Lopez	I	Quintana	R1b		
Flores	Q3	Lucera de Godoy	R1b	Quiros	E3b		
Flores	R1b	Lucero	Q	Rael de Aguilar	R1b		

The mention of the name Luna brings us full circle to the conversion event in southern France mentioned at the beginning of this chapter. The de Luna family can be traced to a French nobleman named Bon de Lunel from a town in the kingdom of Septimania near Narbonne.[57] Bon ("Good") received his name from the fact that his pedigree, like all Nesim (Hebrew princes), was believed to go directly back to King David (Appendix A on the "good name"). Our Luna's R1b haplotype is consistent with proposals that the convert Jews of Septimania were of European, specifically western European, origin, although they believed themselves to be of Davidic, hence Middle Eastern, descent. Other forms of the "good" surname are Shem Tov (Hebrew), Kalonymus (a line of rulers of Narbonne in the tenth century), Bonet, Bennetton (Italian), Kalman (German), Boone/Bohun/Bo(w)en (Dutch, as in Daniel Boone), Good or Goode or Goad (English, intermarried with Boones in Tennessee) and Buen (Spanish).

Melungeon and Cumberland Gap Projects

Spain also planted colonies in Florida and the Carolinas. As many have previously noticed, Sephardic DNA profiles and surnames are still evident in the population of the lower Appalachian Mountains, notably among Melungeons, a dark-skinned European ethnic group mixed with American Indians and Africans found dwelling there when the first English settlers crossed the Blue Ridge into Cherokee territory in the 1600s. Melungeon Y-chromosome data invoke the Cuban pattern with R1b again far outstripping all the other haplogroups. Several J and E3b participants have Ashkenazi Jewish matches, while a number of R1b males have matches in South and Central America and the Caribbean, all suggesting Sephardic ancestry. Selected surnames from the authors' project appear below.

The much larger Cumberland Gap Y chromosome data echo these results and indicate that both Appalachian populations (which overlap to some degree) incorporate a combination of Sephardic and Ashkenazic Jewish ancestry. Melungeon mitochondrial (female lineage) figures lend support to this hypothesis and show that the first Melungeons tend to be families and couples, not solitary, scattered shipwrecked Portuguese sailors, as has sometimes been suggested. In sum, Melungeon DNA is similar to Latin American with the exception of a heavy Scots-Irish component.[58]

Melungeon Surnames and Y Chromosome Types

Surname	Type	Notes on Jewish connections
Adair	J2	Probably the same as Dare, either from Hebrew Adar or Darius
Adkins	R1b	"One from Aix/Aachen"
Alexander	R1b	Scottish clan name, from Alexander the Great, hero to Jews
Austin	E3a	Sub-Saharan-African type, perhaps from times of Roman occupation
Baggett	I1a	Arabic surname
Blevins	E3b1	Ashkenazi Jewish
Boone	R1b	Davidic "good name" like Buen, Bon
Brown	R1b	Border Country clan, common American Jewish surname
Bunch	E3a	Sub-Saharan African type
Caldwell	R1b	From Ashkenazic place-name Kahlwil, matches Wallen, Rodriguez
Campbell	R1a	Y Chromosomal Levi, Ashkenazi Modal Haplotype
Carter	R1b	Compare Cartier, "transporter, wheelwright"
Caudill	R1b	Rare, matches only other Caudills, Israel
Chaffin	I1a	Probably from Cohen, matches Ortiz, Klein, Goodheart, Marrero, Canary Is.
Christy	R1b	Puerto Rico, 24 marker match with Cuban, Chile, 23/25 match with Azores
Collins	E3a	Sub-Saharan African type
Cooper	R1b	Hebrew form of Jacob, meaning "merchant," Ashkenazi matches
Cowan	R1a/b	I.e., Cohen, Scottish clan, two septs
Flores	R1b	Sephardic name, haplotype Portuguese, family claimed to be Huguenot

Surname	Type	Notes on Jewish connections
Forbes	R1b	Scottish clan, compare Sephardic surname Febos
Givens	R1b	Rare, matches Munoz, Parish, Massey, Macedonia
Good	R1b	Davidic "good name," family from Cornwall, recently practiced Judaism
Goins	E3a	Sub-Saharan African type
Gordon	J2	Scottish clan, name a corruption of Cohen, matched Russian Jews
Hale	I1b	Rare Balkan Jewish type, matches only other Hales
Houston	R1b	25/25 match with Samuel Houston, 12/12 with Africa, Cuba, etc.
Kennedy	R1b	From Khan-a-dey "place of the Khan," cf. Candia, Candiano, Canada, Candy
Leslie	R1b	Scottish clan, from Hungarian Ladislaus, matches in Africa, Morocco, Chile
Looney	I1a	Sephardic name Luna, Hebrew Yareakh "moon," matches Isle of Man
McAbee	I	Scottish name similar to McBeth, from Maccabeus (Mi chamocha baeilim)
Moore	G	Rare, matches Hammar, Wilde
Morgan	B	Welsh name, Sub-Saharan African DNA type, perhaps from Roman times
Morrison	I1b	SNP tested, Balkan Jewish type
Newberry	I1a	Danish and Norman family, rare, matches in Canary Islands
Ney	E3b	Ashkenazi, matches Deutch, Gelley, Cantor, Raphelly, Shapiro, Levy
Perry	G	Compare Perez, Peres, Peirara, 23/25 match with Canter in South America
Powers	R1b	Close to Wallen, Hale, Houston, Payne ("payin"), Ozmet (Arabic name)
Saylor	R1b	Atlantic Modal Haplotype
Sizemore	Q3	From Hebrew Sismai (?), American Indian DNA type alongside R1b
Stewart	R1b	Scottish clan, originally Norman, means "keeper of the kingdom"
Talley	I	Hebrew name
Tankersley	I or T	Extremely rare, no matches
Wallen	R1b	"Foreigner," matches in Azores, Rezente, Schaefer, Ven, Talley, Nagle, Kranz
Wampler	R1b	R1b, matches Hernandez, Zimmerman
Wolf	E3b1	Ashkenazi Jewish
Yates	R1b	Close to Atlantic Modal Haplotype, center Northern Portugal, Ashkenazi name

Haplogroup	Canary Islands	Azores	Cuba	Puerto Rico	Mexico	New Mexico	Cumberland Gap	Melungeon
R1b	56	62	73	49	56	56	64	49
E3b	18	0	9	12	12	10	4	6
I	9	31	9	13	12	8	17	17
J	0	0	2	12	12	18	5	4
G	9	8	2	5	5	3	3	4
Other	9	0	0	9	2	1	7	19

Some significant genetic consistencies emerge from these studies. Across the board R1b is the overwhelming type, with an average representation approaching 60 percent. R1b is the bedrock male DNA of Western Europe, centered in Spain. If the core Sephardic Jewish population of Spain came from North Africa, as proposed by Wexler, one would not expect it to dominate. It is the most common male type in modern-day Europe, accounting for approximately 40 percent of all European males, with a cline of distribution that reaches its height in Ireland and shades off as one goes eastward. J. F. Wilson and his team call it the Atlantic Modal Haplotype.[59] Its ubiquity suggests large-scale conversions of locally persisting populations in the Middle Ages as the genesis of Spanish Jewry rather than intrusions of Middle Easterners or North Africans. To be sure, E3b, G and I are also represented among these communities of New World Sephardim, as are J haplogroups as well as T and R1a1. But given the pattern, it appears that the majority of Sephardim relocating to New World communities were descendants of converts drawn from the southwestern Atlantic and western Mediterranean regions of what are present-day France, Spain and Portugal, and that only a small minority were of Semitic ancestry. Interestingly, those proving to have Semitic DNA do not necessarily bear Hebrew, Arabic or Berber surnames, while those demonstrably carrying European DNA often do have such surnames. One can only conclude that Middle Eastern, or Semitic, roots did not carry a compelling cachet among Sephardic Jews, nor did the authorities distinguish such an ethnicity in their attempt to eradicate Jewish blood from Catholic realms. Only modern "scientific" or nationalistic definitions of Jewish have made Middle Eastern genes pertinent — or problematical, since Middle Eastern Jewish and Palestinian DNA are indistinguishable.

In general, the genetic profile of New World Sephardim closely resembles that of modern Spain. We believe it is likely that what has come to be viewed as quintessentially Jewish DNA was introduced by Hebrew males carrying the J haplogroup out of the Middle East who spread it to various parts of the Greek and Roman Empires. These Semitic-haplogroup-bearing males seem to have served as stimuli for establishing Jewish faith and practices in distant lands and were joined by non–Semitic-haplotype-bearing males whose descendants now compose the majority of both Sephardic and Ashkenazic Jewry.

Autosomal DNA Findings

Autosomal DNA tests examine markers scattered across a person's entire genome, not just those located on the sex chromosomes or female-inherited mitochondrial DNA. With them we can estimate a test subject's overall ancestry and detect contributions that lie outside the direct male or female lines. A small study utilizing self-identifying Melungeons testing with a commercial firm (DNA Consultants) confirms the previous findings of organic chemist James Guthrie, who used blood groups to tackle this ethnic group.[60] The top population matches or presumed regions of ancestry for the participants indicate elevated levels of Jewish (primarily Sephardic, but also Ashkenazi) and Middle Eastern ancestry mixed with Native American and Sub-Saharan African. The European matches have Spain and Portugal in the top ten, behind of course Northwestern European populations like Scotland, revealing a submerged element of Iberian genetics in the predominately Scots-Irish Appalachians. This picture is confirmed by averaged frequencies for meta-populations. Two specifically Jewish populations — Spanish Sephardic and Hungarian Ashkenazic — appear time and again in Melungeons' profiles.

Melungeon Sample European-only matches. **DNA Consultants.**		*Top Meta-Population Frequencies for Melungeons.* **DNA Consultants.**	
Rank	*Population*	*Rank*	*Population*
1.	Scotland/Dundee	1.	Caucasian
2.	Denmark	2.	Portuguese
3.	Ireland	3.	Polish
4.	Belgium	4.	Michigan Native American
5.	France/Toulouse	5.	Lumbee Native American
6.	Spain	6.	Serbian
7.	Switzerland	7.	Brahmin
8.	Portugal	8.	Spanish
9.	Italy	9.	Romani
10.	England/Wales	10.	Belarusian

Social Historical Perspectives

Based on these results the original Melungeon settlers, like many other New World colonists, probably were not primarily Christian. Native Americans, Berbers and Sub-Saharan Africans held, and hold, religious beliefs of an animistic form that invoke solar, lunar, water, earth, fire and seasonal deities and traditions. Arab and Turkish-descended settlers brought Muslim traditions of a syncretistic blend of Sunni and Shi'ia theology. The Romani or Sinti people (Rom, Gypsy, Romechal, Travelers) followed Jewish traditions in a surprising number of parallels with Levitical law, with some influence of Zoroastrianism and elements of fire worship from their sojourn in Mesopotamia but not the slightest tincture of Hindu or Buddhist beliefs, despite having migrated from India and speaking an Indic language (see Appendix D, Customs and Beliefs of the Roma and Sinti). Iberian and Polish/Balkan Jews would have been able to blend their Sephardic and Ashkenazic religious practices. The emerging picture of mixed folkways is clear.

A good overview of the role of Sephardic Jews in the history of modern-day mercantilism can be gleaned from *Sephardic Genealogy* (2002) by Jeffrey Malka (46, 48). This study observes that "Dutch Sephardim in the Netherlands ... were small merchants or shopkeepers. They dealt in tobacco and fish; worked as tailors or goldsmiths, physicians and money-changers, and ran grocery stores. But some ... such as the Pereira, Barrios, and Pinto[61] families ... rose to great wealth. Sephardic merchants dominated the lucrative trade in sugar, tobacco, silk and precious stones.... Wealthy Sephardim were very important both in the founding and running of the Dutch East India and West India Companies"—a role we shall later show had great significance for the early history of the Dutch colony of New York. Malka further notes that the Sephardim usually traded with their relatives, who lived as secret Jews in Spain, Portugal and their possessions, e.g., the Canary Islands, Brazil, Florida, Cuba and Mexico. They used aliases in order to protect their kinsmen from the Inquisition, for example:

Samuel Abrabanel	→	Samuel de Sousa
Samuel Aboab[62]	→	Antonio Sanches de Pas
Yosef Cohen	→	Jeronimo Henriques
Isaac Franco	→	Francisco Mendes de Madeiros
Isak Gaon	→	Philipe Diaz
Menasseh ben Israel	→	Manuel Diaz Soeira
Salomon Naar	→	Manuel Ramirez de Pina
Joshua Sarfati[63]	→	Thomas Nunes de Pina
Jacob Semach	→	Antonio Hidalgo Cortissos
Aron Musafia	→	Manuel Nunes
Michael Nahmias	→	Miguel de Crasto
Josue Nehemias	→	Antonio Lopez

Jewish merchants had an important advantage in being able to do business with, and draw bills of exchange on, relatives, friends, or business associates they could trust.[64] Often, and especially in England, they used the names of local citizens who were sympathetic to their cause as a front for their activities, giving the new associate stock in a joint venture. If the partner married into the family (a frequent outcome), he became an adopted member of the clan, subject to its rules of secrecy and code of commerce.[65]

Malka also notes that some Sephardic surnames originated as early as the Babylonian Exile (586–538 BCE). Among these are Abenzur,[66] Sason, Ben Sushan, Malka,[67] Gabbai[68] and Hasdai.[69] We will encounter a Sasson entering the Virginia Colony prior to 1624. He further notes that Sephardic Jewish families who claimed descent from King David often used the Biblical ruler's name as their surname, e.g., ben David, Ibn Daoud, Dauod, David, Davies, Davidson, Davis, Dawes, Dowd, Dodds, etc., and he adds that during the Middle Ages, Sephardic surnames in Spain and France were frequently translated into their Latin equivalents: Hayim = Vital or Vidas (Life), Shemtob = Bonhomme, Yom Tob = Bondia or Bondion, Tob Elam-Bonenfant, Bonfils or Bonfill (good child), Sarfati = Frances or Frank, Zennah + Crescas or Berdugo (branch).[70]

Other Sephardim carry Berber surnames, for example, OHanna, OHara, Oknine, Assouline, Malkaar, Narr, Montel, Tavora, Pardo (Brown), Nekim and Akbam. Many names come from Hebrew words, for instance, Eliahu or Adoniram, Deborah, Yonah, and Yael. Recalling their Babylonian exile and subsequent emancipation and release by Cyrus of Persia, Sephardim often used Cyrus as a given name. Memories are old among Jewish families. One of Daniel Boone's female ancestors was named Persis, an allusion to a line of Persian exilarchs. Sephardic Jews also adopted geographical surnames, for example Asturia (as in the American Astor family), Belmonte, Cordovera, Frank, Marroquin, Medina, Rhoads/ Rhodes, Roma/Romi (Rome), Russo (Russian), Soriano, Toledana, Turq (Turkey).

Caribbean Jews

Mordechai Arbell in *The Jewish Nation of the Caribbean* (2002) brings us closer to the North American colonies. He notes that as the Conversos moved away from Iberia, they formed concentrations initially in nearby Spanish possessions such as Madeira, the Azores and the Canaries. Thus one clue to the Sephardic ancestry of North American colonists would be trading ties to these places. Conversos also congregated in the French cities of Bordeaux, Bayonne and Rouen. Arbell devotes specific chapters in his book to Barbados, Belize, Berbice, Colombia, Costa Rica, Curacao, the Danish West Indies, Demerar, Dominican Republic, El Salvador, Essequibo, Gyana, or Cayenne, Haiti, Honduras, Jamaica, Martinique and Guadeloupe, Nevis, Panama, Pomeroon and Surinam (Elias Ashmole was governor here), St. Eustatius, Tobago, Trinidad, Tucacas and Venezuela. Sephardim pioneered the rum, sugar cane and orange juice industries. According to Arbell, they were prominent in growing and refining coffee, cocoa, vanilla, indigo, vermillion, coconuts and eggplant. Thus when we encounter North American colonists engaged in these trades, we should view it as a possible sign of Sephardic ancestry.

Arbell also stresses that Sephardic Jews considered themselves one community ("nacion") whether they openly practiced their faith or were privately observant but publicly Protestant or Catholic. It was considered a distinct advantage to have relatives and friends on "both sides of the fence," so to speak, to insure security and protection from potential harassment or persecution. We shall see when we get to New York that several prominent "Christian" families were in fact Conversos and that some members of these families married openly Jewish spouses.

Among the Sephardic surnames in the Caribbean identified by Arbell are Houel/ Howell,[71] Parquet/Parke, Periera, Athias, Molina (Miller),[72] Le Tov, Barjuda, Pinshiron, d'Andeade/Andrews (sometimes Andrus), Louis, daGama, Bueno/Good, Cohen, Lopez,

Gabay, Israel, Vaz/Vass, Nunez, Flores, Betancourt, Sale (Morocco), de La Roche, Beekman, de Vries,[73] Lorenzo, Enoch, Ely, da Sylva (Forest, Woods), Brandon,[74] Henriquez (Henry), Britto, Arrias, Polak ("from Poland," Polk, Pogue), Naar/Narr, Montel, Tavora, Pardo (Brown), Melo, Alva/Alba, Farro, Welcome, Hebron, Cappe, Massle/Massiah, LeBarr/Labatt, Milan, Petit, Yulee, Bernard, Ravel, Robelle (Robles),[75] Nard, and Valencia. Nearly all these names are documented in Faiguenboim and collaborators' surname dictionary.

Marcus' Series

With its three large volumes, Jacob R. Marcus' *The Colonial American Jew 1492–1776* (1970) is the most substantial work on the Sephardic presence in British North America. Marcus traces the roots of American Jews to the important French crypto–Jewish Sephardic community beginning about 1550. He emphasizes that many of the Iberian refugees publicly belonged to Huguenot, Walloon or other Protestant denominations. He also acknowledges the crypto–Jewish, and openly Jewish, Sephardic communities in the Netherlands, which served as the seed bed for the large-scale return of the Jews to England beginning about 1650, as well as for the foundation of the New York colony. As does Katz later, Marcus focuses attention on the underground Jewish community that flourished in England from the reign of Henry VIII (1509–1547). He suggests — as we noted in Chapter One — that Cristobal Colon was a Converso Jew whose family resettled in Italy, and that not only Columbus' navigator but also five additional crew members were Jewish: Alonso de La Calle; Marco, a physician (who bore the same surname as Marcus himself), Mastre Bernal, a physician, Rodrigo Sanchez de Segovia, the controller, and Luis de Torres, the interpreter.

Sephardim in the New World had a wide variety of occupations and lived at all levels of the socioeconomic spectrum, according to Marcus. They were shoemakers, tailors, blacksmiths, tavern keepers, peddlers, mariners, masons, ship captains, factors, barkers, gold and silver smiths, butchers, tanners, physicians, notaries, mine and mill owners, merchants, candy manufacturers, slave dealers, city mayors, priests, bishops, bankers, tax collectors and provincial governors. Judaic religious traditions were usually observed in private. Worship services were held in the homes of anyone where a group would gather on Shabbat. Because no copies of the Torah were available, these secret Sephardim would use the Biblical Old Testament and the Psalms, sometimes also books like Josephus' *Ancient History of the Jews*.

Marcus paints a revealing picture of Jewish mercantile activities involved with Spanish and English economic interests:

> Some of the Jewish Barbadian firms were family partnerships which maintained offices in London where a brother, son, or other relative lived permanently.... Many of the Caribbean consignees, agents, and factors of the London Jewish suppliers were fellow Sephardim. These Jews in the English Caribbean islands either did business with their fellow colonists or by one means or another transshipped goods to the Spanish possessions. Speaking Spanish and Portuguese, they soon established commercial relations with American Marranos and New Christians, and furthered a traffic that brought hard specie into the coffers of the London merchants.

> Jewish importers and exporters in the British West Indies also had substantial dealings with Europe and the British North American colonies. The islands were particularly dependent on the North American colonies for provisions, and there was a steady economic traffic between the Jews of the two areas. Actually, the Jews of the islands, trading local slaves against Pennsylvania flour, had been in touch with Philadelphia merchants as early as the late 1600s when not even one open Jew lived in Philadelphia. The islands sent sugar, molasses, rum, and specie to

North America in exchange for fish, fodder, grain, other foodstuffs, and lumber. Ever since the second half of the seventeenth century, West Indian Jews had traveled back and forth as far north as New England. In 1679, for instance, twelve Jews had left Barbados: Nevis and Surinam claimed one each; two went to Jamaica; two to Antigua; two to London; one to New York; and three probably to Rhode Island.

Among openly Jewish colonists in North America it is perhaps Asser (i.e., Assyrian) Levy, a New York Colony entrepreneur, who is the most prominent, at least in Marcus' opinion. His cohorts and contemporaries include a Pollock family, Moses Lyon, Haym Salomon, Mordechai Mordechai, Uriah Hendricks and numerous Hayses (named for the Hebrew letter). Moreover, several Dutch New York families, including the Beekmans, de Vries and Van Cortlands, are likely crypto–Jewish, a point we will revisit in a later chapter.

Marcus notes Anglicized names among the Jew like Valverde (Greene), Moreno (Brown) and Baruch/Baruh (Barrows, Boroughs, Brookes). Many of these crop up in the ranks of incoming settlers in Virginia, Pennsylvania, New York and other colonies. He documents that Jews coming to the American Colonies from Britain typically bear Anglicized names: Franks, Barnett,[76] Henry, Simson ("son of Simon"), Valentine, Michaels, Phillips, Oaks, Hart, Mears, Russell, Ettings and Lyons. Several of these reappear on the census rolls in the colonies. He also establishes that Ashkenazic Jews from Eastern Germany and Poland figure among the immigrants of the 1700s, some passing through Ireland and England on their journey to North America. It must not be forgotten that Hamburg and Bremen, Germany's two major ports, lay at that time in the English-held provinces of Brunswick and Hanover.

In our view, Marcus underestimates the total Jewish population in the Colonies, which he places at "no more than twenty-five hundred" in 1816. In later chapters, we will argue that there were many persons of Jewish ancestry who resided in British North America but who did not openly practice their religion. Often they were crypto–Jews and crypto–Muslims. Marcus at least devotes a great deal of space to Lancaster, Pennsylvania, as having a large and prosperous Jewish community by the 1700s.[77] From here Jewish merchants such as the Gratzes[78] pioneered land companies and trading routes that stretched far into the interior of the continent. We will argue that several other communities and specific religious congregations in Pennsylvania were clearly crypto–Jewish in character, even if on the surface they seem to be Quaker or Lutheran.

Marcus does not neglect Canadian Jewry. In painstaking detail, he reconstructs the trade correspondences and intermarriages between French Jews and Sephardic families such as the Lopezes of Newport, Rhode Island. A list of the surnames from DNA studies associated with the English colonies' northern neighbor is given below.

Eli Farber's *A Time for Planting: The First Migration 1654–1820*, part of the series *The Jewish People in America* (1992), augments Marcus' survey of Colonial Jewish life with case histories of Caribbean and Brazilian Jews, the Savannah colony of 1733 and Curaçao colonists who arrived in New Amsterdam in 1664.[79] His approach is to present these scattered communities as a paradigm for "the development of the United States as a multiethnic and multiracial society." Although he correctly assesses the religious currents of the day and alliances with the English land-owning families back home as major factors, he seems to miss the larger picture of the Sephardic diaspora and support network which underlie these developments. By the same token, although Todd Endelman's 1979 study of the Anglo-Jewish elite in contemporary Georgian England does not deal with America, his work fails to grasp the deeper motives for Sephardic participation in the ever-enlarging English sphere of influence. Neither Farber nor Endelman considers the possibility that the religious currents and goodwill of certain English families may have been driven by lingering crypto–Jewish tendencies. In common with Jacobs and others, Farber traces a gradual decline in Sephardic Jewish impact in the late eighteenth century, a time when ostensibly it culminated and was most vigorous and influential.

Much of the slack in colonial Jewish studies is taken up by Rabbi Malcolm Stern's *Americans of Jewish Descent* (third edition, 1991). This is exactly what it says, a compendium of genealogy, but it is also an indispensable source for tracing surnames and the intricate interrelationships among Sephardic merchant families. Included are 25,000 individuals. The appearance of a given surname is a virtual guarantee that the family was Jewish or at least crypto–Jewish. Its spotlight is largely on Sephardic Jews, with Ashkenazi families playing only a minor role in the charts, and Stern purposely sets the *terminus ad quem* by which families had to be established in North America at the year 1840. After that date it is the Ashkenazim who are in the ascendancy.

Omitting the obviously Hebrew and European Jewish surnames in Stern, some of the surprising entries into the annals of Colonial American Jewry include Adams, Alexander, Allen, Andrews, Ball (Aramaic "lord"), Barnett (from Issachar),[80] Barrett, Blackwell, Brandon, Brown, Bruce,[81] Bryan(t), Bush, Callahan, Campbell,[82] Carter (Cartier), Cheson, Clark(e), Cooper (a form of Jacob), Davenport ("David's Port"), David, Davis, De Lancey, Ellis (Alis), Etting, Falk, Forbes,[83] Franklin, Goodman, Goodwin, Gordon (a corruption of Cohen), Gregg (i.e., "Greek, Byzantine"), Hamilton ("from Hammel-town"), Harby, Hart (similar to German Hirsch), Hawkins, Hays, Henry, Houston, Howard (from Hereward, one of William the Conqueror's retainers), Hunt, Jackson, Johnson, Labatt, Langley (L'Anglais, English), Lawson, Lewis, Lloyd, Mann,[84] Martin (Spanish: warlike), Michaels, Mitchell, Moore, Morrison, McBlair, Newberry (another aristocratic Norman name), Newhouse, Newman, Nichols, Phillips, Price, Rice, Robinson ("son of Rueben"), Rogers, Russell, Shaw (Hebrew letter), Sim(p)son, Steel, Stewart,[85] Story,[86] Thompson, Valentine, Watson, West, White (Hebrew Labon), Whitehead, Williams, Wilson, Wood, Yates[87] (anagram YZ, Ger Zedek, "righteous convert") and Young. Of course, the appearance of a surname in this list does not mean that everyone bearing it is Jewish anymore than having a name like Cohen necessarily means that person is of Jewish faith or ancestry (the famous songwriter George M. Cohan claimed he was neither). But inclusion is a clue, and it is instructive that some of the sturdiest Anglo-Saxon sounding surnames (for instance, Yates) make the rolls with multiple entries. Some are even borne by rabbis.

Recent scholarship has also brought to light the presence of Converso Jews among the French colonists in North America. We shall see several of these — such as Arnau, Alexander, Brandon, Cassel (Casal, a sept of Clan Kennedy), and Noble — in the British colonies as well.

Some French Canadian Sephardic Surnames

Allaire	Charpentier	Gauvrit	Lovers	Plante
Bellemare	Chollete	LaFleur	Marion	Trottier
Bernard	Dockes	Lafond	Martin	Vaudrin
Bilodeau	Dube	LaMont	Michaud	Vigil
Boucher	Dugas	LaRochelle	Moores	Vizenor
Bourgeois	Eblinaer	LeBlanc	Payeur	Wisener
Case	Forcier	Levinge	Pelland	

Traditional scholarship in the fields both of genetics and history has had the effect of dispossessing the Sephardim of their true character and place in Jewish civilization. In world population figures, Sephardic Jews outnumbered Ashkenazic Jews until about 1800. With the destruction of Eastern European Jewry in the Holocaust, followed by the founding of the state of Israel, Sephardim — now defined as including those Middle Eastern Jews like the Yemeni community who have mostly returned to Israel — have begun regaining their prominence.[88]

Elizabethan England harbored not only a growing level of pro–Sephardic sentiment but, just as likely, a continuing element of crypto–Jews. Let us proceed now to the first of England's colonies in America to see how Sephardic Jews and crypto–Jews numbered in the vanguard of its leaders as well as rank and file.

CHAPTER THREE

Virginia: First — and Not So English — Colony

A volume of documents edited by Stephen B. Quinn on the Roanoke settlements begins by discussing Richard Hakluyt, the Younger, and his older kinsman Richard Hakluyt.[1] The two men helped provide the cartography, justification and promotion for English colonization in America. Of interest is that the elder Hakluyt corresponded with contacts living in Spanish-held Mexico and Portuguese-held Goa in India during the 1560s. We maintain that given Britain's staunch anti–Catholic position at the time, his contacts could be of no other persuasion than crypto–Jewish. Of interest as well is that he learned Italian from his friend John Florio (Sephardic surname)[2] in order to read navigational documents in that language. He then worked with Stephen Parmenius to compile a multilingual set of documents on Eastern North America; Parmenius was the son of converts to Christianity from Turkish-held Hungary — whether of Jewish or Moslem faith is not mentioned, although knowledge of Hebrew argues for the latter — and sailed with Sir Humphrey Gilbert, dying like Gilbert at sea in 1582. Not content with this, Hakluyt also gathered information from botanist Pierre Pena (Sephardic surname)[3] as well as merchants and navigators in Paris and Rouen — two crypto–Jewish hotbeds. He then produced the document that was to make the winning case for English colonization in the New World. The stock he proposed as settlers of this new frontier were "English men and women who might be regarded as surplus to the needs of their own land." These "surplus" persons we will show are those recently driven to England by religious persecution in Iberia and France, Conversos and Moriscos who were adamantly anti–Catholic and desperate enough to climb aboard a cramped, unsafe boat to settle in a faraway *terra incognita* inhabited by ravening beasts and treacherous natives.

In this respect they followed the example of their co-religionists who remained in Iberia, and who under cover of Christian conversion eagerly boarded vessels bound for the new Spanish colonies in the Americas. A crypto–Jewish refuge in northern New Mexico lasted from 1579 to 1591.[4] Perhaps these early forerunners of the Eastern European Jews who embraced America as the golden land at a much later date learned through surreptitious correspondence that life was endurable there despite the forbidding environment. They must have calculated that better fortunes lay in making the journey than in remaining in some Protestant-held way-station such as England, France or Holland, especially when the

British colonies in the southern part of the Eastern Seaboard focused on Virginia, which was charted to go sea-to-sea and laid claim to most of the Ohio Valley (1755) (The Lionel Pincus and Princess Firyal Map Division, The New York Public Library, Astor, Lenox and Tilden Foundations).

Counter-reformation dragnet seemed to be tightening its control in Europe. Part of the resurgence of Catholicism was the confinement of Jews in ghettoes.[5] Jews were ghettoized in Rome by Pope Julius IV in 1555, and in Florence in 1571, setting off a new wave of expulsions in Italy, the Holy Roman Empire and France. The Age of the Ghetto would last until 1796.

Hakluyt's efforts to promote the planting of Virginia were assisted by his friend Martin Basanier (Sephardic surname), a Parisian printer.[6] He also obtained permissions from cartographers Laudonniere and Mendoza (Sephardic surname)[7] to reprint portions of their navigational tracts on the New World. This type of an international effort to direct "surplus" persons to a new homeland was quite unlikely to be undertaken except by organizers who had a personal interest in the matter. The monopolization of the British colonization effort by a handful of interconnected, intermarried families in Cornwall and Devon (Chapter One) is best explained as a massive refugee relocation effort. Just as Zionists finally succeeded in establishing the state of Israel after the Holocaust, it seems probable that a similar plan underpinned the attempt by British crypto–Jews, Sephardic Conversos and Moriscos to establish a New Jerusalem on the Atlantic shores of North America.[8]

Over the past two decades Jewish scholars have gradually recognized that it was Sephardic Jews, not the better-known Ashkenazim of Central Europe, who acted as "avatars of modernization"[9] and laid the groundwork for a collective identity and the eventual emancipation of Jews. Tracts such as Amsterdam chief rabbi Menasseh Ben Israel's *The Hope of Israel* stirred popular yearning for such a utopia of religious tolerance and American Indian-styled sovereignty and self-reliance. According to Ben Israel's biographer Cecil Roth, "The Sephardic Messianic manifesto beat a royal way through the steppes, forests, and villages of the Ashkenazi Jews."[10] It was, one must remember, an era of messianism and false Messiahs—Asher Lelein (1500–1502), Martin Luther (seen by Jews as a precursor to the Messiah), David Reuveni (1523), Solomon Molcho (burned at the stake, 1532), Dona Gracia Nasi (resettled Jews in Palestine, 1560) and Luis de Carvajal (killed in Mexico, 1596).[11] The name Mikve Israel (Hope of Israel) became the top choice for some of the first Jewish congregations in the New World, Curaçao (1654), Savannah (1733) and Philadelphia (1773). Virginia exercised a fascination and magnetic pull for Jews similar to the Antilles, Virgin Islands (St. Croix, Nevis and St. Thomas), Barbados, Jamaica, the Guianas, Curaçao, Surinam and other locations outside the grip of Spanish control.

The first voyage to Roanoke in 1584 had as captains Philip Amadas and Arthur Barlowe, both of whom, to judge by their surnames, were almost certainly Sephardic. The ship's company included William Greenville/Greenfield (brother of Richard mentioned above, perhaps originally Campo Verde), John and Benjamin Wood (perhaps Silva), James Browewich, Henrie Greene, Nicholas Petman, John Hewes and Simon Ferdinando, a known Portuguese Converso. The second voyage in 1585, undertaken again by Sir Richard Greenville at the request of Sir Walter Raleigh, carried as its principal company Master Rafe Lane, Master Thomas Candishe ("from Candy"), Master John Arundell (Aaron's Dale), Master Reymond/Raimund, Master Stukely, Master Bremige, Master Vincent, Master John Clarke and others. Over the years, in instance after instance, Jewish-sounding or Spanish-sounding names have been Anglicized to Christianize, and specifically Anglicanize, the history of English colonization. Grenvil was soon written as Granville or Grandville, Simon was transformed into Symonds, Baruch became Brookes, and Lok acquired the more familiar appearance of Locke. We have seen how Drake's arms and origins were whitewashed by historians.

As before, the ships stopped first at the Canary Islands, a land with a large Converso/Morisco population (Chapter Two). Upon reaching the North American mainland near Cape Fear, the ship's log discusses Captain Aubry and Captain Boniten (Sephardic surname, a trading family later active in Jamaica).[12] The list of colonists left to settle at Roanoke is given in Appendix E in the original spelling of the time; with a bit of decipherment, the pattern seems clear. Can names such as John Gostigo, Anthone Russe (Rousse), Thomas Parre, Joseph Borges (Spanish surname) and Bennett (Baruch) Chappell—not to mention Doughan Gannes (our friend Joachim Ganz)—be those of typical Britons? Obviously not.

After the voyage to Virginia, Thomas Harriot wrote a glowing promotional report of the discoveries, noting that the metallurgist Ganz had not only found rich copper ore, but also "silk worms ... flaxe and hempe ... pitch, tarre, rozen and turpentine ... sassafras ... cedar ... lushious sweete [grapes] ... oile ... iron ... pearle."[13] He argued that the climate was entirely suitable for growing sugar cane, oranges and lemons, and that a new kind of grain, "mayze," had been found. The effort proved unlucky, however. In a few months, the settlers became homesick and discouraged. Walter Raleigh asked Francis Drake—busy raiding Spanish New World settlements in an anti-papist rage—to check up on the venture.

James McDermott provides some insight into the machinations connected with these voyages:

> Raleigh, the chief promoter of the Roanoke colony, was also a backer of Drake's expedition and so must have had the opportunity to discuss the matter with him.... The most lasting service that Drake could provide to them was that which he undertook from the moment he discerned Spanish activity upon the Florida coast: to remove the greatest potential threat to any English colonial presence on the North American coast. On 27 May, the ships' watchers made out a beacon on the Florida shore. Behind it, they found a fortified Spanish settlement: that of St. Augustine. Ostensibly, there seems little reason for Drake to investigate this place further (whose existence, until that moment, had not been suspected). His men's prior experience at Santo Domingo and Cartagena, the probability that the settlement ... would not be worth the plunder, his captains' growing urgency to return to England — all suggest that the English fleet would have been inclined to ignore the new challenge. Yet not only did it pause here, but after attacking and dispersing the Spanish garrison (in an assault in which Frobisher and Drake personally led twenty men into the fort and repulsed a subsequent attempt by local Indians to recapture it for their Spanish masters), the English force razed the town and fort so thoroughly as to render it uninhabitable.
>
> Only Bigges's Summarie provided the reason for such brutal treatment: In this place called S. Augustine, we understood the [Spanish] King [i.e. Philip II] did keepe as is before said, one hundred and fiftie souldiers, and at an other place some dozen leagues beyond to the North-wardes, called S. Helena, he did there likewise kepe an hundred and fiftie more, serving for no other purpose, then to keepe all other nations from inhabiting any part of that coast.[14]

Having thus wreaked revenge on the Spanish King, Drake proceeded to the Roanoke settlement, where he intended to set down hundreds of slaves freed from the enemy in Santo Domingo and Cartagena to serve as laborers for the colony. "There remained the small matter of finding it." Though the 1584 voyage of Amadas and Barlow had explored the Carolina Banks, the precise latitude had not been made available to Drake prior to his sailing. In addition, he was ignorant of whether the colony had actually been established, for Grenville's 1585 Roanoke expedition had returned to England more than a month after he himself had embarked. Let us continue in the words, again, of McDermott:

> St. Helena was the northernmost extent of the Spanish presence on the eastern American continent. The Englishmen saw no other trace of "civilized" habitation until 9 June, when a large bonfire on the shoreline of Hatarask Bank signaled the presence of their countrymen. Leaving the ships outside the so-called Port Ferdinando (the colony's landing place, a small island in a shallow inlet just north of Cape Hatarask), Drake and his captains took their pinnaces into Roanoke Sound, and were greeted by the colony's commander, Ralph Lane.[15]

As McDermott points out, Drake's rescue mission suggests a premeditated plan to assist the colony. He had previously sent Lane a letter with Captain Edward Stafford in which he offered to supply provisions necessary to the colony.

Meanwhile, the promised supply ship from England and the relief expedition under Grenville were delayed. During this time, the goodwill of the local Algonquian Indian tribes had evaporated. Next, as Giles Milton well summarizes in his account, "The powerful chief Wingina refused to provide any more food to the settlers. Lane, the grim veteran of the Irish wars, marched on his village and treacherously put the chief along with all his deputy chiefs to the sword. A threatened attack by an alliance of tribes aimed at wiping the Englishmen out was thus prevented. But now only one group of native Indians, those of Croatoan Island, were friendly to the Englishmen, and the Croatians' own supply of corn was also exhausted. Drake's offer was a godsend."[16]

The colonists decided in a council convened on June 16 to ask Drake to transport them all back to England, as none believed that the promised relief from England would arrive in time. They decamped with such haste that they piled their equipment higgledy-piggledy into the boats and three colonists absent on business somewhere in the bush were simply abandoned. The fleet made its getaway on June 18, 1584, ending the first chapter of England's colonization in the New World on a note of defeat and ignominy.

Second Roanoke Colony

Two years later, another colony was established at Roanoke. Its leader was a civilian named John White, an artist and adventurer known to speak Spanish who evidently had Spanish connections. He was quite familiar with the coastal interior and the Spanish who attempted in 1571 to establish a mission there. Of this foray by the Spanish, William B. Cridlin, a Virginia historian, writes:

> The documents record that one year after the exploration of the peninsula by Verrazano, Lucas Vasques de Ayllon, a lawyer and judge of Santo Domingo, obtained a patent from King Charles (Carlos) of Spain, authorizing him to explore and plant a settlement on the American mainland.... It was in June, 1526, that de Ayllon set sail, with three small vessels, from Puerto de la Plata, Santo Domingo. Accompanying him were six hundred men, women and children, with sufficient supplies and 150 horses. De Ayllon entered the Chesapeake Bay, which he named Madre de las Aguas (Mother of Waters), and ascending the Guandape (James) River, landed at a place he called St. Michael (San Miguel).

St. Michael was the second colony attempted on the mainland of North America after that established by Ponce de Leon, at Charlotte Harbor, Florida, in 1521. De Ayllon soon died of fever and the settlement passed through a deadly winter marked by plague, Indian attacks and a slave insurrection. Not soon afterwards, its savior, Francis Gomez, gathered together the survivors on two ships and sailed for Santo Domingo. Only one hundred and fifty of the six hundred original colonists ever reached safety.

Cridlin continues the story of Spain's thwarted efforts at establishing a presence in the region:

> No further attempt at colonization was made until 1570, when Menendez, Governor of Florida, desirous of a colony on the Chesapeake, fitted out an expedition headed by Fathers Segura and Louis Quiros, assisted by six Jesuit Brothers, named Soli, Mendes, Linares, Redondo, Gabriel Gomez and Sancho Zevalles [all Conversos]. The expedition planted its little colony on the banks of the Rappahannock, but was soon betrayed by a supposedly converted Indian who had received the baptismal name of Don Louis de Valasco [Sephardic name]. De Valasco, conspiring with other Indians, massacred the unsuspecting Spaniards to a man, and it was not until the following spring that Mendes learned of the disaster through a pilot he had sent with supplies. He immediately sailed for Axacan, as the settlement was called, captured and hanged the murderers....
>
> When Captain John Smith of Jamestown explored the Rappahannock, he found an Indian, "Mosco" [i.e., "mosque," a Muslim name] with whom he could converse [presumably in Spanish] and use as an interpreter. Mosco was of lighter complexion than the other natives and wore a beard. Evidently he was a descendant of the ill-fated colony. Smith and Newport also had found an Indian, whom they used as interpreter, on their voyage to the falls of the James, just ten days after landing at Jamestown, and it is reported they also saw a youth of light complexion and an old Indian with a beard. Presumably they were descendants from the Spanish settlement at St. Michaels.

Raleigh's second expedition had ninety-four colonists, including women and children. The families were supposed to be planted farther north at Chesapeake Bay, but the transport ships peremptorily abandoned them at Roanoke in order to pursue their preferred business of raiding Spanish treasure fleets in the Caribbean. White quickly returned to England to obtain supplies and reinforcements, but it was the year of the Spanish Armada's invasion and England was focused on repelling the attack. He was not able to return until August 1590, when he found the entire settlement abandoned. The only trace left by the second colonists was the word "Croatoan" carved into a tree. As before, they present a markedly un–English impression. The occupations of lawyer, professor, mathematician and the like, as well as the Mediterranean foodstuffs they carried as provisions, do not appear anything like the norm for Northern European pioneers in the New World. The settlement date of 1587 was only one year before the well-announced Spanish invasion of England. These "surplus" persons who had hardly gotten their feet on the ground in England were willingly enlisted, as a voyage to America provided the means to escape the feared arrival of the Inquisition.

Numerous studies of the so-called Lost Colony of Roanoke have attempted to locate survivors among the mixed tribes of North Carolina, including the Occaneechi, Lumbee, Tuscarora, Cohaire and various Algonquian groups in the area.[17] C. D. Brewington, "a distinguished native of Sampson Co.," wrote *The Five Civilized Indian Tribes of Eastern North Carolina* with "historical facts about these Indians whose descendants are still here" and "evidence of their intermarriage and life with the Whites from Sir Walter Raleigh's Lost Colony." Yet an equal number of books and articles have attempted to demonstrate that the English men and women from the Roanoke colony could not have survived for long in the wilderness and so never managed to join together with local Indians.[18] They claim that Virginia Dare (probably a Jewish surname in origin; see Chapter One), the first "white" child born in English America and John White's granddaughter, probably died of starvation in the woods or fell with an Indian tomahawk in her skull.

There are significant genealogical indications of the Lost Colony's blending with the Indians, however. The 1790 federal census includes a fourth column between the number of females and slaves in the household designed to enumerate "Other Free Persons." It was left to the census taker how to interpret this category. In Sampson County, North Carolina, home of the Cohairie Indians, one of the claimed descendant groups of Roanoke settlers, the enumerator seems to have used it for Jews and Indians. Brewington's ancestors, for instance, are listed as "other" in the household of Ann Brewington, where there are three "others" and nobody else — a whole household of "others." Individuals listed only by first name like Hannah and Old Natt can probably be identified as "taxed Indians," mixed breeds living in the settlements rather than with other Indians in the interior. This was certainly an odd direction for Indians of any sort to be moving, and taxed Indians are found in only a few other locations in early America (the Virginia frontier in Pittsvylvania County was one). More "other" households from Sampson County with their numbers of members included are: Joseph Williams, 4, Hannah Williams, Nathaniel Revil,[19] 13, Jack Waldon, Crecy (Lucretia) Williams, Old Natt, 2, Molly Clewis, 3, Rachael Green, Cloeraly,[20] 4, Mary Wiggins, 6, Levi Emmanuel,[21] 5, Becky Cobb, 3, David Terry, 4, Ephraim Emmanuel, John Flowers, Abraham Jacobs,[22] 3, John Emmanuel, Jack Mainor,[23] (John Cooper,[24] white), Jesse Emmanuel, Nicholas Emmanuel, 5, Moses Carter, 9, Henry Carter, 8, and Patty Wiggins[25], 5.

Neighboring North Carolina counties Duplin, Bladen, Brunswick, Johnston, Onslow and New Hanover have heads of household falling in the same category, although not as many. We mark names that are likely Jewish or crypto–Jewish with an asterisk: Davis,* Isabella Jones, with 2 slaves, Boon,* Samuel Bell,* (many Joneses),[26] Barfoot,* Jacob(s),* 39 altogether, Pages,*[27] Burnet,*[28] Johnston, Perry,* Chas. and Collop, 15, Demery (from Tamar),* Cumbo,* James Sweet,*[29] Green,* Freeman,*[30] Williams,* Grice (may be Grimes*), Hannah,*[31] with 1 slave, Catherine Wren, Powell, Hesse,* with 3 slaves, Cavers* (Chavis),[32] Sanders,* Jemboy (Genoy?),* with 6 slaves, Aithcock,*[33] and Scott.

Many of these names are either Melungeon or Sephardic Jewish or both. A common name in the Lumbee tribe that probably derives from a medieval Jewish name is Braveboy. A 1292 census of Paris lists numerous wealthy Jews from Brabant, a Flemish city with ties to the cloth, weaving and woolen industry of Lombardy (de Brabant, Brébois). Bradby, a family that supplied multiple chiefs to the Pamunkey Indians of Virginia, may be a corruption.[34]

Jamestown Colony 1607

After the failure of the Roanoke colony, interest in establishing a foothold in the New World waned with the deaths of Raleigh, Grenville and ultimately Elizabeth herself. Even before the queen's final years, however, Raleigh and his party had fallen out of favor. In 1594, public sentiment turned against Sephardic Jews when intriguers trumped up charges of treason against Elizabeth's court physician, Rodrigo Lopez. A decade later a brief peace treaty with Spain scrapped most of the new colonization plans. But in 1606 Elizabeth's successor, James I, granted a charter to the Virginia Company to attempt a new beginning in North America. A commercial venture from the outset, the corporation was subscribed to and underwritten by the major merchants and lawyers of London, many of which had financial ties with Amsterdam's bustling Sephardic enclave (1598).

On May 13, 1607, three small English ships reached the mouth of the James River on the Virginia coast after being diverted from their original goal of Chesapeake Bay.[35] One was commanded by Captain Christopher Newport and carried seventy-one persons; a second under Capt. Bartholomew Gosnold bore fifty-two persons; and the third, captained by John Ratcliffe, had twenty-one persons aboard. No list of these original settlers survives, but we know that among them were Edward Wingfield, John Martin, who had accompanied Sir Francis Drake in earlier days, John Smith, George Kendall, George Percy, the earl of Northumberland's brother, the Rev. Robert Hunt and Gabriel Archer, an attorney and explorer. A resupply vessel arrived in 1608 carrying 70 additional settlers, among whom were Matthew Scrivener/Scribner and two women — a Miss Forrest (perhaps da Silva) and her maid, Ann Burras (Boroughs, Sephardic surname). A few months later, Ann Burras was married to one of the settlers, John Laydon (likely "from Leyden, Holland," a Protestant and crypto–Jewish seat of learning).

In summer 1609, another ship arrived with four hundred unnamed settlers who were taken on from among the impoverished and criminal element in England. During the ensuing winter of 1609–1610, the colony was decimated by disease and starvation and its numbers fell from five hundred persons to around sixty. In May 1610 a new governor, Sir Thomas Gates (Goetz, Yates)[36] arrived with reinforcements apparently from Poland and the Netherlands — both were countries to which Jews were pouring in at this time, Sephardim to newly liberated Low Lands and Scottish crypto–Jews to Poland, especially from Aberdeen.[37] In the meantime Lord De La Warr stopped by to observe the colony. Dr. Lawrence Bohun (Boone, Sephardic) was on hand experimenting with medicinal herbs and botanicals. A list of the known passengers aboard Gates' ship the *Sea Venture* is given in Appendix E.

In May 1611 Sir Thomas Dale arrived in the Virginia Colony with supplies, farm animals and three hundred settlers. During this time, Samuel Argall (Anglo-Norman Jewish name based on Greek *argos*, "treasure"), the Rev. Alexander Whitaker, and Ralph Hamor (Arabic name, "ass seller") had also arrived. In 1616 Abraham Piercey (i.e., Perse, Persian), cape-merchant, took over management of the Virginia Company store in the colony while in 1619 John Pory (perhaps from Porat, Moroccan for Joseph)[38] was secretary. Several of these surnames are Sephardic. Epidemics still swept the colony. Some three hundred persons died during the 1618 winter. A critic back home charged, "Instead of a plantacion, Virginia will shortly get the name of a slaughterhouse." New management was chosen. Sir Edwin Sandys (Sands, from Alexander) became treasurer of the Virginia Company in 1618 and Sir George Yeardley became governor of Virginia in 1619. John and Nicholas Ferrar ("smith," Sephardic) became members of the Virginia corporation the same year.

By 1620 the Virginia colony had another new governor, Francis Wyatt (Arabic surname, Wayad), who put a premium on obtaining female settlers. Economic efforts included timber production, wineries, an iron works and glass manufacture. Mulberry trees were planted to foster silkworms and silk making. All these industries were ones in which Sephardic Jews, Moriscos and Ottoman Turks excelled. Sericulture in particular was a secret art jealously guarded and known only to them. The flight of Huguenots from Catholic France beginning about 1575 brought silk manufacturing to England so that by the end of the seventeenth century Huguenots numbered as high as 80,000 in London. Many of them were silk weavers or skilled craftsmen in the other textile arts in Shoreditch and Spitalfields only two or three generations removed from being Spanish or Italian Jews.[39]

The constitution of the Virginia Company was rewritten in 1621. Named now as proprietors were[40]:

> sir Francis Wyatt, governor, captain Francis West, sir George Yeardley, knight, sir William Neuce, knight, marshal, Mr. George Sandys, treasurer, Mr. George Thorpe, deputy of the college, captain Thomas Neuce, deputy for the company, Mr. Powlet, Mr. Leech, captain Nathaniel Powel, Mr. Christopher Davidson, secretary, Doctor Potts, physician to the company, Mr. Roger Smith, Mr. John Berkeley, Mr. John Rolfe, Mr. Ralph Hamer, Mr. John Pountis,[41] Mr. Michael Lapworth, Mr. Harwood,[42] Mr. Samuel Macock.[43]

Over the course of these arrivals, the surrounding Indian tribes had become increasingly disenchanted with the behavior of the colonists. They attacked the settlement in 1622, killing between one quarter and one third of the inhabitants. Only a year later, Captain Henry Spelman (Spielmann, "jester, actor," especially in Purim plays) and his company were killed, among others. In 1624 James I dissolved the Virginia Company and declared Virginia a royal colony. By that time settlements in Virginia had moved well beyond Jamestown. Elizabeth City, for example, had approximately three hundred fifty residents. The glass factory was re-established in 1624. Individual persons were permitted to establish their own settlements, bringing in colonists of their own choosing. For example, Samuel Argall was assigned 2,400 acres for recruiting twenty-four settlers. To settle in Virginia at that time, one need only swear allegiance to the British monarch and be sponsored by one of the landowners. Thus, persons from any country were eligible to immigrate. Many became landholders after working off their indenture, usually in seven years' time.

One of the first of these outlying settlements was Berkeley Hundred. Established in 1619, it included 35 colonists. Another group arriving in 1620 aboard the *Supply* included Nicholas Heale, the ancestor of one of the authors, who was descended from the same Heale family in Bristol that married into the Drake family, as mentioned earlier. Others founding plantations and estates were Richard Pace, Nathaniel Causey, John Rafe, Isaac Madison, Samuel Maycock, Edward Liske (Czech name), Richard Biggs, Grivell Pooley ("Pole"),[44] Isaac Chaplin (Chapman, from Jacob, the patriarch, who was a traveling merchant),[45] Edward Gourgany (Gurganus, Ashkenazi), Nathaniel Powell, Thomas Harris (English Jewish),[46] Samuel Jourdan, and Mary Tue (Toohy). Again we see the appearance of Jewish surnames.

In 1619 the Virginia Company sent a hundred and fifty people to set up three ironworks under the charge of Captain Bluett. Eventually these were taken over by John Berkeley and his son Maurice. At George Sandy's plantation there was a French man, Daniel Poole (Sephardic name), and twenty "Italians." At Hugh Crowder's plantation, we find a Richard Pace ("peace," perhaps originally Shalom or Solomon), William Perry (Sephardic), Richard Richards and a Thomas Garses (Garcia). Christopher Lawne's plantation was furnished with a hundred immigrants and supplies sent to him by Richard Wiseman (Moroccan name)[47] and Nathaniel Basse (Byzantine or Romaniot Jewish). Basse eventually moved to Virginia himself, as did Edward Bennett, a well established London merchant.

At Newport News there was Daniel Gookin (perhaps the same as German "Guggen," as in Guggenheim),[48] a friend of Sir William Newce in Ireland, and at Mulberry Island, Anthony Baram (Arabic), William Capp (Copp, from Jacob) and Joachim Andrews (Andros, Byzantine Greek or Romaniot).

Taking Stock

What have we learned about Virginia's earliest colonists from 1587 to 1621? First, the majority of the settlers planted by Raleigh and Grenville at Roanoke — from the evidence provided by their surnames, motives of their sponsors and the known ethnicity of Joachim Ganz and Simon Ferdinando as Jews and Conversos — were most likely not of English ancestry. They were Sephardim and Moriscos willing to come to North America to escape what they viewed as an even larger threat, the menace of Spain's invasion of England with the Inquisitorial apparatus following behind it. The initial colonists of Jamestown ten years later do not appear to be all very Anglo-Saxon either, although the later-arriving four hundred "renegades" likely were British in that they probably did not enlist but were tricked by those desirous of getting them out of the country. Many of these were spirited away from alehouses where bounty hunters got them drunk and packed them off in the middle of the night before they knew what had happened. In any event, most of the two groups of early colonists perished unknown and unnamed, leaving no lasting legacy. The arrival in 1610 of Governor Gates finally does provide some names. Such persons as Silvester Jourdain, Joseph Chard (Card), Francis Pearepoint (Pierpoint), Edward Eason (Jason) and the like do not appear to be ethnically English either, but rather Sephardic refugees from France or Holland.

In 1621 a total of 227 Walloon and French immigrants arrived to join a crowd of colonists emptied from the English port of Bristol the year before. The majority of these also were not persons of English descent. Bristol had a large Sephardic community, one member of which — Nicholas Heale — is known to have been dark enough in coloring to have descendants classified as free persons of color some generations later. The Walloon and French Huguenot colonists, following the reasoning of such social historians as Lavender, were probably at least fifty percent Converso and Morisco.[49] By 1624 we have the names Paul Sarrett compiled of several communities then extant in Virginia. In this listing there is an abundance of names that seem to be Morisco, Islamic or Moorish — for example, Daynan (Arabic, "judge"), Fedam (Arabic, "coins, mint"), Hamor and Halam (Arabic, "wise"), while others would seem explicitly Jewish, Bagsell (Hebrew anagram),[50] Brocke (Baruch, "blessed"), Ely, Gouldsmith, Juiman, Levet and Moises.

These observations contradict the received notion that the first Jews to arrive in North America were a boatload of Sephardic refugees from Recife, Brazil, who (illegally) came to the Dutch colony of New York from Curaçao in 1654.[51] As mentioned above, Jews and Muslims were present in North America from Columbus' arrival at Hispaniola in 1492, long before the English arrivals at Roanoke and Jamestown. Indeed, we believe that even the promoters Drake, Raleigh, Grenville and other West Country gentlemen evince Jewish roots. In sum, the larger part of the early English colonization effort in the New World was a Jewish enterprise, one whose overriding purpose was to relocate refugees from the Iberian diaspora and its fallout in other countries.

Immigration patterns in Virginia after 1624 suggest an even stronger picture of the Sephardic and Morisco presence. The aptly named *Abraham* leaving London in 1635 had onboard Walter Piggott, Henry Dobell, Alexander Symes (Simons) and Simon Farrell (see Appendix E). The *David* that same year carried Robert Alsopp, Robert Barron (Varon/Baroun)[52] and Gurtred Lovett ("Levite").[53] The *Bonaventure* (1635) listed as passengers, among others, Bazill (Greek Basil) Booke (Hebrew anagram), Robert Perry, James Mayser and Thomas Hyet (Arabic/Hebrew for "tailor"), each bearing a Sephardic surname. More and more persons of likely Sephardic and Morisco descent continued to arrive. The *Elizabeth* (1635) of London carried John Bagby,[54] George Trevas (i.e., "from Trèves in Alsace") and Ellen Shore (Hebrew *shor*, "bull," related to the name Joseph)[55]; the *Globe*, also in 1635, brought Robert Coppyn (diminutive of Jacob), William Savoy, Michell Hayms and Ann Levyans (which seem obvious enough not to call for comment); and the *Alice* had onboard Robert Haggara and Sophia Rottric (Roderick, Rodrique, Rodrigues). In 1700 several boatloads of Huguenot refugees arrived in Virginia from England. Many of these persons were likely of Sephardic and Morisco ancestry.

The reader is invited to take a look at the complete lists in Appendix E and consider their implications for the ethnicity of the Virginia Colony and Colonial America. The names Jean Vidau and Jean Moreau are Jewish and Moorish, respectively. Jacques Roy means that the ancestors of this Jacques/Jacob were in the employ of the King (Roy), or else played the part of the King in a Purim play. Francois Sassin bears a famous Jewish surname (Sassoon, Sussan) dating from the Babylonian captivity (586 BCE).[56] Abraham Moulin was the ancestor of the Melungeon Mullins family. Francous du Tartre has a surname implying the person's ancestors were Tatar. Jaques Broussee is a French cousin of the once–Jewish Brusse/Bruce family of Scotland. Isaac Symon Jourdan bears a common French Jewish given and surname. Then there is Etienne Ocosand, a Turkish surname. Abraham Remi is a member of the French Jewish Melungeon family Remy/Ramey.[57] Pierre Sarazia's last name means literally Saracen or Muslim in French. Unrecognized and unacknowledged, these are the persons who helped to create the Old Dominion.

Famous Figures

How about the really prominent Virginians, the aristocrats, the first families of Virginia, the Byrds, Lees, and Henrys? Our first glance at these families should be to see what they looked like. Images of prominent people suggest that there lies hidden a large Mediterranean, Middle Eastern and Iberian component in Virginia's colonial-era population and their descendants.

William Byrd

William Byrd, the ancestor of the Byrds of Virginia, was the son of John Bird, a London goldsmith.[58] The earliest firm genealogical record for the family is mention of a Thomas Bird, apprenticed to Henry Sacheverell (Hebrew anagram),[59] vintner, in 1608, subsequently admitted to the Wine Merchants Company in 1616. Thomas Bird married his first cousin Elizabeth Bird. It was Thomas' son John who became a goldsmith. What is transparent from these records, given the occupations of wine merchant and goldsmith and the first cousin marriage, is that the Birds/Byrds were Jewish. Byrd was not an English name before this family became prominent. The first of that name probably came to England as a court musician like the Sephardic Anthons mentioned earlier: a relative was William Byrd, the Renaissance court composer (circa 1540–1623). Publicly they were not Jewish, as Jews were officially banned from England until 1664. They were privately Jewish or crypto–Jewish as were so many other persons in London at the time. It is likely that at least the first generation officially practiced Catholicism, the religion of their parent country. English custom in London and other major cities allowed Spanish and Portuguese Jews as foreigners to worship at their own parish churches, which were presumed to be Catholic.

William Byrd came to Virginia at the request of his uncle Captain Thomas Stegge, who was childless and designated William his heir. Although the exact date is unknown, his arrival was probably around 1670. The Stegges were traders with the Indians, primarily Catawbas and Cherokees, another profession markedly Jewish. Upon reaching adulthood and receiving his inheritance, Byrd entered the lucrative triangular trade between Virginia, Barbados and Africa. Tobacco, deerskins, sugar, rum, and slaves were the primary commodities of exchange. Typically, those who plied this trade imported slaves from Portuguese middlemen off the Guinea Coast of Africa. In Barbados, rum and sugar were taken onboard to be transported to Virginia. American planters paid for rum, sugar and slaves in tobacco or deerskins and received credit in England or Scotland paid out to them in manufactured goods supplied on the steady stream of ships carrying new colonists. Except for the profit margins of the merchants, frequently Jews, no money changed hands, this only in England, thus preserving the mother country's prohibition about allowing specie to flow into the colonies or accumulate there.

George Mason (Emmet Collection, Miriam and Ira D. Wallach Division of Art, Prints and Photographs, The New York Public Library, Astor, Lenox and Tilden Foundations).

In 1673 Byrd married Mary Horsmanden, whose lineage goes back to the St. Leger family of Cornwall

mentioned in Chapter One. Very importantly, biographer Alden Hatch tells us that this St. Leger family traced its ancestry back to Baudoin III, King of Jerusalem during the Crusades, who was evidently of Jewish descent. Byrd soon became receiver general of the king's revenue, as well as auditor of Virginia. As Hatch notes, he both collected the taxes and audited them.

There are other strong cues regarding Byrd's ancestry and religious leanings. Hatch states that Byrd "regarded Catholics as but one degree above the devils from hell." In 1699 when the Huguenots were under attack once again by a Catholic monarch, it was William Byrd of Virginia who championed their cause. About three hundred of them were brought to safety in Virginia and another two hundred the following year. "Largely as a result of the arguments presented by William Byrd to the Board of Trade, between 700 and 800 [Huguenots] settled in Virginia."[60] Such activities are in complete conformity with the efforts begun in the late 1500s by Raleigh and Drake to settle their Sephardic and Morisco kinsmen in the New World. Both Raleigh and Drake had assisted the Huguenots in France before and after the infamous St. Bartholomew's Day Massacre in 1572. In the 1705 edition of his *History*, Robert Beverley wrote of "the Goodness and generosity of Colonel Byrd toward these distressed Huguenots." Beverly goes on to say,

> Upon their first Arrival in that country, he [Byrd] received them with all the tenderness of a Father, and ever since has constantly given them the utmost assistance ... employing all his Skill, and all his friends to advance their interest both publickly and privately.... What Liberties has he not all along allowed them on his own plantations to furnish themselves from thence Corn and other necessaries? His Mills have been at their Service to grind their Corn toll-free.... With what Zeal did he represent their Cause to the Assembly? And with what earnestness did he press all his Friends in their favor"?[61]

Byrd was attended in his final days by one of them, his valet Jean Marat — who bears a common Sephardic/Arabic surname.

William Byrd's son William II was educated in England, where he learned Hebrew, Greek and Latin. Micajah Perry (nearly invariably a Sephardic name, as we have seen) was William Byrd, Sr.'s factor and agent in London and looked after William Byrd, Jr.'s welfare as a student abroad. In 1705 young William returned to Virginia and took over the family's several mercantile and milling interests. He had an avid interest in medicine and special fascination with the properties (and profits) in ginseng. This was a root gathered by Melungeons and shipped as far away as China during the late 1700s by Daniel Boone and John Jacob Astor ("from Asturia"). William Byrd II married Lucy Parke. Lucy's sister Frances would later marry John Custis (Costas), probably of Sephardic ancestry.

Hatch also reports from transcriptions of Byrd's private diary that he would read one or two chapters of the Bible in Hebrew every morning. Since the Hebrew Bible does not contain the New Testament, we must assume that William was reading the Torah. Hatch continues, "Byrd was very strict about keeping the Sabbath. He would allow no work to be done that could possibly be avoided; and even when it could not be helped ... he was uneasy in his conscience and sought a Biblical excuse." Also according to Hatch, Byrd "frequently ducked going to [Christian] church." In our view, these descriptions illustrate crypto–Jewish behavior (Appendix B).

Lees of Virginia

The Lee family of Virginia is perhaps most noted for producing General Robert E. Lee, commander of the Confederate Army during the Civil War. But the family's history in Virginia goes back much far-ther.[62] The genealogy shown below indicates that the founder Richard Lee was born in England in 1618 and immigrated to Vir-ginia in 1640. His wife was Anne Constable. By the first genera-tion, one daughter, Anne, had married a man very likely Se-phardic Jewish, Thomas Youell (Yoel). The next generation sees Richard Lee marrying Martha Silk (also a Sephardic surname) and Phillip marrying Sarah Brooke (Baruch). By the third generation Lees are marrying their close cousins the Corgins (Cohens) and the sisters, prob-ably also Jewish, Mary and Annie Aylett (Eliot, Arabic for "promi-nent person"). Fourth generation Lees twice marry into the Liv-ingston, Grymes and Ball fami-lies elsewhere in this book identi-fied to be of Sephardic origin. By the fifth generation, they are marrying only close of kin: three other Lees and another Fendall,

Richard Lee II (Emmet Collection, Miriam and Ira D. Wallach Division of Art, Prints and Photographs, The New York Public Library, Astor, Lenox and Tilden Foundations).

with a Sephardic Hite (Hyatt, Arabic) and William Byrd Page (Jewish surname) tossed in for good measure. By the sixth generation they have married Carters and another Custis (Costas).

Although it was claimed at one time that the Lee family was sprung from Norman knight Reyner de Lega, who arrived in England circa 1200, Richard Lee actually came from a modest Worcestershire family. Its founder was John Lee/Lies/Lyes, "a clothier whose busi-ness was … in the West Midlands." His mother was Jane Hancock, whose family were also cloth merchants. Richard Lee's older brother, John, was apprenticed to a Hancock kinsman who was a wine merchant in London—an origin similar to the Byrds. The exact date of Richard Lee's arrival in Virginia is unknown, but by 1643 he was named attorney general for the colony. Very much like the first Byrd, he "began to profit not only from the income brought by his public offices, but also by trading with the Indians for fur and skins." Richard's factor in London was John Lee, probably his brother. By 1650 he had risen to become secretary of state for Virginia. By this time he had also established a trading con-nection with the Netherlands, the center of Sephardic commerce. Lee sponsored thirty-eight indentured servants from Holland, whom he settled on headright land granted to him for bringing them over as colonists. Repetitive exploitation of the headright system was only open to the very wealthy. Lee continued to sponsor Dutch (evidently Sephardic) inden-tured servants and reaped increasingly large rewards.

One of Lee's sons, Francis, returned permanently to London in 1677, where he helped manage the family's international trading ventures. Another, Thomas, negotiated in the 1740s with the Iroquois Indians to obtain rights to 500,000 acres west of Virginia, forming the Ohio Company. The company had Laurence Washington, brother to George, as one of its presidents and was operated by the Lee family for several generations. The surveyor used to map the company's land grant boundaries was Christopher Gist (1705–1759), Indian agent, guide and spy for Gov. Edmond Atkin in Maryland and later for generals Washington and Braddock. Gist was the son of Capt. Richard and Zipporah Morray Gist and grandson of Christopher Richard Gist, who was married to Edith Cromwell, a granddaughter of Sir Oliver Cromwell, lord protector of the Commonwealth. Gist's descendants became openly Jewish and joined the Reform Synagogue in Cincinnati, Ohio.[63]

Patrick Henry

Our final nominee is Patrick Henry, staunch patriot and one of the primary architects of the American Revolution. It is William Byrd's diary which provides us with some initial clues about his ancestry. Patrick's mother was born Sarah Winston; she first married Col. John Syme (Hebrew, Simon), who died shortly after their marriage. On October 7, 1732, Colonel Byrd dropped in to see her and wrote later in his diary, "She was a portly, handsome dame, of the Family of Esau, and seemed not to pine too much for the death of her husband, who was of the Family of Saracens."[64] Byrd's testimony firmly establishes that Mrs. Syme was a Jewess and her late husband a Muslim.

Shortly after that visit, Mrs. Syme married a close kinsman of her late husband's, John Henry of Aberdeen, Scotland.[65] The Symes and the Henrys were first and second cousins, and members of both families immigrated to the Virginia Colony. In 1736 the Henrys' son Patrick was born on the family's plantation in Hanover County, where six out of twelve of the governors were kinsmen. As acknowledged by the author of *The Faiths of Our Fathers*, a study of the religious beliefs and practices of the men who were most prominent in the

Patrick Henry (Emmet Collection, Miriam and Ira D. Wallach Division of Art, Prints and Photographs, The New York Public Library, Astor, Lenox and Tilden Foundations).

founding of the United States, Henry's father, Col. John Henry, had "the most distinguished formal education," being a graduate of "the rigorous classical curriculum of Scotland's famous Aberdeen University."[66] His son went on to become an eminent lawyer and delegate to the Virginia House of Burgesses and Continental Congress and achieve fame as one of the most outspoken champions of American independence. He was also the fourteenth largest landholder in Virginia.[67] His first wife was Sarah Shelton,[68] his second, the woman known to history as Dorothea Spotswood Dandridge Henry Winston, but neither marriage produced any children, and so we can trace his genealogy no further.

These observations about the settlement of Virginia and its First Families strengthen suspicion that the Virginia Colony's leading promoters, founders, early settlers and later its statesmen were not the white Anglo-Saxon Protestants paraded through the pages of traditional American histories, but at least partially Sephardim, Moriscos and others. These figures should be recognized as her cultural and political architects.

Alexander Spotswood (Emmet Collection, Miriam and Ira D. Wallach Division of Art, Prints and Photographs, The New York Public Library, Astor, Lenox and Tilden Foundations).

CHAPTER FOUR

Massachusetts: Pilgrims, Puritans, Jews and Moors

The outline of early Massachusetts history is familiar to most Americans. The first settlers arrived on the *Mayflower* in 1620 with the Pilgrims. The Puritans followed within a decade, setting up the towns of Salem in 1628 under John Endicott and Boston in 1630 under John Winthrop. In that same year, the Massachusetts Bay Colony was founded. It absorbed the former colony and brought a large amount of self-government. Within the next decade came more than 20,000 immigrants, almost entirely British, it is said, with East Anglians setting the tone. Counties were formed that echoed the rural regions of England — Hampshire, Berkshire, Essex, Middlesex, Suffolk and Norfolk. Although the northern, hilly land of dense forests, stony soils and a short growing season bore little resemblance to the Puritans' land of origin, farming became the main enterprise of the colony. When the new inhabitants' hard work and zeal had tamed the wilderness, towns with sturdy Anglo-Saxon names like Cambridge, Bristol, Springfield, Salisbury, Boston, Andover, Dorchester, Framingham and Gloucester dotted the countryside with their typical green commons, trim fields surrounded by fences and peaceful church spires. When one thinks of Massachusetts, one conjures up images of devout men and women clothed in "sad" (subdued) colors carrying Bibles and walking solemnly to church on Sunday. Or maybe one envisions the first Thanksgiving, in which these same cheerlessly dressed men and women are gathered around long trencher tables with friendly Indians partaking of wild turkey, venison, corn, potatoes and yams. Such is the nostalgic mythology of Early America.

To describe the founding forefathers and foremothers the author of one standard account, R. C. Simmons, uses the words "pious," "good," "godly," "Calvinistic," "poor," "learned," "staid and orderly," "saintly," "disciplined," and most revealingly, "homogenous."[1] According to another author, David Hackett Fischer, one of the foremothers "wears a sad brown dress ... and her image combines the strength, resolve, seriousness, dignity, virtue and gravitas" typical of the Puritans. Fischer stipulates that this small, uniform group of settlers grew into the regnant population that has essentially lasted to the present day: "The emigrants who came to Massachusetts in the great migration became the breeding stock for America's Yankee population. They multiplied at a rapid rate, doubling every generation for two centuries. Their numbers increased to 100,000 by 1700, to at least one million by 1800, six million by 1900, and more than sixteen million by 1988 — all descended from 21,000 English emigrants who came to Massachusetts in the period from 1629 to 1640."[2]

Pilgrims Holding Bibles Walking Down Path, by James C. King (Library of Congress).

Social historians contrast the simple, rural folkways and purposefulness of Massachusetts families with the Middle Atlantic colonies settled by frivolous cavaliers gambling all on an adventure and independent-minded bachelors running away from responsibilities. Most commentators point to the middle-class pragmatic nature of the Puritans and emphasize their religious mission to "purify" the Protestant faith in a new setting where privilege and medieval tradition counted for less than individualism and good works. One might ask, however, what the reformers sought to purify society of and what drove them to withdraw into their own secret congregations in England and the Netherlands and then take the unusual step of immigrating to a raw, empty wilderness. The focus on purity reminds us of contemporary Spain, with its obsessions about pure-bloodedness and heresy. What radical bent made the Puritan authorities impose a new system of rule and oppression, forcing many autonomous Separatist congregations to steadily splinter in their beliefs and practices? What caused the breakaway settlements soon launched in Rhode Island, Connecticut, New Hampshire, Maine and Nova Scotia? And why anyway did people join in this effort to plant a colony in the bleak, cold North devoid of any promise of crops, minerals or valuable exports other than, perhaps, fish and timber?

An alternative image of Massachusetts begins to emerge if one is bold enough to discard the preconceptions and dig deeper into the original records of the time, probing the historical backdrop in England and the Netherlands. The great majority of the passengers on the *Mayflower* were not actually "Pilgrims" in the first place. Only thirty-five of the original 102 passengers were from the congregation in Leiden; the rest were "miscellaneous persons" picked up in London and Southampton.[3] The financier behind the voyage was the merchant Thomas Weston (English Jewish surname). With this and other similar considerations, the Pilgrim mothers and fathers may not end up so dowdy and redundant after all. Their complexions become darker than previously envisioned. Many of the conscripts for Massachusetts appear to be what we call today persons of color. They came from North African, Semitic and Mediterranean ancestry and preserve distinctly non–Christian religious traditions. Gradually we begin to suspect that one of the strongest motivations uniting this disparate throng of settlers was the resolve to escape certain institutions in the Old World, that they galvanized around such enemies as popery and economic oppression. The common denominator was a resurgence of crypto–Judaism, a long-dormant strain in English society fanned into life again through the influence of Spanish and Portuguese Jews taking refuge in the British Isles and Low Countries.

William Bradford

The new version begins like the old with the writings of the founding fathers, foremost the history composed by William Bradford, first governor of Plymouth Plantation in 1620–1647. Bradford was born in 1590 at Austerfield, Yorkshire, and he joined the Congregational Church there in 1606. Later he moved to Leiden in the Netherlands, where he learned Dutch, Latin and Hebrew. He and his Dutch wife, Dorothy May (Jewish surname),[4] sailed to North America aboard the *Mayflower*, which landed in December 1620. In Plymouth, Bradford supported his family through fur trading with the Indians, setting up stores in Buzzard's Bay and Kennebec. With his death in May 1657, Bradford left furniture and clothing, including "a red Turkey grogram suit of clothes, a red waist coat with silver buttons ... an old violet colored cloak" and "two hats — a black one and a colored one." The will of Jane Humphrey in 1668 makes mention of a scarlet petticoat worn beneath the matron's gray exterior. So much at least for the drab tastes and killjoy nature of the Pilgrims.

Morison states that Bradford's history opens with folios "occupied by Bradford's Hebrew exercises which he wrote circa 1650" in Hebrew:

Though I am grown aged, yet I have had a longing desire to see with my own eyes something of that most ancient language and holy tongue in which the Law and Oracles of God were writ, and in which God and Angels spake to the holy patriarchs of old time; and what names were given to things from the Creation. And though I cannot attain to much herein, yet I am refreshed to have seen some glimpses hereof, as Moses saw the land of Canaan afar off. My aim and desire is to see how the words and phrases lie in the holy text.[5]

Thus Bradford was most interested in the Torah and Nevim, the law and the prophets. This is surely a remarkable sentiment for a man widely perceived as a student of the New Testament and champion of the Gospels. In the same work, Bradford recounts how the French Walloons were persecuted by the Catholics in

William Bradford (Emmet Collection, Miriam and Ira D. Wallach Division of Art, Prints and Photographs, The New York Public Library, Astor, Lenox and Tilden Foundations).

the Netherlands, about which his editor comments in a footnote, "many thousand Protestants among the French-speaking Walloons immigrated across the border to the United Netherlands. Some of them joined the Christian Church in Leiden[6]; one of these was Phillippe de La Noye [from Noë, French for Noah], who came to Plymouth in the Fortune in 1621. This name, Anglicized as Delano, has descended to a host of Americans, including President Franklin Delano Roosevelt. De la Noye is a well-documented Sephardic surname, and this protestant De La Noye family was therefore likely crypto–Jewish.[7]

Bradford's history recounts how the *Mayflower* passengers were originally intended to settle in Virginia and carried letters from Sir Edwin Sandys and John Ferrar to that effect. Underwriter Thomas Weston[8] issued them the Pierce Patent in June 1621 from the Council for New England sponsored by the dukes of Lennox and Hamilton, earls of Warwick and Sheffield, and Sir Ferdinando Gorges (Jorges).[9] Ultimately, they were swept off course — or purposely misled — to the North Atlantic coast. As will be established shortly, these men cannot be explained away as the pillars of English Christendom they might at first appear to be. Thomas Weston admitted that foreigners ("strangers") had to be recruited to act as laborers and help defray its expenses. They came from London and Southampton, the first and second largest Jewish communities in England at the time.

In the aftermath of the Indian massacre of the Jamestown settlers, the Plymouth settlers had built a fort by 1622. Virginian John Pory, the friend of Richard Hakluyt who translated the first description of North Africa into English for Queen Elizabeth, and who bears what is probably a Moroccan surname, visited Plymouth that year and wrote Bradford a letter of gratitude for the hospitality extended to him. Bradford loaned Pory some books during his visit described as "Mr. Ainsworth's elaborate work upon the five books of Moses." These works constitute the Hebrew Torah or Pentateuch, corresponding to Genesis through Deuteronomy in the Old Testament. "Both he and Mr. Robinson do highly commend the authors as being most conversant in the Scriptures.... What good it may please God to work by them through my hands ... who finds such high content in them." Many of the trade channels used by Massachusetts as well as Virginia were evidently Jewish, usually Sephardic or British crypto–Jewish, or both. Marranos typically partnered with London merchants who lent their names to the venture for appearance's sake. As the Plymouth colonists set about trading with the Indians for furs and fish, they used two factors in London to sell their exports. Bradford reports of this arrangement, "[We] appoint James Shirley, Goldsmith, and John Beauchamp, Salter, citizens of London, our true and lawful agents, factors and assigns...."[10] Both these agents bear Sephardic surnames rooted in Anglo-Norman history and are in Jewish-dominated professions.[11] We will encounter a Beauchamp who is probably Jewish in a family in Maryland.

Perhaps even more intriguing given the stereotype of the Plymouth Colony as deeply religious in character is that it functioned entirely without the services of a Christian minister through 1635. The shepherd finally procured for the flock was named, intriguingly, José Glover, but the unfortunate man took ill and quickly died. After securing the services of the Rev. John Norton for about a year, the Pilgrim church ultimately retained John Rayner (Reyner, Ranier, Raina, Sephardic),[12] who arrived in 1635 and remained until 1654.

A final testimony with regard to Bradford's possible crypto–Jewish orientation is another of his addresses to "the people of Israel," that is, the Pilgrims. It is drawn again from his *History* written in 1646:

> Art thou a stranger in Israel that thou shouldest not know what is done? Are not those Jebusites overcome that have vexed the people of Israel so long, even holding Jerusalem till David's days

and been as thorns in their sides, so many ages; and now begun to score that any David should meddle with them? They began to fortify their tower, as that of the old Babylonians; but those proud Anakins are thrown down, and their glory laid in the dust.

The tyrannous Bishops are ejected, their courts dissolved, their canons forceless, their service cashiered, their ceremonies useless and despised, their plots for popery prevented, and all their superstitions discarded and returned to Rome from whence they came, and the monuments of idolatry rooted out of the land. And the proud and profane supporters and cruel defenders of these, as bloody papists and wicked atheists, and their malignant consorts, marvelously overthrown. And are not these great things? Who can deny it? … Hallelujah![13]

Sentiments expressed in such passionate language bespeak a deeply embedded anti–Catholic hostility. We believe that only those whose ancestors had been forced from their homes, as the Sephardic Jews were in Spain, would exhibit such direct and forceful anger. By 1620, England was most emphatically not Catholic, and there was little to fear from Catholic influence. Bradford personally had not experienced the religious persecution necessary to ignite such vehemence.

Although there are thousands of books on the subject of anti–Semitism (even unconscious, transferred and sublimated forms of it), one is hard pressed to find a single study of anti–Christian attitudes or anti–Catholicism in Jews or any other non–Christian group. That it was a persistent theme in Jewish life from the beginnings of the persecution of Jews by the Church of Rome in the early Middle Ages cannot be gainsaid. With the expulsion of Jews from Christian countries (England, 1290; France, 1306; Spain, 1390 and 1492; Portugal, 1497; Provence, 1501; Germany, 1426–1450; Southern Italy, 1541) and their concentration into ghettoes (Venice was the first in 1515, but they lasted until Napoleon around 1800), resentment against their oppressors built in the Jewish people of Europe. It was expressed as disparagement of the tenets of Christianity, including the doctrine of the trinity, virgin birth and Jesus as messiah, as well as criticism of all the pomp and ritual of the liturgy, saints lives and iconography.[14] The Eucharist was mocked as a cannibalistic rite, Our Lady was called Our Stork, and saints' images were denounced as heathen idolatry. It even extended to ridicule of the use of the name Mary (or any patently Catholic name like that of an evangelist or saint), jokes about the Pope, monks, priests and nuns, kneeling postures, ways of walking, haircuts, clothing, house colors, love making and cooking. A diabolical Papist conspiracy was often glimpsed in the tiniest political rumor or trade news brought in by the ships, and the spectacle of Spain's decline and decadence did not go unnoticed.

As twentieth-century Jewish historian Simon Dubnow commented (in tones probably not dissimilar from contemporaries of William Bradford and William Penn), "A people accustomed to the spectacle of the cannibalistic *auto-da-fé* succumbed to savagery; manners grew steadily coarser; the healthy seed of religion was smothered in superstition and fanaticism. The flourishing land of the Arabic-Judaic renaissance was transformed into a lifeless desert of monks."[15] Once Spanish Jews themselves were relieved from the necessity of concealing ancestral sentiments by living in enemy states such as France, England and the Netherlands, they tended to give open vent to anti–Spanish, anti–Catholic sympathies, at the same time maintaining a pride in the Castilian language and other aspects of Iberian culture and history. In the New World, many ingrained predispositions must have surfaced, even if transferred to new circumstances and current events far removed from Inquisitional Spain. Family traditions that were only whispered in France or England were repeated with less fear. As the Spanish emperor distantly insisted that he enjoyed a higher ground in establishing dogma and enforcing laws against heresy as His Catholic Majesty than the Apostolic Church in Rome — presided over by Spanish popes and clergy through much of the sixteenth and seventeenth century even as it was — anti–Catholic and anti–Spanish feeling boiled up and became a frequent theme of public discourse or private commentary. Spain's follies, pretensions and ultimate ruin were the talk of Europe, and it was easy to attribute the cause to an extremist form of Catholicism.

We turn now to Benjamin LaBaree's 1979 work, *Colonial Massachusetts: A History*, which provides a more dispassionate, omniscient narrative of the Massachusetts Colony, one informed by over 350 years of hindsight.[16] By the twentieth century it was well appreciated that the people who were to become known as the Pilgrims originated as an extreme sect of Puritans termed Separatists. They had migrated under the leadership of their minister, John Robinson (i.e., Rueben-son), to Amsterdam in the Netherlands in 1607 and then moved on to Leiden.

In 1606 Sir Ferdinando Gorges (Gorges is Spanish for George and Ferdinando is obviously a Spanish given name) and Sir John Popham, both wealthy Englishmen, formed an alliance of interests with Richard Hakluyt to persuade King James I to charter the Virginia Company. One portion of this charter granted the company the right to colonize between the 38th and 45th parallels. This territory was given to a group termed the Plymouth Company under the command of Raleigh Gilbert (Humphrey's son) and George Popham (English crypto–Jewish),[17] John Popham's nephew. After an attempt to colonize the coast of Maine failed in 1607, the Virginia Colony was set up in 1608 in a location substantially farther south. By a chain of coincidences and accidental events, most of the Puritans originally scheduled to board the *Mayflower* for a second attempt at colonizing the North Atlantic coast were unable to make the voyage. The consequence was that, as LaBarree states, "The majority of the Pilgrims were not even Puritan religious dissidents, per se. They were just persons willing and able to board the Mayflower and head west."

Passengers Aboard the Mayflower

John Carver, Katherine Carver, Desire Minter, John Howland, Roger Wikler, William Lathan, Jasper More (boy)

William Brewster, Mary Brewster, 2 sons, Richard More (boy)

Edward Winslow, Elizabeth Winslow, George Soule, Elias Story, Ellen More (girl)

William Bradford, Dorothy Bradford

Isaac Allerton, Mary Allerton, 3 children, John Hooke (boy)

Samuel Fuller, William Button

John Crackston and son

Capt. Miles Standish, Rose Standish

Christopher Martin, wife, Solomon Prower, John Langmore

William Mullins, wife, 2 children, Robert Carter

William White, Susannah White, 2 sons, William Holbeck, Edward Thompson

Stephen Hopkins, Elizabeth Hopkins, children:

Giles, Constanta, Damaris, Oceanus, Edward Doty, Edward Lester

Richard Warren

John Billinton, Ellen Billington, 2 children

Edward Tilley, Ann Tilley,

Henry Sampson, Humility Cooper

John Tilley, wife, daughter

Francis Cooke and son

Thomas Rogers and son

Thomas Tinker, wife, son

John Rigsdale, Alice Rigsdale

James Chielton, wife, daughter

Edward Fuller, wife, son

John Turner, two sons

Francis Eaton, Sarah Eaton, son

Moses Fletcher, John Goodman, Thomas Williams, Digory Priest, Edmund Margesson, Peter Browne, Richard Britleridge, Richard Clarke, Richard Gardner, Gilbert Winslow

There are several puzzling details in this roster. First, three unaccompanied children surnamed More (Moor) are living with three different families. Jasper More is with the Carvers — a family group that also includes a Desiree Minter and a Roger Wilder — two

Ashkenazic-named persons. Richard More is listed with the Brewster family and their children; Ellen More is with the Winslow family, which also includes George Soule (Sephardic name) and Elias Story (likely from Astoria/Asturia — a heavily Sephardic region of Spain — or a region called Stora in Morocco).[18] Second, the Hopkins family contains children named Giles (French), Constanta (Latin), Damaris (Tamar, Hebrew) and Oceanus (Latin) and is accompanied by an Edward Doty (the Sephardic diminutive for David — Daoudi). Third, the Tilley family includes Henry Sampson (Hebrew). And finally, among the unmarried adult male passengers we find Moses Fletcher, John Goodman (Ashkenazic for Shem Tov), Digory Priest (Kohane), Richard Gardiner (Jardine) and Thomas English (Jews often took their country of residence as a surname). Thus we believe a strong *prima facie* case can be made for the likely presence of many Sephardim and Moors among the Plymouth passengers.

Massachusetts Bay Company

A later incorporation under the auspices of the Council for New England obtained a royal grant for all land lying between 40° and 48° N latitude. By 1628 this venture coalesced into the Massachusetts Bay Colony. It was intended to be a stock company financed by merchants that included Matthew Craddock, Sir Richard Saltonstall and John Venn. Thus in June 1628 John Endicott brought fifty initial settlers to Salem. Then in March 1630 John Winthrop led a fleet of eleven ships carrying seven hundred passengers plus cows, horses and supplies. Soon after that, six more ships arrived bringing the total number of Massachusetts Bay colonists to 1,200 by 1630. The signatories of the 1629 charter were "Mathewe Cradocke, to be the first present Governor of the said Company, and the saide Thomas Goffe, to be Deputy Governor of the saide Company, and the saide Sir Richard Saltonstall, Isaack Johnson, Samuell Aldersey, John Ven, John Humfrey, John Endicott, Simon Whetcombe, Increase Noell, Richard Pery, Nathaniell Wright, Samuell Vassall, Theophilus Eaton, Thomas Adams, Thomas Hutchins, John Browne, George Foxcrofte, William Vassall, and William Pinchion."[19] Several of these persons bear Ashkenazic or Sephardic surnames, e.g., Goffe (Welsh and Borders Jewish),[20] Saltonstall, Ven, Endicott, Noell, Pery, Vassall, Eaton, Adams, Browne and Pynchion.

As LaBaree observes, and contrary to popular belief, most of the Massachusetts Bay colonists made no claim to being Puritans or religious adherents of any shape, sort or fashion. They had simply immigrated to make their fortunes in the New World. The Hutchinson family, for example, traded with the West Indies through their cousin, Peleg Sanford of Rhode Island. Other Boston-based merchants traded with the crypto–Jewish strongholds of Bilbao, Portugal, Malaga, Spain and the Marrano communities of the Canaries, Madeira and Fayal. Some had factors at converso-laden Nevis, Barbados, Antigua and Guadalupe for trading in rum, wine, and sugar. By 1645 Boston vessels were transporting African slaves to Barbados for the sugar plantations. And by 1664 a man named John Leverette, bearing a Hebrew surname, was governor of the colony, which in the meantime had outgrown and now overshadowed the earlier Plymouth Colony, leaving Massachusetts dominated politically and ideologically by Boston and its merchants.

In Appendix F are listed the given and last names of the original Massachusetts Bay settlers. The list contains a vivid cross-section of Sephardic and Moorish nomenclature: Abell is Hebrew, as are Adams and Agar; Alger is Moorish for Algeria; Elizabeth Ballard's child is named Shubael (Hebrew); Jacob Barney bears Hebrew given and surnames; Willam

Barsham's name means "son of Shem"; Samuel Bass (Byzantine Greek for "king," also a Spanish Jewish surname)[21] is married to Ann Savell (Seville). Edward Bendal[22] and John Benham both carry Hebrew surnames, as do the Benjamin brothers; Henry Bright's wife is Beriah (Hebrew), Abraham Browne (designating a brown complexion) is a surveyor — a Jewish/Moorish–dominated trade. Richard Bulgar is likely a Sephard from then Ottoman-held Bulgaria. There is also a Jehu Burr; Bernard Capen and his wife Ruth have a Hebrew anagram surname; William Chesebrough's children bear the names David (Hebrew), Andronicus (Greek), Junia (Latin), Jabez (Hebrew) and Elisha (Hebrew). John Cotton's surname was likely anglicized from the Hebrew/Arabic Caton ("small"); William Dody bears the Hebrew/Arabic diminutive for David as a surname; Edward El Mer's surname translates to "the sea"; George Farr's surname would be rendered Phar in Arabic ("great, mighty"); Samuel Freeman carries a common Ashkenazic appellation; Robert Gamlin likely had his surname shortened from the Hebrew Gamelin; Joshua Hewes married a Mary Goldstone, and onward through the list. The cues and clues of non–Christian, non–English origins of the Massachusetts Puritans grow increasingly evident.

Paul Revere (Picture Collection, The New York Public Library, Astor, Lenox and Tilden Foundations).

LaBaree notes that it was the Huguenots who brought the Jewish-Moorish craft of silver-working to Massachusetts in 1686. Among the best known were Jeremiah Dummer (Dumas), John Coney[23] and Paul Revere.[24] All three of these bear French Sephardic surnames. Another culturally prominent settler was Nathaniel Ames (medieval English Jewish surname from Amos)[25] who simultaneously practiced medicine, ran a tavern and published an almanac. Even the man with whom Paul Revere rode to warn of the British arrival for war in 1775 bore a Sephardic surname — Dawes, as already pointed out, a derivative of David.

The names of some physicians practicing in Boston in 1760–1775 are also informative. They include Abijah Cheever (probably Chiver, "cypher"),[26] John Homans (probably Homem),[27] Nyott Doubt (Dout, David), Nahuja Fry (Ashkenazic), Silvester Gardines, Joseph Gardner, Thomas Mather (Mathew), Josiah Leavitt (Levite), John Sprague (Dutch: "speaker of foreign tongue"), Samuel Adams, Charles Jarvis (Gervaise), John Jeffries (Arabic Jafar), Jean Feron ("iron"), Thomas Kast (Arabic), Isaac Rand,[28] Joseph Calef (Caliph), John Kronenshelt (Ashkenazic), Edmund Dana (Spanish),[29] George Emery (Amir),[30] William Gager (German Jäger, "hunter"), Joshua Gee (Hebrew letter), Giles Heale (discussed in Chapter One), James Jerald, Ebenezer Roby (diminutive for Rueben) and Levi Shepard (that is, Sephard).

Religious and Marital Patterns

No one can deny that Massachusetts religious practices had some peculiar quirks, many of which we believe can be traced to underlying Judaic or Muslim practices (Appendices A and B). Carla Gardina Pestana, for example, reports that Roger Williams, as minister of the Salem Church, "advocated the veiling of women at worship service."[31] Some Puritans became dissenters from the established church in Salem, forming splinter groups. These included Samuel Shatlock, Joshua Buffam and Samuel Gaskill, all carrying Sephardic names. One of the leaders of this new Quaker movement was a John Copland (from Hebrew Koppel, derived from Jacob),[32] who arrived in Salem from England in 1656. Two other prominent Quakers of the period were Nathaniel Sylvester and Eliakim Wardell, both bearing Sephardic given and last names. Still other heretics were Baptists. Pestana reports that one minister, Thomas Gould (German for "money" or "gold" as already discussed), liked to "read Chronicles 1:2 to his congregation: 'Let him kiss me with kisses of his mouth, for your love is better than wine.'" This is an Old Testament passage central to the liturgy of the Kabbalat service of Jews which welcomes the Sabbath as the bride or delight of the bridegroom. Sung Friday at dusk to an ancient Moorish melody as part of the service is the hymn L'cha Dodi ("Come My Beloved") composed in the 16th century by the rabbi Shlomo Halevi Alkabetz. Next to the Shema and the words *Baruch ata Adonai*, this is probably the most familiar part of Jewish Sabbath services. It is not found in Christian services.

In agreement with crypto–Jewish practice, endogamy among the Massachusetts Quaker settlers was carried to extremes. In one case, Pestana reports, "six intermarried families accounted for fully two-thirds of the more than five hundred people known to have been members of the Salem Monthly meeting." Among these congregants were Benjamin Bagnall, Sarah Flood[33] Bassett and the Estes family. All bear Sephardic surnames. A listing of the early settlers in Salem is given in Appendix F. Of these, several would appear to be French Huguenot or Sephardic. For example, John Abbey (Abbe = Aramaic, "fathers"), John Barrow (Baruch), Edward Beauchamp, Roger Conant, Jeffrey Eastey/Esty, Thomas Gardner (Jardine), Edward Giles, Thomas Goldthwaite, Robert Goodale (Godell), Henry Herrick, John Horne (after the Jewish *shofar*), Alice Ingersoll, George Jacobs, Elisha Kibbey, Richard Ober, Samuel Parris (Perez, Pharez, Neh. 11:4), Richard Raymond, Daniel Rea (Rey),[34] John Swasey, John Sweet (for sugar, or candy, a Jewish/Arab monopoly), John Symonds (Simons) and Abraham Temple.

Non-Christians have been acknowledged even in traditional histories to have been present in Massachusetts from a very early date. Historian T.H.H. Breen, for example, quotes a colonist named Roger Clapp who hoped that Massachusetts would "knit together the hearts of all who feared God, whether rich or poor, English or Indian, Portugal [i.e., Sephardic Jewish] or Negro." Others alluded to social distinctions between Christians and "Turkes [i.e., Muslims and Sephards], Heathens, Barbarians and Infidels," confirming that such groups were socially recognized in the ranks of the colonists.[35]

In the early sixteenth century, there were more Englishmen living in Muslim North Africa than Massachusetts and Virginia together.[36] England had signed a trade treaty with Morocco in 1580, there was a Muslim community in London and Plymouth, and it was not unusual for Englishmen to "turn Turk" and take up residence in North Africa in the service of some Muslim potentate, even converting to Islam. The Caribbean trade triangle is familiar to most students of colonial history, but it is not generally known that "the most dominant triangle linked England to Moorish North Africa and North America." "Before the *Mayflower* carried the so-called 'pilgrims' to Plymouth, it had traded in the Muslim Mediterranean." Such adventurers and promoters as George Sandys, William Strachey, Sir Thomas Roe, Ralph Lane, John Smith, George Carteret (founder of New Jersey), John Pory, Sir Thomas Smythe, Sir Thomas Arundel, and John White were in North Africa before they went to America. The ties between England and North Africa were as strong as her antipathy was toward Spain, an orientation enthusiastically endorsed by Sephardic Jews for whom Morocco had been one of their first places of refuge after expulsion from the Iberian Peninsula.

Yet another category included Papists (i.e. Catholics). The latter, especially those identified with Spain, were commonly depicted as archenemies of England and its colonies. Denouncers include Lord Saye and Sele, as well as those refugees from the Iberian Peninsula presumed here to be Sephardic or Muslim fellow travelers of the Puritans. Interestingly, Breen singles out a certain faction of settlers who were especially liberal in their religious views, and who were heavily intermarried with one another:

> Thomas Clark … and William Tyne … were … champions of a wider toleration. Clark would go so far in 1658 as to protest with Edward Hutchinson the harsh laws passed against the Quakers; and Tyne, with Leverett, objected to the Cambridge Platform. Valentine Hill, a landowner and trader to the "eastern parts," was connected to the Hutchinson family because his first wife, Frances Freestone, was a cousin of William Hutchinson. Hill's second wife, Mary Eaton, a daughter of Theophilus Eaton of New Haven, connected him through her stepmother, Anne Eaton, to David Yale (Anne Eaton's son), a Boston merchant who agitated, with Robert Child, for a more flexible form of Puritanism.
>
> Francis Norton … came to the New World initially as an agent for the Mason family of New Hampshire, rather than as a devoted Puritan; he gravitated toward Sedgwick's more expansive vision of Puritanism and was married to Mary Stetson, the daughter of Sedgwick's partner in a Charlestown cider mill. Joshua Hewes, nephew of the prominent English merchant and iron-monger Joshua Foote, was involved closely in business dealings with Edward Hutchinson and other tolerationist forces in the colony. Finally Robert Child himself, also an investor, became infamous as the author of the pro-tolerationist Remonstrance of 1546.[37]

These patterns of interwoven business, religious and marital bonds are typical of crypto–Jewish communities, and we believe they helped to perpetuate a private form of religious practice within the community that endured from generation to generation.

Gloucester and Ipswich

A 1984 study by Christine Heyrman focuses on two Massachusetts maritime communities.[38] She starts by discussing a late seventeenth century minister, the Reverend John Wise, who "supplemented the income from his farm with returns from his investments in two trading vessels. One of his sons, Joseph, set up as a shopkeeper in Boston, and another son, Ammi Ruhammah, became a major merchant in Ipswich." In 1721 the same Reverend Wise compared Gloucester, a flourishing center of the fishery, to the ancient Biblical seaport of Tyre "that was but a rock … yet by merchandize became the Queen of the Seas, the metropolis of the world." This description raises several questions. First, why does a Puritan minister have the Jewish surname Wise?[39] Second, why does this Puritan minister — ostensibly from a sect that eschews materialism — laud the value of commerce and operate not only a farm but two trading ships? Third, why does this same purportedly Christian minister use the ancient Biblical city of Tyre as a metaphor for his congregation's locale? And finally, why would such a minister have a son bearing the Muslim appellation of Ammi Ruhammah? Clearly there was more going on in colonial Massachusetts than traditional history books have recounted.

Gloucester, Massachusetts, was built upon its position as a leading cod-fishing entrepôt trading with the Marrano-dominated areas of the Caribbean, Spain and Portugal. Among the most successful of the town's entrepreneurs were miller Jacob Davis and tanner Isaac Eveleth. Other residents included Christian Marshman (de Soto in Spanish), William and Naome Sargent and Jonathan Springer. Springer held partial interest in four small sloops together with Quakers John Maule and Walter Newberry.

Contrary to their modern-day image of modesty and simplicity, Christine Heyrman comments that Quakers were typically viewed as "unscrupulous, litigious sharpsters" by the other early Massachusetts settlers, a description not inconsistent with anti–Semitic stereotypes of the day.

Witchcraft

A defining attribute of the Massachusetts Colony was the phenomenon of witchcraft. This type of panic broke out much more frequently in New England than the other colonies. One writer finds that more than 95 percent of all accusations and 90 percent of death sentences occurred among the Puritans. The reason most often given is the provincial Anglian origin of Puritans: the eastern counties of England had the highest number of witchcraft cases.[40] This may be only half the story, though, for there appears to be a xenophobic aspect to witch-hunting in both Massachusetts and places like Essex, England.

The town of Gloucester experienced several charges of witchcraft against both ministers and townspeople. In Salem, of course, the witchcraft hysteria had begun in 1692. Three daughters of William and Johanna (Blessing, i.e., Baruch) Towne,[41] Sarah Cloyes, Mary Easty and Rebecca Nurse (Norris, Arabic for "light")[42] were accused, arrested, examined and either imprisoned or executed on charges of "scandalouse evil [and] miscarryage inconsistent with Christianity." Sarah alone escaped punishment after obtaining high powered legal counsel and moved to Framingham, where she and her husband were eventually counted among the town's most illustrious citizens. It is likely that the charges were motivated by jealousy of the Towne family's wealth, attitudes perhaps not unmixed with anti–Semitism.

In Ipswich, witchcraft charges were first directed only toward those in the community already viewed as deviant — Martha Carrier, Mary Parker and Samuel Wardwell — but they soon spread to encompass "nearly forty Andoverians who were all solid and respectable members of the community": the wife of deacon Jon Frye, wife of militia captain John Osgood, two of the Reverend Francis Dane's daughters, his daughter-in-law and several grandchildren, and the wife of Dudley Bradstreet. The defendants pleaded guilty to several charges, including "rebaptism by Satan himself, who preferred full immersion to sprinkling, in the Shawskin River"— which sounds much like the Judaic mikvah bathing ritual.

Arrested in Gloucester were Elizabeth Dicer, Margaret Prince (Judeo-Arabic surname, Amir), Phebe Day (Dias) and Francis Norwood. As Heyrman notes, many of the accused were Quakers, viewed by the Puritans as heretics. In addition to the Quaker affinities of Rebecca Nurse, she mentions the Proctor family, of which five members, John, his wife, Elizabeth, and three children were charged with witchcraft. "What made the Proctors suspect in the eyes of their neighbors," she speculates, "was less that John ran a tavern on the Ipswich Road than that his wife's family, the Bassets of Lynn, included a large number of Quakers.

Joining the Proctors in prison were two members of the Basset family, along with four members of Lynn's Hawkes,[43] Farrar, and Hart families, all of whom had Quaker connections" and bore solid Sephardic surnames.

The same was true of Andover residents Samuel Wardwell, a relative of the Quakeress Lydia Wardwell (Ward, Arabic for "rose," plus the suffix -el), who appeared naked in the Newbury meetinghouse to protest persecution by the Puritans in 1663. Among those accused of witchcraft later in the trial were a large number of people who shared with Rebecca Nurse the same kind of indirect Quaker links of kinship and friendship with religious dissidents.

Another accused witch, Job Tookey (Touhey, already discussed) of Beverly, was at pains to refute charges that his father, an English clergyman, was "an anabaptistical quaking rogue that for his maintenance went up and down England to delude souls for the Devil." In at least one instance in Salem, an accusation of witchcraft figured as a way for an afflicted girl to dissociate herself from the Quaker community.[44] Ann Putnam, Jr., described to the court how "an old gray head man" whom "people used to call Father Pharaoh" tormented her by insisting that he was her grandfather. The old man whom Ann Putnam publicly denied as a blood relative was Thomas Farrar, Sr., the father of a leading Lynn Quaker. Shortly after the trials, one of Salem's chief Friends, Thomas Maule, hinted that some linkage existed between dissenting affinities and the witchcraft prosecutions, comparing the trials to the Quakers' sufferings and expressing relief that none of his relations had been charged. Other alleged witches include George Jacobs, Sr., and Giles Corey (Cori).[45] Heyrman continues, "Testimony on behalf of John and Elizabeth Proctor signed by several of their Quaker neighbors probably helped to seal their fate. And when the condemned witch Sarah Good stood on the scaffold, she threatened Salem's assistant minister Nicholas Noyes, 'if you take away my life, God will give you blood to drink.'"

We believe that many, perhaps most, of those accused of witchcraft were actually secret Judaizers. Whereas their practices may have been successfully hidden or winked at from others in their often remote home villages in England, acts of burning candles, kosher slaughtering, housecleaning rituals and the like were unfamiliar to the majority of their new neighbors. The Massachusetts collective branded their behavior as beyond the pale. Sarah Good's bloody curse, for example, makes the most sense when viewed from the Jewish proscription against consuming blood of any kind.[46] In most of Christian Europe at this time, blood puddings and black/blood sausages were commonplace foods, although, significantly, this was not the case in Scotland with its large population of Jews and crypto–Jews. *Kashrut* of a sort must still have been alive in parts of England. In our view, it is likely that a least part of the heretical appearance of the Quaker sect was due to the fact that a large portion of the membership was drawn from Sephardic Jews and Moors. Of course, there were congregants and ministers among the Puritans who also were very likely of Sephardic descent, e.g., Samuel Parris and Nicholas Noyes.

The Quakers were set apart from the Puritans in Massachusetts not only by virtue of their religious practices but also by their international business connections and greater financial acumen. They were highly endogamous and self-sufficient as a community, both spiritually and financially — sociological characteristics of the Sephardim. Heyrman writes:

> So close was the connection between sectarian membership and daily subsistence for some men that the sundering of ties to the Quaker community meant a loss of livelihood. Ostracized by the fellowship for failure to attend meetings regularly, Richard Oakes [Ochs, "ox," Ashkenazic surname] of Marblehead protested that "the Friends had denied him for Nothing, and that they have Ruined him and his family." The Salem Meeting's ability to supply members' needs for

relief, education, employment, and credit served to reduce the influence of both civil government and orthodox society over the lives of the dissenters.

In some ways, the self-containment of the Quaker community gave the Puritan Congregationalists just what they wanted — as little as possible to do with religious dissidents. But on another level, the development of Quakerism from an anti-authoritarian aberration into an effective, self-governing community made the sect threatening. For what the Quakers had created was not just an alternative to the Congregational church but also to the local community itself. This pattern was analogous to those found among the numerous Sephardic communities after the Iberian Diaspora. Even the ideology of religious persecution within the Quaker community echoed that of these Diasporic communities. Heyrman points out,

> The Quaker fellowship was not just indifferent to geographic boundaries — its essential ethos was anti-localistic. The Salem Meeting not only limited and discouraged its members' engagement in the town community, but also fostered actively their antagonism to local society itself by the ritualized accounting and recounting of "sufferings." Obligations like paying the [Puritan] minister's rate, contributing to the [Puritan] meetinghouse fund, and participating in militia training that the [Puritan] orthodox accounted as identifying badges of membership within the community, the Quakers styled as "sufferings" extracted from dissenters. The Salem Meeting's leading laymen made regular "inspections" of these losses and entered "what friends suffered, when and at whose hands" in a ledger that it "may not be forgotten, but that it may stand upon record for generations yet unborn to see how faithful Friends took joyfully the Spoyling of their goods for the answer of a good Conscience towards God.

Those goods were ample. Most citizens within the Quaker community were extremely competent merchants and international traders. Even Quaker women were astute in business affairs and would upon occasion run their late husband's business — behaviors matching only those in the Sephardic Jewish community. Famously, there was Gracia the Nasi, the "woman who defied kings" in the sixteenth century and took over after her husband's death the largest bank in Europe. The Jewish prophetesses Deborah, Anne, Huldah and Hannah were popular namesakes among the Quakers, as were Biblical heroines like Judith, Esther and Miriam.[47] Puritans seemed to prefer docile names like Ruth, Abigail, Rachel, Sarah and Rebecca.

Of the entrepreneurial qualities of Quaker women, Heyrman writes:

> Nor was Elizabeth Browne the only woman in town involved in business. Miriam Gross [clearly an Ashkenazic surname] invested in a fishing vessel after the death of her merchant-husband and continued his local trade. More reluctant about personally managing her legal affairs than Madame Browne, Miriam appointed her relative, Captain John Stacey, to act as her attorney.... Widow Tabitha Woods took over her husband's tavern and, along with Captain John Stacey [from Eustace], John Edgcomb, and their Boston partner James Pitts, owned a merchant ship, the *Dragon*.... Quaker-run transports traded with Spain by using reshipment stations in England, Jersey (island), and Holland.

These business, marital and trading patterns are indications of a crypto–Jewish presence in those Massachusetts townships that prospered the most, both socially and economically, during the 1600s to 1700s.

Since 2001 with the advent of DNA surname projects we can go beyond the paper trail of genealogy. More than 2,000 of these genetic probes are underway, many devoted to regions or ethnic groups (for instance, Melungeons) rather than surnames. Selecting one of these at random for Massachusetts, the Chelsea DNA Project, we were struck, as was the project administrator, by the "diversity" of local Y chromosome pedigrees. True, the majority

(58 percent) of male haplogroups or lineages were R1b, the leading type in Europe overall, especially on the Atlantic Coast, but there were 8 percent E3b (considered a North African, Middle Eastern and Jewish haplogroup, sometimes called "Moorish"), 3 percent G (another minor Jewish type, believed to be Central Asian), 20 percent I (predominately Scandinavian in origin but important also in Spain), 4 percent T (suspected to be Phoenician and recently proven to be the type of Thomas Jefferson),[48] 5 percent J (the classic Jewish male type, including one family with the surname Cohen) and 2.5 percent R1a (an Ashkenazi, including also one Cohen).[49]

Thomas Paine

An examination of one of America's most influential citizens, the orator and patriot Thomas Paine, provides additional support for the surmise that there might have been a not inconsiderable number of Jewish and Muslim-descended persons living in early Massachusetts. Paine was born on January 29, 1737, to a tradesman's family residing about seventy-five miles from London. The family surname is derived from "pagan, payin" (heathen, infidel) and as we have seen, it is instanced several times among Virginia colonists. Thomas' mother was Francis Cocke; her father was a lawyer. His own father, Joseph, was a Quaker. There are no records of Thomas being baptized. Paine regarded himself as a Quaker and according to Paine biographer Jack Fruchtman hoped to be buried in their cemetery.[50] He attempted to work as a corset maker, apprenticing himself to a John Pronis (Peronnes), but soon abandoned this occupation to sail on the *King of Prussia*, a privateer commanded by a Captain Mendez. Mendez is a Sephardic surname and Pronis seems to be an Italian form of the French Peronne.

By age 22, Paine had acquired a close male friend, Cleo Rickman (Ashkenazic surname), and a wife, Mary Lambert, whose father was a customs tax collector. He himself became a tax collector, an office which entailed "collecting an internal customs duty, mainly on alcoholic beverages, but also on salt, soap, tobacco and other goods." He proved to be slipshod in this line of work, however, and was fired after a year. By 1766 he was back in London,

Thomas Paine (Emmet Collection, Miriam and Ira D. Wallach Division of Art, Prints and Photographs, The New York Public Library, Astor, Lenox and Tilden Foundations).

Quaker meeting house (Robert N. Dennis Collection of Stereoscopic Views, Miriam and Ira D. Wallach Division of Art, Prints and Photographs, The New York Public Library, Astor, Lenox and Tilden Foundations).

where he worked at a "Sabbath-keeping academy" run by a Daniel Noble (Nobel, Norbel). Such an institution would have resembled a Jewish yeshiva and the governing master's name is distinctly Sephardic.

By February 1768 he had returned to being a tax collector, this time in Lewes, Sussex, a sharply anti–Catholic town. Paine lodged at the home of a tobacconist and grocery store owner, Samuel Olive, who had a decidedly Sephardic surname and occupation. In 1771 he married Olive's daughter Elizabeth. One of the witnesses was Henry Verral, a colleague of the father who also bears a Sephardic surname. In 1774 Paine — by now politically radicalized — sailed for Massachusetts, where he fell in with a group of revolutionary thinkers. Among them was Benjamin Rush of Philadelphia, a physician and writer. Rush came from Scotland and was an adherent of Calvinism, a theology having many affinities with Judaic thought.[51] Another was David Rittenhouse, astronomer and instrument maker, and yet another, George Clymer, a prosperous Philadelphia merchant, president of the Bank of Philadelphia, later a partner with financier Robert Morris in the Bank of North America.

To judge a man by the company he keeps, Paine moved in a circle that had all the marks of crypto–Judaism.

Genealogical Analyses

We have thus far examined some of the contemporaneous social relationships among the Massachusetts Colony settlers, especially religious memberships, marital patterns, business dealings and friendships. Such patterns provide a window into the social history of the early decades. We turn now to a longitudinal analysis of some genealogies for persons involved in the colony either as financial-political supporters in England or as founders of prominent colonial lineages. Given below is the genealogy of Lord Saye and Sele, an ardent anti–Catholic English peer and strong supporter of the migration of Protestants to the Massachusetts Colony — Protestants whom we have demonstrated, or attempted to demonstrate, to contain significant amounts of Sephardic and Moorish ancestry.

Genealogy of Lord Saye and Sele

James Fiennes of Hever and Knole in Kent Fought at Agincourt, 1415 1st Lord Saye and Sele, 1447 Treasurer of England, d. 1450	Spouse unknown
Sir William Fiennes 2nd Lord Saye and Sele Killed at the Battle of Barnet, 1471	Margaret Wykeham
Henry Fiennes 3rd Lord Saye and Sele, d. 1476	Anne Harcourt, dau. of Sir Richard Harcourt of Stanton, Harcourt
Richard Fiennes 4th Lord Saye and Sele, d. 1501	Elizabeth Croft, dau. of Richard Croft of Chipping, Norton
Edward Fiennes 5th Lord Saye and Sele, d. 1528	Margaret Danvers, dau. of Sir John Danvers of Deuntsey, Wiltshire
Richard Fiennes 6th Lord Saye and Sele, d. 1573	Ursula Fermoor, dau. of Richard Fermoor of Easton Neston, Norton
Sir Richard Fiennes 7th Lord Saye and Sele, d. 1613	Constance Kingsmill, dau. of Sir William Kingsmill of Sidmanton
William Fiennes 8th Lord Saye and Sele Created Viscount, 1624 One of the Leaders of the Parliamentarians before and during the Civil War, d. 1662	Elizabeth Temple, dau. of John Temple of Stowe, Bucks

James Fiennes 9th Lord Saye and Sele and 2nd Viscount, d. 1674	Frances dau. of Viscount Wimbledon	1. Elizabeth dau. of Sir John Eliot of Cornwell	Nathaniel d. 1669	2. Francis

John Twisleton	Elizabeth	William 3rd Viscount Saye and Sele, d. 1698	Mary dau. of Hon. Richard Fiennes	Celia F. Thavelle
Cecil Twisleton 10th Lord Saye and Sele, d. 1723		George Twisleton of Womersley, Co. York	Nathaniel 4th Viscount Saye and Sele, d. 1710	
Fiennes Twisleton 11th Lord Saye and Sele, d. 1730.		Mary Clarke of Ireland		
John Twisleton 12th Lord Saye and Sele, d. 1763		Anne Gardner of Little Bourton, Oxon		
Thomas Twisleton 13th Lord Saye and Sele, d. 1788		Elizabeth, dau. of Sir Edward Turner of Ambrosden, Oxon		
Gregory William Twisleton 14th Lord Saye and Sele, d. 1844		Maria, dau. of 1st Lord Eardley of Belvedere, Kent	Thomas James Twisleton d. 1824 = Anna dau. of Benjamin Ashe	
Frederick Benjamin Twisleton 15th Lord Saye and Sele		Emily, dau. of Viscount Powers		

The first thing we should take note of the Saye and Sele lineage is that their surname was originally Fiennes. James Fiennes was a descendant of Rollo, the ancestor of William the Conqueror, in the same bloodline as Makhir, Narbonne's King of the Jews, Charlemagne, the Scottish Sinclairs and the kings of Jerusalem. Secondly, we should note that the primary ancestor was treasurer of England, a post often held by Jews throughout Europe during this period. When we reach the 6th Lord, Richard Fiennes, we learn that his wife is Ursula Fermoor — both her first and last names are indicative of non–English ancestry. The surname Fermoor suggests graphically that her ancestry was Moorish and iron-working related.

By the early 1600s, at the time of the Massachusetts Colony's founding, William Fiennes, the 8th Lord, has married Elizabeth Temple, a woman whose surname evokes Jewish ancestry. By the late 1600s the title has passed to another line through the marriage of Mary Fiennes to John Twisleton. Yet we believe that the practice of Judaism — likely in crypto form — has still continued. That this is the case can be inferred from the marriage of Thomas James Twisleton to Anna Ashe, the daughter of Benjamin Ashe, for Ashe is another name strongly suggestive of Jewish affiliation.

Massachusetts Leavitt Family

We turn now to the genealogy of the Levet/Leavitt family, a prominent Massachusetts lineage that is also likely Jewish in ancestry. Why? First, because the name Levet is itself Hebrew, signifying Levite, one from the tribe of Levi. England in 1524 did not have any Jews living openly as such, so the Levet family was likely crypto–Jewish. Note that their naming pattern in England is "English," e.g., William, Elizabeth, not Hebrew or Mediterranean. Perhaps they have become sincerely Christian? Let's look what happens when the family arrives in the colonies.

Nicholas Levet
Born: 1524, Died: 1578
Parents: William Levet, Elizabeth Wentworth
Spouse: Ann Westby
Children: Ralph Levet
NOTES: Normanton and Melton, Eng., Rotherham, Eng.

Ralph Levet
Born: 1541, Died: 3 January 1581
Parents: Nicholas Levet, Ann Westby
Spouse: Elizabeth West
Children: Thomas Levett, Sr.
NOTES: Melton, England

Thomas Levett, Sr.
Born: August 1572, Died: 16 February 1622
Parents: Ralph Levet, Elizabeth West
Spouse: Elizabeth Mirfin, wed 2 July 1593, Eng.
Children: Thomas Levett
NOTES: Melton, England

Thomas Levett
Born: 23 July 1594, Died: 1655
Parents: Thomas Levett, Sr., Elizabeth Mirfin
Spouse: Margaret Lindley
Children: Thomas Leavitt
NOTES: Melton, England

Thomas Leavitt
Born: 1616, Died: November 1696
Parents: Thomas Levett, Margaret Lindley
Spouse: Isabella (Bland) Austin, wed 1644
Children: Hezron, Aretas, John, James
NOTES: Born in Lincolnshire, England, died in Hampton Falls, New Hampshire. Isabella was from Colchester Co., Essex, England

Thomas Leavitt, having been born in England and immigrating to New Hampshire (then part of Massachusetts Colony), marries a woman bearing a Ladino name, Isabella, and has children the couple names Hezron and Aretas ("virtue"). These are Hebrew and Greek names respectively and typical of Sephardic naming customs; they represent an abrupt departure from the previous four generations of Leavitt names.

Massachusetts Generation 1

Hezron Leavitt
Born: 1645, died January 14, 1739
Parents: Thomas Leavitt and Isabella (Bland) Austin
Spouse: Martha Taylor, wed 25 September 1667
Children: Thomas, Lydia, John, James, Moses, Mary, Abigail, Sarah
NOTES: Mother, Isabella, was from Colchester Co., Essex, England.

Hezron Leavitt maintains this new ethnic naming practice, using Lydia (Greek), Moses, Abigail and Sarah as names for his children and carrying forward the James and John names.

Thomas Cushman
Born: February 8, 1607, Died: December 11, 1691
Parents: Robert Cushman, Sarah Leavitt
Spouse: Mary Allerton, wed 1636
Children: Thomas, Sarah, Lydia, Rev Isaac, Elkanah, Feare, Eleazer, Mary.
NOTES: Thomas was raised and educated in the family of Gov. Bradford of Plymouth, Mass.

The Cushman line (Ashkenazic surname) enters at this point, with Thomas Cushman being the son of Robert Cushman and Sarah Leavitt. Thomas and his wife, Mary Allerton, appear to be consciously Jewish, naming their children Lydia, Isaac, Elkanah and Eleazer. Her brother John Leavitt follows this same pattern, marrying two Jewish-surnamed women (Lovet and Gilman) and naming his children Israel, Samuel, Jeremiah, Abigail and so forth.

John Leavitt
Born: 1608, Died: 20 November 1691
Spouses: Mary Lovet; wed 1637, Sara Gilman of Caston, England; wed 1646
Children: John, Hannah, Samuel, Elizabeth, Jeremiah, Israel, Moses, Josiah, Nehemiah, Sarah, Mary, Hannah, Abigail
NOTES: Came over with the Pilgrims (possibly from Derbyshire) in 1630.

Generation 2

Thomas Leavitt
Born: 1677, Died: 1749
Parents: Hezron Leavitt and Martha Taylor
Spouse: Elizabeth Atkinson
Children: Joseph, Samuel, Sarah, Jonathan, Mary

Thomas Cushman II
Born: 1637
Parents: Thomas Cushman, Mary Allerton
Spouses: Ruth Howland (1674), Abigail Fuller (1679)
Children: Robert, Job, Bartholomew, Samuel, Benjamin

Israel Leavitt
Born: 23 April 1648, Died: 26 December 1696
Parents: John Leavitt, Mary Lovit
Spouse: Lydia Jackson
Children: John, Israel, Solomon, Elisha, Abraham, Sarah, Lydia, Hannah, Mary
NOTES: Lived in Hingham, Massachusetts.

At this point several family members have moved to Hingham, Massachusetts, a town shown to have harbored a crypto–Jewish community.

Generation 3

Joseph Leavitt, Sr.
Born: 1704, Died: 1764
Parents: Thomas Leavitt, Elizabeth Atkinson
Spouse: Bethia Bragdon
Children: Joseph, Jr., Thomas, Samuel, Elizabeth, Daniel Jeremiah, Sarah

Benjamin Cushman
Born: 1691
Parents: Thomas Cushman II, Abigail Fuller

Spouse: Sarah Easton
Children: Jabez , Caleb, Solomon, Jerusha, Benjamin, Sarah, Abigail, Thomas, Jerusha, Huldah
NOTES: later Married Sarah Bell

John Leavitt
Born: 6 July 1678, Died: 29 July 1749
Parents: Israel Leavitt, Lydia Jackson
Spouse: Joanna Brisbee
Children: Solomon, John, Jacob, Joanna

Generation 4

Joseph Leavitt, Jr.
Born: 1739, Died: 1809
Parents: Joseph Leavitt, Sr., and Bethia Bragdon
Spouses: Sarah Bradbury, wed November 10, 1763; Anna French
Children: Samuel, Sarah, Joseph, Thomas, William, Betsy, Benjamin, Anna, Bradbury, True.
  Capt. Thomas Bradbury's grandmother Mary Perkins moved from Warwick, England to Amesbury, Mass., in the 1600s. Here she was tried and convicted of witchcraft in 1692. Her execution was delayed when her husband and clergyman testified for her and 117 of her neighbors signed a petition praising her character.

The entry for Joseph Leavitt above ties the family into the Massachusetts witchcraft trials, which, as we have seen, appear to reflect a reaction to crypto–Jewish religious practices.

Benjamin Cushman II
Born: May 25, 1722, Died March 5, 1813
Parents: Benjamin Cushman, Sarah Easton
Spouse: Zeruiah Sampson, wed August 27, 1747
Children: Caleb, Jacob, Benjamin

Solomon Leavitt
Born: 12 March 1708
Parents: John Leavitt, Joanna Brisbee
Spouse: Tabitha Crane, wed 25 November 1731
Children: Jacob, Elizabeth, Abijah, John, Tabitha, Mary

Generation 5

Samuel Leavitt
Born: 18 March 1770 Died: February 1853
Parents: Joseph Leavitt, Jr., and Sarah Bradbury
Spouses: Hannah Garland, wed January 24, 1793, then Mary Ayer, wed 1803, then Dorcus Ridlon
Children: William P. Leavitt, John, Joseph

Caleb Cushman
Born: January 24, 1750, Died March 16, 1833

Parents: Benjamin Cushman II, Zeruiah Sampson
Spouse: Lucy Sinclaire
Children: Caleb, Alvan, William, Mary, Benjamin, Sally, Elias, Chandler, Eliza, Eunice
NOTES: 3 wives: Hepsibah Bolster (4 children), Lucy Sinclaire (6 children) and Abigail Oldham. Moved from Plympton about 1780 to Hebron, Israel, then to Paris, Maine, 1783

This generation is perhaps the "smoking gun" signaling the continuation of Judaism within the Cushman-Leavitt family in the New World. Caleb Cushman, born and raised in the Colonies, departs for Hebron, Israel, in 1780, apparently making an *aliyah* on behalf of his family, perhaps the first in several hundred years.

Jacob Leavitt
Born: 4 February 1732, Died: 25 January 1814
Parents: Solomon Leavitt, Tabitha Crane
Spouse: Sylvia Bonney, wed 15 March 1753
Children: Joseph, Seriah, Abijah, Sylvia, Tabitha, Jacob II, Isaiah, Sarah, Cyrus, Isaac
NOTES: Sylvia was a descendent of *Mayflower* passengers. Her mother, Elizabeth, had a sister Lydia Hamlin. Lydia was the great-grandmother of Hannibal Hamlin; Abraham Lincoln's vice president.

Generation 6

William P. Leavitt
Born: May 27, 1797, Died: August 7, 1844
Parents: Samuel Leavitt, Hannah Garland
Spouse: Anna Berry, wed December 25, 1832, in Buxton, ME.
Children: William Henry Leavitt, Elizabeth, Charles

Nathaniel Fickett Jr.
Parents: Nathaniel Fickett, Susanna Brown
Spouse: Hannah P. Curtis
Children: Loring Curtis, Richmond, Sarah Persis, Martha Jane, Ai Jackson, Nancy, Enos, Elbridge, Hannah Augusta, Olive Gross

As discussed earlier, the given name Persis is Sephardic and means "from Persia." It was adopted in honor of the matriarchs who produced the Babylonian exilarchs.

Chandler Cushman
Born: February 29, 1804, Died: August 19, 1840
Parents: Caleb Cushman, Lucy Sinclaire
Spouse: Mary Jael Prince
Children: Eliza H., Jeanette Dorcas, Mary Francis, Eunice Mellon

Jacob Leavitt II
Born: 31 March 1765 Died: 7 October 1845
Parents: Jacob Leavitt, Sylvia Bonney
Spouse: Rhoda Thayer, wed 1 January 1788
Children: Jesse, Martin, Albert, Orren, Silas, Lovina, Phebe, Almira

In addition to the Ashkenazic given and surname of Jacob Leavitt's spouse, the given name Almira marks them as Jewish. In the seventh generation we encounter a Roxanna, the name of Alexander's Persian wife popular with Jews down the ages, often allegorized as Rosh Hashanah.

Generation 7

William Henry Leavitt
Born: 1834, Died: 1881
Parents: William P. Leavitt, Anna Berry
Spouse: Roxanna Harmon
Children: Joseph E. Leavitt, Alice, Anna, Albert, Arthur, Nellie

Massachusetts Lowell Family

Let us now take a look at the Lowell family of Massachusetts, about whom the saying goes, "The Cabots speak only to the Lowells, and the Lowells speak only to God." We suspect that the God the Lowells are speaking to is Hebrew, not Christian. Let us consider their genealogy. The first member of whom we have record is a Percival Lowle, born in 1571, a successful merchant in England. The relatively late date of 1571, his wife's name of Rebecca (Hebrew), and his occupation as a merchant all suggest the possibility of Judaic heritage. This presumption is strengthened by the marriage of his daughter Joanna to John Oliver, this surname being of Sephardic origin. Further, John is an importer, meaning he has international trade connections. Lowell probably originates as Low, a French form of Levi, plus the theophoric -el so common in Anglo-Norman surnames. Moreover, according to medieval legend, the two Arthurian figures of Percival/Parsifal and Lancelot were Jewish.

Percival Lowle
Born 1571 in Somerset, England. Died January 8, 1664, age 93, in Newbury, MA.
Occupation: Merchant. In England he had a large mercantile establishment.
Married Rebecca
Children:
John 1595–1647
Married Mary, who died in 1639 soon after the birth of their 5th child and the year of her arrival in New England. 2. Elizabeth Goodale in Newbury, MA, 1639.
Joanna, 1609–1677. Married: John Oliver in England. He was an importer of English goods.
Married 2. Captain William Garrish (1617–1687).
Children:
Mary 1640–?, born in Newbury to Joanna and John, born to Joanna and William
Richard, 1602–October 5, 1682

Richard Lowle
Born: 1602 in England.

Died: October 5, 1682, age 80, in Newbury, MA.
Married: 1. Margaret, who died 1642 in Newbury, MA.
2. Margaret in Newbury, MA.
Children:
Percival of Richard and first wife.
Rebecca with second wife.
Samuel
Thomas

Percival Lowle
Born: in Newbury, MA.
Married: Mary Chandler on September 7, 1664, 2. Sarah ___, probably in 1709
Children:
Richard
Gideon
Samuel
Edmund
Margaret
Johanna

In the entry below, we see that Gideon Lowell has married a Sephardic-named woman, Miriam Swett (Sweet); this surname is one found among the Melungeons of Appalachia.

Gideon Lowell
Born: 1672 in Newbury, Massachusetts.
Died: 1763 in Amesbury, Massachusetts.
Married: Miriam "Mary" Swett (1672–1734) in 1692.
 Widow Elizabeth Colby in Amesbury, MA
Children of Gideon and Miriam:
 Mary
 Gideon
 Stephen
 Moses

 Hannah
 Joseph
 Abner
 Jonathan
 Samuel
 John
NOTE: Gideon was a sea captain. He sailed widely and often took his wife, Miriam, with him. Probably some of his children were born at sea. He amassed a considerable fortune.

Gideon's son John was born in South Carolina in 1696 and married Rachael Sargent, a woman carrying Sephardic first and last names.

John Lowell
Born: February 1, 1696, in South Carolina, probably aboard one of his father's sailing vessels.
Married: Rachael Sargent in Amesbury, Massachusetts.
Children:
 Jacob
 John
 Rachael
 Gideon
 Eliphalet
 Alice

John Lowell
Born: 1724 in Amesbury, Mass.
Married: Mary (or Martha) Currier in S. Hampton, N.H., in 1749.
Children:
 Paul
 Dorothy
 Joseph
 Jacob

 Sarah
 Mary
 Ellice
 Martha
 John, Jr.
 William
 Lydia
 Eliphet

Joseph Lowell
Born July 6, 1751, in Amesbury, MA.
Died 1832
Married: Abigail Danforth on November 7, 1773, in Wiscassit, Maine
Children:
 Joseph
 John
 Noah
 Samuel
 David
 James

The marriage partners, occupations and child naming patterns of the Lowell family suggest, as with the Leavitts, that the family was well aware of their Jewish ancestry and acted in ways to preserve that heritage.

Until the end of British rule, despite its small size Massachusetts occupied the position of most populous and best-governed of the colonies. Boston may not have answered to its billing as Hub of the Universe in the eyes of the mother country but it was the uncontested commercial and intellectual capital of the American colonies. Harvard College opened its doors in 1636. The first books in English in North America were printed there, and the earliest American writers came from there. It is understandable that the rebellion against England was planned and launched there. Later it was Massachusetts that led the nation in the development of manufacturing and mechanized assembly lines, especially guns, engines, agricultural equipment and armaments. Transcendentalism, the first distinctively American philosophy, arose in the circles of Boston Brahmins, where a form of deism not unlike the Averroeism of Spanish Jews had long been engrained. And was it an accident that Massachusetts became the center of the abolitionist movement? The success of the so-called Massachusetts experiment in utopianism and American freedom itself can hardly be fortuitous but rests firmly on the shoulders of the prominent families described in this chapter.

Even today, as Boston polishes its reputation as the "Athens of America," having become the leader in the country's high-tech revolution, the city's rank as sixth-largest Jewish community is far out of proportion to its impact on American Jewry and America as a whole. Elie Wiesel, Louis Brandeis, Rabbi Levi Yitzhak Horowitz, Rabbi Stephen S. Wise, Molly Picon, Theodore H. White, Arnold Auerbach, Arthur Fiedler, Leonard Bernstein, Justin Kaplan, Edward Bernays, Oscar Handlin, Barbara Walters, Mike Wallace, Leonard Nimoy, Ellen Goodman, Alan Dershowitz ... one has only to drop the names of some new founding fathers (and mothers) who set the tone in contemporary culture to realize Massachusetts' pioneering qualities and socio-political prominence in American history are unchanged.

CHAPTER FIVE

New York Colony:
Dutch, British and Jewish

New York has the distinction of being the only one of the thirteen original colonies started as a non–English settlement. New Netherland additionally served as a magnet for non–English immigrants such as Germans and Scandinavians, to say nothing of Europeans already transplanted elsewhere in the New World like South American Jews. It was established by the Dutch with outposts at Fort Orange (Albany) in 1624 and New Amsterdam on Manhattan Island the following year. To understand its history, we must first become familiar with the Dutch East India and West India Companies instrumental in its creation. The former was founded by nine merchants who met at a wine tavern in Amsterdam in 1594 at exactly the same time as the formal establishment of the Marrano community there.[1] They included Hendrik Hudde,[2] Reinier Paun,[3] Pieter Hasselaar, Arent ten Grootinhuis, Hendrik Buych,[4] Sejvert Sem (Semah, Hebrew for "descendant," also a form of the first name Shem),[5] Jan Poppin (Sephardic, diminutive of Jacobo), Jan Karel and Dirck van Os.[6]

Of the founders of the Dutch East India Company, most can be described as dark and Mediterranean in appearance — not one is a blond, ruddy cheeked Dutchman we might picture. Several were men who had fled from the southern Netherlands when Antwerp fell to Spanish control in 1585, and it is reported that two of the nine, Jan Karel and Dirck van Os, were Flemish.[7] Their intention was to poach the spice and tea trade in the East Indies established earlier by the Portuguese. From 1594 until as late as 1793, the Dutch East India Company traded with India, China, Japan, Persia, southern Africa, Java and Ceylon, transporting over one million passengers, soldiers, craftsmen and sailors eastward and constructing a remarkable Occidental presence in the Orient. Lead, vermillion (a dyestuff which appears as a Jewish surname) and cochineal were exported to Asia. Cloves, cinnamon, pepper, coffee, nutmeg and mace were imported to Europe, as were silk, cotton, opium, coral and tin.

Alone among the countries of Europe, the Dutch Republic around this time was moving toward declaring Jews citizens of the state. As a first step in this direction, the Dutch Parliament asked eminent legal scholar Hugo Grotius to draw up ordinances governing their treatment. Grotius presented his report concerning the admission of Jews to the Estates of Holland in 1619. With the renewed outbreak of war with Spain in 1621, many Marranos in the United Provinces left Amsterdam and settled in Hamburg for the safety of their import businesses.[8] The year 1639 saw most of them return and a unified Portuguese Jewish community was finally founded in Amsterdam. The Dutch capital now became a magnet for Judaizers fleeing the Spanish Inquisition. The exodus included physicians, merchants and financiers like the Da Costa, Cardozo and Mendoza families. Dutch Jews finally achieved emancipation in 1657, the same year as English Jews. The milestone owed its success to the same campaign, centered on the petitions of Amsterdam rabbi Menasseh ben Israel.

New York differed from the other colonies in another respect. Its purpose was neither high minded nor expedient; it was not to provide a refuge for religious dissidents nor to act as an outlet for restless Northern European *drang*. Because of the Sephardic merchants who founded it, the New York colony was imbued from the

Joan Blaeu, by J. van Rossum.

start with a commercial spirit and innovative intellectual currents of freedom and secularism. We have seen already the importance of Averroism for Spanish and Dutch Jews. The Dutch Republic was not only the world's greatest maritime power but its most enlightened government, championing freedom to such an extent that it welcomed the ideas of René Descartes, John Locke and Benedict de Spinoza. All immigrated there to escape attack in their own countries. The English journalist and novelist Daniel Defoe aptly observed of the Dutch economic spirit: "The Dutch must be understood as they really are, the Middle Persons in Trade, the Factors and Brokers of Europe.... They buy to sell again, take in to send out, and the greatest Part of their vast Commerce consists in being supply'd from All Parts of the World, that they may supply All the World again."[9]

The cartographers for the East India Company were commercially minded Sephardic Jews of the same mold. They included Petrus Plancius (Vlatfoete, from Flanders)[10] and the Blaeu (probably from the name for indigo dye, an Arab and Jewish specialty item)[11] and Van Keulon ("from Cologne") families.

In 1641 the company succeeded in taking the port of Malacca from the Portuguese, gaining an important trade route between Europe and East Asia. No doubt, this prize was considered a type of reprise avenging the expulsion of the members' ancestors from Iberia a hundred and fifty years earlier. Between 1619 and 1629 the company's director was Jon

Pieterszoon Coen (Cohen, Kohane). Coen handpicked and then groomed much of the leadership that followed him, and many of his protégés appear to have been fellow Jews. Under his direction the company built a "trade network stretching from the Cape of Good Hope and Persia in the West, via India, Ceylon and Malacca and the Indonesian Archipelago to China and Japan in the Far East…. The network encompassed some thirty settlements and made the company the most powerful merchant in Asia, as well as largest trading company in the world at the end of the seventeenth century. By 1750, 20,000 civil servants and soldiers resided in the company's Asia settlements." The company's list of imports grew to include indigo, cashmere, elephants, horses, diamonds, lacquer work and porcelain, which significantly impacted European material culture and aesthetics.

One of the best-remembered directors of the Dutch East India Company was Cornelis Speelman (1628–1684, "actor, buffoon").[12] Upon his death King William III created the Speelman baronetcy in Great Britain, and his mother was given the rank of widow of a baronet of England even though he had never, strictly speaking, acceded to the title. A descendant is Jewish chess champion Jonathan Speelman (born 1956).

Dutch West India Company

Meanwhile on the other side of the world Western Europe was experiencing dramatic increases in prosperity, strengthening the demand for luxury goods.[13] The Muscovy Company of England was created in 1570 to trade with Russia for animal pelts used in fashionable hats of the day as well as for warm clothing. French incursions into the fur-rich St. Lawrence region of North America were much envied by the Dutch. The North American fur trade grew to such a scale and magnitude that it charted half a continent and shaped the destinies of every Indian tribe in what is now Canada. It went far toward building the reputation for riches and luxurious living of the French monarch Louis XIV, styled the Sun King for the golden splendor of his court. Significantly, one of the explicit aims of the West India Company was "to remove the resources which Philip IV, king of Spain and Portugal, drew from his American possessions." According to Jewish Caribbean chronicler Mordechai Arbell, it was "in a way an instrument of war against Spain, and this purpose dictated many of the company's decisions when sending colonists to the new world."[14]

Soon an Antwerp-born merchant whose family had fled to Amsterdam in 1585 after the Spanish Invasion entered the fur trade arena in North America by joining with two French partners. His name was Arnout Vogels (Hebrew Zipporah "Bird").[15] Participants in this effort to make inroads on one of the most lucrative markets of the day included persons named Sijmen (Simon) Mau (Moses, Maurice),[16] Francous and Leonnaert Pelgrom ("pilgrim, wayfarer"),[17] Cornelius Ryser ("traveler"), Adriaen Black, Thys Mosell ("from Moselle"), and Hans Hungar ("Hungarian"), names suggesting that this was largely an international and Jewish undertaking. A second set of merchants from Hoorn in the Netherlands included Cornelis Jacobz May,[18] Simon Nooms (Yiddish Nochem),[19] and Jonas Wilsen. Yet a third group included Jacob and Henrick Eelckens (Elkanah)[20] and Adriaen Jansz Engel (i.e., Angel).[21]

By 1626 the West India Company had been formed with Isaac de Rasieres serving as its chief commercial agent in New Netherland. Its corporate charter divided it into five chambers or branches: Amsterdam, Zeeland, the Maes cities, the Noorderquartier and Friesland-Groningen. Its board of directors consisted of nineteen men termed simply "the XIX" in company documents. From the beginning it functioned as a mercantile-military arm of the Netherlands, attacking, plundering and otherwise harassing the hated enemy Spain and her colonies. The Dutch, under Jan de Moor (literally, John the Moor), established colonies in Guiana, the Amazon and Esquibo during the early 1600s and vied for the rich trade in Brazilian sugar. They contemplated conquering Brazil because "in their view the Portuguese were neither able nor willing to offer effective resistance, especially as many of them were Jews, sworn enemies of the Spanish Inquisition."[22]

Isaac De Rasieres was born in Middleburg in the Netherlands in 1595. Little is known of his early life until 1626 when he came to New Netherland as a chief trading agent for the Dutch West India Company and secretary for the province. William Bradford, in the *History of Plymouth Plantation*, describes him as "their upper commis or chief merchant, and second to the governor, a man of fair and genteel behavior; but who soon after fell into disgrace amongst them, by reason of their factions." This rupture is believed to have occurred between November 1627 and September 1630, when de Rasieres' successor began to officiate as secretary.

Rasieres was married in Amsterdam in 1633 to the niece of one of the directors of the West India Company. Certain members of the company tried to make him governor of New Netherland (replacing Wouter van Twiller), but this attempt failed. He afterwards moved to Brazil, home to many Jews and crypto–Jews, where one of his sons was born in 1637 and a second in 1641. Upon his second son's marriage in Amsterdam in 1669, the record simply reads "parents departed to Barbados" (again a center of Marrano settlement). It is a family legend that Rasieres became governor of Tobago.[23]

In 1624 the West Indies Company made the decision to plant colonies in North America. Not surprisingly, given what we have already seen of the English strategy, the company used Sephardim as antagonists in the first onslaught. The earliest settlers were Walloons, "Protestant refugees from the Southern Netherlands [who displayed] willingness to risk wives and children ... towards emigration."[24] As we have witnessed happening repeatedly from Roanoke to Jamestown, from Plymouth Rock and Boston to the shores of South Carolina and Maryland, former Sephardim and Moors, now surfacing in various hues of Protestantism, were placed aboard ships and transported from Western Europe to North America. In addition to the Walloons came French Huguenots recruited by one Jesse de Forest (Jesse Sylva).[25] All these incoming ostensibly Dutch settlers received free passage and an allotment of land to cultivate for their own usage. Conscripts were permitted freedom of conscience in religious matters so long as the public aspect of religious worship adhered to the reformed Protestant practice of the Netherlands.[26] This, of course, left the way clear for continuation of Judaic and Islamic practices in the privacy of their homes.

Also in 1624 the West Indies Company revised its charter to launch the patroon system. Under such auspices an entrepreneur, the patroon, collected twenty families as settlers, provided them with all needed equipment and passage to North America and received a thousand acres of land. Jan de Moor played an important part in gathering colonists for these ventures in South America, the Caribbean and North America. Other prominent patroon colonizers were David de Vries, Samuel Godyn, Johannes de Laet, Samuel Blommart (Flowers, Flores), Kilian van Renssalaer, Albert Conraets, Cornelius Bicker, Gommer Spranger and Hendrick Hamel (Hebrew letter shaped like a "camel").[27]

Jewish mercantilist motives were also instrumental in the formation of New Sweden. This colony was another offshoot of the Dutch West India Company, one spearheaded by its Baltic base in the west Swedish port of Gothenberg where Marranos and other ex-patriots

Peter Stuyvesant (Print Collection, Miriam and Ira D. Wallach Division of Art, Prints and Photographs, The New York Public Library, Astor, Lenox and Tilden Foundations).

of Spain and Portugal dominated the merchant community. Two ships under the command of the disaffected former governor of New Netherland Peter Minuit reached the mouth of the Delaware River near present-day Wilmington in 1638. They established Fort Christina, named in honor of the Swedish queen. Five years later the Amsterdam investors sold out. Finland was the eastern third of the Swedish nation at the time. A reorganization brought thousands of Finnish farmers, but they were too few to hold the colony against attack from their Dutch neighbors to the north. The Swedish colony surrendered to Pieter Stuyvesant, the governor of New Amsterdam. Most of the Finns, however, remained. The design of pioneer log cabins became one of their enduring gifts to America. The Swedes also attempted to establish three colonies in the Caribbean, all inspired by similar commercial motives.

The island of Tobago had a similar early history of links to Marranos in Amsterdam.[28] It was founded by the obscure Baltic duchy of Courland, whose ruler, Duke Jekabs (Jacobus), was related by marriage to shareholders of the Dutch West India Company. Having ventured first to plant a colony in Gambia in Africa, Courland with its Latvians became in 1639 the tiniest European state to boast a colony in the new world. Tobago lasted until 1693 and earned fame as one of the first international settlements of freemen, drawing settlers from Latvia, Lithuania, Amsterdam, Zeeland, the semi-autonomous Jewish state in Livorno, France and its colonies, Germany, Brazil, Africa and even the native population of Caribs on the island itself. All these plans were laid down by investors in Amsterdam and carried out on Dutch shipping with Jewish interests at heart.

Revealingly, non–Dutch settlers composed nearly half of the colonists at New Netherland. It became the most religiously and ethnically mixed colony in North America. Freedom was such a byword that the dissident Anne Hutchinson, declared a heretic in Massachusetts, moved there from exile in Rhode Island. She met an unfortunate death at the hands of an Indian insurrection in 1643.

Marriage Patterns Among Early Dutch Colonists: Marie Taine/Tayne/Toynie

Let us take a closer look at some of these non–Dutch Huguenot and Walloon settlers.[29] Marie Taine married Jean LeRoy in 1671. Her brother Isaac had immigrated to New

Amsterdam some years before her own voyage in 1660. Isaac was made a burgher of New Amsterdam. On 24 June 1666, he obtained a grant of land at New Castle, Delaware, and married Sarah Reson (a name that is Persian for "prince," as previously noted). Marie and her husband, Philippe Casier, sailed directly for Manhattan from the Texel in the Netherlands on 27 April 1660 on board the *Gilded Otter* and settled at Harlem. On 23 July 1664, seventeen Harlem residents had their names transferred to the register of the church at Fort Amsterdam, to which several of them had previously belonged:

> Jan La Montagne, Jr., and Maria Vermeille his wife
> Daniel Tourneur and Jacquline Parisis, his wife
> Johanes Verveelen and Anna Jaersvelt, his wife
> Joost Van Olbinus, Sr., and Martina Westin, his wife
> Joost Van Oblinus, Jr., and Maria Sammis, his wife
> Glaude le Maistre and Hester du Bois, his wife
> Pierre Cresson and Rachel Cloos, his wife
> Jaques Cresson and Maria Renard, his wife
> Jean le Roy (the Royal, a common Sephardic surname)
> Isaac Vermeille and Jacomina Jacobs, his wife
> Resolved Waldron and Tanneke Nagel, his wife
> Pieter Jansen Slot and Marritie Van Winckel, his wife

Former residents or landholders in the same community included Nicholas de Meyer and Lydia Van Dyck, his wife, Jacques Cousseau and Madeline du Tulliere, his wife, Philip Casier and Marie Taine, his wife, Willem de la Montagne, Anna Verveelen, Arent Jansen Moesman and Juriaen Hanel. After the death of her husband, Philippe Casier, Marie sold the lot in Harlem and moved within New Amsterdam. Her sons Jean and Jacques had a bakery there. In 1671 she married Jean Le Roy.

The preceding account of the Taine/Tayne/Toynie family reveals probable Sephardic or Moorish roots. Note that Isaac Taine married a woman named Sarah Reson. As discussed elsewhere, the surname Reson claims linkage to the royal family of Persia as a retainer or chamberlain. The surname of one of their co-passengers, Jacqueline Parisis, is also of Persian origin, meaning Pharsee or Persian. Jan La Montagne (Mountain/Montana/Montanha) was likely originally Juan Montana in Spanish.[30] Sammis is Arabic for "descendant." Jacomina Jacobs bore Hebrew first and last names. Tanneke is Hebrew for Tanakh, the first five books of the Bible. Arent Moesman carried the surname Moses. Finally, Marie Taine remarried to Jean LeRoy ("of the King"), another surname attached to Jews or Moors in the service of the royal family.

Philippe Casier

Phillippe Casier of Calais in France is first mentioned in the Huguenot settlement of the French West Indies.[31] Phillippe and Marie (Taine) Casier's first two children, Jean and Marie, were born on Martinique. In 1645 he and others left the island and returned to Europe. He went first to Calais, then to Sluis in Flanders, where his daughter Hester was born. Many French and Walloon exiles from England and the Dutch seaboard fled to Mannheim in Germany, drawn there by assurances of freedom and protection under the government of the Protestant Elector Karl Ludwig. Sometime after 1652 he moved to the

Lower Palatinate along with a number of professed Protestants. By 1652 David Demarest (Greek) and other Huguenot refugees arrived to join in forming a French church. In it were Phillippe Casier and his family, Simeon Cornier, Meynard Journee (Diaz?) from Mardyck, Flanders, Joost Van Oblinus also from Walloon Flanders and Pierre Parmentier from Walslant, equally Walloon country.

Philippe's daughter Marie Casier married David Uzille/David Utzille (Uziel)[32] about this time, and in 1660 their son Peter was born. But Casier was not content at Mannheim. His wife's brother Isaac Tayne had gone to the New World earlier and become a burgher of New Amsterdam. And so, the Casier family, Uzilles included, followed. The same ship carried Mattheus Blanchan ("white") and others from Mannheim, including a band of soldiers among whom were Jacob Leisler and Joost Kockuyt.

Phillippe Casier, David Uzille and their families settled in Harlem on Manhattan Island. By the end of 1661 there were over thirty adult males settled in the same place. These were Michael Zypergus ("from Cyprus?"), Jan Sneden, Jan La Montagne, Jr., Michael Janse Mayden, Daniel Tourneir, Jean Le Roy, Pierre Cresson, Jacques Cresson, Phillippe Casier, David Uzille, Jacques Cousseau, Phillippe Presto, Francois Le Sueur, Simon De Ruine (Rouen), Gerritsen, Meynden Coerten, Aert Pietersen Buys, Sigismundus Lucas, Jan Pietersen Slot, Nicolaes De Meyer, Jan Laurens Duyts ("German"), Jacob Elderts Brouwer, Nelis Matthysen, Monis Peterson Staeck, Jan Cogu (Cohen), Adolph Meyre, Adam Dericksen, and Hendrick Karsens.[33] The common denominator was again Jewish roots. The list provides three additional Hebrew-Arabic surnames—Uzille, Lucas and Meyer. Two others appear to be Turkish, Buys (Bey, Bay, "king, lord") and Karsen (Khar-son).

David Uzille

The Uzille surname is clearly Sephardic/Hebrew, meaning "God is my strength." David Uzille's family came originally from near La Moussaye in lower Brittany. He married Marie Magdalena, the eldest daughter of Phillippe Casier from Calais. The Reformed Church at Nantes and La Moussaye was supported by the Le Maistres and Uzilles. In Henry G. Bayer's *The Belgians, First Settlers in New York and in the Middle States*, we read: "A little colony of Walloons, flying before the troops of the Duke of Alva, had come to settle within the territory of the Palatinate, at Frankenthal, near Mannheim, its capital, where we find many families that later moved to New Netherland: David de Marest, Frederic de Vaux, Abraham Hasbroucq, Chretien Duyou, Methese or Matthew Blanchan, Thonnet Terrin, Pierre Parmentier, Antoine Crispel, David Usilie, Phillippe Casier, Bourgeon Broucard, Simon Le Febre, Juste Durie, and others."[34]

Also found in Flanders are Robert de Toeni ("from Tunis"),[35] Ilbert de Toeni, Jumel de Toeni, Raoal de Toeni, Auvral de Toenie, Berenger de Toeni and Guillaume de Toeni. De Toeni is considered to be the original name of the Taine family. Magdalen's brother Peter Uzille married Cornelia Damen (Dutch Jewish surname)[36] in 1685, the sister of Lysbeth Damen, who married Jan/Jean Casier, son of Phillippe and Marie (Taine) Casier. Another daughter, Marie Usile, married Leonard Tremi, also known as Jonar Le Roy, in 1703. Adopting a pseudonym to disguise a Sephardic name—Jonar Le Roy—was a common practice among Marranos and Conversos wishing to avoid the attention of the Inquisition.

With this account we are beginning to see another marker of Sephardic-Moorish ancestry, marriage to first and second cousins across multiple generations. There is a strong gravitation toward Amsterdam and thence to the New World of Sephardic families already inter-related in Spain and living in exile in scattered places such as Calais, Rouen, Normandy, Brittany, Tunisia, Flanders, Greece, Turkey and Germany. This was an international set of allied families united by their Jewish (or perhaps better said, crypto–Jewish) faith.

Founding of New Amsterdam

A broader analysis of the Dutch presence in New Amsterdam lays bare some of the motives for Jews and Moors to immigrate to the New York colony. From Harlem historian James Van der Zee we learn that the Amsterdam fur traders who initiated explorations into the interior of North America had contacts with the French in Rouen, a Sephardic-Moorish stronghold encountered by us again and again.[37] Among the Amsterdam fur traders were William Usselinx (corruption of Uzille) and Killian van Renssalaer, both very wealthy; Renssalaer was a jeweler. When New Amsterdam was colonized initially in 1625, the only stone building was its counting house, or bank. Other buildings were wood. Any church remained to be built for a long time. These are sure signs that the colony was a mercantile venture with not even lip service being paid to religion. It is also reported that the Dutch ambassador to England at this time was an Albert Joachime (Dutch Jewish).[38] He was replaced by Jacob Cats, of an openly Jewish family (Katz, anagram of Hebrew *Kohane Tzadek*, "righteous priest").[39]

Remembered today as a poet and humorist, Cats was born at Brouwershaven in Zeeland on the tenth of November 1577. After losing his mother and being adopted with his three brothers by an uncle, he was sent to school at Zierikzee. He went on to study law at Leiden and Orleans. Returning to Holland, he settled at The Hague and began to practice as an advocate. In 1602 he married the wealthy Jewess Elisabeth von Valkenburg.[40] In 1627 Cats visited England on a mission to Charles I, who made him a knight.[41]

Within New Amsterdam proper was a motley array of residents. There was the mulatto Anthony Jansz van Salee from Morocco, son of a Dutch buccaneer who had worked for the sultan Muley Zidan. By 1633 the West India Company found it hard to recruit anymore Dutch settlers and made its colony available to everyone, promising free land to any who would cultivate it. A variety of interlopers arrived including James Farrett, a Scot claiming to be the agent of Henry Alexander, earl of Stirling; Lionel Gardiner, who acquired an island nearby; and a group of Swedes under the supervision of John Printz (Jewish surname).[42] Colonial New York historian Michael G. Kammen reports that "in 1657 ... thirty-one residents of Flushing, New York sent a remonstrance home [stating], 'the law of love, peace and liberty in the State extends to Jews, Turks and Egyptians, as they are considered the sons of Adam, which is the glory ... of Holland.'"[43] This was the same year Jews were officially recognized with decrees of tolerance in both Holland and England.

The Dutch were never able to make a success of their New Amsterdam colony.[44] In 1664 when it was captured by the English, the total population numbered only 1,500 persons. Of these, three hundred fifty dwelt in New Amsterdam city proper. Some of the residents listed in Joyce D. Goodfriend's book are "surgeon Hans Kierstide, brewer Isaac de Forrest [da Silva?], cooper Jan Bresteede,[45] glazier Evert Duycking, merchant Johannes de Peyster ["from Pyzdry" in Poland],[46] baker Laurens van der Spiegel ["mirror," a Jewish specialty like crystal],[47] blacksmith Cornelis Clopper [Cooper?], tailor Boele Roelfsen, mason Paulus Turck [Sephardic surname: many Sephardic Jews took refuge in the Ottoman Empire after the Inquisition began][48] and sword cutler Hendrick Bosch."[49] Goodfriend, in her account of early New Amsterdam, lists many names we will return to shortly. Let us introduce them briefly at this time, beginning with Balthazar Bayard, a brewer, and his brother Nicholas. Balthazar married Marite Loackermanns (Louk/Lok)[50] in 1664, daughter of a wealthy merchant. Abraham de la Noy (already discussed as a Sephardic surname) had two sons, Abraham and Peter. Mention is also made of Albertus Ringo, shoemaker; Peter Jansen Messier, carpenter; Denys Isacksen, another carpenter who arrived in 1659; Jacob Danielsen; Jacob Maurits (Moses), ship captain; Jeronimus Ebbingh, a merchant from Hamburg (another safe-haven for Sephardic Jews at the time); Jacob Abrahamsen, cooper; Martinus Hoffman, who resided in Kingston, Jamaica; Teunis ("from Tunis") Cray; Cornelis Barentsen (compare Berenson), measurer; Peter Jacob Marius, trader; Simon Janszen Romeyn ("from Rome"); Allard Anthony; Isaac de Peyster (Peiser), merchant; Isaac Brasier, carpenter; and Jacob Marius Groen (Green), silversmith.[51] Most of these surnames appear in the genealogies published on the Internet as "Dutch Jewry," and many are in the Family Tree of the Jewish People project.

Around four hundred Huguenots immigrated to New York around 1680. Numbering among them were Francois Bouquett, Josue David, Elie Boudinot (whose grandson would be elected the president of the first Continental Congress, and whose mother was Marie Suire, i.e. Sueiro, of Marans, Aunis, France),[52] Suzanne Papin (Papo),[53] Andre Laurent, Marie Luca, John Magnon, Jacob Rattier, Jael Arnaut, and the Tangee ("from Tangier"), LaFon and Grazillier families. Auguste Jay was a very successful merchant from that crypto–Jewish stronghold La Rochelle, France, which lent its name to New Rochelle north of New York. Like Kay, Bea, Gimbel/Hamel and Vee, the letter Jay was probably adopted as an expedient *kinnui* or secular name. The original *shem hakodesh* or sacred name could have been Judah or Jacob.

Jews Labeled as Such

Only three residents — all with Portuguese or Spanish names — are publicly identified as Jews during this period: Joseph Bueno (the "Good" name), merchant, Isaac Rodrigues Marques (Marks), merchant, and Joseph Isaacs, butcher. Other Jews had successfully adopted Dutch surnames, customs and associates to better blend with the populace. The lives of persons who were publicly branded as Jews were difficult in New Amsterdam, a fact which no doubt stimulated many to practice their religion in private. Van der Zee describes this situation as an extension of the attitude that the Dutch had toward openly Jewish persons in Holland. Remember, Jews had received permission to establish their first congregation in 1605, barely thirty-five years before. The Amsterdam Jewish community was "not loved, but was at least left in peace." They were protected by their wealth.

> The West India Company, struggling to stay afloat, needed Jewish money badly.... [Jews] had been free to go to Brazil. To call them back now "would be unreasonable and unfair, especially because of the considerable loss, sustained by the Jews in the taking of Brazil," the Heeren XIX piously wrote to Stuyvesant, adding more honestly: "and also of the large amount of capital which they have invested in shares of this Company." The letter was sent on April 26, 1655, and on its receipt Stuyvesant had to hastily revoke a resolution, handed over to the burgomasters of New Amsterdam by Van Tienhoven on March 1, in which the Jews [in New Amsterdam] were ordered to depart "forthwith."[54]

Permission to stay did not mean that Stuyvesant considered them normal burghers. The company had instructed him to give the Jews "the same privileges, as they have here [in Amsterdam] only as far as civil and political rights are concerned, without giving the said Jews a claim to the privileges of exercising their religion in a synagogue." But Stuyvesant thought even that too generous. Van der Zee continues,

> From the start he obstructed the Jews in every way possible. When two of them leased houses in December 1655, he tried to stop them and at the same time forbade them to trade on the Delaware River and at Fort Orange. On November 29 the Jews petitioned him not to restrict their activities, but Stuyvesant rejected the request "for weighty reasons." A new petition followed in March 1656 in which the Jews reminded the governor of the rights the company had granted them. They told him they were "willing and ready ... to contribute according to their means," if they were allowed to enjoy the same liberties as the other citizens. Stuyvesant turned to Amsterdam for advice, and on June 14 the lords directors made it clear that the Jews were indeed free to trade and purchase real estate. They were highly displeased with the general and told him reprovingly: "We wish ... that you had obeyed our orders, which you must always execute punctually and with more respect."[55]

A number of restrictions were upheld, however. No Jew could be employed in any public service, nor were they allowed to have "open retail shops." They could exercise their religion only "within their houses." Stuyvesant added to this list of company instructions one of his own. He refused Jews the right to join the militia of the city. Instead they were to pay an exemption tax of sixty-five *stuivers* a month. The Jews were not resentful, and they were more generous than the governor. When in the aftermath of the Indian massacre of 1655 the burgomasters asked for a contribution for the strengthening of the city wall, now Wall Street, five Jews gave five hundred guilders between them, one twelfth of the total. This might have influenced Stuyvesant's decision shortly afterward to grant them a concession he had refused a year earlier — they were now allowed to have their own burial place outside the city (at what is now Chatham Square in Chinatown), a mile from the wall. These restrictions continued into the New York era, as Kammen makes clear.

> By 1706, when the Jews of New York City prepared a kind of "constitution" for their own regulation, they enjoyed economic as well as some civil rights. They voted (if no one challenged them to take a Christian oath) and conducted public worship. In 1718 they won the privilege of naturalization through special acts of the Assembly, a privilege that enabled them to own land. By 1727 they seemed to have won full suffrage, and by 1731, when there were some seventy-five Jewish families in New York, they had dedicated the first synagogue to be constructed as such in British North America, had erected a separate school building, and had been allowed to expand their burying ground.
>
> At the election of 1737, however, their right to vote was successfully challenged. William Smith, Sr., played heavily upon anti–Semitic prejudices in persuading the Legislature to disallow Jewish votes for assemblymen, as well as Jewish testimony in court. Between 1748 and 1761 these privileges were regained and the Constitution of 1777 finally gave Jews (as well as Roman Catholics) full political equality. That document was to be a genuine benchmark in New York's movement toward complete secularization. It declared "that the free exercise and enjoyment of religious profession and worship without discrimination or preference, shall forever hereafter be allowed, within this state, to all mankind.[56]

Thus Jews were not fully enfranchised in New York until after the Revolutionary War. By the 1730s Ashkenazi Jews from Poland and Germany had begun to outbalance their openly Jewish Sephardic brethren. Goodfriend writes,

The Jewish immigrants who joined their coreligionists in New York City during the first three decades of the eighteenth century assembled from places all over the map of Europe, as well as in the West Indies. In 1712, Anglican chaplain John Sharpe cited as one of the advantages of New York City that "it is possible also to learn Hebrew here as well as in Europe, there being a Synagogue of Jews, and many ingenious men of that nation from Poland, Hungary, Germany &c." Ashkenazim outnumbered Sephardim among these newcomers, and by 1728 they formed a majority of the congregation Shearith Israel.[57]

Most of the Jewish immigrants engaged in some form of retail trade, but Valentine Campanal was a butcher and Uriah Hyam was a tallow chandler. Two merchant families that put down roots in the city in the early years of the eighteenth century came to tower over more recent arrivals — the Franks family and the Gomez family. Jacob Franks, whom we will encounter in the Pennsylvania chapter, was an Ashkenzi Jew born in England; he settled in the city about 1708 and commenced his mercantile career. He prospered, attaining high status in the city, and served in a number of important offices. With property assessed at £140 on the 1730 tax list, he ranked in the top five percent of the economic elite.[58]

The grandee Luis Moses Gomez occupies an unusual position in colonial American history. Born in Spain in 1660, he escaped the Spanish Inquisition to live in France and England, where he was a known Judaizer. After spending several years in the West Indies, he moved to New York City about 1703. There he purchased 6,000 acres of land on the Hudson River, at a spot where several Indian trails converged, later known as Jews Creek. He built a stone house with walls three feet thick into the side of the hill. Continuously occupied for more 300 years, Gomez Mill House is today the oldest surviving Jewish resi-

dence in North America. In 1729 Gomez used the right of British citizenship that had been granted him by Queen Anne to purchase a plot of land in lower Manhattan that would become the first cemetery of Congregation Shearith Israel. In 1730 the taxable property of retailers Lewis, Mordecai, Daniel and Moses Gomez totaled £305. The eminence of the Gomez family is illustrated by the fact that a special enclosure of the synagogue gallery was reserved for the Gomez women.[59]

The social and political restrictions on Jews in New York pressured many to abandon public identification with their faith and marry into ostensibly Christian (though in not a few instances, crypto–Jewish) families. Kammen, for

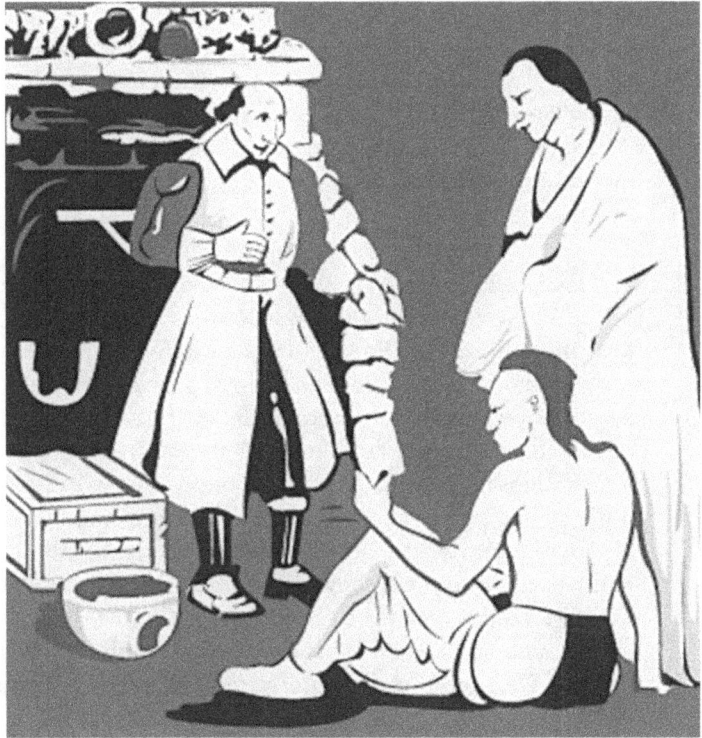

Luis Gomez trading with Indians (illustration by Kim Green).

example, declares: "The Sephardic Jews intermarried with Gentiles to such an extent that by the century's end a discrete Jewish community barely survived. When Phila Franks married Oliver De Lancey in 1742, her family was shocked and disappointed. Realistically, however, the number of eligible young Jewish men was small, and mother Abigail Franks had previously expressed a low regard for most of them. In succeeding years the union of Christian with Jewish families became increasingly common."[60]

We will argue below that what appear to be Jewish-Christian unions often are, in fact, Jewish or crypto–Jewish marriages. Jewish descent and inheritance patterns were maintained in private, though they were invisible in public.

Crypto-Jewish Families in New York

Let us take a closer look at the families believed to be crypto–Jewish and their points of origin.[61] One group arrived from the Palatine region of Germany in 1710. While the majority were directed onward to Livingston Manor on the Hudson River, a few made their way to New York City, including Hans Yure Bloom, John Reupel (Rubel) and John Peter Zenger. Zenger would open the first printing press in the colony. Peter Van Dyck and Myer Myers, both famed silversmiths, became investment bankers in New York City. There were also the prominent family of Daniel Kissam (Arabic) in Queens and the Lott (Hebrew) family of Kings County. Openly Jewish Uriah Hendricks (Henriques) became a leading copper, brass and iron manufacturer. In Albany during the 1730s, Barent Sanders (after Alexander) traded with Surinam, Curaçao, Jamaica, Barbados and Antigua — all Sephardic outposts in the Caribbean. On the upper Hudson, John Henry Lydius (the masculine form of the Sephardic Greek Lydia) was a large-scale fur trader during the 1730s. But surely the primary players were four families that from 1675 to 1725 provided the principal leadership for the New York commercial community. These were the Philipses, the Van Cortlands, the De Lanceys and the Schuylers. A strong case can be made that each of these families was Jewish in private practice, if not in public perception.

Philipse Family

Frederick Philipse (1627–1702), the founder of the Philipse family in the colonies, arrived in New Amsterdam about 1650 as the official carpenter and builder for the Dutch West India Company. Before long he extended his activities and became a trader with the Five Nations. In a few years he had risen to a pinnacle of success as a merchant. His commercial career was aided by both his first wife, Margaret Hardenbrook, and second, Catharine Van Cortlandt, whose families were also active in the Indian trade. By 1674 he was listed as the richest man in the New York colony. His worth of 80,000 guilders far surpassed that of his nearest two rivals, both of whose estates combined were valued at 50,000 guilders.

By the turn of the century when Frederick's only surviving son Adolph took over the family business, records show that the family owned in whole or part at least seven ships — the *Abigail, Diamond, Eagle, Phillipsburg, Charles, Hopewell* and *Mayflower* (the last in partnership with Stephen DeLancey). When Adolph took charge there was an increase in trade with the West Indies and greater variety in both exports and imports. Philipse exported to the West Indies and to the other mainland colonies a growing number of New York products, especially flour, lumber and horses. He also engaged in the Guinea trade, which entailed importation of slaves from the West Coast of Africa. For example, he received a shipload of 128 slaves on March 29, 1718. From about 1712, trade with the West Indies and the Madeira Islands began to loom large, and great quantities of rum and wine were imported. As previously discussed, such trading patterns are strong markers of Marrano-Converso connections.

Van Cortlandt

The founder of the Van Cortlandt family, Oloff Stephen Van Cortlandt (1600–1684), came to New Amsterdam in 1638 as a soldier in the service of the Dutch West India Company. He was appointed to the post of commissioner of cargoes and soon became the owner of a brewery, also launching other ventures such as the Indian trade. In 1642 he married Anneke Lookermans, a woman of ample means. By 1645 he was serving as a member of the councils advising the Dutch governors. He twice held the post of burgomaster of New Amsterdam. In 1674 Van Cortlandt was described as the fourth-richest man in the colony, his worth estimated at 30,000 guilders. He had two sons, both of whom served as his partners in business affairs. Stephen Van Cortlandt (1643–1700) married Gertrude, the sister of Peter Schuyler. Jacob (1658–1739) married Eva DeVries, the adopted daughter of Frederick Philipse. This pattern of endogamy should ring familiar.

Early Van Cortlandt shipping activities were markedly similar to those of Frederick Philipse. The two families jointly owned a ship named the *Beaver*. Jacob Van Cortlandt was especially active in the provisioning trade between the West Indies islands and mainland towns. His accounts for the period from 1699 to 1705 indicate that most of his trade was to Jamaica, Curaçao and Barbados, while other ports of call include Surinam, Madeira, Amsterdam and London. Once again a pattern of Converso-Marrano trading partnerships is evident.

DeLancey

New York's third great mercantile family was founded by Stephen DeLancey (1663–1741).[62] He fled Caen in France as a Huguenot refugee in 1681, going first to the Netherlands and then on to London. In March of 1686 when he was twenty-three years old, he set sail for New York, arriving in June 1686 with a nest egg of £300 from the sale of family jewels. He rose rapidly in New York City society, partly no doubt because of his marriage to Anne Van Cortlandt, daughter of Stephen Van Cortlandt. In 1699 Governor Bellomont (Belmonte)[63] accused DeLancey along with other leading New York City merchants (including both Frederick and Adolph Philipse) of trading in pirated goods smuggled from Madagascar. The African pirates of this period were almost exclusively Conversos and Moriscos. By 1711 DeLancey was prosperous enough to speculate in cocoa to the extent of some £3,000. He also purchased wheat and flour and was active in the Indian trade. From the beginning of the eighteenth century his name appears frequently on shipping records showing that he received wine from Madeira, rum and European goods from the West Indies, and European goods from England. He was accounted as "one of the richest men of the Province."

James DeLancey, the eldest son of Stephen and Anne (Van Cortlandt) DeLancy, was born on November 27, 1703, and grew up in patrician comfort, being groomed for leadership in accordance with the family's expectations. As was the case with William Byrd of Virginia, his father sent him to England at the age of eighteen, where he entered Cambridge in October 1721. He read law for a brief term at Lincoln's Inn, returned to New York at the end of 1725 and prepared to take his position in society. Upon admission to the New York bar, he began his practice with a £3,000 gift from his father. At the age of twenty-six, he was appointed a member of the Governor's Council, and by 1731 he was commissioned second judge of the New York Supreme Court.

Schuyler

The Schuyler (i.e., "scholar") family was founded by Philip Pietersen Schuyler, who settled at Albany about 1650. From modest beginnings as the son of an Amsterdam baker, he chose to concentrate on commerce in the New World, trading furs with the Indians and helping to regulate that trade as one of the Albany Indian commissioners after 1656. His son Peter (1657–1724) extended the family interests by means of two prudent marriages, first to Engeltie Van Schaack of the Albany merchant family, and secondly to Marie Van Rensselaer, granddaughter of the powerful patroon of Rensselaerswyck. Peter Schuyler became the dominant figure in the Albany fur trade. At age twenty-nine he was appointed the first mayor of Albany. His preeminence was based on two main factors. By learning their language and respecting their traditions, he gained a position of influence with the Iroquois equaled by no other white man until William Johnston came to Albany County in 1738. They called him by his first name (Quidor in their language).

The other source of Schuyler's power was his political connections.[64] He was mayor of Albany from 1686 to 1694 and a member of the Governor's Council from 1692 until 1720. He emerged as a strong advocate of the interests of Albany, the fur traders and the Indians. It seems to have been these commercial and political roles that led to his involvement with the Philipse–Van Cortlandt–DeLancey group in the early decades of the eighteenth century. Cathy Matson, who has studied these trading families, lists the London factors they did business with. These include several Jewish surnames — Starkey, Blackall, Lodwick, as well as Micajah Perry, the factor for William Byrd of Virginia.

Morris and Livingston

Two more dynastic families of New York possessed an eminence stemming from land and agriculture rather than trade — the Morrises and Livingstons. We propose they too were crypto–Jewish. The first member of the Morris family in the New York colony was Richard Morris, a captain in Oliver Cromwell's army who sought safety abroad with the Restoration. His son Lewis (1671–1746) was less than a year old when orphaned.[65] For two years the child was "entirely in the hands of strangers," until paternal uncle Lewis Morris arrived from Barbados in 1674 to assume responsibility for him. When the uncle died in 1691 Lewis inherited the family lands and estates. The Westchester County tract of around 3,000 acres was made into the Manor of Morrisania in 1697. The other estate, 3,500-acre Tinton Manor, was located in Monmouth County, New Jersey. From 1691 to 1710 Morris concentrated on his activities in the New Jersey colony, becoming a prominent member of its council. During those years he resided on his Monmouth County estate, which had an iron foundry and sixty or seventy slave workers. Once Robert Hunter became governor of New York and New Jersey in 1710, he shifted his attention to New York, where he was appointed chief justice of the Supreme Court in 1715. Morris also had a seat in the New York Assembly. He assumed the New Jersey governorship in September 1738.

Morris's son, Lewis Morris, Jr. (1698–1762), became the second proprietor of the Manor of Morrisania. It was not until after the middle of the eighteenth century that any member of the Morris family entered directly into a commercial career. This move occurred only when Lewis Morris III won a contract to provision William Shirley's Niagara expedition against the French in 1755–1756. The social apogee of the Morrises came with Gouverneur

Morris, the financier and rakish member of the Constitutional Congress of 1787 credited with authoring the words, "We the People of the United States, in order to form a more perfect Union...."

The Livingston family offers an even more adumbrated exemplar of crypto–Judaism. The earliest form of this Scottish clan name is Levinston (Levite Town[66]), an indication of its Jewish roots. They are considered archetypes of the landed gentry of New York and the name appears among the glitterati in social directories to this day (Appendix G). The great estate they built in Albany County, Livingston Manor, the substantial family holdings they amassed in Dutchess and Ulster counties, as well as close ties forged with other Hudson Valley landowners, cemented their reputation as land barons. But the original Livingston to settle in New York was of humble origins. Robert Livingston (1654–1728) was first and foremost a merchant; only after making his mark in trade and politics at Albany did he successfully recast himself as an aristocrat. He was the son of a Scottish Presbyterian minister forced into exile like many after the reinstatement of Stuart Charles II as king of England. The family settled in Rotterdam where Livingston learned Dutch and began his career as an international trader. Three years later he decided to turn his attention to North American ventures. By 1674 he had immigrated to Albany, where his fluency in Dutch soon made him indispensable to the colonial government. He married Alida Schuyler in 1679.

By surname evidence, there are other New York residents who fall into the category of crypto–Jewish. These include Isaac Gabay (Hebrew, "treasurer"), Abraham Juneau, Jacob de Kay (Hebrew letter), Lucas Santen, Hay (Hebrew letter) M. Solomon,[67] Benjamin, Balthazar and Matthias de Hart, Cornelius Jacobs, Abraham Ver Planck, Jacob Lucena (town in Spain),[68] Nicholas de Meyer, John Barberie, Abraham de la Noy, Abraham Staats, Symon Gilde, Dirck de Wolff (emblem of tribe of Levi),[69] Gerard Beekman, Moses Michael Hays, Myer (Hebrew Meïr) Polock ("Polish") and Caleb Heathcote. About the latter, Cathy Matson writes,

> Caleb Heathcote arrived in New York City in 1691 at the age of twenty-six and quickly established himself as a diversified trader with interests not only in English dry goods importing, but in the Antilles, Madagascar, and Madeira trade as well. From his profits in wine and other luxury imports, Heathcote purchased extensive city lots and an estate at Scarsdale; but he continued to spend most of his time in New York City and his assessment of £640 in 1695 was based upon his owning several warehouses and shops, which he rented to other city merchants.[70]

One of the principal earmarks of crypto–Judaism is intricate and overlapping commercial relationships across families and countries. With regard to several of the families of interest, Matson observes,

> These New Yorkers maintained close liaisons with four prominent partnerships in Amsterdam. A few colonists knew the bankers John de Neufville (i.e., Newhouse) & Son from London introductions, and John Hodshon had moved to Amsterdam after years of doing business in England. Daniel Crommelin & Son had been founded about 1735, after the firm's major partner, a Huguenot refugee from France, had lived in both the West Indies and New York. Crommelin had facilitated and backed shipments between Amsterdam and New York since about 1720, doing business as the Holland Trading Company with bankers like Willincks, Ten Broeck, and Schemmelpennick.... After 1755, the Dutch firm became a banking house, Crommelin & Zoon, which lasted until Crommelin's death in 1768. His son Robert kept commercial liaisons with New Yorkers over these years, and his daughters married the New York merchants Gabriel Ludlow and Gulian Verplanck. John Ludlow [Dutch Jewish family],

Gabriel's brother, bought over 25 percent of his imports from agents of the Crommelin family; in 1757, he exported over five times more to Crommelin than to any English merchant.[71]

Levinus [Dutch Jewish surname[72]] Clarkson, the fourth Dutch liaison, had the double good fortune to have been raised the son of a well-to-do New York City merchant, Matthew Clarkson, and to be related to Charles Lodwick, a successful New York trader, who returned to London after 1710. Levinus visited the Lodwick household and met many of the metropolis's commercial elite; by 1736, he was prepared to join his uncle in Amsterdam, where they launched a vigorous export trade to New York that also involved an elaborate service in converting bills of exchange and extending credit. Occasionally, Clarkson imported New York goods and bills in Daniel Crommelin's name. Through his connection with Lodwick in London, Clarkson also secured goods and credit for Francis Goelet [Huguenot], Anthony Rutgers, and the Roosevelt [Rosenfeld[73]] brothers in New York; until the end of his career, he also held on to his portion of a 5,000-acre colonial estate that had been granted to his relatives, the Van Cortlandts.

Note the recurrence of London and Amsterdam firms and combination again of Huguenot, English and Dutch commercial partners. Clearly despite language and geographic differences, there was an overarching ethnic bond that permitted these relationships to be established and maintained. Similarly, Rodrigo Pacheco, a Spanish crypto–Jew,[74] and James Alexander, a Scottish crypto–Jew,[75] formed a joint venture and worked together. During the 1730s they were friendly rivals aiming to capture a prominent dry-goods position in the New York market. They regularly discussed their cargoes, according to Matson's research. "Rice last year did very well at London, but prices have been declining, and it would sell better at Lisbon," Pacheco predicted in 1732. In order to get the rice — not a commodity that New Yorkers grew — to its destination, Alexander outfitted the ship *Albany* to sail with "flour, bread, pork, pease, tarr, staves, and other goods to Jamaica, buy Sugar, Rum, Lime-juice, Negroes, and Cash to the value of about £800," then to sell the New York goods, and proceed to South Carolina to acquire a full load of rice for Lisbon.

According also to Matson, the firm of Perry and Ludlow and the businesses of John Harris Cruger and Henry Livingston also depended on family connections. It was a network embracing the Curaçao merchants Telemon Cruger, Philip Livingston, John Cuyler, Myndert Lansing, Nicholas and Isaac Gouverneur, and members of the De Peyster, Duyckinck, Bowen, Lefferts, and Remsen families. Cornelius Kortright and Nicholas Cruger had counting houses in St. Croix. David Beekman, whose older brother Gerard lived in New York, became a sugar planter there. William Livingston and Peter van Brugh Livingston went to the West Indies as young men to learn the business before they started out "on their own account" in New York. Alexander Hamilton clerked for the West Indian firm of David Beekman and John Harris Cruger.

Such trading and financial relationships can be interpreted as representing the classic model of a community of Iberian Diaspora Jews. These particular families capably established themselves in the New World through their connections in Amsterdam.

Genealogical Analyses

The family annals of the Morrises and Livingstons illustrate many of the themes presented thus far. The Morris family of New York and New Jersey was one of the most affluent and powerful in Colonial America, producing governors, a signer of the Declaration of Independence and state Supreme Court justices. Supportive of our thesis are the murky origins of the family. What is known is that the Morrises were likely from Wales (a large source of Sephardic immigrants to the Colonies), that they favored the given name Lewis (the Hebrew tribal name of Levi), that they carried a Sephardic/Moorish surname (Morris) and that they spent considerable time in Barbados as sugar planters and refiners. All these characteristics point to Sephardic origins.

Richard Morris (1616–1672) married a woman named Sarah Pole (fairly obviously of Polish-Jewish origin) in Barbados. In the next generation we see marriages to Norris (Arabic for "light") and Isabella (Spanish first name) Graham (often Jewish). Here begins that revealing pattern — cousin-to-cousin marriages. Wesley and West pairings become numerous by the fourth generation. The Staats family provides two consecutive wives for Lewis Morris by the late 1700s. Further, Sarah, Isabella and Euphemia become concretized as daughters' names, creating a publicly-evident link to Mediterranean ancestry. In this generation also, two Jewish surnames enter the family — Ashfield and Antill. There is an additional marriage to a Graham cousin. By the fifth generation the Woolley, Antill, and Ashfield families have re-entered the Morris line as cousin marriages, and the Lawrence family has provided two marital partners. The given names Isaac, Jacob and Rachel have proliferated in the family. Lewis Morris Ashfield has married his cousin Ann Morris, and Vincent Pearce Ashfield his cousin Sarah Morris. Not to be outdone, Sarah Antill marries her cousin John Morris, while John Antill marries two consecutive Colden sisters, Margaret and Alice, whose children then marry a Van Horne cousin and William Davies, who bears a Jewish surname and operates a mercantile business. Toward the close of the genealogy, Morris descendant John Graham marries a cousin, Julia Ogden, as does fellow Morris descendant Amos Borden in the person of Rachel Woolley. Morris descendant Thomas Lawrence closes out the lineage by marrying as his second and third wives two Morris sisters, Mary and Catherine. A child of these unions then marries back into the Shee family, which entered the Lawrence lineage a generation earlier. It is hard to imagine a more stunning record of endogamy.

As we have seen, the Livingston family comes from Scotland. The clan claimed to have traced its line back to a Saxon thane who settled in Scotland late in the eleventh century. Other sources give the Saxon's name as Leving.[76] This appears to be the sort of bogus genealogy we have witnessed already with the Byrds and Lees of Virginia, who also came to the colonies from decidedly middle-class origins in England, and who, then, having made their fortunes, manufactured a glorious ancestry. First of all, Saxons did not bear surnames such as Leving. Second, it would make little sense for a Saxon aristocrat to make his way from England to the Scottish borders simultaneously with the arrival of the Normans in those same regions. Third, the earliest form of the name was Levinston, as we have seen above. According to Livingston historian Cynthia A. Kierner, Robert's father, John, was a third-generation Presbyterian minister "who could not accept the [religious] reimposition ... that accompanied the Stuart Restoration of 1660.... During the English Civil War, he emerged as a leading Scottish advocate of radical ecclesiastical change." Livingstone refused to subscribe to the oath of allegiance in Scotland and was banished.

Not mentioned by Kierner is the fact that Robert's mother was Janet Fleming, an indication that she may have had relatives in Holland/Flanders. The family moved to Rotterdam when Robert was nine. At the age of sixteen Robert began his trading career. He returned to Scotland for a year in 1672 and left it again to sail for Massachusetts. By 1675 he had resettled in Albany. As sketched previously, here he connected with the prominent Dutch landowners and merchants, serving as an estate manager and attorney. It is not explained by Kierner where or how his legal skills came to him. Soon he was acting as a fur wholesaler with Huguenots John Pynchon and Timothy Cooper. He made a propitious marriage to the young widow of Nicholas Van Rennssalaer, Alida (Spanish for "noble-born") Schuyler. According to Kierner, Alida was an accomplished businesswoman and fur trader — something quite unusual for a Dutch woman, but not for a Jewish one. Through marriage, Robert allied himself with the van Cortland family to boot since Alida's sister married Stephen van Cortland.

By 1683 Livingston was factor for London merchants Jacob Harwood and John Blackall, and by 1690 he had a half interest in the ship *Margriet,* which carried slaves, sugar and tobacco between Madagascar, Barbados and Virginia. He had by then acquired enormous acreage in the Hudson Valley, building Livingston Manor. There he opened two mills and built several general stores. Two thousand Palatine refugees were settled at Livingston Manor to serve as the work force — and customers for the mills and stores. An iron works, bakery and brewery were managed by Alida Livingston. The names of the "Palatines" settled at Livingston Manor are most informative. They include Simon Coen, Bastian Lesher, Harme Koon (that is, Koons), Johannes Myer, Isaac Decker,[77] Andries Frans Brusie, Barent Dutcher ("German"), James Barnet (from Issachar),[78] Israel Kniffen, Charles Mead, Catherine Petrie, Nehemiah Purdy, Jacob Blatser ("gold foil worker"), Samuel Coeymans, Philip de Forest, Hendrick Douw (from David), Cornelis Esselsteen ("ass's castle"), Abraham Fonda, Hitchen Holland, Phillip Koons (Hebrew anagram K-N-Z),[79] Omy LaGrange, Jacob and Thomas Mesick (that is, Maszig, Hebrew "successful"),[80] Johann Plese, Johan Muche,[81] Jacob Schermerhorn, Martin Shoeck,[82] Johan Rosman,[83] Abraham Slingerland, Anthony Ten Eyck, Jacob van Alen, Robias Van Duesen, Ariantie Van Voerdt and John Yates (Hebrew anagram). Obviously most of these are not native Germans but rather French, Dutch and Ashkenazic Jews.

In keeping with our thesis, the Livingston genealogy in America shows a pattern of marriage to crypto–Jewish Dutch families in the first generation, including the Vetch, Van Brugh, Beekman and Van Horne families. The Vetch descendants marry into the Bayard family and the subsequent generations show an increased crypto–Jewish marital pattern, including Moffat (Mophat, Arabic), Arnold (Jewish), Cornell (Coronell),[84] Van Horne and Simmon. In one we see a descendant of Philip Livingston marrying his close cousin Gertrude Van Rensselaer Schuyler. In others we encounter two Alexanders , de Peyster, Ten Broeck (crypto–Jewish Dutch), two Huguenots, French and Lawrence, and Hoffman (Dutch Jewish). At a later stage, Robert Livingston of Clermont and wife Mary Beekman have sons who marry two sisters, Eliza and Mary McEvers, and we see also a Sheaffe (likely Huguenot) and Marie Louise Valentine D'Azezac Castra Moreau, the latter very likely openly Jewish. Later the descendants of Gilbert Livingston and Cornelia Beekman marry two close cousins, a Van Cortland and a Van Rensselaer, the Huguenot Joy Darrell, and a Dutchman who seems also Jewish, Jacob Rutsen. Still later we see the descendants of Robert Livingston, Jr., marrying two close cousins, a Livingston and a Schuyler, and two likely Huguenot Jews, Valentine Gardiner and Mary Ann LeRoy. Finally we have William Livingston and Susannah French's children, who marry close cousin John Livingston and two more likely openly Jewish persons, John Cleve Semmes[85] and Catharine Kelkta.

Some Residents of Livingston Manor

The names of male Palatine Germans above twenty-one years old in Livingston Manor, N.Y., in the winter of 1710 and summer 1711 are provided by *A Collection of Upwards of*

Thirty Thousand Names of German, Swiss, Dutch, French and other Immigrants in Pennsylvania from 1727 to 1776; Prof. I. Daniel Rupp, Second Revised Edition, 1876, Philadelphia (http://searchforancestors.com/passengerlists/kocherthal.html).

Names, Age and Occupation of Those Who Accompanied the Rev. Joshua Kocherthal, in the Spring of 1709

The Rev. Joshua Kocherthal, age 39; Sibylla Charlotta, his wife, 39; their children, Benigna Sibylla, 10; Joshua, 7; Susanna Sibylla, 3.

Lorents Schwisser, age 25, husbandman and vinedresser; Anna Catharina, his wife, 26; their daughter, Johanna, 8.

Henrich Rennau, age 24, stocking weaver, husbandman and vinedresser; Johanna, his wife, 26; their children, Lorentz, 1; Heinrich, 5 months old, and two sisters of Mrs. Rennau, Susanna Liboscha, 15; Maria Johanna Liboscha, 10 years old.

Andreas Volck, age 30, husbandman and vinedresser; his wife, Anna Catharina, 27; their children, Maria Barbara, 5; Georg Hieronymus, 4; Anna Gertrauda, 1.

Michael Weigand, age 52, husbandman; his wife, Anna Catharina, 54; their children, Anna Maria, 13; Tobias, 7; Georg, 5.

Jacob Weber, age 30, husbandman and vinedresser; his wife, Anna Elisabeth, 25; their children Anna Maria, 5; Eva Elisabeth, 1.

Johan Jacob Plettel, age 40, husbandman and vinedresser; his wife, Anna Elisabeth, 29; their children Margaretha, 10; Anna Sara, 8; Catharina, 3.

Johannes Fischer, age 27, smith and husbandman; his wife, Maria Barbara, 26; one child, Andreas, 6 months old.

Melchior Guelch, age 39, carpenter and joiner; his wife, Anna Catharina, 43; their children, Magdalena, 12; Heinrich, 10.

Peter Rose, age 34, cloth weaver; his wife, Johanna, 45.

Marie Wemarin, widow, 37 years of age; her daughter, Catharina, 2.

Isaac Feber (Le Fever), age 33, husbandman; his wife, Catharina, 30; their son, Abraham, 2 years old.

Daniel Fiero, age 32, husbandman; his wife, Anna Maria, 30; their children, Andreas, 7; Johannes, 6.

Herman Schuneman, aged 28, clerk, unmarried.

Isaac Turck, aged 23, husbandman, unmarried.

As is clear from the surnames and given names above the congregation of the Rev. Kocherthal was probably Jewish in religious orientation, not Christian.

Roosevelts

The crypto–Jewish character of New York becomes evident also when we examine the genealogy of the Roosevelts. Claes Rosenvelt entered the cloth business in New York, and was married in 1682. He accumulated a fortune. He then changed his name to Nicholas Roosevelt. Of his four sons, Isaac died young. Nicholas married Sarah Solomons. Jacobus married Catherina Hardenburg.

According to an old clipping from the *Corvallis Gazette Times* of Corvallis, Oregon, "The Roosevelts were not a fighting, but a peace-loving people, devoted to trade. Isaac became a capitalist. He founded the Bank of New York in 1790. The first Roosevelt came to America in 1649. His name was Claes Rosenfelt. He was a Jew. Nicholas, the son of Claes was the ancestor of both Franklin and Theodore. He married a Jewish girl, named Kunst, in 1682. Nicholas had a son named Jacobus Rosenfeld."

Roosevelt Genealogy

Marten Van Rosenfelt
Claes Martensen Van Rosenfelt
Nicholas Roosevelt

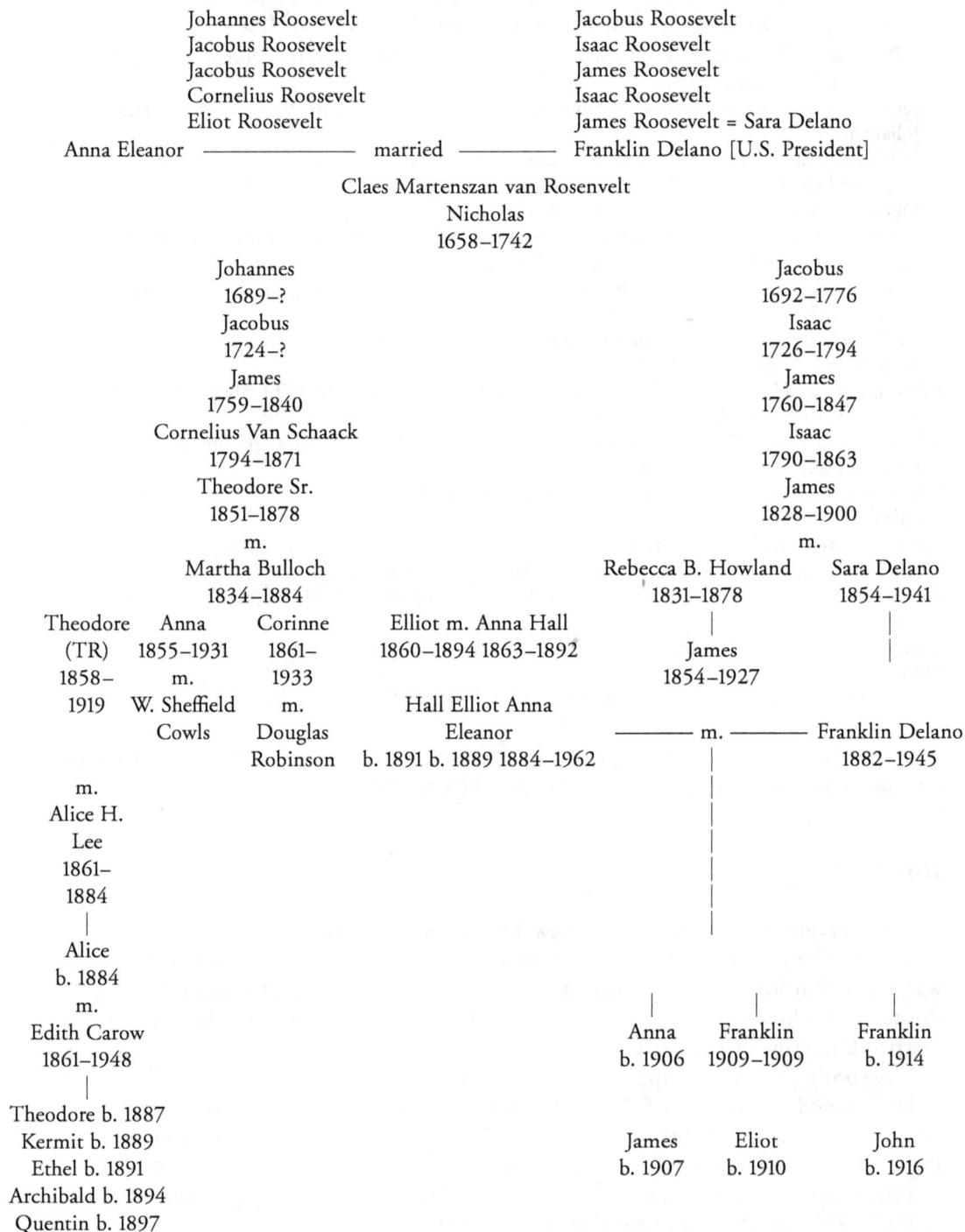

Johannes Roosevelt	Jacobus Roosevelt
Jacobus Roosevelt	Isaac Roosevelt
Jacobus Roosevelt	James Roosevelt
Cornelius Roosevelt	Isaac Roosevelt
Eliot Roosevelt	James Roosevelt = Sara Delano

Anna Eleanor ——————— married ——————— Franklin Delano [U.S. President]

Claes Martenszan van Rosenvelt
Nicholas
1658–1742

Johannes	Jacobus
1689–?	1692–1776
Jacobus	Isaac
1724–?	1726–1794
James	James
1759–1840	1760–1847
Cornelius Van Schaack	Isaac
1794–1871	1790–1863
Theodore Sr.	James
1851–1878	1828–1900
m.	m.
Martha Bulloch	Rebecca B. Howland Sara Delano
1834–1884	1831–1878 1854–1941

Theodore   Anna   Corinne   Elliot m. Anna Hall   James
(TR)   1855–1931   1861–   1860–1894 1863–1892   1854–1927
1858–   m.   1933
1919   W. Sheffield   m.   Hall Elliot Anna
      Cowls   Douglas   Eleanor   ——— m. ——— Franklin Delano
          Robinson   b. 1891 b. 1889 1884–1962   1882–1945

m.
Alice H.
Lee
1861–
1884
|
Alice
b. 1884
m.
Edith Carow   Anna   Franklin   Franklin
1861–1948   b. 1906   1909–1909   b. 1914
|
Theodore b. 1887
Kermit b. 1889
Ethel b. 1891   James   Eliot   John
Archibald b. 1894   b. 1907   b. 1910   b. 1916
Quentin b. 1897

What can we glean from the pages of *Town & Country*, America's foremost social register? As might be expected, the vast majority of names come from the higher ranks of New York society; many are Dutch in origin. In support of our thesis, sixteen out of twenty-three of the social lions can be placed in the column of "possibly, but not necessarily Jewish," while one-fourth of the "rank and file" socialites satisfy the required criteria. Among names harvested by such rough and ready means are Adams, Astor, Beekman, Belmont, Biddle, Carnegie, Chase, Cooper, de Acosta, de Frise, de Forest, de Peyster, De Lancey, Firestone, Forbes, Fraser, Gardiner, Geist, Gimbel, Howell, Jay, Lowell, Pereira, Phillips, Sayre, Van Courtlandt, du Pont, Field, Fish, Gould, Livingston, Mellon, Morgan, Pulitzer, Rockefeller, Roosevelt, Vanderbilt and Yale. We view these coincidences as suggestive of an untold story of ethnic origins in America's colonial past, in particular that of New York.

In sum, the blind spots of historians in the case of the New York colony are particularly glaring. New York's Sephardic antecedents are studiously ignored by textbooks and traditional accounts, even those specializing in Jewish history or genealogy. The story of Jews in New York is almost exclusively focused on the first boatload of Brazilian Sephardic refugees who made landfall there and planted the Shearith Israel congregation in New York City. These Jews, however, were poor and small in number. The group was immediately marginalized in the life of the colony. As we argue in this chapter, it is Scottish, Dutch and Portuguese Jews or crypto–Jews of means in positions of leadership who made the most important contributions to the planting and nurturing of the colony. That New York became the financial capital of the world as well as intellectual nerve center of America is no accident.

CHAPTER SIX

Pennsylvania:
Quakers and Other Friends

When we think of colonial Pennsylvania the images that come to mind are William Penn dressed in his sober black hat and cloak and congregations of Quakers or the Society of Friends sitting on wooden pews in their plain houses of worship. Or we may conjure up scenes of earnest Pennsylvania Dutch farmers recently emigrated from the German Palatinate.

Using immigration records, church rolls and family genealogies, we are going to paint a different picture of Colonial Pennsylvania — one that includes many settlers of Sephardic and Ashkenazic Jewish, Ottoman Turkish and other types of Moorish descent. We are going to argue that prior historians have inadvertently overlooked — or perhaps purposely ignored — evidence that many of the "Protestant" sects arriving in Pennsylvania, e.g., the Mennonites, were crypto–Jewish congregations led by a rabbinical-styled minister. We will provide detailed genealogies of specific families to document endogamy across generations, one of the marks of a crypto–Jewish community.

Deconstructing Penn

Little is known about the early life of William Penn (1644–1718). William Byrd of Virginia, a contemporary, wrote that he was a randy young man who got an aristocrat's daughter pregnant — not

William Penn (Emmet Collection, Miriam and Ira D. Wallach Division of Art, Prints and Photographs, The New York Public Library, Astor, Lenox and Tilden Foundations).

104

Plain dress of Quakers is contrasted with that of the New York aristocracy in a 1680 engraving (Picture Collection, The New York Public Library, Astor, Lenox and Tilden Foundations).

marrying her or legitimizing their child — and who then turned publicly to religion as a way of salvaging his reputation. We should perhaps be a bit circumspect in taking Penn's declarations of Christian zeal at face value. Although Penn today is perceived as a champion of the oppressed and impoverished, he was in actuality wealthy and from a privileged family. His first known ancestor was John Penne, born in Gloucestershire, England, in 1500.[1]

Penn Genealogy

1. John Penne was born in 1500 in Minety, Gloucestershire, England, and died in 1550 in Minety, Gloucestershire, England.
　　Children:
　　　i. William Penn was born in 1525 in Minety, Gloucestershire, England, and died on 12 March 1591 in Minety, Gloucestershire, England. See 2 below.

• **Second Generation** •

2. William Penn was born in 1525 Minety, Gloucestershire, England, and died on 12 March 1591 in Minety, Gloucestershire, England. He was the son of John Penne.
　William must have been quite an important figure, for when he died in 1591 it is believed that he was buried in front of the altar at Saint Leonards Church, Minety. A plaque commemorating his life was erected in the church. All evidence of this was destroyed during repairs and alterations at the turn of the 19/20th centuries.
　　　i. William Penn was born in 1548, lived in Bristol, Gloucester, England, and died on 12 March 1610 in Malmesbury, Minety, Gloucestershire, England. See 3 below.

• **Third Generation** •

3. William Penn was born in 1548, lived in Bristol, Gloucester, England, and died on 12 March 1610 in Malmesbury, Minety, Gloucestershire, England. He was the son of William Penn.
　William married Margaret Rastall in 1570. Margaret was born about 1547/1556, lived in Bristol,

Gloucester, England, is the daughter of John Rastall and Anne George.

William was a law clerk at Malmesbury, Wiltshire, and chief clerk to counselor at law, Christopher George. (Sources: 1)

Children:

    i. George Penn was born in 1571, lived in Birdham, Sussex, England, and died on 4 November 1632 while living in Plymouth See 4 below.

    ii. Giles Penn was born in 1573 and died in 1641/1656 in Fex Or, Morocco. See 5 below.

4. George Penn was born in 1571, lived in Birdham, Sussex, England, and died on 4 November 1632 while living in Plymouth; he was the son of William Penn and Margaret Rastall.

George married Elizabeth. Elizabeth was born about 1587, lived in Birdham, Sussex, England.

Children:

    i. Christian Penn was born about 1606 in England and died in July 1684 in Middleborough, Plymouth, MA.

5. Giles Penn was born in 1573 and died in 1641/1656 in Fex Or, Morocco. He was the son of William Penn and Margaret Rastall.

Giles married Joanne Gilbert on 5 November 1600 in St. Mary Redcliffe church in Bristol.

On December 28, 1635/6, Charles I King of England, with the advice of Captain Rainsborough and Giles Penn, made the decision to besiege the pirates in port in Morocco. Rainsborough departed with four ships February 20, 1636/7. Upon departure the instructions were to take all Turkish frigates and block up the port of Sallee, Morocco. They destroyed 28 ships and hemmed in the port. The governor of the port began to lend assistance, and the port was delivered into Raisborough's hands July 28, 1636/7.

There was an alliance formed with King Charles I and a treaty was reached insuring that the Moroccans never infested the English ports again. Initially 300 [English?] captives were handed over to the English forces. Captain Carteret promptly returned to England with the newly freed British. Rainsborough stayed; he continued to try and free another 1,000 captives who had been sold to Tunis and Algiers. Rainsborough returned to England with the new ambassador November 5, 1636–7. A procession at night with much pomp was noted to have taken place. Captive English and Irish who were missing as long as 30 years were finally returned to their homeland.

The capture and return of English and Irish is noted in various literature of the time. Henry F. Waters, in *Genealogical Gleanings in England* in 1901, notes a sermon, found in Oxford's records by the Rev. Charles Fitz-Geffry of St. Dominic in Plymouth taken from Hebrew 13:3, "Remember them that are in bonds, as bond with them; and them which suffer adversity, as being yourselves also in the body," the sermon titled "Compassion towards Captives, chiefly towards our Brethrn & Countryman who are in such miserable bondage in Barbary." Waters also recollects another document from the same period as reading, "It is certainly known that there are five Turks in the Severne, where they weekly take English or Irish; and there are a great number of their ships in the Channel upon the coast of France and Biscay."

Penn Family History and Genealogy

Children:

    i. Admiral Sir William Penn was born on 23 April 1621 in St. Thomas Parish, Bristol, and died on 16 September 1670 in Essex. See 7 below.

• **Fifth Generation** •

6. Christian Penn was born about 1606 in England and died July 1684 in Middleborough, Plymouth, MA. She was the daughter of George Penn.

Christian married Francis Eaton in 1624/1625 in Plymouth, MA. Francis was born on 11 September 1596 in St. Thomas Parish, Bristol, England. He was the son of John Eaton and Dorothy Smith. He died on 18 November 1633 in Plymouth, MA.

Francis Eaton was one of the Mayflower Company and a carpenter. The following copyrighted information was found at Genealogical Register of Plymouth Families, page 100.

FRANCIS came in the Mayflower 1620, with wife Sarah, and son Samuel. He had a 2d wife by whom he had Rachel, m. Joseph Ramsden; and a 3d, Christian Penn, before 1627, by whom he had BENJAMIN, 1627.

Colonial Families of the United States of America: Volume 5, p. 607.

Francis Eaton. Died at Plymouth, Mass., between 4 and 18 November, 1633. He married, first, Sarah, who died at Plymouth, Mass., early in 1621, but after 11 January. His second wife, whom he married at Plymouth, Mass., in 1624, or 1625, Christian Penn, who died at Middleborough, Mass., about 1684. She had married, second, Francis 2 Billington.

Then Christian married Francis Billington in 1634.

BILLINGTON, FRANCIS, son of John, came with his father in the *Mayflower*, 1620, and m. Christian (Penn) Eaton, widow of Francis Eaton, 1634, by whom he had Martha, m. Samuel Eaton; Elizabeth, m. a Patte of Providence; Rebecca, 1647; Mary, m. Samuel Sabin of Rehoboth; Isaac; Mercy. M. John Martin; Desire, Joseph, and Francis. FRANCIS, son of above, m. Abigail, d. of Eleazer Churchill, and had Sarah, 1702; Sukey, 1704; Francis, 1708; Jemima, 1710; Content, 1712, m. Francis Merrifield; Abigail, 1716; and Joseph, 1718. ICHABOD, with wife Polly, owned an estate in Plymouth, 1774. ISAAC, son of 1st Francis, m. Hannah, daughter of James Glass, and had a son Seth. JOHN, came in the Mayflower, 1620, with wife Eleanor and two children, Francis and John. The son of John died young, the father was hanged, 1630, for the murder of John Newcomen, and the widow married Gregory Armstrong, 1638.

Genealogical Register of Plymouth Families, pg. 28.

7. Admiral Sir William Penn was born on 23 April 1621 in St. Thomas Parish, Bristol, and died on 16 September 1670 in Wanstead, Essex. He was the son of Giles Penn and Joanne Gilbert.

Admiral Sir William married Margaret Jasper. Margaret was born about 1624 in England.

At the time of her marriage to William Penn, Margaret was a Dutch widow, having been married to Nicasius Van der Schure. Margaret Van der Schure was the daughter of Jan (Johann, John) Jasper merchant of Rotterdam (Sietz, 1719, & Burke, 1929) and Alet Pletjes, whose family was from Kempen, Prussia (Lutz, 1988, & Miller, 1991).

Children:

i. William Penn, Jr., was born on 28 October 1644.

William is known as the founder of Pennsylvania. Also known as a famous Quaker for his Great Treaty with Delaware. He was in Pennsylvania only three and a half years. But from 1681, when he received the king's charter at the age of thirty-seven, to 1718, when he died, Pennsylvania was one of his chief preoccupations. The growth and well-being of his colony was based on a tradition of religious toleration and freedom under law, fundamental principles of American civil life. Thomas Jefferson called Penn "the greatest law-giver the world has produced."

In 1681, there came a golden opportunity to make his dreams come true. King Charles II, out of "regard to the memorie and merits of his late father," gave the younger Penn a huge tract of land in North America and named it, in honor of the Admiral, "Pennsylvania," or Penn's Woods.

Examining the genealogical chart provides some significant clues as to Penn's ethnic ancestry. First, his earliest ancestor can be traced to only 1500 and by the mid–1500s had moved to that hotbed of crypto–Judaism, Bristol, England. The family married into the Gilbert and Rastall families, the former of which may have been of Jewish descent. By the fifth generation we encounter a girl, Christian Penn, born 1606, who married Francis Eaton, a *Mayflower* passenger, in Massachusetts. Christian later married Francis Bellington, by whom she had a daughter, Martha, who married back into the Eaton family; Elizabeth, who married a Patte (Sephardic surname of Providence, Rhode Island, the "Bristol" of the Colonies); Rebecca; and Mary, who married Samuel Salsch (Jewish surname) of Rekoboth, Massachusetts. A grandson married Hannah Glass (Jewish surname). William Penn's father, Admiral Sir William Penn, was born in Bristol, England, and married a widow, Margaret Jasper (Sephardic surname) who was the daughter of a Dutch merchant (Rotterdam) and had been married to Nicasius Van der Schure (Nicasius being a Greek shortened form of Nicholas, also the capital of Cyprus). We would not expect to see this type of marriage pattern unless the family was self-consciously attempting to perpetuate a crypto–Jewish tradition.

Penn's Writings

If we look at some of William Penn's writings to his financial backers and his family, we can detect other signs of Judaism.[2] In the constitution for the Colony of Pennsylvania, Penn states in Title 12:

> That this government may appear equal in itself, and agreeable to the wisdom God gave unto Moses and the practice of our best ancestors; and that we may avoid heart burnings in families and the foundation of much misery and beggary or worse. I do for me and mine hereby declare and establish for the 12th Fundamental of the government of this province, that what estate every person dying has in it (through he or she die elsewhere), having children, shall be equally shared, after such person's decease, among the children of the said person, saying only that the eldest if the first born shall have (according to the law of God by Moses given to the Jews) a double portion for his inheritance and not otherwise.

Penn not only adheres to Mosaic Law in inheritance bequests but also appears to state that he and his ancestors were of the original covenant with God, i.e., Jews.

In a later portion of the Constitution, he alludes to the Jewish religious notion of the "coming of the second Adam," or Adam Kadmon, as "the Lord from Heaven": "Daily experience tells us that the care and regulation of many other affairs, more soft and daily necessary, make up much the greatest part of government; and which must have followed the peopling of the world had Adam never fallen, and will continue among men or earth under the highest attainments they may arrive at, by the coming of the blessed second Adam, the Lord from Heaven. Thus much of government in general, as to its rise and end." It may be significant that Penn speaks of the "second Adam" not as Jesus Christ but as a messiah whose coming lies in the remote future.

To attract financial backing for the Pennsylvania Colony, Penn established the Free Society of Traders in 1682. This organization received 20,000 acres, called the Manor of Frank (Freeman House), and recruited craftsmen and tradesmen for the colony. The principals in the society included several persons we would propose, based on their surnames and occupations, were of Sephardic descent.

> And whereas I have by my several indentures of lease bearing date the two and twentieth, and of release bearing are the three and twentieth day of the first month called March in the four and thirtieth year of the said now king's reign, granted unto Nicholas More of London, medical doctor, James Claypoole, merchant, Philip Ford [Faure, Huguenot], William Shardlow of

London, merchants, Edward Peirce of London, leather seller, John Simcock and Thomas Brassey of Cheshire, yeomen, Thomas Barker of London, wine cooper, and Edward Brookes [Baruch] of London, grocer, and their heirs, to the use of themselves and their heirs and assigns, twenty thousand acres of land, parcel of the said province of Pennsylvania, in trust nevertheless for the Free Society of Traders in Pennsylvania and their successors, as soon as the said Free Society should be by me incorporated or erected, as in and by the said indentures (relation being thereunto had) more fully does appear.

Many, if not most, of these names of merchants appear to have Hebrew roots.

Although few letters survive from Penn to his wife and children, biographer Jean R. Soderland does reprint one from 1682 that reads in part:

Remember your Creator in the days of your youth. It was the glory of Israel in the 2d of Jeremiah: and how did God bless Josiah, because he feared him in his youth. And so He did Jacob, Joseph, and Moses. Oh! My dear children, remember and fear and serve Him who made you, and gave you to me and your dear mother, that you may live to Him and glorify Him in your generations....

Remember David, who asking the Lord, "Who shall abide in Thy tabernacle; who shall dwell in Thy holy hill"? answers, "He that walks uprightly, works righteousness, and speaks the truth in his heart; in whose eyes the vile person is condemned, but honors them who fear the Lord"....

In your families, remember Abraham, Moses, and Joshua their integrity to the Lord; and do as [if] you have them for your examples. Let the fear and service of the living God be encouraged in your houses, and that plainness, sobriety, and moderation in all things, as becomes God's chosen people. And, as I advise you, my beloved children, do you counsel yours, if God should give you any. Yea, I counsel and command them, as my posterity, that they love, and serve the Lord God with an upright heart, that He may bless you and yours, from generation to generation.

The same letter continues,

Oh! The Lord is a strong God, and He can do whatsoever He pleases. And though men consider it not, it is the Lord that rules and overrules in the kingdoms of men; and He builds, up and pulls down. I, your father, am the man that can say, he that trusts in the Lord shall not be confounded. But God, in due time, will make His enemies be at peace with Him.

If you thus behave yourselves, and so become a terror to evildoers and a praise to them that do well, God, my God, will be with you, in wisdom and a sound mind, and make you blessed instruments in His hand for the settlement of some of those desolate parts of the world — which my soul desires above all worldly honors and riches, both for you that go and you that stay, you that govern and you that are governed — that in the end you may be gathered with me to the rest of God.

Finally, my children, love one another with a true an endeared love, and your dear relations on both sides; and take care to preserve tender affection in your children to each other, often marrying within themselves, so [long] as it be without the bounds forbidden in God's law. That so they may not, like the forgetting and unnatural world, grow out of kindred and as cold as strangers; but, as becomes a truly natural and Christian stock, you and yours after you may live in the pure and fervent love of God toward one another, as becomes brethren in the spiritual and natural relation.

So my God, that has blessed me with His abundant mercies, both of this and the other and better life, be with you all, guide you by His counsel, bless you, and bring you to His eternal glory, that you may shine, my dear children, in the firmament of God's power, with the blessed spirits of the just, that celestial family, praising and admiring Him, the God and Father of it, forever and ever. For there is not God like unto Him: the God of Abraham, of Isaac, and of Jacob; the God of the Prophets, the Apostles, and Martyrs of Jesus; in whom I live forever.

So farewell to my thrice dearly beloved wife and children. Yours, as God pleases, in that which no waters can quench, no time forget, nor distance wear away, but remains forever.

William Penn

In the tradition of Presbyterian Reformer John Knox, Penn and many other Quakers — despite the use of Jesus' name — may well have been of Sephardic (and perhaps Moorish) leanings. The reader will note that the theology he teaches to his children is grounded in the Hebrew Torah, not the Christian New Testament. Penn describes his ancestors and current family not as like the children of Israel, but as being the children of Israel. We interpret this text as overtly stating that the Penn family is of Jewish/Hebrew descent in fact, not in a metaphorical sense. This is the reason why he admonishes his children to marry with their close kin, not merely with other Christians or even Quakers, in order to preserve unadulterated their direct heritage from the Jewish patriarchs and matriarchs. Penn's position is directly analogous to that of Moriscos during the 1560–1750 period in Spain. A mufti (religious leader) in one fatwa (responsum, legal opinion) composed specifically to answer the quandaries faced by crypto–Muslims living in Christian Spain during those times, wrote: "If they oblige you to give your daughters in marriage to them, then you should cleave firmly to the belief that that is forbidden, were you not under duress, and abhor it in your hearts, so that you would do otherwise, if you were able."[3]

Such opposition to marrying outside Islam was founded on belief that Muslims could trace their descent back to an Arab tribe, companion of the prophet, emir or caliph (see Appendix C, Muslim Rituals and Beliefs).[4] The children of the prophet, as much as the children of Israel, were quite literally a bloodline, one that must not be adulterated. The Spanish Catholics, of course, had their own obsession with ethnic exclusivity, *limpieza de sangre* (purity of blood), but this differed by not being tied to the concept of deep ancestry and distant genealogies. Clearly, Penn was not following the Christian model.

In a 1683 letter to Jasper Batt (Greek/Hebrew surname and given name), a Quaker minister, Penn writes:

5 February 1683

That the entailment of the government of this province may be to David's stock, the tribe of Judah, I close with thee with all my heart. But tell me, how that shall be? It has been the earnest desire of my soul, that it might ever anchor there. Show us the way, and thou shall be the man. The power I have by patent runs thus: that I and my heirs, with the assent of the freemen or their deputies, from time to time may make laws so [long] as they be not repugnant to the allegiance we owe to the king as sovereign.[5]

Once again, this passage does not appear to be intended as metaphor, but rather as an ancestral assertion; that is, Pennsylvania is intended to be a community of Davidic-descended Jews like medieval Narbonne (Chapter Two).

Who Lived in Pennsylvania?

Let's now take a look at who arrived to settle the New Israel of Penn's Woods. The standard histories of Pennsylvania stress that due to the colony's liberal ordinances on religion, settlers came who were not only Quakers but also adherents of several other religious sects from a variety of countries. Unlike South Carolina and Rhode Island, however, Pennsylvania — on paper, at least — seemed to limit its settlers to Christians. We will now document through colonist surnames and genealogies that, despite being from a diverse cross-section of seeming Christian sects and denominations, the majority of early Pennsylvanians were of Judaic descent — in keeping with Penn's sentiments.

But before doing so, it is important for us to review some of the essential facts relating to Quakerism and its founder, the English dissenter George Fox (1624–1691). There are indications that Fox's family were rather recent immigrants to Leicester, where he was born. The Fox surname was not rooted in England but rather in Ireland (a translation of Gaelic *sionnach*) and Germany (Fuchs, a common Sephardic name). George Fox's mother was Mary Lago, the name of a Jewish family denounced to the Inquisition of Lisbon around 1580. He later referred to his mother's origins as "the stock of the martyrs," evidently a gloss on the Mediterranean background she shared with the earliest saints of the Catholic Church. He married Margaret Askew (Ayscough, Hebrew), the widow of Thomas Fell (Sephardic surname).[6] Growing up, he attended a local Presbyterian church. Although it is not clear exactly when the new movement crystallized (some say in 1648), in 1650 Fox was imprisoned for blasphemy. During the trial a judge mocked Fox's exhortation to "tremble at the word of the Lord," calling him and his followers "Quakers." This was the source of the common name of the Society of Friends. Before, they were known as "children of the light." As for the word "friends," Muslims believed they could be a "friend" of God and regarded all other Muslims as brothers (Appendix C).

Fox became a radical preacher in and out of jail before securing an edict of tolerance for Quakers in 1689, partly through the intercession of William Penn, whom he had met at the beginning of his career. Fox traveled extensively in the various American colonies and America increasingly emerged as the Promised Land in the eyes of Quakers. The sect thrived there. It spread like wildfire with more and more meetings (congregations) branching off from each other. A division was made between "birthright friends" and "convinced friends." The former were Quakers born into families that were members of a Friends meeting, while the latter were latecomers who professed the religion and converted to Quakerism without blood ties to members. In this, we can see some of the same Jewish and Muslim thinking described above as well as the traditional Jewish distinction between Jews descended from the patriarchs (*kohanim* and Levites) and the children of Israel seen as having adoptive or undetermined ancestry.

Appendix H presents the surnames in the *Bucks County Quaker Records, Volume 2* by Watring and Wright which we believe stem from or are related to Jewish surnames and given names.[7] Let's consider why this may be the case.

Addams: Adams/Addams is a Hebrew surname, quite plainly. It has become naturalized as English-Christian because two American presidents (cousins) bear the name. Yet it would be more historically sensible to consider that Adams presidents were likely of Jewish descent than to assume, as has generally been done, that the Adams surname is Christian. In the case of this specific Quaker family in Pennsylvania, the use of Talmudic rabbinic names such as Ephraim would seem to be further evidence of crypto–Jewish practice.

Alexander: Alexander was one of the most common Jewish surnames of the medieval period; Esther is a deeply Jewish name for a woman, often used in Orthodox families.

Armor, Ames, Bagley: These three surnames are French Jewish (Amor, Ames) and Turkish (Bagley), respectively.

Bayly: This surname is found on the French Huguenot list, as is Barry. Further, the Bayly family (and Bethulia Barry) carry distinctly Hebrew-Aramaic names, e.g. Bethulia is Hebrew for "virgin," Tamer, "date palm."

Beares, Bears, Bidardike: Members of these two families carry Hebrew/Talmudic names, e.g., Elhanah, Robena (fem. for Ruben), Jael ("female goat").

Buckman[8]: This is a very common Ashkenazic surname. Note the very unusual Hebrew given names, e.g., Abden, Mahlon, Phinchas. Lydia is a Greek given name favored by medieval Jews.

Bunting: Here we see the use of given names that are largely meaningless for a Christian, but redolent of Jewish culture and tradition, e.g., Tamison, Septema, Abner.

Cadwalader: This surname would seem to come from the Arabic Kadwalada, "first born son." Note also the use of the given name Cyrus, the Persian king who freed the Jews from the Babylonian exile, and Judah, a Hebrew tribe, the name also for the Jewish homeland.

Chapman and Cary: Both are on the French Huguenot lists and again we see Jewish-historic names such as Lydia and Mariah.

Eleazar, Ely: These are strongly Jewish-Hebrew surnames. There is a very low probability of non–Jewish ancestry for someone carrying this surname.

Gades: This is the French spelling of Cadiz, Spain — a primary Muslim and Sephardic stronghold.

Le Noir: This name means "the dark" in French; commonly used to designate Moors.

Moon: A common Sephardic surname was Luna, Moon (Hebrew: Yarach).

Pharrow: This is Arabic for "king, ruler," i.e. Pharaoh.

Rhoads: After the expulsion from Spain, a large Sephardic community settled in Rhodes.

Shin: This is a Hebrew letter ( ); other examples include Gemmel (Gimbel), Sin, Tough, Kaph, and Bat that became surnames.

Silver: Surnames which alluded to Jewish and Moorish dominated trades or crafts are strong clues to these ethnicities; examples include Silver/Silber/Silberman, Gold/Golden/Goldman/Goldsmith, Kristeller (crystal trader), Elphinstone (ivory), Silk, Pepper, Zaltman, and Vermillion (a red dye).[9]

Walley: This is the French rendering of the Arabic Wali, "friend, client," a common Moorish surname. In this case, the Hebrew and Greek naming pattern suggests Sephardic (not Islamic) religious affiliation.

Lutherans

In 1728 a congregation of German Lutherans accompanied their pastor, Johann Casper Stoever, to Pennsylvania. Stoever was well educated and could read Latin, Greek, Hebrew and French in addition to his native German. A second table in Appendix H presents the surnames of most of Stoever's congregation. We believe all of those listed are likely Jewish in ancestry. Examples of our reasoning are given below:

Acker/Ackerman: This surname references "one from Acre," an important city in Syria-Lebanon.

Aras: An Arabic surname.

Baasz: An Arabic surname.

Bartholomaie: The Italianized rendering of Bartholomew, a Hebrew surname.

Binzwanger: A prominent colonial-era Jewish surname.[10]

Bubar: A version of a Hebrew surname, e.g., Jewish philosopher Martin Buber.

Canaan: A Hebrew surname for the land between Israel and Egypt.

Canter: Singer/chanter in a Jewish service.

Cantz/Cuntz: Kuntz: an acronym for Kohane Tzadik, "righteous priest."[11]

Cowen: A form of Cohen, the Jewish priestly caste.

Danin: Hebrew for "judge."

Engel: The German form of Angel, a common Sephardic surname.[12]

Fabian: Italian Jewish surname.

Ferrar/Ferry: Common Sephardic surname, means "smith, iron-worker."

Fuchs: German for "fox."[13]

Gross/Grossman: Means "large" in German. Very common Ashkenazic surname.[14]

Gur: Turkish and Arabic for "foreigner, stranger."

Hammon/Ammon: Hebrew surname meaning "that which is hidden."

Hart/Hartman/Hertz: Versions of "deer," a Hebrew tribal totem for Naphthali.

Israel, Jacobi, Jacobs: Hebrew ancestral surnames.

Kapp: Hebrew letter.

Katz/Kintz/Kuhn: Another acronym for Kohen Tzedek.[15]

Lauer, Levan, Lewers, Levandt, Low, Loew: Versions of Levi, with a play on the German for "lion."[16]

Mauer/Moor/Murr/Murhead: Moor or Islamic.

Mooser, Moser, Mosser: Alternative forms of Moses.

Ohr: "Gold" in Latin and French.

Phillippy: A form of the Greek name Phillip; like Alexander, very common among medieval Jews.

Saladin: Arabic for "Light of Religion," as in the famed Muslim general Saladin.

Scheretz: Hebrew word.

Simon, Solomon: Hebrew given and last name.

Sinn, Thau, Tauth: Hebrew letters.

Sonntag: German for "Sunday." Common Ashkenazic surname.[17]

Spanhauer: German for "refugee from Spain"; i.e., one who fled the Inquisition.

Wolf: Hebrew tribal totem for Levi.

Zeh: Hebrew letter.

Some More

Gaeiss: A version of Gess, Gass/Giss/Goss, which is Turkish for "holy warrior."

Gans/Gantz (German for "goose"): The surname of the German Jewish metallurgist on the Roanoke Expedition in 1587.

Gemmel: A Hebrew letter.

Glasick and Glasser: Indicate the bearer is a glazier — a Sephardic and Moorish dominated craft.

Haman and Hammann: Persian-Arabic surnames, as is Hari/Harry.

Hay, Hayes and Hey: The Hebrew letter standing for Hayim, "life."

King and Koenig: Jewish surnames denoting that the bearer was in service to the monarch, as were Kron and Kronin ("crown").

Lora, Lohra, Loray and Lore: Versions of the Sephardic surname Lurie/Luria, as exemplified by Rabbi Isaac Luria.[18]

Maurer: German for "mason."
Morgenstern (Morning Star): A common Ashkenazic Jewish surname.[19]
Sangree: Spanish for "blood."
Valentine: A common Sephardic surname meaning that the bearer was from Valencia.

Names such as these should cause us to rethink just who the early settlers of Pennsylvania were. If they were truly German, why were they carrying surnames such as Saladin, Solomons and Kuntz? Henry Frank Eshleman's excellent *Historic Background and Annals of the Swiss and German Pioneer Settlers of Southeastern Pennsylvania* (1917) can provide some clues. Eshleman traces non-conformity in Christian Europe back to the 800–1400 C.E. time period. During these centuries there were numerous challenges to Catholic orthodoxy — including, but not mentioned by Eshlemann — the resurgence of Judaism. Among the most prominent of these nonconformist Christian sects were the Iconoclasts,[20] Paulicians,[21] Bogomils,[22] or Friends of God, Waldensians,[23] known as the Israelites of the Alps, Cathars and Albigensians[24] and Lollards.[25] One religious sect dating from 1340, according to Eshleman, was actually named Hager (a Sephardic Jewish surname). The Caucasus people called Khazars converted to Judaism in the tenth century and moved eastward into the Ukraine and Poland during the twelfth to fourteenth centuries, bringing a confusion of religions, so that the term for "heretic" in Catholicism became the same as the German word for Khazars (*kertzer*). The fifteenth and sixteenth centuries saw the birth of the Moravians and Anabaptists.

In 1496, four years after the Inquisition began and Jews were banned from Spain, a man named Menno Simon was born in Holland. As both his given and surnames indicate Hebrew affiliation, we believe it is very likely that Menno Simon was of Sephardic descent.[26] By 1525, he had founded the Mennonites, a sect that plays a prominent role in German, Dutch and Hungarian Protestantism. A 1901 book by Kuhns, *The German and Swiss Settlement of Colonial Pennsylvania,* estimates that over 100,000 immigrants from these two countries arrived in colonial Pennsylvania.[27] Several Protestant sects were represented among them: "Swiss Mennonites, the Walloons and the Huguenots." Quakerism, Kuhn notes, had been introduced to Germany by a "William Ames [Sephardic] in 1655" and that another Quaker, William Caton (Hebrew/Arabic word meaning "small, little"), had visited the German Palatinate at a later date.[28] Another, Johann Jacob Zimmerman, one of the founders of the Germantown Colony in Pennsylvania, was an esteemed astrologer, magician and Cabalist. And still another early minister, Johann Kelpius, "believed he was to be taken up into heaven alive like Elijah."[29]

Let us look beyond appearances now at these German settlers. Keith Dull compiled a list of the early German settlers of York County, Pennsylvania.[30] It is given in Appendix H. Among the names already discussed, e.g., Acker, we find some new entries suggestive of Jewish or Islamic ancestry. Amma and Amman are both Arabic, as are Barr and Bentzel. Bless is likely the Anglicized form of Baruch ("Blessing"). Bone and Boner are forms of the Spanish and French words for "good," a common Sephardic surname (see Appendix A).[31] Buatt is Arabic/Turkish; Cappell is Ashkenazic (i.e., as in television reporter Ted Koppel). We find also several French Huguenot names, e.g., de Bus, de Graff, among the German entries. Dewes, Dodd, and Doudel are various forms of David. Duenkel means "dark" and is the German equivalent for Moreno: i.e., dark skinned. Elsasser is Hebrew-Arabic meaning "from Alsace-Lorraine." Eyseck is a form of Isaac. Fiesel is Arabic (i.e., Feisal). Florentina denotes one from Florence, Italy, which had a large post-expulsion population of Jews and

Moors. Blum (Flower) is an Ashkenazic surname.[32] Foucks and Fuchs are the German equivalents of Fox, commonly Ashkenazic, alluding to Feibus/Phoëbus. Frank, Frantz and Frensch describe the bearer as being from France or Frankish lands in the Levant; the Franks family was one of the most prominent Colonial Jewish families in Pennsylvania.

The Franks surname belongs to one of the first families of American Jewry. It shows a similar trajectory to many other Portuguese Jewish families: exile in German or Dutch lands, mercantile activities with London as one of their seats, a branch sent to the Colonies to be naturalized under the new citizenship rules of Queen Anne, prosperity as merchants and partial return to England, where they intermarried with nobility. According to historian Charles Henry Hart,[33] "It seems to be conceded that the American emigrant of the family was Jacob Franks, who came to this country according to one account, circa 1705, and according to another account, circa 1711. His father is variously stated to have been Aaron Franks and Naphtali Franks, of Germany the former of whom it is claimed went to England, with George of Hanover, in 1714, to be crowned king of Great Britain. Jacob Franks (1) was born in 1688 and died in New York, January 16, 1769. In 1719 he married Bellah Abigail Levy, daughter of Moses Levy, and had children, David, Phila, and Moses. David Franks, b. in New York, September 28, 1720, removed to Philadelphia circa 1738, and married there, December 17, 1743, Margaret Evans, daughter of "Peter Evans of the Inner Temple, gentleman, Register General of Pennsylvania." David Franks died in England in 1794, having had 5 or 6 children, viz:

Abigail Franks, b. January 6, 1744/5; baptized in Christ Church, April 12, 1745; m. January 6, 1768, Andrew Hamilton, son of the councilor of the same name who was brother of Governor James Hamilton, son of Andrew Hamilton, the great lawyer and elder brother of William Hamilton of the Woodlands. She died September 11, 1798, leaving one child, Ann, who married James Lyle, whose daughter Ellen married Hartman Kuhn of Philadelphia.

1. Jacob, b. January 7, 1746/7; baptized at Christ Church, April 20, 1747; m. ____. Jacob Franks was living in England in 1781, d. ___.
2. John , b. _____. d. _____. Styled of Ilesworth, Middlesex, England, member of parliament.
3. Mary, b. January 25, 1748; baptized at Christ Church, April 10, 1748; d. August 26, 1774.
4. Moses
5. Rebecca, b. 1760?; m. January 24, 1782, Henry Johnson. Colonel Johnson became a general in 1809 and was created a baronet in December 1818, when his wife became Lady Johnson. She died March 1823. Her son Henry Allen Johnson m. Charlotte Elizabeth, daughter of Frederick Phillipse of New York.

2. Phila Franks, b. June 19, 1722; m. 1742 Oliver Delancey of New York. They had 6 children: Susanna, Charlotte, Phila, Anna, Oliver and Stephen.

1. Susanna (3) m. Lt. Gen. Sir William Draper
2. Charlotte (3) m. Field Marshal Sir David Dundas
3. Phila (3) m. Stephen Payne Galwey
4. Anna (3) m. John Harris Cruger
5. Oliver
6. Stephen. His son was General Sir William Howe De Lancey who fell at Waterloo, where he was on Wellington's staff.

3. Moses Franks, m. Sarah. Had issue Isaac b. May 27, 1759; m. July 9, 1782, Mary Davidson, and d. March 4, 1822. They had issue 4 children, 2 of whom died young, and

1. Samuel D., judge of the court of common pleas for the counties of Schuylkill, Lebanon and Dauphin, PA

2. Sarah Eliza, m. September 9, 1806, John Huffnagle.

David Solebury Franks, who was aide-de-camp to Benedict Arnold, is believed to have been also a son of Moses Franks.

4. "Aunt Franks" is mentioned in the letter from Rebecca Franks to her sister Abby Hamilton, *Pennsylvania Magazine of History and Biography*, Vol. 22, and must have been either her father's sister or the wife of her uncle Moses.

The 1767 tax list for Berkshire County, Pennsylvania, is also enlightening as to the settlers' likely ethnicities.[34] It begins with a Michael Algeier (i.e., Algiers, the North African city inhabited by Moors and Sephards). We find here also the Hebrew-Arabic Haga. There is an Isaac Levan resident in the county and also an Adam Schmael (i.e., Ishmael). Oseas would likely be the Turkish "Osias," and Roads would be Rhodes. Safred is from Safed, the Middle Eastern city. Mr. G. Haal carries a Hebrew-Arabic name. Hans Moser's surname is a rendering of Moshe, and we have Daniel Zacharias and Lloyd Abel, two more Hebrew favorites. There is also Henry Acre (Syrian city), John Terck (Turk), and Nicholas Saladine (the Muslim conqueror of the Holy Land in 1210). Henry Hava has a surname that means "life" in Hebrew. The Romig/Romich surname designates "one from Rome." Yacam is the common Sephardic surname of Yoachim.

In *First Families of Chester County, Pennsylvania*, we find community leaders Zebulon and Israel Hoopes (i.e., Chupa, the Judaic marriage canopy).[35] There is also Ann Ash and Abraham and Esther Ashton. An Allen family in Chester has the following consistently Hebrew-named children: Dinah, Ellis, Emey, Emmor, Espra, Esther, Isaac, Levina, Morral, Orpha, Reuben and Tamer. Similarly, a Baldwin/Baudoin family in Chester named their children Caleb, Deborah, Isaac, Israel, Levina, Lydia, Rachel and Ruth. Traditional historians have proposed that these are simply Old Testament names used by ardent Christians, but such explanations fail to account for the presence of Greek names, e.g., Lydia, which are non–Biblical, and names such as Tamer which are simply Hebrew-Arabic.

We also find in Chester, Pennsylvania, a settler named Frances Bethel, Hebrew for House of God, and Sylvanus Day,[36] whose surname was perhaps Anglicized from the Spanish Dias. There are also Rebecca Eachus and John Faddes who bear Arabic surnames. John Gracey's surname was likely recast from the Spanish Gracia. The Hibberd family in Chester has members named Aaron, Abraham, Caleb, Deborah, Enos, Esther, Hezekiah, Israel, Jacob, Joel, Josiah, Naomi, Orpha, Phineas, Silas and Rhoda, Hebrew for "Rose" (not found in the Bible). Further down the list of Chester residents we find Michael Israel, Isaac Jacobs, Archibald Job, Janny Abel, Judea King, Henrietta Levis and Hannah Lea. These persons are very unlikely to be Christian.

The Maris (Mares means sea, ocean) family has members named Aaron, Barclay, Caleb, Ellis, Esther, Jehu, Jemima, Judith, Lydia, Mordecai, Norris, Phebe, Ruth and Tacey. The presence of Greek names Phebe and Lydia, together with an Arabic name, Norris ("light"), make it very unlikely, again, that the family is Christian. The Marshall family exhibits the same pattern: Abner, Abraham, Armitt, Benjamin, Eli, Israel, Levi, Mabel, Massey,[37] Mira, Moses, Pennock, and Savery. Additional Chester, Pennsylvania, residents include Baroch Michener, Levis Pennock, Hannah Rhoads, Abraham Roman, Issachar Schofeld, Esther, Rachel and Sarah Temple, Sarah Titus, Abraham Widdos and Elhanan Zook (Zug). It is difficult to construe these as Christian names.

We close our discussion of Chester with the Sharpless (Charpeles) family, whose members carry the names Aaron, Abi, Abraham, Abner, Beulah, Caleb, Casper, Danie, Diniah, Eli, Enos, Jonathan, Lydia, Mira, Naomi, Rubene and Ruth. Such a pattern would not be appropriate for a Christian family but would be very meaningful for a Sephardic family aware of its Mediterranean heritage.

Some additional likely Sephardic/Moorish settlers in Pennsylvania are found in the book *Emigrants to Pennsylvania*.[38] These include Anna Habacki, Emanuel Hyams, Isaac Moss, Henry Sharick, John Zinn ("tin"), Israel Morris, William Athens, Joachim Lucke (Fortuna/Tov), Joran Duffua, Turckelson Timmerman, Anders Gedda (a city in Saudi Arabia), John Tizack, L. Anatta, Phillip Mayow, T. Alferry (Alfari), Dyamond (a trade always monopolized by Jews), Benzien (Ben Zion), Lorenz Bagge (Turkish for "ruler, king"), John Arbo, Salome Steinman, Jacob Bechtell, Abigail Pedroe, Ebenezer Zanes, Daniel Jappie, Phillip Hime (Chaim), David Tishell, Alexander Forrentine (Florentine), Moses Hayman (Hyman), Isacher Prise, Maurice Nihil, Pyramus Green, Baltzer Elslegal, Samuel Hasell, William Fagan, Joseph Saull, Patrick OHassan (Berber), Anthony Siddon, Michael Jirael, William Gammon, Susanna Fassell (Judeo-Arabic), William Geddes (Cadiz/Gades), Barak Wright, Anne Canide, Tobias Nile, James Abraham, Mathew Gamalise, Rowland Judd, James Benzet, Mary Hymen (Hyman), Wandel Zarban, Jacob Diamond, Mary Shiekell (Shekel, Hebrew money), Stephen Carmuk, Anna Dingasey, Salome Albright, Patrick Taaffe, David Solomon, Thomas Darrah, Caspar Singar ("cantor"), Levy Marks and Frederick Castill (Castile).

Swedish Naturalization

Another rich source for Sephardic immigrants to Pennsylvania were the Swedes, many of whom were already in place from the former colony of New Sweden (Chapter 5). When the Philadelphia County Court held its first session on 11 January 1683, seventeen Swedish settlers came forward and asked for the rights and privileges of citizenship. The Act of Naturalization passed by the Assembly in December 1682 gave landowning foreigners residing in Pennsylvania or the lower counties three months to be naturalized. The Swedes swore allegiance to the king of England and obedience to Penn as governor, and paid a fee of twenty shillings sterling. By doing so, they received the same rights as their English-born neighbors. They were Lasse Cock, Peter Rambo, Swan Swanson, Andrew Swanson, Wolle Swanson, Lasse Anderson, Mouns Cock, Eric Cock, Gunnar Rambo, Peter Nilsson Laykan, Christian Thomas, Eric Mullica, Peter Cock, Jr., John Boules, Andrew Salem, John Stille, and Lasse Dalbo.

Several of these Swedish settlers appear to be of Sephardic and Moorish ancestry, as indicated by their names. Rambo (Rambeaux) is a French Sephardic surname, Mullica is Spanish; Dalbo is French, and Salem is Arabic. We already noted how the venture that briefly flourished as New Sweden was organized by the same Sephardic merchants as New Amsterdam, so it is not surprising to see familiar types in this list.

Additionally, from the *Bucks County Church Records, Volume 3*, one should note early settlers Elizabeth Hibron (Hebron, city in Palestine), Ann Gomery and Penquite Chapman (Appendix H).[39]

The Quaker commercial atmosphere of Pennsylvania attracted a number of Jewish Indian traders to its hinterlands. A snapshot into the names of traders can be gleaned from documents in the Pennsylvania Archives covering the years 1743–1775 (Appendix H). This ignores, of course, all the unregistered peddlers and "fly by night" merchants. Some of the more overt Jewish names are: Christopher Jacob, Benjamin Spyker (Specker, "swine"), George Crohan (Krohn, "crown"),[40] Lazarus Lowry (Luria), James Lowry, Simon Girtee, John Hart, Samuel Cross, Jacob Cressman, Nicholas Swamp (Soto), Bartholomew Tool (Toule), Jacob Kline, Abraham Moses, Francis Hair, Elias Bender (German: "hoop worker"),[41] George Ray, Jacob Barr, Isaac Wolfe, Joseph Solomon Cohen, Michael Hart, David Shilleman (Schülermann), Abraham Levy, Jacob Isaiah Cohen, Michael Hay, John Barron,[42] Joseph Solomon, Isaiah Cohen, Ephraim Abraham, Abraham Levi, John McCowen and Lyon Nathan.

Case History: Wampler Family

The Wampler family from Sparsbach, Alsace, represents one of the authors' ancestral lines (Elizabeth Hirschman's). They pose an archetypal instance of the crypto–Jewish Pennsylvania Dutch/Deutsch phenomenon discussed in this chapter and so can constitute a good case study.[43] Hans Peter Wampler was born in 1701 in Sparsbach and died in 1749 in Lancaster County, Pennsylvania. He was a linen-weaver by trade. The Wampler family seems to have "appeared" in the 1500s in Zwischefluh, Switzerland, and to have taken their surname from a tiny village there called Wampflen. The earliest church records for them date from 1559.

In the year 1561 two male children, Hans and Anthony Wampler, were christened. The witnesses were "Jacob Flogerey, Niclaus Tuscher, old lady Kammer, and Niclaus Juttziler's wife." At a later christening for a child named Jacob, witnesses included Ull Hala, Heiny Wytter, Christian Wirthi and Margarett Ashler. Later witnesses to other christenings included an Ottmar (Turkish) Stali, (illegible) Zappali, Margret Cuntz, Peter Murer, Jacob Augustein, Eva Zapati, Jacob Stucki, Petter Pierry, Jacob Aegler, Batt Aleman ("German") and Barbara Wolff.

As should now be expected, we are going to argue that the Wampler family was crypto–Jewish while living in Switzerland. What are the clues? First, the family has taken on a local "place" surname, which was common for incoming Jews but not usual for long-term residents or immigrating non–Jews. Second, Wamplers do not appear in the records prior to 1559, suggesting immigration to that locale at a time coinciding with the spread of the Inquisition to France and Holland. Third, their children are given Mediterranean and Hebrew names, e.g., Anthony and Jacob. Fourth, the witnesses to the christenings (christenings were required to establish legitimacy) bore several Jewish surnames, e.g., Tuscher, Kammer, Hala, Ashler, Cuntz, Murer, Zapati, Akman, Wolff and Pierry. Fifth, the family apparently was skilled in linen weaving, a trade strongly associated with Huguenots (and thus Sephards and Moors). Sixth, the family had migrated by the 1700s to Alsace, the location of a large, open crypto–Jewish community. Alsace was the place where they lived before going to America.

The Wampler family immigrated to Philadelphia in 1741 aboard the Lydia with several other persons coming from the Palatinate. Hans Peter Wampler, the author's ancestor, settled in Lancaster County, attending the Lutheran Church near Cleona, Pennsylvania. His son, Hans Peter (born 1723) married Barbara Brenneiss in 1743 and had children named Jacob, David, John, Daniel, Joseph, Barbara, Eve, Christina, Philliptenia and Ann. The family then made its way to Frederick County, Maryland. Of the children who married,

David wed a woman surnamed Susseny (Sephardic surname), John married a Garber, Christina married a Gabriel (Sephardic surname), Philliptenia married Philip Engles (Sephardic surname), and Ann married a Hartman (Ashkenazic surname). Several of these family members then migrated to Wythe County, Virginia, a Melungeon community. Michael Wampler together with Martin Kimberling, Michael Steffey (another ancestor of the author) and John Phillippi (recall that this Greek name was widely used by Jews) "were the elders who founded St. Paul's Lutheran Church in Rural Retreat, Virginia." St. Paul's was later renamed Zion Church.

Elizabeth Wampler, daughter of Michael (born about 1752), married (1) Ludwig Abel (Jewish surname) and (2) George Davis (Jewish surname) in Wythe County, having children David, Jonathan and Maria Salme. Later generations in Wythe County married persons surnamed Cobenhagen (i.e., Copenhagen, Denmark, a refuge for Sephardic Jews), Kettering, Sarah See, Mary Magdalena Wolf, Mary Magdalena Koenig/King, and Jacob Kinser. Subsequent marriages were made with the Steffey family (2), the Jacob King family (2) and the Kinzler family. Children's names began to include Israel, Esther, and Leah. We see this same pattern repeated for some Wampler lines that remained in Pennsylvania.

Roy H. Wampler's book *A Wampler Family History* documents a much larger set of ancestors and descendants.[44] We learn that Peter Wampler (born about 1649) married Magdalena Kunz (Kohane Tzedek) and that Anna Magdalena Wampler had married Samuel Mettauer, linen weaver, in 1714. Upon arriving in Pennsylvania and moving in 1770 to Virginia, as Wampler also documents, the family practiced a distinct pattern of cousin-to-cousin marriage. For example, in 1797 Joseph Wampler married his first cousin Esther Kinser/Kinze, and his brother Henry Wampler married Esther's sister, Maria Kinser. It was a common practice among Sephardim and Moriscos. Their older sister Katherine Wampler earlier married her first cousin George Kinser. John Samuel Wampler married his second cousin Mary Catherine Andes (Sephardic surname). Mary Susan Wampler (1863–1923) married her second cousin Joseph Benjamin Wampler, and Virginia Viola[45] Wampler (1879–1961) married her second cousin, Samuel Homer Driver. Estelle Wampler (1857–1932) married her first cousin, Charles Kuhn (Kohane); Alice Victoria Wampler (1862–1932) married her first cousin John McTeer Wampler, and Leftwich Porter Wampler married his first cousin Tabitha Esther Fielder (1851–1929). Multiple marriages were made into the Copenhaven, Etter (Eder),[46] King/Koenig, Fielder and Driver families (all carrying Ashkenazic surnames), as well as the Zumbrum, Rudisill/Rudisel, Kron, Zepp, Lippy, Cline/Kline (Klein),[47] Snyder and Hershey (Hirsch, Zevi)[48] families — all also having Ashkenazic surnames. But the "smoking gun" is perhaps the marriage of Johann Leonard Wampler (1782–1857) to Ann Mary Martin, the daughter of Mathias Martin and Anna Barbara (Troxell) Martin. The Troxells were openly Jewish.

As with the Wamplers, Troxells first surface in post-diaspora Switzerland. The first name known to us is Stephan Trachsel, born in 1536. According to legend, the Trachsel family came to Switzerland over Vienna from Turkey (then the Ottoman Empire). Descendant Rinnah Bonnie Burns says there were several Jewish communities in the southern part of Emmental, Switzerland, in Canton Berne from 1385, when her Yoders or Joders moved to Steffisburg. They came into contact with the Trachsels of Trachselwald, who had migrated from Turkey to Greece to Austria, then Switzerland. Before that, they must have been in Spain. Other Swiss Jewish surnames, all interconnected, are Zook or Zaugg (Zug), Kauffmann,[49] Amman (founder of Amish religion), and Schrock or Schrag.[50] Trachsel/Troxell was not the family's original name: like other Jews, they obviously adopted it from their place of refuge. The village's name is first attested in 1131 when Uffo von Trachselwald was one of the local gentry. Strangely, the village's coat of arms shows a Star of David. The name in German means Turner's Wood (from Drachsler, a Swiss dialect form of Drexel, Drexler, Drechsler).[51] Could it be that the Trachsels/Troxells, whatever their original name, found a haven with a known Swiss Jewish community? This supposition would explain why the town arms bear a Jewish emblem.

Fast forward two centuries and we find the Trachsels (now calling themselves Troxell) living in Pennsylvania. David Troxell and his wife Anna Elizabeth Saenger ("cantor") have two sons, Christian and George Jacob, who form marriages with Native American women, the time-honored way of securing trade agreements with chiefs. Christian married a Shawnee woman in the band of renegade French trader Martin Chartier, and George Jacob, known as Big Jake, married Cornblossom, daughter of Cherokee war chief Doublehead, who was himself part Jewish through a trader's marriage. Troxell was one of George Washington's spies among the Indians. A sister, Elizabeth Troxell, married Benjamin Burke, one of a *minyan* (quorum of ten or more Jewish adults needed to start a congregation) in the Boone settlement in Kentucky. The groups included men by the names of Cooper, Bell, Gregory, Dolan, and Blevins (that is, Ab "son of" Levin, coincidentally spelling the word for Wolf in Welsh). Jonathan and Elizabeth Troxell's son Benjamin married Nancy Cooper, daughter of Isaac Cooper and Cherokee chief Black Fox's daughter Nancy Blackfox. Both authors have these people as ancestors or relatives. Cousin marriage is so convoluted that it would be a tour de force to show all the interconnections on a chart.

Another marker of crypto–Judaism is membership in churches that are ostensibly Christian, but in fact operate as Jewish houses of worship. The Wamplers and their related families belonged to St. David's church in (West) Manheim Township, York County, Pennsylvania, and were buried in St. Jacobs cemetery in Brodbecks, Quickel's cemetery, Conawago, Immanuel Cemetery, Manchester, Maryland, St. Elias cemetery, Emmitsburg, Maryland, Mt. Tabor cemetery, Rocky Ridge, Maryland, and Zion cemetery in Wythe County, Virginia.

Primary surnames associated with

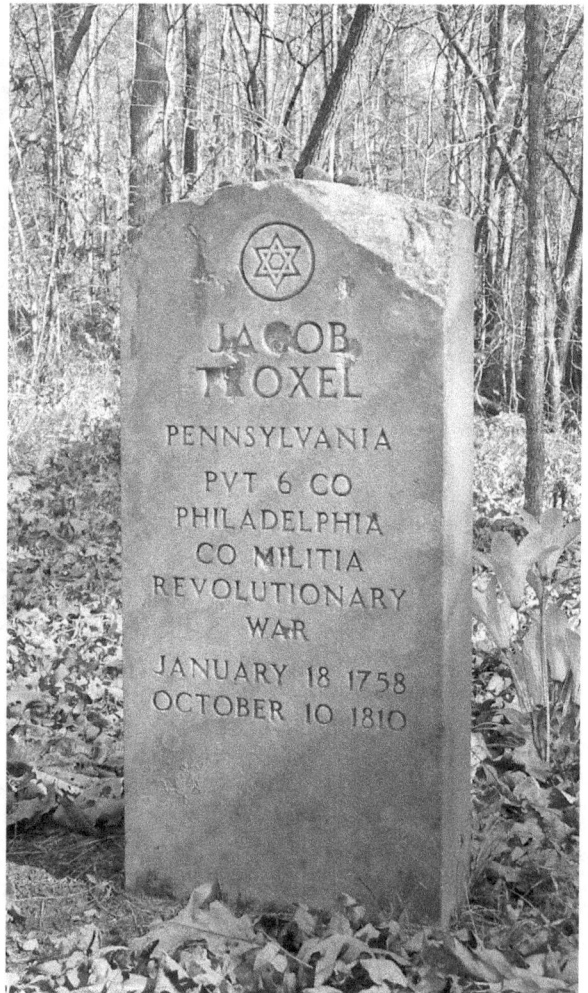

Jacob Troxell grave with Star of David in Daniel Boone Forest in Kentucky (Courtesy of Phyllis and Billy Starnes).

In addition to the "Book of Life" motif, the gravestones of Jewish descended persons in early America sometimes featured a hand pointing to a star, as in this example (author's collection).

the Wampler family in America include the following: Albright, Angel, Brown, Burr, Cooley, Coon (Cohen), Copenhaver, Cramer/Craumer/Croumer (Kremer), Dehoff/deHofe, Derr, Doll, Driver, Eckert, Epley, Fahnestock ("herald"), Feeser, Fielder, Fleischman ("butcher"), Flory (Flori), Fox (Fuchs), Freed (Fried), Frymyer, Fuhrman, Fundenburg, Garber ("tanner," a Jewish trade), Garrett, Glick ("luck," Hebrew Tov), Good (see Appendix A), Grabill, Hagerman, Hancock, Harbrom (Hebron), Hiteshue, Hoover, Horner, Hull, Humbert, Jacobs/Jacoby, Kelly/Kelley, Kemper, King/Koenig, Kinser/Kinsey, Koons (Hebrew anagram KZ), Koontz, Laughman, Lippy, Little, Markle, May, Miller, Myers,[52] Oursler ("bear"), Ruhlman, Scholl (Hebrew *shul*), Sell, Smith, Snyder ("Taylor"), Sterner ("one who wears a — Jewish — star"), Stoner (Steiner), Stonesfer, Streuig, Switzer ("from Switzerland"), Swope, Trish, Utz, Williams, Wolf (e), Yingling, Zepp (compare Zeppelin, Czepler, Polish "warm"[53]) and Zumbrun (m).

Enough has been said that we can draw some conclusions. Although Pennsylvania was the brainchild of the English Quaker William Penn, it was not so much Englishmen, even recently naturalized English, who flocked to the new colony but Germans and other nationalities from the Continent. Penn advertised heavily across Europe.[54] The bulk of those attracted to his international "Asylum for Mankind" were second, third or fourth generation Sephardic Jews. Taken together, the Mennonites, Dunkards and other denominations, many of them mere convenient covers, probably always outnumbered the Quakers. Certainly this was true by the time of the great influx of Scots-Irish Presbyterians after the defeat of the Jacobites at Culloden in 1746. It has been estimated seventy percent of all British immigrants over the past half century were Scots or Irish. The peopling of Pennsylvania took on a life of its own. The ethnicity of the colony became more mixed than any other. But one of the strongest common denominators was the underlying crypto–Jewish roots of the settlers, which fostered a "live and let live" mindset. The desire of William Penn to populate the Colony with the "sons of David and the tribe of Judah" was, in large part, brought to fruition.

CHAPTER SEVEN

Maryland: Catholic in Her Tastes

The most salient aspect of Maryland's colonial era for our thesis is not its history or heroes, per se, for it boasts little in either category, but rather its ordinary colonists. These, as we shall show, resembled a veritable United Nations of immigrants, often non–Christian, eager to avail themselves of Maryland's lax entry laws. The colony's sandy Atlantic shoreline, the endless Chesapeake marshes and numerous inlets served as easy landing places for surreptitious disembarkations, whether of passengers or cargo. Maryland's advantages were not all spiritual. If tobacco figured as the Colonies' biggest cash crop and export, it was Maryland where the bulk of it was grown, for it rapidly outstripped Virginia. Even though the Maryland product was not so fine, it was less expensive. During its heyday it supplied perhaps half the needs of Britain, France and Germany, typically through Scottish factors.[1]

Historians often treat Virginia and Maryland as one. The Chesapeake colonies were a region dominated by scattered plantations. Maryland's population, so goes the orthodox account, was overwhelmingly composed of the drifting poor of England arriving as indentured servants.[2] The colony's whole pattern of life reflected little more than the British county with its parish church and landed gentry transplanted to a New World setting. Underneath the tidy veneer, however, the beginnings of Maryland harbor many mysteries and just plain contradictions. Here we will draw on James Walter Thomas' *Chronicles of Colonial Maryland* (1900) as our primary source for establishing Maryland's chronology and then have recourse to the several extensive *Colonial Families of Maryland* volumes to discuss the settlers.[3]

On the fifth of March 1634 two aptly named ships, the *Ark* and the *Dove,* arrived at the mouth of the Potomac River. On board was Leonard Calvert, who was to govern the province under the proprietorship of Caecilius Calvert, 2nd Baron Baltimore, his older brother. Baron Baltimore reasoned that to make his domain profitable, he needed to acquire colonists whom he could tax and, therefore, under the "Conditions of Plantation" every free man who came to Maryland was to be awarded "one hundred acres of land for himself, a like quantity for his wife, every child over 16 and each servant, and fifty acres for every child under sixteen years of age, to be held by him and his heirs and assigns forever." In 1641 these grants were reduced to 50 acres and 25 acres respectively. Very importantly, no restrictions on the nationality of the settlers were imposed. While it is true that by 1636 the grants were restricted to persons of "British and Irish descent," by 1648 they were reinstated for persons of French, Dutch and Italian descent. Notably, these were countries heavily populated by Sephardic Conversos as well as Moriscos. In 1683 it was reconfirmed that lands were again available to all persons willing to purchase them. Undoubtedly these were the most lenient freeholder opportunities available in British North America. They would — and did — attract many of those displaced by the Inquisition.

Following Thomas' account we learn that William Paca (Pache),[4] Uriah Forrest (Silva)[5] and Clement Hollyday (Yomtov)[6] were appointed state commissioners at the conclusion of the Revolutionary War. St. Clement's Manor, 1659–72, had as landholders Arthur de La Hay (Hebrew Letter),[7] John Gee (another Hebrew letter), John Green ("of foreign complexion"), Benjamin Hamon,[8] Christopher Carnall (Hungarian-Scottish, note the Hebrew theophoric-el/-al suffix), John Goldsmith (a typical Jewish trade), Rowland Mace (i.e., Mays, after the month),[9] and John Mansell (Hebrew, "victor"),[10] among others. By 1760 Anthony Semmes (Hebrew, "descendants"),[11] Moses Tabbs (Hebrew, "cook, butcher"),[12] William Canoday (Canada, Kennedy, Candia, Candiani, Candi)[13] and Leigh Massey (Hebrew) were serving as vestry men of the Poplar Hill parish.

Maryland's Colonists

With that brief introduction to the state, we are going to explore now the identities of some of Maryland's colonial era settlers, the names of whom, we believe, will seem both unusual and familiar by now to the reader. We retain the variable spelling of names to show, among other things, how a Hebrew or Arabic name could gradually become more English-sounding in as short a time as a single generation.

Edaliah Adams married James Dakes on 14 April 1748. Edeliah (Adams) Dakes was mother of the following children: Jesse, James, Daniel, Sabra, Sarah, and Stephen. Adams is a common Sephardic surname. Edeliah Adams Dakes and her husband James Dakes (who bears a Greek surname meaning *minyan*) named a child Sabra, non–Biblical Hebrew for a cactus flower.

Aleefe (Arabic) Joseph Aleefe of Angola Neck died leaving a will dated 13 November 1700. Mentioned are wife Bridgett; son William; daughter Bridgett; wife's son Ebenezer Jones. Witnessed by Thomas Carey, Ledah (Greek) Carey, Roger Corbett, Elizabeth Simmons. The subject, Joseph Aleefe, carries a Morisco/Islamic surname: Alif (first letter in alphabet, "leader"). The name of his township, Angola Neck, suggests this may have been a Portuguese-settled community in Maryland.

Allee (Arabic). The Allee family of Queen Anne County was present in Maryland by 1730. This family married into the Mason family and were indentured for a time to Thomas Ringgold of Chester. Allee is obviously of Sephardic or Morisco origin (i.e., Ali)[14] and the Ringgold family is Sephardic, as we shall later show.

Arey/Aree is a markedly Arabic/Morisco surname: It means "lion," the symbol for the tribe of Judah.[15] David Arey married Hannah Jadwyn in 1695. David Arey, planter, died leaving a will dated 19 January 1714/5. Named were children John, Esther and Deborah. The will stated that if the children were not properly cared for, George Bowers was to take them in charge, and if he be deceased, they were to be under the care of the Quaker Quarterly Meeting. David and Hannah were the parents of John, Deborah (Debrough), who married Benjamin Parrat, and Esther.

Joseph Arey, brother of David Arey, married Jane Clarke, born 1688. She married, first, in 1704, Benjamin Parratt, married, second, Joseph Arey, and married, third, William

Scot. Joseph Arey died leaving a will dated 6 November 1728. The heirs named were sons-in-law Eliazor and William Parratt. Joseph was the father of Mary, David (noted in the will of his cousin Esther) and Jonathan. On 5 November 1762 Jonathan Airey and Enoch Morgan and Sarah, his wife, conveyed to John Jenkinson and Joseph Berry three acres whereon the Tuckahoe meeting house and graveyard came to be "for the use of the people called Quakers." Jonathan Arey died leaving a will dated 8 December 1767. Mentioned were cousins: Sarah, William and John Tillotson and friend, Edward Chetham. Executor was John Tillotson. Witnesses were John Coursey, Michael Green, Philip Saintee and Abraham De la Hunt. Note that these Areys were Quaker and had marital or business dealings with other persons bearing Jewish/Sephardic surnames, e.g., Parratt, Coursey, Green, Saintee and De la Hunt.

Barney (Sephardic). The Francis Barney family carries a Sephardic surname and married into the Perkins family; the wife's given name is Greek, Araminta. The use of Greek names was common among Mediterranean Jews, who had become Hellenized as early as 300 B.C.E. Estate appraisers included William Rasin (Persian for "prince") and Aquila (Spanish for "eagle") Attwix.

Jacob Isaac von Bibber married a woman named Christiana (Converso name). Isaac, Matthias and Henry Van Bibber were brothers, sons of Jacob Isaac Van Bibber, a "Hollander." Isaac Van Bibber, son of Jacob Isaac Van Bibber, was naturalized 25 March 1701. Isaac Van Bebber (perhaps the original spelling) died leaving a will dated 14 September 1723. To son Jacob, daughters Hester (wife of Jacob Goodin), Christina and Veronica, and sons Peter and Isaac, each an equal share. To son Jacob and son-in-law Jacob Goodin, personally. Veronica Van Bebber married John Birmingham; Christina Van Bebber married Peter Lareux; Hester Vanbeber married Jacob Gooding.

The original surname of the Van Bebber family above was Isaacs, a Jewish surname.[16] They were called Van Bebber upon arriving in Maryland, because that is the town in Holland from which they emigrated. Van Bebber is also known to be a Jewish surname (think of the philosopher Martin Beber) and is found among the Melungeons — a Sephardic-Morisco-Native American ethnic group in Appalachia. Notably the family also had business dealings with Edward Cooper of Jamaica, an individual known to be Jewish and denoted in records as mulatto (half–Indian, not half–African, as often imagined).[17]

William Boon, son of John Boone, married Margaret Jump. William died leaving a will dated 22 July 1728 naming sons Jacob, Joseph, Abraham, Benjamin, Moses and daughters Elizabeth, Mary and Rachel.

Boone/Boon was a common Sephardic surname derived from Buen, Bono, Bon, all meaning good, as we have seen.[18] Note the Hebraic naming patterns in this family.

Briscoe Family. Briscoe (Brezca) is commonly accepted by researchers as a Sephardic surname.[19] Philip Briscoe was born about 1647 and died in 1724, having married Susannah Swann, daughter of Edward Swann. Their children were John, Philip, Edward (married Susannah Slye, daughter of Robert Slye and Priscilla Goldsmith, Jewish surnames), George, Sarah, Judith, Susannah, Ann, James, Elizabeth and Izraell. Parmenas (Greek) Briscoe was born in 1749 and married Ann Briscoe, daughter of Gerrard Briscoe and Ruth McMillian. Their children included a son who married Harrison Briscoe, a daughter Elizabeth who married George Cole Briscoe, Sally, Truman, Polly, Gerard, Robert, Fanny, Patsy, Bolivar (Spanish), Rebecca and Hezekiah. Jeremiah Briscoe married Elizabeth Harlan. Their children were Phebe, Silas, George, John, Casander (Cassandra: Greek) and Sarah. With the Briscoe family we have clear evidence of multigenerational endogamy at the first-cousin level — practiced to a great extent among Sephardic Jews and Muslims during this time.

Robert Crouch died leaving a will dated 30 October 1711 naming wife Mary, sons John, Robert, Jacob, daughters Rose (Hebrew Roda), Ann, Ele, Rachell and her son, and grandsons John and Jacob Taylor. The estate of Robert Crouch was administered by Jacob Crouch and the legatees were John Crouch, Alice Layton ("from Leiden" in the Netherlands), Rachell Cary, Anne Disharone, Rose Gording and Robert Crouch. In this entry, Anne Disharone is named as a legatee of John Crouch. Disharone is the Gallicized rendering of Sharon, a Hebrew place-name and surname (e.g., Ariel Sharon, prime minister of Israel).

Davis. There were multiple Davis families in Maryland. Davis was one of the most common Jewish surnames in England during the 1600s and 1700s; later it was the second best known English Jewish surname.[20] Among these, the **Phillip Davis** family married into or had business dealings with several likely Sephardic families: e.g., those of Phillip Raisen (Persian for "prince"), Charles Ringgold, Abraham Ayres, George Copper (Cooper) and Simon Worrell. **John Davis** died leaving a will dated 13 July 1789 naming sons Ruben, Eli, Stephen, and Daniel, and daughters Leah, Tabby, Nelly and Sinah (Hebrew). Also mentioned were William Hopwell, George Disheroon (father-in-law of Ruben Davis), Hetty Sturgis Austin, Nelly Austin, and wife Clare Trower Dias (Portuguese). **Tabitha Davis**, daughter of Beauchamp Davis, married her cousin Levin Beauchamp on 1 May 1765. **Benjamin Davis** and Ishmael Davis witnessed the will of Mathew Rain (i.e. Reyne) on 30 January 1737. Benjamin Davis witnessed the will of Elizabeth Tingell on 18 May 1740. Children of Benjamin and Mary Davis were Ann, Mathias, Leah (Hebrew name for a model mother), Mary, Abijiah, Zipphora and Sophia. **Daniel Davis** died leaving a will dated 7 May 1747. To son William he left a fifty-acre tract, Battle Ridge, to son John, his plantation house, and to the five youngest children, Isaac, Daniel, James, Levin (Levine), and Judah Davis, personal items. **William Davis**, son of Daniel Davis, died leaving a will naming wife Patience and children Spensor, Elizabeth, Selitha (Yiddish, non–Biblical) and Keziah (Arabic/Hebrew "incense"). **John Davis** immigrated to Maryland in 1666. He died leaving a will to maintain younger children John, Tamarlane, David, Frances, Siballa (Sybilla, Greek) and Eliza. To daughters Frances, Siballa and Eliza he left 600 acres; to granddaughter Tabitha (Aramaic, Dorcas in Greek) Davis, he also left some land. To son Tamberlin Davis he left the residue of Tabitha's portion. Son David also received land, and youngest daughter Elizabeth, some personal items. To wife Eliza and her six children, John, Tamberline, David, Frances, Sybilla and Eliza, he gave the residue of his estate.

We propose that these several Davis families were Jewish. What is different about the last one is the use of the Persian given name Tamberlane/Tamarlane for a son. Tamerlane (1336–1405) was born near Samarkand, Uzbekistan. He was an extraordinary conqueror whose domain ultimately spread from Turkey to India. By religion he was Muslim; thus the use of his name as a given name for the Davis family's son strongly suggests that they were, themselves, Muslim or had come from Turkey in the general region in which Tamerlane had lived.[21] Again, naming and marriage patterns tell a story. John Davis, on the other hand, has sons and daughters carrying definitive Judaic names, e.g., Ruben, Ell, Leah and Sinah. He was related by marriage to George Disheroon (de Sharon). Tabitha Davis, his daughter, married her cousin Levin Beauchamp. Within the Benjamin Davis family, Benjamin and Ishmael witnessed Matthew Rain's (Reine)[22] will, and again the naming pattern for children was strongly Judaic, e.g., Abijah, Ziphora, and Sophia (Greek). Daniel Davis also gave his children overtly Judaic names: Isaac, Levin/Levine and Judah. Daniel's son William gave two of his children non–Biblical Hebrew/Aramaic names: Selitha and Keziah (a name also used by Moriscoes) and had Leaven Disharoon be one of his witnesses.

Isaac England. Jews often took their surnames from the countries, provinces or towns in which they lived (e.g., Isaac of York). Here we have an Isaac England who arrived in Maryland by 1714 and married a woman named Rebeckah, a classically Jewish name. They were members of the Cecil Friends Meeting House: Quaker affiliation was a common cover for crypto–Judaism. They had marital or business relationships with William Simcocks (Simchas, Simha, Hebrew but non–Biblical)[23] and Gaspar Hood (Hut, Hud).[24]

Falconar. Falcon/Falco/Falconer were common Sephardic surnames.[25] This family was in Maryland by 1707 and maintained a merchant trade with kinsmen in London. Business dealings included partnerships with Richard Scaggs, Francis Spearman (from Speyer in the Rhineland, a Jewish center),[26] David Barclay in London, Daniel Phillips in London, physician, Joshua Van Sant and Samuel Rue (French for "street"). This family also belonged to the Cecil Monthly Meeting. **Isaac Falkner/Falconer,** son of Isaac and Dorcas Falkner, died leaving a will dated 18 April 1751. To his brother Abraham Faulkner, Isaac left land, giving the bulk of his estate to his wife and children. The will was witnessed by William West, John Barruck and Mary Harwood. **John Falconer** married a woman named Sarah. At November Court 1714 it was presented that Thomas Falconer, laborer, on 15 November in the 12th year of the reign of the queen, at Wye Hundred, committed adultery with Sarah Falconer, wife of John Falconer. Witnesses included Edward Hyett (Arabic)[27] and Ellinor Falconer. A verdict of not guilty was returned. John Falkoner (Falkner) died leaving a will dated 20 March 1727. The will was witnessed by Michael Hussey, Richard Moore and Jane Manner. On 3 February 1767, Henry Casson, merchant, and his wife Esther, and Mary Elles, spinster, conveyed to John Falconer 127 acres of land. **Burton Faulkner** died leaving a will dated 12 December 1774. His son Jonathan and daughter Esther were administrators. Mentioned also were Ruth, Benjamin and a slave named Munday.

Here we have the Falkner (Falconer) family — a common Jewish surname.[28] Isaac and Abraham Faulkner are brothers; Isaac's will is witnessed by John Barruck, whose surname is Hebrew for "blessed." Another Falconer, Thomas, was charged with adultery with his brother's wife (he may have been exercising the duty of Levirate law by which a brother marries his sister-in-law once she is widowed). A witness was Edward Hyett (Hyatt, Hyat/Hayat is Judeo-Arabic for "tailor"). John Falkner's will was witnessed by Michael Hussey, also a Hebrew/Arabic surname.

Freeman. Another very common Jewish surname is Freeman, the translation for Franco, used of merchants free to travel between different countries. In German the word appears as Frank or Friedmann, as in the case of the Holocaust diarist Anne Frank or the Philadelphia/New York aristocratic family of Franks. In Dutch it is Vriedman, and in Spanish, Franco.[29] This usage began with the Crusades, when the Franks and Norman French military carved out a kingdom in the Levant and monopolized trade through the Templar Knights. **William Freeman** was in Maryland by 1668. His son, Isaac, married Hannah Comegys (Turkish). Isaac's executors were William Lovelin, John Falconer and John Scott. Later children married into the Rasin family (twice), the Wilmer and the Ringgold families.

Gale. Also Sephardic is the Gale surname (as in the Colombian actor Gael Garcia Bernal).[30] John Gale was in Maryland by 1699. The family was Quaker and married into the Rasin family. A son married a woman named Barsheba Lamb (i.e., the Paschal lamb of Passover). Children included James, Malachi, Mary, Catherine and Rosamund.

Hebron/Hepburn Family. This family, carrying a Palestinian surname, arrived in Maryland by 1665. They intermarried with the Caselick (i.e., "son of Cassel"), Phillips (Forbes) and Briscoe (Sephardic) families.

Mordecai Jacob was born 24 May 1714 and died about 1771. He was the son of Benjamin Jacob and wife Alice. In December 1745 he married Jemima (Arabic) Isaac. Children were: Ruth, married Isaac Hall, Benjamin, married Elenor Odell (Berber surname), Mordecai, Sarah, Alice, Isaac, George, Jemima and Eleanor. The will of Mordecai Jacob was probated on May 8, 1771. The witnesses were Benjamin Gaither, John Isaac, and Joseph Peach ("Persian").[31]

Clearly this was a self-aware Jewish family, even though living publicly as Christian. A Jacobs man has married an Isaacs woman and many of the children's names are Hebrew. In this case as in the one above, the name Mordecai is likely a direct indicator of a family that is consciously Jewish. Few if any Christians would use this appellation, which derives from ancient Hebrew and has important associations with the legend of Esther celebrated at Purim, Sephardic Jews' favorite high holy day.

Michael Lazel/Lassell (Arabic) married Martha Cook in 1705 and died around 1742. His estate was appraised by P. Kennard and Francis Barney (Sephardic). Nathaniel Lassell, an orphan son, was under age in 1736 when he was bound to Thomas Rouse, plasterer. He died by March 1756. Thomas Ringgold and William Wilmer signed as Michael Lassell's creditors. Nathaniel Lazzel and Alise Reason signed as his next of kin. Martha Lazel filed the inventory on 15 May 1756. Note here the intersection of several Jewish families in financial and estate relationships: Lazzel, Reason, Barney and Ringgold.

Ralph Lowe was transported to the colony of Maryland by 1649 as an indentured servant. He married Rachel Hudson and died leaving a will dated 5 December 1772. John Lowe, son of Ralph Lowe, married Tabitha. On 11 February 1775 John Lowe and his wife, Tabitha, sold land to Benjamin Dashiell. George Lowe (Loe), son of Ralph Lowe, married on 29 December 1754 Sarah Cotman, daughter of Ebenezar Cotman. The father's will was witnessed by Richard Green and Ralph and Hutson Low. Hudson Lowe had children Levin and Samuel.

The Lowe family has a Sephardic surname (i.e. Loewe, a play on Levi: Jacobs 1901–1906 which means "lion").[32] The ancestor arrived as an indentured servant, but we are not sure from what country. His descendant Ralph/Rafe (Rafael) married Rachel Hudson, and the family also intermarried with the Pateys. Two of Ralph's daughters marry into likely Sephardic families, the Henrys (Henriques, the fourth most common Sephardic surname)[33] and the Phillips family, as already mentioned, among the most common Jewish surnames during this time. Ralph's son John also marries a woman bearing a Jewish given name — Tabitha; as does his son George — Sarah Cotman, daughter of Ebenezer Cotman. Tabitha is Aramaic for "gazelle" and was popular in antiquity among the Jews but is a name not found in the Bible.

Massey. The Massey family was in Maryland by 1743. They had business or marital ties with Gilbert Falconer, Daniel Toaes, Aquilla Peacock (Pavo, Pavoncello, a bird popular in Persia and Jewish legend),[34] Samuel Davis, Nathaniel Hynson (son of the deer or hind, the tribe of Naphtali), William Minelly (Italian Sephardic surname), Isaac Bower, Samuel Beck (Baeck, Hebrew)[35] and Zorobabel French. Children's names included Zorobabel (Greek form of Hebrew Zerubbabel), Elisha, Eliza, Nicholas (Greek), Aquilla (Franco–Roman), Rebeccah, Solomon, Ebenezer, Eleazar, Rachel, Enoch, Josiah, Farrah (Arabic: "joy"),[36] Hannah, Johan, Arimenta (Greek), Abigail, Lambert and Louchrisia (Lucretia: Italian). The mixture of Greek, Hebrew, Spanish, Arabic and Italian given names is strongly indicative of Sephardic ancestry, as there were Sephardic communities in all these locations. The name itself is believed to derive from Hebrew *maaseh* "deed, act, tale," used for Marcus in the public realm.[37] Forms of the name include Masse, Massa, Maas, Maxey (Huguenot, common in Virginia) and Mazza (Spanish).[38] It is instanced in Alexandria (Egypt), Port-Said (Arabia), Corfu and Zante (Greece), Florence and Leghorn (Italy) and London, a trail of countries that seems to be commemorated in the first names of the Maryland family. The English branch of the family entered the British Isles with William the Conqueror and goes back to a Hamon (Hebrew Amon: "faithful, true") Massey. Descendants intermarried with the Ashley, Cooper and Gist families, which we have seen to be very probably crypto–Jewish. (Standard authorities Reaney and Wilson explain Massey as "a pet-form of Matthew.")[39]

Branch of Massey Family in England and Colonies

1   Hamon MASSEY
   2   Hamon MASSEY II
      3   Hamon MASSEY III
         4   Hamon MASSEY IV
         5   William MASSEY b: in of Coddington
            6   Robert MASSEY
               7   William De Tatton MASSEY
               +Margery LEGH LEIGH
                  8   Hugh de Tatton MASSEY
                     9   John de Tatton MASSEY
                     10   Hugh MASSEY
                        +Anne BOLD
                     11   Nicholas MASSEY
                     12   Thomas MASSEY
                           +Joan BESWICK
                        13   Alexander MASSEY
                        14   Alexander MASSEY
                        15   Charles MASSEY
                           +Clemence COWDALL
                        16   Alexander MASSEY
                        16   Peter Massey   b: January 01, 1639/40 in Coddington, Cheshire, England
                                 d: December 25, 1719
                              +Unknown
                           *2nd Wife of Peter Massey:
                                 +Lucretia Ashley-Cooper   b: 1647 in Rockbourne, Sham, England
                           17   [4] Lucretia Massey
                                 +[5] John Johnson   b: in Aberdeen, Scotland
                           17   [1] Charles Massey   b: 1668 in Cheshire, England (?)
                                                                d: 1732
                                 +[2] Ann MACON
                           17   [3] John Massey   b: 1673
                           17   [6] Thomas William Massey   b: January 01, 1674/75 in Cheshire, England (?)
                                                                d: March 01, 1731/32 in New Kent Co., Va.
                                 +[7] Martha Mason/Macon
                                 *2nd Wife of [6] Thomas William Massey:
                                 +[8] Mary Walker   b: 1681

*3rd Wife of Peter Massey:

	+Penelope Ashley-Cooper	b: 1647 in Dorset	d: December 25, 1719 in New Kent Co., Va.
17	Sarah Penelope MASSEY	b: 1670	d: 1711
17	[1] Charles Massey	b: 1668 in Cheshire, England (?) d: 1732	
	+[2] Ann MACON		
17	[3] John Massey	b: 1673	
17	[4] Lucretia Massey		
	+[5] John Johnson	b: in Aberdeen, Scotland	
17	[6] Thomas William Massey	b: January 01, 1674/75 in Cheshire, England (?) d: March 01, 1731/32 in New Kent Co., Va.	

+[7] Martha Mason/Macon

*2nd Wife of [6] Thomas William Massey:

+[8] Mary Walker   b: 1681

15 John MASSEY
16 John MASSEY
16 Thomas MASSEY   b: 1589 in Great Budworth, Cheshire, England   d: 1688

+Judith Brereton   b: 1612

13 Thomas MASSEY
13 Nicholas MASSEY   b: in of Ely
14 Richard MASSEY
15 Nicholas MASSEY
16 Elizabeth MASSEY
     +Thomas PELL
15 Richard MASSEY
16 Nicholas MASSEY
     +Anne HERBERT
16 John MASSEY   b: 1616 in Isle of Ell, Shire, England.
     +Sarah BIRDE
     17 John MASSEY   b: in of Ely
     17 Elizabeth MASSEY
     17 Martin MASSEY
     17 JoAnna MASSEY
     17 Anna MASSEY
15 William MASSEY
15 Thomas MASSEY
13 James MASSEY
13 Hugh MASSEY
11 William MASSEY
10 William MASSEY
10 Richard MASSEY
10 Thomas MASSEY
10 Geffrey MASSEY
10 John MASSEY
8 Oliver MASSEY   b: in of Denfield in Tostherne a part of Tatton
     9 John MASSEY

```
        10  William MASSEY
        11  Hugh MASSEY
            +Jane SMITH
        12  William MASSEY
                +Jane PRESTLAND
            13  Hugh MASSEY
                +Elizabeth WHITNEY
            14  George MASSEY                    d: 1666
                +Bridget PEARSALL
            15  William MASSEY
            15  George MASSEY
            15  Thomas MASSEY
            15  Charles MASSEY
            15  Dorothy MASSEY
            15  Bridget MASSEY
            15  Elizabeth
            13  William MASSEY
            13  Richard MASSEY
            13  Geffrey MASSEY
            13  Edward MASSEY
            13  Anne MASSEY
      8  Richard MASSEY
      8  Ellen MASSEY
      7  Hamon de Pontington MASSEY
      8  Thomas MASSEY
          9  Hamon MASSEY
         10  Sir John de Pontington MASSEY
         11  Hamond MASSEY
         11  Thomas MASSEY
         11  Hugh MASSEY
      7  Adam de Rixton MASSEY
      6  Richard MASSEY        Occupation: Justice of Cheshire
      6  Thomas MASSEY
      7  Hamon de Rixton MASSEY
    5  Hamon MASSEY V
      6  Hamon MASSEY VI
    5  Thomas MASSEY          b: in of Grafton
    4  Robert MASSEY
    4  John MASSEY
  3  John MASSEY
  3  Robert MASSEY
2  Robert MASSEY
  3  Geffrey MASSEY
    4  Roger MASSEY
```

Mordechai Moore, a Quaker merchant and physician, died by 1721. He married, first, Ursula and, second, Deborah Hill. The first mention of Mordecae Moore is as a legatee of

Nathaniel Ashcom of Calvert County in 1687. His children were Richard, Deborah, Hannah, Mary, Heather, Elizabeth, and Rachel.

Bryan Omelia, servant, was transported to Maryland about 1665. He married Mary Lewis, 27 June 1676. She was the daughter of William and Sarah Lewis. Jacob Abrahams married Isabel Omelia on 28 May 1685 at Betty's Cove Quaker Meeting House.

Bryan Omelia, above, has married a similarly Jewish-surnamed woman, Mary Lewis. A later child of their marriage, Isabel, married Jacob Abrahams at the Betty's Cove Meeting House. We would argue that this family was Jewish and that the Quaker Meeting House likely conducted Jewish services.

Benony Philips, son of John Phillips, first married Roseannah Elliott, daughter of John and Jane Elliott. Second, he married a woman named Comfort. He died having written a will dated 25 June 1742, leaving to his son Thomas the residue of Glostershire "unless he marry one of the Lewises or Annons, in which case land to go to his brother Jacob." He also left property to his son Solomon, as well as to sons Jacob and Jeremiah. As mentioned earlier, Phillips was a very common Jewish surname during the 1600s to 1800s.[40] Benoni is the Jewish nickname for Benjamin. Interestingly, Benony's will prohibits certain assets from passing to his son John if the latter should marry into the Lewis or Annon families — who would also appear to be Jewish. It may be that he was in the midst of becoming secularized and ceasing to be Jewish.

Elisha Purnell was a witness to the will of Daniel Selbe written 12 December 1694 along with Thomas Smith, John Purnell, John Roussalls and Cornelius Shahan (Arabic). He was father of the following children: William, who married his first cousin once removed, Mary Robins, daughter of Thomas Robins, and Lemual Chessed (Hebrew). William, son of John and Elizabeth (Rackliffe) Purnell, married Mary Elizabeth Fassitt (Fawcett, Facit: Arabic for "lord"),[41] daughter of Lambert and Levinah (Hebrew) Fassitt, and was father of the following children: John, Catherine, Elisha, Benjamin, Mary, William, Lea, Azariah, Levi, Thomas and Jeptha. John Purnell, born 1725, married his first cousin Zipporah Purnell, daughter of John Purnell. Zipporah later married her cousin John Rackliff.

These entries for the Purnell family suggest Sephardic origins. The witnesses to a will include John Roussall (French Sephardic) and Cornelius Shahan (Dutch Morisco). Children are given non–Biblical Hebrew names, e.g., Chessed, as well as Hebrew tribal names, e.g., Levinah and Levi, and there are first-cousin marriages.

Thomas Rasin was born 1640 in England and died in 1687 in Maryland. "Some 90 rebels sailed on the ship Happy Return under Capt. Washam, after the Monmouth Rebellion of 1685. They were delivered to John Browne and Company for Sir William Booth of Barbadoes. Thomas Rason was sold to Col. John Simpson." Here a Thomas Rasin (Persian surname meaning "prince") has entered Maryland as a political prisoner sold as an indentured servant. Thomas and Elizabeth had seven children: Philip, Mary, Thomas, John, Elizabeth, Sarah and Francis. Philip Rasin died in 1717 and was buried at the Cecil Friends Meeting. Note that the Cecil Friends Meeting is the Quaker congregation to which several crypto–Jewish families belonged. At the time of his death, Phillip Reasin was overseer of the Cecil Monthly Meeting.

Thomas Read married Elizabeth and she married, second, Isaac Abrahams. Isaac Abrahams died leaving a will dated 14 October 1674. He gave Elizabeth her dower rights, left personally to George and Benjamin Parret and to Sarah Reed and to son Jacob all land at 19 years of age. Elizabeth Abrahams died leaving a will dated 11 May 1675, giving personal items to William Southbe and his daughter Elizabeth Southbe. **Elizabeth Read,** daughter of Thomas Read, married William Southbee at the house of Isaac Abraham, 29 January 1668. Sarah Read, daughter of Thomas Read, married James Frisbey. On 20 July 1688, James Frisbey and his wife Sarah gave to his brother-in-law Jacob Abrahams power of attorney to acknowledge a parcel sold to John Boram. Thomas Reade, son of Thomas Read, died leaving a will dated 1665. The executor was Jonathan Ashman and his sister Sarah.

The surname Read/Reed/Reid usually meant "red," as in hair or a beard. In German, it was rendered as Roth and in Spanish as Rosa. In the above passages, the wife of Thomas Read has married Isaac Abraham (an obviously Jewish name) with whom she had a son, Jacob. The Parret and Southbe (Sotheby) families are linked to the Read-Abraham family, as are the Frisbey and Ashman families. This pattern of interrelationships would seem to indicate the presence of a consciously Jewish community.

With the **Robins** family below, we find the same pattern of interaction among a group of families bearing Jewish surnames. Robins is an Anglicized form of Rabin/Reuben, a Hebrew tribal name. It is also rendered as Robbins in English and Rabinowitz in Eastern Europe. In the excerpts below we find a Robins marrying a Tilghman. When the husband dies, William Goldsborough marries her in the traditional Jewish Levirate pattern, one we have seen often before. The Daniel Hamer mentioned also bears a Jewish surname, as do the Money sisters, whose surname was likely Anglicized from Gould or Gulder ("money" in German and Dutch) or else Munz. **George Robins** married Henrietta Maria Tilghman, daughter of Richard Tilghman. Anna Maria, daughter of George and Henrietta Maria Robins, married Henry Hollyday (*Yom Tov* or *Shana Tovah* in Hebrew). The will of George Robins was witnessed by William Sharp, Isaiah Parrot, Elinor Robinson and Thomas Ringgold. On 2 September 1747 William Goldsborough married his first wife Elizabeth's halfbrother's widow, Mrs. George Robins, who was then 40 years old and the mother of six children. Her maiden name was Henrietta Maria Tilghman and she was fourth child of Richard Tilghman II and Anna Maria Lloyd. On 2 April 1731 she married George Robins, and five years later she married William Goldsborough. On 28 February 1757 Daniel Hamer and his wife Ann, daughter and heir of Robert Ivy, and great-granddaughter and heir of Robert Smith, conveyed to Susannah Robins 600 acres. William Goldsborough's will was proved 5 November 1760 and it named several of the Robins family members: "To wife Henrietta Maria Goldsborough, late dwelling plantation on Island Creek, at her decease, to nephew Greenbury Goldsborough, son of brother John Goldsborough. To each niece Mary Money and Ann Money, daughters of late sister Mary Money, sum of £20 sterling. To each brother Robert, Nicholas, Charles and John Goldsborough, one mourning ring. To niece Caroline Goldsborough, £20 sterling. To nephew Greenberry Goldsborough, slaves. To son-in-law Thomas Robins, tract lying near Choptank Bridge. To daughter-in-law Anna Maria Holiday, Margaret Robins, Henrtta Maria Robins and Susanna Robins, £10 sterling each. To daughter-in-law, god-daughter Elizabeth Robins, £100 sterling of Great Britain money, when she is age 21. Residue of estate to wife, Henrietta Maria Goldsborough."

Charles Ross, son of John Ross, married Naomey and died leaving a will dated 20 December 1722. Thomas was father of Levin, born about 1744. Peter Ross, possible son of John Ross, married Esther. Peter Ross died leaving a will dated 13 March 1762. Mentioned was Sabra Hammond. Ross, a corruption of Rose, was one of the most common Jewish surnames in England during the 1700s.[42] Here we have Charles Ross marrying a woman named Naomi and having a son named Levin. We then have Peter Ross, likely his brother, marrying a woman named Esther and leaving property to a Sabra (Arabic) Hammond (Hamon,

Amon, Hebrew). These naming patterns suggest a continuation of Jewish identity in Maryland for this family.

Edward Skidmore arrived in Maryland from England in 1657 with a group that included Rhys Bazill (Basil: Greek), Saunders (Alexander) Simmons, Ellinor Abraham, Ursula Duffe and Elias Godfrey. The executor of Edward's will was Theophilus ("Love God," Hebrew Jael) Hackett (Sephardic/Arabic). Inventories on his estate were taken by Ebenezer Blakiston (i.e., "black stone," perhaps a dealer in ebony) and Isaac Harris (Jewish surname). Here again we encounter a group of persons who are likely of Jewish ancestry arriving together as a community.

Samuel Tovey originally came from Bristol, England, immigrated to Maryland by 1675, and transported his wife Elizabeth and two children, Elizabeth and Samuel, to Maryland by 1679. Samuel was indentured to James Ringold in 1676. Samuel's son married Mary Fookes (Fuchs is German for Fox, Jewish)[43] and his son-in-law was Richard Kane (i.e., Kohane). Tovey/Touhey/Tawey is a derivative of the Hebrew letter *toph*, Greek letter *tau*.

Garrett Van Sandt, the son of Stoffell (Ashkenazic) van Sandt, emigrated about 1651 from the Netherlands. He settled in New Utrecht, Long Island, where the records often refer to him as "Gerret Stoffellse" (i.e., Garrett, son of Stoffell). He was the father of Stoffel (Hebrew); Cornelius (Latin); Josias (Hebrew); Harman (corruption of Hebrew Hiram); Alvert; Johannes; Jacobus (Hebrew); George; Jesina (Hebrew); and Garret (French). **Stoffel Van Sandt,** son of Garrett, was born in the colony of New York about 1670 and took the oath of allegiance at New Utrecht in 1687. He moved to Bucks County, Pennsylvania. He married, first, Annetje Stoffels, and, second, Rachel Courson, and joined the Bensalem (Hebrew for "sons of peace") Dutch Reformed Church by certificate in 1710.

Samuel Wickes mentioned in his will Mary Cammell (Hebrew/Arabic: "camel, letter of alphabet"), Sarah Nash, Richard Hill, and Henry Vizard (Arabic). The will was witnessed by Mary Miller and Mary Samuell. His will also mentioned the estate of George Gouldhawke. Legatees named were Rachell Wicks and Richard Marsh (de Soto in Spanish). Joseph, son of Joseph Wicks, married Alice, daughter of Michael Miller. One of their daughters was Mary, who married William Granger. Other daughters were Rachell, who married William Ruock (Arabic: "wind, "open air market"),[44] and Elizabeth, who married James Cumberford.

Francis Willey married, first, Elizabeth Wingate and, second, Rachel Wingate, both daughters of Philip Wingate. Francis and Elizabeth Willey were parents of the following children: Angelo (Spanish or Italian), Elizabeth, Juday and Anestatia (Greek). Francis was also the father of Absolum. Francis and Rachel were parents of the following children: Frances, Molly, Wingate, Judah and William.

Francis Willey had married two Wingate sisters, leaving children named Angelo, Juday, Anestatia, Absolum, Diahaner and Judah, among others. His son, Angelo, later bought land from Edward Numar (Arabic). The naming and marriage patterns above suggest Sephardic-Iberian ancestry, perhaps rather recently, as the name Angelo was used for a first-born son.

Tilghman Family

We have reserved for last the Tilghman family, one of the most illustrious in the history of the Maryland colony. This family produced governors, judges, generals, doctors and merchants. As we shall demonstrate, their history follows a remarkable, not to say egregious, pattern of Jewish endogamy.

Richard Tilghman, physician, born 1626, son of Oswald Tilghman, a grocer of London, married Mary Foxley in England. They were the parents of Samuel, Mary, William, Rebecca, Deborah and Richard. At March Court in 1668 George Heays (Jewish surname, the Hebrew letter that stands for Hayim, "life"), servant to Richard Tilghman, was judged to be 16 years old. Richard Tilghman, son of Richard Tilghman, married Anna Maria Lloyd, daughter of Philemon Lloyd, on 7 January 1700. Richard and Anna were the parents of Mary, who married James Earle, Jr., Philemon; Richard, who married Susanna Frisby; Henrietta Maria, who married, first, George Robins in 1731 and, second, William Goldsborough in 1747; Anna Maria Tilghman, who married, first, William Hemsley and, second, cousin Col. Robert Lloyd; William; Edward; James; and Matthew. Richard served in the Maryland Assembly from 1698 to 1702 and was a member of the Maryland Council from 1711 to 1739. He served as a court justice from 1695 to 1705 and from 1707 to 1709. He was sheriff from 1709 to 1711. In 1722 he was chancellor of the province. In the military he was a captain in 1706, lieutenant colonel in 1711, and colonel in 1716. On 25 June 1766 an indenture quadripartite was made between Richard Tilghman and wife Susanna, James Earle, Edward Tilghman and Richard Tilghman the younger. A marriage was about to be solemnized between Richard Tilghman the younger and Elizabeth, daughter of Edward Tilghman, and Edward agreed to pay a competent marriage portion to his daughter.

William Tilghman, son of Richard Tilghman, was born 22 September 1711 and married his first cousin Margaret Lloyd, daughter of James Lloyd, on 2 August 1736. William and Margaret were the parents of Anna Maria, who married Charles Goldsborough; Richard; James; Margaret, who married her cousin Richard Tilghman, son of Matthew Tilghman; Henrietta Maria; and Mary, who married Edward Roberts. William was a county court justice between 1734 and 1760, served in the Lower House of the Maryland Assembly from 1734 to 1738, deputy commissary, judge of the especial court in 1744, and was a major in the militia by 1744.

Edward Tilghman, son of Richard Tilghman, was born 3 July 1713 and married, first, Anna Maria Turbutt about 1738, second, Elizabeth Chew in 1749, and, third, Juliana Carroll. Edward and Anna Maria had one child, Anna Maria, who married Bennett Chew. Edward and Elizabeth had five children: Richard; Edward; Benjamin; Elizabeth, who married her cousin Richard Tilghman, son of Richard; and Anna Maria, who married Charles Goldsborough. Edward and Juliana had four children: Matthew; Benjamin; Mary, who married her cousin Richard Tilghman, son of Matthew; and Susanna. Edward was high sheriff from 1739 to 1742 and served in the Lower House of the Maryland Assembly from 1746 to 1750. He was a county court justice from 1743 to 1749 and in 1765 was a member of the Stamp Act Congress. From 1776 to 1781 he served in the Senate. In the militia, he was a captain by 1746 and colonel by 1755.

James and Anne Tilghman were the parents of Tench, who married his first cousin Anna Maria Tilghman and served as aide-de-camp to Gen. Washington during the Revolutionary War, Richard, James, William, Philemon, Thomas Ringgold, Anna Maria, who married her first cousin William Hemsley, Elizabeth, who married her cousin James Lloyd, Mary and Henrietta Maria, who married her first cousin Lloyd Tilghman, son of Matthew. James served in the Maryland Assembly, 1762–1763, and then moved to Philadelphia, where he was elected a common councilman in 1764. He served as a member of the Council of Pennsylvania, 1767–1776, and was commissioned secretary of the Pennsylvania Land Office on 1 January 1769.

Matthew Tilghman, son of Richard Tilghman, was born 17 February 1718 and adopted by his childless cousin, Matthew Tilghman Ward, in 1733. He married cousin Anna Lloyd, daughter of James Lloyd and sister of his brother William Tilghman's wife. Richard married his first cousin Margaret Tilghman, daughter of William Tilghman, in 1770. Secondly, he married another cousin, Mary Tilghman, daughter of Edward Tilghman Lloyd and Anna Maria, who had married her cousin Tench Tilghman, son of James Tilghman. Matthew Tilghman was a captain in the horse troops in 1741, served in the Lower House of the Maryland Legislature from 1751 to 1776, in the Maryland Conventions during the Revolutionary War, and was a senator from 1776 to 1783. He also served as a delegate to the Continental Congress and has been referred to as the "Father of the Revolution" in Maryland.

Richard Tilghman, son of Richard Tilghman, was born 11 May 1738 and married his cousin Elizabeth Tilghman, daughter of Col. Edward Tilghman, and had a son Richard Edward Tilghman. Peregrine Tilghman, another son of Richard Tilghman, was born 24 January 1741 and married his cousin Deborah Lloyd, daughter of Col. Robert Lloyd and Anna Maria Tilghman. Peregrine and Deborah were the parents of Robert Lloyd; Anna Maria, who married cousin James Earle; Tench; William Hemsley and Elizabeth, who married John Custis (Costas is Sephardic) Wilson. Peregrine attended the Maryland Convention in 1775, was commissioned a colonel of the 4th Battalion in 1778, and was a state senator, 1787–1794.

These relationships offer a classic case history of crypto–Jewish endogamy. The Tilghmans immigrated to Maryland from London. Oswald Tilghman was a grocer; his son Richard, the immigrant, a physician. Both were occupations favored by Jews in England (crypto–Jews, of course, at this time). Richard's daughters were named Deborah and Rebecca, and Rebecca married Simon Wilmer, whose business dealings intersected with other proposed Jewish families in Maryland. One of Richard's servants, a George Heays, bears a distinctly Sephardic Jewish surname. Richard's son, also Richard, married a Lloyd and the next generation married into the Frisby, Robins and Goldsborough families. The family then embarked on a multi-generational escapade of endogamy that surpassed even that exhibited by the Boones and Bryants and the Chaffins and Hacketts, both of which are Sephardic-Melungeon lineages.[45] Among both Sephardim and Muslims, endogamy, including first cousin and Levirate marriages, was commonly practiced as ways of maintaining "blood purity" and familial secrecy (if needed) regarding religious practices.

Not to belabor the subject, we list other Maryland names thought to be possibly Sephardic or Moorish in Appendix I. By way of conclusion, let us glance at one of those, Adair (Hebrew name for a month),[46] to illustrate a common path to the extreme western frontier taken by settlers landing in Maryland. One of the authors termed this the Great Melungeon Migration.[47] The reasons for this rush to the wilderness do not seem to be the same as those offered commonly by historians such as Alan Taylor, that is, the desire of the small freeholder to avoid taxation by moving gradually beyond the reach of the authorities.[48] Instead, we see a pattern of landing, often illegally, and making a beeline for Kentucky and Tennessee, stronghold of the Melungeons, where breakaway Carolinians had gone so far as to establish the semi-independent state of Watauga, and later, Franklin.

John Adair, Sr., is said to have come to Baltimore with his family in 1760 from Ballymena, County Antrim, Ireland. The family heads straight for the westernmost English settlement in Augusta County, Virginia (later Botetourt, briefly called Fincastle), where the father joins the militia and signs a succession of petitions that today are viewed as signs of a pre–Revolutionary revolt against England.[49] As soon as the way is clear, we find him in the newly-established Watauga Settlement in East Tennessee and Boone Settlement in Kentucky (Wayne County). He eventually builds Adair Station near Knoxville, which becomes a leverage point for removing the Cherokee Indians to their new Lower Towns in Georgia and Alabama. John, Jr., follows in the footsteps of his father, helping defend the frontier around the mouth of the North Fork of the Holsten River in Samuel Brashear's company near present-day Kingsport. In 1789 the North Carolina legislature establishes a storehouse for provisions for the Cumberland Guard, poised to extend European settlements to Middle Tennessee. The storehouse is at the home of John Adair. The road is cut by William Cooper, Daniel Boone's former guide (an ancestor of both authors). John Adair III marries William Cooper's great-granddaughter, granddaughter of Cherokee Chief Black Fox, Sarah Cooper.

The Adairs were among the first Wayne County families, which included Adkins, Burnetts, Barnes, Barriers, Bells, Burks, Blevins, Coopers, Denneys, Davenports, Dobbs, Dolens, Elams, Gregorys, Keetons, Kogers, Lovelaces, Parmleys, Parkers, Phipps, Rices, Ryans, Scotts, Sallees, Sanduskys, Smiths, Sharps, Vaughns and Youngs. Many of these names we have already previewed as being Sephardic. Most of the second generation intermarried with others of the same ilk (often their cousins) or else with the Cherokee Indians, whom they saw as being also of the Tribes of Israel. There was a rudimentary Jewish congregation gathered at one time around Isaac Cooper (about 1775–1845), who had married the daughter of Black Fox. Marriage — and presumably other religious — services were held in his home on Beaver Creek. The names of the leaders of this congregation, which deserves to be called the first west of the Alleghenys, are commemorated in a number of courthouse documents in which the parties cite each other as character witnesses. John Adair, Jr.'s Revolutionary War pension, for instance, names Isaac Cooper, Fleming Gregory, John Bell, Lewis Coffee, Martin Beaty, and William Hardin, all of whom lived in the neighborhood and bear what we have learned to be Sephardic surnames.

DNA analysis demonstrates that James Adair, the Indian trader and author, who was probably a cousin of our John Adair, belongs to male lineage/pedigree J2, a common Mediterranean and Jewish genetic type, to judge from a descendant's test. It can be postulated that he came from Scottish Sephardic stock transplanted to Scotland and Ireland from the lands of the Mediterranean and was in the process (like many of his Jacobite contemporaries) of getting back in touch with the family's Jewish past. His observations on Hebraisms among the Cherokee and Chickasaw Indians in his book *History of the American Indians* (London, 1776) are understandable: they result from ethnic recognition.

Another Maryland family that took approximately the same route to the frontier as the Adairs, although much earlier, were the Gists.[50] The first of the Gists came to Maryland in the 1680s at the time of the Glorious Revolution in England. Christopher Richard Gist was married to Edith Cromwell, a relative of Oliver Cromwell, the Protector. One of his children was Richard Gist, born in Baltimore. Lest the name Christopher seem an odd one for a Jew, let us point out that it was frequently given to the son of a crypto–Jewish family as the perfect "dodge" or cover. Christopher married Zipporah Morray (Sephardic name). Later Gists marry Howards (sisters), a Kennedy (Canada, Candia), a Gratz (Gracia) of the powerful and wealthy Pennsylvania trading company, and other Gists.

Even the family of Sequoyah, the half-breed son of Nathaniel Gist who is credited with inventing a Cherokee writing system, is heavily intermarried with cousins, namely, the Looneys (Luna), a Sephardic banking family which entered the colonies through Philadelphia via the Isle of Man. This island in the Irish Sea off Scotland was at the time a center of piratical activities and "irregular" commerce, a heritage that persists today, as it is, in name at least, a separate and sovereign country. Robert Looney joined Alexander Ross,

Morgan Bryan and seventy other families, including also James and Edward Davis, in a cavalcade down the Valley Road and onto the remote western frontier of Virginia in 1734.

Gist Genealogies

1   Christopher Richard Gist   d: March 10, 1689/90 in Maryland
    +Edith Cromwell   b: Abt. 1660 in Malmesbury, Wiltshire, England
    2   Capt. Richard Gist   b: 1683 in Baltimore, Md.   d: August 22, 1741, in Baltimore, Md.
        +Zipporah Morray   b: 1684 in Maryland   d: April 25, 1760, in Baltimore Co., Md.
        3   Edith Gist
            +Abraham Vaughan
        3   Thomas Gist
            +Susannah Cockney
        3   Ruth Gist
            +William Lewis
        3   Christopher Gist   b: 1705 in Baltimore, Md.   d: July 25, 1759, in Winchester, Va.
            +Sarah Howard b: 1711
            4   Richard Gist   b: September 02, 1729   d: October 7, 1780, in Battle of Kings Mountain
                5   Nathaniel Gist
                    6   Joseph Gist   b: 1748
                        +Mary Ann McNeil
            4   Violette [favorite Sephardic name] Gist   b: July 04, 1731
            4   Nathaniel Gist b: October 15, 1733, in Baltimore, Md.   d: 1796 in Clark Co., Ky.
                +Wurteh ["Margaret"]   b: Abt. 1742 in Tasagi Town, Cherokee Nation, Tennessee
                5   George Gist (Guess, Sequoyah)   b: Abt. 1770 in or near Ft. Loudon, Cherokee Nation, Tennessee
                    +Sallie Waters [of another Indian trader family]
                5   Moses Guest/Gist/Guess b: Abt. 1765 in Tenn.
                    +Dorcas   b: Abt. 1769 in Tenn.
                    6   Martin Guest   b: Abt. 1790
                        +Nancy Looney   b: Abt. 1795
                    6   Mary Guest/Gist/Guess   b: October 17, 1791 in Tenn.   d: January 27, 1857, in Lawrence Co.,
                        `   Ala.
                        +Moses Looney   b: August 06, 1780, in Sullivan Co., Maury Co. or Hawkins Co., Tenn.
                                        d: January 09, 1855, in Lawrence Co., Ala. or Grundy Co., Tenn.
                    *3rd Wife of Nathaniel Gist:
                    +Judith Carey Bell b: Abt. 1750 in Va.
                5   Sarah Howard Gist   b: 1784
                5   Henry Cary Gist   b: 1786
                5   Judith Bell Gist   b: 1789
                5   Thomas Nathaniel Gist b: 1790
                5   Anna Marie Gist   b: 1791
                5   Davidella [!] Gist   b: 1791
                5   Elizabeth Violet Gist   b: 1795
                5   Marie Cecil Gist   b: 1797
                    +Benjamin Gratz   b: September 04, 1792   d: March 17, 1884
                    6   Infant Gratz
                    6   Benjamin Gratz   b: 1821

6	Michael Bernard Gratz	b: 1822		
6	Henry Howard Gratz	b: July 12, 1824	d: September 21, 1913	
6	Hyman Cecil Gratz	b: 1826		
6	Cary Gist Gratz	b: August 09, 1829		

4   Anne Gist   b: 1734
4   Thomas Gist   b: 1735   d: 1785 in Pa.

3 Nathaniel Gist   b: 1707 in Baltimore   d: October 07, 1770
+Mary Howard b: 1713

4   Zipporah Gist
4   Nathaniel Gist
4   Richard Gist
4   Joshua Gist
4   Joseph Gist
4   Thomas Gist
4   Christopher Gist   b: September 24, 1734

3 William Gist   b: 1711
+Violette Howard b: 1716

4   William Gist
4   Anne Gist
4   Sarah Gist
4   Elizabeth Gist
4   Violette Gist
4   John Gist
4   Ellen Gist
4   Joseph Gist   b: September 30, 1738   d: January 22, 1803, in Brooke Co. (now W. Va.)
     +Elizabeth Elder

3 Jemima Gist   b: 1714
+William Seabrook

3 John Gist b: 1722
+Mary Gist

3 Sarah Gist b: 1724
+John Kennedy

Concluding Comments

The philosopher Alfred North Whitehead once remarked that without purpose, human history was "a barren exchange of names." In the case of Maryland we have gone beneath the surface of the names to document marriage patterns, business partnerships, inheritance provisions and other family matters. More than in any other colony, Greek, Ottoman and Turkish roots are exposed once we rub off the English, Dutch or Huguenot veneer. At the base of it all we encounter Spanish, Portuguese, Hebrew, Arabic and Berber, just those elements that imbued the Sephardic world that came to an abrupt end in 1492. We have seen an ingrained pattern of cousin marriage, one that starts even before arrival in the New World, and one that is no respecter of nationalities. Business arrangements were often cemented by these intermarriages, with the effect of keeping money and credit within an extended family. Finally, we have drawn back the curtain of Quakerism to reveal the true motives that dictated where the family settled and where the family moved on to. None of these traits, we suggest, was random or accidental.

CHAPTER EIGHT

Huguenot South Carolina

The crypto–Jewish element in the Carolinas' large French population goes back to the first pogroms against Spanish and French Jews in the 1380s and 1390s. Even before this, however, events had the effect of throwing the two groups together. The union of the two was particularly strong in the Spanish Marches and southwest of France. Here the Babylonian exilarch Makhir (William of Toulouse) had founded a Jewish principate under Charlemagne around the year 770 C.E.

While the Makhiri dynasty suffered increasing inroads on their autonomy by the surrounding Christian barons and soldiers of fortune, and while the Papacy fought incessantly against the legitimacy of the Narbonese government and its nobles, the Jews clung as best as they could to their titles and possessions. Not surprisingly, it was in Toulouse that the Inquisition was first implemented. In 1208, it was claimed that a papal legate was murdered by an agent serving the count of Toulouse. Innocent III declared a crusade against the entire region. Under zealots like Simon de Montfort, earl of Leicester, an estimated 100,000 to 200,000 people were massacred in the name of the purity of Christian doctrine. Despite bell, book and candle, despite the ethnic cleansing and despite the scorched earth warfare of French and English usurpers, however, the rulers of the Babylonian state and its fiefdoms continued to wield influence in the region of Septimania and Auvergne for several centuries. As late as the 1400s there were still Nesim (plural of Nasi, "prince") officially seated in Narbonne. According to Adolph Zuckermann, the historian who rediscovered this medieval Jewish state (the only one ever to have existed outside the Middle East), "The extensive properties held by the Jews and their Nasi (entitled king) at the time of their expulsion in 1306 indicates that they occupied a very substantial portion of the city into the fourteenth century."[1] Even after this, Jews (or better said by now, crypto–Jews) continued to maintain large estates over a broad region ranging from Urgel and Elne in Catalonia to Lunel, Uzès and Orange in Provence. As the state waned and declined, Makhir's great library and academy were transferred to a "Christian" monastery outside Narbonne.

Evidently, many other Jewish institutions and practices gradually went underground at the same time in southern France. Crypto-Jewish expert Abraham Lavender proposes that many Huguenots began as Jews, while Cecil Roth, the chronicler of the Spanish Inquisition, writes that a large number started out as Muslim Moors. Their fortunes were variable. Jews had temporarily returned to France beginning in 1361 at the invitation of Charles V, although they were expelled by his Catholic-leaning successor in 1394. Henceforth even if the border was officially closed to Jews, they took ready refuge with their co-religionists long established around Toulouse and elsewhere in Languedoc. Not until 1501 was there an edict of expulsion in Provence, and even then there remained shifting pockets of freedom in Avignon, Toulon and elsewhere. Quoting Sachar, Lavender notes that although most of Provence's Jews departed in 1481, "a tiny community underwent baptism and remained on. Nevertheless, throughout the sixteenth and seventeenth centuries, augmented by periodic rivulets of Sephardic fugitives, the little enclave of Provençal conversos began to regain something of its former demographic vitality."[2]

We can see in such stories the inevitable blending of Huguenots and Jews. In 1550, a proclamation of French King Henri II allowed Portuguese Conversos to settle in France. This was little more than a concession to political realities. In 1656 Louis XIV issued an edict which in effect confined them to Bordeaux, Bayonne and the surrounding areas. As Lavender notes, the French king no longer believed in "their Catholic camouflage" and began to treat the *merchands Portugais* as Jews. If viewed as Jews, they would have no status, and would have "to pay exorbitant taxes for rights the *nouveaux Chrietiens* had always freely enjoyed." The worst was over, however, and gradually the *nouveaux Chrétiens* returned to practicing Judaism. They became organized enough even to discipline errant members of the community.

In 1685, Louis XIV revoked the Edict of Nantes that had given tolerance to Protestants since 1598. The previous two centuries had witnessed ever-increasing solidarity between Jews and Huguenots or French Calvinists so that it was now hard to tell them apart. As Lavender points out, Protestantism, like Judaism, had a mutual enemy in Catholicism because of the Inquisition. Adherents of both sects were heretics in the eyes of the authorities; indeed, the revocation targeted and penalized both and "the threat of expulsion came to weigh upon the New Christians [i.e., Spanish-Portuguese Jews in France] as well."[3] The rise of Protestantism in Western Europe added to the insecurity of Catholicism, and was one factor leading to the (reinstated) Inquisition. Obviously any road goes in two directions, and if there were Jews in France, we can expect also to find Huguenots in Spain. In 1565 in Pamplona, the capital of Spanish Navarre, French Huguenots were "rounded up" and deported, writes Lavender, while in Toledo during the same year, a tribunal brought charges against individuals who included Protestants. A second reason why Jews and Huguenots found common cause with each other was that "Protestantism, like Judiasm, had a special appeal to merchants and to the financially well-off and well-educated segments of society." Finally, there was sympathy between the two groups because, in the words of Lavender, "in removing many of the trappings of Catholicism (rituals, liturgy, saints, a church hierarchy, etc.), Protestantism returned to a more original Christianity which was closer to Judaism."

It has been estimated that at the end of the period of tolerance toward Huguenots, and beginning of their large-scale flight in 1685, they numbered more than 800,000 people spread across France. Significantly, they were concentrated in the very region where Jewry could boast a continuous presence from Roman times to the High Middle Ages. In a meticulous survey based on contemporary records between 1660 and 1670, Philip Benedict places 80 percent of France's Protestants or Calvinists in the South.[4] Guyenne, corresponding approximately to the province of Aquitaine and former principality of Toulouse, had the highest number—100,000. After the revocation of the edict of Nantes and guarantees of religious freedom were removed, they would come to constitute one-fourth of the population of Amsterdam and practically the entire East End of London. In South Carolina, they would make up about a fifth of the initial colonists.[5]

The tiny island of Ré near the Huguenot stronghold of La Rochelle was an important place of refuge from 1681 to 1686. Although it was only sixteen miles long, Ré was "almost wholly Protestant" and had several Huguenot "temples" on it.[6] The names of those from Ré who settled in America strongly hint at their Judaic background and Iberian origins. We can easily trace in these the transformation of Spanish or Occitan surnames as well as the persistence of favored Jewish given names. The former can often be recognized by the addition of -eau or -ault or like-sounding suffixes to a Hebrew or Arabic name (a phenomenon we have noticed with the so-called theophoric -el / -al in Norman names such as Riddell/ Riddle, Cantrell and Tunnell). Lavender draws especial attention to the naming of children with Old Testament names instead of New Testament or medieval saints' names. He finds that by the end of the 1500s in Rouen, seven of the ten most frequent Protestant male names (numbers 4 through 10) were Old Testament names (Abraham, Isaac, Daniel, David, Jacob, Salomon and Samuel. He observes,

> This pattern of Huguenot naming continued, although weakening with time, in the United States. As late as the 1700 period, for example, Ester and Judith remained among the nine most frequent female Huguenot names in Charleston, South Carolina, while Abraham, Daniel, Isaac, and Jacob were frequent male names. Even as late as 1790 in the United States, Huguenots, despite rapidly assimilating and generally following non-traditional Christianity, were more likely than most other Protestant groups to have Old Testament names. The exceptions were in the Puritan areas of New England, areas which were the most traditional in their following of Christianity. Among the sixteen most frequent Huguenot male names in 1790, seven (Benjamin, Samuel, Jacob, Daniel, Abraham, Isaac, David) were Old Testament names. There clearly is a connection between naming patterns and ethnic/religious identity.[7]

Huguenot Refugees from the Island of Ré. Source: Baird.

Names of Refugees	Colony	Possible Origin (and Reference in Faiguenboim)
Adam de Cheseau	Mass.	Arabic chess
Ezéchiel Carré	Mass.	
Pierre and Daniel Ayrault	Mass.	Ayr
Nicolas Filoux	Conn.	Philo
Paul Collin	Conn.	Colina
Pierre Collin	S.C.	Colina
Pierre and Abraham Jouneau	N.Y.	Jonah
Ezéchiel Barbauld	N.Y.	Barbalha 190
Elie and Guillaume Cothoneau	N.Y.	Arabic coton
Etienne and Esaie Valleau (Vallos)	N.Y.	Valle 414
Du Tay	N.Y.	see Chapter 5
Coulon	N.Y.	see Chapter 5
Jacques Targé	N.Y.	Tajer, Tadzhes, Tagger 401
René Rezeau (wife Anne Coursier)	N.Y.	Arabic rezin prince, khouri priest
Jean Belleville	N.Y.	
François Martineau	N.Y.	Martin 320
Jacques Guion	N.Y.	Guillen? 274
Paul and Marie Regreny	N.Y.	
Jacques Erouard	N.Y.	Heroy, Heouida 285

Names of Refugees	Colony	Possible Origin (and Reference in Faiguenboim)
Elizabeth Brigaud	N.Y.	
Elie Mestayer (Metayer)	N.Y.	Matityah (Hasmonean priest) 321
Daniel Jouet	N.Y.	
Jacques Bertonneau	N.Y.	Barton
Jean and François Vincent	N.Y.	Vicente 416
Ann Guerry	N.Y.	Guerra 274
Oliver Besly	N.Y.	Basil
Grégoire Goujon	N.Y.	Gideon 270
Renée Marie Graton	N.Y.	
Jean and Marie Gallais	N.Y.	Gales 268
Pierre and Daniel Bontecon	N.Y.	
Rappe	Penn.	
Ribouleau	Penn.	
Paul Bernard	Va.	Bernal, Bernar 205
Janvier and Abraham Sallé	Va.	Saya? 386
Jacques and Jean Barbot	S.C.	Barbas? Bereby? 191, 205
Moïse Le Brun	S.C.	
Daniel Garnier	S.C.	
Elizabeth Fanton	S.C.	
Horry	S.C.	Arabic Hori 285
Arnaud France	S.C.	
Daniel Huger	S.C.	
Daniel Jodon	S.C.	
Anne Rassin	S.C.	Arabic *rezin*
Sara Bertonneau	S.C.	Barton
Isaac Mazicq	S.C.	Mahzig 322 (Berber: Musick)[8]
Pierre Mounier	S.C.	Munir 334
Louise Robinet	S.C.	Rueben
Etienne and Ester Tauvron	S.C.	Tavares, Tavarez 402

Another place in France especially sought out by refugee Jews during the Diaspora was Bordeaux, the major Atlantic port of Languedoc. To invoke again Lavender, "In Bordeaux as elsewhere in southern France, an indeterminate scattering of conversos remained behind. And after 1481, the Sephardic remnant was quietly enlarged by an uninterrupted infusion of New Christians from Spain and Portugal. Virtually all of them were Judaizers — Marranos." France continued to bar Ashkenazic Jews from entry into the country even while it allowed the settlement of these Portuguese Jews in Bordeaux. Bordeaux, Bayonne and nearby towns, only fifty miles from the Spanish border, developed strong Sephardic communities that served as gateways to northern France, the Netherlands, England and Scotland. In other parts of France, too, certain accomodations and recriminations were made. In 1632, for example, in Rouen, thirty-seven New Christians were arrested for their "Jewish ways." An auto-de-fe seemed imminent. The Jews declared their fidelity to Catholicism, however, paid money, and were released.[9]

From France to the Carolinas

We have already made mention of South Carolina's very early Sephardic and Moorish history. In 1526, Lucas Vasquez de Ayllon, a prominent settler and sugar grower on Hispanola, sent an expedition to the North Atlantic coast. The colony of 500 settlers, including Ayllon, landed somewhere on the South Carolina coast but met with several disasters. A year later, a hundred and fifty of the colonists managed to straggle back to Hispanola. The fate of the remaining ones is unknown.[10] We would argue that these settlers were very likely Sephardim and Moors, as there is little else to justify their being willing to leave the settled prosperity of Spanish Hispanola to venture to the mosquito-ridden unknown coast of North America — unless the recently arrived Inquisition had caused them to recalculate their odds in a Catholic colony. In 1563, the Frenchmen were aided by Sir John Hawkins, an English privateer (Chapter 1). Ayllon is a Sephardic surname.[11] The settlers named the place where they first made landfall River Jordan (present-day Cape Fear River). We would advance the same reasoning for Hernando de Soto's (a Sephardic surname[12]) 600-person expedition in 1540 through the southeastern region of North America.

The very first attempts at planting French colonies in the New World were inspired by Huguenots who landed in the area of Rio de Janeiro in Brazil in 1555. It came to naught, and the same Huguenot faction planted a short-lived colony named Charlesfort on the South Carolina Coast. Charlesfort was organized by Admiral Gaspar Coligny and Jean Ribaut. In 1564 Coligny attempted a second French Huguenot colony at Fort Caroline on the St. John's River, but the settlers were massacred by the Spanish. Finally in 1566 the Spanish succeeded in establishing the Santa Elena Colony near the present day border of South Carolina and Georgia at Beaufort. The settlers numbered 1,500 men and fourteen women.[13] From Santa Elena, Captain Juan Pardo (Sephardic surname, Brown[14]) set off on two expeditions, establishing forts as far westward as Knoxville, Tennessee. Santa Elena was a thriving seaport colony with craftspeople, families and a Morisco pottery-making facility. Santa Elena craftsmen and merchants traded with Mexico, Italy and Spain; some even owned Chinese porcelain. Soldiers stationed in the town were drawn from a cross-section of Spain: Marchena, Gibraltar, Cades, Sevilla, Bilbao, Leon, Salamanca, Toledo and Palencia, notably all areas with substantial Sephardic and Morisco populations. A list of names of settlers is given in Appendix J. As is readily apparent, most are almost certainly Sephardic Jewish or Converso families.

In 1587, after Sir Frances Drake had attacked and destroyed Saint Augustine in Florida, Phillip II of Spain ordered the Santa Elena residents to abandon their colony and resettle to the south in St. Augustine. The records are unclear on how many actually did so. The position of several Melungeon researchers is that the Santa Elenans did not move en masse to Florida but rather migrated inland toward the Appalachians.[15] If many were indeed of Jewish and Islamic descent this would have been the wisest course of action, as La Florida was becoming increasingly pressured by the Inquisition. Simultaneously, as has been suggested, the colonization of Roanoke was joined by British Sephardim and Moriscos who feared the upcoming Spanish Invasion of England (Chapter 3).

By 1600, no doubt, the southern Atlantic Coast was teeming with a pastiche of Spanish, French and English colonial deserters, castaways and abandoned souls. The presence of Europeans — and their pathogens — on mainland North America caused a general population collapse among the indigenous tribal peoples. Entire sectors of land south of the Chesapeake Bay and westward to the Mississippi had been emptied of native populations due to European-borne infectious diseases like bubonic plague, cholera and typhoid. It is probable that many, if not most (and possibly all) of the "Indians" encountered by the English colonists at Jamestown were actually hybridized, i.e., the surviving descendants of earlier Native-European unions who had passed varying degrees of immunity to their offspring. By the mid–1700s, it can be argued that no unmixed Native peoples were left along the Eastern Atlantic Seaboard.

South Carolina proper was not settled by the English until after 1670, but as has been frequently pointed out, the paradigm for its plantation economy was established over sixty years earlier in British Barbados. Barbados was first settled by the British in 1627, and its economic and social life was revolutionized in the 1640s by the importation of sugar cane cultivation from Brazil. Within a decade or so, Barbados became fabulously wealthy by producing not only sugar but also its much-valued byproduct, rum and molasses. Dutch Jews from Brazil were in the forefront of all these developments.[16] The Barbadan landowners formed a nouveau riche aristocracy whose wealth and materialism was built on African slave labor and international trade. In 1663 a group of settlers in Barbados, the Barbadian Adventurers, hired William Hilton to explore the Carolina coast and locate a hospitable area in which to establish a colony. Significantly, a certain John Yeamans (Yemen, a Middle Eastern country then under Ottoman control), one of the adventurers, helped draft the constitution for the colony, which provided "self-government, freedom of religion, and generous land grants."[17] Barbados also sent forth an exploratory expedition in the area of the former Santa Elena colony under Robert Sanford (Sephardic surname) and Dr. Henry Woodward, a physician who spoke Spanish. After some shaky efforts at establishing the colony at Cape Fear in 1666, Sir Anthony Ashley-Cooper (a crypto–Jew, English peer and Freemason) exercised his rights as lord proprietor of Carolina and sent three ships and a hundred English men and women to settle in Carolina.

Anthony Ashley-Cooper, 1st Lord Shaftesbury and one of the lords proprietor of the Carolinas (Emmet Collection, Miriam and Ira D. Wallach Division of Art, Prints and Photographs, The New York Public Library, Astor, Lenox and Tilden Foundations).

Ashley-Cooper and his secretary, philosopher John Locke (Hebrew Loach, "tariff"), who had spent many years in Holland among Sephardic Jews, then drafted the Fundamental Constitution of Carolina used to govern the colony, making Carolina the most religiously and socially liberal in North America. It expressly mentioned "Jews, heathens, and dissenters." As Edgar writes,

> In matters relating to religion, the Church of England would be the tax-supported church in the colony. That would satisfy hard-core Anglicans. For dissenters from the Church of England there was the promise of religious freedom to anyone who believed in God. Not only could

non–Anglicans settle freely in Carolina, but seven individuals could form a "church or pro-fession [of faith]" that would be officially recognized. Religious toleration meant more than freedom to establish a congregation: "No person whatsoever shall disturb, molest, or persecute another for his speculative opinions in religion, or his way of worship." In legal matters an affirmation, in lieu of an oath, was an invitation to Quakers. Not only could Huguenots worship as they wished, but upon subscribing to the Fundamental Constitutions they could become naturalized citizens. And the stipulation of a belief in God, not Christ, meant that Jews [and Muslims] were welcome. The only religious profession not tolerated was Roman Catholi-cism, a view quite in keeping with the politics of Restoration England. With the exception of Rhode Island, this was the most tolerant religious policy in English America.[18]

The right to vote in South Carolina, however, was dependent upon possessing land. The lords proprietors and their associates controlled most of that, roughly forty percent of each county, while the remaining sixty percent was divided among freemen. Both the Pro-prietors and settlers originated largely in British-held Barbados and other Caribbean islands. South Carolina historian Edgar lists prominent settler names as Beadon, Colleton, Daniel, Drayton, Fenwicke, Gibbs, Godfrey, Ladson, Middleton, Moore, Schenckhingh and Yea-mans, all of Barbados; Amory, Parris, Pinckney and Whaley of Jamaica; Lucas, Motte and Perry of Antigua; Lourdes and Rawlins of St. Christopher's; LaMotte of Granada, and Wood-ward of Nevis. Notably about half these names are identifiable as Sephardic or Moorish.

Besides recruiting their fellow British-Caribbeans, the Lords Proprietor also sought out Huguenots as settlers, due, one may surmise, to their Sephardic-Morisco affinity and enmity toward Spain, the colonial power to the south. Pamphlets were distributed in French to Huguenot refugee communities in Ireland; see Appendix J for a listing of Huguenot refugees in Ireland. When Louis XIV repealed the Edict of Nantes in 1685, which had pro-vided religious freedom to non–Catholics in France, thousands of Huguenots fled France; fifteen hundred of them made their way to South Carolina. Edgar reports that prominent surnames among these colonists were Bonneau (the Davidic "good" name; see Appendix A), Cordes, de Saussure, Deveaux, du Bose, Foret (da Silva), Gaillard, Gendron, Guerard, Horry (Moroccan), Huger, Laurens, Le Gare, Manigault, Marion, Peyre, Porcher, Pricoleau, Ravenel, Simons and Timothy.[19] Again, several are identifiable as Sephardic/Morisco.

In 1764 an additional 300 Huguenot settlers arrived in hopes of developing the silk and wine industries, the same two Sephardic-Moorish dominated industries attempted in the Virginia Colony. Most of the incoming settlers were drawn from La Rochelle and Bor-deaux, two French cities with large Sephardic-Morisco populations. Earlier in the 1720s, Purrysburgh on the left bank of the Savannah River had been settled by around eight hundred French-Swiss settlers, which we have argued elsewhere were primarily of Jewish and crypto–Jewish ancestry.[20]

The 1740s and 1750s saw an influx of 1,500 German Protestants from the Palatine region. In Chapter 6 on Pennsylvania we developed a detailed proposal that the majority of incoming German-Palatine Protestants were of Sephardic, Ashkenazic and Morisco origin. The surnames among these which Edgar lists as predominant in the South Carolina com-munity are Amaker, Boozer,[21] Geiger ("violinist"),[22] Harmon (Dutch), Hutto, Inabinet, Kalteisen, Lever (Levor, Levot),[23] Lorick (Lorich, Lorig),[24] Rast, Sheeley (Schiele),[25] Shuler,[26] Theiis, Wannamaker and Ziegler.[27] Again we are seeing a preponderance of Jewish names.

A group of Scots-Irish settled in the Waxhaws region in 1767, chiefly and foremost among them the Adairs, and the same argument can be made for these families, whose sur-names include Adair, Bratton, Caldwell, Calhoun, Kuykendal, Logan, Montgomery, Moore,

Ross and Wardlaw. A large group of Scots had preceded them in 1746: Abercromby, Allen, Buchanan, Bullock, Dias, Kinloch, Logan, Michie and Pringle. Similarly, when some Welsh settlers arrived in South Carolina, they named their parish St. Davids. Among their surnames were Aymand, Fickling, James, Pawley, Pigues and Wild.

Many of the surnames just mentioned are not typical Celtic or Welsh surnames. Rather they are the names of Sephardic or Moorish persons who in our view migrated to Ulster, Scotland and Wales from Iberia or France from 1500 onward and were now making their way to South Carolina's promise of free land and freedom of religion. Even the settlers whom Edgar identifies as being Dutch sound suspiciously Sephardic: Gillon, Haes,[28] Ioor and Rhett.

As with most traditional historians, Edgar is quite miserly in acknowledging a Jewish presence in colonial South Carolina.

Church with Jewish and Arabic architectural motifs in Oliver, Georgia, across the river from Purrysburgh. Of unknown date, the structure was reportedly for sale in October 2010 (author's collection).

The number of Jewish residents of colonial South Carolina was never large, probably no more than several hundred. With few exceptions they lived in Charleston. Because of its policy of religious toleration, South Carolina attracted a sizable percentage of the Jewish residents of British North America. They were primarily Sephardic Jews who had been expelled from Spain and Portugal, and they came to South Carolina via the Netherlands, England, or the West Indies. A few, however, even in the early years, were Ashkenazic, that is, from central or eastern Europe. In 1697 the names of four [Jews] appear among those of Huguenots who were naturalized under the Alien Act. One of them was Simon Valentine, "an alien of the Jewish nation," who had emigrated from Jamaica.[29]

Others included Avila, Cohen, DaCosta (i.e., Costa, Custis), D'Oliveria, Lindo,[30] Salvador[31] and Tobias.[32]

Historians have missed one of the Jewish families in the early colony, Cooper. This, as it happens, is a family with ancestors common to both authors. The brothers William and Joseph Cooper came to Charleston from Barbados in 1698. Joseph was a translator ("linguister") and operated the counting and customs house on the waterfront while William was stationed on the frontier in Cheeowee, the trading post in Cherokee territory located across the river from present-day Augusta, Georgia. The Board of Commissioners of the Indian Trade met at Joseph Cooper's.

William facilitated the visit of Sir Alexander Cummings (Comyns, thought to be possibly a crypto–Jewish clan)[33] to the Middle and Upper Towns on his quest in 1730 to win the Cherokees' allegiance to Britain. He snatched seven Cherokee braves, including the boy Attakullakulla, ferried them to London and had them lay the Crown of Tennessee (the priest-king's otter hat) at the feet of King George II. Later Cummings came up with another scheme involving the Carolina Cherokees. He sold shares in a company organized to resettle 500,000 European Jews among the Indians in the midst of the Appalachians. Although nothing came of the venture, it is interesting that the number corresponds rather well to the estimated contemporaneous population of Ashkenazi Jews in Poland, Lithuania and Russia, where Cummings had served in the army. His proposal can be viewed as one Jew's advocacy plan to rescue fellow Jews.

In 1700 James Moore became governor of South Carolina. Only two years later he led a military expedition to invade Catholic Spanish Florida, capturing, looting and burning the town of St. Augustine. Then again in 1703–1704 Moore led an "army of 50 whites and a thousand Creek (Indian) allies on a rampage through the Spanish [Catholic] mission settlements in Central and Western Florida.... South Carolina's military successes ... severely damaged Spain's prestige and greatly enhanced England's standing among the Indians of the Southeast."[34] In our view, the South Carolinian attacks on Spanish Florida were likely motivated by revenge — two centuries after the fact — for the Sephardic and Moorish exile from Iberia. Among other governors of South Carolina with likely Sephardic or Morisco ancestry are Seth Southell, Thomas Boone (the "good name" again), William Campbell, Charles Greville Montagu and William Bull (Toro,[35] Schorr). Also, South Carolina's planter and merchant elite was drawn almost exclusively from persons bearing Sephardic or Morisco surnames: Bull, Drayton, Izard (Norman and Arabic),[36] Austin, Beale, de la Conellier, Van der Dussen and Wragg. All of these were at least publicly Christian due to the South Carolina Election Act of 1721. This "defined a voter as a free, white, Christian male, twenty one years of age, who owned fifty acres of land or paid 20 shillings currency ($25.50) in taxes and had lived in South Carolina for [at least] one year."[37] The result of such a law would be to prompt most persons of Jewish or Muslim ancestry to be circumspect about practicing their faiths, to say the least.

Yet despite their crypto status, Jews, Moors and their descendants made important contributions to South Carolina's culture and economy throughout the colonial period. One of South Carolina's major agricultural crops during this time was indigo. The dye plant was introduced by Elizabeth Lucas and its processing was developed by Andrew Deveaux, both of whom have likely Sephardic ancestry. Moses Lindo, an openly Jewish settler, was the colony's indigo export inspector in 1762, and key producers included John Bee, James Stobo, Robert Sams, George Mitchell, Isaac Hayne, Charles Pinckney and John Hudson, most of whom bear Sephardic/Morisco surnames. It is largely the same story with Carolina's silk industry.

Many French Huguenots and newly minted "English" colonists entered South Carolina (and North Carolina) via Ireland. Thus they swelled the ranks of the so-called Scots-Irish settlers, who are estimated to account for about one-third to half of the whole population of the South.[38] The largest migration of Irish and Scottish people occurred after the Battle of Culloden in 1745 when Prince Charles Edward Stuart was defeated and the Jacobite rebellion against England was lost for good. But the roots of Irish immigration to the Amer-

Huguenots had long memories. The date 1598 in this tercentennial program commemorated the Edict of Nantes, when Henry IV of France granted them equal rights with Catholics (Rare Books Division, The New York Public Library, Astor, Lenox and Tilden Foundations).

icas were much deeper. The process can be said to have been jump started when William III (1682–1702), son of William II, prince of Orange, Stadtholder of the United Provinces of the Netherlands, began his campaigns against Irish Catholics. Spoils of war went to Presbyterian Ulster Scots and French Huguenots. This Celtic fringe, however, as it has become known in the nostalgia inherited from the Victorian era, was not altogether Celtic or even British in ethnicity or uniformly Christian in faith. The tolerant Carolinas acted as a magnet for all sorts of nationalities. Those who were better off sailed straightway to Charleston, while those of modest means took the Great Wagon Road that led from the Potomac down the Shenandoah Valley. It is said that the first wave of arrivals in Hillsborough District just across the Virginia line were almost 100 percent Celtic. The road cut through the Piedmont to Fayetteville and was so busy, day and night, that previous travelers had provided it with carved signposts that could be read with the fingers on a dark night.[39]

That many of these Irishmen were of recent French Huguenot provenance, and before that of Spanish Jewish origin, can be seen in a compilation of genealogies covering some of South Carolina's famous colonial surnames. In fact, as historian Lyburn repeatedly points out, the Scotsmen changed their way of identifying themselves as it suited them, alternating between Irish, Ulster, Scottish, English, British and other designations such as Presbyterian or Quaker.

Abbadie James Abbadie, doctor of divinity, was a native of Nay, in Bearn. He was born in London in 1727 and became Dean of Killaloe in Ireland.

Barre A Protestant family of Pont-Gibau, near Rochell, members of which settled in Ireland. Peter Barre married Miss Raboteau, a refugee; he was an alderman of Dublin and carried on a large business as a lines draper. His son Isaac was adjutant-general of the British forces under Wolfe at Quebec. In 1776 Colonel Barre was made vice-treasurer of Ireland and privy councillor.

Batz Three of the sons of Joseph de Batz, seigneur of Guay, escaped from France into Holland and entered the service of the Prince of Orange, whom they accompanied in his expedition to England; two of those sons, who were captains of infantry, were killed at the Boyne.

Bayley This Huguenot name is derived from Phillippe de Bailleux, a French refugee who settled in the neighborhood of Thorney Abbey, circa 1656. Since then the name has assumed the following forms: Balieu, Balieul, Bayly, Bailly, and Bayley.

Belcastel Pierre Belcastel de Montvaillant was a refugee officer from Languedoc who entered the service of William of Orange.

Blaquire John de Blaquire took refuge in England in 1685. He married Mary Elizabeth de Varennes, the daughter of a refugee. One of his sons settled at Lisburn, and his sister married John Crommelin ("chrome worker").[40] The fifth son, John, held various public offices, was made a baronet in 1784, and in 1800 was raised to the peerage as Lord de Blaquire of Ardkill in Ireland.

Boileau Charles, son of Jacques Boileau, served in the English army as captain of infantry and afterwards settled as a wine merchant in Dublin, where he died. His son Simeon was succeeded by Solomon Boileau.

Bonnell Thomas Bonnell took refuge in England and settled in Norwich, where he became mayor. His son was Daniel Bonnell, merchant of London, father of Samuel Bonnell, who became accountant-general for Ireland and was succeeded in that office by his son.

Bouherar Elias Bouherar, medical doctor and doctor of divinity, settled in Dublin, where he was appointed librarian to Marsh's (now known as St. Patrick's) Library. One of his sons, John, entered into holy orders, and another became town-major of Dublin; this town-major, Bouherar, changed his name to Borough (Baruck).

Brocas (*bracha*, **Hebrew prayer**) The Very Rev. Theophilus Brocas was a scion of this family, which held numerous lordships in the South of France, mostly in the neighborhood of Bordeaux. He escaped from France at the Revocation, and having taken holy orders was appointed by the Crown to the Deanery of Killala and vicarage of St. Anne's, Dublin.

For his valuable services in promoting the arts and manufactures of Ireland, he was presented with the freedom of the city of Dublin. He died in 1766 and was interred in St. Anne's Churchyard, Dublin.

Burges A member of this family, Valery, or Valerien de Burgeois, came to England with one of the earliest bodies of immigrants and settled at Canterbury. Most of the earliest Huguenot refugees in England landed in Kent. From successive intermarriages, the name became almost unrecognizable as of Huguenot origin and so was then changed to Burgess, but the pedigree of the family can be clearly traced back to the Burgeois family of Picardy, who were seigneurs of Gamache and d'Oye and of de la Fosse. A Burges was soon found as an Indian trader in the Carolinas.

Caillemotte La Caillemotte, younger son of the Marquis de Ruvigny, commanded a Huguenot regiment at the battle of the Boyne, where he was killed.

Cambon A refugee French officer, who commanded one of the Huguenot regiments raised in London in 1689, fought at the Boyen and at Athlone, and died in 1693.

Carre Of this family of Poitou, several members emigrated to England and others to North America. In Ireland the name has changed to Carry and Carrey.

Chaigneau Louis, John, and Stephen Chaigneau were refugees from St. Sairenne, in the Charente, where the family owned landed estates; they settled in Dublin and prospered. Louis sat for Gowran in the Irish Parliament; another held a benefice in the church. John had two sons — Colonel William Chaigneau and John, who was treasurer of the Ordnance. The great grandson of Stephen was called to the Irish bar in 1793 and eventually purchased the estate of Berown in the county Westmeath.

Chamberlaine Peter Chamberlayne, a physician of Paris, fled into England at the massacre of French Calvinists on St. Bartholomew's Day, August 24, 1572. He was admitted a member of the College of Physicians and obtained extensive practice in London, where he died.

Champagne Robillard de Champagne, a noble family in Saintonge, several of whom took refuge in England and Ireland. The children of Josias de Robillard, chavalier of Champagne, under charge of their mother, escaped from La Rochelle, concealed in empty wine casks, and arrived safe at Plymouth, England. Their father went to the Netherlands.

Chenevix A distinguished Lorraine family, dispersed at the Revocation of the Edict of Nantes in 1685. The Rev. Phillip Chenevix fled to England, and the family afterwards settled in Ireland. Phillip's son entered the King's Guards. His grandson became bishop of Killaloe in 1745 and afterwards of Waterford and Lismore.

Collot Collot de L'Escury, a refugee officer from Noyon, who escaped from France at the Revocation and joined in Holland the army of William of Orange, was major in Schomberg's regiment at the Boyne. His eldest son, David, was a captain of dragoons; another, Simeon, was colonel of an English regiment.

Cousin This name is now often rendered Cussen, as well as Cousins (as in the television producer's name, Norman Cousins).

Dargent A refugee family from Sancere, some members of which settled in England and Ireland at the Revocation. Two of them served as officers in the guards of William III. The name has been changed to Dargan.

De Laval Vicomte de Laval possessed estates in Picardy, but at the Revocation took refuge in Ireland, settling at Portarlington.

De Lavalade Several members of this family settled in Lisburn in the North of Ireland.

Des Voeux Vinchon des Voeus, second son of De Bacquencourt, took refuge in Dublin, where he became minister of the French church. In conjunction with the Rev. Peter Droz, he commenced about 1742 the publication of the first literary journal which appeared in Ireland.

D'Olier Bertrand D'Olier was "capitoul" of Toulouse as early as 1364. Edward Olier was made marquis of Nointel in 1656. His third son eventually settled in Dublin.

Dombrain Other forms of this name were D'Embrun and D'Ambrain. Jacques D'Embrun fled from the town of Embrun, near Gap in the Hautes-Alpes, in 1572 and, escaping to Rouen, crossed the channel in an open boat on 19 August 1572 and settled in Canterbury.

Drelincourt Peter, son of Charles Drelincourt, came to England where he entered the English Church and eventually became dean of Armagh.

Du Bedat The head of this family was the Marquis Du Bedat, some of whose descendants are now living in Ireland.

Dubourdieu A noble family of Bearn. Isaac Dubourdieu was for some time minister of the Savoy Church, London.

Du Port A family of Poitou, several members of which took refuge in England. In Ireland the name has been changed to Porte.

Dury Paul Dury was an eminent officer of engineers who entered the service of William III and afterwards passed into the service of the Elector of Hesse. Two of his sons served in the English army, the elder of whom belonged to the regiment of La Melloniers and was killed at the Boyne.

Duval Many refugees from Rouen of this name settled in England.

Fausille Rene de la Fausille belonged to an ancient Angevine family, entered the service of the Prince of Orange and became captain of Grenadiers in the regiment of Callemotte-Ruvigny and fought with it at the Battle of the Boyne. King William appointed him governor of the port, town, and county of Sligo.

Fleury Louis Fleury, protestant pastor of Tours, fled into England in 1683; his son Phillip Amuret came to Ireland as a Protestant and settled there. The son of Phillip Amuret became vicar-general of Lismore, and his son George Lewis Fleury became archdeacon of Waterford.

Foret Marquis de la Foret, a major general in the British army, served in the Irish campaign of 1699.

Gaussen There were several branches of the family in France. David Gaussen, who took refuge in Ireland in 1685, came from Lunel in Languedoc; descendants of his lived at Antrim, Belfast and Dublin. The Gaussens, who settled in England, were also from Languedoc.

Geneste Louia Geneste took service under the Prince of Orange and fought at the Battle of the Boyne in the regiment of Lord Lifford.

Gosset (Goss, Gist, Guess, Guest, Gozzi, Costa) A Huguenot family originally from Normandy which first settled in Jersey, from where some of the younger branches passed over into England. Among the members of the elder branch of the family was Matthew, for many years vicomte of Jersey, who died in 1842; Major General Sir William Gosset, who held the office of under secretary of state for Ireland, was some time member of parliament for Truro, and for several years sergeant-at-arms to the English House of Commons.

Gost John, son of Daniel Gost, a French Protestant refugee, settled in Dublin about 1684. His son John was born in that city in 1715, and having entered into holy orders was selected to perform the duty of pastor to the French Protestant congregation at Portarlington.

Goyer (Goya[41]**)** Peter Goyer, a refugee manufacturer from Picardy, settled at Lisburn in Ireland.

Gually (Guale[42]**)** Peter Gualy, son of the Sieur de la Gineste of Rourgue, fled to England at the Revocation with his wife and three children. This became the name of a remote "tribe" of mixed African and Indian people on adjacent islands.

Guillot (Berber)[43] Several members of this family immigrated to the Netherlands at the Revocation and received from the Prince of Orange commissions in his Navy. Their descendants settled in Lisburn in Ireland.

Guyon William de Guyon de Geiss (Guest)[44], son of the Sieur de Pamplona, fled the Netherlands at the Revocation and took service under William of Orange, in which he lost an arm.

Hamon An ancient Norman family.[45] Two brothers Hamon who settled at Portarlington in Ireland were of that family. The name has in some cases been changed to Hammond.

Hazard (Arabic)[46] Peter Hazard or Hasaret fled from the persecutions in the Low Countries under the Duke of Parma during the Spanish occupation. Returning on a visit to his native land, he was seized and burnt alive in 1568. Descendants of his still survive in England and Ireland under the name of Hassard.

Labat, or **Labatt (Lobato)**[47] A branch of this family has been long settled in Ireland. The first Labat came over with William III as an officer in his army. Labats became important Indian traders on the American and Canadian frontier.

Langlais ("the Englishman") This Normandy family name has been changed to Langley.

La Rive This refugee who settled in Ireland escaped from France with his wife by pretending to be sellers of oranges (a traditional Jewish occupation) and going about with a donkey and panniers. When they reached the Netherlands, the Prince of Orange gave him a commission, and La Rive fought bravely in the Irish campaigns. By some of the family this name has been changed into Reeves (a Melungeon name). Huguenots often escaped by disguising themselves as servants, gypsies, travelers from foreign countries and the like.

La Roche A refugee from Bordeaux originally named Crothaire, whose son became a member of parliament for Bodmin in 1727.

Larochefoucauld Frederick-Charles de Larochefoucauld, count de Roye, left France at the Revocation and entered the Danish service, attaining the post of grand-marshal. He afterwards settled in England and died at Bath in 1690. His son Frederick William was made a lifetime peer under the title of earl of Lifford in Ireland.

La Trobe Jean la Trobe, a refugee from the south of France, came to Ireland by way of the Netherlands and settled in Waterford about the year 1690.

Layard An ancient Albigensian family whose original name was Raymond (Spanish), De Layarde (near Montpellier) being merely their *nom de terre*, as in many other similar cases.

Le Fanu (Da Fano?)[48] Etienne Le Fanu of Caen married in 1657 and after some time made his escape into England and eventually settled in Ireland.

Lefroy (Froes, Fois)[49] Antoine Leffroy, a native of Cambrai, took refuge in England from the Low Countries about the year 1587 and settled in Canterbury, where his descendants followed the business of silk dyeing until the death of Thomas Leffroy in 1723. Anthony Lefroy settled at Leghorn (once a Jewish port) in 1728 and died there in 1779.

Logier Jean-Bernard Logier, a refugee musician, inventor of the method of musical notation which bears his name, settled as a teacher of music at Dublin, where he died.

Mangin Several refugees of this name settled in Ireland. Paul Mangin became established at Lisburn, and there married Madelaine, the daughter of Louis Crommelin.

Mathy was a celebrated physician and author. After a residence in Holland, he settled in England about the middle of the eighteenth century. He was secretary of the Royal Society in 1758, and was afterwards appointed librarian of the British Museum in which office he was succeeded by his son. This name has been changed into Matthew.

Mazieres Peter de Mazieres was a lieutenant in the French army and afterward joined the army of William of Orange. He settled at Youghal in Ireland, where he died in 1746.

Mercier ("fabric worker") Philip Mercier, a portrait painter born at Berlin of a French refugee family, settled in London, where he died in 1760. In Ireland the name has been changed into Mercer.

Morell[50] Daniel Morell was born in a village in Champagne about the period of the Revocation and lost his parents at an early age. His foster brother Stephen Conte fled with him into the Netherlands under the guidance of a party of refugees. On reaching manhood, both entered the army of William III and fought under him through the Irish campaigns.

Normand Now Norman.

Perrin Count Perrin was a Huguenot refugee from Nouere, where he had large possessions. He originally settled at Lisburn in Ireland, from which he afterwards removed to Waterford.

Raboteau John Charles Raboteau, a refugee from Pont-Gibaud near Rochelle, settled in Dublin and prospered as a wine merchant.

Reynet, or De Reynet (Reyne,[51] **Raina)** A refugee family which settled at Waterford, the freedom of which city was conferred in perpetuity on the descendants of Henri de Reynet. But Henri's youngest son returned to France, and having professed the Roman Catholic religion, he was placed in possession of the family estate, which his descendants of the female line still hold.

Roche (Rocca,[52] **La Roche, Roccas)** Louis Roche, a refugee manufacturer, settled in Lisburn. He became an extensive merchant and descendants of his are now living in Belfast.

Teulon or **Tholan (Toulouse, capital of Jewish principate)** An ancient family of Nîmes, descended from Marc Tholon, sieur de Guiral. Peter and Anthony fled from France at the time of the Revocation and settled at Greenwich. Peter came into Ireland and founded the County Cork branch of the family.

Thorius (from Toro, a city in Spain[53]) Raphael Thorius was a physician born in France, but a refugee in England. He died in 1625, leaving behind him a son, John, who studied medicine at Oxford and became fellow of the College of Physicians of Dublin in 1627.

Victoria Queen Victoria is descended from Huguenot ancestress Eleanore D'Esmiers, marquise d'Olbreuse, who was her great-great-great grandmother. (A great-grandparent was also a Seixas,[54] hence the name of her duchy and dynasty, Saxe-Coburg — which the royal family is said to have hated).

Additional insight can be gleaned into the private lives of Carolina's crypto–Jews also by scanning the names of brides and grooms from the Old 96 and Abbeville Districts (Appendix J).

The given and surnames are markedly Sephardic/Morisco. At least one Levirate marriage (Lipscomb) is reported. Some names such as Mahaffa, Sherriff, Alamza, Alladin, Mahallah, and Arcajah appear to be straightforwardly Arabic, while others such as Vashti, Toccoa, Palestine, Israel and Brazil would seem to be unequivocally Sephardic.

Among the Irish forebears of one of the authors are the Denneys, said to have immigrated to Pennsylvania and Virginia and to have passed through South Carolina on their migration south. Once in Georgia and Alabama, they set up mills and stores. Ultimately (or rather intermediately) the Denney name can be traced to a Robert Denney, who lived in seventeenth-century Ireland. Then it disappears — often a sign it came from elsewhere. Indeed there is a coat of arms claiming a French origin for the name, Denis, which may in turn lead to Spanish roots in the Berber/Arabic surname Danan/Danna.[55] First names in the Denney family tree excerpted below seem decidedly Jewish: Suddarth, Asenith/Seneth, Shered (all Arabic), Azariah, Benjamin, David, Elisha, Joshua, Josiah, Jeremiah, Lazarus, Noah, Samuel, Zachariah, Obediah, Orpha, Rebecca, Rachel, Sarah, Sinaia, Tabitha (all Hebrew), Irby, Effie (Eva), Adeline, Lillian (all Yiddish), Lala, Lula, Cenus Rosa (all Portuguese, i.e. Sinais Rosa, "rose of Sinai"), Irene, Eunice, Bernice, Melita, Adelphia (all Greek), and Cornelia and Lesina (both Italian). Many of the marriage partners bear Jewish surnames: Sarah *Wise* Felton, Lucy Storer/*Storey*,[56] Henry Yates (co-author Donald Yates's great-grandfather), Rebecca Vanderpool,[57] Ann Fulk (form of Raphael),[58] Martha Birchum (Berghoum, Tunisian),[59] Thomas Elihu Hand, Josiah Francis Raines (Reynes), Polly Hanna,[60] Nonnie Gay[61] and Margaret Cohorn (Cohen).

Descendants of Samuel Denney

1   Samuel Denney b: Abt. 1715 in Albemarle Co., Va.
    +Sarah Suddarth/Southard
    2   Azariah Denney   b: Abt. 1750 in Virginia
        +Sarah (Sally) Wise Felton
        3   Joshua Denney   b: Abt. 1778 in Surry Co., N.C.
            +Jane Watkins   b: Abt. 1785
            4   Irby Denney   b: 1801 in South Carolina
                +Lucy Storer (Storey)
                5   Daughter Denney
                5   Daughter Denney
                5   John Callan Denney   b: 1825
                    +Mary Jane (Nancy) Ellard   b: Abt. 1841 in Alabama or Georgia
                    6   Katy Denney
                    6   Mary A. Denney   b: Abt. 1857
                    6   Thomas Newton Denney   b: March 22, 1861 in Randolph Co., Ala.
                        +E. L. -----   b: August 20, 1859
                    6   John W. Denney   b: Abt. 1862
                    6   Sarah A. Lucinda Denney   b: February 18, 1867 in Clay Co., Ala.
                        +Henry Yates   b: September 16, 1862 in Heard Co., Ga.
                    6   T. Lesina Denney   b: May 1870
                    6   Arrena (Irene) Denney   b: Abt. 1873
                        +----- Kelley
                    6   Henry Denney   b: Abt. 1876
                    6   Noah Denney   b: Abt. 1878
                5   Irby Denney   b: Abt. 1830
                    +Nancy T. Kelly   b: Abt. 1832

6	Matilda Denney	
6	Henry Cleveland Denney	b: Bet. December 12, 1848–1854
	+Frank Moore	
6	Martha M. Denney	b: Bet. September 1854–1856
	+Clem C. Sterling	
6	John Wesley Denney	b: January 20, 1861
	+Effie A. -----	
5	Thomas Jefferson Denney	b: February 03, 1844 in Henry Co., Ga.
	+Anna Francis Ellard	b: October 1844 in Georgia
6	S. J. Denney	b: Abt. 1868
6	M. A. Denney	b: Abt. 1870
6	John Thomas Denney	b: March 14, 1870 in Carroll County, Georgia
	+Martha Jane Mitchell	b: May 13, 1876 in Randolph County, Ala.
6	James Yearby Denney	b: Abt. 1873
	+Rosie Hardin	
4	Jane Denney	b: 1828
4	Obediah Denney	
	*2nd Wife of Joshua Denney:	
	+Adeline/Adelphia -----	b: Abt. 1796
3	James Denney	b: 1777 in Pilot Creek, Surry Co., N.C.
	+Rebecca Vanderpool	
4	Orpha Denney	
4	Lewis Denney	
4	Winnie Denney	
4	Jeremiah Denney	
4	Josiah Denney	
4	Sarah Denney	
4	Zachariah Denney	
4	James Denney	
4	Azariah Denney	
4	John Denney	
3	Harrell Denney	b: 1778
	+Nancy -----	
	*2nd Wife of Harrell Denney:	
	+Elizabeth Hill	
3	Louis Denney	b: 1779
3	Rachel Denney	b: Abt. 1781
3	Henry Denney	b: 1782
	+Mary -----	
3	Elizabeth Denney	b: April 04, 1784
3	Sarah Denney	b: Abt. 1788
3	Polly Denney	b: Abt. 1789
3	William Felton Denney	b: March 18, 1792
	+Ann Fulk	
3	Nancy Denney	b: Abt. 1793
3	Asenith (Seneth) Denney	b: Abt. 1794
	+Elisha Gentry	

        4   Azariah Denney Gentry   b: 1812 in Anderson Co., S.C.

   3   Jordan Denney   b: August 29, 1799

       +Martha Birchum

       *2nd Wife of Jordan Denney:

       +Polly Gibson

2   William Denney

2   John Denney

   3   Samuel Denney

       +----- Wooten

   3   William Denney

       +Sally Hill

       4   John Denney

       4   Obadiah Denney

2   Charles Denney

2   Henry Denney

2   Lazarus Denney

2   Benjamin Denney

2   Shered Denney

2   Keziah Denney

      +John Robertson

2   Nancy Denney

2   ----- Denney

      +Britton Meeks

2   James Denney

   3   Azariah Denney

      ----- Denney

      +Richard Pilson

The classical architecture of Beth Elohim in Charleston, the country's fourth oldest congregation, acknowledges both the ancient roots of Judaism in Greek civilization and democratic values of America (author's collection).

Huguenots set the tone of the Carolina colony. With their wealth, professional backgrounds and gentility, it is sometimes hard to distinguish them from Sephardic Jews. Charleston became the fourth oldest Jewish community in the American Colonies after New York, Philadelphia, and Savannah with the establishment of Beth Elohim in 1749. The old DaCosta family plot served as the location of the Coming Street Cemetery founded in 1764. Charleston's overtly Jewish population of five hundred constituted the largest, wealthiest and most cultured Jewish community in the Colonies. Until about 1830 it had the largest Jewish population of any city in the United States. Unlike New York, Philadelphia or most other American Jewish communities with the notable exception of Savannah, it never experienced the slightest repugnance from its host city. Part of that goodwill undoubtedly came from the Jews' fellow travelers — the Huguenots. Was it surprising then that Charleston became the birthplace of the Reform Judaism movement in the 1840s, or that South Carolina voted the first Jew to public office (Francis Salvador, a newly arrived immigrant, in 1774, elected to the First Provincial Congress)? As we have seen, South Carolina's Jewish roots are very deep indeed. Its Muslim elements in the colonial period, moreover, are not insignificant.

CHAPTER NINE

Georgia, the Last Colony

Georgia was the last and most elaborately planned of the British colonies, but in many respects it was the most lawless and least controlled of them. It was the only colony to be planted on soil claimed by a foreign power (Spain), it encompassed at first the settlements of a third nation, France (which maintained scattered towns in the Mississippi, Red River, Missouri and Ohio River valleys), and its territory conflicted with another British colony, South Carolina. Georgia was both remote and vast; it extended in theory to the South Seas, or Pacific Ocean.[1] All these circumstances combined to open the doors to a diversified stream of immigrants, ranging from London Jews and the debtors emptied from England's poorhouses to the Protestant refugees from Catholic Salzburg and Scottish Highlanders in the tidewater enclave named Darien. Although most of those just named were sponsored and official, there were an equal number of surreptitious settlers.

The extreme western part of Georgia was the scene for an attempt on the part of the French to settle Jews and Gypsies on the lower Mississippi in the years from 1717 to 1722. The venture was launched by the Compagnie des Indes and a Scottish entrepreneur named John Law (evidently a Jew himself). Whether for good or ill, it

John Law, from a print by Leon Schenk in 1720 (Mackay, 1841).

159

was Law who introduced paper money, deficit spending, government bonds and many of the methods of state finance in use today. Historians are divided in opinion as to whether he was a "knave or a madman."[2]

Born at Edinburgh in 1671, Law carried on his ancient Fife family's business of gold-smithing and banking before becoming an international gambler and having the ill luck to shoot a rival dead in a London duel. He was arrested, but he somehow managed to escape to the Continent, where after a checkered career he ended up at the court of Louis XIV. A reward for his apprehension described him as "Captain John Law, a Scotchman, aged twenty-six; a very tall, black, lean man; well shaped, above six feet high, with large pock-holes in his face; big nosed, and speaking broad and loud."[3] Law overhauled the strained finances of the kingdom and established the Royal Bank of France. He also acquired the state monopoly on tobacco; the exclusive privilege of trading to Mississippi, Louisiana, China and the French East Indies; and the minting of the coin of the realm, printing of money and issuance of government paper.

Under the scheme that came to be known as the Mississippi Bubble, the poor of Paris and Alsace — overwhelmingly composed of Jews and Gypsies — were to be gathered up and sent as colonists to New France. The land agent was Elias Stultheus, a Jew.[4] Parisians subscribed in a frenzy to the various stock issues. Fortunes were made on speculation. The first fleet of ships set sail and deposited its human cargo several hundred miles up the Mississippi, between Natchez and Memphis. There the Jews and Gypsies, without arms or provisions, were supposed to hold the territory for France and combat the threat of Indian uprisings. After they realized they had been abandoned, however, many of them threw themselves on the mercy of the Natchez, Choctaw and Chickasaw. Others became part of the Old Settlers in today's Northern (formerly Western) Cherokee Nation of the Old Louisiana Territory, later known as the Lost Cherokees.[5] The crash at home came in 1721 when it was discovered that the "junk bonds," as we would say today, were worthless. Law fell from grace and went into exile, giving up his titles and chateaux to take up a gambler's career again in the casinos of Europe.

There are indications that this secret colony was not so secret. James Adair (Hebrew name), the Indian trader, made a beeline for Chickasaw territory shortly after arriving in South Carolina. He developed a strong connection to the Chickasaw, winning the tribe over as staunch allies of the British. Around 1745, he established operations in Piomingo in north Mississippi, then a mixed Choctaw and Chickasaw town. He later wrote, "I have the pleasure of writing this [his famous book, *History of the American Indians*] by the side of a Chikkasah female, as great a princess as ever lived." Elsewhere, he notes that there were already adults in that country who were octoroons, or one-eighth Indian.[6] The Indian-white intermarriage necessary to produce a half-breed of this description must have occurred at least three generations before, about 1720, the time of the Mississippi Bubble. We have already seen how Adair's contemporary and countryman the Scottish adventurer Sir Alexander Cummings proposed to settle Eastern Europe's Jews in the same area.

The *Encyclopedia of Southern Culture* confirms that the oldest Jewish communities in the South were not on the Atlantic or Gulf coast but in the middle Mississippi river valley. The first Jews lived on the St. Francis and Arkansas River in outposts originally Spanish or French — Natchez, New Madrid, Kaskaskia, Cape Girondeau and Memphis.[7] These are all Jewish ghost towns now, like ruins on the Caribbean Islands that once held the first synagogues of the New World. Today there are only twenty-five Jews in Natchez. The city's Museum of the Southern Jewish Experience stands as a lonely tribute to Mississippi's Jewish pioneers.

Plot Thickens

A connection between Jews on the Mississippi and Georgia emerges from a stray reference in the Board of Governors' records of 1750. The "Frenchmen" Isaac Labon (Hebrew for "white," or "blond"),[8] Leonard Bowdle (Beaudel, Bodell), Anthony Pages[9] and Anthony LeSage (Wise, Weise, Sage, Wiseman, Ouizman) are recorded as arriving in Savannah on the ship *The Charming Martha* from London. The Board of Governors "had appropriated a choice piece of Land fitting for their Purposes ... and had also desir'd Mr. Jean Sack [Hebrew anagram for *Zera Kodesh* "holy seed"][10] an old Inhabitant of this Colony, a Country Man of theirs, to ... assist them."[11] One might ask why "Frenchmen" were granted lands in Georgia at a time when Britain was engaged in a bitter struggle with France, one that would only end with that country's surrender and complete withdrawal from North America. Although these "Frenchmen" may have been outwardly Huguenots, it is apparent from their names that they were Sephardic Jews underneath the Protestant veneer.

The subsequent history of one of them will illustrate this. Isaac Labon was a half-breed, believed to be the son of a French or English trader Jean (or John) Lebo (or Leebow) and the daughter of a Choctaw chief. His sister Malea (Hebrew name meaning "full, ripe, buxom")[12] married William Cooper, the Jewish scout and guide for Daniel Boone (William and Malea are common ancestors of both authors).[13] Isaac later moved to Philadelphia and then to Watauga Country, where he signed a petition from the "North of Holston Men" to the president in 1777. There the Labons changed the family name to White. Isaac White, Isaac Labon's son (born 1752), settled in Jonesborough in Washington County and fought as a lieutenant at Kings Mountain in October 1780.

When Chickasaw lands were returned to Spain in 1781, the Coopers (Americanized, but still able to speak Spanish) received grants and operated profitable tobacco plantations in what is now the tri-state area of Mississippi, Alabama and Tennessee. Both the Coopers and Labons provide good examples of crypto–Jews' chameleon-like ability to adopt different personae to suit the occasion. The Coopers alternated between claiming to be British, Portuguese, French, Spanish and American and gave their origin variously as Virginia, Georgia, North Carolina, South Carolina, Pennsylvania, Tennessee and Kentucky. They explained the Indian admixture in the family as Choctaw, Chickasaw, Cherokee, Black Dutch and Black Irish. Cooper is considered a Melungeon surname, as is White.

By 1800, there was just one town of Halfbreeds left — the term used for Chickasaws in British treaties and trade records since about 1720. It is mentioned in the memoirs of a steamboat captain as still in existence at the former French fort below what the steamboat captains called the fourth bluffs on the Mississippi, just south of Memphis: "Fort Pickering ... stands on the left side of the river, in the Mississippi Territory. The United States have a factor here, but the settlement is very thin; it generally consists of what is called the half breed, which is a mixture of Indians and whites."[14] Significantly, the earliest name given to this region by the Cumberland and Watauga Country settlers was Moro District — the "Moorish District." It may be this colony that Choctaw chief Apunkshunnubbee refers to in the 1790s when he tells the Indian agent: "You Americans were not the first [white] people who got this country from the red people. We sold our lands, but never got any value for it."[15]

Under the name Halfbreeds, Chickasaws helped found Augusta and secure the Indian trade from both the Spanish and French. Halfbreeds also defended Augusta in the Cherokee War of 1759–1760. To reward them for fighting the Spanish in 1735 and later rebuffing the Cherokee, Georgia gave them large grants of land on the north bank of the Savannah River.

The Halfbreeds — mixed Chickasaws, Jews and Gypsies — held these plantations until the 1790s. Today, the descendants of this colony in North Augusta, South Carolina, compose one of the largest Romani (Gypsy) communities in the United States — perhaps a vestige of William Law's pool of settlers. Significantly, Roma people regard Memphis as one of the most desirable places to be buried in the United States, possibly because their ancestors were interred in that area following France's Mississippi Bubble colony.

These developments on the frontier can be better understood if we look at some of the standard historical accounts of Georgia. It was a colony long in search of itself. The early years can be divided into three periods: Trusteeship (1733–1748), Interim (1748–1754) and Royal Period (1755–1776). Although established with high-minded ideals, the Georgia colony repeatedly seemed to go awry. Under its charter, colonists enjoyed the free exercise of religion ("except papists"), but the first Anglican church was not dedicated until 1750. In the meantime, Jews, Salzburgers and others had created their own places of worship. There was to be no slavery, rum or swearing. But the outpost of Augusta was a law unto itself. Half of Georgia's population were slaves by the time of the American Revolution. At first, outright ownership of land was prohibited. All grants were made in *tail male*, meaning property could not be transferred to anyone other than the first grantee's male heirs. This simply encouraged squatters, illegal homesteaders and even fraudulent speculators. Quitrents were supposed to be paid to the king, but no one bothered to do so.

The colonists revolted over the land policies of the trustees as early as 1738, and in 1742 sent Thomas Stephens to lay their complaints before Parliament. England turned a deaf ear, and blind eye, to all.

Absentee Government

The founder James Oglethorpe stayed in Georgia for ten years until the border with Spain was secured. Except for him, no trustee ever laid eyes on Georgia. The trustees were, in fact, prevented by the by-laws from visiting the colony or having any financial interests in it. After about 1740, they met infrequently and often could not muster a quorum. Who exactly were these overseers of the last colony? According to the charter of King George II, they were, at the outset, "John Lord Viscount Percival ... Edward Digby, George Carpenter [Carpentier], James Oglethorpe, George Heathcote, Thomas Tower [Tauer, from the letter *tau*], Robert Moor [from "Moor"], Robert Hucks [from Jacob], Roger Holland ["from the Netherlands"], William Sloper [Polish],[16] Francis Eyles [Isles, Arabic], John Laroche [Rocca], James Vernon, William Belitha [Arabic][17] ... John Burton ... Richard Bundy [Bondi][18] ... Arthur Bedford ... Samuel Smith ... Adam Anderson, and Thomas Coram [Hebrew].[19, 20]

Others were added to the list later on, including Anthony Ashley-Cooper (Jewish name, 4th earl of Shaftesbury), Henry L'Apostre (French Huguenot), Samuel Smith and Stephen Hales (Arabic name). The secretary throughout the years was Benjamin Martyn. The accountant was Harman (Dutch Jewish form of Hiram, a name from Jewish legend and Freemasonry) Verelst.

From the list of 115 individual names representing the first arrivals on the *Anne* in February 1733 (Appendix K), one can discern many that could potentially point to Jewish and crypto-Jewish roots. Note Bowling (Hebrew "bath keeper"), Cooper, Fox, Gordon (a corruption of Cohen), Hughes, Ellis (Arabic), Littel, Muir (Moor), Pratt, Sammes, Symes, Wallis and West. Henry Ellis, known as the "second founder of Georgia," was the colony's second governor, 1757–1760.

"An Audience Given by the Trustees of Georgia to a Delegation of Creek Indians (1734–35," oil painting by William Verelst. Donald N. Panther-Yates states the models were apparently Cherokee, not Creek, despite the title. See "A Portrait of Cherokee Chief Attakullakulla from the 1730s? A Discussion of William Verelst's *Trustees of Georgia* Painting," *Journal of Cherokee Studies* 22 (2002), 5–20. (Winterthur Museum).

Silk was to be Georgia's mainstay. As early as 1732, the trustees approached the London silk manufacturer Thomas Lombe ("Lombard")[21] for advice.[22] After some difficulty, they secured the services of Paul Amatis, "Italian Silk Man, Gardner and Silk Care." Amatis introduced silk worms to the colony and taught others the proprietary art of silk manufacture. But did they realize that the Amatis family was not so much Italian, although domiciled in Livorno, Rome, Florence and Genzano, but Sephardic Jews?[23] Another silk expert brought to the colonies was Joseph Solomon Ottolenghi. He began life as a kosher butcher in Italy, and although he converted to Christianity in Georgia, the rest of his family and descendants remained Jewish.[24]

Wherever we look, silk formed part of a triad along with wine and olive oil, which was supposed to be the salvation of the Southern colonies. All these occupations were developed and dominated by Spanish Jews. Silk manufacture was established by medieval Jews who learned the art on the famous Silk Road to China. Their secrets were passed after 1492 to the "Huguenots"—a denomination superficially espoused by Paul Amatis. In South Carolina, a number of families including the Hugers, Legares, Legendres, Manigaults, Mazycks

(Mazhig, Algerian),[25] and Mottes (Mota/de la Motta, Portuguese Jews who also came to Savannah)[26] settled under the pretext of introducing the silk-manufacturing industry. They became Charleston's leading moneylenders, factors and shippers — professions that once again point to Jewish roots. Two apparent Jewesses or crypto–Jewesses involved in the silk profession in Georgia were the "Italian" silk winder Jane Mary Camuse (French Camus)[27] and the mixed breed interpreter-diplomat and trader Mary Musgrove, who passed into history as Creek Mary.

Savannah's Jews

The boatload of 42 Jewish settlers who landed in Savannah on July 11, 1733, and immediately established North America's third Jewish congregation (after New York and Newport, Rhode Island), was the exception to the trustees' policies that proved the rule (see Appendix K, Table 2). There was nothing specifically excluding Jews in Georgia's charter. Only Catholics and slaves were prohibited. Hence in the spirit of "What the law does not forbid, it permits," a group of wealthy merchants of London's Spanish-Portuguese congregation at Bevis Marks collected funds and sponsored their fellow Jews' passage. There were Sephardim (34) and Ashkenazim (8), rich and poor, men, women and children, granted either permanent or temporary residency. This occurred only five months after the arrival of the first one hundred fifteen settlers. Upon disembarkation, the Jews formed about one-quarter of the colony. They are gratefully remembered for introducing standards of hygiene, building housing and providing rudimentary medical services.

At the time, however, the Jews were not greatly appreciated. The trustees wrathfully summoned those held responsible, Alvaro Lopez Suasso, Francis Salvador Junior and Anthony Da Costa (others[28] say the three who spearheaded the development were Moses da Costa, Joseph Rodrigues Sequeira and Jacob Israel Suasso). The trustees' language, however, shows they were willing to accept wealthy merchants, just not "certain Jews."[29] They pretended to "conceive the settling of Jews in Georgia will be prejudicial to the Colony, and as Some have been sent without the knowledge of the Trustees," they demanded that the "Jews be removed from the Colony of Georgia ... for such an Indignity offer'd to Gentlemen acting under his Majesty's Charter."[30] That the Savannah Jews were not deported suggests that their London counterparts were able to iron out the situation with diplomacy (and probably a timely transfer of money to the Trustees' charities).

The history of Savannah Jewry lies beyond the purview of this book. But to lend weight to the suspicion that Georgia may have been the "most Jewish" of the colonies, let us recount some of the famous Jews in its history. We have already noted the silk experts Paul Amatis and Joseph Ottolenghi, who, strictly speaking, were crypto–Jews. A practicing Jew, Abraham de Lyon (De Leon), who arrived with the Bevis Marks Jews, was hired to nourish viniculture after the first vintner failed.[31] His wife was Esther Nunes, daughter of Moses Nunes,[32] a prominent Mason and customs officer for the port.[33] Their children married into the Jewish mercantile aristocracy of the Colonies — Levy, Cohen, Moses, Mordecai, Brandon, Seixas, Hendricks, Machado, Phillips and Russell.[34] One descendant, Raphael Moses of Columbus, Georgia, is considered "the father of Georgia's peach industry."[35]

Benjamin Taliaferro fought in the Revolution and a county was named for him. The "Scottish" Telfair family (a name derived from Taliaferro) was one of Savannah's wealthiest, bequeathing to the city their mansion, now the Telfair Museum of Art. Edward Telfair was governor, 1786–87 and 1789–1793. Dr. Patrick Telfair fled Savannah with the Sephardic Jews at the threat of a Spanish invasion and the return of the Inquisition in 1740[36]— an indication, perhaps, of his religious affinity. David Emanuel was justice of the peace in St. George Parish in 1766 and later became the sixth governor of Georgia, also having a county named after him. James Lucena[37] was justice of the peace in Christ Church Parish in 1773. All these swore Christian oaths of office, an indication that the road to integration in American society lay through conversion — or apparent conversion.[38] That did not change the fact, however, that their roots were Jewish.

Mordecai Sheftall,[39] the son of Ashkenazi parents Benjamin and Perla from Frankfurt, Germany, stood out from the rest by remaining unapologetically Jewish. He was, in the words of his biographer Rabbi Levy, a Jewish American, not an American Jew. He helped provision the Continental Army, a patriotic act for which he asked no recompense. There is a story told at Savannah's Mickve Israel that over a century later his heirs were asked why they never called due the promissory notes given to them by George Washington and others, notes displayed today in the temple museum. The Sheftalls replied they did not wish to bankrupt the United States. A similar story is told of Hyam Saloman, the Polish Jewish émigré who loaned Robert Morris, superintendent for the new government's finances, the requisite funds for feeding and paying Washington's army in the North.

After 1733, more Jews arrived in Georgia, some to stay in Savannah, some to settle in the hinterland. The officials in London mistakenly attributed every Jew's arrival to the date 10 July 1733, when the first boatload of Jews made landfall. For instance, they recorded the Aberdaun/Bandenoon family under that date. Their name comes from Abennomen, a town near Toledo.[40] According to the trustees' notes, Heyman Aberdaun, "Jew inmate," came with Abigail, his wife, Solomon, their son, and Simon Aberdaun, also called "a Jew inmate," with Simon's wife, Grace. Heyman and Simon Aberdaun were fined "for scandal" and "defamation," 27 September 1734.[41] They and their families fled Savannah in 1740 during the War of Jenkins' Ear, when it seemed the Spaniards would take over the colony and introduce the Inquisition.

Another was Moses Ledesma, also said to have arrived with his family 10 July 1733.[42] Altogether, chroniclers Coulter and Saye count 92 of the settlers who paid their own passage as Jews, more than twice the number of Jews (42) who came in 1733. Some of the names of these unstudied Georgia Jews are Isaac Deval (settled at Hampstead), David and Hester Frocis, John, Benjamin and Thomas Levi, David Mendoza and Abraham Monsonte (Monsanto).[43]

By 1738, only five years after its establishment, Georgia had 1,110 inhabitants.[44] Official settlement hugged the coast, particularly the environs of Savannah. There were twenty plantations within a radius of twenty miles inland. A notable village in the interior was Abercorn, fifteen miles north. The Salzburgers' grant of land, called Ebenezer, was thirty-five miles upriver. There were only about 200 residents at the time. "At a considerable distance" was Augusta, "the great resort of Traders & Indians."[45] To the south lay the lonely Scottish outpost of New Inverness on the Altamaha River (renamed Darien).

Salzburgers

The story of Purrysburgh has been told before. It is suspected that some, if not many, of the "Swiss" colonists were crypto–Jews or converted Jews.[46] Georgia's answer to South

Carolina's Purrysburgh was Ebenezer, a colony formed by "transports" (groups of refugees traveling together) of German Lutherans whom the trustees rescued from wandering exile after their expulsion from Salzburg by the Catholic archbishop. As Rubin notices, there was a good deal of similarity and sympathy between the Salzburgers and the Jews. In the first place, although not commonly appreciated, the Salzburgers were not all from Salzburg. Second, the original refugees wandered for years throughout Central and Western Europe before the trustees took on their cause. In the meantime, they were helped along the way by German Jews who collected money for them, fed and clothed them. In one town, local Jews presented them with a gift of four thousand thalers. The Salzburgers were also received kindly by Jews in Frankfurt, Coburg, Wurzburg and Bamberg, all thriving centers of German Jewry at the time.[47]

It seems some of the Jews who identified with the Salzburgers went beyond good wishes and actually joined the swelling exodus, whose numbers may have included crypto–Jews and Huguenots from the start. Their chronicler George F. Jones lists fifteen transports to Ebenezer between 1734 and 1752, only four of which are specifically labeled Salzburgers. The remaining eleven carried Moravians, Palatines, Swiss and Swabians, although even these designations were very rough, and "there were a number of Ashkenazim or German Jews."[48] The Sanftleben[49] party came over en masse from Silesia in Poland in 1739. Table 3 in Appendix K lists the names of some of the Ebenezer colonists we have reason to believe were of Jewish extraction, and perhaps still of Jewish faith and practices, although secretive about it.

One of the first things we notice from the list is intermarriage between certain families. We suggest families like Brandner, Flerl, Helfenstein, Unselt, Treutlen, Zorn, Heinle, Fischer, Dasher and Schubdrein were descendants of Jews who superficially converted to Christianity in response to late medieval pogroms in the Rhineland and Bavaria. Some of those labeled Swiss or Swabian or Salzburgers are obviously not from Switzerland, Swabia or Salzburg except in an adoptive sense. This must certainly be the case with the large "Gunter" (actually Guindre) family said to be Palatines. That they are French Huguenots who originated as Spanish-Portuguese Jews is suggested by the marriage partner of one "Gunter," Anna Monfort. Their name may once have been Guindi/Gundi.[50]

Some of the Salzburgers have transparently Sephardic surnames, for instance, Fahm (Fāo), Lion (De Leon) and Faesch (Fez). Others have names documented to be German, Scottish, French, Flemish or Alsatian Jewish. What is most striking is how these various nationalities converged on Ebenezer, Bethany and the resulting satellite communities within such a short span of years. We find instances of communication and trade between the Salzburgers and the Savannah Jews. At least one "Swiss Baptist" goes back to Germany and then returns to Georgia (with more immigrants?). Some of those arriving in Ebenezer gravitated to it from Pennsylvania Dutch territory and their families had been in the colonies since 1710. Those of Sephardic surname marry those of Ashkenazic surname. "Frenchmen" marry "Germans" despite the traditional antipathy between the two countries. Some settlers defect from the British army, others arrange their own passage with a ship captain, and a large number move in from Purrysburgh. And then, as often happens, once gathered together, they move on. Two Jewish settlements in what became Florida — Flatow[51] and Grunau — owe their existence to the Salzburgers and their kin.

"Prior to the surrender of the charter," writes Rabbi B. H. Levy, "the Trustees had sent to Georgia over fifty-five hundred colonists, of whom about thirty-five hundred had come at their own expense."[52] The first list in Coulter and Saye covers those "who went to Georgia at the Trustees' charge," while the second contains the names of those "who went from

Europe to Georgia on their own account." Levy notes that "by 1752, many of these colonists had either died or left Georgia, but about three thousand people remained in the colony, including approximately eight hundred Negroes." From these figures, it is apparent that the bulk of Georgia's settlers were not the charity cases the Trustees had in mind at the beginning. Moreover, many colonists disembarking at Savannah moved on. Like Maryland with its lax religious restrictions, Georgia with its absence of central authority seemed to beckon to those of a fluid background.

Although the original charter was set to expire in 1753, interest on the trustees' part in their distant experiment became so vaporous that Parliament abruptly eliminated their budget and dissolved the company two years early. Georgia became a royal colony. The Interim Period of 1748–1754 saw an overweening disregard for any directives from the mother country. In 1750, all titles to grants previously made in *tail male* were converted to fee simple. In the months prior to June 23, 1752, when the King was supposed to take control, 75,000 acres of land were granted by the board of governors in Savannah to all manner of takers.[53]

Slice of Colonial Life

Volume VI of the *Colonial Records of the State of Georgia* covering the years 1741–1754 provides us a window on this type of immigrant. In the following list are the names of persons, usually land grantees, whom we regard as of possible or probable Jewish or crypto–Jewish origins. We make reference to two of the authorities on Jewish names, Faiguenboim, et al., and Menk, as well as to Stern's 1991 compendium of Colonial American Jewish genealogy.

Names from the Board of Governors' Minutes, 1741–1754.

Stephen Adye (Adjaj),[54] merchant, St. Kitts

Francis Arthur, merchant

John Ashmore

Walter Augustine

William Backshell (Bäcksel, "bakery item"?)

William Barbo (Barbeaux)

Isaac Barksdale (formed from Baruch), Indian trader

Edward and John Barnard[55] (Bernhard), Creek traders

Richard Benison (French for "prayer," Hebrew *tefilla*), Augusta

Mark Benz (Ashkenazi)

Abraham Bosomworth, Indian agent

Thomas Bosomworth, Indian agent

Benedict and Henry Bourquin (Berber form of Jacob)[56]

Leonard Bowdle (Bodell), Frenchman

Elizabeth Bowling (Hebrew *balin*, "bathkeeper")

Isaac Brabant (town in Flanders), silk

Joseph Burges (Borges),[57] trader originally from Darien, p. 498

Shem (Jewish nickname for Samuel) Butler (Boutellier), South Carolina, many Butlers[58]

Henry Calwell (Caldwell),[59] from Darien

John Calwell (Caldwell), trader and Cherokee Indian agent

Anthony and James Camus, silk

Daniel Clark[60] (Hebrew *sofer*), Augusta trader, originally from Darien

John Coffee (Cohen)

Thomas Collins,[61] Melungeon name

Richard Cooper,[62] Ogeechee River

Jeremiah Courtong (Courtonne), Indian trader

Richard Cox, merchant, Nevis

Thomas Cross (Cruz), bricklayer

George and Philip Delegal (Delegado?)[63]

Daniel Demetres (Demetrius, owner of boat in Frederica)

Peter Destemple ("of the Temple")

Elizabeth de St. Julian, widow

John Deveaux (Devaux, from Chauny, France[64]; Defoe)

William Dews (Dues, "from Douai" in Flanders), Cherokee trader

David Dicks[65] ("stout," Scottish)

Daniel Dourouzeaux (De Rousseaux)[66]

George Dresler ("lathe turner")[67]

Maurice Dullea (Dooly, "black" in Irish)

William Elliott (Arabic)

Thomas Ellis (Arabic)

Mr. Eycott, Indian trader

Anthony Fahie (Arabic), merchant, St. Kitts

Abraham Fezer ("from Fez" in Morocco)[68]

John David Fisher[69]

George Fowle (Vogel, Raphael),[70] Germany

David Fox (Fuchs, adaptation of Phoebus)[71]

William Francis ("from France"), trader, silversmith

Jacob Franks[72]

James Fraser,[73] Augusta trader

Abraham and John Gabel (Gable)[74]

James Galache (Galas)[75]

George Galphin (Galprin), Augusta trader

Samuel Gandy (Candy, Candia,[76] Canada, Kennedy), trader

John Germany, Augusta trader

Isaac Gibbs[77] (from Gabriel)

Thomas Goldsmith

John Goldwire, ferryman

Cuthbert and John Gordon[78] (corruption of Cohen)

Simon Guerin

Matthias Gugul (Kugel)

Peter Guirard

Henry Hamilton[79]

John Hamm, St. Kitts

William Harris[80]

Richard Hazard (Arabic)

Jacob and Jeremiah Helvinstine (Elphenstine, Elphinstone,[81] "ivory dealer")

Alexander Heron

Thomas Hird (Hurd, Heard), Scottish

John Michael Hirsh[82]

Richard I'on

Captain Isaacks[83]

Abraham Jeanneret

James Jeansack

Lewis Johnson,[84] merchant, St. Kitts

John Kays[85]

Donald, Hugh and William Kennedy (Canada, Candia), Darien

Isaac Labon (Lebon, Lebo, Laybon),[86] Frenchman

Samuel Leon (de Leon)[87]

Isaac Lines (Lions)[88]

Alexander Low,[89] merchant, St. Kitts

Samuel Marcer, board of governors

Daniel Martyn,[90] kinsman of trustees' secretary

John McBean,[91] from Darien

Lachlan McGillivray, Creek Indian trader

William Mears[92] (Meïr)

Lowis Michel (Michael), since 1736

Abram Minis (Ashkenazi)[93]

David Montaigut

Peter Morrel[94]

Lewis Motteair, or Muttear

Mr. Millim (Millam), Indian trader

James and Samuel New (Neu),[95] merchant, Nevis

George and Robert Noble,[96] Maryland

Joseph Ottolenghe, silk

Anthony Pages (Pagès),[97] Frenchman

James Papot ("big Pope")

James Paris, Augusta trader

Francis Lewis Parry[98]

Joseph Pavey ("from Pavia" in Northern Italy)[99]

Capt. Joseph Phillips (from Phoebus, Febos, Forbes), merchant

John Place, pilot, and Seth Place[100]

Jacob Plessy

John Rae (Rey, Reis)[101]

Joseph Reymond, South Carolina

Matthew Roche (Rocca)[102]

Jean Sack (Sachs, Sax),[103] Frenchman

Oliver Shaw[104] (Persian for "king")

Benjamin Sheftall[105] (Ashkenazi)

John Sherause (Sherouse, Cherouse)

John Sherif (Arabic), tanner

Peter Sliterman (Sluijterman), Dutchman

James Stewartt (Stuart),[106] Indian agent

Jeremiah Swan,[107] North Carolina

Edmund Tannatt (Tennant), merchant, St. Kitts, became Indian trader

Samuel Tomes[108]

Peter Tondee (Tonti)

David Truan (Trujan)

Adriaan Van Beverhoudt ("from Beverhoud" in Belgium) and three sons, from St. Croix, Virgin Islands, Dutch

Edward, Moses, Nathaniel and Pamenus Way[109]

Thomas Wiggin (Ouizgan, Wizgan,[110] Berber for "black"), relative of Indian trader Eleazar Wiggans, who was openly Jewish

William Wise (Wiseman, Berber Izman, German Weise, Weiser, Weisner),[111] estate, 1741, p. 11

The presence of so many of these surnames in Stern's genealogies is striking to say the least. Stern devotes whole pages to the Frankses, Harrises, Clarks, Coopers and others in the list. It is possible to trace a strong Scottish Jewish or crypto–Jewish presence with names such as Gordon, Kennedy, Stewart and Fraser. Georgia was apparently the prime meeting place for Scottish and Iberian Jews.

Several of these newcomers arrived from Caribbean islands. On British-governed Nevis, one-fourth of the inhabitants were Jewish. Sephardic Jews named Senior, Rezio, Israel, Mendez, Lobatto, Arrobas and de Mesquita had been leaders in the development of the sugar industry on that island. As Jewish historian Mordechai Arbell notes, however, the "decline of the Nevis Jewish population began in the second half of the 18th century. The sugar trade declined, and Nevis Jews had to look for new prospects."[112]

Portuguese and Dutch Jews constantly had to relocate as islands changed hands. Moreover, Jewish commercial competition was so greatly feared that when British merchants first entered a new field they often imposed tariffs on the Jewish traders that forced them to close their doors.[113] Similar reasons probably motivated groups from St. Kitts, which was British, and St. Croix, which the Danes had recently purchased from the French, retaining and encouraging the former Dutch settlement. These were international merchants whose only common denominator seems to be Jewish roots or connections. Anthony Fahie, John Hamm, Lewis Johnson, Alexander Low and Edmund Tannatt (Tennant) arrived as a single party from St. Kitts. Likewise, the four "Frenchmen," Isaac Labon, Leonard Bowdle, Anthony Pages and Anthony Lesage took passage from London together, evidently at the urging of a fellow Jew already established in the vicinity.

Many of the land grantees during these years simply crossed the river from the Purrysburgh Colony in South Carolina. Some of the names found both in Purrysburgh and Georgia are Bourquin/Bourguin, Coste (Costa), Roche, Faure, Franck, Galache, Jeanneret, Jindra (Abraham, a trader, perhaps Guindre), Michel, Nichols/Nicholas, Perry, Shepard and Tanner. The names and gravestone treatments in the Purrysburgh Cemetery testify to a blending of Scottish and Continental Jews in the settlement.

Augusta: Settled or Unsettled?

The frontier town of Augusta had a different character from the rest of Georgia. It actually preceded the foundation of Savannah by several decades, having taken shape as Savannah Town on the north side of the river where Ft. Moore was built in 1715. In 1720, as we have noted, Chickasaws (Halfbreeds) living in northern Mississippi were invited by the South Carolina Assembly to occupy the area. They stayed until after the Revolutionary War.

The trade monopoly called the "Company of Seven Persons at Augusta" ran the outpost as a private fiefdom.[114] As trade history scholar Kathryn Holland Braund has written, this monopoly underwent numerous name changes as new partners came on board but remained basically the same inner sanctum of Scotsmen (we would say crypto–Jewish Scotsmen). Its best known phase was probably Brown, Rae & Company.[115] In later years, it produced what became the behemoth Pensacola-based trading house of Panton, Leslie & Co., reorganized as John Forbes & Co. All these Scottish (presumably Jewish) families were heavily intermarried across generations.

Among the Augusta Indian traders known from Hicks's work are Isaac Barksdale, Edward, John and Timothy Barnard,[116] Joseph Burges, John Caldwell, Daniel Clark, William, Joseph and Richard Cooper, Jeremiah Courtonne, William Dues, Josiah Francis, James Frazer, George Galphin (Galprin), Robert Gandy, James Germany, John Guerard, Lachlan McGillivray, Richard Parris, John Rae, Jordan Roche, William Tennent, John Stuart and Eleazar Wiggan. As is apparent, many of these are Sephardic surnames. An example of Scottish-Portuguese Jewish alliance occurs in the career of George Galphin (1700–1780). Probably originally Galprin, an Ashkenazi name, Galphin was born in County Armagh, Ireland, left a wife and immigrated to Georgia, where he married the illegitimate quadroon daughter of Moses Nunes in Savannah. With various partners, he formed the Augusta trading company Galphin, Holmes & Co.[117]

Another trader who was apparently crypto–Jewish was Francis Harris.[118] He arrived in Savannah shortly after its foundation, about 1740, becoming the manager of the trustees' store until the trustees discontinued the business. In the mid-forties he formed a trading firm in partnership with James Habersham, a close friend. Harris and Habersham is generally seen as the first mercantile and shipping firm in Georgia, although the Jew Abraham Minis maintained a store in Savannah and owned one or more ships. Such operations were frowned upon by the trustees, at least in theory.

Indian traders active in Georgia also include John and Daniel Ross, Christian Russel ("a Silician," i.e. Silesian, Ashkenazi), Nicolas White ("a native of Mersailles [sic], but resident in this nation [Creek Confederacy] 30 years"), Abraham M. Mordecai ("a Jew of bad character" according to Indian agent Benjamin Hawkins, but "an intelligent Jew" according to Albert James Pickett, author of *The History of Alabama*[119]), Mrs. Durant (a female trader), Obediah Low, Cornelius Dougherty (a Jacobite, said to be the first trader, or one of the first, among the Cherokee), John Van (Vann, later an important Cherokee mixed blood family), James Lessle (Leslie), James Lewis, Aron Harad (Harrod), Zachariah Cox (a land developer), Richard Sparks (a captain at Tellico Blockhouse in Cherokee upcountry; Cox is considered a Melungeon name), Davis (a blacksmith), John Marino[120] ("a Spaniard"), John Beamor (a Huguenot, whose original Sephardic name was probably Benamour, and whose Cherokee son was known as a "mustee," or mixed breed),[121] Thomas Nairne (Arabic), James McQueen (corruption of MacKuen, "son of Cohen"), John McKee, Alexander Long, Robert Bunning (Bondurant), Greenwood Leflore (Lefleur, Flores[122]), Benjamin Perryman (mixed blood), Hardy Perry (introduced cattle among the Choctaw), William Dixon Moniac (originally Jacob Monaque, "from Munich," Germany) and John Sheppard (also considered a Melungeon name).

To defend the southern frontier against the Spanish, Oglethorpe planted a military colony of Highlanders at the mouth of the Altamaha River. Called New Inverness, the settlement was later renamed Darien after a failed Scottish colony in Panama.[123] The Scotsmen who became pioneers there reflect the clans we have suggested as having Jewish roots on the basis of DNA analysis and other factors. Among these apparently crypto–Jewish family names are Bain (Bean, McBean), Caldwell, Campbell, Forbes, Fraser, Mackay, Morrison, Sinclair and Stewart (see Appendix K, Table 4). We have noted several times how the British relied on Jews and crypto–Jews' deeply embedded hatred of the Spanish. Many of the Darien settlers and Augusta traders were from Aberdeen, where refugee Spanish Jews and Muslims were, as we have argued, welcomed by the largely crypto–Jewish city leaders. The Scottish Jews were evidently still fighting these old battles, to judge from the rallying cry of Darien they chose for their new town.

In the Interim Period between rule by the trustees and a royal governor, land speculation went wild. Large grants were made to new arrivals. A group of Germans led by John G. W. DeBrahm lost no time in slipping through the gap. They settled at Bethany (a place-name made famous in the Holy Land during the Crusades), not far from the Salzburgers. In 1768, a group of Irish Protestants founded Queensborough on the Ogeechee River. The settlement was co-sponsored by traders George Galphin, John Rae and Lachlan McGillivray. As such, it was not so much Irish as Scottish (and crypto–Jewish)—although this characterization of its history is probably unwelcome news to the Center for Irish Studies at Georgia Southern University, which is excavating the site. Not far behind them came a colony of Quakers who occupied a forty-thousand acre grant north of Augusta they named Wrightsboro in honor of governor James Wright.

Wrightsboro's Quakers

Many of the settlers at Wrightsboro evidently adopted Quakerism as a cover for Judaism. Perusal of the list in Appendix K, Table 5, reveals surnames, among others, like Cooper, Hart, Blevins and Guest which we have encountered elsewhere. Given names are also telling. Although we find, as may be expected, a preponderance of Hebrew names, many are not Biblical: Aden, Asahal, Benejah, Menoah, Rezin and Zimri, for instance. Others are Greek and hark back to the centuries preceding the common era and continuing through the Roman Empire when most Jews were Greek in speech and cultural traditions: Archelaus, Axia, Cassandra, Chloe, Ferreby (from Pharabus, Phoebus), Lydia, Phillipini, Phineas, Phoebe, Rhoda, Sibilla and Theodate. Avarilla, Priscilla, Latia and a few others are Latin or Roman.

We can gain some insight into the business relationships, and evident crypto–Jewish identities, of these Quakers by looking at the will of Israel Robinson, or Robertson, or Roberson, or Robeson ("son of Rueben"), made in Wrightsboro in 1773.[124] After distributing numerous horses and cattle among family members, Robeson gives one hundred acres lying on the head of Beaverdam "in South Carolina [more likely North Carolina][125] where it is thought there is a Iron Mine" to son and executor David Robeson, Sr. The will was witnessed, and the probate witnessed as well, by Benjamin Cooper, Isaac Cooper and Mary Brown. Isaac Cooper was born in the Norfolk area, was related to our William Cooper, the guide and scout for Daniel Boone, migrated through Granville and Bute counties, North Carolina, and received a land grant at Wrightsboro in 1774. The Roberson family produced James Robertson, a leader in Watauga in East Tennessee and founder of Nashville and the Cumberland Settlement in Middle Tennessee. Scottish in origin (and we would suggest Sephardic Jewish: the line cannot be traced farther back in Scotland than the sixteenth century), the family lent their name to Robeson County, North Carolina. Robersons intermarried with persons of surname Bean, Cox, Gower (Goar, Hebrew), Marks (Marx),[126] Nichols, Sevier (Xavier,[127] Sephardic, as in John Sevier, first governor of Tennessee), Shelton and Spann (Spain), as well as other Robersons. Many of these names are considered Melungeon. Both Robersons and Coopers were involved in land speculation and mining—the latter often a Jewish activity, as we saw with Joachim Ganz (Chapter 1). David Cooper (1725–1792) was a mineral surveyor.

E Pluribus Unum

Because of its exposed location on the southern frontier, its ambiguous charter and lack of control by the authorities, the colony of Georgia had points of entry that were easily breached and borders that leaked like a sieve. Its situation allowed all manner of immigrants to cross its boundaries or be offloaded in Savannah, Darien, the Sea Islands or Frederica.

Some of its first settlers actually came from the West — the halfbreeds who settled outside Augusta. Many of these immigrant groups stayed only long enough to bring over others like themselves and consolidate their numbers before heading for greener pastures. Not a few of the recruits for the Melungeon experiment that arose in Daniel Boone's Kentucky and Tennessee after 1763 once lived in or passed through Georgia. The character of the colony changed from decade to decade. Land policy was not fixed until after the Revolutionary War. Georgia never managed to settle the Creek Indian claims nor define its boundaries precisely until the early nineteenth century. It long remained the least populous colony of the original thirteen. With its thin population it nearly fell to the British during the Revolution. Throughout all these developments the ties that bound people together appear to have been Jewish, anti–Catholic and anti–Spanish. Georgia thus became the only colony where it was possible, like Mordecai Sheftall the Savannah merchant and patriot, to be a Jewish American and not just an American Jew.

CHAPTER TEN

Beacon of Freemasonry: Elias Ashmole, John Skene and Early American Lodges

One of the social mechanisms through which Jews and Muslims learned about their opportunities in the New World was Freemasonry. By way of concluding this work, and drawing together the various strands of Jewish and Muslim biography in the American colonies, let us examine the origins and spread of Freemasonry along with the story of its coming to the Colonies. Taking a long view, Freemasonry evolved out of the experiences of the Knights Templar as they became acquainted, allied and befriended with Jews and Muslims over the course of the Crusades (1100 to 1360 C.E.). Although seen often today as bitter enemies, Jews, Muslims and Christians frequently intermingled in the Holy Land in the pre-modern period. Marriages and conversions to one another's faiths were not uncommon occurrences. In his book *The Magus of Freemasonry*, Tobias Churton offhandedly remarks that in 1200 the Templar Knight Ormus LeGuidon returned home from the Crusades to Lichfield, England, accompanied by a group of *paynim* (pagans or Saracens/Muslims). The foreigners stayed and put down roots. Three and a half centuries later a female descendant of the knight, Ann Bowyer, would wed Simon Ashmole in the same town. Their son was Elias Ashmole (1617–1692), an early English Freemason and founder of the Ashmolean Museum in Oxford.[1]

Elias Ashmole (Wikimedia Commons).

Ashmole has not only an unusual name but an extraordinary history. In our view his surname was most likely originally Ishmael.[2] He sprang from a Muslim or Jewish ancestor who arrived in England either with the group accompanying the Templar knight Ormus Le Guidon or in a later influx of Jews and Moors that began arriving in England disguised as Christians shortly after the onset of the Spanish Inquisition. Ismaili Muslims follow Shiia beliefs. Throughout the course of Islamic civilization they have been prominent in Syria, Persia, India, and especially Egypt during the Fatimid Dynasty — a timeframe and locale overlapping with the first Crusades. Since the earliest Ashmole of which there is any record in England dates only to Elias' grandfather Thomas, it is most likely that the family arrived in England around the mid–1500s. We have seen this clue before: A genealogical line appears out of the blue in a new country. Thomas Ashmole was mayor and senior bailiff of Lichfield, England. He had two sons, Thomas, Jr., and Simon (born 1589), the latter bearing a Hebrew given name. He seems to have suffered from manic-depression, for he failed in a string of occupations, including saddler and soldier. Nonetheless, he married a woman of prestigious ancestry, Ann Bowyer, the descendant of the Templar knight Ormus LeGuidon. They had but one child, a son. Elias became not only a leading Freemason but noted Cabalist and astronomer. As a crypto–Jew, he vigorously promoted the immigration of like-minded souls to North America.

Allegedly, Elias' Hebrew given name was assigned to him on a spontaneous impulse by his godfather, Thomas Ottey. But this explanation seems designed to serve as a safe cover for familial Jewish affiliation. Elias/Elijah is one of the most revered names in Judaism — the name of the prophet called upon to attend in spirit every male Jewish newborn's birth and every Jewish family's annual Passover Seder. We might further note that Mr. Ottey bears an Arabic surname, *attiya*, meaning "gift."[3] Shem Tov Attia (1530–1601) was a famous rabbi and Cabalist, a contemporary of Elias Ashmole's grandfather.

The men in the Ashmole family were leather workers, a largely Moorish/Sephardi craft, making saddles and shoes. At age 15 Elias was apprenticed in the same trade,[4] but not for long. As it happened, Elias' mother had a sister, Bridget, who married James Pagit/Paget, the baron of the exchequer in London, that is, royal accountant, a post often filled by Jews. Through the Pagits, Elias was invited to live in London. He enrolled in the study of law, becoming admitted as a barrister in London in 1638. At age 21, he married his cousin, Eleanor Mainwaring, whose family had come to England with the Norman Conquest. The surname meant "one from Varenne/Warenne Manor," in other words, it implied that the family was serving the owner of Warren Manor. By 1644, at the age of 27, Elias was named tax collector for Staffordshire.

Two years later, in 1646, Elias Ashmole was initiated into the Freemasons — at that time a completely secret organization whose origins trace back to the Templars and which included many Sephardic Jews. Elias entered the secret lodge with his cousin Col. Henry Mainwaring. The members were listed as Richard Penket/Pinket, James Collier, Richard Sankey, Henry Littler, John Ellam, Richard Ellam and Hugh Brewer. At least three of these names — Penket (Pinquet, from Pincas/Pinhas, a Biblical name),[5] Sankey (from Spanish Sanco)[6] and Ellam (El-lahm, Elahmi, a reference to Bethlehem)[7] — are of French/Sephardi/Moorish origin. Edward Sankey wrote the origins of their organization as follows in the "The Old Charges":

> Good brethren & ffellows, our purpose is to tell you, how and in what manner this Craft of Masonrie was begun; and afterwards founded by worthy Kings and Princes; & many other worshipful men; and also to ye that are heare; wee will declare to [whom] the Charge yt doth

belonge to every true Mason to keep for good sooth if you take heede thereunto it is well wor-thie to bee kept; or a worthie Craft and curious science, ffor there bee seaven liberall sciences;

Before Noes flood was a man called Lameth [Hebrew letter] as it is written in ye 4 chapt of Genesis, and this Lameth had 2 wives; ye one was called Adar; ye other Sella; and by Adar hee begot 2 sonnes. The one was called Jabell ye other Juball; And by ye other wife hee had a sonne & a Daughter; and these foure children found ye beginninge of all Crafts in ye world; This Jabell was ye elder sonne; and found ye Craft of Geometry;

And these children did knowe that God would take vengeance for sinne eather by fire or water; Wherefore ye writ ye Sciences wch weare found in 2 pillars of stone; yt ye might be found after the flood; The one stone was called Marble that cannot burne wth fire: The other was called Lether that cannot drowne with water; Our intent is to tell you truly how & in what manner these stones weare found; where these Crafts were written in Greek; Hermenes that was sonne to Cus, & Cus was sonne to Shem [Hebrew letter] wch was ye sonne of Shem wch was ye sonne of Noath: The same Hermenes was afterwards Hermes; the ffather of wise men, and hee found out ye 2 pillars of stone where ye Sciences weare written, & taught him forth.

When Abraham and Sara his wife went into Eygpt; there weare taught the seaven sciences unto ye Egyptians; And hee had a worthy Schollar called Euchlid and hee Learned right well and was Maister of all ye 7 Sciences; And there was a King of an other Region yt men called Hyram and hee loved well Kinge Solomon; and gave him timber for his worke; And hee had a sonne that was named Aynon & he was Mr of Geometry; and hee was chiefe Mr of all his Masons; and Mr of all his graved works; and of all other Masons that belonged to ye Temple; & this Witnesseth the Bible in Libro 2 Solo capite 5.

And soe it befell that a curious workman; who was named Numus Graecus & had beene at ye makeinge of Solomons Temple; and came into ffrance; and there taught ye Craft of Mason-rie; to ye man of ffrance that was named Charles Martill [Charles Martel]; And all this while England was voyde both of any charge or Masonrie; until ye time of St. Albans; And in his time ye King of England that was a Pagan; and hee walled ye Towne sch is now called St. Albans;

Until ye time of King Athelstone; yt was a worthy King of England; and hee brought ye Land into rest and peace againe; and hee builded many great workes & Castles & Abbies; and many other Buildings; and hee loved masons well; and hee had a sonne yt was named Hadrian:

And hee held himself assembly at Yorke and there hee made Masons, and gave ym Charges and taught them Mannrs of Masons; and commanded that rule to bee holden ever after: And to them took ye Charter & Commission to keepe; And from time to time Masonrie until this day hath beene kept in yt forme & order, as well as might gov'ne ye same; And furthermore at dyvrs assemblies hath beene put to and added certaine Charges; more by ye best advices; of Mastrs and fellows; Heare followeth the worthie and godly oath of Masons; Every man that is a Masonn take Heede right well to this charge; if you finde yo'self guilty of any of these; yt you amend you; againe especially you yt are to bee charged take good heed that you may keepe this Charge; for it is a great peril for a man to foresweare himselfe on a book[.][8]

This garbled tale is essentially a Sephardic Jewish-mediated synthesis of Gnostic-Her-metic-Cabalistic esoteric traditions dating to Ptolemaic Egypt (ca. 300 BCE).[9] Allied to these were rituals connected to Greek priests serving Dionysus/Bacchus. The name Bacchus will recur among Elias Ashmole's associates.

Roots of Freemasonry's Esoteric Traditions

Romanian scholar Felicia Waldman links European esotericism of the type practiced by Ashmole to the Judaic-Cabalistic notion of "As above, so below," meaning that the earthly material world is an imperfect reflection of divine, spiritual perfection. The doctrine obviously has Platonic and neo–Platonic origins as well. Judaism — while not originating these ideas — acted as a fusion for them from the Greco–Roman world to Western Europe from 500 CE onward. Waldman notes that the rise and spread of Islam served the same function. She writes, "There seems to be evidence for at least two different kinds of Hermetic worship: one group centered in Egypt, possibly around Hermopolis, which has some very traditional Egyptian beliefs ... and another type of group similar to Gnostic or ascetic Jews, engaging in religiously-significant meals and other practices in communities." The term Hermeticism is believed to originate with a historical figure, sometimes called Hermes Trismegistus, or Thrice-Greatest, who lived prior to the rise of Greek civilization ca. 500 BCE. Among Muslims he is named Idris and is mentioned in the Quran. Among Jews his name is Enoch. Hermes/Idris/Enoch was deemed the originator of all sacred texts and mathematical equations, the arts and the sciences, including writing, arithmetic, geometry, astronomy, medicine and alchemy. At an even earlier date he was linked to the Egyptian god Thoth, the inventor of writing and all cunning arts, whose symbol was the moon.[10]

Several historians agree that Charles Martel of France (688–741) played a key role in introducing Hermetic-Cabalistic traditions to Western Europe. Martel was the illegitimate son of Pepin, mayor of the palace of Frankish Austrasia under the declining Merovingian dynasty. Upon his death in 714 C.E., a power struggle ensued in which Charles Martel ultimately triumphed to seize control of the Frankish empire. In 732 at Poitiers, he defeated an Arab force from Spain, a victory that turned back the tide of Islam in Europe and allowed the Pepinid mayors of the palace to pursue the reconquest of southern France. He was known as Martel ("the Hammer") for his insistence in beating back the foe in battle. What is usually ignored in history books is that Charles Martel's great-grandmother was a noblewoman from Aquitaine in the far south of present-day France named Itta, a Jewish name.[11] We do not know her origins in any detail, but her birth land at the time was held by the Visigoths, Barbarian invaders of the Roman Empire who had absorbed many Jews, settled in the southwest of France and won most of Spain by 550 C.E. Medievalists have generally glossed over her name as a form of Ida, making it sound Germanic to fit the mold of the

Charlemagne (Print Collection, Miriam and Ira D. Wallach Division of Art, Prints and Photographs, The New York Public Library, Astor, Lenox and Tilden Foundations).

Franks. But in actuality it is derived from Yehudit or Judith, the archetypal Hebrew feminine name. Charles Martel's grandfather Ansegisèle, son of Arnulf of Herstal, married Itta's daughter by Pepin the Older (585–639), Begga (Rebecca), another name strongly indicative of Jewish roots. Accordingly Charles Martel's father Pepin II of Herstel (653–714) was born of a woman who was Sephardic Jewish, as was her mother. Charles Martel was the son of a Jewish father.

The Frankish kings and their Pepinid successors often married or had for concubines women evidently of Jewish backgrounds. Charlemagne, Charles Martel's grandson, took as his last concubine a woman known variously as Adeline, Adelaide or Adela. She is believed to be the *Ur* mother of all lines of European royalty, the direct female ancestor, for instance, of Marie Antoinette.[12] Here again history has bowlderized the original name in the interests of painting a pleasing picture of royal genealogies. In all likelihood, her name was Adel, from Hebrew Adinah. Einhard and the court chroniclers who followed him in the reign of Charlemagne's son Louis the Pious pretended to derive the name from the Germanic word Adel ("noble") and even confabulated it to Adelheid ("nobility"). That this etymology is false is shown by the popularity among later Jews, both Sephardic and Ashkenazic, of Adel in its many forms of Ada, Edna, Eida, Ethel, Adela, Dela and Etalka.[13] When Sephardic Jews began to intermarry with Europe's aristocratic families in the eighteenth century, the choice of Adelaide as a royal name re-emerged as an avataristic choice. Princess Adelaide of Saxe-Meiningen (1792–1849), for instance, became the queen consort of English king William IV and thereby Queen Victoria's aunt. The Pepinid and Carolingian dynasties' Jewish strain may account for why they self-consciously styled themselves a sacred royal line, the first in Europe. Charles Martel was proclaimed a new Joshua for his conquests in the south of France, and the sovereigns of this new Israel were declared a new Moses, a new David and a new Solomon. Charlemagne adopted the nickname David in his circle of intimates. The emperor's portrait was used for that of the Biblical king and Psalmist by manuscript illuminators and other artists. As medieval scholar Alessandro Barbero observes, "Pepin brought into use the ritual recorded in the Old Testament, in which it is told that Saul took control of the kingdom by being anointed by the prophet Samuel. After him, David and Solomon took the throne by being anointed."[14] The institutions of both the Cabala and priest-king seem to have entered France through the influence of foreign queens from the Jewish south of the country.

Elias Ashmole's Social World

Having described Ashmole's origins and membership in Freemasonry, let us now turn to a consideration of his social milieu. We will argue that (1) his contacts and friendships were overwhelmingly Jewish and Muslim, (2) that Freemasonry, alchemy, astrology and astronomy were dominated by persons of Jewish and Muslim ancestry and (3) that subsequently these same patterns were carried over to England's colonies in North America.

Dudley Wright's 2005 biography of Ashmole lists a rather remarkable set of social contacts for a man of common birth who worked as a tax collector.[15] For example, in 1662 Ashmole dined with Hamet (i.e., Mohammet), the ambassador of Morocco. He was close friends with William Lilly (Sassoon, Lilie)[16] and Jonas Moore, both noted mathematicians and astrologers, diarist Samuel Pepys (Pepe, Pepi),[17] alchemist Dr. Robert Fludd (Flood),[18] Rosicrucian and hermeticist William Backhouse (Bacchus), Dr. Richard Napier (French

Huguenot), Dutch botanist John Tradescant, Sir William Glasscock, and Sir Edward Bysshe (Bises, Beziz),[19] among others.

Biographer Tobias Churton provides a more comprehensive list and description of Ashmole's friends. They included the king's master mason Nicholas Stone and royal architect Inigo (Basque for Ignatius) Jones, physician Robert Childe, Sephardic Rabbi Solomon Frank (from whom Elias learned Hebrew), Izaak Walton, iron worker and author of *The Compleat Angler: The Contemplative Man's Recreation* (1676), Anthony Dyott, first president of the British Royal Society, Robert Moray of Scotland, Scottish scientist Samuel Hartlib (Hart, an emblem of the tribe of Benjamin), Sir Edward Bagot (Moroccan Bagoh, a type of grape),[20] Dr. Thomas and Judith Dod (David), Zachary Turnepenny, architect Sir Christopher Wren, painters Charles and Nathaniel Pollard, and John Dee's son, Arthur Dee, who was physician to the "emperor" (czar) of Russia.

In addition to these persons, Ashmole's own diary describes some additional connections. He notes that on May 14, 1645, he "christened Mr. Fox's son at Oxford," on another date, he "christened Mr. Buttler, the goldsmith's, son William," on another date, he "christened Captain Wharton's daughter, Anne, and in late May of one year, "I christened Mr. Timothy Eman's [Arabic *imam*] son of Windsor." The following year on March 17, "I christened Secundus, son to Mr. Lacy, the Comedian." What are we to make of Elias' christening activities? Ashmole was not an ordained minister and, in fact, did not even attend church. Our assumption is that he was essentially acting as a rabbi, perhaps even circumcising the boy children and overseeing Judaic rituals appropriate for newborns. This hypothesis is strengthened when we read in Ashmole's diary that his cousin is named Moyse (Moses), surely a remarkable appellation (as is Elias) in a country with ostensibly no openly practicing Jews at the time.

Ashmole had extensive international contacts suggestive of a linkage with crypto–Jewish/Muslim communities. He was friends not only with the Moroccan ambassador, but also the Spanish governor of Florida, Count Magalotti, and others in service to the prince of Tuscany, Monsieur Lionberg, who was the Swedish envoy to Britain, Count de Monroux, who was the envoy from the duke of Savoy, and additionally the diplomatic agent of Venice (Italy), the duke of Saxony (Germany), the king of Denmark, Monseur Swerene, the envoy of the prince of Brandenburg (Germany), Monsieur La Mere, the envoy of Prince William of Orange, Monsieur Spanheim (a name meaning "from Spain"), the envoy from the prince elector of the Palatinate (Germany), and the envoy of the king of Spain. We believe that what all these contacts have in common — and which could explain their interest in communicating with a British tax collector who spoke Hebrew — is that they represented communities where Sephardic Jews and Muslim Moors had fled after the institution in 1480 of the Catholic Inquisition in Spain. One must remember also that the final expulsion of all Muslims in the Iberian Peninsula was decreed and carried out in 1609–1614, resulting in the exodus of 300,000 people forced to leave their homes.[21] Elias Ashmole himself in 1661 was awarded the governorship of Surinam, a British colony in the West Indies filled with crypto–Jews and Moors.

In Ashmole's later years, we find deeper relationships formed by him with obviously and overtly Jewish and Muslim individuals. In 1682, he not only paid a visit to Mohamet, the Moroccan ambassador, he also had "Alcade, Abdelloe and Bomonzore [of Morocco] to my house, and [they] dined with me" on several occasions. As Muslims, we would anticipate that these gentlemen were being served *halal* foods or ritual dishes by their host.

Later that same year, a Frenchman, Job Ludolph, and his son dined with Elias. And in October of 1682 he mentions giving a book and "gold buckles" to a Mr. Heysig (Sephardic surname, Isaac).[22] Other visitors included "Polander, Johann Chodowiesky,"[23] "Sir Thomas Duppa," "Mr. Haak" (Hayak),[24] "Mr. Negos," "Mr. LaBadie," "Monsieur Bessor," John Faulconer of Scotland and Joshua Barnes — all of whom bear Jewish or Muslim names.

Imagery and Portraits

Let us take a look now at some of the images associated with Hermeticism, the Cabala and Freemasonry during the 1600s in Ashmole's lifetime during the founding of England's colonies in North America. The author of the Hermetic text *Microcosmus Hypochondriacus*, Malachias Geiger, has both a Jewish given and surname.[25] An engraving from this very influential book features the Tetragrammaton in the heavens, the tree of life (arbor vita), a phoenix rising from the fire, a peacock, astrological signs, Solomon's seal, a right triangle and additional Hebrew writing in the lower right corner. The theme *in uno omnia* "all in one" was used by Ashmole as his own credo. An engraving by Achille Bocchi from 1574 features Mercury/Hermes holding a lighted menorah. The *Fasciculus Chemicus* was translated and published by Elias Ashmole in 1650. It features two columns representing the arts and sciences, Jachin and Boas in Freemason lore, as well as solar, lunar and tree of life images. The *Speculum Sophicum Rhodostauroticum* (Rosicrucian Philosopher's Mirror) from numerous editions in several countries around 1618 shows the Tetragrammaton, complete with vowels, indicating a non–Hebrew audience, at the top center. Additional Hebrew lettering, this time without vowels for a Hebrew-fluent audience, appears on the shields of the heralds in the tower. Six-pointed stars are in each top corner. Many esoteric texts copied the Sefer Yetzirah, or Book of Creation, a primer on the Cabalah published in Hebrew by Sephardic Jews in exile in Italy, the Netherlands and Greece.

The landmark book by Meric Casaubon edited by John Dee, *A True and Faithful Relation of What Passed for Many Years Between Dr. John Dee ... and Some Spirits* was published in London in 1659 . It depicted Mohammed, Apollonius of Tyana, Edward Kelly, Roger Bacon, Paracelsus and John Dee as learned men contributing to the knowledge embraced by Freemasonry. Many of the books sampled here were printed in Germany in cities known to have large Sephardic populations. Note the use of Judaic symbolism: the Tree of Life, Star of David, and Lion Rampant.

The English philosopher and statesman Francis Bacon (1561–1626), a contemporary of William Shakespeare, served as a major conduit of Sephardic Jewish intellectualism from the south of France into the British Isles and the American Colonies. It is possible that he came of British Jewish ancestry, as the name Bacon was not used in England before the fourteenth century, and then apparently as a racial epithet for Jews or Muslims, somewhat as Maranno in the sense of "pig" in Iberia. His father, Sir Nicholas Bacon, was lord keeper of the Great Seal of England. As a young man, he lived in Paris with Sir Amias Paulet, the English ambassador. He then served a diplomatic apprenticeship at the court of Navarre, a Protestant kingdom on the Spanish border then thronged with Cathars and Jewish Cabbalists. Returning to England, he brought word of the impending invasion by Spanish king Phillip II and formed a secret society of Freemasons "designed to keep intelligence secrets from being penetrated by Spanish spies."[26] Freemasonry was thus nakedly linked with a political, anti–Spanish agenda. By 1586, Bacon was publishing esoteric books such Whitney's *Choice of Emblems* and had created, and presided over, the Order of the Knights of the Hel-

יְהוָֹה

Et vidit Deus lucem   *quod esset bona*

Mundus Intellectualis

SYLVA SYLVARVM
or
A NATVRALL HISTORY
In ten Centuries.
Written by the right Honble Francis
L^o: Verulam Viscount St Alban.
Published after y^e Autho^rs Death
by W: RAWLEY D^r of Divi-
nity. &c

Tho: Cecill sculp:

LONDON
Printed for W: Lee and are to be sould at
the Great Turks head next to the Mytre
Taurne in Fleetstreet.

Anne   1651

Francis Bacon's *Sylva Sylvarum*, a natural history compendium from 1656 (Wikimedia Commons).

met, reviving the style of learning he imbibed in the South of France. This secret society spawned the Rosi Crosse Society, a reorganization of the Knights Templar, "suggesting that Bacon had met refugee Templars in Navarre," with a new rite of Freemasonic brotherhood.[27] His *Novum Organum* reformed logic and popularized what we now know as the scientific method. On Bacon's sixtieth birthday in 1621, the poet Ben Johnson delivered a Masonic ode composed in his honor. His *New Atlantis* about a Utopia in the New World ruled by Rosicrucians was widely read. Nicholas Hagger detects its influence in the plans of the promoter Bartholomew Gosnold and others. Another author wrote a book with the blatant title *Freemasonry Came to America with Captain John Smith in 1607*. The tangled threads extend to Nathaniel Bacon, Puritans ("actually Rosicrucian"), Skene, Jonathon Belcher, an American who became a Freemason during a visit to England in 1704, Franklin and Jefferson and were apparently grafted together with the Stuarts and Jacobeans.[28]

Jews, Muslims and Freemasonry

In the present day, Freemasonry attracts adepts from all countries and religious backgrounds; its scope is international (although it is banned in many Muslim countries because of its Jewish orientation). However, in the 1400s through 1600s, that is, in its formative period, its members were largely drawn from non–Christian or non–Catholic backgrounds — especially Jewish, Muslim, Gnostic, Cathar, Albigensian, Walloon and similar sects. The reason is because the central premises of the group are monotheistic, focused on a supreme deity who created the world, man and universe. There is no notion of Messianism, a trinity, saints, demigods and the like. Medieval Arabic philosophers such as Avicenna and Jewish philosophers such as Maimonides, both of whose philosophies fed into Freemasonry, espoused beliefs consistent with a neo–Platonic worldview grounded in movement toward human perfection reflecting that of God to be achieved through a sense of oneness, communality and rationality. In Jewish tradition this idea is encapsulated in the phrase *tikkun olam* or "perfecting the universe." These principles transcend the various religious orthodoxies prevailing at the time, whether promulgated by Christianity, Judaism or Islam. Thus adherents forswore ethnic, religious and political boundaries to strive toward the essential unity of human experience and seek knowledge through rationality. Francis Bacon, a freemason, writing in *The New Atlantis* (1607) describes such a utopian community. The Royal Society was founded after Bacon's death by Charles II (believed to be of Jewish descent). Elias Ashmole was a member. It had as its purpose to bring into being a new civilization called Saloman's House. Churton writes:

> The potent image of Saloman's House was derived from Sir Francis Bacon's allegorical fable New Atlantis, which first appeared as an addendum to his *Sylva Sylvarum, or Naturall History in Ten Centuries*, published a year after Bacon's death in 1627....
>
> New Atlantis tells ... of a ship that arrives at a mysterious island called Bensalem [Arabic for "sons of peace"]. The voyagers are greeted cautiously by a people of enviable educational and psychological endowments. The narrator is informed of how they came to be a people of such advanced attainments. An ancient patriarch had established an order on the island, and the islanders had proved faithful to his inspiration. The patriarch's name was Solamona.
>
> Inhabitants of Bensalem ... seem familiar with Rosicrucian imagery. A scroll first delivered to the travelers before they are permitted to land is "signed with a stamp of cherubin's wings, not spread, but hanging downwards; and by them a cross." This image is reminiscent of those under the protective eye of the Rose Cross Brothers: Sub umbra alarum tuarum Jehova ("under the shadow of Jehovah's wings")....
>
> Bacon's aim was to get people from the known to the unknown: from worshipping God in his "House" (church) to examining God's creation in his "other" house: the universe, or Temple of Nature. This idea goes back to Hermetic and natural philosophic sources that Bacon shared with Elias Ashmole....
>
> To return to Bacon's story: Having been permitted to land on the island, the travelers to Bensalem are informed of a king, the island's lawgiver Solamona, who had established the island's distinctive organization 1,900 years earlier [which would place this at the time of the

fall of the Second Temple in Jerusalem]: Ye shall understand, my dear friends, that amongst the excellent acts of that king, one above all hath the pre-eminence. It was the erection and institution of an order, or society, which we call Saloman's House; the noblest foundation, as we think, that ever was upon the earth and the lantern of this kingdom. It is dedicated to the study of the works and creatures of God. I find in ancient records this order or society is sometimes called Saloman's House, and sometimes the College of the Six Days' Works; whereby I am satisfied that our excellent king had learned from the Hebrews that God had created the world, and all that therein is, within six days: and therefore he instituted that house, for the finding out of the true nature of all things (whereby God might have the more glory in the workmanship of them, and men the more fruit in the use of them).

The prevailing philosophy embraced by Freemasons at the time of the English colonization of the New World went beyond conventional religions and ethnic divisions to embrace the universality of human brotherhood — essentially, an Islamic and crypto–Muslim concept (Appendix C). This enlightened perspective played a large role in opening the door for persons of diverse — and often persecuted — origins to make their way to the New Atlantis of North America.

John Skene

One particular Freemason who made that journey was John Skene. The name derives from the family's hereditary office at the Scottish court of regulating the measure of wool known as skeins. John Skene is the first Freemason to set foot in North America and coincidentally an ancestor of co-author Elizabeth Caldwell Hirschman. He arrived in 1682 in the New Jersey colony from Aberdeen, Scotland. As Hahn writes, "John Skene, made a [Free]mason in 1682 in Aberdeen, Scotland and who migrated to Burlington, New Jersey shortly thereafter, is the first known Mason in America."[29]

Cerza provides additional discussion, noting that several Masons and their families immigrated to New Jersey from Scotland with Skene. All those named are probably of crypto–Jewish descent.

Among those attracted by the liberal [colonization] terms was John Skene. In October, 1682, he came to the area with his wife and several other men who were members of Aberdeen Lodge; he settled at Burlington, in West Jersey, one of the two provinces of New Jersey. The others did not remain, but returned soon thereafter to the old country. The list of members of Aberdeen Lodge for the year 1670 named Harrie Elphinston, as the master; he was the booking agent who arranged passage on the vessel *Henry and Francis*. The arrangement for the trip was made under the sponsorship of the Earl of Perth, a Freemason, John Forbes, a Freemason, and others. John Forbes came to New Jersey in 1684; he settled in Plainfield, but returned to Scotland the following year. John Skene remained, however, and soon after his arrival was elected to the Assembly; later under Governor Edward Bylinge he became deputy governor, and also presided as judge of the court at Burlington. John Skene continued to serve as deputy governor until his death in 1690.[30]

As is widely appreciated, Scotland was the first country to establish Freemason lodges. Naudon states:

In Scotland, the two lodges in Edinburgh, Mary's Chapel and Kilwinning, held the privilege of forming new lodges. Kilwinning was given the significant title of "mother lodge" and practiced a unique rite that has become known as the Rite of Kilwinning. There are a number of lodges in Scots Freemasonry that grew out of the Kilwinning Mother Lodge and formed in various locales throughout the region, even in Edinburgh....

The Schaw Statutes make mention of another lodge, that of Stirling, which also held authority over a certain number of workshops. A fourth very old Scottish lodge, one which the Schaw Statutes does not mention but which can be found in city documents of 1483, is the Lodge of Aberdeen.[31]

The Scottish lodges had as their judges and hereditary patrons, who would now be called grand masters, the Saint Clairs, barons of Roslyn and earls of Orkney and Caithness. This hereditary privilege went back to the Scottish king James II who, in 1438, granted the right of jurisdiction to the masters of the Scottish lodges. They were authorized by him to establish personal tribunals in all the large cities, using the proceeds from a four-pound tax levied on each mason graduating to the rank of master, so that the privileges of freemasons would be protected. Furthermore, the lodge masters were authorized to impose an admission fee on each new member. A document delivered by the masons of Scotland

Washington as a Mason (Print Collection, Miriam and Ira D. Wallach Division of Art, Prints and Photographs, The New York Public Library, Astor, Lenox and Tilden Foundations).

in 1628 and signed by all the lodge representatives confirmed to William Saint Clair's successor the dignity and hereditary rights of this same position.

We can still find a trace in Scotland of other officers exercising jurisdiction over several lodges. For example, a charter granted by King James IV on November 25, 1590, conferred upon Patrick Copland of Udaught the right to exercise the office of first warden of the Freemasons in the districts of Aberdeen, Banff and Kinkardine.

Colonial Freemasonry Symbols

It is no secret that Freemasons were involved in the founding of America. According to one writer who has delved into the subject, "Of the 56 who signed the Declaration of Independence, nine according to some, 53 according to others, were Freemasons."[32] Masonic imagery appears on the seal of the United States as well as its money, in addition to those of the states of Connecticut, Delaware, New Jersey, North Carolina and South Carolina. These display the same familiar images of the Cabala, Gnosticism, Hermetic symbols and alchemy, esoteric traditions introduced into European thought by Sephardic Jews and Muslim thinkers. We notice the two pillars of Jachim and Boas, the sun or all-seeing eye representing God, a book that could be the Torah, Qu'ran, Bible or recorded learning, circle with central dot, Pythagorean right angles, moon (Thoth, Luna) and stars. Clearly the images and philosophy of the Sephardic Diaspora were carried over to North America. All bore a distinctly anti–Spanish and anti–Catholic stamp.

We review now three books discussing the American colonists conventionally identified as Freemasons. The first, Ronald F. Heaton's book on the founding fathers,[33] provides biographical information on prominent Colonial Freemasons. We place the initials *SJ* after those we propose to be of Sephardic Jewish descent (simply *J* for Jewish). Among those listed by Heaton are Benedict Arnold (SJ), Mordecai Gist (SJ), Rufus King (SJ), Benjamin Lincoln (an ancestor of President Abraham Lincoln — SJ) and George Washington.

Hodapp's more recent book, *Solomon's Builders*,[34] lists Daniel Campbell (SJ), the grand master of Virginia, the Marquis de Lafayette and Andrew Jackson (SJ), Benjamin Franklin (Frankeln, SJ),[35] Paul Revere (Rivera, SJ),[36] John Hancock, Dr. Joseph Warren (SJ), James Otis, James Galloway, Peyton Randolph, Richard Henry Lea (SJ, ancestor of Robert E. Lee of the Confederacy), William Dawes (who rode with Revere, SJ), James Monroe, John Jay, Robert Livingston (SJ), John Marshall, William Paterson, John Blair (J), Jacob Broom, Daniel Carroll, John Dickinson, Nicholas Gilman (J), John Wise (J), David Stewart (J), Elisha Cullen Dick, John Duffey (J), Valentine Reintzel (J), Haym Salomon (SJ), Eliphas Levi (J), Benjamin Latrobe, Morgan Lewis (J), Arthur St. Clair (J), Elias Boudinot (J), Nathan Gorman (J) and John Sevier/Xavier (SJ).[37]

In *Colonial Freemasonry* edited by Lewis Cook,[38] various authors discuss the Masonic membership of famous figures throughout the original thirteen American Colonies. Connecticut Freemasons were led by Master Mason Jehosophat Starr (Arabic and Hebrew for "promissory note," SJ).[39] Another Connecticut freemason is Benjamin Isaacs, who, although known to be Jewish, nonetheless attached himself to the local Episcopal Church to avoid anti–Jewish legislation then in force. He is remembered as the designer of the Great Seal of the United States.[40] Other Connecticut Masons include Joel Clarke, Joseph Perry, Daniel Moulton, Samuel Mott, John Barrett, Jonathan Hart, Bilious (Hebrew Bilhah) Ward, Israel Putnam, Seth Warner, Ezra Stiles and Dr. Sall (Saul) Pell — all of whom we propose to be of Jewish ancestry and orientation.

Delaware had as Freemasons Col. Charles Pope, Peter Jaquett, Caleb Bennett, Thomas Mendenhall (from Portuguese Mendes), Dr. Joseph Capelle and Joseph and Israel Israel.

In Georgia the preeminent lodge was Solomon's Lodge #1 of Savannah. It was derived from the Grand Lodge in London and organized by Georgia's founder, James Oglethorpe, together with a group of men led by Moses and Daniel Nunes in 1734, part of the original boatload of Jews in Savannah. According to Micke Israel rabbi-historian Rubin, it was "the second constituted Masonic Lodge in North America."[41] The lodge counted among its members Roger Holland, Elisha Dobree, known Jews Moses and Daniel Nunes, James Habersham, Gray Elliott, Peter Tondie, Thomas Elfe, Oliver Lewis and Belthasar Schaffer (Ashkenazi "steward, trustee")[42]— all of whom likewise were of probable or certain Jewish ancestry. Benjamin Sheftall was a past master of the lodge. Among its most active members were heroes of the American Revolution. The overtly Jewish Masons of this lodge created the Union Society, an early interfaith organization headed by an Episcopalian, a Catholic and a Jew.

Massachusetts has a lengthy and detailed history of Freemasonry. Its first grand master was Henry Price. Members included Isaac de Costa/er (SJ), Dr. Joseph Warren, Jeremiah French, Seth Deane (De Ane), Paul Revere, Joel Stark, Jonathan Hart,[43] Benjamin Tupper, John Lowell, Thaddeus Harris, Moses Mordecai Hays, William Schollay, Thomas Dennie (Deni, Dionysios), Job Prince, Caleb Swan (Jewish house sign)[44] and Samuel Barratt. All may be presumed to be of probable Jewish or Muslim ancestry and cognizant of it.

New Hampshire's first Freemason's Lodge was formed in 1739. Among its charter members was Charles Facy (Fassi, from Fez, Morocco), likely either a Sephardic Jew or Muslim Moor. Elias Ashmole had close connections with Morocco in the mid to late 1600s, as already pointed out. It also included Nicholas Gilman, who signed the Constitution, and Revolutionary War hero James Betton, as well as Samuel Cherry and Amos Emerson (e.g. Emir/Amir-son "prince's son"),[45] Luther Emes, Benjamin Ellis, Josiah Goldsmith, Benjamin Keene, Bezaleel Woodward, Nathaniel Adams, Joseph Bass, Nathaniel Folsom and Alpheus (Arabic) Moore. All these again were likely Jews, crypto–Jews, Muslims or crypto–Muslims.

New Jersey Freemasons included William Tuckey/Tukey (Ashkenazic Tuch, Tuchman, "cloth, rag," J),[46] David Jamison, John Blanchard, Isaiah Wool, John Motte (J), William Patterson, William Makissack ("son of Isaac," J), Moses Ogden (J), John Jacob Faesch (Fez, J), and Jonathan Rhea ("king," J). One of the early lodges in New Jersey was named Nova Caesarea, after the Roman city in Israel, now Beit Shean. Nova Caesarea, in fact, became a sobriquet for the entire state of New Jersey.

The seal of the lodge of New York displays several figures from the Cabala: the ark of the covenant, guardian cherubim and the lion rampant, eagle, bull and man surrounded by acacia leaves. Among its colonial-era members were Francis Goelet (J), Sir Henry Moore, Abraham Savage (J), Isaac Heron (J), Henry Francken (J), Philip Livingston (J), Theodore Van Wyck, Peter van Brugh Livingston and William Tuckey/Tukey (Tukey, J). Tuckey composed a choral version of the 133rd Psalm in Hebrew to commemorate their meeting (below). Other New York Freemasons included Seth Warner (J), John Chapman (from Jacob, J), Morgan Lewis (J), Moses Michael Hays (J) and Moses Sproule (J).

The book *The Ahiman Rezon* used by all colonial lodges (rezon means prince) was authored by Francois Xavier Martin, a native of Marseilles who immigrated to North Carolina and served as grand master of Freemasons in that state. He was very likely Jewish, as was, without a doubt, Thomas Cooper, the provincial grand master, a carpenter and the son of William Cooper, the scout for Daniel Boone. Thomas Cooper founded one of the earliest lodges in North Carolina, Greenville Masonic Lodge at Crown Point in Pitt County in 1776. His mother was Elizabeth Cannon (Canaan), and his uncle of the same name had married Sarah Anthony of the London Jewish merchant family previously mentioned. The entire Cooper clan moved from the Cooper plantation in Surry County, Virginia, across the river from Jamestown to Buffalo Creek in North Carolina about 1755. There with other Jews, crypto–Jews and Scotsmen in exile after the Battle of Culloden, they helped establish Bute County, named for the freethinker John Stuart, Earl of Bute, lord of the treasury and first Scottish prime minister of Great Britain. Bute County had a courthouse southeast of the present-day city of Warrenton that simultaneously served as the Blandford-Bute Lodge. This was a hotbed of radicalism in the days following the Stamp Act of 1765. Sermons were preached there on Saturdays, and the religious affiliation was clearly not Christian. Nearly every one of the six hundred residents in the county treasonously signed a declaration of independence from George III that predated by ten years the one in Philadelphia. Most of them were Freemasons. Among the obvious Jewish names are Moses and Sampson Myers.

Bute County lay on the Occaneechi Indian Trail and served as a staging area for Daniel Boone's exploration and the eventual settlement of Kentucky and Tennessee. It long continued to have a Jewish and Masonic character. The tiny, remote town of Warrenton attracted Moses Mordecai, one of the first three hundred Jews in the Colonies, whose son married the daughter of well-known New York jeweler Myer Myers. Mordecai and his wife founded an Orthodox Jewish women's academy in Warrenton in 1808. The town today makes the impression of a sleepy backwater, but its ante-bellum homes in a variety of styles ranging from Italianate and Moorish to Colonial and Georgian are considered smart, architecturally significant showpieces of the Old South.

Other North Carolina Freemasons of ostensibly Jewish or Muslim heritage include Cornelius Harnett, Caleb Grainger, Joshua Toomer (Tumar), John Salter, William Tryon (French surname), Daniel Lovel, Silas Arnett (diminutive of Aaron), Patrick Garvey, Hardy Murfree, William Brimage, Stephen Cabarrus (as in the Spanish-Jewish financier Francis Cabarrus), John Mare, Abner Neale, William Muir (i.e., Moor), John Geddy (Gadis, "from Cadiz"), John Ashe and John Macon.

Psalm 133 (King James)

133:1 Behold, how good and how pleasant it is for brethren to dwell together in unity!

133:2 It is like the precious oil upon the head, coming down upon the beard; even Aaron's beard, that cometh down upon the collar of his garments;

133:3 Like the dew of Hermon, that cometh down upon the mountains of Zion; for there the Lord commanded the blessing, even life for ever.

Hebrew Transliteration

133:1 shiyr hamma aloth ledhavidh hinnen mah-thobh umah-na iymshebheth 'achiym gamy-achadh

133:2 kashemen hathobh al-haro'sh yoredh al hazzaqan zeqan-aharon sheyyoredh al-piy mid-dothayv

133:3 kethal-chermon sheyyoredh al-harerey tsiyyon kiy sham tsivvah Adonay ethhabberakhah chayyiym adh-ha olam

This version of the psalm is from the Jewish Publication Society (JPS), a translation of the Hebrew Bible published in 1917.

The Pennsylvania Freemasons were chartered under the Duke of Norfolk, who served as the grand master of England, and who was a social contact of Elias Ashmole. The Duke of Norfolk has always been considered the pre-eminent duke in the English peerage. The roots of the dukedom go back to the Bigod ("Picard"), Mowbray (from Montbrai in Normandy, an important Templar name) and Howard ("high warden") families. Typically the Duke of Norfolk holds the hereditary royal office of Earl Marshall of England. In Pennsylvania, members of the Duke's lodge of probable Jewish or Muslim ancestry are William Pringle, Thomas Boude (French, Budaeus), Benjamin Franklin, Daniel Coxe, Thomas Hart, Thomas Bond (Sephardic Bondi/Biondi), Phillip Syng ("cantor"), Thomas Cadwalader (Arabic for first-born son), William Ball, Humphrey Morrey and Joseph Shippen (Dutch).

Rhode Island was known even in Colonial times as a haven for non-traditional religious adherents such as Roger Williams and Anne Hutchison. It had a large and prosperous Sephardic Jewish population. The presence of Jews and Muslims among its settlers, and Freemasons, is to be expected. Moses, John and Joseph Brown (Pardo), Abraham Whipple, John Waterman, William Ellery, Silas Talbot, Jabez Bowen, Moses Seixas, Peleg Clarke — many of these were members of King David's Lodge.

South Carolina's first freemasons met at Solomon's Lodge in Charlestown, which vied with Savannah for the title of the Supreme Council of Scottish Rite Masonry. Of the nine patriarchs who founded it, four were open Jews — Emanuel De la Motta, treasurer-general; Abraham Alexander, secretary-general; Israel Delieben, and Moses C. Levy, inspector-general. We would categorize others in the membership as crypto–Jewish or crypto–Muslim: James Graeme, Maurice Lewis, James Michie, James Gordon, Thomas Denne, Barnard Elliott and John Geddes.

Finally, in Virginia, we would include among well-known Freemasons Peyton Randolph and John Blair as being of Jewish descent. Notably the first Masonic Lodge in Virginia was created in Alexandria, named for the city in Egypt.

As a coda, let us not forget to observe that as with Judaism, the history of Freemasonry in this country is integrally bound up with the traditions of the Cherokee and other Indians. The common denominator was undoubtedly Sephardic Jews. The name Looney from Spanish-Portuguese Luna, in Hebrew Yareakh "moon," was borne by more than one Cherokee chief. The admixed chief Black Fox, 1805–1811, also known as Henry White and called by Washington "the Cherokee king," had his seat in Creek Path on Sand Mountain in Northern Alabama. His sister married John Looney, a

Moses Looney in old age. While other photographs show him in Cherokee dress, here he wears Masonic regalia (Courtesy of Wanda Looney Buss).

Cumberland pioneer whose forebears entered the Colonies through Pennsylvania from the Isle of Man. His nephew was Chief John Looney, who signed the Act of Union between Eastern and Western Cherokees in 1839. William Webber, also called Redheaded Will, was the son of a British officer father named Webber and Cherokee woman who was the mother also of Ostenaco, a Cherokee chief painted by Sir Joshua Reynolds in 1762 when he visited England. Both chiefs were related to Blackheaded Cooper, recorded as a Chickamauga chief. The Webbers intermarried with the Vanns, prominent in the Cherokee hierarchy before and after Removal. Sarah Webber married John Brown, a family whose surname we have noticed more than once. Chief Will's daughter Betsy Webber married Chief John Looney. Their daughter Eliza Abigail Looney married Daniel Rattling Gourd. Another daughter, Eleanor, married Gen. Elias (Stand) Watie, whose family openly followed the ways of Islam. Yet another daughter, Rachel, married John Nave, the grandson of Daniel Ross and Mary McDonald, parents of Chief John Ross. Wataugan leader John Looney's son by his Indian wife was Moses Looney, who married Mary Guest/Gist, the granddaughter of Sequoyah's father, Nathaniel Gist. Moses pursued warfare until the Cherokee were completely defeated, then settled down on a plantation in Lawrence County, Alabama, were he died in 1855. In a rare print preserved by family members from the earliest days of photography, he is shown in Masonic regalia.

Summing Up

The story of Freemasonry unites many of the themes of this book — the striving of Jews scattered in exile by the forces of persecution to build a New Jerusalem in the absence of a real homeland, the search for a free, harmonious society expressive of the Sephardic Jewish ideals remembered in a collective repression from the long centuries of the coexistence of the three faiths in Moorish Spain and southern France, and the practice of a scientific approach to knowledge and religion grounded in remote antiquity, one that was at once rational and mystical. All these attainments beckoned to the immigrants from every corner of Europe and the Mediterranean who settled and populated what became the United States of America. It must count as no accident that the government's emblems of state, its monuments and national literature reflect those origins, from the Masonic imagery on its money to the classical architecture of its capital city.

Despite the obvious, nobody can fail to raise important questions about the actors in this drama. One concerns the nature of crypto–Judaism. We know that when the Spanish-Portuguese Bevis Marks Synagogue in London was dedicated in 1703 some families in attendance were returning to what they believed the true and correct practice of Judaism after a lapse of three hundred years. In many cases their ancestors had gone underground with the first riots against Jews in Spain in 1391. It is an easy leap to reason that after the expulsion of Jews from England in 1290, there were many who persisted in their traditions until the proper time and place came for revealing themselves. From 1300 to 1600 is a like period of time. A faith with thousand-year-old roots could easily persist and persevere. Moreover, there was a steady drift of Spanish and Portuguese Jews into the British Isles after 1492. The fact that many English Jews, some of them underground since the reign of Henry I, went to Scotland after 1290 can only mean that a lamp of hope always flourished to the north, one that welcomed refugees from France, Spain, Italy, the Netherlands, Poland, Germany and the Ottoman Empire. The persistent patterns of intermarriage and naming documented in this book suggest that Jewish identity survived if it did not grow or flourish. It bore throughout its history the stamp it received from French Jews who accompanied William the Conqueror. Scottish, Irish, French and English Jews were naturally open to being reinvigorated by those of the parent culture.

So why, we might also ask, was there such a gulf in America between the crypto–Jews and those openly branded as such, the "real" Jews with Hebrew names and places of origin like Poland and Lithuania? Why — if the families we have argued to be Jewish actually were Jewish in their sympathies and loyalties, not neutral or anti–Jewish — did the process of consolidation and solidarity fail to crystallize? Why were Sephardic Jews so often at odds with Ashkenazic Jews? Why did so many of both denominations cease to identify as Jews, seizing the expediency of finally converting to Christianity or becoming secularized or agnostic, to the extreme of denying their Jewish roots altogether? The answers to these questions inevitably have to do with the complacency and conservatism of the upper class in the British Isles. Today it is estimated that eighty to ninety percent of the land and its income in England, Scotland, Wales and Ireland is controlled by the aristocracy and gentry. Such a statistic brings into even more telling relief the role of Jews in colonial America, where the revolt against privilege was joined in many cases by the very scions of old English and Scottish families. Jews and Muslims played into this dynamic with leading roles.

These are some of the mega-questions that traditional, mainstream American historians have avoided asking, whether consciously or unconsciously. Undoubtedly it has been for the same reasons that the named and unnamed in our chronicle chose to remain secret and did not openly embrace a Jewish presence or identity. Answers cannot be found until questions are raised. In this spirit we hope that our compilation can inspire others to see colonial history through a different lens. The true vision of our forefathers (and foremothers) will only be clear to us after painstaking research, after numerous new biographies, systematic local histories and countless case studies probing into the long centuries of silence.

APPENDICES

A. Jewish Naming Practices and Most Common Surnames
(Including the "Good Name")

Use this appendix to verify if a surname encountered in records or genealogies has a high likelihood of being Sephardic Jewish in original form or translation. The compilation of common Sephardic surnames in Table A.1 illustrates some origins and meanings of Jewish and Muslim names. They have been extracted from a variety of sources.[1] Most Converso surnames of purely Hispanic origin, such as Rodriguez, Gomez, Mendez, and Henriquez, are not included. Hispanic naming customs are complex, varying from country to country and time to time.[2] Locative names (those originating from place-names) such as the following are largely omitted: Almanzi, Castro, Carvajal, Leon, Navarro, Robles (Spanish), and Almeida, Carvallo, Miranda, and Pieba (Portuguese). Neither of these categories — purely Hispanic or locative names — have any intrinsic Jewish meaning or origin, although any name may acquire Jewish associations through history. The notations "ben…" and ibn…" indicate the variant appears with the ben or ibn prefixes designating "son of." The notes column will contain a page number in Faiguenboim, et al. (2004), if applicable (FVC).

TABLE A1. SELECTED SEPHARDIC SURNAMES: VARIANTS, LANGUAGES, AND MEANINGS

Name	Variants	Original Language	Meaning	Notes
Abenrey	Malka, Ben Rey, ibn Rey, Avenreyna, Ben Melekh, Reyno, Soberano	Judeo-Arabic	Son of king	FVC 163
Abensour	Abensur	Hebrew	Son of rock (tsour)	FVC 163f.
Abitbol	Toboul, Abitboul (see also Bothol)	Arabic	Drummer (taboula)	FVC 164f.
Abouaf	Aboab, Abuhab, Abudarham	Arabic	Dispenser of goods; alternatively, stringed musical instrument	FVC 165
Abravanel	Abrabanel, Barbanel (Polish)	Hebrew	A limb of a limb of God	Ancient family said to descend from King David; FVC 166
Abulafia	Boulafia, Alafia	Arabic	Physician's son (Arabic)	Name also borne by Moslem families; FVC 167
Aknin	Aqnine, ben Aknine	Berber	Jacob	FVC 170
Albaz	Elbaz, Elvas, ben…	Arabic	Falconer, also locality in Spain	FVC 171
Alfasi	Alfassa, Fasi, Elfassi, Defaz	Arabic	From Fez, Morocco	FVC 172
Alhadeff	Alkhadif, Alhadyb	Arabic	Kedif, or chief	FVC 173

Name	Variants	Original Language	Meaning	Notes
Al-Muqatil	Mocatta	Arabic	Mason, soldier	
Alouf	Aluf, Alef	Arabic, Hebrew	Chief, leader, general, lord, city head	FVC 174
Anonios		Greek	Eternal	Found in Janina
Arditi		Spanish	Burnt	FVC 180
Ashkenazi	Eshkanazi, Eskinazi	Hebrew	German	FVC 182
Assouline	Asulin, ben... benasuly	Berber	Rocks, cliff	FVC 182
Attal		Arabic	Porter	FVC 183
Azulay	ben...	Berber	Town of Bouzoulai	FVC 185
Baca/Vaca	Spanish	Cow	FVC 189	
Barcilon	Barchilon, Barcilon, Bargeloni	Hebrew Barshelona (our coast)	Old name of Barcelona	FVC 191
Barmalil		Hebrew	Son of the word	Mostly in Morocco
Behar	Behor, Beja, Bejar, Bechor, Bega	Arabic	First-born (alt. "from the sea")	FVC 194
Benatar	ibn Attar, Abenatar, Alatar	Arabic	Druggist, perfumer	FVC 199
Benbeniste	Benvenist, Abenvenisti, Bensiti	Spanish	Welcome (translation of shalom), alt., the name of a fictional herb	A noted Benvenisti family came from Narbonne. FVC 204
Ben Sushan	ben Sussan	Persian	Ancient Persian capital (Suze)	FVC 203
Bitton	Betoun, Beton	Arabic	goat thorn	FVC 207
Bothol	Tebol, Boutbol (see also Abitbol)	Arabic	Drum maker or seller	FVC 208
Cabalero	Caballero, Cabaliero	Spanish	Knight, horseman	FVC 215
Cardoza	Cardozo, Cartoso	Spanish/ Portuguese	From towns in Guadalajara (Spain) or Viseu (Portugal). Full of thorns.	FVC 219
Carmi	Karmi	Hebrew	My vineyard	FVC 220
Caro	Habib	Spanish	Dear, beloved	FVC 220
Carvalho	Cabalo, Carvajal, Caravajal	Portuguese, Spanish	Town in Portugal, oak woods, forest	FVC 221
Casal		Spanish	Ghetto	FVC 221
Castelnuovo		Italian	Town in Italy, "new castle"	FVC 222 (with arms)
Castorianos		Spanish	Distinguished	FVC 222
Castro	Decastro	Portuguese, Spanish	Roman tower, camp, pre–Roman fortified town	FVC 222
Charbit	Sharbit	Hebrew	Handkerchief seller	FVC 225
Chayet	Hayyet, Hyatt (English), Schneider, Snyder, Taylor	Hebrew	Tailor	FVC 283
Cohen	Al-Haruni ("Aaronite"), Coffin, Coffe, Sanchez, many others, incl. Katz, Kohn, Cowan, etc.	Hebrew	Priest	FVC 227–29 (with arms)
Cohen-Scali		Hebrew-Spanish	From "Scali Sevillan"[3]	Morocco and Egypt
Corcos	Corcoz	Spanish	Town in Castile	FVC 230 (with coat of arms)
Costa	Acosta, Gozzi, many others	Portuguese, Spanish	Coast, rib, backside	FVC 231f.
Crespin	Drispin; aven... ben...	Spanish	Curly (hair)	FVC 233
Dalyan	Dalven	Turkish	Fishnets/fishpond	Found in Ioannina

Name	Variants	Original Language	Meaning	Notes
Danon	Dondon, aben… Abendanno	Hebreo-Spanish, Arabic	Judge, increase	FVC 237
Dayan		Hebrew	Judge	FVC 238
DeAragon	Ragon (see also Aragon)	Spanish	Kingdom in Spain	
De Fez	Alfasi	Arabic	From Fez, Morocco	
Delgado		Spanish	Slim, slender	FVC 240
De Silva	Da Silva	Spanish	From the forest (silva)	FVC 392f.
De Soto	Soto, Del Soto	Spanish	From the woodland	FVC 396
Fakhar	Al-Fakhkhar, Farquarson (Scottish Clan)	Arabic	Nobleman, potter	
Farhi	Hafarhi	Hebrew	From Florenza (perahi = flowered)	FVC 256
		Arabic	From farha (joy)	
Ferreres	Ferares, ben… Ferreira	Spanish	Blacksmith. From towns in Majorca or Zamora	FVC 258f.
Foinquinos	Follinquinos, Foyinquinos, Foenkinos	Greco-Latin	Phoenician	FVC 260
Franco	Franca (also given as first name)	Spanish	One from Eastern Mediterranean or Byzantine lands	FVC 261f.
Gabbay	Gabai, Avin… Cabay	Hebrew	In Talmudic era, alms collectors; in Spain, tax collectors	FVC 267
Gaguin	Gagin, Gagi, Gaguim	Berber	Wagag Tribe (Stutterers)	FVC 267
Galanos		Greek	Blue-eyed	FVC 267
Guedalia	Guadella, Guedalha	Hebrew	God is great	FVC 274
Hakham	Al-Hakham	Arabic	Sage	FVC 280
Hakim	Elhakim, Alhakim, Hakim, Facqim	Arabic	Physician	FVC 280
Halfon	Khalfon, Jalfon, Alfon, Halpen, Chalfon	Arabic	Money changer	FVC 280
Hamu	Hammou, Hamuy	Arabic, Berber	Father-in-law; heat (from hams Hebr.); Berber tribe	FVC 281
Hasdai	Hasday, Chasdai, ben… Acday, Azday	Aramaic	Merciful	FVC 282
Hayyim	Chaim, Haim, Vida, Vidal	Hebrew	Life. Replacement name given to dangerously sick person	FVC 283
Hazan	Azan, Chasan, Ha-Hazan, Fasan, Hassan	Hebrew	Official, cantor in a synagogue	FVC 282
Kampanaris		Greek	Bells	Found in Janina
Kokkinos		Greek	Redhead	FVC 301
Laredo		Spanish	Town in Santander, Castile	FVC 306
Levy	Halevy, Levita, Levit, Levin, many others[4]	Hebrew	Levite	FVC 308 (with arms)
Lombroso	Lumbroso	Spanish	Translation of Hebrew *nehora* or *eir*, meaning luminous	FVC 310, 314 (with arms)
Lopez	Lopes, Seef, Zeeb, Seff, Wolf, Wolff, Wulf.	Spanish	Wolf. Totemistic use for someone of the tribe of Benjamin (Gen. 49:27)	FVC 310–13 (with arms)
Lugasi	Lugashi	Arabic	Berber tribe of Ait Wagassa, Morocco	FVC 314
Machado		Spanish	Axe (seller)	FVC 317
Maimon	ben… Mainonides, Mimon, Maymo	Hebrew	Fortunate, lucky	FVC 318

Name	Variants	Original Language	Meaning	Notes
Malka	ben Melekh, Soberano, ibn Rey, Reino, Malki, Abimelekh	Aramaic	King	FVC 318
		Hebrew	From Malaga (Malaca)	
Malqui	Malka, Almalqui, Almalki, Maleque, Malaki	Spanish	From Malaga (Aramaic) (Malaca = owner)	FVC 318
Mandil		Arab	Apron	FVC 319
Marciano	Martziano	Spanish	From Murcia	Mostly in Morocco. FVC 320
Marcus	Marcos	Spanish	Plural of Marco (measuring weight). Smith's hammer	FVC 320
Medina	De Medina	Hebrew	State	FVC 323
		Arabic	Several towns in Spain. Urban	
Mendes			Son of Mendo	FVC 324f.
Mizrahi	See also Ben Ashurqui, De Levante, Shuraqui	Hebrew	Eastern, Levantine	FVC 329
Montefiore		Italian	From place-name Montefiore. Originates in Montebaroccio in Papal States	FVC 331 (with arms)
Moreno	ben	Spanish, Portuguese; Arabic	Brown, brunette. Our master	FVC 332
Nahman	ben Nahman, Nachmann	Hebrew	Lord will heal (or console)	FVC 337
Nahon		Hebrew/Spanish	From town of Naon in Oviedo, Spain	FVC 337f.
Naor	Noor, Norris (English)	Arabic	Erudite	FVC 338
Navaro	Nabaro	Spanish	Kingdom of Navarre	FVC 339
Obadya	Obadiah, Ovadia, Abdias	Hebrew	Servant of God	FVC 347
Ohanna	O'Hana, Bohana, Abuhana, Abuhenna	Berber	Son of henna seller. Prefix O means "son of" in Berber	FVC 347
Ohayon		Berber Hebrew	Son of Life (Hayon) (hayon)	FVC 347
Oiknine	Waknin, Ouaknin, ben...	Berber	Son of Jacob	
Olivar	Olibar, Olival, Olivares, Olivera, Oliver (English)	Spanish	Olive oil seller	FVC 347
Pardo		Spanish, Portuguese	Brown, mulatto, drab; panther; from El Pardo, Spain	FVC 354
Patish	Betache	Hebrew	Hammer	In Greece and North Africa
Peralta		Portuguese	Dandy, coxcomb, naughty child	FVC 356
Pereira	Pera, Peral	Portuguese	From Perera, Spain, or a place with pears. Many Jews forced to convert to Christianity took on the names of trees	FVC356f. (with arms)
Perez		Hebrew	Grandson of Jacob, son of Judah and Tamar	FVC 357f.
Pinto	De Pinto, Pynto, Pinter	Spanish	Town near Madrid	FVC 359–60
Pisa		Italian	Town in Italy	FVC 360 (with arms)
Rabi	Rebi, ben... Rab, Raban	Hebrew	My rabbi	FVC 369
Rofé	Ha Rofe, Roffe, Rophe, (see also Del Medico)	Hebrew	Physician	FVC 375
Romero		Spanish	Pilgrim; rosemary	FVC 377
Rosales	Rozales	Spanish	Rosary, also a place-name	FVC 377
Sabah	Saba, Caba	Arabic	Morning, early riser	FVC 381

Name	Variants	Original Language	Meaning	Notes
Saltiel	Shealtiel, Chaltiel	Hebrew	I asked God	FVC 383f.
Santob	Shemtob, Sentob, Sento	Hebrew	Good name	
Sasson	Sason, Sasun, Sassoon, ben...	Berber	Joy; from town of Ait Sassoun, Morocco. Lily (?)	FVC 387
Sebag	Sabag, Assabagh, Essebagh	Arabic	Dry cleaner	FVC 387
Senor	Senior, Bonsenyor, Ben Senor, Bonsignour	Spanish	Elder, sir	FVC 388f.
Serero	Cerero	Spanish	Candle maker	FVC 389
Serfati	Sarfati, Zarfati, Ha-Zarfatti, Hasserfaty	Hebrew	Frenchman	
Sevillano		Spanish	From Seville, Spain	FVC 390
Shalom	ben... Chalon	Hebrew	Peace	FVC390
Shuraqui	ben, Souraqi, Shouraqui (see also Mizrahi)	Arabic	Easterner	FVC 226, 392
Soberano	see also Malka	Spanish	Sovereign	FVC 394
Sofer	HaSoffer, Soffer, Sopher, Schreiber (German), Clark (English), Leclerc (French) etc.	Hebrew	Scribe, notary	FVC395
Soriano		Spanish	From Soria in Castile	FVC 395
Sultan	Bensultan, Ibenrey, Malka	Arabic	Sultan, king	FVC 398
Tangier	Tanjir, Tanzir, Tandjir, Tanger	Berber	Clay cooking pot, town in Morocco	FVC 401
Taranto	Toranto	Italian	Town in Italy	FVC 402
Toledano		Spanish	From Toledo	FVC 404
Turqui	El Turqui, Eturki, Atturki	Arabic	Turk	FVC 406
Uaknin	Waknin (see Oiknine)	Berber		
Uziel	Oziel, Uzziel, Ouziel, Uzzielli	Hebrew	God is my strength	FVC 409 (with arms)
Valensi	Balenci, Valensin, Valencia	Arabic, Spanish	From Valencia	FVC 413
Veniste	Beniste, Benveniste	Spanish	Welcome	FVC 415
Verdugo	Berdugo	Spanish	Branch (of a tree)	FVC 415
Vidal	Vital, Vitalis, Bitales	Latin	Life (Hebrew Chaim)	FVC 416
Yahia	ibn Yahia	Arabic	Life, from Chiya (Aramaic) and Haim (Hebrew). Ibn Yahia family descended from Yahia al Daoudi (Yahia of Davidic descent)	FVC 429
Zadoq	Sadoc, Zadoc, Acencadoque, Aben Cadoc, Sadox	Hebrew	Just. Biblical high-priest	FVC 433
Zafrani	Ezafrani, Alzafrani	Arabic and Persian	From Zafaran, in Persia. Saffron seller, yellow	FVC 433

TABLE A2. TOP 100 MOST COMMON SEPHARDIC SURNAMES
SOURCE: Faiguenboim, et al., 143–46

1. Leon (de), Leao
2. Sarfati
3. Rodrigues
4. Henriques
5. Benveniste
6. Gabay
7. Cardoso
8. Attia
9. Castro (de)
10. Perez
11. Eskenazi
12. Nahmias
13. Franco
14. Mendes
15. Pereira
16. Baruch
17. Lopes
18. Toledano
19. Mizrahi
20. Costa (da), Acosta
21. Azulay
22. Nunes, Nuñes
23. Fernandez, Hernandez
24. Amar
25. Benatar
26. Abulafia
27. Paz (da) (de)
28. Tedeschi, Tedesco
29. Vital, Vidal, Vitali
30. Aboab
31. Diaz
32. Modiano, Modigliano, Momigliano
33. Navarro
34. Suarez
35. Behar
36. Errera, Ferreira
37. Gomez
38. Pardo

39. Dayan	51. Carvalho, Car-	62. Aguilar	76. Arditi	87. Salem
40. Finzi	vajal	63. Fano (da)	77. Cassuto	88. Vaz, Vais
41. Menache,	52. Curiel	64. Nahon	78. David, Ben	89. Zacuto
Menasse	53. Bassan, Bassano	65. Salama	David, Daud	90. Baron, Varon
42. Abravanel,	54. Hasson, Has-	66. Uziel	79. Foà	91. Calderon
Abrabanel	souni	67. Valensi	80. Sidi, Cid	92. Ezra
43. Medina (de)	55. Salva (da)	68. Farache	81. Espinosa, Spin-	93. Halfon
44. Molho	56. Moreno	69. Nahum	oza	94. Montefiore
45. Sasson, Sassoon	57. Abendana	70. Russo, Rosso	82. Torres (de),	95. Srur, Soror
46. Fonseca (da)	58. Cattan	71. Sasportas	Torre (della)	96. Ancona (d')
47. Álvarez	59. Forti, Fortes,	72. Barzilai	83. Crespin, Crespo	97. Ergasz
48. Ventura	Fuerte	73. Campos (de)	84. Silvera	98. Padoa, Padova
49. Bezaquen	60. Lumbroso	74. Danon, Dannon	85. Gattegno	99. Segrè
50. Hazan, Hazzan	61. Nigri, Negri	75. Hassan	86. Romano	100. Sequeira

A Good Name

Following are notes based on Andres J. Bonet, "The Bonet-Kalonymos-Shem Tovs. Direct Descendants of King David and the Princes of Septimania," *Sharsheret Hadorot*, Vol. 17, No. 2, June 2003.

Of all the Jewish communities in Western Europe in the first millennium of the Common Era, Narbonne in southern France was the most important. The French city acted as speaker and sovereign representative for the rest of the communities with the king or emperor. Narbonne's leader was called Nasi (prince). The Spanish March or buffer zone between the Carolingians and Muslim rulers of Spain comprised Jaca, Girona, Barcelona and Tarragon and was ruled by the Nasi in the same way as any other king. The Nasi was a semi-independent, semi-dependent vassal of the emperor. He was sometimes referred to as "King of the Jews."

Under the Carolingians from 717 to 900, this province or principality was called Septimania. It was ruled by a Nasi or Gaon (meaning "descendant"). These Geonim claimed to be direct descendants of King David. Their privileges were passed down within the same family. The Nesi'im (plural of Nasi) of Septimania ruled "the most prosperous and influential Jewish community of their time." They were so well known that sources refer to the state as *terra Hebraeorum* in 842, 950, 994, 1004 and 1032, as *terra Israhelis* in documents from Cluny, or the *Villa Iudaica* in the case of Gerona in 982.

Abraham ibn Daud, author of the cabalistic *Book of Tradition*, wrote that Charles Martel requested the caliph of Babylon to send him a Jewish prince. The result was the emigration of the Exilarch Makhir, a magnate and scholar, head of the exiled Jewish community in the Arab capital and descendant of the House of David. Makhir married the daughter of Charles Martel and grandmother of Charlemagne. His daughter Bertrada married Pepin I, king of Italy. Later descendants were to become the consorts of Otto I, king of Germany, and Hugo Capet, Robert II and Louis VI, all kings of France. Other descendants are Sancho III the Elder, king of Navarre, Ramiro I, king of Aragon, and Ferdinand I, king of Leon and Castile. The Davidic-Carolingian lineage blended with the whole of European royalty. All of the royal houses of Europe, as well as the Spanish monarchs in the Reconquest and their successors down to the current king of Spain, Juan Carlos I, are descendants of Charlemagne and the Nasi Makhir Davie, Teodoric I (730–96), also called Thierry de Autun, prince of Septimania.

According to tradition, the Shem-Tov family are direct descendants of the House of David. This name was of Hebrew or even Aramaic origin and means "good" or literally "good name." The line was also known as Yom-Tov or Toviyah. Yom-Tov is literally translated as "good day" and incorporates the meaning "God is good." In all cases, "good" represents the keynote of this line.

The *kinnui* or civil name equivalent of Yom-Tov is Bonet or Bonjorn. The translation of Shem-Tov into Greek is Kalonymos, of Greek origin: *kalon* signifying "nice" or "good," and *onymos* meaning "name."

The "good" line was translated into Medieval Latin as Bono, Bona, or Bonitus. The diminutive of the Romance language form would finally become the name Bonet.

Yom-Tov would morph into Bondia (Narbonne in 1306), Boudia (in Marseille in 1350), Bonus Dian (in Manosque in 1326) or Bondie (in Salon-de-Provence in 1391) and the form Bondie and its variants Bondi, Bondy, and Bonidy. The expression *bonne fete* would, in the same way, transform into Bonfed, Bonefad and Bunefad in the South of France and Spain.

The Greek Kalonymos would vary as the family moved from place to place, appearing in German as Kalonymus, Kalma, Kelman, Kalma, or Kalm, in Polish as Kalmanowicz, Kalmanski, Kielminski, and Kielmanson and in Russian Kalmanson, Kalmanov, Kalmanovich, Kalmanok and Kelmanskij. Many by these names were prominent rabbis.

KALONYMOS GENEALOGY

Rabbi Moses "the Elder" Kalonimos, Jewish king of France (Nasi), 917–?
Kalonymos, son of Moses "the Elder"
Todros, about 1064
Kalonymos "the Great," end of 11th to beginnings of 12th centuries
Todros, about 1130–1150
Kalonymos, from before 1160 to after 1199
Todros, from before 1216 to before 1246
Kalonymos Bonmancip, from before 1246 to after 1252
Astruc-Tauros, from before 1256 to end of 13th century
Momet-Tauros, from the end of the 13th century to 1306

The adaptations of Bon can be glimpsed in the following surnames, all used by Sephardim in Spain: Bon, Bona, Boned, Bonet, Bonet de Lunel, Boneti, Bonhom, Bonhome, Bonjorn, Bonnin, Bono, Bonom, Bonomo, Bonsenior, d'en Bonsenjor, Bonsenyor, and Bonus.

Related surnames documented as Sephardic include: De Bonaboya, Bonacosa, Bonafe, Bonafed, Bonafeu, Bonafill, Bonafilla, Bonafos, Bonafoux, Bonafus, Bonafux, Bonagua, Bonaloc, Bonan, Bonananch, Bonanasc, Bonanasch, Bonanat, Bonanet, Bonastre, Bonastruc, Bonastruch, Bonaventura, Bonavia, de Bonavida, Bondavin, Bondia, d'en Bondieta, Bondoga, Bondogas, Bonfed, Bonfev, Bonfil, Bonfillet, Bonguha, Bonhe, Bonhome, Bonhorn, Boni, Boni, Boniach, Boniel, Bonifant, Bonino, Bonirac, Bonisac, Bonisach, Bonito, Bonitto, Bonjom, Bonjua, Bonjudio, Bonjuha, Bonmacib, Bonmacip, Bonnin, Bono, Bono, Bonom, Bonomo, Bononat, and Bonsucesso.

Sources

Following are some prime sources for Jewish surname research from which some items of interest have been extracted. Many of these names are mentioned in the text.

Abecassis, Jose Maria. *Genealogia Hebraica: Portugal e Gibraltar (Jewish Genealogy: Portugal and Gibraltar.* Lisbon: Author, 1990). Four volumes present carefully documented Jewish family trees from Portugal and Gibraltar, listed alphabetically.

Volume 1: Abeasis, Abecassis, Abensur, Abitbol, Aboab, Abohbot, Absidid, Abudarham, Acris, Adrehi, Aflalo, Albo, Alkaim, Amar, Amram, Amselem, Amzalak, Anahory, Asayol, Askenazi, Assayag, Athias, Atrutel, Auday, Azancot, Azavey, Azerad, Azuelos, Azulay, Balensi, Banon, Baquis, Barchilom, Baruel, Benabu, Benady, Benaim, Benamor, Benarus, Benatar, Benbunan, Benchaya, Benchetrit, Benchimol, Bendahan, Bendelack, Bendran, Benelisha, Beneluz, Benhayon, and Berlilo.

Volume 2: Beniso, Benitah, Benjamim, Benjo, Benjuyal, Benmergui, Benmiyara, Benoalid, Benoliel, Benrimoj, Benros, Bensabat, Bensadon, Bensaude, Benselum, Bensheton, Bensimon, Bensimra, Benslaoha, Bensliman, Bensusan, Bentata, Bentubo, Benudis, Benuunes, Benyuli, Benzacar, Benzaquen, Benzecry, Berdugo, Bergel, Bibass, Blum, Bohudana, Brigham,

Brudo, Buzaglo, Bytton, Cagi, Cansino, Cardoso, Carseni, Castel, Cazes, Cohen, Conquy, Coriat, Cubi, Danan, Davis, Delmar, Elmaleh, Esaguy, Esnaty, Farache, Ferares, Finsi, Foinquinos, and Fresco.

Volume 3: Gabay, Gabizon, Garson, Hadida, Hassan, Hatchuel, Israel, Kadoshi, Katzan, Labos, Laluff, Laredo, Lasry, Lengui, Levi, Malca, Maman, Marques, Marrache, Martins, Massias, Matana, Megueres, Melul, Moreira, Mor-Jose, Mucznik, Muginstein, Muller, Nahon, Namias, Nathan, Obadia, Ohana, Oliveira, Pacifico, Pallache, Pariente, Pimienta, Pinto, Querub, Roffe, Ruah, Rygor, Sabath, Salama, Sananes, Saragga, Schocron, Sebag, Segal, Sequerra, and Serfaty.

Volume 4: Serequi, Serrafe, Seruya, Sicsu, Tangi, Tapiero, Taregano, Taurel, Tedesqui, Tobelem, Toledano, Tuati, Uziel, Varicas, Wahnon, Waknin, Wolfinsohn, Zafrany, and Zagury.

Arie, Gabriel. *Genealogie de la famille Arie de 1766 a 1929.* 1929. (Pamphlet). Gabriel Arie (1863–1939) of Samakov, Bulgaria, was a well-known teacher and director of Alliance Israelite Universelle schools in various countries. Family surnames in his pamphlet include:

Abdala, Acher, Adroxi, Aguilar, Aharon, Alcalay, Almalech, Amada, Arav, Arditti, Arie, Asian, Assa, Baruch, Baruh, Bassan, Behar, Behmoaras, Benaroya, Benyaech, Beraha, Caldron, Calef, Camhi, Canetti, Carasso, Cario, Cohen, Cohen-Hemsi, Conforte, Conorte, Crespin, Decaro, Donna, Elias, Eliezer, Faraggi, Farhi, Fortunee, Gerson, Gueron, Haim, Hananel, Henri, Houromdji, Jacob, Jacobson, Joseph, Kaplan, Koffler, Kokachoeli, Kouyumdjulu, Levy, Maggar, Manoach, Mazaltov, Melamed, Mevorah, Mitrani, Molho, Moscona, Moshe, Ninio, Panigel, Papo, Policar, Presente, Rachel, Rahamim, Raphael, Rivca, Rudiac, Schnur, Semach, Shabetay, Sidi, Soref, Tagger, Uziel, Varsano, Venezia, Weill, Weinstein, and Zonana.

Attal, Robert, and Joseph Avivi. *Registres Matrimoniaux de la Communaute Juive Portugaise de Tunis: XVIII–XIX siecles.* Jerusalem: Ben Zvi Institute, 1989. Names in 1,031 ketubot from the Sephardic Portuguese community (Grana or Leghorn [Livorno] Jews) of Tunis, including the following:

Abdias, Aboccara, Aboucaya, Achour, Adahan, Adi, Albaili, Alban, Alloro, Almaizi, Amar, Amorborgo, Anakas, Arous, Artona, Ascoli, Ashkenazi, Assafar, Assfar, Assuid, Astrologo, Atazouri, Attal, Attia, Attias, Azoulay, Bais, Bargansa, Bargas, Barnes, Baron, Baruch, Basivi, Bassan, Battan, Bekhassen, Bellaiche, Bembaron, Ben Adi, Ben Baron, Ben Simeon, Ben Yaiche, Bendana, Berda, Bessis, Betito, Bijaoui, Bises, Bismuth, Biziz, Boccara, Boiro, Bonan, Bondi, Bonfia, Borcatsa, Borgel, Boublil, Boucarra, Boujenah, Boukhobza, Brami, Buemo, Calo, Calvo, Camio, Campus, Capoua, Cardozo, Cariglio, Carmi, Caro, Carravallio, Cartozo, Cassuto, Castelnuevo, Castro, Cattan, Cavallio, Cesana, Chemla, Cittanova, Cohen, Cohen de Lara, Cohen Solal, Cohen Tanougi, Constantine, Corcos, Coronel, Coronel, Coscas, Coscas, Costa, Crimas, Crimisi, Curiel, Dadoune, Dahan, Daian, Dardour, Darmon, Darmouni, David, De Pas, Delouya, Dias Palma, Dicunia, Diouani, Douali, Elahmi, Elajim, Elfassi, Elhaik, Elkana, Elmalih, Elportogues, Elpronti, Eminenti, Enajar, Enriques, Errera, Espinoza, Etazer, Etouil, Exberro, Fellous, Finaro, Finia, Finiro, Finsi, Finzi, Fitoussi, Flah, Florentino, Forti, Fougi, Franchetti, Franco, Freoa, Funaro, Gabai, Gabay, Gabison, Gandus, Garci, Garsin, Garson, Ghalula, Ghanem, Ghozlan, Gidilia, Gimsi, Gonzales, Grego, Guedalia, Guetta, Guez, Guiguiati, Guttieres, Habalou, Habib, Hacohen, Haddad, Hadida, Hagege, Hakouk, Hakoun, Halevy, Halevy de Albaili, Halevy de Leon, Halevy Sonsine, Halimi, Hanouna, Hasda, Hassid, Hattab, Hayoun, Hazaken, Heskouni, Hiskouni, Houri, Iflah, Isaac, Isaaki, Israel, Israel Enriques, Jami, Jano, Jarmon, Jazo, Jerafa, Josue, Journo, Kali, Khalaf, Khalfon, Khayat, Khrief, Knoshklash, Koresh, Ksabi, Ktorza, Lahmi, Lampronti, Lara, Leon, Leotagi, Leve, Levi, Levy, Levy de Albaili, Levy de Leon, Lodriguez, Lodriguez Dicunia, Lodriguez Enriques, Lodriguez Silvera, Lopes Perrera, Louizada, Louniel, Lumbroso, Lunel, Lussato, Maarek, Malabar, Malka, Margalit, Marini, Marouani, Martassi, Marzouk, Medina, Meimoun, Melloul, Mendes, Mendes Ossona, Mendoza, Messica, Messina, Mizrahi, Moati, Modiliano, Modon, Molco, Molho, Molina, Montefiore, Montillia, Moreno, Moron, Morpourgo, Morpugo, Naccache, Nahon, Nahum, Najar, Namias, Narboni, Nataf, Nounil, Nunes, Nunes Vais, Obadia, Obana, Ossona, Ouaiche, Palatgi, Pansir, Pansiri, Pariente, Pas, Pasanno, Pavoncello, Peres, Perets, Pignero, Pinheiro, Pinto, Piperno, Platero, Polako, Pougi, Priosa, Rignano, Roa, Rodriguez, Rodriques, Saada, Saadoun, Sabban, Sacouto, Sagdoun, Sala, Salom, Saltillana, Samana, Santaliana, Sarbia, Sarfati, Sberro, Sedbon, Semah, Semaha, Senouf, Servadio, Servi, Setbon, Setroug, Settouna, Sfez, Shalajar, Shalazar, Shalom, Sharabi, Sharabia, Sharabig, Shebokh, Shemama, Sicso, Signia, Silvera, Simeon, Sion, Sira, Sitri, Slama, Smaja, Solal, Solas, Solima, Sonino, Sonsine, Soria, Souzine, Spinoza, Spizzichino, Strologo, Suares, Suied, Tabib, Taieb, Taigan, Tanougi, Tapia, Tedeschi, Timsit, Tisignia, Tito, Tivoli, Tolicciano, Toubiana, Uzan, Vais, Valensi, Ventura, Vilariali, Voltera, Yaiche, Yakhia, Yehia, Younes, Zacout, Zacouto, Zafrana, Zaibi, Zaken, Zarka, Zazo, Zazoun, Zegbib, Zeitoun, Zerah, and Ziki.

Laredo, Abraham. *Les noms des Juifs du Maroc.* Madrid: Institut Arias Montano, 1978. This extensive work presents family names of Sephardic Jews of Morocco, including their origins and variants. Lists historical occurrences of the names with a summary of available data with documented sources. Because of its extensive detail, this out of print book is an indispensable source for Sephardic research, even if the family did not originate in Morocco.

Malka, Eli S. *Jacob's Children in the Land of the Mahdi: Jews of the Sudan.* Syracuse, N.Y.: Syracuse University Press, 1997. Includes index. Surnames mentioned in the text include:

Abboudi, Ades, Aeleon, Aghion, Aharoni, Ani, Baroukh, Bassiouni, Battan, Belilos, Bellenstein, Benabssa, Ben-David, Ben-Ezra, Benis, Ben-Lassin, Ben-Malka, Benou, Ben-Rubi, Ben-Sion, Bergmann, Bern- stein, Blau, Bloch, Braunschweig, Braunstein, Btesh, Carmona, Castro, Cattaoui, Cohen, Dahan, Dannon, Daoud, Douek, Dwek, El-Eini, Ezra, Farhi, Forti, Gabbai, Gabra, Gabriel, Gaon, Godenberg, Goldring,

Gwertzman, Haim, Hakim, Harari, Hayon, Hazan, Heiman, Hemou, Hornstein, Inglizi, Ishaq, Israel, Kaminski, Kanarek, Kane, Kantzer, Klein, Kudsi, Levy, Lieberman, Malka, Manfinfeker, Mani, Marcos, Marcovitch, Marnignone, Mashiah, Massoud, Mazuki, Menasce, Menasse, Mendel, Merzan, Metzger, Mosseri, Mousky, Nadler, Nahmias, Nahum, Novecks, Ohanna, Ortasse, Pinto, Polon, Pontremoli, Prato, Qattawi, Reich, Risenfeld, Rodriguez, Romy, Rubin, Safadi, Safra, Saleh, Salem, Salvator, Sasson, Schechter, Schlesinger, Seroussi, Shaoul, Shapiro, Shoua, Siboani, Silvera, Simoni, Sinauer, Smouha, Sokolov, Soriano, Steinhart, Suleiman, Tamman, Toledano, Tueta, Turetsky, Tuval, Weinberg, Wolf, Yacoub, and Yettah.

Appendix I in Eli Malka's book lists all Jewish marriages in the Sudan. Names in the records include: Ab-boudi, Abdalla, Ades, Aeleon, Alon, Ani, Baroukh, Behar, Belilos, Ben Rubi, Benaim, Bennou, Berchmann, Berkowitz, Berlenstein, Bigo, Bossidan, Braunstein, Carmona, Cavaliero, Cohen Coshti, Dannon, Daoud, David, Dayan, Drigg, Dwek, Eini, Feinstein, Franco, Gabra, Gabriel, Gaon, Gershon, Goldenberg, Goldring, Greenberg, Hakim, Harari, Heber, Heimani, Hemmo, Herman, Hindi, Ishag, Ishkinazi, Israel, Kanzer, Khaski, Konein, Kramer, Kudsi, Leilibh, Levitin, Levy, Loupo, Malka, Mannifker, Marcos, Masasini, Mashi, Menovitch, Mizrahi, Moshe, Mourad, Moussa, Ohanna, Ortasse, Palombo, Pinto, Saada, Safadia, Sagrani, Saltoun, Sasson, Seroussi, Shakra, Shama, Shaoul, Shapiro, Shenouda, Shoua, Sidis, Sinai, Soriano, Stulmacher, Tammam, Vago, Wahba, Wais, Weinberg, Yetah, and Yona.

Following are a sampling of notable names from Sephardim.com:

Aalamani, Aba, Abadi, Aelion, Alemano, Alfacar, Al-Fakharmeir, Al-Yamani, Amadia, Amar, Amon Yaari, Amor, Amram, Amzalag, Anashiksan, Anatoli, Andalusi/Fasi/Sikili, Atar, Awad, Ayash, Azar, Azareff, Azaria, Aziz, Azubid, Azulay, Bachi, Bagrat, Barun, Barzilai, Basan, Basilea, Basola, Bassan, Bassani, Basto, Basula, Battat, Bauri, Behar, Beirav, Bejar, Belasco, Belforte, Benas, Benmozegh, Benoliel, Benvalia, Benveniste, Benzaquen, Berab, Beraha, Bertinore, Bertinoro, Berujim, Bessis, Betsalel, Bezalel, Bibas, Bonan, Bonanasco, Bonastruc, Bonchara, Bondabi, Bondavin, Bonet Sarfati, Bonfil, Bonfils, Bonjorn, Bonjuhes, Bordzhel, Botton, Bragadini, Bravo, Brito, Bueno, Bueno/De Mesquita, Cabra, Cabral/Da Gama, Calvo, Candiote, Candioti, Canias, Caro, Carsinet, Carvajal, Carvalho, Carvallo, Cases, Cassin, Cassuto, Castel Huevo, Castiglioni, Castro, Cataui, Cattaui, Cavalleria, Colon, Corsino, Costantini, Cremieux, Cremieux/Moie, Crescas, Crespin, Culi, Curiel, Da Costa, da Fonseca, da Mercado, da Peschera da Pisa da Rosa, da Silva, Dabah, Dabella, Dahan, Dana, Daud, David, de Fulda, de Heart, de Jorena, de Jorjena, de Lattes, de Luna, de Mercado, de Modena, de Montalto, de Pina, de Pina/Sarfatti, de Pisa, de Rossi, de Sequeyra, de Symons, de Tolosa, de Tudela, Del Medigo, Della Torre, Delmar, Delmedigo, Demaestre, Devir, Diena, Dina, Disegni, Ditrani, Divekar, Drago, Drago de Lemos, Dunio, Duran, Durant, Duwayk, Dzhalil, Dzhama, Dzhamil, Dzhian, Dzian, Edni, Efendi, Effendi, Efrati, Ejica, Erera, Ereza, Ergas, Escapa, Escobar, Evans, Faba, Falaquera, Falcon, Fano, Farrar, Fermi, Fernandes, Fernandes/Brandao, Figo, Finzi, Foz, Furtado, Gabay, Gabirol, Gambach, Gaon, Garzon, Gatanio, Gavison, Gedelicia, Gegate, Gilbert, Girondi, Gitakila, Godefroi, Gomez, Gracian, Gradis, Granata, Graziani, Guedalia, Guenun, Guershom, Gurdzhi, ha Cohen, ha Nasi, Hadida, Hagege, Hagiz, Haguiz, ha-Haver, ha-Hazan, Haim, Hakim, Haley/Elie, Halfon, Ha-Maravi, Hamon, Hana, Hananel, Hanasi, Ha-Paytan, Harari, Harizi, Haroma, Harun, Herrera, Hibat/Alah, Hiya, Hoshama, Hoyada, Huino, Hushiel, Jagiz, Jaion, Jais, Jakun, Jalfon, Jalshush, Jamtsi, Jamuy, Janan, Janoj, Jaquete, Jardon, Javilla, Jay, Jayudzh, Jazan, Jezkia, Jida, Jinin, Jushiel, Jushiel/Ben Efrain/Yosef, Juzin, Kadoorie, Kafa, Kafih, Kahani, Kalonimus, Kamaniel, Kamniel, Kanian, Kastoria, Katsin, Kayra, Kazaz, Kehimkar, Khalas, Khalfon, Kiki, Labadon, Labatt, Laguna, Laredo, Laski, Latimi, Lattes, Leao, Leeser, Ligier, Lombroso, Louzada, Lumbroso, Luria, Lusitanus, Luzada, Luzzato, Madmun, Madriaga, Maduro, Madzhani, Magangaki, Magriso, Maimi, Maimon, Majzir, Maleha, Mali, Malka, Mallah, Maracha, Mari, Marini, Marour, Marzuk, Masajaway, Mascaran, Massarani, Massarini, Masud, Matita, Maymeran, Mayques, Mazliaj, Medola, Meiggs, Meiri, Mejzir, Meknes, Mendes, Mendoza, Merman, Mezan, Mier, Migash, Miledi, Milhau, Mishan, Modigliani, Modon, Moha, Monsanto, Monsino, Montagnana, Montagu, Montalto, Montefiore, Morais, Morban, Mordejay, Moresco, Moron, Morpurgo, Mortara, Morteira, Moscato, Mosconi, Musa, Musafia, Nadjara, Nafusi, Nahama, Nahman, Nahon, Nahum, Narro, Nasi, Nata, Natan, Navarra, Navarro, Navon, Nayas, Nedebo, Nedivot, Nicanor, Nicholas, Nieto, Nimir, Nissim, Nissim Gambach, Noah, Nono, Noraim, Nunes De Nattos, Nunes Wais, Nunez, Nunez-Cardoso, Nunez/Carvalho, Nunez De Silva, Olmo, Omar, Orabuena, Orsani, Orvieto, Ossuna, Ottolenghi, Ovadia, Ovadia De Bertinoro, Oz, Ozmo, Pacheco, Pacifico, Palache, Palaggi, Pardo, Paredes, Pariente, Pejiel, Penso, Penso Mendes, Perahia, Pereira, Perez, Perfet, Pinehas, Pinto, Piza, Planes, Porto, Prato, Primo, Proops, Pyrrhus, Querido, Raban, Rahabi, Rajpurkar, Raka, Ramirez, Ratsbashi, Ratshabi, Ravena, Ravenna, Recanati, Reggio, Remos, Reuven, Reuveni, Ribeiro, Ricardo, Ricchi, Rieti, Robles, Rogelio, Romanelli, Romano, Rosanes, Rossi, Rovigo, Rubin, Rubio, Saadi, Sabor, Sacchetto, Sacerdoti, Sada, Sadaga, Sad-Aldawla, Safir, Saguiz, Saieg, Saimen, Sakri, Sala, Salamon, Salamon De Trani, Salamons Salas, Salem, Salem, Salih, Salomon, Salvador, Samama, Samaya, Samlaich, Samolovlio, Samson, Sanitago, Sanu, Sapir, Saportas, Saragosti, Saraval, Sardas, Sarfati, Sarmad, Sarok, Saruk, Sas Portas, Sasoon, Sciaky, Sedacca, Sedequias, Sefas/Alfasi, Seloaf, Semaj, Semior, Senoriu, Senyor, Sequerra, Sereni, Sereno, Serfati, Seror, Sforno, Shabazi, Shabetay, Shabrabak, Shagi, Shahun, Shakri, Shalom, Shaltiel, Shame, Sharabi, Shaul, Shelemo, Shelush, Shemaria, Sherira, Sheshet, Shincook, Shofet, Shoshan, Shushan, Siboni, Sid, Sidi, Sidun, Sieff,

Siesu, Sigmar, Siliera, Slelatt, Sodicky, Sofat, Soiano, Soliman, Somej, Somekh, Soncino, Soriano, Sosportos, Soulam, Spinoza, Stora, Sullam, Sunbal, Sussan, Svevo, Tabit, Tabul, Tadjer, Tagliocozzo, Taitashak, Tam, Tamim, Tartas, Taurel, Taviana, Tawa, Tayb, Tayeb, Teboul, Teixeira, Templo, Terracini, Testa, Teubal, Tibbon, Tiboli, Tivoli, Toledano, Toledo, Tomas, Tores, Torres, Touro, Trani, Treves, Tsahalon, Tsalaj, Tsarefati, Tsemaj, Tsevi, Tsova, Ukba, Ulhoa, Uriah, Usque, Uzan, Uziel, Vadzhar, Vaez, Ventura, Verga, Vetura, Vidash, Viegas, Vital, Volterra, Wakar, Wakasa, Yacob, Yafe, Yahia, Yahuda, Yaish, Yajya, Yakar, Yakub, Yana, Yanez, Yatah, Yayez, Yedidia, Yehiel, Yehoshua, Yejiel, Yekutiel, Yekutiel/Kohen, Yerushalmi, Yesha, Yishag, Yojay, Yom Tov, Yona, Yuda, Zacut, Zahit, Zahula, Zakar, Zakay, Zaken, Zaky, Zeevi, Zelvi, Zemat, Zequi, Zerbib, Zhuli, Zimra, and Zuta.

Toledano, Joseph. *La saga des familles: Les juifs du maroc et leurs noms.* Tel Aviv: Stavit, 1983. This book is less extensive than Laredo's work, but includes photographs of individuals when available.

Abdallah, Abecassis, Abehsera, Abensour, Abergel, Abetan, Abikhzer, Abisror, Abitbol, Abizmil, Aboab, Aboulafia, Aboundraham, Abourbia, Abourmad, Abow, Abrabanel, Adi, Adrotiel, Afalo, Afriat, Akoka, Akrich, Albaranes, Albo Alcheikh, Alfonta, Alloul, Almaalem, Altaraz, Altia, Altit, Amar, Amghar, Amiel, Amor, Amozeg, Amselem, Amsili, Amzallag, Anconina, Anfaoui, Anidjar, Ankri, Annaquab, Arajel, Arama, Arrouas, Asbili, Assabti, Assaraf, Assopr, Assouline, Attar, Auday, Azar, Azencot, Azerad, Azeroual, Aziza, Azogui, Azoulay, Azran, Azuelos, Bahloul, Bahtit, Banon, Barchilon, Barsheshet, Baruk, Belahdeb, Belahsen, Belicha, Ben Baroukh, (Ben) Haco, Ben Waish, Benadiba, Benaim, Benaksas, Benamara, Benamram, Benaroch, Benaudis, Benazeraf, Benchlmol, Bendavid, Bendelak, Bendrao, Benelzra, Benezra, Benghouzi, Bengio, Benhaim, Benibgui, Beniciki, Benisty, Benkemoun, Benlolo, Benmaimon, Bensaude, Benshabat, Bensimon, Bentolila, Benwalid, Benyair, Benzaquen, Benzenou, Berdugo, Beriro, Betito, Bettach, Bibas, Bitton, Bodoch, Bohbot, Bothol, Bouaziz, Boucfti, Bouganim, Bouhadana, Bouskila, Boussidan, Bouzaglo, Cabessa, Candero, Cardozo, Caro, Castiel, Cazes, Charbit, Chetrit, Chkeiran, Chlouch, Choukroun, Chriqui, Cohen, Cohen, Cohen-Scali, Conqui, Corcos, Coriat, Dabela, Dades, Dadia, Dadoun, Dahan, Danan, Danino, Danon, Dayan, Delmar, Deloya, Dery, Diwan, Drihem, Elalouf, Elbaz, Elfassi, Elgrabli, Elhadad, Elharar, Elhyani, Elkabas, Elkayim, Elkeslassy, Elkouby, Elkrief, Elmaleh, Elmekies, Elmoznino, Encaoua, Eskouri, Etedgui, Ezerzer, Fedida, Fhima, Fouinquinos, Gabay, Gagurn, Garzon, Gavison, Ghozlan, Guedalia, Guigui, Hadida, Haliwa, Hamou, Hamron, Harboun, Hassan, Hassine, Hatchwel, Hazan, Haziza, Hazot, Himi, Houta, Ifergan, Iflah, Ifrah, Illouz, Iscini, Israel, Itah, Kadoch, Kakon, Karenti, Katan, Kessous, Khalfon, Khalifa, Knafo, Lahmy, Laredo, Lasry, Lazimi, Levy, Levy-Ben-Yuli, Librati, Loeb, Loubaton, Lougassy, Louk, Lousky, Mahfoda, Maimran, Malka, Mamane, Mansano, Maquin, Marache, Marciano, Mareli, Medioni, Meloul, Meran, Mergui, Messas, Monsonego, Moreno, Moryoussef, Moyal, Mreien, Myara, Nahmany, Nahmias, Nahon, Nahori, Nezri, Nidam, Obadia, Ohana, Ohayon, Ohnouna, Oliel, Ouaknine, Ouakrat, Ouanounou, Ouazana, Outmezguin, Ouyoussef, Ouziel, Pallache, Pariente, Perez, Pimienta, Pinto, Rebibo, Revah, Riboh, Rimokh, Rosilio, Rouach, Rouah, Ruimy, Ruti, Saba, Sabah, Sadoun, Sananes, Saporta, Saraga, Sarfati, Sasson, Sayag, Sebag, Seban, Selouk, Serero, Shoushana, Siboni, Siksu, Sisso, Soudry, Soussan, Suissa, Sultan, Sunbal, Tangui, Tapiero, Tawil, Temstet, Tobali, Tobi, Toblem, Toledano, Torjman, Vidal, Wahnish, Wizgan, Wizman, Ymar, Zabaro, Zafrani, Zagury, Zamero, Zaoui, Zazon, Zekri, Zimra, Zini, Znati, and Zrihen.

Ujlaki, Gyorgy (comp). *Most Common Names from the Sophia (Bulgaria) Jewish Cemetery.* Budapest: Ujlaki, 1997.

Abilash, Adroki, Aftalion, Alabalah, Aladjem, Albalah, Albas, Albasa, Albuhayre, Alfandari, Alhalel, Alkabes, Alkalai, Alkolukbre, Almaleh, Almoznino , Anavi, Anzhel, Apsheh, Arama, Arditti, Aroyo, Arucheti, Arye, Asael, Assa, Asseo, Astrik, Astrug, Astuk, Atias, Avigdor, Avishay, Azriel, Bakish, Barnathan, Baruh, Basan, Behar, Behmoram, Benaroy, Benatov, Benbasat, Beniesh, Benmayor, Benoasat, Bentura, Benvenisti, Benyozef, Beraha, Betzalel, Bidzherano, Biyla, Burla, Cemah, Daca, Dafret, Danon, David, Davitchon , Dekalo, Delareya, Djain, Djaldeti, Djiba, Djivany, Dzherasi, Elazar, Eli, Eshkenazi, Ezdra, Faraggi, Farhi, Faruy, Fintzi, Florentin, Fransiz, Garti, Gershon, Haimov, Hazan, Hazday, Hezkiya, Ilel, Isal, Izrale, Kalderon, Kalev, Kamhi, Kapo, Kapon, Karakash, Katalan, Katarivas, Katzuni, Kemalov, Konfino, Konforti, Konorti, Kordova, Koren, Kovo, Koyen, Krusrin, Levi, Lidzhi, Lossia, Luna, Lupo, Madzhar, Magrilo, Mamad, Mamon, Mandil, Manoah, Mashiah, Mashiyah, Melamed, Menashe, Merkado, Mesulam, Mevorah, Mezan, Mhael, Mizrahi, Molhov, Moscona, Moshe , Nahnias, Nardeya, Natan, Navon, Niego, Ninyo, Oliver, Ovadya, Pandjuro, Panizhel, Paparo, Papo, Pardo, Pardov, Penhas, Perera, Peretz, Pidzhi, Pilosof, Pinctzu, Pinkas, Piyade, Polikar, Prezente, Primo, Rahamim, Rahaminov, Reftov, Rodrig, Ronko, Rosanes, Sabitau, Sabitay, Salmi, Samuel, Sarfati, Sason, Seliktar, Seviliya, Shabat, Shamli, Shaulov, Sidi, Spinadel, Tadzhes, Tagger, Tagjer , Talvi , Taranto, Tchitchek, Uziel , Varsan, Yarhi, Yeroham, Yerushalmi, Yeshua, Yomtov, Yona, Yuazari, Yulzari, and Zaharigy.

B. Rituals and Practices of the Secret Jews of Portugal

The following is a list of practices indicative of Jewish origin assembled from numerous sources, formal and informal.

- Told one is Jewish explicitly by parents, grandparents, or other relatives, a boy when he turns 13, a girl at 12.
- Having Jewish family names: Duran, Lopez, etc.
- Secret synagogues; secret prayer groups.
- Avoiding church.
- Churches without icons.
- Lighting candles on Friday night when the first star appears.
- Clean house and clothes for Shabbat.
- Not allowed to do anything Friday night (not even wash hair).
- El Dia Puro (Yom Kippur).
- Celebrating a spring holiday.
- Fasts: three days of Tanit Esther; every Monday and Thursday, fast of Gedalia.
- Venerating Jewish saints, with celebrations: Santa Esterika, Santo Moises, etc.
- Eight candles for Christmas.
- Circumcision; consecration on eighth day (avoiding circumcision because that would bind child to the laws of Moses).
- Biblical first names, like Esther.
- Women taught Tanakh and ruled on questions.
- Married under huppah/canopy.
- Rending of garments; burial within one day; covering mirrors; spigots in cemeteries.
- Seven days, then one year, of mourning.
- Tombstones bearing Hebrew names, designations such as "daughter of Israel," and Jewish symbols (hand pointing to a star, open book of life, torah, star of David).
- Possessing talit and tefillin, mezuzot, Tanakh, siddurim other Jewish objects.
- Sweeping the floor away from the door (to avoid defiling mezuzah).
- Having Cabalistic knowledge and practices.
- Ritual slaughter (special knives, tested on hair or nails); covering blood with sand; removing sinew.
- Purging, soaking, salting, boiling meat.
- Avoiding pork and shellfish and other non-kosher foods (squirrel, rabbit).
- Avoiding blood; throwing out eggs with bloodspots.
- Avoiding red meat in general.
- Waiting between meat and milk.
- Eating only food prepared by mother or maternal grandmother.

BIRTH RITUALS

- To place a rooster's head over the door of the room where the birth will occur.
- After the birth the mother must not uncover herself or change clothes for 30 days.
- To throw a silver coin into the baby's first bath water, especially a son's.
- To say a prayer eight days after birth in which the baby's name is included.
- Belief that the fairies (*hadas*) preside over a naming ceremony at birth.

WEDDING RITUALS

- Only home weddings.
- To fast on the wedding day (both bride and groom, as well as two male friends of the groom and two female friends of the bride).
- To bind the bride and groom's hands with a white cloth while a prayer is said.
- To follow the wedding ceremony with a light meal consisting of a glass of wine, salt, bitter herbs, honey, an apple and unleavened bread.
- At the wedding ceremony bride and groom eat and drink out of the same plate and glass.
- Marrying your brother's widow (Levirate law).

FUNERAL RITUALS

- To have ritual meals to which a beggar is invited and serve the food the deceased liked best.
- To throw away all water in the home of the deceased.
- To leave furniture overturned to show how a relative's death has upset the family.
- To appear disheveled and careless about your own appearance during mourning.
- To go to the deceased's room for eight days and say: May God give you a good night. You were once like us, we will be like you.
- Not to shave for 30 days after the death of a relative.
- Not to eat meat for one week after a death in the family, then fast on the anniversary.

NAMING RITUALS

- Having two names, a private one in Hebrew (*kinnui*, e.g. Moses) and public one in the vernacular (Morris). Others: Jacob/James, Raphael/Ralph, Hannah/Johannah, Adina/Adelaide.
- Allusions to mascots of Hebrew tribes like deer (Naphthali) and wolf (Levi).
- Belief in being descended from the Biblical King David.
- Naming after religious objects: Paschal, Menorah.
- Translating Hebrew names, especially girls': Hannah into Grace, Esther into Myrtle, Peninah into Pearl, Roda into Rose, Shoshannah into Lillian or Lily, Simchah into Joy, Tikvah into Hope, Tzirrah into Jewel, Golda into Goldie.
- Allusions to Jacob's blessing of his sons and grandsons, e.g., Fishel for Ephraim because he was to multiply like the fish of the sea.
- Use of Hebrew but non-biblical names (e.g., Meir, Hayyim, Omar, Tamarah/Demarice).
- Use of names from Jewish legend and folklore (e.g., Adinah, Edna, Adel, progenitress of the tribe of Levi).
- Use of hypocoristic or pet names within the family alluding to Hebrew ones, for instance Zack or Ike for Isaac, Robin (Rueben) instead of Robert.
- Adding the theophoric suffix "el" to surnames, e.g., Lovell, Riddell, Tunnel.
- Naming after a living relative, preferably the eldest born after the grandfather or grandmother, the next

born after uncles and aunts and only after the
father when these names are exhausted (Sephardic)
or naming only after dead relatives (Ashkenazic).
- Use of double names like Edward Charles and James
  Robert.
- Changing the name of a child who becomes ill to
  foil the angel of death.
- Giving a child an amuletic name like Vetula ("old
  woman") to bring long life.
- Favoring names that begin with Lu- to remind the
  child that the family was once Portuguese (Lusitan-
  ian): Louise, Luanne, etc.
- Belief in gematria (numerology of names, determined
  by Hebrew alphabet)
- Avoiding saint's names (Paul, Peter, Barbara) and
  using Marianne or Mariah instead of Mary.
- Jokes about the virgin birth of Jesus by Mary
- Using names like Christopher or Christina to dispel
  doubts about conversion to Christianity.
- Knowing whether your family belongs to the
  Kohanim (priestly caste), Levite (House of David)
  or Israelite (all the rest) division of Jews.

OTHER

- Swearing an oath with your hat on.
- Not mentioning the name of God. Writing it G*d.
- Washing your hands before prayer.
- A father blessing a son in public.
- Saying grace after the meal.
- Bowing and bobbing during religious service.
- Jokes about the central tenets of Christianity (Im-

maculate Conception of Mary, rising from the dead
of Jesus, etc.).
- Deriding idolatry of saints and ornate decor of
  churches.
- Hatred of the pope.
- Preparing Saturday's meal (often a slow-cooking stew,
  for instance of eggplant) on Friday afternoon so no
  work is performed on the Sabbath.
- Eating preferably fruits that grow in the land of Israel
  (dates, olives, oranges, grapes, peaches etc.).
- Spreading sand from Israel on a grave or in a sanc-
  tuary.
- Eating tongue on Rosh Hashanah to symbolize *head*
  of the year.
- Having Bibles containing only the Old Testament and
  prayer books consisting only of the Psalms.
- Having pictures of rabbis and scholars rather than
  saints in the sanctuary.
- Performing tashlich, letting old clothes float away in
  running stream to mark a new year.
- Forgiving a debt on Yom Kippur.
- Facing Jerusalem during rituals.
- Uttering brief blessings when you see lightning,
  mountains and other natural wonders.
- Using only percussion instruments like the tam-
  bourine and hand clapping in services.
- Silent prayer by congregation after prayers made
  out loud.
- Worship services in the home.
- Having a quorum of 11 elders in a place of worship
  (minyam).

C. Muslim Rituals and Beliefs

Not as well documented as the practices of crypto–Jews are those of their neighbors the crypto–
Muslims, which are listed here for the sake of readers' convenience. These traits are extracted chiefly
from the chapter "Ways of Islam" and other parts of the book *A History of the Arab Peoples* by Albert
Hourani (1991).

- Belief that every Muslim is a Muslim's brother.
- The idea of *silsila*, a chain of witnesses stretching from
  the Prophet to the end of the world.
- Observance of the Pillars of Islam, the first of
  which is the *shahada*: testimony that "there is no
  god but God, and Muhammad is the Prophet of
  God." Repeating this daily in prayers.
- The second is daily affirmation of the basic creed in
  a ritual prayer called *salat*—either twice a day or
  five times a day facing the direction of Mecca.
- Ritual washing (*wudu*) of the hands before prayers,
  followed by bowing, kneeling and prostrating,
  often on a special prayer carpet.
- Beginning of the holy day at sunset on Thursday.
- Noon prayer on Friday.
- The third pillar is *zakat* ("purification"), gift giving
  to the poor and needy.
- *Sawm*, or fasting once a year in the month of

Ramadan, abstaining from sexual intercourse and
food until nightfall.
- Haji, pilgrimage to Mecca at least once in a lifetime,
  especially during the month of Dhu'l Hijja.
- Throwing a stone at the Devil.
- Use of only geometrical forms as ornaments in jew-
  elry, rugs and fabrics. No realistic animal forms.
- Use of the Arabic language. Forbiddance of other
  languages in recitation of Quran or law.
- Belief in *shari'a*, obedience to the laws of God.
- Brief, private ejaculations of praise or blessings.
- The concept that an individual could be a friend
  (*wali*) of God.
- Dancing the *zambra* (flamenco-like dance).
- Hanging votive rags on saints' shrines and natural
  places like springs.
- Celebrating the birthday of the Prophet (*mawlid*).
- The tomb of a saint as a place of refuge.

- Reading the Quran.
- Poetry composing contests, especially on the subject of beauty.
- Fountains and private gardens within courtyards.
- Forbidding of pipes and stringed instruments.
- Belief in astrology, alchemy, the evil eye and *jinns* (devils taking the form of animals).
- Belief in dream interpretation as a high art.
- Belief in angels.
- Knowledge of irrigation works, water wheels, underground pipes and canals.
- Letters of credit, partnerships and *commenda* (stock ventures).
- Calling a judge or leader a *qadi* and a religious authority an *imam*.
- Use of the Arabic language in calligraphy serving as a decoration in the home or on jewelry and clothing.
- Avoidance of pork.
- Wearing of the veil in public by women.
- Verbal divorce by man of his wife by repudiating her in public.
- Public baths (*hamman*).
- Burial within 24 hours of death, female relatives washing the body, wrapping in white cloth. Graves with a mound of dirt on them kept clear of all weeds and with no monument.

- Houses built to be seen within, not from outside, with only the size of the door revealing the owner's wealth. An antechamber or reception room separate from family quarters.
- Wearing slippers rather than shoes and reclining on cushions rather than sitting in chairs.
- Painting houses "Morocco green" or "Tunisian blue."
- Eating lamb rather than beef. Rare inclusion of any meat in a meal.
- Abstinence from alcohol, especially that not diluted with water.
- Belief in lucky numbers.
- Houses with turrets, arches, arabesque designs, submerged levels and courtyards.
- Forgiveness for oaths made before non–Muslims.
- Concept of the family situated within an inviolable space (*harem*).
- Regarding certain trades such as agriculture, tanning and leather working as unclean and unworthy.
- Exclusive use of Muslim butchers and ritual slaughtering.
- Charitable foundations (*awaqf*).
- Use of Spanish and other languages written with the Arabic alphabet (*aljamia*).
- Belief in the ability to trace one's descent back to an Arab tribe, companion of the Prophet, emir or caliph.

D. Customs and Beliefs of the Roma and Sinti

To help judge whether family traditions may have included Roma/Sinti or Romechal (the term used in the British Isles) ancestry, the following list of customs, terms and beliefs has been compiled from good authority.[1]

- Strict monotheism similar to Jews
- Keeping the seventh day holy
- Lighting candles on the evening of Parashat (Friday)
- Blasphemy a sin, as is cursing an elder
- Beng (Satan) the enemy of God and of the Roma people
- The Evil One called *bivuzhó* (impure) and *bilashó*

CODE OF LAW

- No social classes, only a division into Roma and Gadje (non–Roma)
- A court of justice called Kris (Judiciary Council), composed of clan representatives as judges
- Both men and women serving on Kris
- Issues between Roma to be judged only by the Kris, not by Gadje
- All Roma equal before the eyes of the Kris
- Belief in blood revenge and compensatory payment for clan of victim
- Banishment from territory of victim's clan for wrongdoing
- Forfeiture of protection if banished offender re-enters
- Roma not even to acknowledge or greet one who is banished

- Accursed or banished called *mahrimé* (impure)
- Roma not to ask interest for loans to other Roma, only from Gadje

SEXUALITY, MARRIAGE AND CHILDBIRTH

- Nudity is taboo, allowed only with a husband and wife
- Showing naked legs before an elder disrespectful
- Homosexuality an abomination
- Not allowed to wear clothes of the opposite sex, even as a joke or disguise
- Virginity before marriage essential
- Tokens of virginity shown to the assembly after wedding
- Prostitution strongly condemned
- Incest taboo, defined in the same way as Mosaic law (including step-siblings and in-laws)
- Permissible to marry your cousin
- Members of the Kris must be married
- Lack of a spouse makes a man or woman incomplete
- Groom's family pays dowry to the bride's family
- Dowry for a widow amounts to half that for a virgin
- A man dishonoring a woman should pay the dowry to her family anyway

- Runaway couples considered legitimately married
- Marriage endogamic, even within the same clan
- Clan recognized by a common ancestor within a few generations
- Divorce admitted: husband sends wife out or she leaves
- Remarriage expected after divorce
- Levirate law practiced (Deut. 25:5–6)
- Childbirth impure, must take place outside the home
- Mother giving birth isolated with baby for seven days strictly, followed by 33 days of less strict isolation (cf. Lev. 12:2, 4–5)
- New mother cannot show herself in public or attend religious services
- Both sexes marrying very young (child marriage)

Funeral and Mourning Rituals

- Dead to be buried intact (autopsy or cremation sacrilegious)
- Close relatives of the dead impure for seven days
- Not to touch a dead body
- Family and relatives of deceased forbidden to bathe, comb their hair, cut their nails for three days
- On third day after a death, relative must wash thoroughly, and then not again until seventh day
- All food in house where a person died is thrown away as defiled
- On third day after a death, the house is purified ("the ashes of the burning of the sin") and a virgin sprinkles running water
- The same ceremony repeated on the seventh day after a death, with food brought to the mourners from another dwelling place
- Mourners stay at home
- Sitting on low stools
- Covering mirrors
- Not using oils or perfumes or cosmetics
- Not wearing new clothes
- Not listening to loud music
- Not taking photographs or watching television
- Not painting, cooking, and cannot greet people
- Day mourning extended after seventh day remembrance ceremony until thirtieth day
- Another remembrance ceremony on thirtieth day, closing the strict mourning period

Beliefs in Afterlife

- Death is final, no reincarnation or return
- Soul goes to Paradise or Hell

Purity and Impurity

- Concept of *marimé* (similar to *kashrut*)
- Lower body and things associated with it impure
- Sleeping regarded as an impure state
- Not to greet anyone upon waking until washed
- Disrespectful to greet anyone in an impure state
- Dogs and cats impure
- Horses, donkeys or riding animal impure
- Carnivorous animals impure
- Avoidance of horseflesh
- Shoes, pants, hose, skirts, trousers, etc. impure
- The camp pure
- Restrooms built outside the home
- Clothes for the lower body and menstruating women washed separately
- Dishes washed in a different place from clothes

Other Practices

- Custom of *mangel*, asking for favors from Gadje
- Painting doorposts of dwelling with animal blood to protect against angel of death
- Invoking the Prophet Elijah, particularly when seeing lightning or hearing thunder
- Firstborn son considered a special blessing to the family
- Wearing of whiskers
- Left hand related to the public domain (Gadje), impure
- Separate dishes and cups for Gadje
- Only eating ritually slaughtered animals
- Slander considered very a very serious offense, worth taking to Kris
- Lack of belief in divination (contrary to general view of Gypsies)
- Practice of Tarot cards and crystal balls for Gadje only
- Having a Gypsy name besides a civil name
- Names that are Hebrew, Greek, Russian, Spanish, Hungarian, Persian, never Indian or Hindu
- Beef a favorite food
- Interest in bullfighting
- Middle Eastern music and dance with zithers, etc. (Flamenco in Spain)
- Fingernails and toenails filed with an emery board, not a clipper
- Going to a church called Filadelfia (Brotherhood)
- Claiming to be Egyptian in origin
- Making pilgrimages to the burial places of your ancestors

E. Lists of Immigrants to Virginia 1585–1700

Given in this appendix are lists of traditional names for the earliest colonists in Virginia. The names generally are listed in the order and spelling of the source records. Some glosses and annotations have been added in parentheses and notes.

THE NAMES OF LANE'S COLONISTS (1585)

The names of all those ... that remained one whole yeere in Virginia
under the Governement of Master Ralfe Lane.[1]*— National Park Service.*

Master Philip Amades, Admirall of the coun- trie
Master Hariot
Master Acton
Master Edward Stafford
Thomas Luddington
Master Marvyn
Master Gardyner
Captaine Vaughan
Master Kendall
Master Prideox
Robert Holecroft
Rise Courtney
Master Hugh Rogers
Thomas Foxe
Edward Hugen
Darby Glande
Edward Kelle
John Gostigo
Erasmus Clefs
Edward Ketcheman
John Linsey
Thomas Rottenbury
Roger Deane
John Harris
Master Thomas Harvie
Master Smelling

Master Anthony Russe
Master Allyne
Maste Michel Polyson
John Cage
Thomas Parre
William Randes
Geffrey Churchman
William Farthowe
John Taylor
Philppe Robyns
Thomas Phillippes
Valentine Beale
James Skinner
George Eseven
John Chaundeler
Philip Blunt
Richard Poore
Robert Yong
Marmaduke Constable
Thomas Hesket
William Wasse
John Fever
Daniel
Frauncis Norris
Mathewe Lyne
Edward Kettell (Catteil?)
Thomas Wisse
Robert Biscombe

William Backhouse
William White
Henry Potkin
Dennis Barnes
Joseph Borges
Doughan Gannes
William Tenche
Randall Latham
Thomas Hulme
Walter Myll
Richard Gilbert
Steven Pomarie (Pomerie)
John Brocke
Bennett Harrye
James Stevenson
Christopher Lowde
Jeremie Man
James Mason
David Salter
Richard Ireland
Thomas Bookener (Buchener)
William Philippes
Randall Mayne
Thomas Taylor
Richard Humfrey
John Wright
Gabriell North

Bennet Chappell
Richard Sare
James Sare
James Lasie
Smolkin
Thomas Smart
Robert
John Evans
Roger Large
Humfrey Garden
Frauncis Whitton
Rowland Griffyn
William Millard
John Twyt
Edwarde Seklemore
John Anwike
Christopher Marshall
David Williams
Nicholas Swabber
Edward Chipping
Sylvester Beching
Vincent Cheyne
Haunce Walters
Edward Barecombe
Thomas Skevelabs
William Walters

THE NAMES OF THE 1587 VIRGINIA COLONISTS

The names of all the men, women and Children, which safely arrived in Virginia, and remained
to inhabite there. 1587. Anno Regni Reginae Elizabethae. 29.— National Park Service.

John White [Governor]
Roger Bailie [Assistant]
Ananias Dare [Assistant]
Christopher Cooper [Assis- tant]
Thomas Stevens [Assistant]
John Sampson [Assistant]
Dyonis Harvie [Assistant]
Roger Prat [Assistant]
George Howe [Assistant]
Simon Fernando [Assistant]
Nicholas Johnson
Thomas Warner
Anthony Cage
John Jones
John Tydway
Ambrose Viccard
Edmond English
Thomas Topan
Henry Berrye
Richard Berrye
John Spendlove
John Hemmington
Thomas Butler
Edward Powell
John Burden

James Hynde
William Willes
John Brooke
Cutbert White
John Bright
Clement Tayler

Women

Elyoner Dare
Margery Harvie
Agnes Wood
Wenefrid Powell
Joyce Archard
Jane Jones
Elizabeth Glane
Jane Pierce
Audry Tappan
Alis Chapman
Emme Merrimoth
Colman
Margaret Lawrence

[Men]

William Sole
John Cotsmur
Humfrey Newton

Thomas Colman
Thomas Gramme
Marke Bennet
John Gibbes
John Stilman
Robert Wilkinson
Peter Little
John Wyles
Brian Wyles
George Martyn
Hugh Pattenson
Martyn Sutton
John Farre
John Bridger
Griffin Jones
Richard Shaberdge
Thomas Ellis
William Browne
Michael Myllet
Thomas Smith
Richard Taverner
Thomas Harris
Richard Taverner
John Earnest
Henry Johnson
John Starte

Richard Darige
William Lucas
Joan Warren
Jane Mannering
Rose Payne
Elizabeth Viccars
Arnold Archard
John Wright
William Dutton
Morris Allen
William Waters
Richard Arthur
John Chapman
William Clement
Robert Little
Hugh Taylor
Richard Wildye
Lewes Wotton
Michael Bishop
Henry Browne
Henry Rufoote
Richard Tomkins
Henry Dorrell
Charles Florrie
Henry Mylton
Henry Payne

Thomas Harris	Thomas Hewet	Thomas Archard	**Children Born in**
William Nicholes	William Berde	Thomas Humfrey	**Virginia**
Thomas Phevens		Thomas Smart	
John Borden	**Boys and Children**	George Howe	Virginia Dare
Thomas Scot	John Sampson	John Prat	Harvye
James Lasie	Robert Ellis	William Wythers	
John Cheven	Ambrose Viccars		

Original Settlers (May 14, 1607) at Jamestown, Listed by Occupation[2]

Source: *Virtual Jamestown: The First Residents of Jamestown*[3]

Council Members

Master Edward Maria Wingfield,
  President
Captaine Bartholomew Gosnoll
Captaine John Smyth (or Smith)
Captaine John Ratliffe (or Ratcliffe)
Captaine John Martin
Captaine George Kendall

Preacher and gentleman

Master Robert Hunt

Gentlemen

Master George Percy
Anthony Gosnoll
George Flower
Captaine Gabriell Archer
Robert Fenton
Robert Ford
William Bruster (or Brewster)
Edward Harrington
Dru Pickhouse (or Pigasse)
Thomas Jacob, Sergeant
John Brookes
Ellis Kingston (or Kiniston)
Thomas Sands
Benjamin Beast (Best)
John (or Jehu) Robinson (Melungeon name)
Ustis (or Eustace) Clovill
Stephen Halthrop
Kellam Throgmorton
Edward Morish (or Moris)
Nathaniell Powell
Edward Browne
Robert Behethland (or Betheland)
John Penington
Jeremy (or Jerome) Alicock
George Walker
Thomas Studley (or Stoodie)
Richard Crofts
Nicholas Houlgrave

Thomas Webbe
John Waller
John Short (Melungeon name)
William Tankard
William Smethes
Francis Snarsbrough
Richard Simons
Edward Brookes
Richard Dixon
John Martin
Roger Cooke
George Martin
Anthony Gosnold
Thomas Wotton (Wooten), Surgeon
John Stevenson
Henry Adling (or Adding)
Thomas Gower
Thomas Gore
Francis Midwinter
Richard Frith
Stephen Galthorpe (Goldthorp)

Carpenters

William Laxton
Edward Pising
Thomas Emry
Robert Small

Bricklayers

John Herd (Heard)
William Garret

Labourers

William Cassen (or Cawsen)
George Casson
Thomas Casson
Willam Rods (or Rodes = Rhodes)
William White (Melungeon name)
Ould Edward (perhaps a Scot or Irishman)

Henry Tavin (or Tauin: from Hebrew)
George Golding (or Goulding)
William Johnson
William Vnger (or Unger, i.e., Hungarian)

Boys (i.e., servants)

Samuell Collier (Melungeon name)
James Brumfield
Richard Mutton (or Mullon = Mullin: Melungeon name)

Other

Anas Todkill, Soldier
Jonas Profit (Melungeon name), Sailor, Fisher, Soldier
Thomas Couper (or Cowper: Melungeon name), Barber
Edward Brinto (or Brinton), Mason, Soldier
William Loue (or Love: Melungeon name), Tailor, Soldier
Nicholas Skot (or Scot), Drummer
John Laydon (i.e., from Leiden), Labourer, Carpenter
John Dods (Dodds), Labourer, Soldier
William Wilkinson, Surgeon
James Read (Melungeon name), Blacksmith, Soldier
Nathaniel Pecock (or Peacock), Boy, Sailor, Soldier
Mathew Morton, Sailor
John Asbie (Melungeon name) Unclassified
Andrew Buckler
John Capper (perhaps Cooper)
William Dier (or Dye, Melungeon name)
Thomas Mounslie
Thomas Mouton, a Dutchman

Mariners and Others Known to Have Been with the Expedition That Established Jamestown on May 13, 1607[4]

Source: *The First Residents of Jamestown*

Browne, Oliver
Clarke, Charles (Melungeon name)
Collson, John Mariner
Cotson, John Mariner

Danyell, Stephen
Deale, Jeremy
Fytch, Mathew Mariner
Genoway, Richard (from Genoa?)

Godword, Thomas
Jackson, Robert (Melungeon name)
Markham, Robert
Nellson, Francys

Newport, Christopher Captain,
  Councilor
Poole, Jonas

Skunner, Thomas
Turnbrydge (or Turbridge),
  Thomas

Tyndall, Robert Mariner, Gunner
White, Benjamyn (Melungeon
  name)

JAMESTOWN COLONISTS ON THE RESUPPLY SHIP, 1608

SOURCE: National Park Service

Thomas Abbay
Jeffery Abbot
Rob Alberton
David Aphugh
Robert Barnes
William Bayley
Gabriel Beadle
John Beadle
William Beckwith
Richard Belfield
Henry Bell
William Bentley
John Bouth
Thomas Bradley
Richard Bristow
Richard Burket
Anne Burras
John Burras
James Burre
George Burton
William Cantrell
Nathaniell Causy
John Clarke
Thomas Coe
Henry Collings
Robert Cotton

Raleigh Crowhaw
John Cuderington
Robert Culter
John Dauxe
Thomas Dawse
Will Dawson
Richard Dole
William Dowman
David Ellis
Richard Featherstone
Thomas Field
Unknown Floud
George Forest
Thomas Forest
Unknown Forest
Thomas Fox
Thomas Gibson
Post Ginnat
Raymond Goodison
Richard Gradson
Thomas Graves
William Grivell
Edward Gurgana
Nicholas Handcock
Unknown Hardwyn
Harmon Harrison

George Hill
Unknown Hilliard
Thomas Hope
John Hoult
Unknown Hunt
Wil Johnson
Peter Keffer
Richard Killingbeck
Thomas Lavander
Timothy Leeds
Henry Leigh
John Lewes
Michael Lowick
Thomas Mallard
Thomas Maxes
William May
Unknown Michaell
Unknown Milman
Richard Milmer
Unknown Morley
Ralph Morton
Richard Mullinax
Rawland Nelstrop
John Nichols
Thomas Norton
Dionis O'Connor

William Perce
Francis Perkins
Thomas Phelps
Henry Philpot
Michaell Phittiplace
William Phittiplace
Peter Pory
Richard Pots
John Powell
Unknown Powell
John Prat
George Pretty
Richard Prodger
David Pugh
Christopher Rods
Unknown Rose
John Russell
Unknown Russell
William Russell
William Sambage
Richard Savage
Thomas Savage
Unknown Scot
Mathew Scrivener
Jeffrey Shortridge
Michaell Sicklemore

William Simons
John Spearman
William Spence
Dani Stallings
John Taverner
William Tayler
Lawrence Towtales
Daniel Tucker
Nicholas Ven
Unknown Vere
Richard Waldo
Unknown Walker
William Ward
James Watkins
Francis West
Unknown Wiles
Unknown Williams
Hugh Winne
Peter Winne
Hugh Wolleston
Richard Worley
George Yarington
William Younge

SEA VENTURE PASSENGERS

SOURCES: *The Generall Historie of the Bermudas*, by Captain John Smith, 1624,
reprint 1966; and *Bermuda: Unintended Destination*, by Terry Tucker, 1982

Sir Thomas Gates, Governor for Virginia
Sir George Somers, Admiral of the flotilla
Rev. Richard, chaplain to the expedition
William Strachney, Secretary-elect of Virginia Company
Silvester Jourdain, of Lyme Regis, Dorset
Joseph Chard
Mr. Henry Shelly
Robert Walsingham, cockswain
Robert Frobisher, shipwright
Nicholas Bennit, carpenter
Francis Pearepoint
William Brian
William Martin
Henry Ravens, master mate; lost at sea when he sailed for
  help
Richard Knowles
Stephen Hopkins
Christopher Carter, deserted and stayed behind on the
  island
Robert Waters, deserted and stayed behind on the island
Edward Waters
Samuel Sharpe
Henry Paine, shot to death for mutiny
Humfrey Reede

James Swift
Thomas Powell, cook
Edward Eason
Mistress Eason
Baby boy Bermuda Eason, born in Bermuda to the above
John Want
Mistress Horton
Elizabeth Persons, maid to Mistress Horton; married
  Thomas Powell while in Bermuda
Capt. (Sir) George Yeardley, experienced veteran of the
  Dutch wars
Jeffrey Briars, died in Bermuda
Richard Lewis, died in Bermuda
Edward Samuel, murdered by Robert Waters
William Hitchman, died in Bermuda
Thomas Whittingham, lost at sea with Henry Ravens (above)
Edward Chard, who stayed behind on the island
Captain Matthew Somers, nephew and heir of Sir George,
  was aboard the Swallow on the same expedition
Robert Rich*, the brother of Sir Nathaniel Rich, a share-
  holder. Was a soldier. Returned to Bermuda 1617 and
  died there 1630.
Christopher Newport*, captain of the Sea Venture, former
  privateer

Stephen Hopkins*

John Rolfe*, a young man in his twenties and traveling with his wife. Their baby girl was born in Bermuda, christened Bermuda and died shortly thereafter. His

wife died shortly after reaching Virginia in Spring 1610 and he married Pocahontas in April 1614.

Mistress Rolfe, first wife of above

*Royal Naval Dockyard Museum, Somerset, Bermuda (Tucker's Note).

ADDITIONAL PERSONS LISTED AS ARRIVING AT JAMESTOWN IN THE *PATIENCE* AND THE *DELIVERANCE* (AND THEREFORE ASSUMED TO BE ABOARD THE *SEA VENTURE* WHEN IT WRECKED AT BERMUDA)

SOURCE: *Cavaliers and Pioneers* by Nell Marion Nugent (1963)

Henry Bagwell, age 35, in *Deliverance*

Thomas Godby, age 36, in the *Deliverance*

Edward Waters, age 40, in the *Patience*

Elizabeth Joons, age 30, servant

John Lytefoote

John Proctor

VIRGINIA HISTORICAL INDEX BY E.G. SWEM

According to the original records, "As a results of the efforts, Sir Thomas Gates as sole and absolute Governor, with Sir George Summers, Admiral, and Capt. Newport, Vice Admiral of Virginia, and divers and other persons of ran four cke and quality in seven ships and two pinnaces, left Falmouth on the 8 of June 1609, and on the 24 day of July, 1609 they encountered a terrible storm that prevailed from Tuesday noone till Friday noone; that scattered the fleet and wrecked the *Sea Venture* (on July 28, 1609) upon the island of Bermuda."

Francis Michell lived at Elizabeth Citty February 1623 and Josuah Chard, aged 36, who came in the *Sea Venture*, May 1607.

Josuah Chard came in the *Sea Venture*

PURSE AND PERSON

The following came in the *Sea Venture* (from different pages)

p. 15   Henry Baguel

p. 22   Samuel Sharp

p. 30   John Lightfoote

p. 31   Capt. Wm Pierce

p. 32   George Grave

p. 38   John Procter

p. 140   Richard Buck sailed June 1609 with wife, Miss Langley and four Buck children. Marooned for 9 months embarked for Virginia from Bermuda 10 May 1610. Arrived in Jamestown 21 May 1610. He was a minister. The four Buck children, Elizabeth, Bridget and Bermuda were born and died while their parent marooned on Somers Island (1609–1610) Mara born in Virginia 1611 ward of brother-in-law, John Burrows.

p. 374   Stephen Hopkins left England 9 June 1609 among 150 persons cast ashore etc etc then it states "Although there is no complete list of the shipwrecked

party which eventually reached Jamestown in the two pinnaces Patience and Deliverance, built on the islands, Hopkins did not remain on The Somers Islands and the conclusion is that the recalcitrant came to Virginia despite his known wish to return to England. (He went back to England and came on the Mayflower in 1620 to Plymouth, Mass.) No further connection with the Colony.

p. 475   Wm Pierce

p. 507   John Rolfe and wife. 9 months on Somers Island. Wife died on Somers Island or shortly after arriving in Virginia.

p. 590   Wm Strachey from Surrey England b 1572 on SV, marooned 9 mo etc

p. 650   Lieut. Edward Waters on SV and on to Virginia Patience.

p. 724   George Yeardley

Admiral Sir George Somers (1554–1610) was born near Lyme Regis in Dorset, England of modest circumstances. At an early age he took to the sea, and as a captain of the Flibcote he captured Spanish booty, bringing it back to Dartmouth. He became a large landowner by his early thirties. In 1609 he received orders to command an expedition to Virginia, mortgaged his property and outfitted the Sea Venture. He left no direct descendants.

WALLOON AND FRENCH COLONISTS TO VIRGINIA (1621)

SOURCE: W. Noel Sainsbury, ed. *Calendar of State Papers*, pp. 498–99

According to the original records, the settlers swore, "We promise my Lord Ambassador of the Most Serene King of Great Britain to go and inhabit in Virginia, a land under his Majesty's obedience, as soon as conveniently may be, and this under the conditions to be carried out in the articles we have communicated to the said Ambassador, and not otherwise, on the faith of which we have unanimously signed this present with our sign manual." The signatures and the calling of each are appended in the form of a round robin, and in a outer circle the person signing states whether he is married, and the number of his children. The charter is endorsed by Sir Dudley Carleton.

Signature of such Walloons and French as offer themselves to goe into Verginia." The names with an asterisk have only signed their marks. Total 227, including 55 men, 41 women, 129 children, and two servants.

Mousnier de la Montagne, medical student; marrying man

Mousnier de la Montagne, apothecary and surgeon; marrying man

Jacque Conne, tiller of the earth; wife and two children

Henry Lambert, woolen draper; wife

*George Beava, porter; wife and one child

Michel Du Pon, hatter; wife and two children

Jan Bullt, labourer; wife and four children

Paul de Pasar, weaver; wife and two children

Antoine Grenier, gardener; wife

Jean Gourdeman, labourer; wife and five children

Jean Campion, wool carder; wife and four children

*Jan De La Met, labourer; young man

*Antoine Martin, wife and one child

Francois Fourdrin, leather dresser; young man

*Jan Leca, labourer; wife and five children

Theodore Dufour, draper; wife and two children

*Gillian Broque, labourer; young man

George Wauter, musician; wife and four children

*Jan Sage, serge maker; wife and six children

*Marie Flit, in the name of her husband, a miller; wife and two children

P. Gantois, student in theology; young man

Jacques de Lecheilles, brewer; marrying man

*Jan Le Rou, printer; wife and six children

*Jan de Croy, sawyer; wife and five children

*Charles Chancy, labourer; wife and two children

*Francois Clitdeu, labourer; wife and five children

*Phillippe Campion, draper; wife and one child

*Robert Broque, labourer; young man

Philip De le Mer, carpenter; young man

*Jeanne Martin; young girl

Pierre Cornille, vine-dresser; young man

Jan de Carpentry, labourer; wife and two children

*Martin de Carpentier, brass founder; young man

Thomas Farnarcque, locksmith; wife and seven children

Pierre Gaspar

*Gregoire Le Juene, shoemaker; wife and four children

Martin Framerie, musician; wife and one child

Pierre Quesnee, brewer; marrying man

Pontus Le Gean, bolting-cloth weaver; wife and three children

*Barthelemy Digaud, sawyer; wife and eight children

Jesse de Forrest, dyer; wife and five children

*Nicholas De la Marlier, dyer; wife and two children

*Jan Damont, labourer; wife

*Jan Gille, labourer; wife and three children

*Jan de Trou, wool carder; wife and five children

Philippe Maton, dyer, and two servants; wife and five children

Anthoine de Lielate, vinedresser; wife and four children

Ernou Catoir, wool carder; wife and five children

Anthoin Desendre, labourer; wife and one child

Agel de Crepy, shuttle worker; wife and four children

*Adrian Barbe, dyer; wife and four children

*Michel Leusier, cloth weaver; wife and one child

*Jerome Le Roy, cloth weaver; wife and four children

*Claude Ghiselin, tailor; young man

*Jan de Crenne, glass maker? (fritteur); wife and one child

*Louis Broque, labourer; wife and two children

MORE SETTLERS FROM VARIOUS SOURCES

According to the records, in 1635, in addition to those before-mentioned were Jonas Austin, Nicholas Baker, Clement Bates Richard Betscome, Benjamin Bozworth, William Buckland, James Cade, Anthony Cooper, John Cutler, John Farrow, Daniel Fop, Jarvice Gould, Wm. Hersey, Nicholas Hodsdin, Thos. Johnson, Andrew Lane, Wm. Large, Thomas Loring, George Ludkin, Jeremy Morse, William Nolton, John Otis, David Phippeny, John Palmer, John Porter, Henry Rust, John Smart, Francis Smith (or Smyth), John Strong, Henry Tuttil, William Walton, Thomas Andrews, William Arnall, George Bacon, Nathaniel Baker, Thomas Collier, George Lane, George Marsh, Abraham Martin, Nathaniel Peck, Richard Osborn, Thomas Wakely, Thomas Gill, Richard Ibrook, William Cockerum, William Cockerill, John Fearing, and John Tucker.

Moreover, in 1636 were John Beal, senior, Anthony Eames, Thomas Hammond, Joseph Hull, Richard Jones, Nicholas Lobdin, Richard Langer, John Leavitt, Thomas Lincoln, Jr., miller, Thomas Lincoln, cooper, Adam Mott, Thomas Minard, John Parker, George Russell, William Sprague, George Strange, Thomas Underwood, Samuel Ward, Ralph Woodward, John Winchester, and William Walker.

In 1637 were Thomas Barnes, Josiah Cobbit, Thomas Chaffe, Thomas Clapp, William Carlslye (or Carsly), Thomas Dimock, Vinton Dreuce, Thomas Hett, Thomas Joshlin, Aaron Ludkin, John Morrick, Thomas Nichols, Thomas Paynter, Edmund Pitts, Joseph Phippeny, Thomas Shave, Ralph Smith, Thomas Turner, John Tower, Joseph Underwood, William Ludkin, and Jonathan Bozworth.

In 1638 there was a considerable increase of the number of settlers. Among them were Robert Peck, Joseph Peck, Edward Gilman, John Foulsham, Henry Chamberlain, Stephen Gates, George Knights, Thomas Cooper, Matthew Cushing, John Beal, Jr., Francis James, Philip James, James Buck, Stephen Payne, William Pitts, Edward Michell, John Sutton, Stephen Lincoln, Samuel Parker, Thomas Lincoln, Jeremiah Moore, Henry Smith, Bozoan Allen, Matthew Hawke, and William Ripley.

According to our sources, all of those preceding who came to this country in 1638, took passage in the ship *Diligent*, of Ipswich, John Martin, master. In addition to these, the following received grants of land in 1638: John Buck, John Benson, Thomas Jones, Thomas Lawrence, John Stephens, John Stodder, widow Martha Wilder, and Thomas Thaxter.

In 1639 Anthony Hilliard and John Prince received grants of land. The names of Hewett (Huet) and Liford are mentioned in Hobart's diary, in that year, and in the diary the following names are first found in the respective years mentioned: in 1646, Burr; in 1647, James Whiton; in 1649, John Lazell and Samuel Stowell; in 1653, Garnett and Canterbury.

PASSENGERS ON THE *ABRAHAM* BOUND FROM LONDON, ENGLAND, TO VIRGINIA IN 1635

John Barker (perhaps an error for Barber), Master,
Arranged by First Name, Surname and Age

SOURCE: http://www.olivetreegenealogy.com/ships/tova_abraham1635.shtml

Tobie Sylbie 20	Jo: Clark 20	Francis Stanely 23	Patrick Wood 24
Robert Harrison 32	Gabriell Thomas 30	Willm Freeman 46	Tho: Kedby 25
Willm Lawrence 22	David Jones 21	Edward Griffth 33	Riger Greene 24
John Johnson 35	Alexander Maddox 22	Willm Manton 30	Will= Downs 24
W. Fisher 25	Francis Tippsley 17	Owen Williams 40	Jo: Burnett 24
Steeven Taylor 17	Emanuell Davies 19	Tho: Flower 32	Tho: Allen 31
Tho: Penford 30	W=Williams 25	Jo: Bullar 32	Simon Farrell 19
Wm Smith 25	Roger Matthews 28	Jo: Clanton 26	Tho: Clements 30
Tho: Archdin 18	Jo: Britton 23	Alexander Symes 19	Wm Hunt 20
Rich Morris 17	George Preston 20	Anto Parkhurst 42	Kathryn Adwell 33
Walter Piggott 19	Robert Toulban 23	Jo" Hill 36	
Rich Watkyns 20	Henry Dobell 20	Alexander Gregorie 24	
Jo: Brunch 13	George Brewett 18	Martin Westlink 20	

THE *DAVID* FROM ENGLAND TO VIRGINIA, 1635

The under-written Names are to be transported to Virginea, Inbarqued in the
"David," Jo. Hogg, Master, have been examined by the minister of Gravesend, etc.

SOURCE: http://www.olivetreegenealogy.com/ships/tova_david1635.shtml

Edward Browne 25	Jo: Bonfilly 21	Jo: Morris 26	Ann Beeford 25
Samuel Troope 17	Roger Mannington 14	Richard Brookes 30	Martha Potter 20
Wm Hatton 23	Josua Chanbers 17	Robert Barron 18	Gurtred Lovett 18
Daniel Bacon 30	Henry Melton 23	Jonathan Barnes 22	Jane Jennings 25
Robert Alsopp 18	Davod Lloyd 30	Henry Kendall 17	Margaret Bole 30
Teddar Jones 30	Donough Gornes 27	Tho: Poulter 31	Mary Rogers 20
Tho: Siggins 18	Geo: Butler 27	Jo: Lamb 22	Margaret Walker 20
Abell Dexter 25	Addan Nunnick 25	Tho: Nunnick 22	Freese Brooran 20
Rich Caton 26	Jo: Stann 27	Jo: Steevens 19	Eliza Jones 20
Henry Spicer 28	Edward Spicer 18	Edward Crabtree 20	
Tho: Granger 19	Jo: Felding 19	Wm Barber 17	

THE *BONAVENTURE* (1635)

SOURCE: http://www.olivetreegenealogy.com/ships/tova_merchbona1635.shtml

Richard Doll 25	Mary Carlton 23	Richard Champion 1	Rich: Hore 24
Tho: Perry 34	Abram Silvester 40	Abram Silvester 14	Ralph Nichelson 20
Uxor Dorothy 26	Tho: Belton	Elizabeth Nanisk 20	Robert More 20
Ben: Perry	Richard Champion 1	Jo Atkinson 30	Joan Nubold 20

Tho: Hebden 20
Willm Sayer 58
Brazil Brooke 20
Robert Perry 40
Charles Hillard 22
Edward Clark 30
Jo: Ogell 28
Richard Hargrave 20
Jo: Anderson 20
Francis Spence 23
John Lewes 23
Richard Hughes 19
John Clark 19
Wm Guy 18
John Burd 18
James Redding 19
Richard Cooper 18
Andrew Jefferies 24
Wm Munday
Arthur Howell 20
Jo: Abby 22
James Moyser 28
Mathew Marshall 30
Wm Smith 20
Garrett Riley 24
Miles Riley 20
Willm Burch 19
Peter Dole 20
James Metcalf 22
Margerie Furbredd 20
Jo: Underwood 23

Robert Luck 25
John Wood 23
Waltr Morgan 23
Henrie Irish 16
George Greene 20
Henry Quinton 20
Jo: Bryan 25
Robert Payton 25
Tho: Symonds 27
Michell Browne 35
Jo: Hodges 37
Jo: Edmonds 16
Garrett Pownder 19
Jo: Wise 28
Henry Dunnell 23
Symon Kenneday 20
Tho: Hyet 22
Tho: James 20
Jo: Sotterfeyth 24
Emannell Bomer 18
Leonard Wetherfield 17
James Luckbarrowe 20
Tho: Singer 18
Jesper Withy 21
Robert Kersley 22
Jo: Springall 18
Tho: Jessupp 18
James Perkyns 42
Daniell Greene 24
Wm Hutton 24
Jo: Wilkinson 19

Hugh Garland 20
Richard Spencer 18
Humfrey Topsall 24
Tho: Stanton 20
John Fountaine 18
Henry Redding 22
Loughten Bosteck 16
John Russell 19
Tho: Ridgley 23
Robert Harris 19
Willm Mason 10
Victor Derrick 23
John Bamford 28
Margaret Huntley 20
Geo: Session 40
Jo: Cooke 47
Tho: Townson 26
Tho: Parson 30
Tho: Goodman 25
Philip Connor 21
Launcelot Pyrce 21
Uxor Thomazin 18
Kat: Yates 19
Alveryn Cowper 20
Jo: Dunnell 26
Leonard Evans 22
Tho: Anderson 28
Edward Cranfield 18
Jo: Baggley 14
Tho: Smith 14
Willm Weston 30

Tho: Townsend 14
Edward Davies 25
Mary Saunders 26
Jane Chambers 23
Margaret Maddocks 21
Roger Sturdevant 21
John Wigg 24
John Greenwood 16
Andrew Dunton 38
John Wise 30
Wm Hudson 32
Tho: Edmborough 37
John Hill 50
Henry Rogers 30
Robert Smithson 23
Nics Harvey 30
James Grafton 22
Daniell Daniell 18
Reginell Hawes 25
Geo: Burlington 20
Jo: Hutchinson 22
James Crane 17
Richard Hurman 20
Sam: Ashley 19
Geo: Burlingham 20
Elizabeth Jackson 17
Sara Turner 20
Mary Ashley 24

HUGUENOT REFUGEES ON BOARD SHIP *MARY AND ANN*, AUGUST 12, 1700, VIRGINIA, JAMES CITY

SOURCE: http://newsarch.rootsweb.ancestry.com/th/read/CHASTAIN/1999-10/0938965828

Pierre Delome, et sa femme
Marguerite Sene, et sa fille
Magdalaine Mertle
Jean Vidau
Jean Menager et Jean Lesnard
Estienne Badouet
Pierre Morrisct
Jedron Chamboux et sa femme
Jean Farry et Jerome Dumas
Jean Tardieu
Jean Moreau
Jaques Roy, et sa femme
Abraham Sablet, et des deux enfants
Quintin Chastatain et Michael Roux
Jean Quictet, sa femme and trios enfants
Henry Cabanis, sa femme et un enfant
Jaques Sayte
Jean Boisson
Francois Bosse
Teertulien Sehult, et sa femme et deux enfants
Pierre Lauret
Jean Roger
Pierre Chastain, a femme et cinq enfants
Philippe Duvivier

Pierre Nace, sa femme et leur deux filles
Francois Clere
Symon Sardin
Sourbragon, et Jacques Nicolay
Pierre Mallet
Francoise Coupet
Jean Oger, sa femme et trios enfants
Jane or Jean Saye
Elizabet Angeliere
Jean et Claude Mallfant, avec leur mere
Isaac Chabanas, sou fils, et Catharine Bomard
Estinne Chastain
Adam Vignes
Jean Fouchie
Francoise Sassin
Andre Cochet
Jean Gaury, sa femme et un enfant
Pierre Gaury, sa femme et un enfant
Pierre Perrut, et sa femme
Isaac Panetier
Jean Parransos, sa seur
Elie Tremson, sa femme
Elizabeth Tignac
Antoine Trouillard

Jean Bourru et Jean Bouchet
Jaques Boyes
Elizabet Migot
Catherine Godwal
Pierre la Courru
Jean et Michell Cautepie, sa femme et deux enfants
Jaques Broret, sa femme et deux enfants
Abraham Moulin et sa femme
Francois Billot
Pierre Comte
Ettienne Guevin
Rene Massoneau
Francois Du Tartre
Isaac Verry
Jean Parmentier
David Thonitier et sa femme
Moyse Lewreau
Pierre Tillou
Marie Levesque
Jean Constantin
Claud Berdon, sa femme
Jean Imbert, et sa femme
Elizabeth Fleury
Looys du Pyn
Jaques Richard, et sa femme

Adam et Marie Prevost
Jaques Viras, et sa femme
Jawues Brouse, sou enfant
Pierre Cornu
Louiss Bon
Isaac Fordet
Jean Pepre
Jean Gaillard et son fils
Anthonie Matton, et sa femme
John Lucadou et sa femme
Louiss Orange, sa femme et un enfant
Daniel Taure, et deux enfants

Pierre Cupper
Daniel Roy
Magdelaine Gigou
Pierre Grelet
Jean Jovany, sa femme, deux enfnans
Pierre Ferrier, sa femme, un enfant
La vefve faure et quatre enfants
Isaac Arnaud, et sa femme
Pierre Chantanier, sa femme et son
    pere
Jaen Fonasse
Jaques Bibbeau

Jean March
Catherine Billot
Marie et Symon Jourdon
Abraham Menot
Timothy Moul, sa femme un enfant
Jean Savin, sa femme un enfant
Jean Sargeaton, sa femme un enfant
Claude Philipe, et sa femme
Gabriel Sturter
Pierre de Corne
Helen Trubyer

LIST OF PASSENGERS FROM LONDON TO JAMES RIVER IN VIRGINIA INBARQUED IN THE SHIP YE *PETER AND ANTHONY*

Galley of London, Daniel Perreau, Commander (viz't) 20th of Sept. 1700

SOURCE: http://www.olivetreegenealogy.com/ships/hugship02.shtml;
http://huguenot_manakin.org/manakin/brock2.php#LIST2

Jean Pilard
Estienne Ocosnad (Turkish)?
Abraham Remis, sa femme = Ramy
Jean Le Franc Vudurand
Daniel Maison Dieu
Pierre Baudry
David Menestrier
Jacob Fleurnoir, sa femme 2 garsons
    & 2 fille avid Blevet sa femme &
    6 enfants
Elizabeth Lemat
Abraham Le Foix, sa femme & 4
    enfants
Jean Aunant, sa femme & un fille
Jean Genge de Melvis
Monsieur Je Joux, minister
Francois de Launay, & un enfant
Gaspart, sa femme & 7 enfants
Jacques Corbell
Jacob Capen
Isaac Iroc (Iraq?)
Elie Gastand
Anthonie Boignard
Nicholas Mare, sa femme & 2 enfants
Jaques Feuillet & sa femme
Pierre Sarazin
Jean Perrachou
Phillippe Claude
Simon Hugault
Samuel Barrel
Gaspar Gueruer, sa femme & 3 enfants

Jean Soulegre
Jean Morroe (possibly Moreau)
Louis Desfontaine & sa femme
Pierre Masset
Solomon Jourdan
Estienne Chabran, sa femme
Susanne Soblet & 3 enfants
Jean Hugon
Michel Michel
Mheodore de Rousseau
Pierre Cavalier, sa femme & un
    garson
Pierre Anthonie Eupins
Isaac Le ffeure (now Lefew in Virginia)
Jean Martain
Pierre Renaudd
Marthien Roussel
Augustin Coullard
Jean Coullard
Jaques du Crow, sa femme & une fille
Paul Laurion
Moise Broc.
Jean Pierre Bondurand[5]
Pierre La Badic
Jean Bossard, sa femme & 3 enfants
Guillaume Rullett
Anthony Gioudar
Anne Carbonnet & un enfant
Guillemme Guervot, sa femme & un
    garson
Louis Robert, & un fille

Estienne Tauvin, sa femme & 2
    enfants
Paul Castiche
Jean Mazeris
Noel Delamarre, sa femme & un fille
Jean Le Vilain
Jean Marisset
Jean Maillard & 3 enfants
Thimotthree Roux
Gaspart Guamondet & sa femme
Daniel Rogier
Pierre Gosfand
Soloman Ormund
Louis Geoffray
Maize Veneuil, sa femme & 5 enfants
Joseph Oliver (probably from Niort,
    in Poitou)
Jaques Faucher
Pierre La Grand, sa femme & 5 enfants
Pierre Prevol (Prevat, Prevatte[6])
Daniel Riches
Francis Clapie
Jacob Riche, sa femme & un enfants
Mathier Passedoit
Pierre Hiuert
Michel Fournet, sa femme & deux
    enfants
Jean Monnicat
Simon Faucher
Jean Combelle

F. Lists of Settlers in Massachusetts

The following lists are transcribed in alphabetical order with annotations on date of arrival, marriage (M.) and other pertinent details from traditional records. The names of family members, along with notes on the meaning/origin of some names, may appear in parentheses.

TABLE 1. CONGREGANTS AT THE SALEM MEETING

SOURCE: www.usgenweb.org

Ancestor with Date of Arrival in Salem

John Abbey 1637
Samuel Aborn (Aborne, Eaborn) 1636
John Barrow (Barrowe) 1637, aboard the *Queen Anne*
Edward Beauchamp (Beachem) 1636
John Becket (Beckett) 1656
Henry Birdsall (Birdsale) 1639
Edward Bishop 1646
Richard Bishop 1628
Jeremiah Butman (Bootman) 1651
Anthony Buxton 1637, from England
William Clark (Clarke) 1637
Peter Cloyes (Cloyce) 1677, from York, Maine
Roger Conant 1626, one of the "Old Planters"
Henry Cook (Cooke) 1638
William Dixy 1638
William Dodge 1629, aboard "The Lion's Whelp"
Jeffrey Eastey (Esty, Estey) 1636
Nathaniel Felton 1633
Thomas Flint 1650
William Flint 1642
John Friend 1637
Robert Fuller 1639
Thomas Fuller 1638

Thomas Gardner 1626, one of the "Old Planters"
Edward Giles (Gyles) 1634
Thomas Goldthwaite 1630
Robert Goodale
Thomas Graves 1629, aboard *George Bonaparte*
Edmund Grover 1628
Henry Haggett 1642
John Hathorne 1634
Henry Herrick 1629
John Horne 1639
Joseph Houlton (Houghton) 1652
Richard Hutchinson 1634
Alice Ingersoll 1629
Richard Ingersoll 1629
George Jacobs 1674
Hugh Jones (Joanes) 1642, from Wincanton, England
Elisha Kebee (Kibbe, Kibbey) 1667
Lawrence Leach 1628
John Marston 1637
Richard Norman 1626, one of the "Old Planters"
Francis Nurse 1640
Richard Ober Unknown
The Rev. Samuel Parris 1689, from the West Indies
James Patch 1648

Robert Pease 1634, aboard *The Francis*
John Putnam 1638
Richard Raymond 1629
Daniel Rea 1631
Thomas Read(e) 1630, with the Winthrop fleet
Capt. John Seamans 1643
Ephraim Sheldon 1691
James Smith 1635
Lawrence Southwick 1639
John Swasey 1640
John Sweet 1632
Job Swinerton 1637, from England
John Symonds (Simonds) 1636
John Talbie (Talby) 1635
Abraham Temple 1637
John Thorndike 1637
William Towne 1640
Capt. William Traske 1626, one of the "Old Planters"
Thomas Trusler (Tresler) 1629
Peter Twiss 1680
Jonathan Walcott 1634
William Walcott 1634
Bray Wilkins 1628
John Woodbury 1626, one of the "Old Planters"
William Woodbury 1636

TABLE 2. MASSACHUSETTS BAY SETTLERS

SOURCE: www.winthropsociety.com/settlers.php

Daniel Abbott
Robert Abell
Jeremy Adams
William Agar
George Alcock
Thomas Alcock
Andrew Alger (Algiers)
William Allen (children Persis, Bethiah)
Isaac Allerton
Mathew Allyn
Samuel Archer (child Bethia)
William Aspinwall
Stephen Bachiler (child Theodata)
John Baker
William Baker (Bethia)
John Balch
Eliz. Ballard (Shubael)
William Ballston (Mehitabell, Meribah)
Jacob Barney
William Barsham
Robert Bartlett
Thomas Bartlett (Bathshua, Mehitable, Abiah)

Samuel Bass   M. Ann Savell (Seville)
Edward Bates   M. Lydia
Gregory Baxter (Bethia)
William Beamsley   M. Martha Hallor (Habbakuk)
Alexander Beck   M. Eliz. Hinde (Ephraim, Manassah)
Edward Belcher
Edward Bendal (Ephraim)
John Benham
John Benjamin   M. Abigail Eddy
Rich. Benjamin (Simeon, Priscilla)
John Bennett
Will. Bennett (Moses, Aaron)
John Black (Persis, Lydia)
Will. Blackstone
Mary Blott
Jon. Bosworth (Bethia, Bathsheba)
Zaccheus Bosworth
Garrett Bourne
Nathaniel Bowman (Dorcas)
Rich. Brackenbury
Will. Brackenbury
Rich. Brackett

Simon Bradstreet
Will. Bronton (Mehitabel, Jaleham, Ebenezer)
Daniel Brewer
Will. Bridge   M. Persis Pierce (Persis)
Clement Briggs
Francis Bright
Henry Bright (Beriah)
Abraham Browne   M. Lydia "surveyor"
Edmund Browne   M. Eliz. Okiye
Hugh Browne
James Browne
James Browne (Abraham)
John Browne
Richard Browne
William Browne
Judith Bugby (Bagby?) (Rachel)
Richard Bugby
Richard Bulgar (Bulgaria)
Jehu Burr (Jehu)
John Burslyn
Edward Burton (Phebe, Ruth) M. Margaret Otis

Richard Butler
John Button
Matthias Button
John Cable (Cabel)
Thomas Cakebread
Bernard Capen (Ruth)
John Carman (Carmen)　M. Florence
Edward Carrington
Joshua Carter (Joshua, Elias, Elisha)
Charles Chadwick
Amy Chambers (Camera)
John Chapman
Will. Chase
Will. Chesebrough (David, Andronicia, Junia, Jabez, Elisha)
Leonard Chester (Dorcas, Eunice)
Ephraim Child
Thomas Chubb
Garrett Church (Samuel, David)
Richard Church
Roger Clap
Nicholas Clarke
George Cleeve　M. Alice Abrood
Will. Coddington　M. Mary Moseley (Bediah)
James Coggan　M. Mary Jourdain (Lydia)
John Coggeshall (Hananiel, Bedaiah)
Will. Colbron
Anthony Colby (Isaac)
Thomas Coldham (Enoch)
Rice Cole
Samuel Cole
Robert Coles
Richard Collicott (Bethiah, Ebenezer)
Roger Conant
Edward Convers
Aaron Cooke (Aaron, Miriam, Moses)
William Cornwall (Jacob, Esther)
John Cotton　M. Eliz. Horrocks
Mathew Cradock (Camaris)
Griffin Craft (Moses)
Benjamin Crisp (Eleazar, Zachariah, Mehitable)
Thomas Crocket (Ephraim, Elihu)
William Curtis　M. Sarah Eliot (Isaac)
William Dady
Rich. Davenport (name signed with a "true cross" or saltire)
Will. Denison
Will. Denning (Obediah)
Nich. Denslow
John Devereux (Bethiah)
Thom. Dewey (Douai) (Josiah, Israel, Jedediah)
Thom. Dexter
Anthony Dike (Dyck)　M. Tabitha
John Dillingham　M. Sarah Caly (Calle)
Ed. Dix
Will. Dixy
Will. Dodge

John Doggett (Hepzibah)
Mary Downing (Benjamin, Solomon, Samson)
Thomas Dudley
Richard Dummer　M. Jane Mason (Shubael)
Nathanial Duncan　M. Eliz. Jourdaine
George Dyer
John Eddy (Ruth)
John Eeles
Beget Eggleston
Jacob Eliot (Mehitable, Asaph)
John Eliot
John Ellet
Edward Elmer (El Mar)
John Endecott　M. Anne Gower, Eliz. Cogan (Zerubabel)
Richard Fairbanks (Zacheus)
George Farr (Phar)
Thomas Fayerweather
Henry Feake (Judith)
Robert Feake　M. Eliz. Fones
George Felt (Aaron, Moses)
Walter Filler　(Zerubabel)
Daniel Finch (Abraham)
John Finch (Isaac, Abraham)
John Finman (Josias, Judith)
Giles Firman
Ed. Fitzrandolph　M. Eliz. Blossom
Cotton Flack (Deborah)
Ralph Fogg (Ezekial, David)
Elizabeth Fones
Thom. Ford　M. Eliz. Charde (Hepzibah)
Thom. Fox　M. Rebecca (Jabez)
Rich. Foxwell　M. Susanna Bonython (Esther, Luretia)
Samuel Freeman　M. Apphia Quick
Alice French
Stephen French
Thom. French (Ephraim)
Nicholas Frost
Will. Frothingham (Bethia)
Samuel Fuller　M. Elsie Glascock
John Gage　M. Sarah Keyes
Will. Gager (Yager)
Humphrey Gallop
John Gallop　M. Chistobell Brushett
Robert Gamlin (Gamelin)
Thom. Gardner (Miriam, Seeth)
Richard Garrett
Will. Gaylord
Ambrose Gibbons
Edward Gibbons (Jerusha, Jotham, Metsathiell)
Gyles Gibbs
Edward Giles (Mehitabell, Eleazer) dau. M. Henry Moses
Jonathan Gillett (Cornelius, Josiah)
Nathan Gillett (Abiah, Elias, Rebecca)
Edward Godfrey　M. Eliz. Oliver
Thom. Goldthwaite (Mehitabel)

Rich. Goodman
Will. Goodwin
John Gosse (Phoebe)
Charles Gott (Deborah)
Matthew Grant (Priscella, Tahan)
Seth Grant
Thomas Graves
Bartholomew Green (Phebe)
John Green (Jacob)
John Greenaway (Ursula)
Rich. Gridley (Abraham)
Edmund Grover (Nehemiah, Naomi, Lydia, Deborah)
Thom. Grubb　M. Ann Salter
Jarrett Haddon
Robert Hale (Zacharias)
Thomas Hale　M. Mary Nash
John Hall　M. Bethia ____ (Shebas, Nathaniel, Gershom, Elisha)
Phillippa Hammond
Will. Hammond　M. Eliz. Paine
Robert Harding
Thomas Hardy　M. Lydia
Anthony Harker
Thom. Harris
Edmund Hast (Elisha)
Stephen Hart (Rachel)
Henry Harwood
Will. Hathorne
Henry Haughton
Timothy Hawkins　M. Anna Hammond (Mehitable)
John Hayden (Ebenezer, Nehemiah)
John Haynes　M. Mabel Harlakinden (Ruth)
Will. Heath　M. Mary Perry (Peleg)
Will. Hedges
Ralph Hemenway
Henry Herrick　M. Edith Laskin (Zachariah, Ephraim)
Joshua Hewes　M. Mary Goldstone (Joshua)
Francis Higginson (Theophilus, Neophytus)
John Hill (Ebenezer, Mehitabel, Ruth)
Will. Hill　M. Sarah Jourdaine (Ruth, Rebecca)
Will. Hills　M. Phyllis Lyman (Benone) (Abraham, Hestea)
Edward Hilton　M. Katherine Shapleigh
Will. Hilton
Edmund Hobart　M. Margaret Dewey (Nazareth, Anthony, Rebecca, Joshua)
Thom. Holcombe (Benejah, Deborah, Nathaniel, Joshua)
John Holgrave (Joshua, Lydia)
John Holman　M. Anne Bishop
Thomas Hooker　M. Susanna Gargrand
John Horne　M. Francis Stone (widow, Greece Simon)

Will. Horsford

John Hoskins

Thom. Hosmer (Hannah, Clemence, Esther)

Atherton Hough

Robert Houlton (Jakey)

Daniel Howe

Thom. Howlete   M. Alice French

Simon Hoyte   M. Susannah (Moses, Joshua, Miriam)

Benjamin Hubbard

William Hudson

Will. Hulberd

George Hull   M. Thomasine Mitchell (Josias, Cornelius, Joshua, Naomi)

*John Humphrey   M. Lady Susan Fiennes (Theophelus, Lydia, Dorcas)

Simon Huntington (Christopher, Simon)

Christopher Hussey   M. Theodata Bachiler (Theodata, Huldah)

Edward Hutchinson (Inchabod)

George Hutchinson

Richard Ingersoll   M. Agnes Langlye (Bathskola, Nathaniel)

Edward Ireson (Rebecca, Hannah, Reith, Eleazar, Benoni)

Mathias Iyans   M. Anne Browne

Nicholas Jacobs   M. Mary Gilman (Deborah)

Thomas James   M. Olive Ingoldsby (Nathaniel)

Will. Jefferay   M. Mary Gould (Priscilla, Susannah)

Edward Johnson   M. Priscilla (Benjamin, Deborah)

Francis Johnson (Naomi, Ruth)

John Johnson   M. Mary Heath (Isaac, Hannah)

Richard Johnson

Edward Jones

Will. Kelsey (Hestor, Priscilla)

Rich. Kettle (Ketal)   M. Hester Ward

Robert Keyes (Solomon, Rebecca, Phebe, Elias)

Henry Kingsbury   M. Margaret Alabaster

John Kingsley (Eldad)

Nicholas Knapp (Joshua, Caleb, Ruth, Moses, Lydia)

Will. Knapp   M. Judith Tue (Judith)

George Knower (Knauer?)

Thom. Knower

Edward Lamb (Pascal?)

Thom. Lamb (Abel, Benjamin, Joshua Abiel)

Henry Langster

Lawrence Leach (Rachel)

Will. Learned   M. Goodith Gilman (Bethia, Isaac)

Will. Leatherland (Zebulon)

John Legge

John Leavens   M. Rachel Wright (Rachel)

Thomas Leverette   M. Anne Fitch

Will. Leveridge (Caleb, Eliazar)

Thomas Lewis   M. Elizabeth Marshall (Judith)

Will. Lewis

Edmond Lockwood

Thomas Lombard (Jemima, Caleb, Jobaniah, Jedediah, Benjamin)

Richard Lord

Roger Ludlow

Richard Lyman

Henry Lynn   M. Sarah Tilley (Ephraim)

John Mason   M. Ann Peck (Israel, Priscilla, Rachel)

Jeffrey Massey

John Masters (Lydia)

Thom. Matson   M. Amy Chambers (Joshua)

Elias Maverick (Mayerick)   M. Anna Harris (Elias, Ruth, Rebecca)

John Maverick   M. Mary Gye (Samuel, Elias, Aaron, Moses, Antipas)

Moses Maverick (Aaron, Rebecca)

Samuel Maverick   M. Amias Cole

Thom. Mayhew   M. Jane Gallion (Hannah, Behtia)

Abraham Mellowes (Oliver, Abraham)

John Mills

Thomas Minor (Ephraim, Manasseh)

John Moore

John Moore (Jerusha, Ephraim)

Richard More (Caleb, Joshua, Christian)

Isaac Morrill (Isaac, Abraham)

Robert Moulton

Thom. Moulton (Jacob)

Ralph Mousall (Muslim/Mousel)

Roger Mowry (Mehitalde, Apphia)

Thom. Munt

Ann Needham   M. Thom. Helt (Hannah, Eliphalett, Mehitalde, Israel)

Rich Norman

George Norton (Mehitalde)

Walter Norton

Increase Nowell (Noel)   M. Parnell Gray (Jasper, Eleazer, Mehitalde, Alexander)

John Odlin (Elisha)

Thom. Oliver

James Olmstead   M. Joyce Cornish (Mabel, Nehemiah)

Frances Onge (Simon, Isaac, Moses, Jacob)

John Page   M. Phebe Paine

Peter Palfrey (horse) (Jehoidan)

Richard Palgrave (Rebecca, Lydia, Bethia)

Walter Palmer   M. Rebecca Short (Nehemiah, Moses, Bershon, Rebecca)

Will. Parke (Theoda, Deborah)

James Parker   M. Mary Maverick (Azricam)

Robert Parker   M. Judith Bugby (Rachel)

Daniel Patrick   M. Anneken van Beyeren (from Bavaria) (Beatrice)

Henry Pease

James Pemberton

James Penniman   M. Lydia Eliot (Lydia, Bethia)

John Perkins   M. Judith Gater (Gaither?) (Jacob, Lydia)

Will. Perkins (Tobijah, Rebecca)

Francis Perry   M. Jane Cash (David, Elisha)

John Perry

William Phelps (Phillips)   M. Anne Dover (Cornelius)

George Phillips (Zorobabel, Theophilus)

John Phillips

John Pickrum   M. Esther

John Pickworth (Ruth, Rachel)

John Pierce   M. _____ Parnell (Nehemiah)

Will. Pierce

Anne Polland

Eltweed Pomeroy   M. Johana Keech (Dinah)

M. Margery Rocket (Eldad, Medad, Caleb, Joshua)

John Poole (Poulet, chicken)

Walter Pope

Phineas Pratt   M. Mary Priest (Cohen?) (Aaron)

Valentine Prentice

Will. Pynchon

Edward Rainsford (Ranis, Nathan, David, Solomon)

Thom. Rawlings (Nathaniel)

Daniel Ray (Rey) (Bethia, Joshua)

Richard Rayment   M. Judith (Bathsheba, Joshua, Lemuel, Daniel)

Thomas Read   M. Priscilla Banks

Joseph Redding   M. Annice

Robert Rice/Royce (Joshua, Nathaniel)

Ezebial Richardson   M. Susanna (Phebe, Theophelus, Josiah)

Will. Rockwell   M. Susana (Capen, Ruth)

Edward Rossiter

Will. Royal   M. Phebe Green (Isaac)

Simon Sackett   M. Isabel (Simon)

John Sales   M. Phillipa Soales (Phebe)

Richard Saltonstall   M. Grace Kaye

John Sanford (Eliphal, Peleg, Esbon, Elisha)

Will. Sargent   M. Eliz. Perkins
Robert Scott
Thomas Scruggs (Rachel)
Robert Seely   (Nathaniel)
Samuel Sharpe   M. Alice Stileman
  (Elias)
Robert Shelley
Rebecca Short (Nehemiah, Moses,
  Gershon, Rebecca)
Richard Silvester   M. Naomi (Lydia,
  Israel, Dinah, Naomi, Hester)
John Simpson   M. Susanna
Samuel Skelton   M. Susanna Travis
Judith Smead
Henry Smith   M. Ann Pynchon
  (Elisha, Rebecca)
Frances Smith
William Spencer   M. Agnes Harris
Ralph Sprague (Phineas)

William Sprague   M. Millicent
  Eames (Persis)
Isaac Stearns   M. Mary Barker (Isaac)
Elias Stileman   M. Judith Adams
  (Elias)
Samuel Stone (Lydia)
Israel Stoughton   M. Elizabeth
  Knight (Israel, Susanna, Rebecca)
Thomas Stoughton   M. Margaret
  Barrett
Nicholas Stowers
John Stratton
John Strickland
John Sweet
John Talcott   M. Dorothy Mott
Will. Talmage   M. Eliz. Pierce
John Tatman (Jabez)
John Taylor   M. Rhoda
Gregory Taylor

Stephen Terry
David Thompson   M. Anrias Cole
  (Priscilla)
John Thorndike
Hugh Tilly/Hillier   M. Rose (Debo-
  rah)
Timothy Tomlins
William Trask
Morris Truant   (Mehitable)
Nathaniel Turner (Rebecca, Isaac)
Robert Turner   M. Penelope
  (Ephraim)
Thomas Ufford   M. Isabel
John Underhill   M. Helena de Hooch
  M. Eliz. Feake (Deborah, Nathaniel)
Nicholas Upsall   M. Dorothy Capen
William Vassall   M. Anna King
  (Judith)

G. Names from *The Town & Country Social Directory,*
1846–1996

These names have been gleaned from the listings in a volume celebrating 150 years of *Town &
Country* magazine.[1] Not only were the alphabetized listings scanned but also the names of distinguished
ancestors and related families that might have been included to impress readers. Most of the pedigrees
came from colonial New York. Fortunes typically came from banking, less often from mercantile
companies or manufacturing. By this means, one might arrive at an estimate of how many of America's
socially prominent, wealthy families, despite what was often the Dutch-sounding cachet or Anglo-
Saxon appearance of their last name, potentially (but not necessarily) have Jewish or crypto–Jewish
roots. Of course, not everyone bearing a certain surname follows the rule for that surname. Many
surnames were passed over as ambiguous. Still, the names selected constitute about one-fourth of all
entries. Nearly all are discussed in one place or another in the text with references.

From Family Portraits					
Adams	Alexander	Byrd	Dana	Dyer	Grant
Astor	Ames	Caldwell	Davis	Eliot/Elliott	Gray
Belmont	Anthon	Card	de Acosta	Ellis	Green
Biddle	Anthony	Carnegie	de Bassano	Ely	Guggenheim
du Pont	Auchincloss	Carter	de Braganca	Fahnestock	Haggin
Field	Ball	Cassell	de Forest	Firestone	Haines/Hanes
Fish	Barlow	Castellane	de Frise	Fleischmann	Hale
Gould	Barnes	Chase	De Lancy	Flood	Hamilton
Livingston	Barrett	Chrysler	Delano	Forbes	Hanna
Mellon	Barton	Clemens	de Menil	Ford	Harrison
Morgan	Beekman	Clews	Denny	Fox	Harte
Pulitzer	Belin	Coffin	de Peyster	Fraser/Frazier	Hartshorn
Rockefeller	Bell	Collins	Devereux	French	(Hirschhorn)
Roosevelt	Berlin	Colt	de Wolfe	Gardiner	Hawkins
Vanderbilt	Bernheimer	Cooper	Dick	Gates	Hay/Hayes/Heye
	Bigelow	Copley	Dinsmore	Geist	Hazard
From Listings	Bok	Cotton	Dodge	Gibbs	Heine
	Bolling	Cravath	Douglas	Gibson	Hewitt
Abraham	Bowles	Cromwell	Dows	Gimbel	Hitchcock
Adair	Brokaw	Cronin	Drake	Goldsborough	Homans
Aitken	Burnett	Curtis	Drexell	Gordon	Horwitz
	Burney	Cushman	Duer	Graham	Hough

Howe	Law	Mendl	Pereira	Ross	Spears
Howell	Lazarus	Mercer	Perry	Rubinstein	Speyer
Hunt	Leas/Lee	Meserole	Peters	Russell	Spotswood
Isham	Leatherman	(de) Meyer	Phillips/Phipps/	Sage	Stearns/Stern
Isaacs	Leavitt	Miles	Phelps	Sanford	Stewart/Stuart
Izard	Lehman	Miller	Polk	Samuel	Storer
Jackson	Levy	Miner	Porter	Sands	Straus
Jacobs	Lewis	Moore	Potter	Saunderson	Strycker
James	Little	Morison	Price	Sayre	Thaw
Jarvis	Loeb	Morris/Morse	Prince	Schell	Travers
Jay	Loew	Morton	Proctor	Schenck	Tripp
Jesup	Loubat	Murray	Rauh	Schermerhorn	Untermyer
Jewell	Lovett	Nathan	Ravenel	Schuchardt	Valentine
Jordan	Low	Neuhaus	Rawle	Schuyler	Van Courtlandt
Kahn	Lowell	Newberry	Rea	Sears	Van Meter
Kane	Mackay	Noble	Rhodes	Seligman	Wanamaker
Kean/Keene	Macy	Norrie	Rice	Shaw	Warburg
Kennedy	Manigault	Norris	Riddle	Shepard	Weems
Keteltas	Markoe	Olin	Robb	Shoemaker	Weir
Keyes	Martin	Oliver	Robbins	Short	White
Kip	Mather	Osborn	Robinson	Simon/Simmons/	Wise
Kissel	Massie	Page	Robertson	Simonds	Wood
Knox	Maxwell	Paine/Payne	Root	Simpson	Yale
Kounce/Koontz	May	Parker	Rose	Sinclair	Yulee
Laidlaw	Meeker	Parrott	Rosekrans	Singer	Zimbalist
Lasker	Mendes	Peck	Rosenwald	Smith	

H. Pennsylvania Names

TABLE 1. BUCKS COUNTY QUAKER RECORDS

SOURCE: *Bucks County, Pennsylvania Church Records of the 17th and 18th Centuries*, Vol. 2, Anna Miller Watring & F. Edward Wright

Adams/Addams: Benjamin, Ephraim, Jedediah, Obadiah, Zedidiaty, Seemey

Alexander: Esther

Ames/Amis: Merebe/Meribah

Amor: Richard

Bagley: John

Banges: Hannah

Barracliff (Barak-lif): Ann

Barry: Bethulia

Bayly: Howard, Deborah, Israel, Latitia, Merriot, Ozmond, Phebe, Tamer

Beaks: Abraham, Robena, Ruth, Samuel

Beans: Elhanah, Sarah, Seneca, Benjamin

Bickerdike: Jael, Gideon, Esther

Boz: Cassandra

Briten/Briton: Lionel

Buckley: Deborah, Elias, Israel, Phinehas, Ruth

Buckman: Aaron, Alsden, Abner, Amos, Benjamin, David, Deborah, Esther, Isaac, Jacob, Jesse, Jonathan, Lydia, Mahlon, Penquite, Phinchas, Rachel, Ruth, Stacy

Bunting: Abner, Amos, Abejah, Asa, Benjamin, David, Esther, Isaac, Israel, Jeremiah, Job, Letitia, Phebe, Rachel, Septema, Tamison

Buress: Aaron, Amos, Amy, Dan., Dav., Edith, Ellin, Lidia, Moses, Priscella, Rachel

Cadwalader/Kadwalada: Benjamin, Cyrus, David, Jacob, Judah, Phebe, Isaac, Jacob....

Canby: Benjamin, Beulah, Hanameel, Joshua, Letitia, Lydia, Oliver, Phebe

Carinthus: Rachel

Cary: Asa, Asaph, Bethula, Beulah, Hanameel, Hephzi-bah, Joshua, Phineas, Sampson, Samuel, Sarah

Chapman: Abraham, Marah, Ruth, Seth

Comfort: Aaron, Beulah, David, Ellis, Ezra, Josiah, Lydia, Moses....

Copock: Aaron

Cowfill: Cowgial, Septmea, Nehemiah, Abner, Ebeneser, Eleasar

Craft: Beulah

Croasdale: Aaron, Abe, Abijah, Achsah, Deborah, Elser, Ezra, Macre, Marah....

Davids: Hannah

Day: Elizabeth

Doan/Doane: Abigail, Daniel, Eleasar, Elizah, Ephraim, Israel, Mehetabal, Miriam, Tabitha, Tamar

Dubre: Armelle, Sarah

Dymoike: Tobias

Eleazar: Lundy

Elkton: Zebulan

Ellicott: Nathaniel

Ely: Ann
Farmer: Barzilla
Gades: Elizabeth (Cadiz)
Gilbert: Benjamin, Jesse, Jonathan, Phebe, Rachel, Rebeccah, Sarah, Simon
Gill: Agnes, Joshua, Uri
Gillam: Isaac, Jeremiah, Joseph, Joshua, Lucas, Sarah, Simon, Susanna
Gummery (Gomeri): Hannah
Harvey: Abraham, Elhena, Hannah, Moses, Rebecca, Sarah
Hough: Benjamin, Bernard, Daniel, Deb., Edith, Hezek, Is., Latitia, Oliver, Rachel, Septimus
Jacobs: Mary
James: Dinah
Janney family
Jesse: Zachariah
Jessup: Samuel
Kaper: Caleb
Kinsey: Alcesta, Benjamin, David, Hannah, Samuel.
Ebenezer (Large, Gross): Esther, Gemima, Hestor, Jacob
Lenoir (the dark): Ann
Liddle: Isaac
Livesay: Daniel, Deborah, Ezra, Isaac, Jonathan, Samuel
Longshore: Abi, Abner, Abraham, Aza, Asher, Cyrus, Euclidus, Phebe, Rachel, Ruth, Sara, Ursula
Lovet(t): Daniel, Susannah, Cassandra, Jesse, Joseph, Magdalena, Mahlon
Lucas: Benjamin, Esther, Grace, Isabel, Mahlon
Margerum: Abraham, Benjamin, Isabel, Phebe
Mendinhall
Merrick: Deborah, Enos, Hannah, Deborah, Jacob, Jason, Mercy, Naomi, Pheby, Priscilla, Ruth, Rachel
Milner: Armin, David, Elvira, Hannah, Harriet, Isaac, Jonathan, Joseph, Mahlon, Narina, Nathan, Phebe, Pleasant, Priscilla, Rachel, Virena
Moon (Luna): Agnes, David, Isaac, Jasper, Jonas, Moses, Rebeccah, Samuel, Sarah, Simon
Moss: Abraham

Myers: Jacob & Rachel
Palmer: David, Jonathan, Rachel, Abner, Amos, Asenath, Benjamin, Caleb, Christian, Daniel, Dinah, Esther, Jael, Jonathan, Joseph, Joshia, Latitia, Moses, Naomi, Priscilla, Rachel, Ruth, Tacy, Tamar, Theodocia
Patte: Abi, Alcesta, Benjamin, Eucloidas, Jolly, Levi, Martha, Rachel
Pharrow: Gove
Preston: Aror
Rhoads: Silas
Robbins: Mary
Salkeld: John
Sands (Alexander): Abigail, Abraham, Benjamin, Esther, Isabella
Shin: Elizabeth
Siddel: Esther
Silver: Sarah
Sison: Rachel, Rebecca
Solomon: Elizabeth
Stapler: Achsah, Esther, Hannah, Latitia, Rachel
Starr: Sarah
Walley: Damoris, Hananiah, Naomi, Shadrach
Watson: Abner, Amos, Beulah, David, Hannah, Isaac, Isaiah, Jacob, Joel, Levi, Phebe, Rachel, Rebeccah, Ruth, Tamer
Wharton: Abigail, Abner, Daniel, David, Hannah, Israel, Joseph, Mahlon, Moses, Nehemiah, Phebe, Phineas, Rachel, Rebeccah, Sarah, Samuel
Wiggans: Bezaleel
Wildman: Abigail, Amos, Enos, Hannah, Isaac, Jacob, Jonathan, Joseph, Joshua, Mahlon, Marah, Rachel, Rebeccah, Sarah, Solomon
Wilson: Achilles, Agnes, Amos, Anthony, Asa, Asaph, Benjamin, David, Christopher, Dinah, Ezra, Isaac, Jacob, Jesse, Jonathan, Joseph, Joshua, Latisha, Lydia, Macy, Oliver, Phebe, Sidney
Yardley: Achsah, Enoch, Hester, Isaac, Latitia, Lydia, Mahlon, Mararetta, Samuel, Sarah

TABLE 2. INDEX NAMES OF STOEVER CONGREGANTS AND BAPTISMS

Since this was essentially a Jewish congregation, the baptisms are assumed to be a legal formality to permit the families to vote, own land, etc. as "Christians." In many crypto–Jewish congregations in Catholic countries, such practices are followed (Gitlitz 2002).

Acker/Axer	Benin	Cuntz	Fiedler	Hartman
Ackermann	Bich, Jacob	Cypher	Flory	Heilman, Adam
Adam(s)	Bickel	Daniel	Franck	Hertz
Albrecht	Bischoff	Danin	Frey	Hey
Anspack	Biszwanger	David	Fuchs	Heydt, Abr., Jost
Appel/Apfel	Blanck	Davies	Gebhardt	Hill
Aras	Blum	Diller	Geiger	Hoffman
Auman	Boger/Buger	Eisenhauer	Goldman, Jacob	Holtzman
Baasz	Braun	Eli	Gross	Honig
Bach	Brosius (Ambrose)	Engel	Grossmann	Huber, Abr.
Bachman	Bubar	Ermentrout	Gruber	Israel, Eva
Bamberger	Canaan	Espy	Gur	Jacob, Phillip
Bartholomaei	Canter	Essel	Gurman	Jacobi, Adam
Bauer	Cantz	Faber	Haag	Jacobs
Baumgartner	Cassel	Falck	Haasz	Joho
Bayer	Cavet, Moses	Favian	Hammon	Jung
Beans	Cowen	Ferrar	Hanna, Isaac	Kalliah
Bechtel	Cumru, Sabina Roth	Ferry	Harry	Kally

Kapp	Levandt	Murhead	Saber	Tempelmann
Karmenie	Lew	Murr	Saladin (3)	Teuber
Karr	Lewers	Nagel	Saltzer (Jacob)	Thani
Kasie	Lips	Ochs	Schaeffer (Mary)	Thau
Katz	Loewe	Ohr	Scheretz	Voelcker (Jacob)
Kau	Loewenstein	Olin	Schindel	Vogel
Kaufman	Low	Oliphants (Rebecca)	Schmelser	Von Beber (see also
Keller	Lucas	Pannel	Schnabele	Maryland chapter)
Kemp	Mack	Parry	Schneider	Wagner
Kessinger/Kissinger	Mackey	Patz	Simon (Mary)	Wegman
Kintz (el) (er)	Manck	Petry	Sinn	Wolf (Mary)
Klee	Mann	Phillippy	Solomon (Adam)	Wunderlich
Klein	Maurer	Pressler	Sonntag	Zartman (Jacob)
Koenig	Maxell	Ralph (Zacharios)	Spanhauer	Zeh
Kraft	Merck	Reiss	Stern (Mary)	Zeller
Kuhn	Meyer (Mary)	Roessel	Stober/Stoever	Ziegler
Kuntz	Moor	Rosenbach	Suess	Zimmerman
Lauer	Mooser	Rosenbaum	Taffeler	Zorn
Lehmann	Morgenstern	Rosenberger	Tauber	Zoth
Levan Stonesifer (i.e.,	Moser	Roth	Tauth	Zuber
stonecutter/mason)	Mosser	Ruth	Tauzing	

TABLE 3. EARLY GERMAN SETTLERS OF YORK COUNTY, PENNSYLVANIA

SOURCE: www.usgenweb.org Transcribed by Keith A. Dull

Acker	Cappell	Florentina	Haas	Katzenbach
Adam	Cline	Flower	Hachar	Kaufman
Ager	Coffman	Fortune	Hackmann	Keentz
Albrecht/Albright	Coldenty	Foucks	Haffner	Keller
Amelot	Corel/Correll	Frank	Hagge	Kiefaber
Amendt	Couli	Frantz/Frensch	Haines	King/Koenig
Amma	Cresap	Free/Frey	Haman/Hammann	Kissel
Amman (capital of	Cronebach	Freitag/Freytag	Hari	Kissinger
Jordan)	Dagen	Frick	Harry	Klee
Andreas	Dantzler	Friend	Hart/Hartman	Klein
Appel	Davies/Davis	Frolich	Hassler	Kobel
Appelmann	Debus	Fry	Hauck	Koch
Babb	Degraff	Fucha	Hauser	Kohler
Bachman	Dehoff	Gabel	Hay	Kontz
Barr	Dewes	Gaeiss	Hayes/Heys	Koonsin
Bartel	Diller	Galatin	Heck	Kraemer
Barth/Barthel	Dodd	Gans/Gantz	Heilman	Krantz
Bayer	Doudel	Garden/Gardner	Heintz	Kroll
Bechtel	Droxel	Gauch/Gauesch	Hellman	Kron/Kronin (crown)
Becker	Duenkel	Geiselmann	Herring	Kruger
Beherin	Easum	Gemmel	Hershey	Kuhn/Kuntzel
Bensin	Eby	Gerber	Hertzog	Lantz
Bently/Bentzel	Eckart	Gess/Giess/Gotz	Hoffman	Lau/Lauer/Laumann
Berlin	Ellmore	Glasick	Homel	Lederman
Beroth	Elsasser	Glasser	Honas	Lefeure
Bickel	Emmerich	Goafman	Honig (honey)	Leib
Bischoff	Engelman	Gobble/Gobel	Horn	Leonhardt
Bless (Baruch)	Engels	Gottlieb	Hornig	Liebenstein (Living-
Blum	Eschelbach	Gottwald	Hose/Hosi	stone)
Bone	Eyseck (Isaac)	Graibill/Graybill	Huber	Lischy (many)
Boner	Fackler	Grimm	Ickes	Lora/Lohra/Loray/
Bindel	Farne	Grippel	Imell	Lore
Brotzman	Ferree	Gross	Jacob/Jacobs	Low
Bruner/Brunner	Fettro	Gruen	Jacobi	Lowenstein
Buatt	Fiesel (Fisal)	Grunblad (Green-	Jullus	Lucas
Bucher	Fink	leaf)	Kabel	Luchenbach
Bushong	Fischborn	Grunwald	Kann	Maak
Canto	Fischel/Fissel	Gutjahr (good year)	Kapp/Kappler	

Maas	Neiman	Reidel	Sasseman	Simon
Maier/Mayer/Meier/ Meyer	Neuman	Rein	Schaffer (many)	Stein
Markey	Neyswanger	Ritter	Seherer	Uly
Maurer	Ob	Roser	Shindel	Valentine
Menges	Palle/Palli	Rothermel	Sehlegal	Venus (Venice)
Merckel	Peissel, Peizel	Rothrock	Schleppi	Vogel/Vogeler
Metzgar	Petri/Petry	Rubel	Schneider	Wolf/Wolff (many)
Michel	Quickel	Rudisill (many)	Schramm	Zauck/Zouck
Morganstern	Rader	Sabel	Schwartz	Ziegler (many)
Moser	Ranck	Sangree	Schwob	Zimmerman
	Rausch	Sappell	Seitz	

TABLE 4. TAX LIST OF BERKS COUNTY, PENNSYLVANIA, 1767 (unalphabetized)

Michael Algeier (Algiers in Algeria)	Kuns	Weiser	Hoffman	Conrad Menges
Alder	Korrel	Gutman	Jacob Joder	Eneas Noel
Berer	G. Lilly	Mosser	Nich. Jacoby	Romig
Bingeman	Jacob Hagabuch	Jacob Hamm	Lobach	Hertzog
Braun	Jacob Bechore	Hawk	Lentz	Daniel Golden
Baum	Isaiah Cushwa	Sheeler	Barrel	Jac. Gelbach
Anthony Blum	Adam Daniel	Bryan	Bachman	Dan. Levan
Abraham Bleistein	Ad. Kassel	Dunkle	Jacob Fux	John Terck
Dewees	Dan. Kabel	Eckell (Echol)	Kline	Jacob Sylvius
Eisenbeis	Dav. Mercki	Mordecai Lee	John Rey	Jacob Sharadine
Feather	Caspar Schebele	Jacob Zech	Sheth	Saseman
Fry	Lor. Sambel	Abram Huy	Adam Schmael (i.e., Ishmael)	Baron
Gross	John Gabriel	Dan. Beean	Jacob Sammet	Henry Hava
Geisler	John Goheen	Th. Berry	Silver	Haman
Haga	Jacob Frey	Ed. Goff	Schwartz	Ley
Haag	Hans Moser	Geiger	Zanger	Trautman
Haas	Boone	Jackson	Oseas	Jac. Zettlemayer
Hartman	Bechtel	Elias Ratge	Bastian Fucks	Flicker
John Jacob	David	Levers	Bucher	Lewis
John Judy	Feager	Keys	Guldin	Stoner
Isaac Levan	Lincoln	Peter Aman	Lober	Van Horme
Maurer	Israel Ritter	Simon Brosius	Tobias Mauck	Biddle
Marx	Finck	Abert Hey	Roads	Isenhower
Naugle	May	Adam Jacobi	Beck, Becker	Romich (Rome)
Rose	Starr	Jacob Levengud	Lor. Krone	Baltas Simon
David Rein	Abram Luckinbill	Valentine Ney	Dav. Kintzig	Yocam
Jacob Seider	Adam Ares	Reys	Geo. Lora	Akker
Snyder	Christian Deppy (from Dieppe, France)	Reidel	Dan. Zacharias	Davis
Wolf		Shuler	Peter Ashelman	Lorah
Manus Sasamanhous	Jacob Erb	Schoch	Lloyd Abel	Marsteller
Safred	Fassler	Anspach	Jacob Blessing (Baruch)	Paine
Peter Schaen	Haine	Jacob Bich		Rhoads
Nich. Ely	Kuhn	Felty Mogle	Phil. Gabel	Sands
J. Glass	Lebo	Jacob Mast (Mast & Cohen store in Asheville)	Harry	Curry
David Kamp	Laur		G. Jacob	Parvin
Baltzer Moon	Nich. Saladine (Muslim conqueror)	Yarnal	Koenig	Zug
G. Nuz	Smeal	Zimmerman	Isaac Sailer	Zaber
Nich. Beron	Yost Sugar	Scherer	Jacob Zinn	Jacob Stein
George Rab	Kapp	Kuhn	Jon. Zerbe	Peter Schamo/ Schomo
Jacob Donat	Blanck	Albrecht	Pet. Ruth	
G. Haal		Emrich	Henry Acre	

TABLE 5. PENNSYLVANIA ASSEMBLY 1683

Kent	*Bucks*	*Chester*	*Philadelphia*	*New Castle*	*Sussex*
John Briggs	William Yardley	John Haskins	John Songhurst	John Cann	Luke Watson
Simon Irons	Samuel Dark	Robert Wade	John Hart	John Darby	Alexander Draper
Thomas Hassold	Robert Lucas	George Wood	Walter King	Valentine Holl-	William Futcher
John Curtis	Nicholas Waln	John Blunston	Andros Binkson	ingsworth	Henry Bowman
Robert Bedwell	John Wood	Dennis Rochford	John Moon	Casparus Herr-	Alexander Mo-
Qilliam Winds-	John Clowes	Thomas Brassey	Thomas Wynne	man	lestine
more	Thomas Fitzwater	John Bezar	Griffith Jones	John DeHaes	John Hill
John Brinkloe	Robert Hall	John Harding	William Warner	James [Williams]	Robert Brassey
Daniel Brown	James Boyden	Joseph Phipps	Swan Swanson	William Guest	John Kipshaven
Benoni Bishop				Peter Alricks	Cornelius Ver-
				Henrick Will-	hoofe
				iams	

TABLE 6. PENNSYLVANIA INDIAN TRADERS, 1743–1775

SOURCE: USGenWeb Archives, Pennsylvania Archives. 2nd Series, pub. Matthew S. Quay, ed. John B. Linn & William H. Egle. Vol. II (Harrisburg: Meyers, 1876). Transcribed by Brenda Paullo.

Indian Traders: 1743–1748

1743
March 9 John Duguid
March 9 Thomas Wood
March 9 Dougal Ferguson
May 4 Benjamin Specker
June 2 Robert Anderson
June 8 John Harvey
June 13 Leonard Smith
June 16 Nicholas Haupt
June 21 John Speaker
June 21 James White
June 21 John Savanner
June 21 Charles McMichael
June 21 Christopher Jacob
December Henry Plat

1744
January Peter Wylt
February James McKnight
February James McAlister
February John Muckle-
waine

March Robert Syer
April Benjamin Spyker
June Michael Sprongle
July John Duguid
July Thomas Wood
July James Wilson
July Robert Anderson
July Florian Povinger
May Thomas McGee
May George Croghan
May Alexander Moorhead
May Peter Chartier
May Peter Sheaver
May Peter Tostee
July Henry Smith
July Samuel Cousans
July John Galbreath
July John Potts
July Lazarus Lowry
July James Lowry
July Simon Girtee

July John Hart
July James Denning

1745
Peter Chartier, for 1744
Peter Sheaver, for 1744
_____Finley, for 1744, 45, 46
Alexander Moorhead, for 1744, 45, 46
August John Specker
August Samuel Cross
October Charles McMickell
October William Clark
October Henry Platt
October Florian Povinger
October Philip Coleman
October James Stewart
December William Clark

1746
September Philip Coleman
December Henry Platt

1747
Robert Taggart
John Duquid
Samuel Cross
June William Wallace
June John Buiser
June Jacob Power
December Martin Cleaver
December Philip Coleman

1748
March 3 Robert Taggart
March 3 John Dougell
March 3 Thomas Woods
April William Dixon
June George Arentz
June Peter Moyer
June Bernard Packer
July 2 George Graham
July 2 Andrew Englehart
November 1 Bernard Atkinson

Traders Licenses Dispensed in the Secretary's Office: 1762–1768

1762
March 1 Nicholas Workhyser
March 11 Jacob Faust
March 12 John Simpson
April 15 Bartholomew Tool
June 5 Philip Jacob Young
June 30 Jacob Cressman
July 12 Andrew Grager
September 10 Alexander McDougal
September 23 James Scott
October 2 Nicholas Swamp
October 29 Robert Carson
November 18 John Morrison
November 19 Frederick Lytick
December 2 Alexander McCurdy
December 2 Robert Patten

1763
February 12 Alexander Ramsey
February 17 John Great
March 9 Nicholas Workhiser
March 23 Adam Ulrick
April 12 Bartholomew Tool
May 5 John McQuaid
May 13 Josiah Lockart
June 6 Charles Conner
June 6 Adam Stoll
July 9 Thomas McClan
July 22 Robert McDonal
August 13 Andrew Bellfour
September 12 John Pechin
September 16 Jacob Cressman
September 17 Alexander McMichael

September 30 Joseph Mitchell
October 1 Jacob Kline
October 4 John Ramsey
November 23 William Smith
November 29 John Hill
December 1 John Trebell
December 6 Andrew Hopkins
December 6 Robert McDurmont

1764
March 1 Daniel Boyle
March 5 Nicholas Werkhyser
April 6 Mathew Henderson
April 21 Bartholomew Toole
June 2 Adam Stoll
June 4 Josiah Lockhart
June 9 Adam Platto

June 12 Thomas Ashton
June 14 Charles Campbell
July 10 James Harbeson
August 7 William Carr
September 5 Alexander McMun
September 6 John Ramsey
September 24 Alexander Sinclair
September 28 Jacob Cressman
November 6 Thomas Davit

1765
January 4 Alexander Campbell
February 8 James Kinnear
March 1 James Alexander
March 4 Nicholas Workhyser
March 4 Bartholomew Tool
May 3 James McFarland
June 4 Moses Abraham
June 4 Abraham Moses
June 4 Thomas Bamford
June 5 Robert Russel
July 29 William Orr
September 2 Jacob Smith
October 12 Allen Ramsey
October 12 Josiah Lockhart
October 14 David Mitchell
October 21 Francis Hair
October 28 Frederick Rorer
October 31 John Barclay

1766
May 19 James Kenneaur
July 28 Bartholomew Tool
August 12 Jacob Strewer
October 9 George Ray
October 12 Preston Menassey
October 14 Peter Seen
November 3 Robert Buchannan
November 6 John Campbell
November 26 Thomas McFarland
December 2 Robert Patton
December 4 Patrick Cary
December 5 David Humphra
December 6 Thomas Carr

1767
March 2 Henry Magill
March 3 Christopher Boyer
March 5 John Richards
March 14 William Minnes
March 17 Bartholomew Tool
May 15 Francis Hair
May 18 Jacob Cressman
June 4 Elias Bender
December 9 John Zean
December 10 John Willson

1768
March 3 Bartholomew Tool
April 13 Francis Hare
June 8 Matthew Bonner
June 13 John Richards
June 27 James Mullen
August 26 James Kinneaur
September 8 Mannassah Preston
September 9 William Mackey

October 10 George Ray
October 18 John Barren
December 5 Patrick Hare
December 5 John Simpson
December 6 William Gibson
December 10 Robert Anderson
December 13 Josiah Lockhart
December 29 Bartholomew Tool
December 30 Thomas Kerr

1770
4 December Andreas Steel

1771
January 15 Alexander Ewen
February 1 Bartholomew Toole
February 4 Martin Frank
February 11 Peter Gallagher
March 7 Michael Meyer
March 21 William Kerr
April 19 Jacob Baar
April 30 John Barron

1771
May 15 Joseph Scott
June 14 John Grate
June 18 Francis Hare
June 24 James Alexander
July 20 Robert Lilley
August 7 Barnet Runey
August 14 James Brown
August 17 David Burnside
September 5 John Henry
September 14 Peter Fiss
October 10 Daniel Gillin
October 19 Matthew Thompson
November 1 John McCartney
November 9 James Horner
November 13 Isaac Wolf
November 16 John Shedden
November 29 William McCandlass
December 13 John Rankin

1772
January 2 Andreas Steel
January 13 Jeremiah Pickering
January 13 William Shields
January 25 John Bell
February 11 Robert Thompson
February 11 James Costello
March 1 John Fairservice
March 6 Joseph Solomon Cohen
March 13 Alexander Ewen
March 17 Andrew Cowpland
April 1 David Collins
April 1 Hugh Dean
April 2 Patrick Hare
April 4 William Parker
April 4 Daniel Mullan
April 4 Peter Gallagher
April 23 Michael Hart
April 25 John Richards
April 27 John Watt
May 5 Andrew Walker
May 5 John Hood
May 6 John Graham

May 12 Henry Lane
May 19 George Peendle
May 25 Edward Holland
May 26 David Shilleman
June 1 John Barron
June 3 Peter Gill
June 6 Charles McHenry
June 15 John Michael Kuch
June 20 John Barclay
August 7 Benjamin Wolf
August 13 John Taylor
August 14 George Butz
August 31 Joseph Galbreath
August 31 Adam Thompson
September 18 John McFarland
September 22 Robert Hutchinson
October 12 Edward Pennell
October 12 Alice Herbert
October 16 Francis Hare
October 20 John Stuart
November 2 Isaac Wolfe
November 13 John Vaughan
December 8 Abraham Levy
December 11 James Horner
December 16 Peter Fiss
December 22 Jacob Sleer

1773
January 2 James Brown
January 4 William Steel
February 8 David Cowpland
February 20 Bartholomew Tool
March 6 Henry Dill
March 15 William Linton
March 21 David Brooks
April 14 Patrick Hare
April 24 William McDermott
April 26 John Richards
April 29 James Fiddes
May 10 Joseph Solomon Cohen
May 12 Jacob Isaiah Cohen
May 17 Michael Hay
May 18 John Graham
June 1 Ephraim Abraham
June 25 Andrew Robeson
August 10 Andreas Stahl
August 24 William Steel
August 26 John Grantzer
September 6 Daniel Stahlman
September 27 Michael Patterson
October 5 Robert Thompson
October 6 William Currie
October 11 Henry Lane
October 30 Hugh Thompson
November 30 Abraham Levy

1774
February 24 John Barron
March 15 Peter Fiss
March 22 Francis Hare
March 25 William Miller
March 30 Jeremiah Sullivan
May 10 Bernard Vanderin
May 20 Joseph Solomon
May 24 Richard Markey

June 7 James Clark
June 13 Robert Young
July 8 James Mulloy
July 20 Peter Gill
September 7 John Wright
October 6 Isaiah Cohen
October 6 Ephraim Abraham

November 24 Paridon Ernst Peterson
December 2 John McCowen
December 8 Abraham Levi
1775
March 6 Patrick McGill
March 8 Joseph Ramsay
April 21 George Helm

May 5 Lyon Nathan
May 20 Michael Hulings
August 8 Andrew Stahl
August 8 Mary Henry
November 11 Joshua Bourne

I. Maryland Names

Below are listed other surnames and residents in colonial Maryland beyond those given in Chapter 7 which are believed to be of possible Jewish or Muslim affinity. A date in parentheses after a name indicates when the name was documented in local records.

James Adair (1770s)
James Alans (1763)
Abraham Alexander (1770s)
Burch Allison (1765)
Benjamin Amos (1777)
Valentine Arnett (1780s)
Darius Ayer (1755)
Jonathan and Elias Barber (Berber) (1794)
Barron
Basille
Batz
Rezin Beall (prior to 1800)
James Berry (1691)
George Black (a) More (1760)
William Bohner/Bonner (1775)
Bonamy
Bonnell
Boze (Boaz)
Robert Brashear (Brassier) (1704)
Jacob Brazleton (1749)
Brevard family
Brunneau (Brown)
Zacharriah Cadle/Caddle (1688)
Solomon Cole (1753)
Barachias Coop (1760)
Nicholaus Copple/Kappel (1778)
William Crabtree (1758)
Crockett family (Tangier Island) (1728)
Zachariah Cross (Cruz) (1761)
Lewis de Moss (1715)
de Sailly (after Sallee in Morocco)
des Romanes ("from Rome")

du Roy
Enoch Enochs (1766)
Ferrer
Jacob Fifer (Pfeifer, German for "piper") (1754)
Fleury
George Forbush (1743)
Nathan Frizzell (1759)
Bazil Gaither family (1771)
James Gassaway (1770)
Gibbon/Gibbens family (1685)
Mordecai Gist family (1740s)
Givan/Given family (1709)
Gost (Gist)
Orlando Griffith family (1766)
Aaron Guyton (1761)
Aaron Hale (1785)
Hayes
Hazard
Farel Hester (1774)
William Highat (Hayat) (1766)
Jacob Holland family (1754)
Henry Horah (1750s)
Benjamin Howard (1755)
Rezin Howard (1731)
Rachel Jacob (1770s)
Emory Jarman (1763)
Isaac Julian (1690)
La Mott
LaVie (similar translation into French)
Rezin Keziah Lazenby (1777)
Daniel Lewis (1755)
Louzada (after Lausitz, Germany; see Faiguenboim et al 314)

Basil Lowe family (1749)
William Lucas (1754)
Ezekiel and Angell Mace (1794)
Phillip Maroney (1776)
Elijah Minor (1739)
James Monet (1782)
Jacob Moser (1778)
Francis Mosier (1763)
Isaac Nichols (1790s)
Moses Payne (1764)
Perron
Samuel Perry (1771)
Isaac Perryman (1745)
Polk family (Pollock) (1729)
Hezekiah Posey (1751)
David Reese
Reeves
Rey
Alexander Rhodes (1739)
Rueben Ross (1752)
Moses Ruth family (1781)
Rutledge family
Sarasen (i.e. Muslim)
George Silver family (1751)
Abraham Stoner (1770s)
Elias Amos Veatch (1760s)
Jesse Vermillion (1752)
Vidal (translation into Spanish of Hebrew Hayim)
Vivian (similar translation into English)
Wiseman (Moroccan).
Aaron Wood family (1776)

J. South Carolina Names

TABLE 1. NAMES OF SANTA ELENA COLONY
DURING 1560S AND 1570S (unalphabetized)
SOURCE: Eloy J. Gallegos, *The Melungeons*

Names listed in Faiguenboim, et al., as Sephardic are marked with an asterisk

Antonio de Padilla	Migue Molina*	Niculas de Vurgos (Burgos)*	Rodrigo Madera*
Diego Casca* de Salazar*	Domingo Lopes*	Alonso Guerra*	Francisco Ecija*
Gomez de Santillan*	Pedro Garcia*	Francisco Rico*	Gaspar Nieto*
Alonso Martines* Espadero	Pedro Aguilera*	Juan Remon*	Andres de Viveros*
Diego de Cumiga	Marcos Garcia*	Diego de Orgina	Pedro de Ariniega
Lopes* de Sarria	Juan Fernandes*	Migual Palomar	Francisco de Ybar
Gomes* Henao	Pedro Solis*	Juan Jil*	Francisco Molgado
Lope de Vaillo*	Juan Gomez Fialo*	Francisco Deibar	Florian Mosquera*
Tomas Vernaldo	Andres de Simancas	Anton de Pena* Vaira	Juan de Noriega
Alvaro Flores*	Juan Martin*	Bartolome de Medina*	Juan Batista*
Francisco de Hecija	Simon Bega*	Juan Navarro*	Alonso Torres*
Valtesar de Oserno	Juan Calvo de Zamora*	Domingo Quadrado	Cristoval de Uzeda
Alonso Dias*	Francisco Olmos*	Pedro de Ariniega	Alonso de Baena*
Domingo Hernandez*	Gonzalo Vicente*	Hernando Silva*	Alonso Garcyn*
Blas Palomar	Andres Vigero*	Juan Sanches Moreno*	Diego de Cardenex*
Gaspar Perete	Francisco Rodriguez*	Pedro Santana	Pedro del Arrazabal
Prudencio Arrieta	Alonso Diaz*	Pedro de Rueda*	Juan de Rivero*
Juan Mes*	Antonio Ruiz*	Juan Baldes*	
Juat Garcia*	Caspar Arias*	Ganzalo Herrera*	

TABLE 2. HUGUENOTS TO ENGLAND, SCOTLAND,
WALES & IRELAND PRIOR TO 1643
Source: *Huguenots-Wallons-Europe-L Archives*

Alexandre	Briot	Crawley-Boevey	De Lallee	Des Bouveries	Folkstone
Alix	Buchanan	Daigneux	De la Melloniere	Des Colombiers	Fontaine
Anthonie	Bulteel	D'Ambrun	De la Motte	Des Galles	Francois
Ashtown	Bustein	Dangy	De la Place	Des Granges	Gamier
Banet	Byrt	D'Aranda	De la Pryme	Des Moulins	Garin
Banks	Calamy	D'Arande	De Lasaux	D'Espagne	Garrett
Baptiste	Calmady	D'Assigny	De Laune	D'Espard	Garth
Baro or Baron	Cappel	D'Aubon	De Lidge	Des Serfs	Girard
Bassens	Cargill	De Beauvais	Delme	Des Travaux	Grafton
Baudoin	Carlier	De Cafour	Radcliffe	De Vendome	Greville
Beaufort	Cartanet	De Carteret	De Lobel	Dobree	Groslot de l'Isle
Beevey	Casaubon	De Catteye	de Maligny	Dolbel	Gualter
Bennet	Castanet	De Chambeson	De Marsilliers	Dolin	Guerin
Beny	Castol	De Chatillon	De Mayerne	Dombrain	Guyneau
Berku	Caveler	De Cherpont	De Melley	Dubais	Hamlyn
Bertram	Chamberlaine	De Coulosse	De Mompouillan	Du Cane or Du	Hayes
Bignon	Chappelain	De Cugnac	De Montfossey	Quesne	Henice
Bisson	Chartres	De Ferrieres	De Montgomery	Du Faye	Herault
Blondell	Chastelin	De Freiderne	De Montmorial	Du Moulin	Houblon
Bonespair	Chaudrom	De Garencieres	De Moynerville	Du Perron	Howie
Bongenier	Chestes	De Grasse	De Nielle	Du Poncel	Howitt
Bonhomme	Chevalier	De Gronville	De Nouieville	Du Quesnel	Huard
Bonnell	Chrestien	De Haleville	De Pouchel	D'Urfey	Hunsdon
Bothan	Clancarty	de Heez	De Rache	Du Val	Inglis
Bouillon	Conant	De la Barre	Deroche	Ellice	Janssen
Bourghinomus	Conyard	De la Branche	De Sagnoule	Emeris	Jeffrey
Bouverie	Coquel	De la Courte	de St. Michael	Eyre	Jeune
Bowthand	Cossyn	De la Fontaine	De St. Voist	Falconer	Johanne
Brevin	Courtney	De la Fortrie	De salvert	Famas	Johnstone
Brevint	Cousin	De la Haye	De Saules	Fitzroy	Joret

Kells	le Jeune	Marie	Niphius	Richier	Valpy
La Grande	le Keux	Marmet	Paget	Rime	Van Lander
Laignaux	le Macon	Marny	Painsec	Rodulphs	Vashon
Lamie	le Pine	Marriette	Palmerston	Rosslyn	Vasson
Lamott	le Quien	Martin	Papillon	Countess of	Vauville
La Motte	le Roy	Marvey	Parent	Roullees	Vernevil
Langlais	le Thieullier	Matelyne	Penzance	Rowland	Vignier
Lart	levart	Maurois	Perruqut de la	St. Michel	Vignon
La Tranche	levet	Maxwell	Melloniers	Saye	Vincent
le Blancq	Lixens	Medley	Perucel la Riviere	Sayes	Vouche
le Blane	Lodowicke	Merlin	Philip	Selyn	Waldo
lebon	Lompre	Merrit	Pincon	Sibthorp	Walke
le Bouvier	Longford	Mesnier	Ponsonby	Sicard	Wheildon
le Burt	Loulmeau	Millet	Portal	Strype	Weldon
le Cat	Machevillens	Monange	Presot	Talbot	Wiseman
le Chevalier	Machon	Monceau	Pryme	Tayler	Wolstenholme
le Churel	Maignon	Monier	Pusey	Tovilett	Wood
le Duc	Malaparte	Moreau	Radnor	Treffroy	Wybon
lefroy	Malet	Moulinos	Earl of Ratcliffe	Trench	
le Grimecieux	Marchant	Mulay	Regius	Tryon Tullier	
le Gyt	Maret	Muntois	Riche	Ursin	

TABLE 3. LISTS FROM *IRISH PEDIGREES*

SOURCE: *Irish Pedigrees*, Vol. 2, by John O'Hart, published in 1892, New York

Abanzit	Angier	Ausonneau	Basmenil	Belafaye	Berlemeyer	Bibal
Abelain	Angoise	Austin	Basset	Belcastel	Bernaon	Biball
Abraham	Annaut	Autain	Bastell	Belet	Bernard	Bibbant
Acque	Anviceau	Aveline	Batailhey	Beliard	Bernardeai	Bichot
Adam	Arbunot	Aviceau	Battier	Belin	Bernardon	Bidley
Adrien	Archbaneau	Ayland	Baudertin	Bellanaer	Bernaste	Bieisse
Agace	Ardauin	Ayrault	Baudevin	Bellemarte	Berney	Bielfeld
Ageron	Ardesoif	Azire	Baudoin	Belleroche	Berniere	Biet
Aissailly	Ardesoife	Barbaud	Baudouin	Bellet	Bernieres	Bignon
Alart	Arnaud	Barbe	Baudovin	Belliard	Bernou	Bigot
Alavoine	Arnaudin	Barber	Baudowin	Bellin	Berny	Billon
Albers	Arnauld	Barberis	Baudrie	Belliville	Berslaer	Billonart
Albert	Arnoult	Barbet	Baudris	Belloncle	Bertau	Billop
Albin	Artieres	Barbier	Baudry	Belon	Berthe	Billot
Alden	Artimot	Barbot	Bauer	Belorn	Bertheau	Billy
Aleber	Assaire	Barbotin	Bauldevin	Belton	Bertie	Binand
Alexandre	Asselin	Barbule	Bauldouin	Beluteau	Bertin	Binet
Allaire	Astory	Barbur	Baume	Belvere	Bertonneau	Bino
Allais	Auber	Bardeau	Baurru	Bemecour	Bertran	Bion
Allard	Aubert	Barel	Bauzan	Benard	Bertrand	Bire
Allat	Aubertin	Bargeau	Baver	Benech	Beschefer	Blagny
Allen	Aubin	Bargignac	Bazire	Beneche	Besnage	Blanc
Allix	Aubourg	Barian	Beauchamp	Benesot	Bessier	Blancar
Allotte	Aubri	Baril	Beaufills	Benet	Bessin	Blancard
Alvant	Aubry	Barion	Beaufort	Benezet	Besson	Blanchard
Amail	Audebert	Barle	Beaujeu	Benezolin	Bessonet	Blanzac
Amelot	Audeburg	Barnege	Beaulande	Bennet	Best	Blaquiere
Amiand	Auduroy	Barnouin	Beaulieu	Benoict	Bethencour	Blefeau
Amiot	Aufrere	Baronneau	Beaumont	Benoist	Beule	Blennerhasse
Amonnet	Augel	Barqueno	Beaune	Benoitt	Beuzelin	Blommart
Amory	Augibant	Barrau	Beaurepere	Benouad	Beuzeville	Bloncour
Amyand	Augnier	Barron	Beauvois	Beranger	Bewkell	Blond
Amyraut	Aure	Barset	Becher	Beraud	Bezenech	Blondeau
Andart	Aurez	Barsselaer	Beckler	Berault	Bezier	Blondell
Andre	Auriol	Bartalot	Beekman	Berchere	Bezin	Blondet
Andrieu	Aurios	Barvand	Bege	Berens	Biagnoux	Blondett
Anes	Ausmonier	Bashfeild	Begre	Beringhen	Biard	Bobin
Angelier	Ausol	Basille	Beiser	Berionde	Biart	Boche

Bockquet
Bocquet
Bodrd
Bodvin
Boehm
Boileau
Boisbeleau
Boisdeschesne
Boismotet
Boisnard
Boisragon
Boisribeau
Boisrond
Boisseaux
Boissonet
Boiste
Boitoult
Bonafons
Bonamy
Bonard
Boncoiron
Boncourt
Bondoi
Bondvin
Bonel
Bongrand
Bonhomme
Bonhoste
Bonier
Bonin
Bonine
Bonmot
Bonneau
Bonnel
Bonnell
Bonnelle
Bonnet
Bonneval
Bonomirier
Bonouvrie
Bontefoy
Bonvar
Booth
Borchman
Borderie
Boreau
Borie
Borneman
Borough
Borrowes
Bos
Bosanquet
Bosch
Bosquetin
Bossairan
Bossis
Bosy
Bouche
Boucher
Bouchet
Bouchett
Boucquet
Boudet

Boudier
Boudin
Boudinot
Boudoin
Boudrie
Bouet
Bouhereau
Boulanger
Boulier
Boullard
Boullay
Bouillier
Beauregard
Boullommer
Bounin
Bouquet
Bourdeaus
Bourdet
Bourdier
Bourdillon
Bourdin
Bourdiquet
Bourdon
Boureau
Bourgeais
Bourgeois
Bourgeon
Bourges
Bourginignon
Bourian
Bourn
Bournack
Bournet
Bourreyan
Boursiquot
Bouryan
Bousar
Bousart
Bousquet
Boussac
Boutelleir
Boutet
Boutilier
Boutonnier
Bouverie
Bouvet
Bovey
Bowden
Boy
Boyblanc
Boycoult
Boyd
Boye
Boyer
Boygard
Bozey
Bozuman
Bracquchaye
Braglet
Braguier
Bragvier
Brasselay
Bratelier

Breband
Breda
Bredel
Brehut
Brement
Breon
Bretellier
Breval
Brevet
Brevint
Brian
Brianceau
Briand
Bridon
Brielle
Briet
Brievinck
Brigault
Brinquemand
Briot
Brisac
Brissac
Brissau
Brisson
Brithand
Brocas
Brodeau
Broha
Brossard
Brouard
Brouart
Brouchet
Brouino
Brozet
Brugierres
Bruke
Brule
Brulon
Brun
Brunant
Brunben
Bruneau
Brunet
Bruneval
Brunier
Bruquier
Brus
Brusse
Brussear
Brusson
Brutel
Bruyer
Bryon
Bucaile
Buissieres
Bulmer
Bumet
Bunel
Bunell
Buor
Burear
Bureau
Burges

Burreau
Burtel
Buschman
Bush
Bussat
Bussereau
Bussiere
Bustin
Butel
Butetell
Buteux
Byles
Cabibel
Cabrol
Cadet
Cadett
Cadroy
Cagrou
Cahuac
Caillabueuf
Cailland
Caillard
Caille
Cailleau
Cailletiere
Caillobeuf
Caillon
Cailloue
Cain
Caldevele
Callarde
Callifies
Callivaux
Calmels
Camberland
Cambes
Cambon
Cambrelar
Campredon
Cancellor
Canole
Cantier
Cannieres
Caovet
Cappel
Capper
Carbonel
Cardel
Cardes
Cardins
Cardon
Careiron
Cari
Carlat
Carle
Carles
Carlier
Carnac
Carnegie
Caron
Carpentier
Carre
Carriere

Carron
Cart
Cartier
Carus-Wilson
Cashaw
Casie
Casier
Cassart
Cassaw
Cassel
Casset
Castagnier
Castaing
Castanet
Castelfranc
Castin
Castres
Cauchie
Caudaine
Cauderc
Caulet
Cauon
Caussat
Causson
Cautin
Cavalier
Cavallie
Cazalet
Cazals
Cazaly
Cazautnech
Cazeneusne
Cazenove
Ceaumor
Cellery
Cene
Cesteau
Ceyt
Chabanei
Chabaud
Chabet
Chaboissan
Chabossan
Chabosse
Chabot
Chaboussan
Chabriers
Chabrol
Chabrole
Chadaigne
Chaieler
Chaigneau
Chaille
Chale
Chalie
Challe
Challion
Chalopin
Chalvet
Chameau
Chamier
Champagne
Champfleury

Champion
Champlaurie
Champon
Chapelier
Chapelle
Chapellier
Chaperon
Chapet
Chapon
Chappell
Charas
Chardavoine
Chardin
Chardon
Charier
Charle
Charles
Charlie
Charlot
Charon
Charpe
Charpenelle
Charretie
Charrier
Charron
Charters
Chartier
Chartres
Chaseloup
Chasgneau
Chasles
Chasselon
Chasserea
Chassloup
Chastagnier
Chastelain
Chastelier
Chateauneuf
Chatterton
Chaudrec
Chauveau
Chauvet
Chauvin
Chauvit
Chavalier
Chave
Chaver
Chef d'Hotel
Chelar
Chemonon
Cheneu
Chenevie
Chenevix
Cheradaine
Cheseau
Chesneau
Cheval
Chevalier
Chevalleau
Chevallier
Chirot
Chotard
Chouard

Chouy
Chovard
Chovet
Chrestien
Chretien
Chrispin
Christian
Chupin
Cigournai
Clairvaux
Clamouse
Clancherie
Clari
Clark
Clarke
Clarmont
Clary
Claude
Claus
Claveie
Clavier
Clement
Clerembault
Clerenbault
Clerenceau
Clervaux
Clinton
Cloakie
Cloquet
Cocker
Coderk
Coenen
Cogin
Cognand
Cohen
Colgnand
Colebrant
Colet
Colineau
Coliner
Coliveau
Colladon
Collet or Col-
  lottt
Collett
Collette
Collier
Collineau
Collon
Colom
Colombies
Colomies
Colomiez
Columbine
Colvile
Colville
Combauld
Combe
Combrune
Compan
Cong
Constantin
Constantine

Conte
Contet
Contreau
Convenent
Cooke
Coqueau
Coquerel
Corbiere
Cordelon
Cordes
Cormier
Cornand
Cornet
Corniere
Cornish
Carraro
Correges
Corso
Cortey
Cossard
Cossart
Cosson
Costat
Coste
Cothoneau
Cothonneau
Cotigno
Cottibi
Cottin
Cotton
Courdain
Coudert
Couillano
Coulombieres
Coulon
Coupe
Couppe
Courage
Courallet
Courand
Courcelles
Coureau
Courson
Courtaud
Courtauld
Courteil
Courtet
Courtin
Courtion
Courtis
Courtois
Courtonne
Courtris
Cousin
Coussirat
Cousteil
Coutart
Couterne
Coutet
Coutois
Couturier
Couvelle
Couvers

Couvreue
Covillart
Coyald
Cozun
Cramahe
Cranstown
Crespigny
Crespin
Crespion
Cresse
Cretes
Creuse
Creusean
Crispeau
Crispin
Criyger
Crocheron
Crochon
Crohare
Cromelin
Cromer
Crommelin
Crothaire
Crouard
Croyard
Croze
Cruger
Crull
Crusins
Culeston
Cuny
Curnex
Curoit
D's here
D'Abadie
Dacher
Dafancell
D'Agar
Dagar
Dagenfeldt
Daignebere
D'Aiguesfon
Daillon
Dainhett
Dalbey
Dalbiac
D'Albon
D'Allain
D'Allemagem
D'Allemagne
D'Allone
Dallons
Dalton
Damascene
Damboy
Danear
Daney
Dangirard
Daniel
Dansay
Dansays
Dantilly
D'Antragnes

Darasus
Darby
D'Arcy
Darel
Darenes
Dargent
Dariette
Darill
D'Arrabin
Darrac
D'Arreche
Darrigraud
Darticues
Daubussar-
gues
Daubuz
Dauche
Daude
Daulnix
D'Aumale
Daure
Daval
D'Avene
Davi
David
Davisme
Davois
Davy
Dawson
D'Ayrolle
De Aernac
De Bancous
De Barbut
De Bariso
De Barry
De Bat
De Batilly
De Bearlin
De Beauheu
De Beaulier
De Beaure-
gard
De Bees
De Belcastel
De Bernier
De Bernieres
De Bernon-
ville
De Bey
De Blagney
De Blanchet
De Blaquiere
De Boisraon
De Boissobre
De Boiville
De Bonneval
De Boos
De Bordet
De Bostaquest
De Bouexin
De Bourbon
De Bourdeaux
Debox

De Boyville
De Bre
De Brevall
De Brissac
De Bruse
De Bussy
De Calvirac
De Camp
De Carbonne
De Carbonnel
De Cardon
De Carron
De Casaliz
De Casaubon
De Case
De Castle-
franc
De Cautepye
De Caux
De Cazenove
De Chabert
De Cham-
brun
De Champ
De Charine
De Charines
De Chefbou-
tonne
De Cherville
De Cheusse
De Clene
De Cluset
De Cogny
De Comarque
De Conninck
De Constan-
tin
De Conu
De Conuig
De Cosne
De Costa
De Courceill
De Courceille
De Courcelles
De Courcey
De Coursel
De Crouchy
De Cussy
De Dibon
De Diepe
De Durand
De Falaise
Deffray
De Foissac
De Fonvive
De Forges
De Fossi
De Fossiac
De Fouquein-
bergues
De Gaillardy
De Gaschon
De Gastin

De Gaume
Degenfeldt
De Gennes
De Ginest
De Gouvernet
De Graffen-
ried
De Grand
De Grandges
De Grassy
De Grenier
De Gually
De Gualy
De Guerin
De Guion
De Gulhc
De Gulhon
De Hague
De Hane
De Hause
De Hausi
Dehays
De Heucourt
De Heule
De Heulle
De Hogbet
De Hogerie
De Hombeau
De Hubac
De Jages
Dejean
De Joncourt
De Joux
De Joye
De Jurnac
De Kantzow
Delabadie
De la Barbe
De la Barre
De La Barre
De la Basti
De la Bastide
De labatt
De Labene
De la Billiere
De la Bla-
chiere
De la Bois
De la Bor
De la Burri-
erre
De la Bye
De la Chasse
De la Chau-
mette
De la Cherois
De La Ches-
naye
De la Clar-
tiere
De la Combe
De la Conda-
mine

De la Couldre
De la Cour
De la Cou-
tiere
De la Croix
De la Fausille
De la Faville
De la Faye
De lafon
De la Fond
De la Fons
De la Force
De la Foreste
De la Foresti-
rie
De la Fuye
De la Grange
De la Greliere
Delahaize
De la Haize
De la Hays
De la Heus
De la Heuze
De Laine
De Lainerie
De Laire
De la Jaille
De Lalende
Delaleu
De Lalo
De la Loe
De Lamaindre
De la Marre
De la Maziere
De la Meja-
nelle
Delamere
De la Misegle
De la Motte
De la Musse
De Lancey
De Lande
Delandes
Delandre
De la Neuvu-
maison
De la Newf-
mason
De l'Angle
De la Nove
Delapier
De la Pillon-
niere
De la Place
De Lardiniere
De la Reve
De la Rive-
rolle
De la Riviere
De la Roche-
foucauld
De la Salle
De la Touche

De la Tour
De Lausat
De Laval
De la Vala
Delavau
De la Viverie
De l'Espine
De l'estabiere
De l'Estand
De l'Estang
De lestrille
Delgardir
De l'Hermi-
tage
Delhomme
De Lhoumeau
De Limage
Delize
Delmaitre
Delmas
De Lo
De Loche
De Loches
De Lommeau
Delon
De l'Orme
De Lorme
De l'Orthe
De Loumea
Deloumeau
De Louvain
Delpech
Delpeth
De Lussi
De Luvigny
De Maffee
De Magny
De Maistre
De Malacare
De Malanze
De Manoir
Demarais
De Marance
De Margueri
De Maricourt
De Marinville
De Mar-
maude
De Marton
De Massanes
De Maxuel
De May
Demay
De Melher
De Menondue
De Merargues
De Millon
De Milon
De Miremont
De Mirmar
De Missy
De Miuret
De Moasre

De Moivre
De Molien
De Moliens
De Mombray
De Mommare
De Moncal
De Monceaux
De Money
Demons
De Montandre
De Montault
Demonte
De Montigny
De Mouginot
De Mount-
mayor
Denandiere
De Nauton
De Neafvrille
De Neufville
De Neuville
De Nipeville
Denis
Denise
Dennis
De Noyer
Denys
De Pages
De Pampe
De Paris
De Passy
De Paulin
De Paz
De Pecheis
De Pelissier
De Penna
De Perroy
De Petigny
De Petit
De Pierrepont
De Poncet
De Pond
De Pont
De Pontereau
De Ponthier
D'Eppe
Deppe
De Prades
De Prat
De Pront
De Puissar
De Puy
De Raed
De Rambou-
illet
De Rante
Derby
De Renet
Dergnoult
D'E Ricq
De Rideau
Derignee
De Riols

Derit
De Rivals
De Rivery
De Robillori
De Roche-
blave
De Romaignac
De Rossiers
De Roucy
De Rouredes
De Roye
Derrier
De Ruvigny
Desagulier
De Sailly
De St. Colome
De St. Ferreol
De St. Her-
mine
De St. Julien
De St. Leu
De St. Phili-
bert
De Savary
Desbordes
Des Brisa
Desbrisay
Descamps
Des Carrieres
Deschamps
De Schelandre
De Schirac
Des Clouseaux
Desdeuxvilles
De Selincourt
De Sene
Deseret
Deserre
Desessars
De Sicqueville
Des Lands
DesMaizeaux
Desmarets
DesMarets
D'Esmiers
Des Moulins
Desnaes
Desodes
Des Orme
Desormeaux
Des Ouches
D'Esperan-
dieu
Despere
Desperon
Despommare
Dess Easarts
Dessebues
De Surville
DesVoeux
De Tarrot
De Tugney
De Urie

De Val
De Vallan
De Vandar-
gues
De Varengues
De Varennes
De Vassale
Devaux
Devaynes
De Veill
Deveryt
Devesmo
De Vicouse
De Viere
De Vigneul
De Vignoles
De Viletts
Devins
De Virasel
De Virby
Devisme
De Vivaris
De Vivens
Devoree
De Wael
De Walpergen
De Wicke
Dezieres
D'fervart
D'Haucourt
D'Herby
D'Hervart
Diband
Didier
Dien
Die Port
Digard
Diharce
Dinard
Dioze
Diserote
Divorty
Dixon
Dobertin
Dobier
Doland
D'Olbreuse
Dolep
Dollond
D'Olier
D'Olon
Domerque
Donnell
Donut
Dor
D'Ornan
Dornan
Dornaut
Doron
Dorrien
D'Ortoux
Doruss
D'Orval

Dorvall
Dossein
Doubelet
Doublet
Douillere
Douissiner
Douxain
Dove
D'Oyon
Drelincourt
Droilhet
Drouet
Drovett
Drovillart
Droz
Drummond
Dubare
Dubarle
Du Bedat
Du Beons
Dubison
Du Bois
Du Boist
Du Borda
Du Bordieu
Dubosoq
Du Bourdieu
Du Brevie
Dubrois
Dubuer
Dubuisson
Ducasse
Du Charol
Duchemein
Du Chemin
Du Ches
Du Chesne
Duchesne
Du Chesoy
Duchier
Duclos
Du Clou
Du Cloux
Du Commun
Du Coudray
Du Could
Du Cros
Dudessart
Dueno
Du Faa
Du Fau
Du Fay
Dufay
Du Four
Dufour
Dufray
Dufresney
Dugard
Du Gat
Dugua
Du Gua
Du Guernier
Du Claux

Du Hamel
Du Jardin
Du Lac
Dulamon
Dulamont
Dulivier
D'Ully
Dulon
Du Lorall
Du Maistre
Dumaresq
Dumas
Dumay
Dumolin
Dumons
Du Mont
Dumont
Du Monte
Du Monthel
Du Montie
Dumore
Du Moulin
Dumoulin
Dumoustier
Du Pain
Du Parc
Duperon
Du Perrier
Du Perrion
Du Perron
Du Petit
Du Pin
Dupin
Duplessay
Du Plessis
Duplessy
Duplex
Du Pont
Duport
Duprat
DuPratt
Dupre
Du Pre
Duprey
Du Pu
Du Pus
Du Puy
Du Quesne
Durand
Durans
Durant
Durban
Durell
Durie
Duroure
Du Roure
Durrell
Du Rousseau
Du Roy
Du Ru
Durval
Dury
Dusoul

Du Souley
Du Soutoy
Du Tens
Du Teron
Du Thais
Du Thuille
Dutry
Duval
Du Val
Duvivier
Du Viviere
Edwards
Eele
Eland
Elibank
Elliott
Emerelle
Emet
Emly
Endelin
Enoe
Equerie
Ermenduiger
Erraux
Esmont
Espaignet
Espinasse
Espinet
Esquier
Essart
Estienne
Estivall
Estive
Estrance
Eversley
Excoffier
Eyme
Eynard
Faber
Fache
Faget
Fagett
Faitout
Falaiseau
Falch
Fald
Fallet
Fallon
Famoux
Fanevie
Fanevil
Farcy
Fargeon
Farinel
Farly
Faron
Farquhar
Farquier
Fasure
Faucerreau
Faucon
Fauconnier
Faulcon

Fauquier
Faure
Favet
Favin
Favnec
Favnc
Favre
Feerman
Feilloux
Felles
Fellowe
Felster
Fennvill
Ferdant
Fermend
Ferment
Feron
Ferrant
Ferre
Ferrer
Ferret
Ferry
Feuilleteau
Fevilleteau
Fiesill
Fish
Fleureau
Fleuriot
Fleurisson
Fleury
Flournoys
Flurian
Flurison
Flury
Foissac
Foissin
Folchier
Fongrave
Fonnereau
Fontaine
Fontijuliane
Forcade
Forceville
Forent
Forestier
Foretier
Foriner
Forister
Forit
Forme
Formont
Forrester
Forrestier
Fortanier
Fouace
Fouache
Foubbert
Foubert
Foucaut
Fouchard
Fourchars
Fourche
Fouchon

Fougeron
Foulouse
Foulre
Fountaine
Fouquerell
Fouquet
Fourdrinier
Fourgan
Fournier
Fourreau
Fovace
Fox
Foy
Fradin
Fraigneau
Frallion
Francia
Francillon
Francis
Francois
Francq
Frau
Frayelle
Frazier
Frement
Fremont
Freneau
Fresne
Fresneau
Fresnot
Fret
Friell
Friend
Frigont
Frisquet
Fromenteau
Fruchard
Frushchan
Fumeshau
Furon
Fury
Gabelle
Gabet
Gabrier
Gaches
Gagnier
Gaillardine
Gaillon
Gain
Gaindait
Gaiot
Gairand
Galabin
Galand
Galdy
Galhie
Galineau
Galissard
Gallais
Galland
Galliard
Galloway
Galway

Gambier
Garache
Garcelon
Gardien
Gardies
Garin
Garinoz
Gario
Gariot
Garnault
Garnier
Garon
Garrard
Garrie
Garrick
Gaschere
Gasherie
Gashlie
Gastaing
Gastigny
Gastily
Gastine
Gaston
Gau
Gaubert
Gaugain
Gaultier
Gaussen
Gautie
Gautier
Gaution
Gautron
Gavot
Gaydan
Gayot
Geaussent
Gebert
Gedouin
Gelien
Genays
Gendrant
Gendrault
Gendreu
Gendron
Geneste
Genhemiere
Gentilet
Geoffrey
Georges
Gerbier
Gerbrier
Gerdaut
Germaine
Germen
Geruy
Gervais
Gervaise
Gervaizet
Ghiselin
Giberne

Gibson
Gideon
Gignons
Gignooux
Gignoux
Gilbert
Giles
Gilles
Gillois
Gillot
Gilman
Gimlette
Ginonneau
Girandeau
Girard
Girardot
Giraud
Giraurd
Giraux
Girod
Glanisson
Glenisson
Gloria
Gne
Goayquet
De Gobert
Gobs
Godard
Goddard
Godeau
Godefroy
Godet
Godfrey
Godfroy
Godin
Godins
Gohier
Goilard
Goisin
Goldevin
Gomar
Gomart
Gomeon
Gontier
Gorin
Gorion
Goslin
Gosseaume
Gosselin
Gosset
Goubert
Goudron
Gouffe
Gougeon
Goujon
Goulain
Gouland
Goulle
Goulon
Gourbie
Gourbould
Gourdon
Gourdonnel

Goutelles
Gouvernet
Gouy
Govin
Govis
Govy
Goyon
Grabem
Grancay
Granger
Grangier
Grasset
Grasvellier
Grateste
Gravelle
Gravelot
Graverol
Graves
Gravisset
Grazeillier
Greene
Grellier
Greneau
Grenier
Grenot
Greve
Griberlin
Griel
Griet
Griffin
Grignion
Grignon
Grillet
Grimault
Grogan
Groleau
Grolon
Gron
Gronguet
Grosart
Groslet
Grossin
Grote
Grosteste
Gru
Grubb
Grueber
Gruider
Grunpet
Gually
Gualtier
Gualy
Geunard
Geunault
Guenon
Geupin
Geurin
Geurineau
Guerrier
Guery
Guesher
Guesnard
Guesnaud

Guespin
Guetet
Gueyle
Gui
Guibal
Guibald
Guibert
Guichard
Guichardiere
Guichenet
Guichery
Guichinet
Guiday
Guidon
De Guiennot
Guigner
Guigver
Guilhen
Guill
Guillandeau
Guillard
Guilleaume
Guilleband
Guillebert
Guillein
Guillermin
Guillon
Guilloneau
Guillot
Guimard
Guinand
Guinard
Guion
Guioneau
Guirand
Guirod
Guisard
Guitan
Guitton
Guive
Guizot
Gukllet
Gullet
Gulry
Gunge
Guoy
Gusset
Gutton
Guy
Guyon
Habberfield
Hager
Hagger
Hain
Haines
Hall
Hallee
Hallinguis
Hamelot
Hamlet
Hammel
Hamon

Hanbury
Hanet
Haquinet
Harache
Hardossin
Hardouin
Hardy
Harenc
Harris
Hartman
Hasbrouk
Hassard
Hastier
Hattanville
Hautkwits
Hautot
Havee
Havet
Havy
Hayes
Hayrault
Hays
Headley
Hebert
Helin
Hellot
Helot
Hemard
Hemet
Henault
Herache
Herbert
Herbot
Hercontaud
Herison
Hermand
Hersand
Hervart
Herve
Herviett
Hervieu
Hesdon
Hesne
Hesse
Hester
Heude
Heurteleu
Heurtley
Heurtin
Heury
Heuse
Heuze
Hewett
Hewlett
Hibon
Hierome
Hioll
Hirzel
Hobler
Hodshon
Hogelot
Hoissard
Holdernesse

Holl
Holzafell
Honze
Horeau
Horion
Horry
Houssay
Houssaye
Hovell
Hubert
Hudel
Huelins
Huet
Huger
Hugues
Huguetan
Hugueton
Hulen
Hullin
Huyas
Igon
Ilamber
Ieremonger
Jacques
Jalabert
Jamain
Jamart
Jambelin
Jame
Jamin
Jamineau
Jammard
Jammeau
Janse
Jappie
Jaquand
Jaqueau
Jardeau
Jarsan
Jarvey
Jastrain
Jaubert
Jaudin
Jaumard
Jay
Jeard
Jeay
Jegn
Jenne
De Jerome
Jerseau
Jesnouy
Jeverau
Joiry
Jolin
Jolit
Jolivet
Jollan
Joly
Jonneau
Jonquiere
Jordan
Jordis

Jortin
Jouanne
Jouillot
Jounne
Jourdain
Jourdaine
Jourdon
Journard
Journeau
Jousselin
Jousset
Jouvenel
Joyay
Joyeux
Juglas
Juibert
Julien
Juliet
Jullian
Justamon
Justamond
Justel
Justenier
Jyott
Kay
Keller
Kemp
Kenny
King
Kinnoull
Knigg
Knight
Kugelman
La Bachelle
La Barthe
La Basoche
Labasti
De La Basti
De Labatie
La Batie
Labe
Labelle
la Besse
De La Billiere
La Boissonna
Laborde
De Labouch
Labouchere
La Bouche-
tiere
La Boucille
La Boulaye
La Brosse
La Brousse
La Bussa
De La Caillem
Lacam
Lacan
La Cana
La Capelle
La Casterie
La Caterie
La Caux

La Clide
La Cloche
La Colombino
La Combe
La Conde
La Coste
La Coude
Lacour
Lacoze
L'Advocat
La Fabreque
Lafausille
La Fertie
Lafeur
L'afite
Lafitte
LaFont
Lafont
La Force
Laforey
Laghacherie
Lagis
La Grangerie
La Guarde
La Hautville
Lailleau
Laine
Laisne
La Jaielle
Lakeman
La Lande
Lallone
Lalon
Lalone
La Loubiere
La Lovele
La Malquiere
La Marie
Lamb
Lambert
Lame
La Melonniere
Lamouche
Lamp
La Mude
Landes
Landon
Lane
Langelier
Langlois
Langue
Laniere
Lapiere
La Place
La Plaigne
Laporte
La Postre
Larcher
Lardeau
Lardien
La Rivie
La Riviera
La Roche

Larpent
Larrat
La Salle
Laserre
Lasson
La Tourte
Lauber
Lauran
Laurand
Laure
Laureide
Laurens
Laurent
Lauze
Lavaine
Lavanotte
La Vie
Lavie
Lawrance
Lawrence
Layard
le Anglois
le Bailli
le Bas
lebas
le Bayeant
le Bayent
leber
le Berginer
le Berquier
lebet
le Blanc
le Blank
le Blaus
le Blon
De Bonneval
le Bour
le Boytevy
le Breton
le Caron
le Carron
le Castile
le Cene
lecerf
lechabrun
le Challeur
le Cheaube
le Chenevix
le Cheva
Lechigaray
le Clercq
le Clere
le Clereq
le Comte
le Conte
le Coq
le Coste
le Court
le Cras
le Creu
le Croil
Ledeux
le Doux

Lee
Leeson
Lefabure
La Fabure
le Febre
Lefebure
le Febure
le Ferre
le Feure
le Ficaut
le Fort
le Fourgeon
le Franc
L'Egare
Leger
Legrand
le Grou
Leguay
Lehad
Leheup
le Homme-
hieu
le Jeune
le Large
Lelarge
le Lordier
le Macon
le Maistre
Lemaitre
le Maitton
le Mann
Lemasle
le Mer
le Mesurier
le Moine
le Moleux
le Monnier
le Moreux
le Moyne
Lenglache
le Noble
le Noir
le Page
le Pin
le Plaistrier
le Plastrier
le Porte
le Poulveret
Lequesne
le Quien
Leriteau
Lermoult
Lernoult
le Roux
le Rouz
le Roy
le Royer
Lerpiniere
le Sage
le Saye
lesclure
lescure
le Serrurier

le Sombre
le Souef
Lespine
Lestocart
Lestrille le
Sueur
le Tavernier
le Tellier
le Tondu
Leturgeon
Leufoes
le Va
De le Vasseur
le Vassor
Levesque
Levi
Levielle
le Vieux
Lewis
Lexpert
L'heureux
Liege
Liegg
Lievrard
Liger
Ligonier
Limousin
Linard
Linart
Liron
Lisns
L'jomedin
Lloyd
Loffting
Lofland
Lombard
Longuet
Longuevil
Lope
Loquin
Lorens
Lormier
Lorrain
Lortie
Losweres
Loubier
Lougviguy
Louzada
Loveres
Lovis
Lucadou
Lucas
Lulo
Lunel
Luquet
Lussan
Lusson
Lutra
Luy
Luzman
Lyon
Lys
Macaire

Machet
Madder
Magniac
Mahaut
Mahieu
Maigne
Maigre
Maillard
Maillet
Main
Mainard
Maintru
Maintry
Maion
Maittaire
Majendie
Malacarte
Malegne
Malense
Malet
Malevaire
Malherbe
Malide
Malie
Mallet
Malpoil
Malre
Manin
Manvillain
Mar
Marandel
Marbeust
Marboeuf
Marc
Marchais
Marchand
Marchant
Marchay
Marche
Marcherallier
Marchet
Marchett
Maret
Margas
Maricq
Marie
Mariet
Mariette
Marignac
Marin
Marinville
Marinyon
Marion
Marionneau
Mariot
Marissal
Marmot
Marot
Marplay
Marriet
Marseille
Martel
Martell

Martil
Martinauz
Martineau
Martines
Martinet
Maryon
Maseres
Masfagnerat
Masly
Mason
Masse
Massey
Massienne
Massiot
Masson
Massoneau
Massu
Mastes
Mataver
Mathe
Mathias
Matte
Matthews
Matthias
Maudet
Maudon
Mauger
Maunier
Maupetit
Maurice
Maurin
Mauze
Mayen
Mayer
Maymal
Maynard
Maze
Mazenq
Mazick
Mazicq
Mazieres
Meffre
Meldron
Melier
Melinet
Mell
Melun
Memerdiere
Menage
Menanteau
Menard
Mendez
Menet
Menil
Mercie
Mercier
Merisseterit
Merlin
Meroist
Mervilleau
Mery
Merzeau
Mesgret

Meslier	Mougine	Pain	Perdriaux	Pollock	Raoul	Roberdeau
Mesmin	Mouginot	Paisible	Pere	Polran	Rapillard	Robert
Mesnard	Moulong	Paissant	Pereira	Poltais	Rapillart	Robethon
Mesnier	Mounier	Palot	Peres	Pontardant	Rappe	Robin
Messieu	Mousnier	Pandereau	Peridier	Pontitre	Ratier	Robineau
Metair	Mousset	Panier	Perigal	Poppin	Ravart	Roch
Metivier	Moxon	Panthin	Perlier	Porch	Ravaud	Roche
Meure	Moyne	Papavogn	Perpoint	Portail	Raveau	Rocher
Meyer	Moyon	Papin	Perrandin	Pouchon	Ravel	Rodet
Michael	Moze	Paquet	Perrault	Poulveret	Ravenel	Rodier
Michel	Mullett	Paravienne	Perreat	Poupe	Raymondon	Rodriguez
Michon	Mussard	Pare	Perreau	Pourroy	Raynaud	Roger
Midy	Mutel	Parett	Pertineau	Pousset	Raynaut	des Romaines
Mignan	Muysson	Pariolieau	Pertuison	Poussett	Reale	Rowland
Minet	Myre	Parmenter	Pertuson	Povillon	Rebecourt	Roy
Minnielle	Narbonne	Parquot	Pesche	Prat	Reberole	Royer
Minuel	Nau	Pascal	Peschier	Prestrau	Redoutet	Rubbatti
Minvielle	Naudin	Pasquereau	Petioiel	Preux	Reed	Rucault
Mirassoz	Neau	Pasquinet	Petit	Prevenau	Regard	Ruel
Mire	Neel	Pastre	Petitot	Prevereau	Regnaud	Ruffane
Misson	Neusrue	Pastureau	Peyret	Prevost	Regnauld	Russeler
Mogin	Nezereau	Patot	Peytrignet	Pringel	Regnier	Russiat
Moiseau	Nisbet	Pau	Phelippon	Prioleau	Reignier	Ruvigny
Moizy	Nobillieau	Paucier	Phellipeau	Prion	Rembert	Rybott
Molet	Noblet	Paul	Philbrick	Pron	Remousseaux	Sabatieres
Molinier	Noguier	Paulet	Picaut	Prou	Remy	Sabattier
Moller	Noiray	Paulmier	Pien	Pryor	Renaud	Saint
Monbocvil	Nolleau	Paulsen	Pierranc	Puech	Renaudet	Saint-Amen
Moncousiet	Normand	Pauret	Pierre	Puisancour	Renaudin	Saint Faver
Monet	Normani	Paustian	Pierresene	Puitard	Renaudot	Saint-Pe
Monfort	De Norris	Pautins	Pigou	Pujolas	Renault	Salnau
Monhallier	Nouaille	Pavet	Pigro	Pulley	Renaust	Salomon
Monier	Nourcy	Payen	Pillot	Pusey	Renaut	Samon
Monileau	Nouretier	Payrene	Pilon	Puxen	Reneau	Samson
Monnerat	Nourtier	Peau	Pilot	Pyron	Renee	Sandham
Monnerian	Novel	Pechel	Pilote	Quache	Renie	Sandrin
Montagu	Novell	Pechell	Pillart	Quarante	Rennys	Sange
Montague	Nurse	Peek	Pinandeau	Quenis	Renue	Sangeon
Montallier	Nyort	Pegorier	Pineau	Quern	Renvoize	Sanseau
Montebr	Obbema	Peinlon	Pinot	Quesnel	Resse	Sanselle
Montelz	Obert	Pele	Pinque	Quet	Retz	Sanson
Monteyro	Odry	Pelerin	Pinquet	Quille	Reverdy	Sapte
Montier	Offre	Pelet	Piozet	Quinault	Rey	Sarasin
Montil	Ogelby	Peletier	Piquet	Quintard	Reynard	Sarazin
Montolieu	Ogier	Pelissaly	Piron	Rabache	Reynaud	Sartoris
Montressor	Ogilby	Pelisson	Pitan	Raboteau	Reynell	Sartres
Moore	Oliver	Pellisonneau	Pittar	Racine	Reyners	Sasportas
Morand	Orian	Pellotier	Planarz	Raddisson	Reynous	Sasserire
More	Orion	Peloquin	Planck	Radiffe	Rezeau	Satur
Moreau	Oriot	Pelser	Plastier	Radnor	Riboteau	Sauinier
Moret	Osmont	Peltrau	Plate	Raimond	Ribouleau	Saureau
Morgas	Oufrie	Penault	Play	Rainbaux	Richard	Saurin
Morgat	Ouranneau	Peneth	Plison	Raine	Richer	Sausoin
Morgue	Ourse	Penigault	Pluet	Rainel	Rigail	Sauvage
Morin	Outand	Penny	Plumier	Rambaud	Rigaud	Sauze
Morion	Ouvry	Pensier	Poignet	Rame	Riolet	Savary
Morisseau	Pacquereau	Pepin	Poince	Ramier	Riou	Savignac
Morisset	Paetts	Peraud	Poitevin	Ramoudon	Risley	Savoret
Mortier	Page	Perblin	Poitevoin	Ranaule	Risteau	Savory
Motet	Pages	Percey	Poitier	Rand	Rivand	Sbuelen
Moteux	Paget	Perchard	Poitiers	Randeau	Rivard	Scholten
Mouchet	Pagnis	Perdereau	Polerin	Rane	Robain	Schomberg
Mougin	Paillet	Perdreau	Poletier	Ranel	Robateau	Schonburg

Schozer	Soignon	Taillett	Tiel	Trillet	Vaucqet	Voier
Schrieber	Solon	Tanqueray	Tiercelin	Trinquand	Vauriguad	Vollier
Schut	Sonegat	Taphorse	Tillon	Triquet	Vautier	Vome
Schwob	Sotie	Tardy	Tiphaine	Tristan	Vautille	Vorer
Scoffier	Souberan	Target	Tiran	Trittan	Vauvelle	Vouliart
Segouret	Soufflet	Targett	Tirand	Tudert	Veel	Vourioh
Segournay	Souhier	Targier	Tirel	Tuley	Verdetty	Vrigneau
Seguin	Soulart	Tartarin	Tissier	Tulon	Verdois	Vrigno
Seheult	Soulegre	Taudin	Tixier	Turquand	Vere	Vuclas
Sehut	Soullard	Taumur	Tonard	Turst	Verger	Wagenar
Seigler	Soureau	Tavernier	Torin	Tutet	Verhope	Wagner
Seigneur	Soux	Teissier	Torquet	Vaillant	Verigny	Waltis
Seigneuret	Soyer	Telles	Tostin	Vaille	Verit	Ward
Seignoret	Sozze	Tellier	Totin	Valet	Vernezobre	Ware
Selmes	Sperling	Temple	Toton	Valleau	Vernous	White
Senat	Stahelun	Tenderman	Touchart	Vallett	Veure	Wieten
Sene	Stample	Ternac	Toulchard	Vanderhulst	Vialars	Wilcens
Senecal	Stanley	Tessereau	Toullion	Vanderhumek	Vidal	Wildigos
Senecat	Steger	Tessier	Touray	Vandernedon	Videau	Wilkens
Setirin	Stehelin	Testard	Tourneur	Van Deure	Viet	Willaume
Severin	Sterel	Testas	Tourtelot	Van Hattem	Vievar	Williamme
Sevestre	Stockey	Testefolle	Tousaint	Van Juls	Vignault	Williams
Shipeau	Stokey	Teulon	Tousseaume	Van Lester	Vignoles	Winsor
Shoppee	Stone	Thauvet	Toutaine	Vannes	Villars	Wooddeson
Sibron	Streing	Thaveau	Toutton	Van Somer	Villeneusne	Wyndham
Siegler	Suire	Thercot	Touvois	Vare	Villepontoux	Yon
Sieurin	Sureau	Theron	Tovillett	Vareille	Villette	Yoult
Sigourney	Surville	Theronde	Travers	Vareilles	Villier	Yvonet
Silvestre	Suyre	Thesmaler	Traversier	Varine	Villiers	Yvonnet
Simeon	Sylvestre	Thibaut	Treiber	Vashon	Villotte	Zinck
Simon	Tabare	Thiboust	Trevigar	Vassall	Vincent	Zurichrea
Simonneau	Tabart	Thierry	Treville	Vatable	Voileau	
Simpson	Tacher	Thomas	Tribert	Vatier	Viroot	
Sion	Tadourneau	Thomeaur	Trible	Vattelet	Visage	
Smart	Tahourdin	Thomeur	Trigan	Vattemare	Vivian	
Sohnms	Taillefer	Thouvois	Triller	Vauchie	Vivier	

TABLE 4. LIST OF SOUTH CAROLINA COLONIAL SURNAMES COMPILED BY PAUL R. SARRETT, JR., OF THE STATE ARCHIVES

SOURCE: www.usgenweb.org

Able	Barber	Biddy	Burk(e)	Chawes/	Cubela	Dennie/
Adair	Barden	Bird	Burney	Cheves	Cumine	Denny
Addis	Barksdale	Block	Burnit	Chiver	Cummings	dePia
Adkins	Barlow	Boby	Burrough(s)	Clark(e)	Curry(ie)	De Roch
Akin(s)	Barnwell	Boelthe	Butler	Clockler	Daniel(l)	deSaussure
Alair	Baron	Boone	Cain	Cocks	Darquior	deTrivers
Alexander	Barrett	Borus	Caldwell	Coffer	Daugherty	deVall
Alis	Barry	Bosomworth	Calis	Cogan	Davenport	Dial
Allein	Barton	Bourdeaux	Campbell	Collins	Davids	Dick
Allison	Beamor	Bourke	Canedy/Can-	Commander	Davidson	Dominick
Argo	Bean	Bowlin	nada	Comyne	Davies	Dorff
Ash	Bee	Box	Cannon	Conn	Davis	Dosda
Aspenal	Beels	Brabant	Cantey	Cook(e)	Day	Drake
Bacon	Belin	Brazel/Brazeal	Cargill	Cooper	Deal	Ducat
Bacot	Bell	Breshar	Carlisle	Copai	Dean	Durant
Badjeaw	Below	Brooks	Carmichael	Cotton	Deas	Duryn-
Bagley	Benn	Brown(e)	Carne	Cowan	Dee	mayer
Bags	Bennett	Bugnion (Bon-	Carter	Cox	deLas	Eakins
Balir	Benson	durant)	Cassells	Crane	delPonte	Ecolier
Balote	Berry	Bull	Castle	Crise	deMonclar	Egnia
Baptistere	Biddis	Bunel	Catarina	Cronenberger	Dendey	Ellis(son)

Elvin	Gombze	Jay	Manigault	Odam/Odom	Rivers	Taggart
Emrey	Good(e)	Jeannerette	Mansell	Oliver	Robertson	Taverson
English	Gordon	Jerman	Margarita	Osborne	Robeson	Temple(ton)
Erwin	Gore(y)	Jevelah	Mark(s)	Osgood	Robinson	Tennant
Eskridge/	Gorman	Joel	Marte	Ottalia	Roche	Towns
Etheridge	Grant	Jolley	Martin	Otterson	Roderick	Townsend
Fabian	Gray	Jones	Mazyck	Paarcy	Rolipo	Troup
Fannin(g)	Green(e)	Jordan	McBee	(Pharsi?)	Roper	Tunno
Fares	Greenwood	Kaill	McCall	Pace	Rose	Turk
Farquharson	Greer	Kays	McDaniel	Page	Ross	Valentine
Farris	Greg(ory)	Keith	McDavid	Paget	Ruble	Valoars
Faucounet	Grey	Keller	McDonald	Palmer	Russell	Vanay
Faure	Grimes	Kempe	McDowell	Pamer/Pamor	Sacby	Vander Heyd
Fee	Grob(er)	Kennedy	McGee	Papot	Sadler	Van der Horst
Field	Groce/Gross	Key	McGown	Parish	Sakker	Van Horn
Fish(er)	Haliday	Kirran	McKee	Parrot	(Sachar)	Vann
Flar	Hallems	(Koran?)	McKeown	Parry	Sanders	Vasseks
Fload/Flood	Halloway	Kueffer/Kuif-	McleMarr	Payne	Sanderson	Verdier
Forbes	Hames	fer	McLochlin	Pearis	Sandys	Verdiman
Ford	Hamilton(el)	L'Argent	Meguinas	Pelow	Satur	Verjen
Fort	Hammett	LaBord	Messer	Perrin	Saunders	Verrays
Fortune	Hannah	Lang	Metsger	Perry	Saussy	Vessels
Foxe	Harkins	LaRoche	Michall	Pew	Selby	Veuve
Foy	Harmon	Lasles	Michel	Phillips	Shepard	Wales
Franck(k)	Harry	Laurans	Michie	Pindkney	Shereiff	Wallace
Franklin	Hawkes	Lawrence	Miles	Pope	Sibella	Waly
Fraser/Frazer	Hawkins	Lea(y)/lee	Miller	Prince	Sigler	Ward
Fraylick/Free-	Hay(es)	LeMar	Mims	Proctor	Simmonds	Wardlaw
lick	Hazzard	Lesley/leslie	Minchen	Pugh	Simms/Sims	Waters
Frederucj	Heard	Letcher	(Munchen)	Purry	Skene	Weems
Freeman	Hepworth	Lewis	Mingin	Queen	Smiley	West
Galache	Hext	Liddle	Mires	Rachie	(Ismaeli)	White
Galphin	(Hoechst?)	Liles	Mitchell	Rainey	Spears	Wild
Gamble	Hindra	Livingston	Mock	Rambo (Ram-	(Spiers?)	Williams(son)
Garratt/Garet/	Holiday	Lodge	Moore	beaux)	Stanyarne	Winn
Garrot	Holloway	Loucoss	Mosely	Raphel	Starns	Wise
Geimball	Hollum	(Lucas?)	Moss	Rattray	Stebens	Wiseman
Genbretz	Hossey	Loundes	Mounts	Ravelel	Steel	Wragg
Ghent	Howard	Lowery	Murray	Rawlings	Sterns	Wright
Gist	Hudson	Luckie	Musgrove	Ray	Steward	Wunderlich
Glasgos(w)	Hyle	Mabry	Nichols	Recorder	Stewart	Yanam
Glaze	Inglis	Mach	Nicholson	Rees	Storey	Yates
Gobbooane	Irving	Mackey	Nickels	Rey	Stuart	Zouberbuker
Goings	Irwin	Maens	Noble	Rhodes	Susam/	
Golding	Istes	(Mainz)	Norman(d)	Richey	Susanns	
Gollman	Izard	Man(n)	Norris	Rippur	Tabor	

Table 5. Marriages from Old 96 and Abbeville Districts

Source: http://files.usgwarchives.org/sc/marriages/scm_96th.txt (Listed below are several marriages occurring within the Old 96/Abbeville district during the colonial era in South Carolina.)

James Able + Eleanor Fox
Will. Acker (Acre, Palestine) + Dewanes Barmore
John Adams + Elmira Martin
Adoniram Judson Agnew + Emma Agnew
James Agnew + Mahala Dodson
Sam. Alex. Agnew + Alice Zelene Sullivan
Augustus Aiken + Mayme Agers
Joseph Kar Aiton + Mary Wilson
John Darby Alewine + Miriam Pearman
George Allen + Sophronia Hodges
Oliver Perry Anderson + Arabella Brownlee

Elihu Franklin Andrews + Emma Sims
John Argo + Peggy Adamson
Archibald Arnold + Mahala Reynolds
Thomas Arnold + Ellen Traxler
David Atkins + Sarah Short Lomax
Thomas Atkins + Eve Feltman
Alpheus Barnes + Jane Zimmerman
Samuel Benjamin + Isabel Major
Aiken Breazeal + Louisa Pace
James Henry Brooks + Lily Marilla Wingo
John Wesley Brooks + Taphones Lipscomb

Stanmore Butler Brooks + Taphones Lipscomb
Alladin Buchanan + Nancy Roman
(illegible) Burriss + Vashti Sharp
R.W. Cannon + Toccoa Fair
David Capeland + Belle Arnold
Benjamin Cason + Amelia Cason
Reuben Clinkscales + Isabella Cowan
Lazaraus Covin (Calvin) + Susan David
Letitia Alamza Cowan + Wesley Black
Marcus Crews + Isabella Ross
Emziah Davis + Lucinda Young
Isaac Banta Davis + Henrietta Sassard
Robert Elgin + Machanie Arcajah
Livingston Fair + Toccoa Roubin
Jehu Foster + Margaret Perrin
Nimrod Gaddis (Cadiz) + Ella Davis
Jonadab Gaines + Jennie Gaines
Thom. Graham + Zolacus Rothrock

Nathaniel Harris + Bersheba Cain
James Hester + Lena Hester
John Hester + Callie Cofer
M. Israel + Rebecca Elias
Paschal Dawes Klugh + Emma Syfan
Alonzo Lawton + Buena Vista Welch
Adolphus Mahaffa + Arabella Winn
Samuel Elias Mays + Elvira Moseley
John Morrah + Emma Morrah
Henry Mouzon + Sarah Mouzon
Samuel Paschal + Pherreba Ward
Thomas Pharr + Elizabeth Rasor
William Ricketts + Palestine Delilah Armstrong
Alfred Sheriff + Jane Drake
James Shillito + Mahala Wardlaw
George Syfan + Nina Augusta Isaacs
James Vermillion + Anna Stone

TABLE 6. CAROLINA INDIAN TRADERS, COMMISSIONERS AND AGENTS (alphabetized)

SOURCE: Theresa M. Hicks, *South Carolina Indians*; authors' research

James Adair (Hebrew)
Ephraim Alexander
James Alford
Shippy/Sheppy Allen
Captain Allick
Thomas Andrews
Peter Arnaud
John Ash
Edmund Atkin (from Aix)
Joseph Axson
Thomas Ayers
James Baldridge
Charles Banks
William Bannister
Isaac Barksdale
John Barnwell
Thomas Barton/Burton
William Bates
James Beamer (Beaumour)
Thomas Beamer
John Bee
Bench (Benge)
Samuel Benn
Richard Beresford
William Bennet (Baruch)
Jethro Bethridg
John Blackluck
William Blakeway
John Boone (Good)
Thomas Bosomworth
Edward Brailsford
Brannon
William Bray
William B. Brett/Britt
William Broadway
Edward Broody
Thomas Broughton
Alexander Brown
James Brown

Patrick Brown
Daniel Bruner
John Buckles
Stephen Bull
William Bull
James Bullock
Dr. Charles Bunham
Robert Bunning (Bondurant)
Butler (Boutellier)
Joseph Cain
Nathaniel Cain
Daniel Callaham/Callahane
Alexander Cameron
John Campbell
Martin Campbell
William Cantey
Robert Card
John Chaplin (form of Jacob)
John Chester
George Chicken (Gallo?)
Daniel Clark (Sofer)
James Cochram
Capt. John Cochran
John Crockett (Croquetaine)
James Colbert
Joseph Cooper (form of Jacob)
Joseph Cornel (Coronel)
Jermyn Courtong/Jerome Courtonne
James Craford
Capt. Craft
Charles Craven
David Crawley
Childermas Croft
Jess Crosley
Joseph Crosley
Joseph Cundy
George Cussings
William Dalton (D'Alton)
Nicholas Day

Anthony Deane (D'Eanes?)
John Dickson/Dixon
Cornelius Doherty/Dougherty
James Douglas
David Dowie
(David) Downing
Jonathan Drake (Dragon)
William Drake
Thomas Duvall
John Edinburgh
Thomas Edwards
Samuel Elchinor (El Senor?)
John Elliot (Arabic)
Edmund Ellis (Arabic)
Samuel Elsnear/Elshanner
Henry Evans
John Evans (1)
John Evans (2)
Nathaniel Evans
Samuel Eveleigh
John Fenwick
Robert Fenwick
Tobias Fitch
William Ford (Faure)
Stephen Forest/Forrest
James Francis
William Franks
John Fraser
John Frazier
Robert French
George Galphin
Robert Gandey (Canada)
James Germany
Barnaby Gilbert
Barnabus Gillard
Phillip Gilliard
Guess/Gist (Costa, Gozzi)
Charlesworth Glover
Richard Goer/Gower

Robert Gowdie/Gowdey/Gowdy
   (Gandey)
Hugh Grange
Ludowick Grant (Grand)
John Graves
Edward Griffin
Joseph Griffin
John Guerard
George Haig
George Haines/Haynes
Charles Hart (Naphthali)
Thomas Hasfort
Theophilus Hastins/Haistings/
   Hastings
Richard Hacher/Hatcher
John Hatton
Rachel Hatton
William Hatton
Thomas Hawkins (Haquim)
John Herbert
Robert Hicks
Samuel Hilden
Charles Hill
John Hilliard
Jacob Hite/Height (Arabic)
John Hogg
Holford
John Hook
Capt. Job Howe
Bernard Hughes
Price Hughes
John Hutton
James Ingerson
Ralph Izard (1) (Arabic)
Ralph Izard (2)
John Jones
Richard Jones
Martin Keane
John Kelly
John Kennard
Alexander Kilpatrick
Jeremy Knott
Thomas Lamboll
Anthony Lantague
John Lawson (Levi)
John Legrove
Cornelius Le Mott (Motta)
Louis Lentiniat
Even Lewis
Col. George Logan
Alexander Long
James Lucas
Cornelius Maccarty/Macarty/
   Meckarty
Alexander Mackey
Maurice Matthews
Robert Matthews
Arthur Middleton
William Mitchell
James Moore
John Moore
Abram Mordecai[1]

William Morgan
James Morson
John Abraham Motte
Isaac Motte (Motta)
Captain/Colonel John Musgrove
Francis McCartin
John McCord
James McCormick
George McCullough
Richard McCully
Daniel McDonald/ McDaniel
David McDonald/McDaniel
Archibald McGillivray
Charles McGunningham
Lachlan McIntosh
George McKay/McKoy
Charles McLamore
Barnard McMullen (Molina)
William McMullian
Charles McNaire (Arabic)
Alexander McQueen (Cowan)
William McTeer
Thomas Nairne
John Nel(l)son
William NewburyAlexander
   Nicholas
Charles Nicols
Edward Nichols/Nicols
Thomas Nightingale
Anthony Park(s)
Richard Pearis/Parris (Perez)
Lewis Pasquereau
James Patteson/Paterson/Pattison
Abraham Peirce/Pearce or
   Poythress, Poyers, Pyers
Andrew Percival
William Pettypoole
Charles Pierce
William Pinckney (Pinhas)
John Pight
Christian Gottlieb Priber
Moses Price
Richard Prize/Price
Anthony Probat/Probert
Benjamin Quelch
John Rae (Reye)
Major Repele
William Rhett
Richardson
James Risbee
John Roberts
William Robertson
William Robinson
Jordan Roche (Rocca)
John Ross (Rose, red)
Charles Russell
Bryan Sallmon/Salmon (Solomon)
William Sanders
Roger Saunders
John Savage
Peter Scarlet
William Scarlet

Samuel Scott
Thomas Seebrook/Seabrook (Sebog?)
Benjamin Sealey (Sallé)
George Sheel or Sheed (Shilo?)
Thomas Shubrick
Thomas Simond/Simonds (Simon)
Peter Slann
William Sludders
Mathew Smallwood
Abraham Smith
Augustine Smith
George Smith
John Smith
Richard/Dick Smith
Thomas Smith (1 and 2)
William Smith
James Stanyarne (steel worker)
William Stead
Robert Steill/Steel
George Sterling/Sterland
George Stevens
Robert Stevens
Charles Stuart
John Stuart (Stewart)
George Summers/Sommers
Thomas Summers
David Taitt (Tate)
Henry Tally
John Tanner
Samuel Taurence (Torrence)
William Tennent
Samuel Terron
William H. Thomas (white chief
   of Cherokee)
Thurston
Robert Tool (Toule)
Richard Tranter (Tarento)
Patrick Troy
Trumbal
Francis Underwood
David Vann
Samuel Warner
Warrin
William Waties (Arabic)
Weaver
James Welch
Thomas Welch
Jack Welsh
Caleb Westbrook
Andrew White
Eleazer Wiggin(s) (Wizgan)
Henry Wiginton
John Williams
Dove Williamson
Francis Wilson
Alexander Wood (Silva?)
Henry Woodward
   (Duboisgarde)
George Wright
John Wright
Samuel Wyly
Francis Yonge

K. Lists of Settlers in Early Georgia

TABLE 1. ORIGINAL GEORGIA SETTLERS, FEB. 1733

SOURCE: *A List of the Early Settlers of Georgia*, Coulter and Saye, 106–111[1]

- Amatis, Paul, Italian silk man, gardener & silk care
- Bowling, Timothy, 38, potash maker
- Calvert, William, 44, trader in goods
  Calvert, Mary, 42, wife of William
  Greenfield, William, 19, nephew
  Greenfield, Charles, 16, nephew
  Greenfield, Sarah, 16, niece
- Cannon, Richard, 36, carpenter
  Cannon, Mary, 33, wife to Richard
  Cannon, Clementine, 3, daughter
  Cannon, James, 7 months, son, died en route, 26 November 1732
  Cannon, Marmaduke, 9, son
  Hicks, Mary, servant
- Carwell, James, 35, peruke maker
  Carwell, Margaret, 32, wife
- Causton, Thomas, 40, calico printer
- Christie, Thomas, 32, merchant
  Johnson, Robert, 17, servant
- Clark, Robert, 37, tailor
  Clark, Judith, 24, wife
  Clark, Charles, 11, son
  Clark, John, 4, son
  Clark, Peter, 3, son
  Clark, James, 9 months, son, died on *Ann*, December 22, 1732
- Close, Henry, 42, cloth worker
  Close, Hanna, 32, wife
  Close, Ann, 2, daughter to Henry
- Coles, Joseph, 28, miller and baker
  Coles, Anna, 32, wife
  Coles, Anna, 13, daughter
  Wellen, Elias Ann, 18, servant
- Cooper, Joseph, 34, writer[2]
- Cox, William, 41, doctor
  Cox, Frances, 35, wife
  ?Cox, William, 12?, son of William
  Cox, Eunice, 3, daughter
  Lloyd, Henry, 21, servant
- Fitzwater, Joseph, 31, gardener
- Fox, Walter, 35, turner

- Goddard, James, 35, carpenter and joiner
  Goddard, Elizabeth, 42, wife
  Goddard, John, 9, son
  Goddard, Elizabeth, 5, daughter
- Gordon, Peter,[3] 34, upholsterer
  Gordon, Katherine, 28, wife
- Gready, John, 22, farmer
- Hodges, Richard, 50, basketmaker
  Hodges, Mary, 42, wife
  Hodges, Mary, 18, daughter
  Hodges, Elizabeth, 16, daughter
  Hodges, Sarah, 5, daughter
- Hughes, Joseph, 28, cider trade
  Hughes, Elizabeth, 22, wife
- Jones, Noble, 32, carpenter, surveyor[4]
  Jones, Sarah, 32, wife
  Jones, Noble W., 10, son
  Jones, Mary, 3, daughter
  Cormock, Mary, 11, servant
  Ellis, Thomas, 17, servant
- Little or Littel, William, 31, understands flax and hemp
  Little or Littel, Elizabeth, 31, wife
  Little or Littel, Mary, 5, daughter
  Little or Littel, William, 2, son
- Milledge, Thomas
  Milledge, Elizabeth, 40, wife
  Milledge, John, 11, son
  Milledge, Sarah, 9, daughter
  Milledge, Richard, 8, son
  Milledge, Frances, 5, daughter
  Milledge, James, 2, son
- Mugridge, Francis, 39, sawyer
- Muir, James, 28, peruke maker
  Muir, Ellen, 38, wife
  Muir, John, 2, son
  Satchfield, Elizabeth, 24, servant
- Overend, Joshua, 40, mercer
- Parker, Samuel, 33, heelmaker
  Parker, Jane, 36, wife
  Parker, Samuel, Jr., 16, son

  Parker, Thomas, 9, son
- Penrose, John, 35, husbandman, pilot at Tybee, Georgia
  Penrose, Elizabeth, 46, wife
- Pratt, Thomas, 21
- Sammes, John, 42, cordwainer
- Scott, Francis, 40, military
  Cameron, John Richard, 35, servant
- Stanley, Joseph, 41, stockingman
  Stanley, Elizabeth, 35, wife
  Mackay, John, 25, servant
- Symes, George, 55, apothecary
  Symes, Sarah, 52, wife
  Symes, Ann, 21, daughter
- Thibaut, Daniel, 50, understands vines
  Thibaut, Mary, 40, wife
  Thibaut, James, 12, son
  Thibaut, Diana, 7, daughter
- Wallis, John
  Wallis, Elizabeth, 27, wife
- Warren, John, 34, flax & hemp dresser
  Warren, Elizabeth, 27, wife
  Warren, William, 6, son
  Warren, Richard, 4, son
  Warren, Elizabeth, 3, daughter
  Warren, John, 2, son
  Warren, Georgius Marinus, born on ship, Oglethorpe was godfather.
- Waterland, William, 44, mercer
- West, John, 33, smith
  West, Elizabeth, 33, wife
  West, Richard, 5, son
- Wilson, James, 21, sawyer
- Wright, John, 33, vintner
  Wright, Penelope, 33, wife
  Wright, John Norton, 13, son
  Wright, Elizabeth, 11, daughter
- Young, Thomas, 45, wheelwright

TABLE 2. FORTY-TWO JEWISH SETTLERS ON THE SHIP *WILLIAM AND SARAH*, 1733

SOURCE: Stern in Rubin, *Third to None*, 3–4

Ashkenazi Jews
- Benjamin Sheftall
  Perla Sheftall (his wife)
- Jacob Yowel (Joel)
- Abraham Minis
  Abigail Minis
  Leah Minis (daughter)
  Esther Minis (daughter)
  Simon Minis (Abraham's brother)

Sephardic Jews
- Dr. Samuel Nunes Ribeiro
  Zipporah Nunes (his mother)
  Moses Nunes (son)
  Daniel Nunes (son)
  Sipra (Zipporah) Nunes (daughter)
- Abraham de Lyon
  Shem Noah (servant)
- Isaac Nunes Henriques

Abigail Sequeira Henriques (wife)
Henriques (child, died at sea)
Shem Henriques (probably Samuel Sequeira)
- Raphael Nunes Bernal
  Rachel Bernal (his wife)
- David (Lopez) Olivera
  Jacob Lopez Olivera
  Judith Velha Olivera (his wife)

David Olivera (son)
Isaac Olivera (son)
Leah Olivera (daughter)
• Aaron De Pivia (De Paiba?)
• Benjamin Gideon
• Jacob Lopez De Crasto

• David Lopez De Pass (De Paz)
Zipporah De Pass (his wife)
• Isaac De Costa Villareal
• Abraham De Molina
• David (Rodrigues) Miranda
Jacob (Rodrigues) Miranda

• David Cohen Delmonte
Rache Delmonte (his wife)
Isaac Delmonte (son)
Abigail Delmonte (daughter)
Hannah Delmonte (daughter)
Grace Delmonte (daughter)

TABLE 3. SELECTED NAMES OF SALZBURGERS

SOURCE: George F. Jones, *The Germans of Colonial Georgia*, 1986

Adam,[5] Abraham
Ade (Adjaj), Salomo[6]
Bacher (carpenters)
Bender[7] (Palatinates, since 1695)
Blessing (Baruch)
Blume[8] (Palatines, from 1710)
Brabant (from the town in Flanders), Isaac
Brandner (intermarry with Flerl)
Briest[9] (deserter from British army)
Burgi (Swiss)
Denny,[10] Walter (discharged soldier)
Depp (i.e., "from Dieppe, the Netherlands," from Purrysburgh)
Ernst[11] (Bavarian, one is a physician)
Faesch, Andreas (Fez, "en route from London to Georgia")
Fahm (Sephardic surname Fam, Fão, Faão)[12]
Fasan ("from Fasano," Italy, near Bari),[13] Benjamin Heinrich (Swiss)
Fetzer ("from Fez"; Swabians)
Fischer[14] (Swabians)
Flerl (Florel), Israel, Judith, Hanna, etc.(Salzburg)
Francis (German woman married by a Lt. Francis)
Francke (from Purrysburgh)
Gabel, Abraham (settled in Abercorn)
Geiger ("fiddler"),[15] Abraham (Swiss)
Gimmel (Gimpel,[16] "bullfinch"), Balthasar
Goering, Simon (Palatinate, since 1706)
Gress (Swabian)
Gronau (from Kroppenstedt, near Magdeburg in Lower Saxony)[17]
Gugel (Kugel[18])
Gunter, Guinere, Guindre, Gurndre (French)
Haisler, David ("late from Germany")
Hamilton, Regina Charlotte, wife of Henry Hamilton (from Silesia)
Hamm,[19] Johann, gentleman
Hammer[20] (Saxons from Chemnitz)
Handley, William (intermarried)
Harmann
Hart (Palatinate)
Hartstein
Hauge ("from The Hague," Netherlands), Georg (settled in Abercorn)
Heidt (Salburgers and Palatinates)

Heinle,[21] David, Israel, Salome, etc. (Swabian, from Gaerstetten, married with Meyer)
Helfenstein (Elphinstone, Palatines, settled in Abercorn)
Herseberger (Herzberger),[22] Francis
Hirsch (from Augsburg)
Hirschmann (including a Rosina, Salome and Sophia, settled in Halifax, 1752)
Holland, Johann Georg (1716, Palatinate)
Hundredpound, Jacob
Jackocho, Abraham Friedrich (wife, Jenny Kain=Kohan)
Jedermann, Yeter, Yeterman, Yeaterman, Martin
Jett, Caspar
Kieffer[23] (Palatines, since 1716, married with Flerl, Depp, Zant, Schubrein)
Klein (from Alsace)
Kraemer ("keeper of retail booth")[24]
Kronberger (from Purrysburgh, married Kieffer, Schrempff, Roesberg)
Kuhn (Cohen),[25] Balthasar (ran away and joined the Congaree Indians)
Kusmaul ("kissy mouth"),[26] Jacob, wife Sevila ("from Sevile," Spain; Palatines)
Lackner ("lacquerer"; Salzburgers from Goldeck, a place-name meaning "gold village, or district," married Schubrein)
Lebey (Liebe, Ashkenazic "dear one"),[27] Judith
Lemke
Lion (Lyons), Martin
Lion (Lyon), Samuel (Palatine, sold and moved to Skidaway)
Mack (Mock, from Mordecai)[28]
Mann (from Menachem),[29] Johann (granted land on Briar Creek and Prethero's Bluff)
Marks, Anna, Hugh, Levi and Isaac, Ashkenazi Jews (arrived 1738)
Meyer, Adrian (from Purrysburgh, became butcher in Savannah)
Meyer (including Judith, Juliana, Sara, William and Jacob, several families, married Unselt, Treutlen, Zorn, Heinle, Fischer, Dasher)

Minis (Minz,[30] Savannah Jews, several were mentioned in wills)
Monfort, Anna (Southern French, married Gunter, also French)
Mott, Abraham (married Sara Scruggs) and Isaac
Neibling, Aleander (Swabian, from Langenau near Ulm)
Ochs (married Neibling, Fetzer)
Plessi
Ramsett, Ramsut, Ramshard, Remshart
Regnier, Reiner, Ranier, Jean François (Swiss Baptist, went back to Germany, then returned)
Rieser (Riess,[31] Salzburgers)
Rose[32] (Moravians)
Roth[33] (from Wurzburg, married Fetzer)
Rothmaler, Job
Sanftleben (Silesians)
Schad ("shame," Swiss, Margaretha married Friedrich Treutlin)
Schubrein ("drifter, vagrant," Daniel, David, Hanna, Jacob, Josef, Samuel, Judith, Salome, Israel, etc. (came over as servants for Zouberbuhler, originally from Alsace)
Sheftall (Savannah Jewish family, had dealings with Salzburgers)
Solomon, Coleman, German Jew (arrived 1736, daughter Hannah married Benjamin Sheftall)
Staeheli, Stehlen, Staley (originally Swiss, as in Madame de Staël)
Stein, Justus Grayson (army)
Steiner
Stierlin, Sierle (Swiss)
Strohbart (from Purrysburgh)
Taissoux, Daniel, German
Taylor (Schneider), Abraham (Palatine, 1722)
Thilo[34] (from Lauchstedt, near Leipzig, 1708, married Helfenstein, Heile)
Tonnewan, Jeremias and Sara
Treutlen[35] ("from Treuchtling," Bavaria), Johann Adam (Palatine, 1733, later governor of Georgia, married Margaretha Dupuis and, secondly, Anna Unselt; daughters married Schad, Provost, Kennedy)

Tubear (T'Bear), David, gunsmith in Savannah, formerly in Charleston (Dutch)

Tullius ("from Toule, France"), Josua Daniel, skilled man from Purrysburgh

Unselt (Palatines from Purrysburgh, originally from Ulm in Swabia; one married Henry Bishop)

Voegli[36] (Swiss)

Wagner ("cartwright"),[37] Abraham and Samuel (1735, settled in Hampstead, mentioned in a French will)

Wannamacher (Wanamaker,[38] "van maker, cartwright")

Weinkauf ("wine merchant," Swabian, from Wurttemberg, married Mack)

Yowell (from Joel), Jacob, German Jew

Zant (from Alexander), Bartholomaeus (wife Sibilla, grandson Benaja, etc.; Swiss)

Zorn, Barbara (Palatinate), married Ludwig Meyer

Zuericher ("from Zurich," in Switzerland), Anna Maria, married Nikolaus Schubrein, 1758

TABLE 4. LIST OF EARLY SETTLERS OF DARIEN, GEORGIA, 1735–1741

Compiled by Bessie Lewis from: Colonial Records of Georgia (published and unpublished); *A List of the Early Settlers of Georgia*, edited by E. Merton Coulter and Albert E. Saye; Charleston County wills, Charleston, S.C.; mesne conveyances, Charleston, S.C.; Deed Records, Liberty Co., Ga.

Baillie, James, servt. to Kenneth Baillie, age 33

Baillie, John, of Fortrose, farmer

Baillie, Kenneth, age 20, farmer, ensign to the Darien Company

Bain, Jo, of Lochain, age 45, trustee's servant

Bain, Kenneth, age 18, servt. to Alex Tolmie

Bain, Will, of Thuso, age 19, tailor

Burges, Joseph

Burges, Margaret, wife of Joseph

Calder, Will, age 20, tr. servt. for 4 yrs., at expiration of his services was made a soldier of the Highland Independent Company by General Oglethorpe

Calwell, John

Cameron, Alex'r, slain at siege of Inverness, age 20, servt. to Farqr. Macgilivray

" , widow of Alex'r.

Campbell, Colin, gentleman, age 17

Campbell, John, 24, woodcutter

Chisholme, Alex'r, of Inverness, age 10, servt. to Farqr. Macgilivray

Chisholme, Alex'r of Dronach, age 17, servt. to Mr. Mackay of Scourie

Chisholme, Margt., age 22, servt. to J. Sinclair

Clark, Donald, age 23, of Dorris, farmer

Clark, Donald, age 42, of Tongie, slain at St. Augustine

" , Barbara Grey, age 40, wife of Donald

" , Alex'r, son, age 15

" , Angus, son, age 5

" , Barbara, dau.

" , Geo., son, age 13

" , Hugh, son, age 12, a soldier in the Highland Independent Co.

" , Will, son, age 8

Clark, Hugh, age 21, of Dorris, Farmer, sgt. in the Independent Co.

Clark, Hugh, born in Ga., 3 yrs., 3 mos. old, May 6, 1741

Cleaness, Alex'r, age 24, tr. servt.

Cogach, Jo., age 33, laborer and cowherd

" , Ann Mackay, wife

" , Angus, son, age 7

" , Christiana, dau., age 16

" , Isabel, dau., age 13

" , William, son, age 11

Crookshanks, Rob., servt. to Farqr. Macgilivray

Cuthbert, Geo., of Inverness, farmer

Cuthbert, Jo, age 31, of Draikes, gent.

Denune, Jo, age 26, tr. servt.

Douglass, Geo., age 28, laborer

" , Margaret Munro, wife, age 29

Dunbar, Capt. George

Dunbar, John, age 36, Inverness, farmer

Forbes, Hugh, servt. to Will and Hugh Sterling

Forbes, John, age 26, servt. to Jo. Cuthbert of Draikes

Fraser, Donald, of Abercour, servt. to Patrick Grant

Fraser, Donald, of Inverness, age 20, servt. to Alex'r McIntosh

Fraser, Donald, of Inverness, age 22, servt. to Jo. Cuthbert of Draikes

Fraser, Jennet, age 18, servt. for 4 yrs.

Fraser, John, age 21, tr. servt.

Fraser, Margaret

Frazer, Donald, of Kingussie, age 25, servt. to Jo. Mackintosh

Glass, John, age 18, servt.

Grant, John, age 18, servt. to Patrick Grant

Grant, John, age 22, laborer

Grant, Margaret

Grey, Margaret, age 24

Joliffe, Mary, age 22

Kennedy, Will, age 22, tailor, servt. to Jo. Cuthbert of Draikes

" , Elizabeth, wife, age 24, servt. to Jo. Cuthbert of Draikes

Lossley, Christian, age 30, widow, Highlander

Macbean, Archibald, age 26, of Aberlaur

" , Catherine, wife, age 21

" , Alexander, son

Macbean, Duncan, age 21, servt. to John Mackintosh, Holmes' son

Macbean, McWillie, Jo, age 27, servt to Jo. Spence

Macbean, Will, age 17, tr. servt.

Macbean, Will, age 27, tr. servt.

Macdonald, Alex'r

Macdonald, Donald, age 22, servt.

" , Alvine Wood, wife, alias Winwood Macdonald

Macdonald, Elizabeth, age 19, servt. for 4 yrs., by 1741 was called Hellen

Macdonald, George, age 19, of Tar., tr. servt.

Macdonald, George, age 22, laborer

Macdonald, Georgia, born in Ga., age about 6 yrs., 1741

Macdonald, Hugh, age 37 of Tar., laborer

Macdonald, Janet, born in Ga. (Darien), 4 yrs. old in 1741

Macdonald, Jo, age 32, Hunter

" , Marian Cadach, wife, age 29, died Aug. 1742

" , Donald, son, age 2

" , Elizabeth, dau., age 6

" , William, son, age 4

Macdonald, Norman, age 32, laborer

" , Elizabeth Mackay, wife, age 29

" , Catherine, d. age 9

" , John, son, age 6

Macdonald, Ranald, died in S.C. after 1741

Macgilivray, Farquar, age 30, servt. to J. Cuthbert of Draikes

MacInver, Murdow (Murdoch?), servt. to J. Cuthbert of Draikes

Mackay, _____, of Strothie, Gent.

Mackay, _____, of Scourie, Gent.

Mackay, Alex'r, age 28, of Lange, laborer, tr. servt.

Mackay, Angus, age 19, of Tonge, laborer, tr. servt.

Mackay, Angus, age 21, tailor

Mackay, Angus, age 28, of Andralichlis, tr. servt.

Mackay, Bain Donald, age 39, of Tar, Laborer, tr. servt.

Mackay, Barbara McLeod, wife of James, age 36

" , Barbara, dau., age 17 or 11

" , Donald, son, age 9

" , Jeanne, dau., age 6

Mackay, Catherine, dau. to widow Christian Lossley

Mackay, Cha., age 17 of Tar, ensign to the Highland Co.

Mackay, Donald, age 21, laborer

Mackay, Donald, 32, laborer

" , James, son, age 8

" , Margaret, dau., age 12

Mackay, Donald, age 39, of Tar, tr. servt.

Mackay, Elizabeth, age 20

Mackay, George, age 20, cowherd

Mackay, George, age 20, of Tar, trustee's servt.

Mackay, Lt. Hugh, made capt. in Oglethorpe's regiment

Mackay, Isabel, age 18

Mackay, James, age 17, of Tar, slain at St. Augustine

Mackay, Jo., age 50, of Lairg.

" , Jannet Mackintosh, wife, age 40

" , Donald, son, age 6

" , Jeanne, dau., age 2

" , Patrick, son, age 7

Mackay, John, age 22, of Tonge, laborer

Mackay, John, age 56, of Durnes, farmer

" , Jannet, wife, age 32

" , Elizabeth, dau.

" , Hugh, son, age 18

" , John, son, age 3

" , Mary, dau.

" , Will, son

Mackay, Marian, age 16

Mackay, Neil, age 40, of Tar, tr. servt. (age may have been 22)

Mackay, Will, age 21, of Lavig, servt. to Mackay of Scourie, soldier in the Independent Co. of Highlanders

Mackay, Will, age 24, tr. servt.

Mackay, William, age 18, servt. to Mackay of Strothie

Mackay, William, age 21, cowherd

Mackennie, Alex'r, age 50, laborer

Mackenzie, Tho., age 23, trustee's servt.

Mackenzie, Will, age 17, trustee's servt.

Mackintosh, Adam, age 22, of Lange, laborer, tr. servt.

" , Catherine Monro, wife, age 25

Mackintosh, Benj., age 50, of Dorris, farmer

" , Catherine, w, age 45

" , Eliz., d. age 20

" , Jannet, d. age 18

" , Lachlan, son, age 12

Mackintosh, Donald, age 17, servt. to John Mackintosh of Inverness

Mackintosh, Donald, age 20, of Inverness, servt. to Alex'r Mackintosh

Mackintosh, Geo., age 21, of Durnes, tailor

Mackintosh, Hugh, born in Darien 1739

Mackintosh, Jo. Holmes

Mackintosh, Jo., age 15, farmer, of the Highland Rangers

Mackintosh, Jo., age 21 of Dorris, farmer

Mackintosh, Jo., age 21 of Inverness, laborer, tr. servt.

Mackintosh, Jo., age 50, senr. of Dornes

" , Cath., wife, age 47

" , Alex'r, son, age 8

" , Will, son, of the Highland Co. of Rangers

Mackintosh, John, age 24, of Inverness, farmer, son of Holmes

Mackintosh, John Mor, age 36, gent.

" , Margaret* (*Marjorie Fraser), wife, age 30

" , John, son, age 8

" , William, son, age 10

" , Lachlan, son, age 9

" , Phineas, son, age 3

" , Lewis, son, age 14 mos.

" , Janet, dau., age 14 mos.

" , Ann, dau., born in Darien, in 1737

" , George, son, born in Darien, 1739

Mackintosh, John, age 50, of Dornach

Mackintosh, Robert, of Moy, age 20, servt. to Jas. McQueen

Mackintosh, Roderick, age 19, farmer, of the Highland Rangers

Maclean, Alex'r, age 32, of Inverness, farmer

Macleod, Angus, age 17, of Apint, tr. servt. of the Highland Independent Co.

Macleod, Angus, age 17, of Hawnick, Weaver, servt. to Mackay of Strothie

Macleod, Donald, of Tar, laborer, servt. to Mackay of Strothie

Macleod, George, age 17, laborer, servt. to Mackay of Strothie

Maclean, George, age 30, of Ardelack, farmer

Macleod, Hugh, age 21, laborer, servt. to Mackay of Strothie, of the Highland Co.

Macleod, John, of the Isle of Skye, Scots minister at Darien

Maclean, John, age 19, of Inverness, servt. to Allen Maclean of the Highland Independent Co.

Maclean, John, age 29, servt. to Robt. Macpherson of Alvie

Macleod, John, age 35, fisherman

Maclean, Simon, of Inverness, servt. to Alan Maclean

Macmurrwick, Alex'r, age 20, servt. to Colin Campbell

Macoul, Alex'r, age 30, servt. to Mr. Mackay of Scourie

Macpherson, Norman, age 24, laborer

Macpherson, Robt., age 24, of Alvie, farmer

Macqueen, Ja., age 19, of Inverness

Macqueen, James, age 19, his servt.

Main, Geo., age 23, servt. to Donald Steward

Miller, David, age 26, servt. to Mackay of Strothie, of the Highland Independent Co.

Miller, James, age 18, servt. to James Anderson

Monro, Alex'r, age 24, of Dornach

Monro, Donald, age 45, of Alnit, Rossit, laborer

Monro, John, age 16, of Alnit, Rossit, laborer

Monro, Robt., age 17, of Dornach, laborer

Monro, Will, age 12, of Dornach, laborer

Monro, Will, age 40, of Durnes, laborer, of the Highland Co. of Rangers

" , Eliz., dau., age 17

" , Margaret, dau., age 14

Morchison, Jo., age 30, of Kildruth, laborer, tr. servt.

Morrison, Cath. of Durnes, age 22, servt. to Will Munro

Morrison, Hugh, age 22, of Tonge, laborer, tr. servt. of the Highland Independent Co.

Morrison, Hugh, age 23, farmer, a Highland Ranger

Munro, James, age 33, cowherd

" , Janet Macleod, wife, 26

Murray, Alex'r, age 17, laborer

Murray, Alex'r, age 28, of Rogart, laborer, tr. servt.

Murray, Jo., age 25, servt. to Mackay of Scourie

Robertson, William, age 21, cowherd

Ross, Hugh, age 36, of Drenach, servt. to Mr. Mackay of Scourie

Ross, James, miller of Waffin

Shearer, Donald, age 16, of Tonge, laborer, tr. servt.

Sinclair, John, servt. to John Mackintosh of Dorres

Spence, John, age 36, servt. to Jo. Cuthbert of Draikes

Stewart, Anne
Stewart, Anne, age 8
Stewart, David, age 23, of Cromdale,
    surgeon

Sutherland, Alex'r, age 30, servt. to
    Mr. Mackay of Scourie
Sutherland, Robert, age 35, of Leath,
    tr. servt.

Tolmie, Alex'r, age 36
Watson, Hugh, age 18, servt. to Tho.
    Baillie, murdered at sea, June 1730

TABLE 5. EARLY WRIGHTSBORO TOWNSHIP LANDHOLDERS, RESIDENTS AND ASSOCIATED FAMILIES, 1768–1810

Hinshaw's *Encyclopedia of American Quaker Genealogy*, Vol. 5; and
"The Story of Wrightsboro, 1768–1964." Transcribed by Sarah Shaw Tatoun.

SOURCE: http://www.geocities.com/heartland/plains/2064/wrightlist.htm

Name Date Born — Spouse/Parents

Angley ("English"), Alexander — Mary Dunn
Anglin ("English"), James
Anglin, John
Anglin, _____ — Mary Jones
Ansley, Abel 1761 — Lydia Morris/Thomas & Rebecca
Ansley, Benjamin 1738 — Amy/William & Rebecca
Ansley, James 1770 — Elizabeth Jones/Thomas & Rebecca
Ansley, Joseph 1775 — Mary Simpson, Mary Adkins
Ansley, Mary 1745 — Job Morris/William & Rebecca
Ansley, Nancy — Joseph Duckworth/Thomas & Rebecca
Ansley, Rebecca 1775 — William Duckworth
Ansley, Samuel 1765 — Mary Tillman/Thomas & Rebecca
Ansley, Thomas 1737 — Rebecca Cox/William & Rebecca
Ansley, Thomas 1767 — Henrietta Ragland/Thomas &
    Rebecca
Ansley, William 1770 — Thomas & Rebecca
Ashfield (Ash=Assur, Assyrian), Henry
Ashmore, Frederick
Atkinson (Atkin, "from Aachen"), David 1797 — Thomas
    & Ruth
Atkinson, Edith 1793 — Thomas & Ruth
Atkinson, Elizabeth 1784 — Thomas & Ruth
Atkinson, Martha 1787 — Thomas & Ruth
Atkinson, Rachel 1788 — Thomas & Ruth
Atkinson, Ruth 1791 — Thomas & Ruth
Atkinson, Thomas — Ruth Crew
Atkinson, William 1782 — Thomas & Ruth
Attery, Alexander
Auglin, John
Austin, Richard
Baldwin, David
Barfield, Solomon
Barnard (Ashk. Bernhard), Edward
Barnes, Jacob
Baskin, Hannah — Isaac Pugh
Battin, Richard — Catherine
Beck, George — Phebe Vernon/(Phillips)
Beck, John 1766 — Rachel Lundy/George & Phebe
Beck, Sarah 1745 — Charles Hobson/(Phillips)
Beddell, Absolom — Ruth Jackson
Bedell, Richard
Beggot, Elisha
Benson, Alice 1754 — Marmaduke Mendenhall
Benson, Robert
Benson, William
Bird (Hebrew Zipporah), Richard
Bishop, James
Bishop, Stephen
Boggs, Joseph
Bowd, Thomas — Esther Stubbs

Bowie, James
Brown, James 1742
Brown, John 1794 — Richard & Mary (Norton)
Brown, Jonathan 1799 — Richard & Mary
Brown, Joseph 1740 — Ann Jones
Brown, Lydia 1790 — Richard & Mary
Brown, Margaret 1776 — Mercer & Sarah (Piggott)
Brown, Martha — Nathan Maddock
Brown, Mary 1765 — Mercer & Sarah
Brown, Mercer 1740 — Sarah/Richard & Mary
Brown, Mercer 1781 — Mercer & Sarah
Brown, Mercer 1792 — Mary Smith/Richard & Mary
Brown, Phebe (Jewish first name) 1778 — Peter Dill/
    Mercer & Sarah
Brown, Rachel — William Patten
Brown, Richard 1767 — Mary Embree/Mercer & Sarah
Brown, Richard 1798 — Martha Stubbs/Richard & Mary
Brown, Samuel 1797 — Margaret Stubbs
Brown, Sarah 1769 — Mercer & Sarah
Brown, Sarah 1789 — Richard & Mary
Brown, William
Brown, William 1796 — Arriah Stubbs/Richard & Mary
Bryan, John
Buffington (Cherokee name), Esther 1756 — Joseph Evans/
    Peter & Hannah (Waite)
Buffington, Peter 1723 — Hannah Waite/Phoebe (Grubb)
Buffington, Peter 1753 — Sarah Mooney/Peter & Hannah
    (Waite)
Buffington, Sarah 1772 — Isaac Hart/Peter & Hannah
    (Waite)
Bull, Jesse
Bullock, Phereby (Jewish first name: Phoebus) — John
    Day/Archibald & Mary (de Veux)
Burdge, Joseph — Sarah Morris
Burke, John
Burns, Andrew
Butler, Beale — Mary Stubbs
Butler, John
Butler, Mary — Jeremiah Mote (La Motte)
Butler, Mary — Beale & Mary
Butler, Samuel 1793 — Rebecca Davenport, Jane Osborne
Butler, Susanna 1795 — Joseph Manifold/Beale & Mary
Butler, William 1798 — Mary/Beale & Mary
Callingham, Morris
Candler, Henry
Candler, William — Elizabeth
Carson, Elizabeth 1753 — John Kelly/John & Esther
Carson, Esther 1765 — John Williams/John & Esther
Carson, John — Esther Stubbs
Carson, John 1759 — Rachel/John & Esther

Carson, Mary 1753 — Samuel Winslitt/John & Esther
Carson, Sarah 1763 — John & Esther
Carson, Thomas
Carter, Margaret 1766 — Isaac Stubbs/Samuel, Mary (Barnes)
Castle ("from Castile"), Jacob
Castle, John — Greathouse
Childrey, Agnes 1768 — William Hodgin
Childre, William
Cloud, Ann 1792 — John Perry/Joel & Hannah
Cloud, Esther 1784 — Joel & Hannah
Cloud, Hannah 1782 — William Pyle/Joel & Hannah
Cloud, Joel 1745 — Hannah Pyle/Joel & Esther (Stubbs)
Cloud, Joel 1793 — Nancy Wilder/Joel & Hannah
Cloud, Lydia 1786 — Samuel Dodson/Joel & Hannah
Cloud, Mary 1779 — Phillip Brantley, Nathan Jefferies
Cloud, Rebecca 1789 — Byrd Perry, Pascall/Joel & Hannah
Cloud, Sarah 1780 — John Perry/Joel & Hannah
Clower, John
Clowers, _____ — Jenny Perkins
Coats, James
Cobbs, James
Cobbs, Mary — Robert Flournoy (French Huguenot)
Cochrane, Cornelius
Collins, Jacob
Conner, Catherine 1798 — John & Rachel
Conner, Jesse 1800 — John & Rachel
Conner, John — Rachel
Conner, John 1801 — John & Rachel
Conner, Mary 1805 — John & Rachel
Conner, Thomas 1803 — John & Rachel
Conner, William 1795 — John & Rachel
Cooper, Absolom 1791 — Sarah/Benjamin & Ferribee
Cooper, Benjamin 1760s — Ferribee Sanders/Isaac & Prudence
Cooper, Benjamin 1787 — Susanna/Benjamin & Ferribee
Cooper, Charity — Benjamin & Ferribee
Cooper, Ferribee 1789 — Merida (place in Spain) Wade
Cooper, Isaac — Prudence
Cooper, Isaac 1774 — Elizabeth/Isaac & Prudence
Cooper, Isaac 1784 — Abigail Thornbrough
Cooper, Joel 1788 — Benjamin & Ferribee
Cooper, John 1793 — Mary Ann Morris/Benjamin & Ferribee
Cooper, Joseph 1796 — Nancy Raney/Benjamin & Ferribee
Cooper, Mordecai — Benjamin & Ferribee
Cooper, Sarah 1799 — W. Harryman, Reb. Blevins (fr. Levin)
Coppock, John 1766 — Anne Jay
Cowin (Cohen), Robert
Cox, Ann 1796 — Asa Hicks/John & Rachel
Cox, John — Rachel Stubbs
Cox, Levi 1790 — John & Rachel
Cox, Mary 1777 — Evans/Richard & Ann
Cox, Peter 1745 — Deborah Maddock/Thomas & Mary
Cox, Peter 1772 — Margaret Marshal/Peter & Deborah
Cox, Rachel 1799 — Borden Hanson/John & Rachel
Cox, Rebecca 1732 — Harrison, Thomas Ansley/(Potts)
Cox, Richard 1750 — Ann Hodgin/Thomas & Mary (Cooke)
Cox, Stephen 1791 — Elizabeth Stubbs/John & Rachel
Cox, Thomas 1775 — Richard & Ann
Cox, Thomas 1786 — John & Rachel

Crew (Cruz?), Littleberry
Curle, Sarah
Curley, Sarah — Abraham Greathouse
Daniel, William
Davies, Abiather 1754 — Lydia Embree
Davies, Amos 1779 — Abiather & Lydia
Davies, Benjamin 1793 — Margaret Fettig/Abiather & Lydia
Davies, John 1787 — Lydia Coate/Abiather & Lydia
Davies, Lydia 1798 — Joseph Coate/Abiather & Lydia
Davies, Mary 1789 — Joseph Iddings/Abiather & Lydia
Davies, Rachel 1781 — Henry Carter/Abiather & Lydia
Davies, Rhoda 1781 — Nathan Calbuth/Abiather & Lydia
Davies, Samuel 1785 — Dorcas Jones/Abiather & Lydia
Davies, Sarah 1796 — Abiather & Lydia
Davies, Sibilla 1791 — Abiather & Lydia
Davis, Abraham — John & Sarah
Davis, Benjamin — John & Sarah
Davis, Elizabeth — John & Sarah
Davis, Gabriel
Davis, Hezekiah — John & Sarah
Davis, Isaac
Davis, Jacob
Davis, John — Sarah Greathouse
Davis, John — Peter & Sarah (Moore) Perkins
Davis, John — John & Sarah
Davis, Joseph — John & Sarah
Davis, Keziah — John & Sarah
Davis, Reuben — John & Sarah
Davis, Sarah — John Jones/John & Sarah
Davis, _____ — Jane Moore
Davis, _____ — Abigail Perkins
Day (Diaz?), Almon — Sarah Sykes/John & Phereby
Day, David 1808 — Amanda F. Daniel/Nathaniel & Hannah
Day, John 1768 — Phereby Bullock/Stephen & Margaret
Day, Jonathan 1776 — Stephen & Margaret
Day, Joseph 1782 — Nancy Ponder/Stephen & Margaret
Day, Joseph 1789 — Mary Hampton, Lincey Dunn
Day, Mary 1810 — John Miller/Nathaniel & Hannah
Day, Mary Ann — Chapman (Jacob) Maddox
Day, Nathaniel 1775 — Hannah Mendenhall
Day, Nathan 1785 — Stephen & Margaret
Day, Nathan — Martha Cole/John & Phereby
Day, Rebecca 1774 — John Kendrick/Stephen & Margaret
Day, Rebecca — Edward Wooding/John & Phereby
Day, Richard — John & Phereby
Day, Robert
Day, Samuel 1788
Day, Stephen 1742 — Margaret Jones/John Day, Ann Hussey
Day, Stephen 1772 — Priscilla Jones/Stephen & Margaret
Day, Stephen 1791 — Mary Hobbs/John & Phereby
Day, Sylvanus 1778 — Stephen & Margaret
Day, Theodate 1769 — Thomas Kendrick/Stephen & Margaret
Day, William
Day, William — Nancy McDonald/John & Phereby
Denison, Patrick
Dennis, Abraham — Elizabeth/Samuel & Ruth (Tindall)
Dennis, Isaac — Sarah (Moore?)/Samuel, Ruth (Tindall)
Dennis, Jacob — Sarah/Samuel & Ruth (Tindall)
Dennis, John — Mary Slater/Samuel & Ruth (Tindall)

Dennis, Rachel — Joseph Maddock/Samuel, Ruth (Tindall)
Dill, Daniel — Peter & Phebe
Dill, Peter — Phebe Brown
Dixon, Eli
Dixon, John
Dixon, Solomon
Dover, John
Drummond, Walter
Duncan, John
Dunn, Benjamin — Sarah
Dunn, Charles
Dunn, John
Dunn, Josiah — Benjamin & Sarah
Dunn, Lincey Jane 1787 — Joseph Day/Nehemiah & Ann
Dunn, Nehemiah — Ann/Benjamin & Sarah
Dunn, Thomas 1776 — Josiah
Durkee, Nathaniel
Echols (Eccles), Edward
Edwards, James — Jane Evans
Edwards, Phebe — Alexander Moore/James & Jane
Elam, William
Embree, Amos 1766 — Sarah
Embree, Anne
Embree, John 1721 — Mary/Moses & Mary
Embree, John 1791 — Amos & Sarah
Embree, Joseph 1796 — Amos & Sarah
Embree, Lydia 1759 — Abiather Davies/John & Mary
Embree, Mary 1769 — Richard Brown/John & Sarah
Embree, Mary 1788 — Amos & Sarah
Embree, Mercer 1801 — Amos & Sarah
Embree, Rebekah 1789 — Amos & Sarah
Embree, Sarah 1794 — Amos & Sarah
Emmett, James
Evans, Aaron 1794
Evans, Adam 1784 — Joseph & Esther
Evans, Hannah 1776 — William Johnson/Joseph & Esther
Evans, Isaac 1778 — Joseph & Esther
Evans, Jane — James Edwards
Evans, John
Evans, John, Jr.
Evans, John 1787 — Joseph & Esther
Evans, Joseph 1749 — Esther Buffington
Evans, Margaret 1782 — Joseph & Esther
Evans, Mary — Thomas Phelan
Evans, Mary 1792 — Levi Hawkins (Hauquin "physician")
Evans, Moses 1780 — Joseph & Esther
Evans, Phebe 1790
Evans, Robert 1789 — Esther, Mary Jenkins/Joseph & Esther
Evans, Samuel 1775 — Joseph & Esther
Evans, Sarah 1797 — John Furnas/Joseph & Esther
Evans, _____ — Mary Cox
Fairchild, John
Farmer, Benjamin
Farmer, Jesse 1783 — William & Rebecca
Farmer, John — Mary
Farmer, John 1776 — William & Rebecca
Farmer, Susannah 1804 — Uriah Bailey/? & Ann
Farmer, William — Catherine
Farmer, William 1751 — Rebecca Hurst
Farmer, William A. 1779 — William & Rebecca
Farmer, William — Ruth Williams
Farmer, William — William & Catherine

Farmer, William 1800 — John & Mary
Few, Benjamin
Few, William
Fleming, David
Flournoy, Robert — Mary Cobbs
Foster, William
Galbreath, Elizabeth — Henry Jones
Galbreath, John — Sarah Sanders
Gardner, Rachel 1772 — Joseph Mendenhall
Gardner, Susanna 1771 — Caleb Mendenhall/William & Susanna
Gilbert, Joel — Elizabeth
Gilbert, Thomas 1800 — Joel & Elizabeth
Gilburger, _____ — Ann Pugh
Gilliland, Thomas
Graham, John
Granade (Granada, place in Spain), Stephen — Charity Sanders
Granade, Timothy — Sarah Sanders
Gray, Isaac
Greason, John
Greathouse (Greditz?), Abraham — Sarah Curley/Jacob & Nancy
Greathouse, Abraham 1790 — Nancy/Abraham & Sarah
Greathouse, Allison 1801 — Mary/Abraham & Sarah
Greathouse, Anna 1766 — William Holden/Jacob & ?
Greathouse, Archelaus — Abraham & Sarah
Greathouse, Catherine — Jacob & ?
Greathouse, Deanna 1760 — Abraham Perkins/Jacob & ?
Greathouse, Hannah 1789 — Benjamin Smithson/Jacob & Nancy
Greathouse, Isaac 1768 — Jacob & ?
Greathouse, Jacob
Greathouse, Jacob — Nancy Perkins/Jacob & ?
Greathouse, John 1790 — Rebecca Williams/Abraham & Sarah?
Greathouse, Sarah — John Davis/Jacob & ?
Greathouse, Sarah 1786 — Jacob & Nancy
Greathouse, _____ — John Castle/Jacob & ?
Green, Amos — Esther Lowe (i.e., Levi)
Green, Amos 1794 — Amos & Esther
Green, Hannah 1792 — Amos & Esther
Green, Jesse 1790 — Amos & Esther
Greene, Edward
Greene, Isaac
Gregg ("Greek"), Silas 1759 — Rhoda
Gregg, William 1797
Grey, Hillery
Guest (Gist, Costa), Baker 1796 — James & Hannah
Guest, James 1755 — Hannah Jones
Guest, James 1793 — James & Hannah
Guest, John 1797 — James & Hannah
Guest, Mary 1790 — James & Hannah
Guest, Sarah 1789 — James & Hannah
Haines, Ellis
Haines, Mary
Haines, Nathan
Hagen, Edward
Haley, Lucy — Benjamin Moorman
Harper, Robert
Harris, Ellis
Harris (Hirsch), Nathan
Harrison, Benjamin — Rebecca (Cox)

Hart (symbol of Napthali), Isaac 1773 — Sarah Buffington/ Samuel & ?

Hart, James

Hart, Peter

Hart, Phineas

Hart, Samuel 1746 — Esther Lowe/Esther (Myles: Fr. Jewish)

Hart, Samuel G. 1799 — Mary Johnson/Isaac & Sarah

Hart, Thomas

Hartshorn, John

Hathborn, _____ — Hannah Sidwell

Hayes, Bailey 1777 — Mary Stubbs

Hayes, Mary

Hayes, Zilpha 1765 — Joseph Stubbs

Hickson, Ann — Jonathan Mote

Hickson, John 1740 — Mary Mooney/William, Sarah Elizabeth

Hickson, John 1800 — Phebe Randall/William & Rachel

Hickson, Kezia 1738 — Henry Jones/William, Sarah Elizabeth

Hickson, Kezia 1774 — Joseph Stubbs/John & Mary

Hickson, Mary 1802 — Joseph Goodwin/William & Rachel

Hickson, William 1715 — Sarah Elizabeth/Timothy or John

Hickson, William 1776 — Rachel Stubbs/John & Mary

Hickson, William 1804 — Sarah Pearson/William & Rachel

Hill, Edward

Hill, James

Hill, John

Hill, Joshua

Hilton, Abram

Hinshaw, Rebecca — Joseph Maddock, Jr.

Hobbs, John

Hobbs, Mary — Stephen Day/John & ?

Hobbs, Matthew

Hobson, Charles 1744 — Sarah Beck/George, Hannah (Kinnison)

Hobson, Lydia 1768 — George Jones/Charles & Sarah

Hobson, Mary 1777 — Thomas Stubbs/Charles & Sarah

Hobson, Sarah 1790 — William Stubbs/Charles & Sarah

Hodgin, Agnes

Hodgin, Amy 1800 — Benjamin Clendenon/Stephen & Elizabeth

Hodgin, Ann 1756 — Richard Cox

Hodgin, Asenath 1796 — Samuel Starbuck/Stephen & Elizabeth

Hodgin, Eli 1798 — Mary Engle ("angle")

Hodgin, John 1735 — Mary Vernon/Robert (Hodgson)

Hodgin, John 1791 — Prudence/William & Agnes

Hodgin, John — John & Mary

Hodgin, Lydia — Dinkins Ivey/John & Mary

Hodgin, Martha 1798 — Elijah Steele/William & Agnes

Hodgin, Mary 1788 — Samuel Berry/William & Agnes

Hodgin, Robert — John & Mary

Hodgin, Sarah 1793 — Amos Davis/William & Agnes

Hodgin, Stephen 1772 — Elizabeth/Abby Williams

Hodgin, William 1766 — Agnes Childrey/John & Mary

Hodgin, William 1795 — Mary William/William & Agnes

Hodgin, William 1802 — Harriet Moore/Stephen & Elizabeth

Hoge ("from the Haag"), Jacob

Hoge, Phebe

Hoge, William

Hokitt, Richard

Holden, William — Anna Greathouse

Holliday (Yom Tov), Ambrose

Hollingsworth, Joseph

Hollingsworth, William

Hollowell, Charity 1722 — Joel Sanders/Thomas & Sarah

Houstown, Patrick

Howard, Benjamin

Howard, John

Howard, John

Howell (Joel), James

Hume, James

Humphrey, Mary 1747 — Daniel Williams/(Embree)

Hunter, John

Hussey, Content — James Vernon

Iddings, Joseph

Jackson, Absolom 1750 — Pharabea Webster

Jackson, Ann — James Morris

Jackson, Benjamin — Elizabeth Clark/(Starkey)

Jackson, Deborah — Robert McGinty/Thomas & Mary

Jackson, Elizabeth — Rezin (Yiddish) Pugh

Jackson, Enoch — Nancy Moore/Isaac & Mary

Jackson, Hugh — Rebecca Morris

Jackson, Isaac — Mary/ Benjamin & Elizabeth

Jackson, Isaac — Mary Miller/Thomas & Mary (Starkey)

Jackson, Isaac — Miriam Pugh

Jackson, Jane — James Moore/Isaac & Mary

Jackson, Joseph — Thomas & Mary

Jackson, Nathaniel 1743 — Isaac & Mary (Miller)

Jackson, Ruth 1748 — Absolom Bedell/Isaac & Mary (Miller)

Jackson, Thomas — Mary/Isaac & Mary (Miller)

Jackson, Walter — Mary Chancey/Benjamin & Elizabeth

James, Alicia — Thomas Jenkins

James, John

Jenkins, Averida — Thomas & Alicia

Jenkins, James — Thomas & Alicia

Jenkins, Robert

Jenkins, Sarah (?) 1797/8 — Richard Moore

Jenkins, Thomas — Alicia James

Johns, Robert

Johnson, Lewis

Johnson, Susannah in minutes, 1786

Johnson, William — Hannah Evans

Johnston, Abraham

Jones, Ann 1741 — Henry Morgan, Joseph Brown

Jones, Ann 1781 — Dilwin Bogue (Turkish)

Jones, Cassandra — Jesse Moore

Jones, David 1780 — Mary Mendenhall/Francis & Rachel

Jones, Deborah 1773 — Francis & Sarah

Jones, Dorcas 1789 — Samuel Davies/Samuel & Mary

Jones, Eleanor 1766 — Nathan Stubbs/Francis & Sarah

Jones, Elizabeth 1768 — Nathan Stubbs/Henry & Keziah

Jones, Francis 1725 — Sarah Jones/(Medcalf Wallis)

Jones, Francis 1753 — Rachel Mote/Francis & Sarah

Jones, Francis 1788 — Samuel & Mary

Jones, George 1770 — Lydia Hobson/Henry & Keziah

Jones, Hannah 1760 — James Guest/Francis & Sarah

Jones, Henry 1742 — Keziah Hickson, Prudence Maddock

Jones, Henry 1756 — Elizabeth Galbreath/Francis & Sarah

Jones, James — John & Mary

Jones, Jane 1764 — John Stubbs/Francis & Sarah

Jones, Jesse 1794 — Samuel & Mary

Jones, John 1717 — Mary Phillips

Jones, John 1750 — Margaret/John & Mary
Jones, John 1758 — Phoebe McDonald/Francis & Sarah
Jones, John 1770 — Sarah Davis/Nathan & Catherine
Jones, John 1781 — Sarah McKee/Samuel & Mary
Jones, John 1798 — Henry & Prudence
Jones, Jonathan 1783 — Deborah Lindley/Samuel & Mary
Jones, Joseph 1769 — Mary Taylor/Francis & Sarah
Jones, Kezia — William Gifford/Henry & Keziah
Jones, Lucius Davis 1802 — Sarah Daniel/John & Sarah
    (Davis)
Jones, Margaret — Stephen Day/John & Mary
Jones, Mary — Anglin/John & Mary
Jones, Mary 1771 — Samuel Stubbs/Francis & Sarah
Jones, Nathan — Catherine Greathouse/(Phillips)
Jones, Newton 1778 — Ann Mote/Francis & Sarah
Jones, Phillipini — Stanfield/John & Mary
Jones, Rachel 1752 — Samuel Maddock/Francis & Sarah
Jones, Rachel 1793 — Joseph & Mary
Jones, Richard
Jones, Samuel 1755 — Mary Mote/Francis & Sarah
Jones, Samuel 1786 — Prudence Mooney/Samuel & Mary
Jones, Sarah 1767 — Francis & Sarah
Jones, Sarah 1775 — Samuel Culbertson/Henry & Keziah
Jones, Sarah 1776 — John Abbott/Francis & Rachel
Jones, Sarah 1792 — Samuel & Mary
Jones, Thomas 1790 — Samuel & Mary
Jones, William 1772 — Elizabeth Culbertson/Henry &
    Keziah
Jourdan, Timothy
Julian, Ruth — Elijah Pugh
Kallensworth, Joseph
Kellum, Anna 1801 — William Dill, Jacob Wolf (Ashk.)
Kellum, Elijah 1797 — Nathaniel & Elizabeth
Kellum, Elizabeth 1786 — Nathaniel & Elizabeth
Kellum, John 1784 — Nathaniel & Elizabeth
Kellum, Joseph 1794 — Nathaniel & Elizabeth
Kellum, Kezia 1805 — Perry Blossom/William & Deborah
Kellum, Nathaniel — Elizabeth
Kellum, Nathaniel 1791 — Nathaniel & Elizabeth
Kellum, Sarah 1788 — Nathaniel & Elizabeth
Kellum, Susanna 1799 — Nathaniel & Elizabeth
Kellum, William 1779 — Deborah Stubbs/Nathaniel &
    Elizabeth
Kendrick, John — Rebecca Day
Kendrick, Thomas — Theodate Day
Kirk, Tamar 1738 — Phineas Mendenhall/ (Buckingham)
Lackey, Mary — Mordecai Moore/(Maynard)
Lacey, Jane — Thomas Mills/(Moore)
Lang, John
Lay, William
Lee, John
LeMarr, William
Lindsay, John
Linn, Thomas
Lockridge, Robert
Louders, Abram
Lowe, Esther 1754 — Samuel Hart, Amos Green/Mooney
Lowe, Isaac — Ann Mooney
Lynn, Thomas
Lynn, William
McCarter, Aaron
McCarty, Daniel
McClen, Robert

McCowen, Bathsheba
McDonald, John 1755 — Affinity Phelan
McDonald, Phoebe — John Jones
McFarland, James
McFarland, William
McKay, James
McKee, John 1764 — Mary Mendenhall
McKee, Sarah 1785 — John Jones/John & Mary
McGinty, Joseph — Deborah Jackson
McGinty, Thomas — Joseph & Deborah
McLen, Robert
McMunn, John
McNeal, John — Mary
McNeal, _____ — Mary Vernon
Maddock, Anna — James Anderson/Nathan & Michelle
Maddock, Benjamin — Polly Franklin/Joseph & Rebecca
Maddock, Benjamin — Joseph & Rachel
Maddock, Chloe — Nathan & Michelle
Maddock, Deborah 1741 — Thomas Stubbs, Peter Cox
Maddock, Eleanor 1787 — James Cook/Samuel & Rachel
Maddock, Elizabeth — Nathan & Michelle
Maddock, Esther 1740 — John Stubbs/Joseph & Rachel
Maddock, Francis 1779 — Phebe Cook/Samuel & Rachel
Maddock, Hannah — Joseph & Rachel
Maddock, Henry — Latia Manru/Joseph & Rebecca
Maddock, Isaiah — Olivia Burnley/Joseph & Rebecca
Maddock, John — Dorcas Mote/Nathan & Michelle
Maddock, Joseph 1720 — Rachel Dennis/ (Nicholls)
Maddock, Joseph, Jr. — Rebecca Hinshaw/Joseph & Rachel
Maddock, Joseph — Mary Vaugn/Joseph & Rebecca
Maddock, Joseph 1775 — Samuel & Rachel
Maddock, Mary — Joseph & Rachel
Maddock, Mary — Nathan & Michelle
Maddock, Nathan — Mitchell, Michelle /Joseph & Rachel
Maddock, Nathan — Nathan
Maddock, Nathan 1778 — Martha Brown, Sarah Fouts
Maddock, Rebecca — Nathan & Michelle
Maddock, Samuel 1750 — Rachel Jones/Joseph & Rachel
Maddock, Sarah — Jonathan Randal/Nathan & Michelle
Maddock, Sarah 1774 — John Seybold/Samuel & Rachel
Maddock, William 1785 — Sarah Huffman, Hannah Stubbs
Matthews, Oliver 1729 — Walter & Mary (Mendenhall)
Mendenhall (fr. Menachem), Abigail 1786 — Phineas &
    Catherine
Mendenhall, Ann 1807 — Nathan Stubbs Jr./Elijah &
    Martha
Mendenhall, Caleb 1769 — Susanna Gardner/Phineas &
    Tamar
Mendenhall, Caleb 1797 — Anna Thomas/Caleb &
    Susanna
Mendenhall, Elijah 1782 — Martha Miller/Marmaduke &
    Alice
Mendenhall, Grace 1766 — Nathaniel Vernon/Phineas &
    Tamar
Mendenhall, Griffith 1793 — Elizabeth Airey/Caleb &
    Susanna
Mendenhall, Hannah 1788 — Nathaniel Day/Marmaduke
    & Alice
Mendenhall, James 1718 — Aaron, Rose (Pierson)
Mendenhall, James 1792 — Mary Brown/Marmaduke &
    Alice
Mendenhall, John 1790 — Margaret Brown/Marmaduke
    & Alice

Mendenhall, Jonathan 1782 — Joseph & Elizabeth

Mendenhall, Joseph — Elizabeth Sell/Robert & Phebe (Taylor)

Mendenhall, Joseph 1772 — Rachel Gardner/Phineas & Tamar

Mendenhall, Joseph 1782 — Joseph & Elizabeth

Mendenhall, Marmaduke 1755 — Alice Benson/(Thomas)

Mendenhall, Marmaduke 1797 — Nancy Griffin/Marmaduke & Alice

Mendenhhall, Mary 1764 — John McKee, John Mooney

Mendenhall, Mary 1785 — David Jones/Marmaduke & Alice

Mendenhall, Mary 1795 — Isaac Brown/Joseph & Rachel

Mendenhall, Miriam 1792 — David Mote/Caleb & Susanna

Mendenhall, Naomi 1784 — Phineas & Catherine

Mendenhall, Phebe 1777 — William Williams/Joseph & Elizabeth

Mendenhall, Phineas 1742 — Tamar Kirk, Catherine Vernon

Mendenhall, Robert 1779 — Joseph & Elizabeth

Mendenhall, Tamar 1774 — John North, Jr./Phineas & Tamar

Mendenhall, William 1795 — Elizabeth Warner/Caleb & Susanna

Middleton, Hannah — Joseph & Phebe

Middleton, Holland, Jr. 1739 — Holland & Sarah

Middleton, Holland, Sr. 1715 — Middleton, Parks/(Tears)

Middleton, Hannah 1778 — Joseph & Phebe

Middleton, Jehu 1776 — Mary Mills/Joseph & Phebe

Middleton, Joseph 1755 — Phebe Vernon

Middleton, Martha 1787 — Joseph & Phebe

Middleton, Mary 1784 — Joseph & Phebe

Middleton, Zachariah 1774 — Mary Wright Livingston/Holland, Mary

Miles, Daniel

Miles, William

Milhouse, Daniel 1800 — Esther Clendenon/Robert & Sarah

Milhouse, Robert — Sarah Williams/Henry, Rebekah (Cook)

Millen, Joseph

Miller, Ezekiel

Miller, Martha — Nathan Maddock

Miller, William — Anne Mooney

Mitchell, William

Mitchell, _____ — Nathan Maddock

Mooney (Muniz, Money), Ann — Isaac Hart

Mooney, Anne 1747/8 — Joseph Stubbs, William Miller

Mooney, Deborah 1762 — Joseph & Mary

Mooney, Grace 1790 — Adam Scott/John & Mary

Mooney, John 1749 — Mary Mendenhall/Joseph & Mary

Mooney, Joseph 1722 — Mary Moore

Mooney, Joseph 1759 — Caroline Mote/Joseph & Mary

Mooney, Mary 1757 — John Hixson/Joseph & Mary

Mooney, Prudence 1752 — Samuel Jones/Joseph & Mary

Mooney, Sarah 1754 — Peter Buffington/Joseph & Mary

Moore, Abigail — Thomas/Richard & Sarah

Moore, Alexander 1760 — Phebe Edwards/Mordecai & Mary

Moore, Amy — John Perryman/John & (Clark?)

Moore, Avarilla 1803 — Joseph & Jane

Moore, Axia — Mordecai & Mary

Moore, Benejah 1802 — Alexander & Phebe

Moore, Dempsey

Moore, Elizabeth — Mordecai & Mary

Moore, Elizabeth 1788 — Jesse Clark/Alexander & Phebe

Moore, Hannah 1807 — Pleasant/Alexander & Phebe

Moore, James 1740 — Alice (Iddings?)/Richard & Sarah

Moore, James 1752 — Jane Jackson/John & Clark?

Moore, James — James & Alice

Moore, James — Hannah Thomas

Moore, James 1798 — Alexander & Phebe

Moore, Jane

Moore, Jane 1783 — Davis/Alexander & Phebe

Moore, Jesse 1786 — Cassandra Jones/Alexander & Phebe

Moore, John — Clark?, Sarah /Richard & Sarah

Moore, John — Margaret Ross/John & Clark?

Moore, Jonas — Richard & Sarah

Moore, Joseph — Jane/James & Alice

Moore, Lydia 1806 — Joseph & Jane

Moore, Mary — Joseph Mooney/Richard & Sarah

Moore, Mary — Mordecai & Mary

Moore, Mordecai 1727 — Mary Lackey/Richard & Sarah

Moore, Mordecai 1791 — Rachel Stubbs/Alexander & Phebe

Moore, Nancy — Enoch Jackson/John & Clark?

Moore, Naomi — Mordecai & Mary

Moore, Phoebe — Mordecai & Mary

Moore, Prudence — James Ryan/Richard & Sarah

Moore, Rachel — Mordecai & Mary

Moore, Richard 1797 — Sarah Jenkins (?)/(Cuerton)

Moore, Richard — Richard & Sarah

Moore, Sarah — Peter Perkins/Richard & Sarah

Moore, Sarah — Mordecai & Mary

Moore, Seaborn 1794 — Rachel Stubbs/Alexander & Phebe

Moore, Thomas — Richard & Sarah (?)

Moorman, Benjamin — Lucy Haley/Andrew & ?

Moorman, Charles — Benjamin & Lucy

Moorman, Elizabeth — Benjamin & Lucy

Moorman, Lishy — Benjamin & Lucy

Moorman, Milly — Benjamin & Lucy

Morgan, Deborah

Morgan, Jesse

Morgan, Sarah — Joel Sanders, Jr.

Morris, Jacob — Elizabeth Ansley/(Porter)

Morris, James 1761 — Ann Jackson/Job & Mary

Morris, Job 1735 — Mary Ansley/Richard & Mary (Porter)

Morris, Lydia 1770 — Abel Ansley/Job & Mary

Morris, Mary 1770 — Abraham Sanders/Job & Mary

Morris, Rebecca 1763 — Hugh Jackson/Job & Mary

Morris, Sarah — Joseph Burdge

Morris, Zilpha 1766 — Henry Williams/Job & Mary

Morrow, George

Morrow, James

Mote, Ann 1785 — Newton Jones/Jonathan & Ann

Mote, Caroline 1795 — Joseph Mooney

Mote, David 1733 — Dorcas Nichols/Jonathan & Sarah

Mote, David 1754 — David & Dorcas

Mote, David 1787 — Jonathan & Ann

Mote, David 1792 — Miriam Mendenhall

Mote, Dorcas 1798 — Jonathan & Ann

Mote, Dorcas — John Maddock

Mote, Elizabeth 1795

Mote, Jeremiah 1769 — Mary Butler/David & Dorcas

Mote, Jeremiah 1803 — Jonathan & Ann

Mote, Jesse 1775 — David & Dorcas

Mote, John 1767 — David & Dorcas

Mote, Jonathan 1758 — Ann Hickson/David & Dorcas
Mote, Jonathan 1791— Susannah Kessler/Jonathan & Ann
Mote, Margaret 1753 — David & Dorcas
Mote, Mary 1760 — Samuel Jones/David & Dorcas
Mote, Mary 1800 — Jonathan & Ann
Mote, Rachel 1756 — Francis Jones/David & Dorcas
Mote, Sarah 1789
Mote, Timothy 1784 — Jonathan & Ann
Mote, William 1763 — David & Dorcas
Mote, William 1793 — Jonathan & Ann
Murphey, Edward
Murray, John
Neal, _____ — Elizabeth Perkins
Nelson, Robert
Nichols, Dorcas — Mote, David
Nipper, Ann
North, Delaney 1801— Welcom Metcalf Capron/John & Tamar
North, John, Jr. 1776 — Tamar Mendenhall
North, Mary (Martha) 1799 — George Walker/John & Tamar
North, Singleton 1804 — Sarah Penny/John & Tamar
Northdike, Abraham 1736 — Mary Rogers/Henry & Rebecca Perkins
Northdike, Aden 1762 — Martha Johnson/Abraham & Mary
Northdike, Benajah 1766 — Abraham & Mary
Northdike, Beulah 1769 — Abraham & Mary
Northdike, Daniel 1775 — Abraham & Mary
Northdike, Hiram 1782 — Abraham & Mary
Northdike, Israel 1764 — Mary ?/Abraham & Mary
Northdike, Micajah 1771— Charity Ellis/Abraham & Mary
Northdike, Phebe 1779 — Jehu Ellis/Abraham & Mary
Odom, Uriah
Oliver, Alexander
Oliver, James
Oliver, John
Oliver, Samuel
O'Maley, Thomas
Owen, Benjamin 1792 — Ephraim & Sarah
Owen, Elizabeth 1799 — Ephraim & Sarah
Owen, Ephraim — Sarah
Owen, Ephraim 1797 — Ephraim & Sarah
Owen, Ephraim 1797 — Samuel & Margery
Owen, John 1790 — Ephraim & Sarah
Owen, John 1800 — Samuel & Margery
Owen, Mary 1795 — Ephraim & Sarah
Owen, Mary 1802 — Samuel & Margery
Owen, Ruth 1803 — Ephraim & Sarah
Owen, Samuel — Margery
Owen, Sarah 1796 — Samuel & Margery
Owen, Sarah 1801— Ephraim & Sarah
Pace, Silas
Pace, Thomas
Parker, Abraham
Parks, Mary 1747 — Holland Middleton, Sr./Benjamin
Parvey, Dial
Patten (Patton), Ann 1782 — Robert Vernon/William & Rachel
Patten, Grace 1784 — William & Rachel
Patten, Isaac 1778 — William & Rachel
Patten, John 1796 — Rebecca Stubbs/William & Rachel
Patten, Mahlon 1787 — William & Rachel

Patten (Patton), Mary 1780 — Amos Vernon/William & Rachel
Patten, Rachel 1793 — William & Rachel
Patten, Sarah 1799 — William & Rachel
Patten, William 1754 — Rachel Brown
Patten, William 1790 — Phebe Embree/William & Rachel
Perkins, Abigail — Davis/Peter & Sarah
Perkins, Abraham — Peter & Sarah
Perkins, Eleanor — Jethro Darden/Peter & Sarah
Perkins, Elizabeth — Neal/Peter & Sarah
Perkins, Jemima — White/Peter & Sarah
Perkins, Jenny — Clowers/Peter & Sarah
Perkins, John
Perkins, John 1770 — Peter & Sarah
Perkins, Nancy — Jacob Greathouse/Peter & Sarah
Perkins, Peter — Sarah Moore
Perkins, Peter — grandson of Peter & Sarah
Perkins, Sarah — William Wilkins/Peter & Sarah
Perrit, John
Perry, John
Perryman, John — Amy Moore
Pewgate, Jasias
Phelan, Affinity — John McDonald/Thomas & Mary
Phelan, Elizabeth — Thomas & Mary
Phelan, Evans 1775 — Thomas & Mary
Phelan, Jeremiah 1777 — Margaret/Thomas & Mary
Phelan, Mary 1787 — Thomas & Mary
Phelan, Thomas 1759 — Mary Evans
Phelan, Thomas 1795 — Jemimah Fowler/Thomas & Mary
Philips (f. Phoebus), Peter
Phillips, Joel
Phillips, Zachariah
Pirks, John
Ponder, Ephraim
Ponder, Nancy — Joseph Day/Ephraim & ?
Powell, Lewis
Pugh (Puah), Achsah 1797 — Amos Robinson, Giles Chapman
Pugh, Alexander 1764 — Jesse, Elizabeth (Stewart)
Pugh, Alviah 1801— Joseph Hall/Elijah & Ruth
Pugh, Ann — Gilburger/Jesse & Elizabeth
Pugh, Deborah 1799 — Alexander & Hannah
Pugh, Elijah, 1760 — Ruth Julian/Jesse & Elizabeth
Pugh, Elijah 1800 — Robert & Alcy
Pugh, Elizabeth 1793 — Alexander & Hannah
Pugh, Elizabeth — David Smith/Robert & Alcy
Pugh, Esther 1791— John Eslinger/Alexander & Hannah
Pugh, Isaac 1785 — Hannah Baskin/Elijah & Ruth
Pugh, Isaac 1801— Margaret Swisher ("from Switz.")
Pugh, James 1695 — Jemima/James M. & Joan (Price)
Pugh, James Kinman — Robert & Alcy
Pugh, Jehu — Jesse & Elizabeth
Pugh, Jesse 1737 — Elizabeth Stewart/(Pugh)
Pugh, Jesse 1795 — Elizabeth Robinson/Elijah & Ruth
Pugh, Jesse 1801— Rachel Conarroe/Alexander & Hannah
Pugh, John — Jesse & Elizabeth
Pugh, John 1797 — Kezia Jones/Alexander & Hannah
Pugh, Kezia 1795 — Peter Moyer/Alexander & Hannah
Pugh, Martha 1800 — David Parham Jones/Robert & Alcy
Pugh, Meredith — Robert & Alcy
Pugh, Miriam 1790 — Isaac Jackson/Elijah & Ruth
Pugh, Nancy — Gideon Alston Macon/Robert & Alcy
Pugh, Olive — Jesse Johnston/Robert & Alcy

Pugh, Rezin (Persian) 1787 — Elizabeth Jackson/Elijah & Ruth

Pugh, Robert 1770 — Alcy Kinman/Jesse & Elizabeth

Pugh, Stephen 1805 — Elijah & Ruth

Pugh, William — Jesse & Elizabeth

Pyle (Pfeil), Hannah — Joel Cloud

Pyle, William — Hannah Cloud

Rees, Benjamin

Rees, Hugh — Elizabeth Newsom

Richards, Watkin

Richardson, Martha — Robert Stewart

Robinson, David

Robinson, Israel

Robinson, Mary — Thomas Sanders/gr. dau. Israel Robinson

Rogers, Drury

Ryan, James — Prudence Moore

Samson, Samuel

Sanders, Abraham 1763 — Mary Morris/Joel & Charity

Sanders, Barbara 1780 — Joel & Sarah

Sanders, Benjamin 1746 — Leah Smith/Joel & Charity

Sanders, Charity 1799 — Stephen Granade ("from Granada")

Sanders, Dempsey 1753 — Joel & Charity

Sanders, Ferribee 1756 — Benjamin Cooper/Joel & Charity

Sanders, Hollowell 1755 — Joel & Charity

Sanders, James 1791 — Sarah Sell/Abraham & Mary

Sanders, Jeremiah — Joshua & Patience

Sanders, Joel — Charity Hollowell

Sanders, Joel 1751 — Sarah Morgan/Joel & Charity

Sanders, John 1748 — Massey (Jewish) Sims/Joel & Charity

Sanders, Joshua — Patience

Sanders, Josiah 1761 — Sarah Smith/Joel & Charity

Sanders, Keziah — Joshua & Patience

Sanders, Lydia 1753 — Chris Wilson, John Scott

Sanders, Mark — Joshua & Patience

Sanders, Mary 1797 — John Thompson/Abraham & Mary

Sanders, Miriam 1744 — Joel & Charity

Sanders, Mordecai 1764 — Margaret Thomas/Joel & Charity

Sanders, Nathan — Joshua & Patience

Sanders, Patience — Joshua & Patience

Sanders, Reuben — Joshua & Patience

Sanders, Sarah 1767 — John Galbreath/Joel & Charity

Sanders, Sarah 1800 — Timothy Granade/Abraham & Mary

Sanders, Thomas 1759 — Mary Robinson/Joel & Charity

Sanders, William 1778 — Amy Williams/Joel & Sarah

Sattan, William

Schofield, Joseph

Scott, Adam 1790 — Grace Mooney

Scott, Deborah — James Jones/William & Deborah

Scott, Henry — Mariah Rees/William & Deborah

Scott, John — Lydia Sanders

Scott, Joseph

Scott, Margaret — Elias Jones/William & Deborah

Scott, Nancy — Robert Parnham/William & Deborah

Scott, Sarah — Elijah Parnham/William & Deborah

Scott, William 1762 — Deborah Sell

Scott, William — Susannah Gassaway

Sell (Ashk. fr. Samuel?), Deborah 1762 — William Scott/Jonathan & Sarah

Sell, Elizabeth 1758 — Joseph Mendenhall/Jonathan & Sarah

Sell, Enos 1760 — Jonathan & Sarah

Sell, Henry

Sell, John 1773 — Jonathan & Sarah

Sell, Jonathon, Jr. 1776 — Jonathan & Sarah

Sell, Jonathon, Sr. 1728 — Sarah Tatum

Sell, Mary 1770 — Jonathan & Sarah

Sell, Patience 1767 — Jonathan & Sarah

Sell, Sarah 1778 — Jonathan & Sarah

Sell, Thomas 1756 — Jonathan & Sarah

Sergison, Patrick

Sherill, Reuben

Sidwell, Amey — Cox

Sidwell, Ann — Nathan & Rebecca

Sidwell, Anne — David & Ruth

Sidwell, Daniel

Sidwell, David — Ruth, Esther Stubbs

Sidwell, David — David & Ruth

Sidwell, Elizabeth — Waggoner/David & Ruth

Sidwell, Gabriel Baker — Nathan & Rebecca

Sidwell, Hannah — Hathborn

Sidwell, John — Catherine Vernon/John & Mary

Sidwell, John — Nathan & Rebecca

Sidwell, Joseph — David & Ruth

Sidwell, Joseph — Nathan & Rebecca

Sidwell, Mary — King/David & Ruth

Sidwell, Nathan — Rebecca/John & Catherine

Sidwell, Nathan — Nathan & Rebecca

Sidwell, Ruth — David & Ruth

Sidwell, Sarah — Nathan & Rebecca

Sidwell, Susan — John & Catherine

Simpson, John

Sims, Massey (Mazza) — John Sanders/Reuben, Jemima (Glenn)

Singuefield, Samuel

Sinquefield, William

Slater, John

Slater, Mary — John Dennis

Smith, John

Smith, Leah — Benjamin Sanders/Thomas & Esther

Smith, Richard

Smith, Sarah — Josiah Sanders

Smith, William

Smithson, Benjamin — Hannah Greathouse

Stanley, Thomas 1757 — Edith, Priscilla Ladd/Thomas & Sarah

Stewart, Elizabeth — Jesse Pugh/Robert & Martha

Stewart, John

Stewart, John, Jr.

Stewart, Robert — Martha Richardson

Stuart, Amos — Robert & Martha

Stuart, Branner

Stuart, Gravener — Robert & Martha

Stubbs, Abisha 1806 — Mary Risk/William & Sarah

Stubbs, Abraham 1793 — Joseph & Zilpha

Stubbs, Achsah 1800 — Samuel Kelley/Isaac & Margaret

Stubbs, Amanda 1798 — Job Talbert/Joseph & Kezia

Stubbs, Anne 1804 — William Gifford, Jonathan Dicks

Stubbs, Arriah 1801 — William Brown/Thomas & Mary

Stubbs, Deborah 1777 — William Kellum/John & Esther

Stubbs, Deborah 1792 — Robert Vernon/Joseph & Zilpha

Stubbs, Elisha 1798 — Elizabeth Townsend/Thomas & Mary

Stubbs, Eliza 1801— Elijah Hanson/Joseph & Zilpha
Stubbs, Elizabeth 1795 — Stephen Cox/Joseph & Zilpha
Stubbs, Esther 1767 — Thomas Bowd, David Sidwell/
Stubbs, Esther 1786 — John Newlin/John & Jane
Stubbs, Hannah 1770— Alexander Pugh/John & Esther
Stubbs, Hannah 1792 — William Maddock/Nathan & Elizabeth
Stubbs, Hannah 1792 — Abner Elliot/John & Jane
Stubbs, Hester 1765 — Joseph & Anne
Stubbs, Iddo 1798 — Mary Patton/Joseph & Zilpha
Stubbs, Isaac 1761— Margaret Carter/John & Esther
Stubbs, Isaac 1790 — Elizabeth Doudney/Joseph & Zilpha
Stubbs, Jacob 1788 — Sophia Coon (Cohen)/Joseph & Zilpha
Stubbs, Jane 1794— John & Jane
Stubbs, Jesse 1782 — Alice Alzana (Arabic) Walker
Stubbs, John 1732 — Esther Maddock/(Minor)
Stubbs, John 1762 — Jane Jones/John & Esther
Stubbs, John 1786 — Rhoda Whitcomb/Isaac & Margaret
Stubbs, John 1796 — Margaret Huston, Margaret Griffin
Stubbs, John Maddock 1801— Eleanor Taylor/Joseph & Kezia
Stubbs, Joseph 1737 — Anne Mooney/Thos. and Mary (Minor)
Stubbs, Joseph 1763 — Zilpha Hayes/Thomas & Deborah
Stubbs, Joseph 1767 — Joseph & Anne
Stubbs, Joseph 1772 — Kezia Hickson, Nancy Harvey
Stubbs, Joseph 1799 — Sarah Townsend/Nathan & Elizabeth
Stubbs, Joseph 1801— Margaret Saunders/John & Jane
Stubbs, Keziah 1790 — Jesse Overman/Nathan & Elizabeth
Stubbs, Keziah 1804 — Alfred Bogue/John & Jane
Stubbs, Margaret 1790 — Samuel Brown, Jr./John & Jane
Stubbs, Martha 1800 — Richard Brown, Jr./Samuel & Mary
Stubbs, Martha 1806 — Merit Pugh/Jesse & Alice
Stubbs, Mary 1763 — Beale Butler/Joseph & Anne
Stubbs, Mary 1784 — Bailey Hayes/Joseph & Zilpha
Stubbs, Mary 1802 — James Allison/Jesse & Alice
Stubbs, Nathan 1759 — Eleanor Jones, Elizabeth Jones
Stubbs, Nathan 1801— Ann Mendenhall/Nathan & Elizabeth
Stubbs, Newton 1798 — Mary Talbert/Samuel & Mary
Stubbs, Rachel 1760— John Cox/Thomas & Deborah
Stubbs, Rachel 1774 — William Hickson/John & Esther
Stubbs, Rachel 1785 — Menoah Hanson/Joseph & Zilpha
Stubbs, Rachel 1798 — Mordecai Moore/Nathan & Elizabeth
Stubbs, Rachel 1798 — Seaborn Moore/John & Jane
Stubbs, Rebecca 1793 — Thomas Brown/Samuel & Mary
Stubbs, Rebecca 1795 — William Talbert, Azariah Denney
Stubbs, Rebecca 1796 — John Patton/Joseph & Zilpha
Stubbs, Rhoda 1802 — James Vernon/Joseph & Zilpha
Stubbs, Samuel 1790 — Rachel Whitacre/Isaac & Margaret
Stubbs, Samuel 1766 — Mary Jones/John & Esther
Stubbs, Sarah 1787 — Benjamin Hall/Joseph & Zilpha
Stubbs, Sarah 1788 — John McDonald, Jr./John & Jane
Stubbs, Sarah 1802 — Nathan Clark, George Haworth
Stubbs, Tabitha 1796 — William Jones/Samuel & Mary
Stubbs, Thomas 1735 — Deborah Maddock/(Minor)
Stubbs, Thomas 1775 — Mary Hobson/John & Esther
Stubbs, William 1789 — Esther Townsend, Mary Stout
Stubbs, William 1795 — Delila Parham/Samuel & Mary
Stubbs, William 1805 — Sarah Hobson/John & Esther

Stubbs, Zephaniah 1803 — Mary Updegraf, Elsie King
Stubbs, Zimri 1797 — Mary Irons/Isaac & Margaret
Swords, James — Rev., war soldier
Taylor, Mary — Joseph Jones
Thomas, Abijah 1793 — Camm & Elizabeth
Thomas, Abisha — Rebecca
Thomas, Anna — Caleb Mendenhall
Thomas, Asahel 1795 — Camm & Elizabeth
Thomas, Camm 1763 — Elizabeth/Rebecca
Thomas, Caty 1800— Camm & Elizabeth
Thomas, Elizabeth — Rebecca
Thomas, Hannah 1716/7 — Mendenhall, Moore/(Atherton)
Thomas, Hezekiah 1798 — Camm & Elizabeth
Thomas, Margaret — Mordecai Sanders/Rebecca
Thomas, Priscilla 1803 — Camm & Elizabeth
Thomas, Rebecca — died 1802
Thomas, Rebecca — Rebecca
Thomas, Sarah
Thomas, William 1791— Camm & Elizabeth
Thomas, _____ — Abigail Moore
Thompson, John — Mary Sanders
Thompson, Laurence
Thompson, Richard
Thompson, Solomon — witnessed Peter Perkins' will 1801
Thomson, Isaac
Tinnen, Hugh
Todd, Rebecca — in minutes 1792
Todd, Robert — Rebecca
Todd, Stephen — Sabilla Williams/Rebecca
Todd, Theodate — Rebecca
Todd, William — Rebecca
Townsend, Hannah 1718 — Isaac Vernon/John & Catherine
Vernon, Amos — Mary Patton/James & Content
Vernon, Ann 1802 — Andrew Bond/Nathaniel & Grace
Vernon, Catherine 1741— Sidwell, Mendenhall/Isaac & Hannah
Vernon, Content 1801— Robert & Ann
Vernon, Grace 1804 — Ezekiel Mote/Nathaniel & Grace
Vernon, Isaac 1715/6 — Hannah Townsend/(Williams)
Vernon, Isaac 1742 — Isaac & Hannah (Townsend)
Vernon, James 1751— Content Hussey/Isaac & Hannah
Vernon, James 1775 — Tamar Davis/James & Content
Vernon, James 1800 — Rhoda Stubbs/Amos & Mary
Vernon, Lydia 1789 — Abram Mott/Nathaniel & Grace
Vernon, Margaret 1787 — Robert McConnell/Nathaniel & Grace
Vernon, Martha 1753 — James Brown/Isaac & Hannah
Vernon, Mary — John Hodgin/Issac & Hannah
Vernon, Nathaniel 1766 — Grace Mendenhall
Vernon, Phebe 1741— George Beck, Joseph Middleton
Vernon, Rachel 1802 — Amos & Mary
Vernon, Robert 1777 — Patton, Stubbs/James & Content
Vernon, Solomon 1779 — James & Content
Vernon, Tamar 1785 — James North/Nathaniel & Grace
Vernon, Theodate — James & Content
Vernon, Theodate 1804 — Jonathan Morris/Amos & Mary
Vernon, Thomas 1796 — Hollingsworth, Ballinger
Vernon, William — Deborah Hanson/Robert & Ann
Waddell, Moses
Waggoner, George
Walden (Walton), Robert

Walker, Alice Alzana — Jesse Stubbs
Walker, Henry
Watson, Jacob
Watson, John
Watson, Thomas, Sr.
Watson, Thomas, Jr.
Weathers, Peter
Webb, Jesse
Webb, Richard
Welch, John
Weldon, William
West, John
Wheat, William
Whigham, Thomas
White, Nicholas
White, Thomas 1753
White, _____ — Jemima Perkins
Whitsett, John
Whitsett, John, Jr.
Whitsett, Joseph
Wilkerson, Adam
Wilkins, John — William & Sarah
Wilkins, William — Sarah Perkins
Williams, Aaron 1795 — Matilda Saffle/Henry & Zilpha
Williams, Abby 1791 — Stephen Hodgin/Henry & Zilpha
Williams, Amy 1782 — William Sanders/Daniel & Mary
Williams, Daniel 1747 — Mary Humphreys (Davis)
Williams, Elias 1798 — Lydia Smith/Henry & Zilpha
Williams, Elizabeth 1778 — Stephen Hodgin/Daniel & Mary
Williams, Henry 1752 — Zilpha Morris
Williams, Isaiah 1797 — Hannah Way/Henry & Zilpha

Williams, Job 1792 — Elizabeth Clendenon/Henry & Zilpha
Williams, John — Esther Carson
Williams, Mary 1787 — Richard Fawcett/Daniel & Mary
Williams, Peter
Williams, Rebecca 1785 — Abel Gilbert/Daniel & Mary
Williams, Ruth 1780 — William Farmer/Daniel & Mary
Williams, Sabilla 1776 — Stephen Todd/Daniel & Mary
Williams, Sarah 1773 — Robert Milhouse, Jesse Bailey
Williams, William 1777 — Phebe Mendenhall/ (Crawford)
Wilson, Chris — Lydia Sanders
Wilson, Samuel
Winslett, David 1779 — Mary Ann Wooten/Samuel & Mary
Winslett, Esther 1788 — John Kimbrough/Samuel & Mary
Winslett, Gibson 1792 — Susannah Coleman/John
Winslett, Joel 1785 — Samuel & Mary
Winslett, Joel A. 1802 — Mary McLeod/John & ?
Winslett, John 1775 — Hattie Ward/Samuel & Mary
Winslett, John Carson 1799 — Susan Stewart, Nancy West Nellams
Winslett, Jonathan 1793 — Gillian Bagley/Samuel & Mary
Winslett, Mary 1783 — Samuel & Mary
Winslett, Richard 1790 — Parthania Bagley/Samuel & Mary
Winslett, Samuel 1749 — Mary Carson
Winslett, Samuel 1787 — Nancy Merritt, Dicey (Jewish)
Winslett, William 1777 — Elizabeth Harp, Margaritt Calhoun Withrow, Henry
Wooddell, Gersham
Wright, Sir James
York, William
Young, Thomas

Notes

Preface

1. Simon Wiesenthal, *Sails of Hope* (New York: Macmillan, 1973), 228–29.
2. Leon Harris, *Merchant Princes* (New York: Harper & Row, 1979), 27f. His remarks are based on interviews with Rabbi Malcolm H. Stern, compiler of *Americans of Jewish Descent*.

Introduction

1. L. G. Pine, *The Genealogist's Encyclopedia* (New York: Collier, 1969), 35.
2. *Ibid.*, 18, citing Robert W. Formhals in *The Augustan* 10/4 (April 1967).
3. *Ibid.*, 40.

Chapter 1

1. See, for instance, John L. Kessell, *Spain in the Southwest* (Norman: University of Oklahoma Press, 2003). David M. Gitlitz, *Secrecy and Deceit* (Albuquerque: University of New Mexico Press, 2002). Stanley M. Hordes, *To the End of the Earth* (New York: Columbia University Press, 2008). Mordechai Arbell, *The Jewish Nation of the Caribbean* (Jerusalem: Gefen, 2002).
2. L. P. Harvey, *Muslims in Spain 1500–1614* (Chicago: Chicago University Press, 2005).
3. Salvador de Madariega, *Christopher Columbus: Being the Life of the Most Magnificent Lord....* (New York: Macmillan, 1939). Simon Wiesenthal, *Sails of Hope: The Secret Mission of Christopher Columbus* (New York: Macmillan, 1973). Jacob Rader Marcus, *Early American Jewry*. Vol. I: *The Jews of New York, New England and Canada 1649–1794* (New York: KTAV, 1973), 3. See also Jack Abramovitz, *They Sailed with Columbus*, E-text available at www.eductrak.com.
4. Wiesenthal, 107.
5. Edward Kritzler, *Jewish Pirates of the Caribbean* (New York: Doubleday, 2008), 75–92.
6. Vol. 1 of *Religions of the United States in Practice* in the series *Princeton Readings in Religions*, for instance, includes a chapter on Jewish worship practices in the early New York colony, "The Amidah in Colonial American Synagogues," by Dianne Ashton, but the essay is restricted to the experi-

ence of open Spanish Jews and cannot be generalized to crypto–Jews or other denominations (ed. Colleen McDannell, Princeton: Princeton University Press, 2001). We have been unable to find any work that throws light on private worship services or family traditions of secret Jews in North America.
7. See, for instance, Jane S. Gerber, *The Jews of Spain* (New York: The Free Press, 1992), 113–14.
8. David Cesarani, "The Forgotten Port Jews of London," in *Port Jews*, ed. David Cesarani (London: Cass, 2002), 11–24.
9. Nabil Matar, *Turks, Moors, and Englishmen in the Age of Discovery* (New York: Columbia University Press), 20–21, citing Andrew P. Vella, *An Elizabethan-Ottoman Conspiracy*.
10. Evidence for the Anglo-Norman Seymour family's Jewish origins is presented in the authors' "Jerusalem's Gate: Jews and Muslims in England." (manuscript).
11. Matar, 19–82. Both authors have in their family tree the Cherokee Nancy Ward, half-blood daughter of Sir Francis Ward. Her name in Cherokee, Tsistuna-gis-ke ("Little Rose"), is a reminder of Arab connections. Other Arabic names in their genealogies are Ashmole (Ishmael), Ridge/Watie (*wadi*), Reece (Riis), Aleef, Ashley (Asseley "honeyman"), Hammett, Hams, Suddarth, Isham, Story (Stora), Hale and Haley.
12. *Ibid.*, 61–62.
13. C. Baurain, and C. Bonnet, *Les Phéniciens: Marins de Trois Continents* (Paris: Armand Colin, 1992). Barry Cunliffe, *Facing the Ocean: The Atlantic and Its Peoples* (New York: Oxford University Press, 2004). C. Shell in M. Ryan, ed., *The Origins of Metallurgy in Atlantic Europe: Proceedings of the Fifth Atlantic Colloquium* (Dublin, 1979), 259–61.
14. D. B. Barton, *Essays in Cornish Mining History*, 2 vols. (Truro: 1968, 1971); *A History of Copper Mining in Cornwall and Devon* (Truro: 1978). Edmund Newell, "The British Copper Ore Market in the Nineteenth Century, with Particular Reference to Cornwall and Swansea," unpublished Ph.D. thesis, University of Oxford, 1988.
15. James F. Wilson, et al., "Genetic Evidence for Different Male and Female Roles during Cultural Transitions in the British Isles," *Publications of the National Academy of the Sciences* 98/9 (2001), 5078–83. C. Capelli, "A Y Chromosome Census of the British Isles," *Current Biology* 13 (2003), 979–984.

16. Glenn E. Markoe, *The Phoenicians* (London: Folio, 2005), 254.

17. Michael Adler, *Jews of Medieval England* (London: Jewish Historical Society of England, 1939). David S. Katz, *The Jews in the History of England* (Oxford: Clarendon Press, 1996).

18. *When Scotland Was Jewish* (Jefferson, NC: McFarland, 2007), 90–96.

19. Bernard Susser, *Jews of South West England: The Rise and Decline of Their Mediaeval and Modern Communities* (Exeter: University of Exeter Press, 1993), 33. German *ganz* means "goose." It was a sign in the Frankfort Jewish quarter (Jacobs, "Personal Names") and appears as a Sephardic surname, Ganso, documented by the Inquisition in Lisbon and Brazil (Faiguenboim, et al., 268). It was also a Jewish masculine given name used as a short form of Yehohana, Johannes, or Elhanan (Menk, 298).

20. No origin has been suggested for Raleigh, the name of the family's manor and eponymous title. It appears first as *Raalega* in the Pipe Rolls for Devon (*DES* 371). *Raalega* has no known French or English elements.

21. John William Shirley, *Sir Walter Raleigh and the New World* (Raleigh: North Carolina Division of Archives, 1985).

22. The Jewish community in Genoa was prominent from the days of Theodoric in the fifth century CE. Spanish refugees arrived there in 1492. By the beginning of the sixteenth century a special office was established in Genoa, "Ufficio per gli Ebrei" (Office for the Hebrews). Shakespeare's Jew Shylock in *The Merchant of Venice* had important connections in Genoa. In the seventeenth century, trade was brisk between and among Genoa and Jewish import-export firms in Amsterdam, the Caribbean, London, Turkey and India. As already alluded to, it has been widely accepted that the Colom family that produced Christopher Columbus were Catalan Jews who settled in Genoa. In modern times, the Jewish writer Primo Levi grew up in the Jewish community in Genoa. See Urbani, Rossana, and Guido Nathan Zazzu, eds., *The Jews in Genoa: 507–1681*, Vol. 1, *Studia Post Biblica, a Documentary History of the Jews in Italy* (Leiden: Brill, 1998).

23. See Gitlitz, 10, 90, 112–14.

24. A readable account is Milton Giles, *Big Chief Elizabeth* (New York: Farrar, Strauss and Giroux, 2000).

25. Perhaps "one from Hagalili," a Moroccan Jewish community meaning "God be celebrated" in Hebrew, rendered into English or Dutch (see Faiguenboim, et al., 279). *DES* (s.v.) derives it from "'hack little,' a nickname for a lazy woodcutter."

26. Perhaps the same as Harots in Amsterdam (Faiguenboim, et al., 281), in turn identical with Harrod (the name of a department store founder in London).

27. Faiguenboim, et al., 256.

28. Portuguese Jewish surname recorded in Leghorn, Genoa and Tunis (Faiguenboim, et al., 258).

29. "Cretan, from Crete." Compare Candia (Faiguenboim, et al., 219), probably also Candiani, Canada, Gundy, Kennedy (Kan-a-dey, "place of the governor").

30. Amado/Amadeus/Amadios (Spanish "beloved") is a Sephardic name recorded in Amsterdam, Pisa, Florence, Lisbon and Marseilles, among other places (Faiguenboim, et al., 176).

31. Faiguenboim, et al., record the names Dias (Portuguese) and Diaz (Spanish) as Sephardic surnames in London, Middelburg, Amsterdam, Curaçao, Smyrna, Bordeaux, Jamaica, Torino, Leghorn, Lisbon, Azores, Dutch Brazil, Venice, Rome, Amsterdam, Lima, Mexico and elsewhere (241–42).

32. "Lowe ... mainly from Great Britain or America," like popular Jewish surnames Loew, Löwen, Löwenberg, Löwenstein, Loewenthal, etc., formed from a play on German Löwe "lion" and Hebrew Levi." The lion was, of course, also the symbol of Judah. See Menk, 495–500.

33. "Lista de Apellidos Judios segun noto de Père Bonnin [*Sangre Judia*]," available online at www.personaes.com/colombia.

34. Virginia Dare, Ananias and Eleanor Dare's daughter, is regarded as the first English child born in North America. The Norman name Dare is attested as early as 1243 in the Somerset Assize Rolls (*DES* 126), where it is derived hypothetically from OE *deor* "wild animal." Its Norman French origins may have more to do with Darius, a favorite name from Jewish legend, than the Anglo-Saxon language of the Norman's subjects, or with Hebrew *Adar*, the name of a month in spring. Dare could have been an accommodation. An etymology for the more common Scottish surname Adair derives it from Gaelic Edzaer (?) meaning "the ford of the oaks," although the phonetic resemblance is not clear. It, too, may have been an accommodation. Ananias is a Greek Sephardic surname, meaning "God's grace." It is also a Biblical name, familiar from the Christian New Testament, where "Peter said, Ananias, why hath Satan filled thine heart to lie to the Holy Spirit, and to keep back part of the price of the land?" in a transaction with the apostle. Ananias "fell down, and died" (Acts 5:1–5). His name became a byword for perfidy, specifically that experienced at the hands of Jews in the Middle Ages. It is unlikely any Christian subject in England would have borne this first name unless he was Jewish.

35. After Alexander's conquest of Judea in 332 BCE, most Jews spoke Greek, even in the synagogue, and Greek names were also favored. For esoteric reasons, Dionysius was a common name in Freemasonry (Chapter Ten). Harvey, Harvie, Hervey, Herveus, etc., are considered Breton names that came to England with the Norman Conquest derived from Old French *Hæruiu*, "battle worthy" (*DES* 219). The etymology underlying the Breton form has never been closely examined. We suggest the original name might have been composed of *har*, Hebrew for "mount," and a suffix to denote a topographical location, as in Har Adar or Har Vered, noble seats often being named in this fashion. A Harvye was the second child recorded to be born in English North America.

36. Sanderson derives from "Alexander's son" (Jacobs 1901–1906). Many Jews of this time period had the surname Alexander or some derivative thereof, such as Saunders, Sand, Sender and Zander. It is said that the high priest in Jerusalem decreed that all male children born in the year after Alexander's visit be named for him; Alexander in modern times is one of the most frequent surnames in lists of Jewish benefactors in the British Isles (Jacobs 1901–1906). Alexander embraced Judaism probably for reasons of diplomacy and "public relations" (Graves 45).

37. Upon the failure of the Guiana mission, Keymis committed suicide. Although condoned in certain situations by halakic law (Torah), suicide is strongly denounced in Christianity, a fact which raises suspicions about his true religious affiliation.

38. The Catholic symbol of the Cross (Crux, Cruz) was often adopted by Conversos to emphasize their new religion (see Faiguenboim, et al., 129). For instance, Juana Inés de la Cruz (1648/51–1695), fully Juana Inés de la Cruz de Asbaje (or Asuaje) y Ramírez de Santillana, was the illegitimate Aztec daughter of a Spanish nobleman born in Mexico and raised as a nun. She became a prominent

poet. Her writings were censured by the Spanish Inquisition.

39. Peter Whitfield, *Sir Francis Drake* (New York: New York University Press, 2004), 15.

40. Davis is the second name in Jacobs' list of Jewish names known for charitable giving in England (1901–1906).

41. Jose M. Brito, "The Inquisition and Crypto-Judaism in the Canaries," Society for Crypto Judaic Studies, www.cryptojews.com/canaries.html, accessed 8/11/2006. Ronald Schneider, "The Jews of Cap Verde and the Azores," www.saudades.org/cverde.htm, accessed 8/11/2006. Landau, Benny, "The Jews of the Canary Islands: Calendar of Calumny," www.saudades.org/Jews%20_Canary%20_Islands.htm, accessed 8/11/2006. Manuel Lobo Cabrera, *La Esclavitud en Las Canarias Orientalis en El Siglo XVI(Negros, Moros Y Moriscos)* (Santa Cruz de Tenerife: EXCMO, 1982).

42. Whitfield, 25.

43. Abraham D. Lavender, "DNA and the Sephardic Diaspora: Spanish and Portuguese Jews in Europe," *HaLAPID* (2003), 10/1:1–7.

44. A golden deer is the emblem of the Hebrew tribe of Naphtali. Like others it goes back to the patriarch Jacob's prophetic blessing of his sons, where it is said of Naphtali, "Naphtali is a hind let loose, which yields lovely fawns" (Gen. 49:21). Jacobs (1901–1906) finds that the following surnames are based on this allusion: Cerf, Harris, Harrison, Hart, Herschell, Hershkovitz, Hertz, Hertzen, Hertzl, Herz, Herzl, Hirsch, Hirschel, Hirschkovitsch, Huzka, and Zewi. To this list may be added the Sephardic surnames Cervo, Corzo, Naphtaly, Naphthali, Tsevi, Tzevi, Zevi and Zvi. Both Harris and Hart are among the top Jewish surnames in Great Britain, according to Jacobs.

45. Faiguenboim, et al., 414.

46. Dourado/Dorato ("golden") was a Jewish surname in Seville (Faiguenboim, et al., 243). Vas/Vaz/Vai, an abbreviated form of Vasco, is the 88th most common Sephardic surname (Faiguenboim, et al., 146, 414–15).

47. Drago(n) is a corruption of d'Aragon, both forms being surnames found in Amsterdam, Portugal and Brazil, among other places, according to Faiguenboim, et al., 244. This may be a pun, however, as Dragón means "dragon" in Spanish. The German equivalent was Drach, a house-sign in the ghetto of Frankfurt am Main (Menk, 244). Draga was the well-known Portuguese form.

48. Sebastian (Greek given name) was the son of the Genoese-Venetian explorer Giovanni Caboto (who became John Cabot when he sailed under English colors). Significantly, Cabot is a Spanish surname on Father Bonnin's list of Jewish surnames.

49. Biographical details are based on James Alexander Williamson, *Sir John Hawkins, the Time and the Man* (Westport, CT: Greenwood, 1969).

50. Hakin is Hebrew for "physician" and a widespread Sephardic surname evidenced in Spain, Turkey, Greece, Damascus, Egypt, Italy, Tunisia, Morocco and London (Faiguenboim, et al., 280).

51. Named perhaps after the Hebrew letter tau.

52. On Melungeons, see Elizabeth C. Hirschman and Donald N. Panther-Yates, "Suddenly Melungeon! Reconstructing Consumer Identity across the Color Line," *Consumer Culture Theory*, Vol. 11 of *Research in Consumer Behavior*, eds. Russell W. Belk and John F. Sherry, Jr. (Amsterdam: Elsevier), 241–59. Hirschman and Yates, "Toward a Genetic Profile of Melungeons in East Tennessee," *Appalachian Journal* (Fall 2010). Elizabeth C. Hirschman, *Melungeons: The Last Lost Tribe in America* (Macon: Mercer University Press, 2005). Brent N. Kennedy, *The Melungeons:*

The Resurrection of a Proud People. Rev. ed. (Macon: Mercer University Press, 1998).

53. Williamson, 24.

54. Borey may be a naturalized form of Borjes. Phillips comes from Forbes/Pharabes/Phoebus (Jacobs 1901–1906). Phillips is a name in the top ten of Jacobs' list of prominent British Jewish surnames.

55. See Norman Golb, *The Jews in Mediaeval Normandy* (Cambridge: Cambridge University Press, 1998).

56. Faiguenboim, et al., 239, 361.

57. Sephardic Martinezes are noted in Spain, Amsterdam and London by Faiguenboim, et al., 320).

58. Probably cognate with Barnal (from Hamburg) and Bernal; see Faiguenboim, et al., 191.

59. Williamson, 52.

60. The name appears to be formed from Lov- ("Levite") and the theophoric suffix -el favored by so many Norman, Italian and southern French Jews (Jacobs 1901–1906). An alternative theory is that the Lov- element imitates Spanish Lobo "wolf" and designates the tribe of Levi.

61. Barrett seems to come from Jacob's son Issachar, for whom Jacobs (1901–1906) lists also the following surnames: Achsel, Bar, Baer, Barell, Barnard, Barnett, Berusch, Beer, Bernard, Berthold. Names incorporating Baer (German for "bear") such as Bernard and Bernstein are popular among Jews in Germany (Menk, 154, 173f.), while Barnett is among the best-known Jewish surnames in Great Britain (Jacobs, 1901–1906).

62. On Luna, one of the most prestigious old Sephardic Jewish names, see Faiguenboim, et al., 314.

63. Spanish Jewish (Faiguenboim, et al., 180).

64. Martin means "bellicose" in Spanish and was a Sephardic surname found in Toledo and London before 1492, according to Faiguenboim, et al., 320.

65. A common English Jewish surname, derived, according to Jacobs (1901–1906) from Feibos, Phaedus, the latter an attribute of Apollo as god of the sun. This in turn translates Aramaic Shraga Feivush, meaning "light, lamp, lantern" (Gorr, 36).

66. See Faiguenboim, et al., 222.

67. Williamson, 165.

68. Probably a Moroccan name; see Faiguenboim, et al., 209, s.v. Boudouk.

69. James McDermott, *Martin Frobisher, Elizabethan Privateer* (New Haven, CT: Yale University Press, 2001).

70. *Ibid.*, 8.

71. See David S. Katz, *The Jews in the History of England* (Oxford: Oxford University Press, 1996).

72. McDermott, 23f.

73. Derived from Isaac (Jacobs, 1901–1906).

74. McDermott, 40.

75. Faiguenboim, et al., 310, 313.

76. See note 59.

77. Williamson, 34.

78. See Bruce Masters, *The Origins of Western Economic Dominance in the Middle East* (Chicago: University of Chicago Press, 1988).

79. Faiguenboim, et al., find the name or one of its variants in Lisbon, Amsterdam, Mallorca, Rhodes, Smyrna, Tangier, London, Bordeux and other cities (256, 258–59).

80. Jacobs, 1901–1906.

81. Millicent V. Hay, *The Life of Sir Robert Sidney, East of Leicester* (Washington: Folger, 1984).

82. No, Noe = Noah (Jacobs, 1901–1906).

83. The family was descended from a Paen Gamedge, who arrived in England with the Norman Conquest from the place called Gamaches, in Normandy. Paen means pagan.

84. Hay, 227.

85. Their surname is taken from a town near the Norman capital of Rouen known to have a substantial Jewish population (Golb, 1998).

86. Boleyn may come from Hebrew Ballin, "ritual bathkeeper" (Jacobs, 1901–1906). Other forms are Bolling, Balen and Bollin. *DES* 52 claims its origin is ME *bolling*, "excessive drinking."

87. It is most likely from Arabic Bakoda, recorded from early times in Toledo (Faiguenboim, et al., 53).

88. Robert Lacey, *Phoenix: Robert Devereux, Earl of Essex, an Elizabethan Icarus* (New York: Phoenix, 1971), 79.

89. "The husband's brother shall go in unto her, and take her to him as his wife, and perform the duty of an husband's brother under." On Levirate law (Hebrew *yibbum*) see Solomon Schechter and Joseph Jacobs, "Levirate Marriage," *The Jewish Encyclopedia: A Descriptive Record of the History, Religion, Literature, and Customs of the Jewish People from the Earliest Times to the Present Day,* pub. by Isidore Singer and ed. by Cyrus Adler, orig. pub. in London, reprint by KTAV Publishing House, 1980. Available online at http://www.JewishEncyclopedia.com/.

90. For Dee, we follow the account of Benjamin Woolley, *The Queen's Conjuror: The Science and Magic of Dr. John Dee, Advisor to Queen Elizabeth I* (New York: Holt, 2001).

91. Menk 567: 1550 London, England, from Portugal; 1553 Bristol, England....

92. It has been pointed out elsewhere that letters with Hebrew portions survive from her hand and she was evidently from a crypto–Jewish mercantile family (Hirschman and Yates, 2007).

93. Woolley, 34.

94. *Ibid.*, 61.

95. *Ibid.*, 63.

96. *Ibid.*, 118.

97. For the Grenvilles, we rely on A. L. Rouse, *Sir Richard Grenville of the Revenge, an Elizabethan Hero* (London: Jonathan Cape, 1937).

98. One St. Leger daughter was named Eulalia, a popular medieval Jewish name.

99. As noted before, Cavendish's surname was originally rendered as Candysh, i.e., from Candia (Turkish Crete).

100. Rowse, 205.

101. *Ibid.*, 270.

102. *Ibid.*, 338.

Chapter 2

1. See Jane S. Gerber, *The Jews of Spain* (New York: Free, 1992), 2.

2. See Paul Wexler, *The Non-Jewish Origins of the Sephardic Jews* (Albany: State University of New York Press, 1996), esp. 12–13.

3. The only study of Machir and his times is Arthur Zuckermann, *A Jewish Princedom in Feudal France, 760–900* (New York: Columbia University Press, 1972). Some ramifications of the Jewish state for the background to the Norman invasion of England and subsequent settling of Jews in Scotland were explored in Hirschman and Yates (2007), 82–85.

4. Thus, for instance, P. Kyle McCarter, *Ancient Israel: A Short History from Abraham to the Roman Destruction of the Temple* (Biblical Archeology Society, 1991). See now Shlomo Sand, *The Invention of the Jewish People* (London: Verso, 2009).

5. See J. T. Shaye Cohen, *The Beginnings of Jewishness: Boundaries, Varieties, Uncertainties.* Hellenistic Culture and Society (Los Angeles: University of California Press, 1999).

6. See L. I. Levine, *Judaism and Hellenism in Antiquity* (Seattle: University of Washington Press, 1998). Erich S. Gruen, "Hellenistic Judaism," in David Biale, ed., *Cultures of the Jews* (New York: Schocken, 2002), 77–132.

7. Wexler, 12–13.

8. Doron M. Behar, "Contrasting Patterns of Y Chromosome Variation in Ashkenazi Jewish and Host Non-Jewish European Populations," *Human Genetics* 114 (2004), 354–65; "Multiple Origins of Ashkenazi Levites: Y Chromosome Evidence for Both Near Eastern and European Ancestries," *American Journal of Human Genetics* 73/4 (2003), 768–79. Almut Nebel et al., "Y Chromosome Evidence for a Founder Effect in Ashkenazi Jews," *European Journal of Human Genetics* 13/3 (2003), 388–91. Karl Skorecki, et al., "Y Chromosomes of Jewish Priests," *Nature* 2/385/6611 (1997), 32. M. G. Thomas, et al., "Founding Mothers of Jewish Communities: Geographically Separated Jewish Groups Were Independently Founded by Very Few Female Ancestors," *American Journal of Human Genetics* 70 (2002), 1411–20. Population data for New World countries are drawn from the following online sources, all available at www.familytreedna.com: Anousim Project (n=55), Azores DNA Project (n=13), Canadian-Anousim Project (n=34), Canary Island Sephardic DNA Project (n=34), Cuban DNA Project (n=44), Cumberland GaDNA Project (n=193), Melungeon DNA Project (n=47), Mexican Genealogy and DNA Project, New Mexico DNA project, Puerto Rico DNA Project (n=67), and Sephardim–New Mexico Project (n=64).

9. Judgment that a surname may be Jewish is based on sources that include: "Adath Yisroel Burial Society Records, Cheshunt Cemetery" (n.d.), Jewish Genealogical Society. Available online Dec. 1, 2002: http://www.jgsgb.org.uk/bury01.htm.; *History of the Jews in Aragon,* by Jean Regne; records of Bevis Marks, London; Barnett and Wright, *The Jews of Jamaica;* Jewish Canadian Surnames; Gitlitz, *Secrecy and Deceit;* Hyamson, *The Sephardim of England; Judios Conversos,* by Mario Javier Saban; Liebman, *The Jews of New Spain;* "Messianic Jews Sephardic Surname Reference List"; Rothenburg, *Finding Our Fathers;* Sephardim.com; Sangre Judia, or *Lista de apellidos Judios publicada por Père Bonnin;* Paul Sebag, *Les Noms des Juifs de Tunisie,* extracted by Lionel Levy; and, finally and most importantly, Faiguenboim, et al. Only surnames of interest not noted elsewhere are marked in this chapter. Many others are passed over without comment.

10. Paul H. Chapman, *Columbus, the Man* (Columbus: ISAC, 1992), 87f.

11. On Canarian history for this and other events, see Salvador Lopez Herrera, *The Canary Islands through History* (Madrid: Madrid University Press, 1978). On U6, see A. M. Gonsalez, "Mitochondrial lineage M1 traces an early human backflow to Africa," *BMC Genomics* 9/8 (2007), 223. N. Maca-Meyer, et al., "Ancient mtDNA Analysis and the Origin of the Guanches," *European Journal of Human Genetics* 12/2 (2004), 155–62.

12. See Alan Taylor, *American Colonies: The Settling of North America* (New York: Penguin, 2000), 30–32.

13. Faiguenboim, et al., 241–43, 244, 270, 285, 341–43, 257–58, 372–75, 405, 240, 369. On T formerly K2, see Kalevi Wiik, "Where Did European Men Come From?" *Journal of Genetic Genealogy* 4 (2008), 35–85.

14. See T. Bentley Duncan, *Atlantic Islands: Madeira, the Azores and the Cape Verdes in the Seventeenth Century*

(Chicago: University of Chicago, 1992). Fatima Dias, "The Jewish Community in the Azores from 1820 to the Present," in *From Iberia to Diaspora: Studies in Sephardic History and Culture*, ed. Yedida K. Stillman and Norman A. Stillman (Leiden: Brill, 1999). P. R. Pacheco, et al., "The Y Chromosomal Heritage of the Azores Islands Population," *Annals of Human Genetics* 69/2 (2005), 145–56.

15. Duncan, 196.

16. Faiguenboim, et al., 256.

17. From Lobato (*ibid.*, 310).

18. Menk, 744. Vogel was a common North German Jewish surname.

19. Faiguenboim, et al., 396, as in John Phillip Sousa, the American composer.

20. *Ibid.*, 377.

21. *Ibid.*, 262.

22. Myrna Katz Frommer and Harvey Frommer, "A Story That Is About to End: The Jews of the Azores," in *Fromer Luxury Travel*. Retrieved February 3, 2010, at http://www.travel-watch.com/azores.html.

23. Siboney, actually a Sephardic surname from the Moroccan tribe Sebayoun (Faiguenboim, et al., 392).

24. See Clifford L. Staten, *The History of Cuba* (New York: Palgrave Macmillan, 1991).

25. Faiguenboim, et al., 331.

26. Carvalho and variants "oak"; *ibid.*, 221.

27. *Ibid.*, 275.

28. *Ibid.*, 184. Teresa of Avila was Jewish before her conversion to Christianity.

29. *Ibid.*, 244.

30. *Ibid.*, 289.

31. Denounced to the Inquisition in Mexico City; *ibid.*, 320.

32. I.e., from Salle, Morocco; *ibid.*, 383.

33. *Ibid.*, 414.

34. *Ibid.*, 416.

35. See Arturo Morales Carrion, *Puerto Rico: A Political and Cultural History* (New York: W. W. Norton, 1983).

36. Osorio, a town in Portugal; *ibid.*, 348f.

37. "One who makes caldrons"; *ibid.*, 216.

38. Denounced to the Inquisition in Mexico City; *ibid.*, 333.

39. Aida R. Caro Costas, "The Organization of an Institutional and Social Life," in Carrion, 32.

40. Faiguenboim, et al., 218.

41. Febos: *ibid.*, 257; on the name, see Jacobs, 1901–1906.

42. Faiguenboim, et al., 334.

43. *Ibid.*, 271.

44. Denounced to the Inquisition in Mexico City; *ibid.*, 328.

45. *Ibid.*, 331.

46. "Olive oil seller"; *ibid.*, 347.

47. *Ibid.*, 353.

48. *Ibid.*, 354.

49. *Ibid.*, 369.

50. *Ibid.*

51. As in Hernando de Soto, the conquistador; *ibid.*, 396.

52. Harriet and Fred Rochlin, *Pioneer Jews: A New Life in the Far West* (Boston: Houghton Mifflin, 2000), 2–9.

53. Angelico Chavez, *Origins of New Mexico Families in the Spanish Colonial Period 1598–1820* (Santa Fe: Historical Society of New Mexico, 1954).

54. See the Great New Mexico Pedigree Database Project at http://www.hgrc-nm.org/surnames/surnames.htm. All these names can be found in Faiguenboim, et al. (2006).

55. Stanley M. Hordes, *To the End of the Earth: A History of the Crypto-Jews of New Mexico* (New York: Columbia University Press, 2005).

56. Haplogroup Q is responsible for about 90 percent of indigenous American male lineages but can also be Jewish.

57. On Narbonne, see Zuckermann, 1972.

58. Luis G. Carvajal-Carmon, et al., "Strong Amerind/White Sex Bias and a Possible Sephardic Contribution among the Founders of a Population in Northwest Colombia," *American Journal of Human Genetics* 67 (2000), 1287–95.

59. Ruiz in the nomenclature of geneticist Stephen Oppenheimer, *The Origins of the British* (Carroll and Graf, 2005), 188ff.; dubbed Oisin by Sykes, *Saxons, Vikings, Celts* (2005). Wiik, 39. J. F. Wilson, "Genetic Evidence for Different Male and Female Roles During Cultural Transitions in the British Isles," *Publications of the National Academy of the Sciences* 98/9 (2001), 5078–83.

60. Donald N. Yates and Elizabeth C. Hirschman, "Toward a Genetic Profile of Melungeons in Southern Appalachia," *Appalachian Journal* 38 (Fall-Winter 2010). The definition of "Jewish" DNA is based on Doron M. Behar, "Contrasting Patterns of Y Chromosome Variation in Ashkenazi Jewish and Host Non-Jewish European Populations," *Human Genetics* 114 (2004), 354–65. Yates and Hirschman, "Multiple Origins of Ashkenazi Levites: Y Chromosome Evidence for Both Near Eastern and European Ancestries," *American Journal of Human Genetics* 73/4 (2003), 768–79; A. Picornell, et al., "Jewish Population Genetic Data in 20 Polymorphic Loci," *Forensic Science International* 125 (2002), 52–8; and A. Pérez-Lezaun, et al., "Allele Frequencies of 13 Short Tandem Repeats in Population Samples from the Iberian Peninsula and Northern Africa," *International Journal of Legal Medicine* 113 (2000), 208–14. Cf. also M. G. Thomas, et al., "Founding Mothers of Jewish Communities: Geographically Separated Jewish Groups Were Independently Founded by Very Few Female Ancestors," *American Journal of Human Genetics* 70 (2002), 1411–20; M. G. Thomas, et al., "Origins of Old Testament Priests," *Nature* 9/394 (6689) (1998) 138–40; M. G. Thomas, et al., "Y Chromosomes Travelling South: The Cohen Modal Haplotype and the Origins of the Lemba — The "Black Jews of Southern Africa," *American Journal of Human Genetics* 66 (2002), 674–86. James Guthrie, "Melungeons: Comparison of Gene Frequency Distributions to Those of Worldwide Populations," *Tennessee Anthropologist*, 15/1 (1990), 13–22.

61. The same name as the English playwright Harold Pinter; Faiguenboim, et al., 359.

62. The name of a place in Tunisia; *ibid.*, 164.

63. "French"; *ibid.*, 386.

64. The Shaltiel family research group has posted an extensive list of names and their aliases on a Web page at maxpages.com/donadeli/Aliases.htm; sources of information for these aliases are not included. An extensive list was also published in the March 2001 issue of the Sephardic genealogy periodical *ETSI*.

65. See Gedalia Yogev, *Diamonds and Coral: Anglo Dutch Jews and Eighteenth-century Trade* (Leicester: Leicester University Press, 1978).

66. Faiguenboim, et al., 163.

67. "King"; *ibid.*, 318.

68. "Treasurer"; *ibid.*, 267.

69. "Merciful"; *ibid.*, 282.

70. One of the authors' ancestors was named Peter Jacobs Branch Kennedy.

71. One of the founding families of Long Island — which demonstrates the links forged by Jewish merchants between Caribbean and New England ports.

72. Faiguenboim, et al., 330.

73. A surname that entered New York with the Dutch.

74. Very numerous, documented in Amsterdam, Bayonne, Bordeaux, Hamburg, Altona, Pernambuco, Bahia, Rio de Janeiro, Brazil, Porto, Portugal, Jamaica, Spanish-town, Hunt's Bay, Kingston, New York, London, Belgium, Tunisia and Dominican Republic; Faiguenboim, et al., 210.

75. Amsterdam, Curaçao, Brazil, Fundâo, Portugal, London, Mexico City, Barbados, Dominican Republic, Panama; *ibid.*, 371.

76. One of the most prestigious English Jewish names, according to Jacobs (1901–1906).

77. Marcus (1973), 116f.

78. Faiguenboim, et al., 273; but cf. Menk, 320, who derives the name from the Polish city of Grätz.

79. Baltimore: Johns Hopkins, 1992, esp. 14.

80. See Jacobs, 1901–1906.

81. See Hirschman and Yates, *When Scotland was Jewish.*

82. See Hirschman and Yates, *When Scotland was Jewish.*

83. Also included in *When Scotland was Jewish.*

84. "Early used by Jews as hypocoristic form of 'Menahem' > Menke, partly also of 'Menasheh' > Manasses" (Menk, 510–11).

85. Also included in *When Scotland was Jewish.*

86. Stora: see Faiguenboim, et al., 397.

87. A contraction like Katz, from Kohan Zedek, "righteous priest."

88. See "Sephardic Population Figures through History," available at www.sephardim.com/html/lore.html.

Chapter 3

1. David Beers Quinn and Alison Quinn, eds., *First Colonists: Documents on the Planting of the First English Settlements in North America, 1584–1590* (Raleigh: North Carolina Division of Archives and History, 1982), esp. xi.

2. Flori, Amsterdam, in Faiguenboim, et al., 260.

3. Faiguenboim, et al., 356. Note there was a Pena in London, as well as many other places.

4. Stanley M. Hordes, *To the End of the Earth* (New York: Columbia University Press, 2005), 72–103.

5. Barnavi, 126–27.

6. Compare Bassani (Faiguenboim, et al., 193).

7. Faiguenboim, et al., 326, with mention of London.

8. Nicholas Hagger, *The Secret Founding of America* (London: Watkins, 2007), goes further and sees a generalized conspiracy linked to Freemasons and Francis Bacon's New Atlantis, which we reject as too much *post hoc* thinking.

9. Cesarani, 2.

10. Cecil Roth, *The Life of Menasseh Ben-Israel: Rabbi, Printer and Diplomat* (New York: Arno, 1961), 164.

11. Barnavi, esp. 22, 256–57.

12. Faiguenboim, et al., 208.

13. Qtd. in Quinn and Quinn, 50–54.

14. James McDermott, *Martin Frobisher, Elizabethan Privateer* (New Haven: Yale University Press, 2001), 316–18.

15. *Ibid.*

16. Milton, 135–40.

17. A fairly comprehensive bibliography on the subject down to 2002 appears in Adam S. Eterovich, *Croatia and Croatians and the Lost Colony 1585–1590.*

18. E.g., Robert Lacey, *Sir Walter Ralegh* (New York: Phoenix, 2001).

19. Perhaps Ravel, from Mallorca and Marseille (Faiguenboim, et al., 370).

20. Probably Clerle, from Venice (Faiguenboim, et al., 227).

21. The Emmanuel family was prominent in London, among other locations (Faiguenboim, et al., 249).

22. Jacob, Jacub, Jacubs, Jacobi: in characteristic denial, Reaney states categorically that the surname "was not Jewish" (251); further, Abraham, he says, "was not confined to Jews" (1). Jacobs in modern times is the tenth best known English surname (Jacobs, "Personal Names").

23. Minor and its variants is a well-established Melungeon surname.

24. Cooper, another Melungeon surname.

25. Probably from Wizgan/Wizegan, derived from Ait Ouezgan, a Moroccan Berber town, meaning "black" (Faiguenboim, et al., 421). The "Irish" Indian trader Eleazar Wiggan was a self-declared Jew on the Carolina frontier active from about 1700.

26. Jacobs, "Personal Names," notes that Jones was a favorite civil name for the sacred name Jonas.

27. Faiguenboim, et al., 353. Stern, 40.

28. I.e., Barnett, a common Jewish surname.

29. Sweet, i.e., sugar merchant, candymaker, often Jewish or Moorish occupations.

30. Freimann or Freymann in German; see Menk, 286.

31. Hannah, as in the industrialist kingmaker Mark Hanna; see Menk, 343; Faiguenboim, et al., 281.

32. Cavers/Chavis, mostly Portuguese (Faiguenboim, et al., 225).

33. Aithcock, Hitchcock, from Isaac, Iztak (Jacobs, 1901–1906).

34. Brébois is perhaps the same as Brebby listed in Faiguenboim, et al., 210.

35. Charles E. Hatch, *The First Seventeen Years: Virginia, 1607–24* (Charlottesville: University of Virginia Press, 1957).

36. Gates, like Yates, derived from the Hebrew anagram GZ *Ger Zedek*, "righteous convert, stranger" (Jacobs, 1901–1906).

37. According to immigration specialist Eric Richards (*Britannia's Children*, London: Hambledon and London, 2004, 52), forty thousand Scotsmen immigrated to Poland in the first half of the seventeenth century. Scottish Jewish names like Gordon and Cooper soon became common among Ashkenazi Jews.

38. Faiguenboim, et al., 361.

39. Richards, 29.

40. Source: http://www.ku.edu/carrie/docs/texts/ordinanc.html.

41. Pountis is perhaps a corruption of Ponte; see Faiguenboim, et al., 361.

42. Harwood: Har is Hebrew for "mountain" and is found in several Jewish names (e.g. Harari, Harboun, Harby).

43. Maycock could designate Mechach, a Jewish surname in Tunisia (Faiguenboim, et al., 317).

44. Poole: Pool/de Sola Pool, in London, New York (Faiguenboim, et al., 361).

45. Chaplin: Jacobs, "Personal Names."

46. Harris, thirteenth most frequent name of Jewish donors to charity in England (Jacobs, "Personal Names").

47. Wiseman/Wizman, a predominantly Moroccan Jew-

ish surname from the town Ait Izman (Faiguenboim, et al., 421).

48. Guggenheim: Menk, 328.

49. Abraham Lavender, "DNA and the Sephardic Diaspora: Spanish and Portuguese Jews in Europe," *HaLAPID* 10/1 (2003), 1–7.

50. Bagsell from BaK, *beney kedoshim,* "descendants of martyrs," with the addition of the so-called theophoric suffix -el. Menk, 150.

51. Eli Faber, *A Time for Planting: The First Migration, 1654–1820; The Jewish People in America* (Baltimore: Johns Hopkins, 1995).

52. Varon/Baroun is a very widespread Sephardic name, even today, as in the British entertainer Sasha Baron Cohen; see Faiguenboim, et al., 191, 414.

53. Clan Lovat is included in *When Scotland Was Jewish.*

54. Bagby is a contraction formed on BaK for Hebrew "bney kedoshim," meaning "children of the martyrs of _____" (Menk, 150).

55. Menk, 671; think of entertainer Dinah Shore and journalist Daniel Schorr. Faiguenboim, et al., 386.

56. It is sometimes objected that Jewish-sounding names were only Biblical and adopted by Christians from their study of the Old Testament. Shoshanah is a good example of a Hebrew name that is non-biblical, based instead on Jewish legends (Gorr 83).

57. He is another ancestor of Teresa Panther-Yates. Family legend has it that the Rameys originated in ancient Egypt.

58. Byrd is perhaps translated from Hebrew Zipporah, used of both males and females. In Germany, the Jewish surnames Vogel, Fogel and Feiglin are examples (Gorr, 87). In general, see Alden Hatch, *The Byrds of Virginia: An American Dynasty, 1670 to the Present* (New York: Holt, Rhinehart and Winston, 1969), esp. 36, 48, 51, 118, 141, 165. William Byrd the composer also married a cousin, Juliana (a favorite Jewish name) Byrd (1568). Their children were Christopher (a good crypto-Jewish name), Elizabeth, Rachel (Hebrew), Mary, Catherine, Thomas and Edward.

59. Sacheverell appears to be derived from a contraction of Hebrew *zera kodesh* "holy seed," as in the names Sachs, Saks and the like (Menk, 641).

60. The respective Huguenot ancestors of author Donald Yates and his wife Teresa, Jean Pierre Bondurant (from Bon and Duran) and Pierre Prevot/Prevatt (Templar name from the Channel Islands) came on the same ship, the *Peter and Anthony.*

61. Robert Beverley, *The History of the Present State of Virginia* (London: R. Parker, 1705).

62. Paul C. Nagel, *The Lees of Virginia* (New York: Oxford University Press, 1990), esp. 11.

63. Gist is the same name as Guest, Gozzi, Costa, Kist, Gass and Gast and seems to go back to the name of one of the noble converts in Khazaria (Hirschman and Yates, 2007); cf. Faiguenboim, et al., 231f. Jean Muir and Maxwell Dorsey, *Christopher Gist of Maryland and Some of his Descendants 1659–1957* (Chicago: Swift). On Guest, see Faiguenboim, et al., 272.

64. Byrd quoted in Moses Coit Tyler, *Patrick Henry* (London: Chelsea House, 1980), 1.

65. On Aberdeen see Hirschman and Yates (2007), pp. 152–91, for a discussion of the Jewish and Muslim presence.

66. Alf J. Mapp, Jr., *The Faiths of Our Fathers: What America's Founders Really Believed* (New York: Fall River, 2006), 88.

67. *Ibid.,* 94.

68. Shelton is possibly from "shell-man," that is, "pilgrim, wayfarer." The Sheltons were aristocratic and intermarried neighbors of the Coopers in the English Midlands. Both families came to Britain as retainers under William the Conqueror. Sheldon, on occasion, is a Jewish first name today.

Chapter 4

1. *The American Colonies from Settlement to Independence* (New York: Norton, 1976), 26–29.

2. *Albion's Seed* (New York: Oxford University Press, 1989), 17.

3. Simmons, 16.

4. Menk, 507.

5. William Bradford, *Of Plymouth Plantation,* ed. Samuel Eliot Morison (New York: Knopf, 2001), esp. xxvi–xxviii, 20n.

6. Recall the earlier colonists we have discussed surnamed Laydon.

7. "Family Tree of the Jewish People," www.jewishgen.com, s.vv.

8. Weston: "Family Tree of the Jewish People," s. v. It was sometimes spelled Westron.

9. Probably originally Jorges; see Faiguenboim, et al., 294.

10. Morison, 199.

11. Shirley: Hebrew *shor* plus *lea,* meadow. "Family Tree of the Jewish People," s.v. Beauchamp is Norman, but that does not exclude the founder from being Jewish, as William the Conqueror brought Jews to England to run its civil administration.

12. A Sephardic Raina family lived in Amsterdam at the time (Faiguenboim, et al., 370).

13. Morison, 352. As in the motion picture series *Star Wars* by director George Lucas (who is Jewish), Anakin is the name of a despotic ruler.

14. See Gitlitz, 88, 100, 118, 135–37, 141, 158–59, 166, 329, 502, 516, 627, esp. Chapter 5, "Attitudes Toward Christian Beliefs."

15. Quoted in Wiesenthal, 228.

16. *Colonial Massachusetts: A History* (New York: Knopf, 1979), 25, 352.

17. "Family Tree of the Jewish People," s.v.

18. Stora: Faiguenboim, et al., 402.

19. Source: http://www.law.ou.edu/hist/massbay.html (accessed April 20, 2010).

20. Many of this name, also spelled Goffe and Gough, in "Family Tree of the Jewish People," s.vv.

21. Bass, Vass: Faiguenboim, et al., 193. A famous bearer of the surname was Saul Bass, American graphic designer and filmmaker known for his innovations in title credits (1920–1996).

22. Probably from Bend (Benedict, "blessed," Hebrew *baruch*) plus the usual theophoric suffix. Cf. Bendix: Menk, 165.

23. Cone/Coni: Faiguenboim, et al., 230.

24. Reveres were numerous in Italy (Faiguenboim, et al., 370). Paul Revere's family was allegedly Huguenot.

25. Ames: "Family Tree of the Jewish People," s.v. Reaney and Wilson conflate Ames with Amies, Amice, Amize, Amis, Amys and Amiss ("friend … a name for the lower classes, especially the slaves"), although they do not explain why the English noblemen and country gentry recorded from 1221 onwards would have borne such déclassé names. They further specify that Amos, "due to the influ-

ence of the Biblical name ... was not used in England before the Reformation."

26. Chiver: Faiguenboim, et al., 226.

27. *Ibid.*, 285.

28. As in the Viennese logician Rose Rand (1903–1980).

29. Dana: named for a Berber tribe (Faiguenboim, et al., 237).

30. Amir (Prince): Faiguenboim, et al., 177.

31. *Quakers and Baptists in Colonial Massachusetts* (Cambridge: Cambridge University Press, 2004), esp. 3, 44f., 73.

32. Koppel: Menk, 434. The popular eighteenth century ballad "Robin Adair" tells the story of an English lady who had a romantic adventure with a dashing and witty young man rejected by her family. Her true name was Lady Caroline Keppel. The offspring of the affair, Sir Robert Adair (1763–1855), was remembered in the will of Indian trader and author James Adair, who, we have proposed, had Jewish ancestry as well.

33. Flood, Flud, Floyd: "Family Tree of the Jewish People," s.vv. In the authors' families, Floods intermarried with Cooper, Massey and Bondurant, proven crypto–Jews, including Moses and Nathan Flood.

34. Rey: Faiguenboim, et al., 370.

35. T.H.H. Breen, *America Past and Present* (New York: HarperCollins, 2001), 7, 51.

36. Matar, 83–108.

37. Breen, 53, 97.

38. Christine Heyrman, *Commerce and Culture* (New York: Norton, 1984), 14, 128, 104, 113–16, 138, 140, 242f.

39. Wise: Adath Yisroel, 87–88.

40. Fischer, 127–30.

41. The family subsequently changed its name to Townsend to escape association with the witchcraft trials.

42. Nurse: yet another relative of Melungeon Teresa Panther-Yates. The Newberrys (Newburgh) trace back to the earls of Warwick, participants in the Norman Invasion of England in 1066. Newberry DNA has proved to be Danish (haplogroup I1a) like so many of the noble Norman families. Descendants founded a college and department store chain in the South. See "Family Tree of the Jewish People," s.v.

43. Hawk is a translation of Falco(n); Farrar means "smith" in Spanish; and Hart is the eleventh most frequent Jewish surname among supporters of English charitable causes (Jacobs 1901–1906).

44. Charles Upham, *Salem Witchcraft*. 2 vols., orig. published 1867 (New York: Unger, 1959).

45. Corey: Faiguenboim, et al., 231.

46. Good(e) is one of the Davidic surnames, also in the family genealogy of Teresa Panther-Yates.

47. Cf. Fischer, 94–95.

48. Nicholas Wade, "Study Raises Possibility of Jewish Tie for Jefferson," *The New York Times*, February 28, 2007. According to Mapp (2–21), Jefferson's religion evolved into a Deist stance that was self-consciously anti–Christian and in sympathy with Jews, sharing many positions with Freemasonry: one of his correspondents was Thomas Cooper (Chapter Ten). Jefferson particularly "deplored the political activities of the Catholic Church" and "rejected the trinitarian concept of Father, Son, and Holy Ghost (Spirit)." He was the framer of the Virginia Statute for Religious Freedom. More than any other founding father, it was Jefferson who fought against an established church.

49. Chelsea, MA, DNA Project at http://www.family-treedna.com/public/Chelsea.Revere.Winthrop.Ma/, James Denning, project administrator.

50. Jack Fruchtman, Jr., *Thomas Paine: Apostle of Freedom* (New York: Basic, 1994), esp. 21.

51. On some similarities of Calvinism and Judaism, see Hirschman and Yates (2007), 192–204.

Chapter 5

1. On the Jews of the Dutch Republic, see Miriam Bodian, *Hebrews of the Portuguese Nation: Conversos and Community in Early Modern Amsterdam* (Bloomington: Indiana University Press, 1997).

2. Hudde, perhaps from *Jude*, "Jew."

3. Paun, i.e., Peacock, Pavon (Faiguenboim, et al., 355), Pfau (Menk, 586), a Persian symbol important to Sephardic Jews, also a house sign in the Frankfort ghetto.

4. Buych is perhaps the same as German Jewish Bueck, Bück (see Menk, 209).

5. On Sem, Faiguenboim, et al., 388; Amsterdam, Dutch Brazil.

6. Van Os was a Jewish family, according to the Web site "Dutch Jewry" at akevoth.org.

7. Els N. Jacobs, *In Pursuit of Pepper and Tea: The Story of the Dutch East Indies Company* (Zutphen: Wahlberg Purs, 1991), esp. 76–77, 86.

8. Many of America's "Sephardic Elite," as described in Stephen Birmingham's book *The Grandees*, passed through Hamburg, long Germany's main port. Hamburg(er) has a full page devoted to it as a Jewish surname in Menk, 340–41.

9. Quoted in Taylor, 248.

10. Amsterdam's Dutch Resistance Museum, formerly a synagogue and Jewish cultural center, bears Plancius' name and a star of David.

11. Cf. Blau in Menk, 174.

12. Menk, 701. The designation "actor" was often given to prominent members of the Jewish community who enacted parts in Purim plays (Jacobs, 1906–1911). For genealogies, see the "Dutch Jewry" Web site at akevoth.org.

13. Van Cleaf Bachman, *Peltries or Plantations: The Economic Policies of the Dutch West India Company in New Netherland, 1623–1639* (Baltimore: Johns Hopkins University Press, 1969).

14. Mordechai Arbell, *The Jewish Nation of the Caribbean* Jerusalem (Gefen, 2002), 59.

15. Vogels: Menk, 744.

16. Mau: Menk, 521.

17. Pelgrom: see "Dutch Jewry" on the Jewish family and descendants.

18. May: Menk, 522.

19. Nochem: Menk, 525.

20. Eelckens: Menk, 257f.

21. Engel: Menk, 261.

22. Bachman, 50.

23. J. Franklin Jameson, *Narratives of New Netherland 1609–1664* (New York: Scribner's, 1909).

24. Bachman, 75.

25. Sylva, Silva: Faiguenboim, et al., 392f.

26. Bachman, 81.

27. Hamel: Faiguenboim, et al., 280f.

28. Tobago: Arbell, 58–66.

29. Taine genealogies are based on http://www.olivetree-genealogy.com/hug/surnames/taine.shtml, by Lorine McGinnis Schulze, 1996.

30. Montana: Faiguenboim, et al., 331.

31. Casier information is drawn from Schulze. See also "Dutch Jewry" Web site.

32. Uzille: Faiguenboim, et al., 409. The family was an important one in Amsterdam.

33. Gerritsen , Buys, Lucas, Slot, Duyts, Brouwer: "Dutch Jewry" Web site.

34. Henry G. Bayer, *The Belgians, First Settlers in New York and in the Middle States* (New York: Devlin-Adair, 1925).

35. Toeni: Faiguenboim, et al., 406.

36. Damen: "Dutch Jewry" Web site.

37. James Van der Zee, *The Harlem Book of the Dead* (New York: Morgan and Morgan, 1978).

38. Joachime: "Dutch Jewry" Web site.

39. Cats: "Dutch Jewry" Web site; Menk, 415; cf. Jacobs, 1906–1911.

40. Van Valkenburg: "Dutch Jewry" Web site.

41. See Jacob Cats, *Complete Works* (1790–1800, 19 vols.), later editions by van Vloten (Zwolle, 1858–1866; and at Schiedam, 1869–1870); Pigott, *Moral Emblems, with Aphorisms, and c., from Jacob Cats* (1860); and P.C. Witsen Gejisbek, *Het Leven en de Verdienstenwan Jacob Cats* (1829). For the name, see Jacobs (1901–1906).

42. Printz: Menk, 600.

43. Michael G. Kammen, *Colonial New York: A History* (New York: Scribner's, 1975).

44. Joyce D. Goodfriend, *Before the Melting Pot: Society and Culture in Colonial New York City, 1664–1730* (Princeton, NJ: Princeton University Press, 1992), esp. 15.

45. Bresteede, Breasted: "Family Tree of the Jewish People." James Henry Breasted (1865–1935) was the first American citizen to obtain a degree in Egyptology and the author of numerous books on the subject.

46. Peyster: Menk, 583.

47. Van der Spiegel: "Dutch Jewry" Web site.

48. Turck, Turk, Türk: Menk, 736.

49. Bosch: "Dutch Jewry" Web site.

50. Loackermanns: Faiguenboim, et al., 313; "Dutch Jewry" Web site.

51. Maurits, Hoffman, Marius, Romeyn, Anthony, Groen: "Dutch Jewry" Web site.

52. Sueiro: Faiguenboim, et al., 397; cf. Soeiro and Suero.

53. Papo or Papini, both diminutives of Giacomo (Faiguenboim, et al., 354).

54. Van der Zee, 292–93.

55. *Ibid.*

56. Kammen, 75.

57. Goodfriend, 151–53.

58. Franks: Faiguenboim, et al., 261f. Franco designated "one from Eastern Europe, or Byzantine lands in the Levant, where Jewish traders were 'free'" to come and go.

59. Gomez from Gomos, "man"; see Faiguenboim, et al., 271f.

60. Kammen, 232f.

61. Based on Kammen, also on Patricia Bonomi, *A Factious People: Politics and Society in Colonial New York* (New York: Columbia University Press, 1971), esp. 60, 63.

62. Bonomi, 145.

63. Bellomont: Faiguenboim, et al., 135.

64. See Cathy Matson, *Merchants and Empire: Trading in Colonial New York* (Baltimore: Johns Hopkins University Press, 1998.

65. Bonomi, 70–71.

66. Levinston: personal communication from a Clan Livingstone member.

67. Solomon: "Dutch Jewry" Web site.

68. Lucena: Faiguenboim, et al., 313f.

69. de Wolff: "Dutch Jewry" Web site.

70. Matson, 61.

71. *Ibid.*, 98.

72. Levinus: "Dutch Jewry" Web site.

73. Franklin D. Roosevelt's ancestor was Clinton Roosevelt, a founding member of the Columbian Lodge of the Order of the Illuminati in New York City in 1785 (Hagger 141).

74. Pacheco Faiguenboim, et al., 353: Amsterdam, London, New York.

75. Matson, 155.

76. George Way of Plean and Romilly Squire, *Scottish Clan & Family Encyclopedia* (New York: Barnes and Noble, 1999).

77. Decker: "Dutch Jewry" Web site.

78. Barnet: Jacobs, 1906–1911.

79. Koons, Kuntz: Jacobs, 1906–1911; cf. Menk, 446f.

80. Maszig: Faiguenboim, et al., 322.

81. Muche: Faiguenboim, et al., 334.

82. Schoeck: Menk, 667, 673.

83. Rosman: "Dutch Jewry" Web site; Menk, 632.

84. Coronel was the honorific title accorded to Abraham Señor when he "converted" to Catholicism (Faiguenboim, et al., 230). In Southeastern U.S. records, a Joseph Cornell was the Indian interpreter in Tallassee in Creek country. His daughter by a Tuckabatchee woman married Alexander McGillvray, known as emperor of the Creeks and Spanish superintendent general of the Creek Nation, a partner of the Pensacola trading firm of Panton, Leslie whose Creek name was Hoboi Hilli Mikko ("Good Child King"). Cornells were prominent for two centuries in Creek and Choctaw affairs.

85. Semmes: Faiguenboim, et al., 387.

Chapter 6

1. For Penn and his family, we have relied on the Penn Family Web: http://www.cems.uwe.ac.uk/~rstephen/living-easton/local_history/Penn/Penn_family_part_2.html; Penn Family History and Genealogy Countee Cullen Web site: http://www.coroinn.com. Genealogical Register of Plymouth Families, William T. Davis, Boston: Damrell and Upham, 1899. *Colonial Families of the United States of America*, George Mackenzie, Norbury, New York, 1907. The Families Bruce Cox Web site: http://awt.ancestry.com/cgi-bin/igm.cgi?op=GETanddb=bcox2899andid=I14160. Gale M. Roberts: http://awt.ancestry.com/cgi-bin/igm.dgi?op=GETanddb=galerobertsandid=I062530. "William Penn in Pennsylvania," Pennsylvania Historical and Museum Commission Web site: http://www.dep.state.pa.us/dep/PA_Env-Her/William_Penn.htm.

2. Jean R. Soderland, *William Penn and the Founding of Pennsylvania* (Philadelphia: University of Pennsylvania Press, 1983), 103, 101, 148, 167, 169–170.

3. Harvey, 62.

4. *Ibid.*, 8.

5. Soderland, 199–200. Faiguenboim, et al., 304.

6. Fell: "trader in furs, hides."

7. Anna Miller Watring and F. Edward Wright, *Bucks County, Pennsylvania Church Records of the 17th and 18th Centuries, Vol. 2, Quaker Records: Falls and Middletown Monthly Meetings* (Baltimore: Heritage, 2003).

8. Buckman: Menk, 209; Faiguenboim, et al., 314.

9. Silbermann, Goldmann, Kristeller, Elfmann, Seidemann, Pfeffermann, Salzmann, Diamant, Färber, Feber, Roth: Menk, 689, 309, 441, 257, 682, 586, 646, 239, 269, 633.

10. Binzwanger: Stern, s.v.; Menk, 181.

11. Kuntz: Menk, 446.

12. Engel: a translation of Malachi; *ibid.*, 261.

13. Fuchs: adopted for Feiss, which comes from Feibus; *ibid.*, 294.

14. There are 9,722 instances of it in the 1998 German telephone book: *ibid.*, 323.

15. See Jacobs, 1901–1906; Menk, 415.

16. Menk, 496.

17. As in Susan Sontag, the American essayist; *ibid.*, 698.

18. It comes from the town of Loria in Italy (Faiguenboim, et al., 314).

19. Morgenstern: Menk, 545. Faiguenboim, et al., 413.

20. Iconoclasts: Robin Cormack, *Writing in Gold, Byzantine Society and its Icons* (London: George Philip, 1985).

21. Paulicians: Nina G. Garsoian, *Armenia between Byzantium and the Sasanians* (London: Variorum, 1985).

22. Bogomils Stephen Runciman, *The Medieval Manichee: A Study of the Christian Dualist Heresy* (Cambridge: Cambridge University Press, 1947).

23. Waldensians: Alexis Muston, *The Israel of the Alps: A Complete History of the Waldenses and Their Colonies* (1978).

24. Cathars and Albigensians: Rene Weis, *The Yellow Cross: The Story of the Last Cathars* (New York: Penguin, 1998).

25. Richard Rex, *The Lollards: Social History in Perspective* (New York: Palgrave, 2002).

26. Simon: Menk, 690f.

27. Oscar Kuhns, *The German and Swiss Settlement of Colonial Pennsylvania* (Baltimore: Genealogical Publishing, 2002).

28. *Ibid.*, 17, 34.

29. Eshleman, 43, 45.

30. Keith A. Dull, *Early Families of York County, Pennsylvania* (Baltimore: Heritage, 1995).

31. Boner: Faiguenboim, et al., 211.

32. Blum: Menk, 186f.

33. Charles Henry Hart, "The Franks Family." *Pennsylvania Magazine of History and Biography* 34/2 (1910).

34. *Tax List of Berks County, Pennsylvania of 1767* (Baltimore: Heritage, 2003).

35. John Pitts Launey, *First Families of Chester County, Pennsylvania* (Baltimore: Heritage, 2003).

36. Day: as in the Irish-English actor Daniel Day-Lewis, whose mother is of Baltic Jewish descent and whose father is the British poet laureate Cecil Day-Lewis.

37. Massey: probably from *mazzi*, Medieval Hebrew for a precocious girl of uncanny knowledge. Henry James titled one of his novels *What Masie Knew*. Barbara Streisand played the part of a *mazzi* in the movie *Yentl*.

38. Michael H. Tepper, ed. *Emigrants to Pennsylvania, 1641–1819: A Consolidation of Ship Passenger Lists from the Pennsylvania Magazine of History and Biography* (Baltimore: Genealogical Publishing, 1975).

39. Anna Miller Watring and F. Edward Wright, *Bucks County Church Records*, Vol. 3 (Baltimore: Heritage, 2003).

40. Krohn: Menk, 441. George Crohan claimed to be Irish.

41. Bender: *Ibid.*, 165.

42. Baron means "son of strength, wealth": *ibid.*, 156. As in British comedian Sacha Baron Cohen, inventor of the character Borat.

43. We draw on Fred B. Wampler, *The Wampfler (Wampler) Family History: The 1500s–1700s* (by the author, 1986), esp. 81, 11, 15.

44. Roy H. Wampler, *A Wampler Family History* (by the author, 1999).

45. Viola, like Violetta, is a common Sephardic girl's name, also the exotic name of the famous world-weary courtesan in Alexander Dumas' book and Verdi's opera *La Traviata*. It occurs repeatedly in the genealogy of the Maryland Gist family (Chapter Seven).

46. Etter, Eder: Stern, 14.

47. Klein: Menk, 426.

48. Hirsch: *Ibid.*, 371.

49. Kaufmann is modeled on the name Jacob, meaning "merchant," a common Jewish occupation; *ibid.*, 471f.

50. Schrag: *ibid.*, 672.

51. *Ibid.*, 245.

52. Myers was once the sixth best known English Jewish name (Jacobs 1901–1906).

53. Czepler: Menk, 229.

54. See Richards, 77, 79.

Chapter 7

1. T. M. Devine, *The Tobacco Lords: A Study of the Tobacco Merchants of Glasgow and Their Trading Activities, c. 1740–90* (Edinburgh: Donald, 1975).

2. Taylor, 138–57.

3. James Walter Thomas, *Chronicles of Colonial Maryland* (Baltimore: Genealogical Publishing, rept. 1995).

4. Pache: Faiguenboim, et al., 353.

5. Silva: *ibid.*, 392f.

6. Yomtov: *ibid.*, 430. Judy Holiday was a Jewish movie actor of the 1950s and 1960s.

7. Hayes: New York (*ibid.*, 283): cf. Stern for Hays family marriages with Gratz, Etting, Michaels, de Lancey, McKenney and Minis (75–77).

8. Hamon: *ibid.*, 281.

9. Mays: *ibid.*, 322; Menk, 522. Elaine May (née Berlin in 1932) is a celebrated screenwriter, actress and director whose parents ran a Yiddish theater in Philadelphia.

10. Mansell: Faiguenboim, et al., 319.

11. Semmes: *ibid.*, 388.

12. Tabbs: *ibid.*, 401.

13. Kennedy: *ibid.*, 218. We propose the original name of the famous Kennedys of Hyannis Port, Massachusetts, may have been Italian Candiani, filtered through the French form Canada — from Candy, the old name for the Turkish capital of Crete. Genealogies of the Irish branch of the Kennedys do not go farther back than Patrick Kennedy, a prosperous farmer of Dunganstown, County Wexford, Ireland, who was born about 1785 and whose son immigrated to America. The family was probably of French origin before it became Irish. Both Cassel (a sept of Clan Kennedy pointing to a region in southern France) and Canady appear on a list of refugee French Huguenots to Ireland.

14. Ali: *ibid.*, 173.

15. Arey/Aree: *ibid.*, 180.

16. Isaacs: Menk, 387f.

17. Edward Cooper was evidently the son of William and Elizabeth Williamson Cooper, a merchant family based in Norfolk. William (d. 1732) was the son of William Cooper and Ann Bailey, a mulatto from the Caribbean. On the confusion between half–Indian and half–African, refer to Theresa M. Hicks, *South Carolina Indians, Indian Traders and Other Ethnic Connections beginning in 1670* (Spartanburg: Reprint, 1998), xiii: "understood to be 'one born of an Indian mother' ... with particular reference to children born of Indian women and the Indian Traders ... 'half-Indian.'" The term is consistently taken out of historical context by Paul Heinegg, *Free African Americans of Virginia*,

North Carolina, South Carolina, Maryland and Delaware,
available online at www.freeafricanamericans.com, leading
him to populate the southern colonies with African men
owning land and marrying white women.

18. Boone, Buen: Faiguenboim, et al., 211; Appendix A.

19. Brezca: *ibid.*, 210.

20. Jacobs, 1901–1906, s.v.

21. The question of the conqueror Tamerlane's religious
beliefs has been a matter of controversy. His veneration of
the house of the Prophet Mohammed, the spurious genealogy on his tombstone taking his descent back to Ali, and
the presence of Shiites in his army led some observers and
scholars to call him a Shiite. However, his official religious
counselor was the Hanafite scholar Abd al Jabbar Khwar-
azmi. Timur's religious practices with their admixture of
Turco-Mongolian shamanistic elements belonged to the Sufi
tradition. Timur avowed himself the disciple of Sayyid
Baraka, the holy man of the commercial city of Timidh.
He also constructed one of his finest buildings at the tomb
of Ahmad Yaassawi, who was doing the most to spread Folk
Islam among the nomads.

22. Reine: Queen (Esther), the part played by a leader
of the synagogue during Purim (Jacobs 1901–1906).

23. Simha: Faiguenboim, et al., 393. For the name as
Hebrew but non-biblical, Gorr, 84.

24. Hud: abbreviated form of Yehudah (Jacobs 1901–
1911).

25. Falco: Faiguenboim, et al., 255.

26. Speyer: Jacobs, 1901–1906. The medieval seat of an
important Jewry gives us one of the most common Jewish
surnames, Shapiro.

27. Hyett, Hyatt, Khiat: Faiguenboim, et al., 283, 301.

28. Falner, Faulkner: Faiguenboim, et al., 255; Menk,
269. Arabs domesticated and bred falcons and hawks for
the first time.

29. Franco: Faiguenboim, et al., p. 261f. Under the rule
of Francisco Franco during World War II, the Spanish borders were kept open for Jewish refugees from Vichy France
and Nazi-occupied territories in Europe. Spanish diplomatic
protection was extended to Sephardic Jews in Hungary, Slo-
vakia and the Balkans. Spain was a safe haven for all Jewish
refugees and anti–Semitism was not official policy under
the Franco regime. Franco's Jewish origins are evident in
the other surnames in his family tree as well: Bahamonde,
del Pilar, Pardo, de Andrade, de la Paz and Villalva. Through
his mother he was descended from Portuguese royalty.

30. Gale: Hebrew Jael, Yehuel, Jehiel and Scottish Yell.

31. The word "peach" is derived from "Persian apple."

32. Cf. Menk, 496–500.

33. Faiguenboim, et al., 143.

34. Peacock: *ibid.*, 355.

35. Beck is formed from the abbreviation BaK, *bnei kedoshim*, "blood of the martyrs," as in Leo Baeck, London
rabbi; Menk, 150f.

36. Faiguenboim, et al., 256.

37. Menk, 520.

38. Mazza: Faiguenboim, et al., 322–23.

39. *DES*, 301.

40. Jacobs, 1901–1906; Adath Yisroel, 63.

41. Facit: Faiguenboim, et al., 255.

42. Adath Yisroel, 69.

43. Menk, 294.

44. Faiguenboim, et al., 377.

45. See Hirschman, 2005.

46. In story and song, the name Adair was connected to
that of Currie (Arabic Khoury, Kori). Currie, who held the
castle of Dunskey, was declared a rebel, robber, and pirate.

A proclamation was made that whoever should produce
Currie, dead or alive, should be rewarded with his fortunes.
Adare killed Currie and presented Currie's head to the king
(Robert I the Bruce, ruled 1306–1329). He got the lands
and the family was known ever afterwards as the Adairs of
Portree. When a castle was built on the spot in Dumfrieshire
where Currie was struck down, it was called Kilhilt. The
beheading of the pirate Currie appears in the Adair crest,
which depicts "a man's head couped and bloody." The
origin of the name Adair is usually explained as Gaelic, cognate with Edzaer, meaning "the ford of the oaks," but the
Celtic etymology of the name from Gaelic *ath* "oak" and
dare "ford," obviously covers up the original Hebrew. Edzaer
does not even sound like Athdare or Adare. Adairs proper
do not appear in Scottish history until the fourteenth
century, long after Gaelic ceased to be the language of the
aristocracy and had been replaced by Scots, a dialect of
English.

47. Hirschman, 2005.

48. Taylor, 140–50.

49. See Archibald Henderson, "A Pre-Revolutionary
Revolt in the Old Southwest," *The Mississippi Valley Historical Review* 17/2 (1930), 191–212.

50. This unusual name was borne by several prominent
colonial Americans, including Joseph Gist, a business
partner of George Washington, and the land agent, spy and
military guide Christopher Gist (1705–1759), whose grandson was George Guest (usually identified with Sequoyah).
It appears to come from Altaic Turkic GWSTṬ/Gosṭaṭā,
Heb. גרסטטא, the name of a line of Khazar nobles who
embraced Judaism as early as the seventh or eighth century
CE (Golb and Pritsak, 35–40). The Byzantine form was
Κώστας. The same aristocratic line later joined the migration to Kiev and the Ukraine when the Jewish empire in
the east moved into Central Europe. Their name was rendered in Latin letters as *Gostou-n/s* as early as the eighth
century. In Spain, after the ninth century, the family
assumed the name Da Costa, which they derived from
"God's rib." Acosta is a variant. This became Kist in Ashke-
naz (*Ger.* "coast," through a pun on *costa*, which could mean
"rib" or "coast"). From Golb and Pritsak's account, then, it
appears likely that the Da Costa and Gist families of Spain,
Italy, the Low Lands, and the British Isles were originally
Turkish. A trait of Khazar Jewry in acknowledgment of their
convert origins was to adopt names that had ritual or mystical significance, such as Pesach and Yomtov, rather than
Judean tribal names such as Benjamin. The Gist name
occurs in the Ragusan/Croatian/Venetian Gozzi family of
traders, explorers, admirals, tax farmers and physicians in
Elizabethan London and the Ottoman Empire. Variants in
Britain and North America are Gass, Guess, Guest and
Goss.

Chapter 8

1. Arthur Zuckermann, *A Jewish Princedom in Feudal
France, 760–900* (New York: Columbia University Press,
1972), 167.

2. Quoting Sachar, Abraham D. Lavender, "DNA and
the Sephardic Diaspora: Spanish and Portuguese Jews in
Europe," *HaLAPID* 10/1 (2203), 1–7.

3. Benbassa, 50.

4. Philip Benedict, *The Huguenot Population of France,
1600–1685* (Darby: Diane, 1991), esp. 8.

5. Jack P. Greene, et al., *Money, Trade, and Power: Evolution of Colonial South Carolina's Plantation Society*

(Columbia: University of South Carolina Press, 2001), 28f., estimates 642 individuals.

6. Charles W. Baird, *History of the Huguenot Emigration to America* (New York: Dodd, Mead, 1885), 302–11.

7. Lavender, 186.

8. Musick: Melungeon surname.

9. Nahon, 340, qtd. in Lavender, 199.

10. Walter Edgar, *South Carolina: A History.* (Columbia: University of South Carolina Press, 1998).

11. Faiguenboim, et al., 184.

12. *Ibid.*, 396, after the Spanish town of Sotto del Barco.

13. See Eloy J. Gallegos, Eloy J. *The Melungeons: The Pioneers of the Interior Southeastern United States 1526–1997* (Knoxville: Villagra, 1997), 27.

14. Faiguenboim, et al., 354 (can also mean "mottled," "panther," and refer to town of El Pardo).

15. E.g., Alther, Kennedy, Gallegos.

16. Abell, 193.

17. Edgar, 40.

18. *Ibid.*, 43.

19. *Ibid.*, 52.

20. Hirschman, 2005.

21. Menk, 196.

22. *Ibid.*, 300.

23. *Ibid.*, 473.

24. *Ibid.*, 495, with reference to the Middle Rhineland and Saarland.

25. Schiele: *ibid.*, 656 (as in the "shocking" Viennese Jewish painter Egon Schiele, 1890–1918).

26. *Ibid.*, 674.

27. *Ibid.*, 792.

28. Haes: "Dutch Jewry" Web site.

29. Edgar, 61.

30. Faiguenboim, et al., 309f., with mention of Amsterdam, Portsea, England, Barbados, Jamaica, Falmouth, Kingston, Lacovia, El Salvador and Panama.

31. *Ibid.*, 384, with mention of Brazil, Viseu, Portugal, Amsterdam, London, Charleston, Montpellier and Buenos Aires.

32. *Ibid.*, 744, with mention of London.

33. See Hirschman and Yates, 2007.

34. Edgar, 93.

35. Faiguenboim, et al., 405.

36. Izard: as in the British Yemen-born comedian and actor Eddie Izzard (b. 1962).

37. Edgar, 212.

38. Grady McWhiney, *Cracker Culture: Celtic Ways in the Old South* (Tuscaloosa: University of Alabama Press, 1968). Another estimate of their numbers appears in James G. Leyburn, *The Scotch-Irish* (Chapel Hill: University of North Carolina Press, 1962), who writes that "millions of Americans have Scotch-Irish ancestors … at least one out of every ten or fifteen Americans was Scotch-Irish" at the time America gained its independence, and that between 1717 and the Revolutionary War some quarter of a million Ulstermen came to America" (xi, 157, 179–83).

39. *North Carolina Guide*, 26.

40. Crommelin: probably the origin of the name Cromwell in England.

41. Goya: Faiguenboim, et al., 273; as in Francisco Goya, the Spanish court painter (1746–1828).

42. *Ibid.*, 274.

43. *Ibid.*, 274.

44. Guest: *ibid.*, 274.

45. Hebrew: faithful, true; see Chapter 7.

46. Hazard: Faiguenboim, et al., 282. There is a Hazard, Kentucky, and Hazard County, Arkansas.

47. *Ibid.*, 345; Menk, 449, with mention of Hamburg and Altona.

48. De Fano: Faiguenboim, et al., 255. Perhaps also the same as Faneuil.

49. Froes, Fois: *ibid.*, 262, with reference to Leghorn.

50. *Ibid.*, 332.

51. *Ibid.*, 370.

52. *Ibid.*, 371f.

53. *Ibid.*, 405.

54. Seixas: Faiguenboim, et al., 388; the German form is Sachs, see Menk, 641.

55. Danan: Faiguenboim, et al., 237. The Denny family in Armagh dealt in foodstuffs and founded a grocery chain.

56. Storey: Stora from de Istora, Algeria (*ibid.*, 397).

57. Van der Pool: De Sola Pool was a Sephardic family in London and New York, according to Faiguenboim, et al., 61.

58. Gorr, 29f.

59. Faiguenboim, et al., 205.

60. Menk, 343.

61. Gay, Gaia, Gayas "happy"; Faiguenboim, et al., 267, 271. The name survives in a large rum distillery on Barbados, as well as in the name of the airplane that dropped the atomic bomb on Hiroshima, the *Enola Gay*.

Chapter 9

1. Allen D. Candler, et al., eds., *The Colonial Records of the State of Georgia*, 28 vols. (Athens: University of Georgia Press, 1970–1989), I 20.

2. Charles Mackay, *Extraordinary Popular Delusions and the Madness of Crowds* with a foreword by Bernard M. Baruch (New York: Barnes and Noble, 1959), esp. 2–5. Adolphe Thiers, *The Mississippi Bubble: A Memoir of John Law* (New York: Townsend, 1959).

3. Mackay, 3.

4. Stultheus lit., "house of fools." See Marcus.

5. Beverly Baker Northrop, *We Are Not Yet Conquered: The History of the Northern Cherokee Nation of the Old Louisiana Territory* (Paducah: Turner, 2001). The name Cooper is among the oldest (around 1720).

6. Adair, 447.

7. Charles Reagan Wilson and William Ferris, co-editors, Ann J. Abadie and Mary L. Hart, associate editors (Chapel Hill: University of North Carolina Press, 1989).

8. Faiguenboim, et al., 307; in the Bible Laban is the father of Leah and Rachel, Jacob's father-in-law (Genesis 24:29–60). It can also mean "from Lebanon" (the "white land"). Spellings vary: LeBon/LaBon/LaBoon (a South Carolina Huguenot gunsmith family from Rochefort, France), Labon (the favored spelling in Nacogdoches, Texas, families, also in Santa Fe, Leabon (English parish registers, Pennsylvania) and Leban (common in German and Polish lands). The name is also given as Lebo (Spanish-American and Pennsylvania Dutch), LaBeau, LaBon, LeBon, Les Baux (French Canada), Leebow, Laybon, Laban, Leban, and Laborn. A famous LaBon married a Capet in France and one of his sons was a Jacobite. The other came to South Carolina with the Gervais (Jarvis, considered a Melungeon name today) family of Maryland. This Pierre LaBon left a sizable family in upcountry Anderson County; they changed their name to LaBoon. Family members married Waters (an Indian trading family connected with Creek Mary and Sequoyah), Riddle (another Melungeon name), Moore, Rodriquez, Durant and (multiply, in cousin marriage) Gervais. The traditional Labon ungrammatically combines a

feminine article with a masculine form of the adjective — it should be either LaBonne or Lebon.

9. Majorcan name: Faiguenboim, et al., 353.

10. Menk, 642.

11. Candler, VI, 351.

12. It is the same name as one of President Barack Obama's daughters. The name was rendered Milla in early English history. Milla was the name of the wealthy widow of the Jew Samuel Mutun of Royston, near Cambridge, who was killed by Simon de Montfort in the Albigensian crusades (Michael Adler, *Jews of Medieval England*, Jewish Historical Society of England, 1939, 22). The name, therefore, was associated with French Jewry as early as 1200. In America, it became common in the tribal hierarchies of the Chickasaw, Choctaw and Creek. For instance, a Mallea (Milly) Francis was known as the "Creek Pocahontas." She was the daughter of Josiah Francis (Hillis Harjo), called the Prophet, hanged by Andrew Jackson in 1818. The Francises ("from France"), like the Coopers, were also Sephardic Jewish Indian traders in Georgia, specializing in gunsmithing and silversmithing. The only mention of Malea Cooper in historical documents is a 1768 land sale in Bute County, North Carolina, in which she appears as a witness, her name recorded as Emelea Cooper (DB-2 p. 101). Perhaps her husband, William Cooper, was away at the time.

13. Another daughter, Elizabeth White, married William Lackey in Rowan County in 1781. William had come from the ancestral seat in Scotland with his entire clan, arriving in Baltimore in 1755 at the age of two. His sons and grandchildren continued to intermarry with mixed American Indian women, settling eventually in North Alabama and forever puzzling Lackey genealogists with the source of a Melungeon identity and dark looks among such staunch Scotsmen. Whites married with Bells, Vaughans, Looneys, Gists, Joneses, Blevinses (all Cherokee families), Shankles (Dutch-Scottish Jews), Rains, a Flippo (Spanish), Phipps and, of course, Coopers (Cherokee-Choctaw-Jewish). They are all in co-author Donald Yates's family tree.

14. Zadok Cramer, *The Navigator, Containing Directions for Navigating the Monongahela, Allegheny, Ohio, and Mississippi River*, 9th ed. (Pittsburgh: Cramer, Spear and Eichbaum, 1817).

15. See Benjamin Hawkins, *Letters of Benjamin Hawkins, 1796–1806* (Savannah: Georgia Historical Society, 1974).

16. Menk, 662.

17. Faiguenboim, et al., 195.

18. Faiguenboim, et al., 208: "good day" (Yom Tov).

19. Menk, 435.

20. Candler, I 12.

21. Faiguenboim, et al., 310.

22. Candler, 1915, 404–5.

23. See Faiguenboim, et al., 177.

24. Stern, cited in Rubin, 351.

25. Faiguenboim, et al., 322.

26. Faiguenboim, et al., 333.

27. As in the Algerian-French philosopher Albert Camus.

28. Rubin, 2.

29. Candler, I 150.

30. *Ibid.*, 151–52.

31. Candler, VI, 3.

32. Faiguenboim, et al., 341–43. In 2007, as the congregation of Mickve Israel prepared to celebrate the 175th anniversary of Savannah Jewry, Nunes heirs in Georgia were contacted after some difficulty. They had no idea their famous ancestor was Jewish.

33. Rubin, 13.

34. Rubin, 13–14; Stern, 222–3.

35. Rubin, 14–15.

36. E. Merton Coulter and Albert B. Saye, *A List of the Early Settlers of Georgia* (Baltimore: Genealogical Publishing, 2001), 98. Variants of the name in England (since the twelfth century): Telfer, Telford, Tailefer, Talfourd, Rilford, Tilfourd, Tolver, Tulliver, Tolliver Talyveer. The Taliaferro family was said to be Italian. Perhaps their name came from the village of Tagliaferro in Tuscany near Florence.

37. De Lucena: Stern, 41.

38. Sheldon J. Godfrey and J.C. Godfrey, *Search out the Land: The Jews and the Growth of Equality in British Colonial America 1740–1867* (Toronto: McGill-Queen's University Press, 1998), 303.

39. A form of Shabtai; see Menk, 654. As an Ashkenazi, Sheftall and his family were the only Savannah Jews not to flee to Beth Elohim in Charleston during the War of Jenkins' Ear (1739–48), for fear of the Spanish prevailing in the conflict and bringing the Inquisition into Georgia.

40. Faiguenboim, et al., 163.

41. Coulter and Saye, 60.

42. Coulter and Saye, 82.

43. Monsanto: Faiguenboim, et al., 330f.

44. Candler, III, 391.

45. *Ibid.*, 402.

46. E.g., Bourquin, Babant, Da Roch, Galache, Huguenin, Marte, Myer, etc.; see Hirschman, 2005, 154–56).

47. Rubin, 8–9.

48. George F. Jones, *The Germans of Colonial Georgia, 1733–1783* (Baltimore: Clearfield, 1986), vi.

49. Menk, 648. Lit. "easy living," an example of a mocking name assigned to Jews.

50. See Faiguenboim, et al., 275. There was also an Indian trader in Georgia named Robert Gandy/Gundy/Gaudy.

51. Founded by the Flatau/Flatow/Zlotow family in 1812 (Menk, 277).

52. B. H. Levy, *Mordecai Sheftall: Jewish Revolutionary Patriot* (Savannah: Georgia Historical Society, 1999), 28.

53. Rubin, 18.

54. Faiguenboim, et al., 169. Ade is not listed in Coulter and Saye (2001); perhaps he came into the colony "under the radar." This is the case with many names which follow.

55. Stern, 115, 118.

56. Faiguenboim, et al., 210.

57. Faiguenboim, et al., 208; Menk, 211 (s.v. "Burgas").

58. Stern 63, 76, 123.

59. Perhaps from Kalwill, an important Jewish city in Ukraine.

60. Stern 56, 103, 111.

61. *Ibid.*, 100.

62. *Ibid.*, 33, 55, 111.

63. Faiguenboim, et al., 240.

64. *Ibid.*, with mention of Curaçao, Jamaica, Dominica, New Orleans, London, etc.; Stern, 39.

65. For Dick or Dicks as a Jewish surname, see Menk, 239. Granny Molly Dick was the wife of Richard Blevins, a pioneer in Marion County, Tenn., and the Dicks were also intermarried with the Cooper and Troxell families (recognized as Jewish).

66. Faiguenboim, et al., 378.

67. Menk, 245.

68. Faiguenboim, et al., 259.

69. Menk, 276; Stern 122.

70. Menk, 271, 294.

71. *Ibid.*, 744.

72. *Ibid.*, 281–2; Stern, 55–61.

73. *Ibid.*, 60, 105, 111, 126.

74. *Ibid.*, 97.
75. Faiguenboim, et al., 67.
76. *Ibid.*, 218.
77. Stern, 98.
78. *Ibid.*, 66, 225; Menk, 313.
79. Stern, 259.
80. *Ibid.*, 68.
81. For a Bishop Elphinstone in Aberdeen, see Hirschman and Yates, 2007, 163–5.
82. Stern, 22, 225.
83. *Ibid.*, 90–93.
84. *Ibid.*, 61.
85. *Ibid.*, 64.
86. Both authors' 7th great-grandfather.
87. Faiguenboim, et al., 307, with reference to Savannah; Stern, 1991, 27, 40, 222; Menk, 467.
88. Menk, 486–7.
89. Stern, 1991, p. 56; Menk, 496ff.
90. *Ibid.*, 200.
91. *Ibid.*, 87.
92. *Ibid.*, 134.
93. Faiguenboim, et al., 328; Stern, 1991, 138, 227.
94. Faiguenboim, et al., 332.
95. New is the Anglicized form of German Neu; Menk, 558.
96. Stern, 1991, 103; Faiguenboim, et al., 340.
97. *Ibid.*, 40; Faiguenboim, et al., 353.
98. Stern, 1991, 35.
99. Faiguenboim, et al., 355.
100. Stern, 1991, 114, 116.
101. *Ibid.*, 126, 146; Faiguenboim, et al., 370.
102. Stern, 1991, 61.
103. *Ibid.*, 22 (Sax); Menk, 642.
104. Stern, 1991, 61.
105. *Ibid.*, 193, 229.
106. *Ibid.*, 61, 74, 11; see also Hirschman and Yates, 2007, pp. 33–34, 62–63.
107. Menk, 2005, p. 676.
108. Faiguenboim, et al., 404f.
109. Stern, 1991, 87.
110. Faiguenboim, et al., 421.
111. Faiguenboim, et al., 421; Menk, 761.
112. Arbell, 2002, 218–21.
113. Rubin, 9.
114. Board minutes, 561.
115. Kathryn E. Holland Braund, *Deerskins and Duffels: Creek Indian Trade with Anglo-America, 1685–1815* (Lincoln: University of Nebraska Press, 1996), 44–48.
116. Edward Barnard later joined the Wrightsboro colony.
117. Braund, 55.
118. Levy, 30–31.
119. *Letters of Benjamin Hawkins 1796–1806*, 168.
120. Faiguenboim, et al., 320.
121. Variants are Bem Amor, Benamou, Ben Hammo, Ben Ammou, Benamu, etc., all formed from Ben Hammo: Faiguenboim, et al., 198, with mention of London, Paris, Lisbon, Madrid and Jerusalem.
122. Faiguenboim, et al., 260. LeFlore was a Choctaw chief who remained in Mississippi after the departure of the rest of the tribe to Indian Territory. He built the showpiece mansion Malmaison. Descendants changed the name back to the Portuguese form.
123. The ill-fated Darien colony was launched when 1200 Scotsmen set sail from Edinburgh in five ships in 1698. It was promoted particularly by Sir James Stuart. Like the South Sea Bubble in London in 1711, it was a harbinger of Law's Mississippi Bubble in 1720. Thousands of Scottish subjects subscribed to its stock. Another 1300 Scotsmen followed in a second expedition before the Spanish extinguished the colony (Thiers, 1859).
124. Colonial Georgia Will Book AA, 105–108. See online version at: http://robertson-ancestry.com/123-will.htm (retrieved February 13, 2010).
125. Beaverdam lies at the intersection of modern-day Virginia, Tennessee and Kentucky. Until the nineteenth-century, many were not sure what state such places as Washington County, Kingsport or Boonsboro belonged to.
126. A Germanized form of Mordecai: Menk, 518–9. The father of Communism Karl Marx was a Rhineland Jew.
127. Faiguenboim, et al., 425.

Chapter 10

1. Giant of English letters Samuel Johnson was also born in Lichfield in the same street as Ashmole a century later and attended the same grammar school.
2. "God listens." Variants: Ismael, Ishmiel, Ischmail, Ismail (Faiguenboim, et al., 290).
3. Attias: Menk, 146. Attie, Attia: Faiguenboim, et al., 183, with reference to the surname in London.
4. For biographical details, we follow Tobias Churton, *The Magus of Freemasonry: The Mysterious Life of Elias Ashmole — Scientist, Alchemist, and Founder of the Royal Society* (Rochester: Inner Traditions, 2006), esp. 36.
5. Faiguenboim, et al., 359.
6. Faiguenboim, et al., 364.
7. Elahmi: Faiguenboim, et al., 305. The vexations of etymology are illustrated by a standard account given for "Elam, Ellams, Ellam, Ellum" in Reaney's *Dictionary of English Surnames* (s.v.). Although it is by no means proven that the four forms of the heading are one and the same, born by descendants of the same forebear, the following scattered persons and locations are cited as though they share a surname and genealogy with an identical derivation: John *Ellam* 1231 (Patent of Calendar Rolls, Lancaster), Henry *de Elham* 1275 (Rotuli Hundredorum, London), Henry *de Elham* 1324 (Feet of Fines, Kent), John *Elum* 1501 (Calendar of Patent Rolls, York), Robert *Elam* 1744 (Register of Freemen of the City of York). Although York, London, Kent and Lancaster are virtually different countries, with different histories, no continuity can be claimed between the first occurrence of the name as Ellam in 1231 in Lancaster and the later forms of Elum and Elam in York three to five hundred years later. Nevertheless, it is maintained that all "variants" derive "from Elham" in Kent (a spelling, without reason, not even listed in the rubric of the entry) or "a lost *Elham* in Crayford" in Kent "or Elam Grange in Bingley." This seems grasping at straws. Setting aside whether all variants came from a place-name called Elham or Elam, the explanation does not address where *that* name originated or make clear whether a bearer received his name from it or gave it the name. Every surname in this work, which represents the accumulation of similar works for over two centuries, is subject to similar doubts and criticisms.
8. Churton, 101–102.
9. See Paul Naudon, *The Secret History of Freemasony: Its Origins and Connection to the Knights Templar* (Rochester: Inner Traditions, 2005) for a more detailed discussion of the Egyptian religious and architectural traditions which fed into Freemasonry.
10. Felicia Waldman, "Jewish Influences in Medieval

European Esotericism." Available at www.unbuc.ro/eBooks
filolgie/hebra/2-7.htm. Accessed May 8, 2010.

11. Itta: Gorr, 89f.

12. Marie Antoinette traced her ancestry back to the
twelfth-century figure Bertha von Putelendorf (Jehaes 1998).
Although most royal genealogies stop with Bertha, we have
found that one authority gives her great-great grandmother
as Judith of Schweinfurt, born before 1050 (Stamp, "Ahnenliste"). Furthermore, Judith's mother was a descendant
of Frederuna of France, consort of Charles the Simple, and
Frederuna herself was a daughter of Count Theodoricus,
an illegitimate younger son of Charlemagne by Adel. Thus
Marie Antoinette's female heritage goes back to the wife or
concubine of Theodoricus (French Thiérry), who according
to Einhard's *Life of Charlemagne* was imprisoned in a
monastery by his half-brother the emperor Louis the Pious
("Achternamenlist").

13. The name of Teresa Panther-Yates's grandmother,
Etalka Good of a Melungeon family from Tennessee.
Etalka's middle name was Vetula ("old woman"), a Jewish
"amulet name" intended to ensure long life (see Gorr, 1992,
p. 52). Etalka named one of her daughters Elzina after her
sister (Arabic for "beautiful").

14. Alessandro Barbero, *Charlemagne, Father of a Continent* (London: Folio, 2006), 16, 20.

15. Dudley Wright, *Elias Ashmole: England's Masonic Pioneer* (Whitefish: Kessinger, 2005).

16. Faiguenboim, et al., 387; Menk, 483.

17. Faiguenboim, et al., 356.

18. Family Tree of the Jewish People at www.jewishgen.
org.

19. Faiguenboim, et al., 205f.

20. *Ibid.*, 189.

21. See Harvey, 1.

22. Ashmole, 368.

23. Polish Jewish surname Choszczewski: Beider, 127.

24. Hyac: Faiguenboim, et al., 286, in reference to
Hamburg.

25. Geiger, lit. "violinist" or "violin maker" (Menk,
300). The violin and other stringed instruments were spe-
cialties of Jews. The Birds, for instance, were invited by
Henry VIII to come to England because of their musical
talents.

26. Nicholas Hagger, *The Secret Founding of America*
(London: Watkins, 2007), 87.

27. *Ibid.*, 87–88.

28. *Ibid.*, "Freemasons in Virginia and Massachusetts,"
84–106.

29. Conrad Hahn, *A Short History of the Conference of
Grand Masons in North America* (New Haven: MSA, 1963),
5.

30. Alphonse Cerza, *A Masonic Reader's Guide* (St. Louis:
Masonic Lodge of Research, 173), 106.

31. Paul Naudon, *The Secret History of Freemasony: Its
Origins and Connection to the Knights Templar* (Rochester:
Inner Traditions, 2006), 203.

32. Hagger 106, citing authorities Paul Bessel and William T. Still.

33. Ronald F. Heaton, *Masonic Membership of the Founding Fathers* (Columbus: Masonic Service Association, 1974).

34. Christopher Hodapp, *Solomon's Builders: Freemasons,
Founding Fathers and the Secrets of Washington, D.C.* (Berkeley: Ulysses, 2007).

35. Frankeln: Menk, 281. The name is a diminutive form
of Frank.

36. Faiguenboim, et al., 371.

37. *Ibid.*, 425.

38. Lewis C. Wes Cook, ed., *Colonial Freemasons* (Fulton: Missouri Lodge of Research, 1974).

39. *Starr* was used in England beginning with the Nor-
mans of any financial instrument involving Jews. It is a good
instance of a term imported by French Jews from the Judeo-
Arabic world in southern Europe. The secret place where
the king kept his IOUs and other contracts became known
as the Star Chamber after Jews were expelled from England.
Starr today is a relatively common Jewish (and Cherokee
Indian) surname, as in Belle Starr, the outlaw who married
Cherokee Sam Starr. Emmett Starr was the author of *Old
Cherokee Families and their Genealogy,* a standard Cherokee
genealogy reference work. The current president of the
Chicago Indian center is Anishnabe/Ojibwe elder George
Starr-Bresette.

40. Paul Foster Case, *The Great Seal of the United States*
(Los Angeles: Builders of Adytum, 1973–1974), 26.

41. Rubin, 94–95.

42. Menk, 561.

43. A prominent Jewish American colonial and London
merchant family.

44. Menk, 676.

45. Faiguenboim, et al., 177.

46. Tuch, Tuchman: Menk, 735. As in author Barbara
Tuchman, daughter of banker Maurice Wertheim and
granddaughter of financier Henry Morgenthau, born a
Bavarian Jew. Ragman or old clothes dealer was a typical
occupation for medieval Jews. From ragman, they sometimes proceeded to peddlers, storekeepers and department
store chain founders.

Appendix A

1. Sources: Abraham Laredo, *Les Noms des Juifs du
Maroc* (*Names of the Jews of Morocco*) (Madrid: Institut
Montano, 1978); Jose Maria Abecassis, *Genealogia Hebraica:
Portugal e Gibraltar, Secs. XVII a XX* (*Jewish Genealogy: Por-
tugal and Gibraltar, 17th to the 20th Centuries*); Joseph
Toledano, *La Saga des Familles: Les Juifs du Maroc et leurs
noms.* (*Family Sagas: The Jews of Morocco and Their Names*)
(Tel Aviv: Stavit, 1983); Joseph Toledano, *Une histoire des
familles: les noms de famille Juifs d'Afrique du Nord* (*Family
History: The Family Names of the Jews of North Africa*);
(Jerusalem: author, 1999); Maurice Eisenbeth, *Les Juifs de
l'Afrique du Nord: Demographie et Onomastique* (*Jews of
North Africa: Demographics and Onomastics*) (Algiers: Im-
primerie du lycee, 1936); Jacobs (1901–1906).

2. We are not aware of a good guide to the subject, so
we will attempt to summarize it briefly. In most Spanish
and Portuguese-speaking countries, people have at least two
surnames, one inherited from the father, the other from the
mother. In most Spanish-speaking regions, parents usually
pass on to their children the name of the father and his surname is written before the mother's (Lopez-Garcia). In Portuguese-speaking countries, however, it is the other way
around (Garcia-Lopez). In Portugal, the Azores and Brazil,
then, it is very frequent for children to get two surnames
from each of their parents, thus having usually the last surname of each of their grandparents.

In Latin American countries when a woman marries,
she may choose to drop her own maternal surname and
adopts her husband's paternal surname, with "de" ("of")
inserted between. Thus if Ángela López Sáenz marries
Tomás Portillo Blanco, she may style herself Ángela López
de Portillo.

The order rule means that the surnames of the female

branch tend to get lost as generations pass, but if the female surname is especially prestigious it may end up replacing the male surname.

Not every surname is a single word. For instance, the former Mexican president José López Portillo, whose mother was a Pacheco, adopted the full style José López Portillo y Pacheco. Other surnames derive from church names, as San José, or were changed when a person of Jewish faith converted to Christianity, as Santa Maria. The patronymic place-name "de" was common for surnames originating from Castile and Álava. In Spain, unlike in neighboring France, the prefix "de" (meaning "of") on a surname does not typically indicate noble origin.

In Spanish, most surnames ending in "-ez" originated as patronymics. Thus "López" originally meant "son of Lopo," "Fernández" meant "son of Fernando," etc. Other common examples of this are "Hernández" (from Hernando, a variant of "Ferdinand"/"Fernando"), "Rodríguez" (from "Rodrigo"), "Sánchez" (from "Sancho"), "Martínez" (from "Martín"), and "Álvarez" (from "Álvaro"). Sometimes, however, the "-ez" suffix simply means the plural (the Cortes), and in Portugal -ez usually becomes -es. Since many Jews fleeing from Spain went to Portugal their surnames were translated into Portuguese; for instance, Cortez became Cortes.

It is quite common in Brazil that someone will prefer to be called by his or her least common surname. Examples of common surnames in Brazil are Silva, Souza (Sousa), [dos] Santos and Cavalcanti (the last one of Italian origin). Therefore, even if someone inherits one of these surnames from his or her father, the maternal surname will be used instead.

3. Scali denotes a gold-thread industry conducted in Seville during the Middle Ages; the numerical equivalent of Saddock, denoting descent from that direct Cohen line.

4. Jacobs (1901–1906ab) gives the following forms: Aleuy, Elvy, Halevy, Ha-Levi, Lavey, Lebel, Leblin, Levay, Leib, Leopold, Leve, Levene, Levenson, Levi, Levie, Levien, Levin, Levinsky, Levinsohn, Levison, Levy, Lewey, Lewi, Lewin, Lewinsky, Lewinson, Lewis, Löb, Löbel, Loewe, Loewi, Louissohn, Lovy, Low, Löwy, and Lowy. To these may be added Lovat, Labat, Lavender, Lyon, Lionell and Louvain, perhaps also McLean and McClowan (Hirschman and Yates, 2007).

Appendix D

1. Abraham Sándor, "Comparison of Romany Law with Israelite Law and Indo-Aryan Traditions." Available at http://www.imninalu.net/Zakono.htm. We have added to Sándor's list from various other sources in different places.

Appendix E

1. Copies of this list in public records, as all the following ones in this appendix and elsewhere in our book, are legion in scholarly and popular literature. As far as we are informed they do not represent copyright materials. Out of convenience, we have followed in this instance the list provided by the National Park Service. Others are published all over the Internet. We make no claim that the list provided here is original, authoritative or definitive. At the same time, we have attempted to harmonize different versions and acknowledge important sources. If anyone holds the copyright to this or similar material used by us, we would appreciate hearing so that we can make the correction.

2. The original group came in May 1607, the first supply group in January 1608, and the second supply group in the fall of 1608. Occupations are given with original spellings. List is based on the records of John Smith, "Proceedings of the English Colony in Virginia" and *Generall Historie*. The record states there were "diverse others to the number of 105."

3. This is the title of the facsimile parchment record in my possession.

4. There were 144 persons in the expedition, including the 105 who remained in Virginia.

5. One of the authors' ancestors from Provence, said to have been of extremely dark appearance. The surname was probably originally a Spanish compound one, Bon-Durante, a form of the "good name" (see Appendix A). Durands/Durants were a prominent Sephardic family of rabbis, physicians and scholars who settled mostly in Provence, Marseilles, Majorca and Morocco after the Expulsion of 1492 (Faiguenboim, et al., 244), where the Bondurants originated. Jean Pierre, the immigrant, was an apothecary and vintner by profession. His mother was Gabrielle Barjon ("son of Jean"). A Barjon relative was one of the organizers of the mass escape from France, which led the Huguenots through Switzerland, Germany and finally, London, to the New World. Jean Pierre's wife, Rhoda Faur (Anglicized as Ford), also bore a Sephardic surname (Faiguenboim, et al., 256). The Bondurant family can be traced back to Génolhac, département Gard, France, to the early sixteenth century, but not before — as we have seen, often a clue invoking the date 1492. They were probably relatively new arrival from Inquisitorial Spain. In Virginia, the Bondurants intermarried again and again with Agee, Maxey, Radford and Ford cousins, a common crypto–Jewish trait.

6. Ancestor of co-author's spouse Teresa Panther-Yates. The family intermarried with Tuscarora and Cherokee Indians and was later known as Black Dutch.

Appendix J

1. Self-proclaimed Jew who married a Creek Indian woman and founded the town of Montgomery, Alabama.

Appendix K

1. As Coulter and Saye's notes make clear, the vast majority of these settlers either died within a year or two or "absconded," i.e., left the colony and moved on.

2. His widow rented out quarters to new arrivals and returned to England.

3. Their servant was Elizabeth Abraham (Coulter and Saye, 1).

4. Untiring servant to the trustees, builder of the home Wormsloe outside Savannah.

5. Menkl, 130.

6. Palatinate shoemaker family "carry'd over by Capt. Thompson at his own risk" in 1738, and "given to the Saltzburgers"; Coulter and Saye, 1).

7. Menk, 165.

8. *Ibid.*, 186–7.

9. *Ibid.*, 202.

10. On the Denneys as a Jewish family, see Chapter 8.

11. Menk, 264.

12. Faiguenboim, et al., 255, with reference to several places in Portugal.

13. *Ibid.*, 256.

14. Menk, 276.
15. *Ibid.*, 300.
16. *Ibid.*, 306.
17. *Ibid.*, 322, with reference to Grunau, Fla.
18. *Ibid.*, 444.
19. *Ibid.*, 341.
20. *Ibid.*, 341.
21. *Ibid.*, 358, with reference to Swabia.
22. *Ibid.*, 363.
23. *Ibid.*, 422. Often regarded as the same as Cooper.
24. *Ibid.*, 438.
25. *Ibid.*, 445.
26. An example of unbecoming or patronizing names given to Jews by authorities when they were ordered to have surnames in the eighteenth century.

27. *Ibid.*, 481.
28. *Ibid.*, 505.
29. *Ibid.*, 510.
30. *Ibid.*, 540.
31. "A South German name": *Ibid.*, 618.
32. *Ibid.*, 625.
33. *Ibid.*, 633, with reference to Fürth, Wurtemburg, and Flatow, Fla.
34. Ashkenazic pronunciation of *tehillah*, "song of praise": *Ibid.*, 729.
35. *Ibid.*, 733.
36. As in the name of Philadelphia's department store founded by John Wanamaker.
37. *Ibid.*, 744.
38. *Ibid.*, 747.

References

Abecassis, José Maria (1990–1991). *Genealogia Hebraica*: *Portugal e Gibraltar sécs. XVII a XX.* Lisbon: Ferin.

Abramovitz, Jack (n.d.). *They Sailed with Columbus.* E-text available at www.eductrak.com.

"Achternamenlist" Web page of Gertjan Broekhoven: http://home.zonnet.nl/broekhoven2/Broekhoven/surnlist.htm.

Adath Yisroel Burial Society Adath Yisroel Burial Societ Records — Cheshunt Cemetery (n.d.). Jewish Genealogical Society. Available online Dec. 1, 2002: http://www.jgsgb.org.uk/bury01.htm.

Adler, Michael (1939). *Jews of Medieval England.* London: Jewish Historical Society of England.

"Die Ahnenliste des bayerischen Königs Ludwig II entspricht...." Web page of Dr. Hans Peter Stamp: http://www.drstamp.de/start/a1613.html.

Arbell, Mordechai (2002). *The Jewish Nation of the Caribbean. The Spanish-Portuguese Jewish Settlements in the Caribbean and the Guianas.* Jerusalem: Gefen.

Arie, Gabriel (1929). *Genealogie de la famille Arie de 1766 a 1929.* N.p. (Pamphlet).

Attal, Robert, and Joseph Avivi (1989). *Registres Matrimoniaux de la Communaute Juive Portugaise de Tunis: XVIII-XIX siecles.* Jerusalem: Ben Zvi Institute.

Bachman Van Cleaf (1969). *Peltries or Plantations: The Economic Policies of the Dutch West India Company in New Netherland, 1623–1639.* Baltimore: Johns Hopkins University Press.

Baird, Charles W. (1885). *History of the Huguenot Emigration to America.* New York: Dodd, Mead.

Barbero, Alessandro (2006). *Charlemagne, Father of a Continent,* trans. Allan Cameron. London: Folio Society.

Barnett, Richard D. (1959). "Tombstones in Barbados," *Tesora de los Judios Sefardies* (Jerusalem) 2:XLV–XLVI.

Barton, D.B. (1978). *A History of Copper Mining in Cornwall and Devon.* N.p.: Truro.

Baurain, C. and C. Bonnet (1992). *Les Phéniciens. Marins de Trois Continents.* Paris: Armand Colin.

Bayer, Henry G. (1925). *The Belgians, First Settlers in New York and in the Middle States.* New York: Devlin-Adair.

Behar, Doron M. et al (2004). "Contrasting Patterns of Y Chromosome Variation in Ashkenazi Jewish and Host Non-Jewish European Populations." *Human Genetics* 114:354–65.

_____. (2003). "Multiple Origins of Ashkenazi Levites: Y Chromosome Evidence for Both Near Eastern and European Ancestries," *American Journal of Human Genetics* 73/4:768–79.

Beider, Alexander (1996). *A Dictionary of Jewish Surnames from the Kingdom of Poland.* Teaneck: Avotaynu.

Benbassa, Esther and Aron Rodrigue (2000). *Sephardi Jewry.* Berkeley: University of California Press.

Benedict, Philip (1991). *The Huguenot Population of France, 1600–1685.* Darby: Diane.

Beverley, Robert (1705). *The History of the Present State of Virginia.* London: R. Parker.

Biale, David, ed. (2002). *Cultures of the Jews. A New History.* New York: Schocken.

Bodian, Miriam (1997). *Hebrews of the Portuguese Nation. Conversos and Community in Early Modern Amsterdam.* Bloomington: Indiana University Press.

Bonet, Andres J. (2003). "The Bonet-Kalonymos-Shem Tovs. Direct Descendants of King David and the Princes of Septimania," *Sharsheret Hadorot* 17/2.

Bonomi, Patricia (1971). *A Factious People: Politics and Society in Colonial New York.* New York: Columbia University Press.

Braund, Kathryn E. Holland (1996). *Deerskins and Duffels: Creek Indian Trade with Anglo-America, 1685–1815.* Lincoln: University of Nebraska Press.

Breen, T. H. H. (2001). *American Past and Present.* New York: HarperCollins.

Brewington, C.D. (1994). *The Five Civilized Indian Tribes of Eastern North Carolina.* Clinton: Sampson Co. Historical Society.

Brito, Jose. M. "The Inquisition and Crypto-Judaism in the Canaries," Society for Crypto Judaic Studies, www.cryptojews.com/canaries.html. Accessed 8/11/2006.

Cabrera, Manuel Lobo (1982). *La Esclavitud en Las Canarias Orientalis en El Siglo XVI (Negros, Moros Y Moriscos).* Santa Cruz de Tenerife: EXCMO.

Camp, Anthony J. (1990). *My Ancestors Came with the Conqueror.* Baltimore: Genealogical Pub.

Candler, Allen D. et al, eds. (1970–1989). *The Colonial Records of the State of Georgia*, 28 vols. New York: AMS and Athens: University of Georgia Press.

Capelli, C. et al (2003). "A Y Chromosome Census of the British Isles." *Current Biology* 13:979–984.

Carvajal-Carmona, Luis G. et al (2000). "Strong Amerind/White Sex Bias and a Possible Sephardic Contribution among the Founders of a Population in Northwest Colombia." *American Journal of Human Genetics* 67:1287–1295.

Carrion, Arturo Morales (1983). *Puerto Rico: A Political and Cultural History*. New York: Norton.

Case, Paul Foster (1973–4). *The Great Seal of the United States*. Los Angeles: Builders of Adytum.

Cerza, Alphonse (1973–4). *A Masonic Reader's Guide*. St. Louis: Missouri Lodge of Research.

Cesarani, David (2002). *Port Jews. Jewish Communities in Cosmopolitan Maritime Trading Centres, 1550–1950*. London: Cass.

Chapman, Paul H. (1992). *Columbus, the Man*. Columbus: ISAC.

Churton, Tobias (2006). *The Magus of Freemasonry. The Mysterious Life of Elias Ashmole — Scientist, Alchemist, and Founder of the Royal Society*. Rochester: Inner Traditions.

Cohen, J. T. Shaye (1999). *The Beginnings of Jewishness: Boundaries, Varieties, Uncertainties*. Hellenistic Culture and Society. Los Angeles: University of California Press.

Cook, Lewis C. Wes, ed. (1974). *Colonial Freemasons*. Fulton: Missouri Lodge of Research.

Cormack, Robin (1985). *Writing in Gold, Byzantine Society and its Icons*. London: George Philip.

Coulter, E. Merton and Albert B. Saye (2001). *A List of the Early Settlers of Georgia*. Baltimore: Genealogical Pub.

Cramer, Zadok (1817). *The Navigator, Containing Directions for Navigating the Monongahela, Allegheny, Ohio, and Mississippi River.*. 9th ed. Pittsburgh: Cramer, Spear & Eichbaum. Available online at http://onlinebooks.library.upenn.edu/webbin/book/lookupname?key=Cramer%2C%20Zadok.

Craven, Wesley Frank (1970). *The Southern Colonies in the Seventeenth Century 1607–1689. A History of the South*, vol. I, ed. W. H. Stephenson and E. M. Coulter. Louisiana State University Press.

Cruciani, F. (2004). "Phylogeographic Analysis of Haplogroup E3b (E-M215) Y Chromosomes Reveals Multiple Migratory Events within and Out of Africa." *American Journal of Human Genetics* 74:1014–22.

Cunliffe, Barry (2004). *Facing the Ocean, the Atlantic and Its Peoples*. New York: Oxford University Press.

Devine, T.M. (1975). *The Tobacco Lords: A Study of the Tobacco Merchants of Glasgow and Their Trading Activities, c. 1740–90*. Edinburgh: Donald.

Dias, Fatima (1999). "The Jewish community in the Azores from 1820 to the Present," in *From Iberia to Diaspora: Studies in Sephardic History and Culture*, ed. Yedida K. Stillman & Norman A.. Stillman. Leiden: Brill.

Dorsey, Jean Muir and Maxwell Dorsey (n.d.). *Christopher Gist of Maryland and Some of His Descendants 1659–1957*. Chicago: Swift.

Dull, Keith A. (1995). *Early Families of York County, Pennsylvania*. Baltimore: Heritage.

Duncan, T. Bentley (1992). *Atlantic Islands: Madeira, the Azores and the Cape Verdes in the Seventeenth Century*. Chicago: University of Chicago.

Durant, David N. (1981). *Ralegh's Lost Colony*. New York: Atheneum.

Edgar, Walter (1998). *South Carolina: A History*. Columbia: University of South Carolina Press.

Edwards, Eric (2004). *Britannia's Children. Emigration from England, Scotland, Wales and Ireland since 1600*. London: Hambledon and London.

Einecave, Nissim (1981). *Los Hijos de Ibero-Franconia*. Buenos Aires: La Luz.

Eisenbeth, Maurice (1936). *Les Juifs de l'Afrique du Nord: Demographie et Onomastique*. Algiers: Imprimerie du Lycee.

Endelman, Todd M. (1999). *The Jews of Georgian England 1714–1830*. Ann Arbor: University of Michigan Press.

Eshleman, Henry Frank (1917). *Historic Background and Annals of the Swiss and German Pioneer Settlers of Southeastern Pennsylvania*. Lancaster.

Esposity, John L. (1999). *The Oxford History of Islam*. New York: Oxford University Press.

Faber, Eli (1995). *A Time for Planting: The First Migration, 1654–1820. The Jewish People in America*. Baltimore: Johns Hopkins.

Faiguenboim, Guilhermo, Paulo Valadares and Anna Rosa Campagnano (2004). *Dictionary of Sephardic Surnames*. Rio de Janeiro: Fraiha.

Feuer Lewis (1987). "Jews in the Origins of Modern Science and Bacon's Scientific Utopia: The Life and Work of Joachim Gaunse, Mining Technologist and First Recorded Jew in English Speaking North America," The American Jewish Archives Brochure Series No. VI.

Fischer, David Hackett (1989). *Albion's Seed. Four British Folkways in America*. New York: Oxford University Press.

Flores, C. et al (2001). "The Peopling of the Canary Islands: A CD4/alu Microsatellite Haplotype Perspective." *Human Immunology* 62/9:949–53.

French Sephardim (n.d.). "Sephardic and Jewish Surname List," available online at http://www.geocities.com/sephardim2003/surnamesA.html.

Fructman, Jack, Jr. (1996). *Thomas Paine: Apostle of Freedom*. New York: Basic.

Gallegos, Eloy J. (1997). *The Melungeons: The Pioneers of the Interior Southeastern United States 1526–1997*. Knoxville: Villagra.

Garsoian, Nina G. (1985). *Armenia between Byzantium and the Sasanians*. London: Variorum.

Gerber, Jane S. (1992). *The Jews of Spain*. New York: Free.

Gitlitz, David M. (2002). *Secrecy and Deceit. The Religion of the Crypto-Jews*. Intro. by Ilan Stavans. Albuquerque: University of New Mexico Press.

Godfrey, Sheldon J. and J.C. Godfrey (1998). *Search out the Land: The Jews and the Growth of Equality in British Colonial America 1740–1867*. Toronto: McGill-Queen's University Press.

Golb, Norman (1998) *The Jews in Medieval Normandy*.

A Social and Intellectual History. Cambridge: Cambridge University Press.

Golb, Norman and Omeljan Pritsak (1982). *Khazarian Hebrew Documents of the Tenth Century.* Ithaca: Cornell University Press.

Gonsalez, A.M. et al (2007). "Mitochondrial lineage M1 traces an early human backflow to Africa." *BMC Genomics* 9/8:223.

Goodfriend, Joyce D. (1992). *Before the Melting Pot: Society and Culture in Colonial New York City, 1664–1730.* Princeton: Princeton University Press.

Goris, J.A. (1925). *Etude sur les colonies marchandes méridionales (Portugais, Espagnols, Italiens) à Anvers de 1488 à 1567.* Louvain: Librarie Universitaire.

Gorr, Shmuel (1992). *Jewish Personal Names. Their Origin, Derivation and Diminutive Forms.* Bergenfield: Avotaynu.

Greene, Jack P. et al (2001). *Money, Trade, and Power: Evolution of Colonial South Carolina's Plantation Society.* Columbia: University of South Carolina Press.

Guthrie, James (1990). "Melungeons: Comparison of Gene Frequency Distributions to Those of Worldwide Populations." *Tennessee Anthropologist*, 15/1:13–22.

Hagger, Nicholas (2007). *The Secret Founding of America.* London: Watkins.

Hahn, Conrad (1963). *A Short History of the Conference of Grand Masons in North America.* New Haven: MSA.

Hale, John P. (1971). *Trans Alleghany Pioneers.* Originally pub.1886.

Harris, Leon (1979). *Merchant Princes.* New York: Harper & Row.

Hart, Charles Henry (1910). "The Franks Family." *Pennsylvania Magazine of History and Biography* 34/2.

Harvey, L. P. (2005). *Muslims in Spain 1500–1614.* Chicago: Chicago University Press.

Hatch, Alden (1969). *The Byrds of Virginia: An American Dynasty, 1670 to the Present.* New York: Holt, Rhinehart and Winston.

Hatch, Charles E. (1957). *The First Seventeen Years: Virginia, 1607–24.* Charlottesville: University of Virginia Press.

Hawkins, Benjamin (1974). *Letters of Benjamin Hawkins, 1796–1806.* Savannah: Georgia Historical Society.

Hay, Millicent V. (1984). *The Life of Sir Robert Sidney, Earl of Leicester (1563–1626).* Washington: Folger.

Heaton, Ronald F. (1974). *Masonic Membership of the Founding Fathers.* Columbus: Masonic Service Association.

Henderson, Archibald (1930). "A Pre-Revolutionary Revolt in the Old Southwest." *The Mississippi Valley Historical Review* 17/2:191–212.

Herrera, Salvador Lopez (1978). *The Canary Islands through History.* Madrid: Madrid University Press.

Heyrman, Christine (1984). *Commerce and Culture.* New York: Norton.

Hicks, Theresa M. (1998). *South Carolina Indians, Indian Traders and Other Ethnic Connections Beginning in 1670.* Spartanburg: Reprint.

Hirschman, Elizabeth C. (2005). *Melungeons: The Last Lost Tribe in America.* Macon: Mercer University Press.

Hirschman, Elizabeth C. and Donald N. Yates (2007). *When Scotland Was Jewish. DNA Evidence, Archeology, Analysis of Migrations, and Public and Family Records Show Twelfth Century Semitic Roots.* Jefferson: McFarland.

Hirschman, Elizabeth C. and Donald N. Panther-Yates (2007). "Suddenly Melungeon! Reconstructing Consumer Identity across the Color Line," *Consumer Culture Theory* (Research in Consumer Behavior, Volume 11), ed. Russell W. Belk and John F. Sherry, Jr. Amsterdam: Elsevier. Pp. 241–59.

Hodapp, Christopher (2007). Solomon's Builders: Freemasons, Founding Fathers and the Secrets of Washington, D.C. Berkeley: Ulysses.

Hordes, Stanley M. (2008). *To the End of the Earth: A History of the Crypto-Jews of New Mexico.* New York: Columbia University Press.

Hourani, Albert (1991). *A History of the Arab Peoples.* Cambridge: Belknap.

Hudson, Charles (1992). *The Southeastern Indians.* Knoxville: University of Tennessee Press.

Hühner, Leon (1911). "The Jews of Virginia from the Earliest Times to the Close of the Eighteenth Century." *Publications of the American Jewish Historical Society*, vol. 20. Cincinnati.

Ibn Ezra (1937, 1970). *Ichay, Imach, Imola, Isaac, Iskandari, Israel, Israeli, Issaev, Isserles* Cambridge: The Mediaeval Academy of America, 1937. Reprint, New York, 1970.

Jacobs, Els N. (1991). *In Pursuit of Pepper and Tea: The Story of the Dutch East Indies Company.* Zutphen: Wahlberg Purs.

Jacobs, Joseph (1901–1906a). "Personal Names." In *The Jewish Encyclopedia. A Descriptive Record of the History, Religion, Literature, and Customs of the Jewish People from the Earliest Times to the Present Day*, pub. by Isidore Singer and ed. by Cyrus Adler. Orig. published in London. Reprint by KTAV Publishing House, 1980. Available online at http://www.JewishEnclopedia.com/.

_____ (1901–1906b). "London," in ibidem.

Jameson, J. Franklin (1909). *Narratives of New Netherland 1609–1664.* New York: Scribner's.

Jehaes, E. et al (2001). "Mitochondrial DNA Analysis on the Putative Heart of Louis XVII, Son of Louis XVI and Marie Antoinette." *European Journal of Human Genetics* 9/3:185–90.

_____ (1998). "Mitochondrial DNA Analysis on Remains of a Putative Son of Louis XVI, King of France and Marie-Antoinette." *European Journal of Human Genetics* 6/4:383–95.

Jones, George F. (1986). *The Germans of Colonial Georgia, 1733–1783.* Baltimore: Clearfield.

Kammen, Michael G. (1975). *Colonial New York: A History.* New York: Scribner's.

Katz, David S. (1996). *The Jews in the History of England.* Oxford: Clarendon.

Katz, Solomon (1937). *The Jews in the Visigothic and Frankish Kingdoms of Spain and Gaul.* Boston: Mediaeval Academy of America.

Kessell, John L. (2003). *Spain in the Southwest.* Norman: University of Oklahoma Press.

Kennedy, N. Brent (1998). *The Melungeons. The Resurrection of a Proud People.* Rev. ed. Macon: Mercer University Press.

Kierner, Cynthia A. (1992). *Traders and Gentlefolk: The*

Livingstons of New York, 1675–1790. Ithaca: Cornell University Press.

Koestler, Arthur (1976). *The Thirteenth Tribe: The Khazar Empire and Its Heritage.* New York: Random.

Kritzler, Edward (2008). *Jewish Pirates of the Caribbean. How a Generation of Swashbuckling Jews Carved Out an Empire in the New World in Their Quest for Treasure, Religious Freedom — and Revenge.* New York: Doubleday.

Kuhns, Oscar (2002). *The German and Swiss Settlement of Colonial Pennsylvania.* Baltimore: Genealogical Publishing.

LaBaree, Benjamin Woods (1979). *Colonial Massachusetts: A History.* New York: Kraus.

Lacey, Robert (2001). *Sir Walter Raleigh.* New York: Phoenix.

_____ (1971). *Phoenix: Robert Devereux, Earl of Essex, an Elizabethan Icarus.* New York: Phoenix.

Landau, Benny, "The Jews of the Canary Islands: Calendar of Calumny," www.saudades.org/Jews%20_Canary%20_Islands.htm. Accessed 8/11/2006.

Laredo, Abraham (1978). *Les Noms des Juifs du Maroc.* Madrid: Institut Montano.

Launey, John Pitts (2003). *First Families of Chester County, Pennsylvania.* Baltimore: Heritage.

Lavender, Abraham D. (2003), "DNA and the Sephardic Diaspora: Spanish and Portuguese Jews in Europe." *HaLAPID* 10/1:1–7.

Leon Tello, Pilar (1979). *Judios de Toledo.* Madrid: Institut Arias Montano.

Levy, Lionel (n.d.). "Commentary on Paul Sebag: *Les Noms des Juifs de Tunisie* (Appendix 'Les noms des Livournais')." Available online at: http://www.ortho-help.com/geneal/levyseba2.htm.

Levi, Israel (1904). "Le roi juif de Narbonne et le Philomene," *Revue des Etudes Juives* XLVIII:19–207.

_____ (1895, 1896). "L'origine davidique de Hillel," *Revue des Etudes Juives,* XXXI.

Levine, L.I. (1998). *Judaism and Hellenism in Antiquity.* Seattle: University of Washington Press.

Leyburn, James G. (1962). *The Scotch-Irish. A Social History.* Chapel Hill: University of North Carolina Press.

"Lista de Apellidos Judios segun noto de Pere Bonnin [*Sangre Judia*]," available online at: http://www.personaes.com/colombia.

Lot, Ferdinand (1924). "Les tributes aux Normands et l'eglise de France au IX siècle," *Bibliot l'Ecole des Chartes,* LXXXV.

Maca-Meyer, N. et al (2004). "Ancient mtDNA Analysis and the Origin of the Guanches." *European Journal of Human Genetics* 12/2:155–62.

Mackay, Charles (1989). *Extraordinary Popular Delusions and the Madness of Crowds,* with foreword by Bernard M. Baruch. New York: Barnes & Noble.

McCarter, P. Kyle (1991). *Ancient Israel. A Short History from Abraham to the Roman Destruction of the Temple.* London: Biblical Archaeology Society.

McDannell, Colleen, ed. (2001). *Religions of the United States in Practice.* Princeton Readings in Religions, series ed. Donald S. Lopez, Jr. Princeton: Princeton University Press.

de Madariega, Salvador (1939). *Christopher Columbus: Being the Life of the Most Magnificent Lord....* New York: Macmillan.

Malka, Eli S. (1997). *Jacob's Children in the Land of the Mahdi: Jews of the Sudan.* Syracuse: Syracuse University Press.

Marcus, Jacob Rader (1973). *Early American Jewry.* Vol. I: *The Jews of New York, New England and Canada 1649–1794.* Vol. II: *The Jews of Pennsylvania and the South 1655–1790.* New York: KTAV.

Markoe, Glenn E. (2005). *The Phoenicians.* London: Folio Society.

Masters, Bruce (1988). *The Origins of Western Economic Dominance in the Middle East: Mercantilism and the Islamic Economy in Aleppo, 1600–1750.* Chicago: University of Chicago Press.

Matar, Nahil (1999). *Turks, Moors, and Englishmen in the Age of Discovery.* New York: Columbia University Press.

Matson, Cathy (1998). *Merchants and Empire: Trading in Colonial New York.* Baltimore: Johns Hopkins.

McCarter, P. Kyle (1991). *Ancient Israel. A Short History from Abraham to the Roman Destruction of the Temple.* London: Biblical Archeology Society.

McDermott, James (2001). *Martin Frobisher, Elizabethan Privateer.* New Haven: Yale University Press.

McWhiney, Grady (1988). *Cracker Culture. Celtic Ways in the Old South.* Tuscaloosa: University of Alabama Press.

Menk, Lars (2005). *A Dictionary of German-Jewish Surnames.* Bergenfield: Avotaynu.

Miles, David (2005). *The Tribes of Britain.* London: Phoenix.

Milton, Giles (2000). *Big Chief Elizabeth.* New York: Farrar, Strauss and Giroux.

Mira, Manuel (2001). *The Portuguese Making of America: Melungeons and Early Settlers of America.* P.A.H.R. Foundation.

Muston, Alexis (1867). *The Israel of the Alps: A Complete History of the Waldenses and Their Colonies.* Vol. I. London: Blackie. Accessed through Google Books: http://books.google.com/books?id=__5fAAAA-MAAJ&dq.

Nagel, Paul C. (1990). *The Lees of Virginia.* New York: Oxford University Press.

Naudon, Paul (2006). *The Secret History of Freemasonry: Its Origins and Connection to the Knights Templar.* Rochester: Inner Traditions.

Nebel, Almut et al (2003). "Y Chromosome Evidence for a Founder Effect in Ashkenazi Jews." *European Journal of Human Genetics* 13/3:388–91.

Netanyahu, B. (1999). *The Marranos of Spain from the Late 14th to the Early 16th Century, According to Contemporary Hebrew Sources.* 3rd ed., updated and expanded. Ithaca: Cornell University Press.

Newell, E. (1988). *The British Copper Ore Market in the Nineteenth Century, with Particular Reference to Cornwall and Swansea.* Unpublished Ph.D. thesis, Oxford.

The North Carolina Guide, ed. Blackwell P. Robinson (1955). Chapel Hill: University of North Carolina Press.

Northrop, Beverly Baker (2001). *We Are Not Yet Conquered. The History of the Northern Cherokee Nation of the Old Louisiana Territory.* Paducah: Turner.

Nugent, Nell Marion (1963). *Cavaliers and Pioneers: Abstracts of Virginia Land Patents & Grants 1623–1800.* Richmond: Dietz.

O'Hart, John (1888). *Irish Pedigrees.* New York: Benziger.

Pacheco, P.R. et al (2005). "The Y Chromosomal Heritage of the Azores Islands Population." *Annals of Human Genetics* 69/2:145–56.

Panther-Yates, Donald N. (2002). "Shalom and Hey, Y'all: Jewish-American Indian Chiefs in the Old South." *Appalachian Quarterly* 7/2:80–89.

_____ (2001). "A Portrait of Cherokee Chief Attakullakulla from the 1730s? A Discussion of William Verelst's 'Trustees of Georgia' Painting." *Journal of Cherokee Studies* 22:5–20.

Patterson, Jerry E., Anthony T. Mazzola and Frank Zachary, eds. (1996). *The Best Families. The Town & Country Social Directory, 1846–1996.* New York: Hearst.

Pérez-Lezaun A. et al (2000). "Allele Frequencies of 13 Short Tandem Repeats in Population Samples from the Iberian Peninsula and Northern Africa," *International Journal of Legal Medicine* 113:208–14.

Pestana, Carla Gardina (2004). *Quakers and Baptists in Colonial Massachusetts.* Cambridge: Cambridge University Press.

Picornell A. et al (2002). "Jewish Population Genetic Data in 20 Polymorphic Loci." *Forensic Science International* 125:52–8.

Pine, L. G. (1969). *The Genealogist's Encyclopedia.* New York: Collier.

Planas, Silvia (2002). *The Jewish Communities of Catalonia: Girona and surrounding area In: Jewish Catalonia, catalogue of the exhibition at the Museu d'Historia de Catalunya.* Ambit. Barcelona.

"Portuguese Translation of Names from Sephardim List," e-mail discussion group postings, available from sephardicforum@yahoogroups.com.

Quinn, David Beers and Alison M. Quinn, eds. (1982). *First Colonists: Documents on the Planting of the First English Settlements in North America, 1584–1590.* Raleigh: NC Division of Archives and History.

Read, Piers Paul (2001). *The Templars: The Dramatic History of the Knights Templar, the Most Powerful Military Order of the Crusades.* London: Da Capo.

Reaney, P.H., ed. (1997). *A Dictionary of English Surnames.* Rev. 3rd ed. with corr. and add. by R.M. Wilson. Oxford: Oxford University Press.

Regne, Jean (1978). *History of the Jews in Aragon, Regesta and Documents 1213–1327.* Jerusalem: Magnes.

_____ (1912). *Juifs de Narbonne et etude sur la condition des Juifs de Narbonne du Ve au XIVe siecle.* Narbonne: 1912.

Rex, Richard (2002). *The Lollards: Social History in Perspective.* New York: Palgrave.

Romano Ventura, David (1988). *Per una historia de la Girona Jueva.* Girona, Ajuntament de Girona.

Roth, Cecil (1961). *The Life of Menasseh Ben-Israel: Rabbi, Printer and Diplomat.* New York: Arno.

_____ (1937). *The Spanish Inquisition.* New York: Norton.

_____ (1929). "Les Marranes à Rouen," *Revue des études juives* X:113–55.

Rowse, A. L. (1937). *Sir Richard Grenville of the Revenge, an Elizabethan Hero.* London: Jonathan Cape.

Rubin, Saul Jacob (1983). *Third to None. The Saga of Savannah Jewry.* Savannah: Congregation Mickve Israel.

Rubinstein, W. D. (1996). *A History of the Jews in the English-speaking World: Great Britain.* London: Macmillan.

Runciman, Stephen (1947). *The Medieval Manichee: A Study of the Christian Dualist Heresy.* Cambridge: Cambridge University Press.

Sainsbury, W. Noel, ed. (1864, rept. 1964). *Calendar of State Papers,* Colonial Series, Volume 1: *America and West Indies, 1574–1660.* Vaduz: Kraus.

Sand, Shlomo (2009). *The Invention of the Jewish People.* London: Verso.

Sándor, Abraham. "Comparison of Romany Law with Israelite Law and Indo-Aryan Traditions." Available at http://www.imninalu.net/Zakono.htm.

Santos, Richard G. (2000). *Silent Heritage. The Sephardim and the Colonization of the Spanish North American Frontier.* San Antonio: New Sepharad.

Shaftesley, John M. (1977). "Jews in Regular Freemasonry, 1717–1860." *The Jewish Historical Society of England University College, Gower St, London, Transactions, Sessions 1973–1975* 25.

Shaltiel, Moshe, "An analysis of some Judeo-Spanish families," *Newsletter of the Worldwide Congregation Charlap/Yahya,* 11–3, 2000.

Shaltiel-Gracian, Moshe (February 2002). "Tracing a Davidic Line from Babylon to the Modern World." *Sharsheret Hadorot. Journal of Jewish Genealogy* 16/2.

Shell, C. in M. Ryan, ed. (1979). *The Origins of Metallurgy in Atlantic Europe. Proceedings of the Fifth Atlantic Colloquium* 259–61. Dublin.

Simmons, R. C. (1976). *The American Colonies from Settlement to Independence.* New York: W. W. Norton.

Simonsohn, Shlomo (1986). *The Jews in the Duchy of Milan.* 4 vols. Jerusalem: Israel Academy of Sciences and Humanities.

Skorecki K, Selig S, Blazer S, Bradman R, Bradman N, Waburton PJ, Ismajlowicz M, Hammer MF (Jan. 1997). "Y Chromosomes of Jewish priests." *Nature* 2/385(6611):32.

Schneider, Ronald, "The Jews of Cap Verde and the Azores," www.saudades.org/cverde.htm. Accessed 8/11/2006.

Smith, John (1624, reprint 1966). *The General Historie of Virginia, New England, and the Summer Isles.* Ed. A. L. Rowse and Robert Ormes Dougan. Cleveland: World.

Staten, Clifford L. (1991). *The History of Cuba.* New York: Palgrave Macmillan.

Stern, Malcolm H. (1991). *First American Jewish Families, Third Edition.* Baltimore: Ottenheimer.

Story, D. A. (1931). *The DeLanceys. A Romance of a Great Family.* London: T. Nelson & Sons.

Susser, Bernard (1993). *Jews of South West England. The Rise and Decline of Their Mediaeval and Modern Communities.* Exeter: University of Exeter Press.

Swem, E. G. (1965). *Virginia Historical Index.* Glouster: P. Smith.

Sykes, Brian (2006). *Saxons, Vikings and Celts. The Genetic Roots of Britain and Ireland.* New York: Norton.

Tax List of Berks County, Pennsylvania of 1767 (2003). Baltimore: Heritage.

Taylor, Alan (2000). *American Colonies: The Settling of North America.* New York: Penguin.

Telushkin, Joseph (2002). *The Golden Land; the Story of Jewish Immigration.* New York: Random.

Tepper, Michael H., ed. (1975). *Emigrants to Pennsylvania, 1641–1819: A Consolidation of Ship Passenger Lists from the Pennsylvania Magazine of History and Biography.* Baltimore: Genealogical Pub.

Thiers, Adolphe (1859). *The Mississippi Bubble. A Memoir of John Law.* New York: Townsend.

Thomas, M.G. et al (2002). "Founding Mothers of Jewish Communities: Geographically Separated Jewish Groups Were Independently Founded by Very Few Female Ancestors." *American Journal of Human Genetics* 70:1411–20.

_____ et al (2000). "Y Chromosomes Travelling South: The Cohen Modal Haplotype and the Origins of the Lemga — The "Black Jews of Southern Africa," *American Journal of Human Genetics* 66:674–86.

_____ et al (1998). "Origins of Old Testament Priests," *Nature* 9/394(6689):138–40.

Thompson, Gunnar (1994). *American Discovery.* Seattle: Argonauts Misty Isle.

Toledano, Joseph (1999). *Une Histoire des Familles: Les Noms de Famille Juifs d'Afrique du Nord.* Jerusalem: By the Author.

_____ (1983). *La Saga des Familles: Les Juifs du Maroc et Leurs Noms.* Tel Aviv: Stavit.

Tovey, D'Blossiers (1738/1967). *Anglia Judaica, or the History and Antiquities of the Jews in England.* Oxford: At the Theatre. Repr. New York: Burt Franklin.

Trevelyan, Raleigh (2003). *Sir Walter Raleigh.* New York: Penguin.

Tucker, Terry (1982). *Bermuda — Unintended Destination 1609–1610.* Bermuda: Island.

Tyler, Moses Coit (1980). *Patrick Henry.* London: Chelsea.

Ujlaki (comp). *Sophia (Bulgaria) Jewish Cemetery.* Budapest: Ujlaki, 1997.

Upham, Charles (1959). *Salem Witchcraft.* 2 vols. orig. published 1867. New York: Unger.

Urbani, Rossana and Guido Nathan Zazzu, eds. (1998). *The Jews in Genoa: 507–1681.* v. 1. *Studia Post Biblica, a Documentary History of the Jews in Italy.* Leiden: Brill.

Van der Zee, James (1978). *The Harlem Book of the Dead.* New York: Morgan and Morgan.

Wall, Moses (1987). *Menasseh ben Israel, The Hope of Israel. The English Translation by Moses Wall, 1652.* Ed. with intro. and notes by Henry Méchoulan and Gérard Nahon. Oxford: Oxford University Press.

Wampler, Fred A. (1986). *The Wampfler (Wampler) Family History: The 1500s–1700s.* By the author.

Wampler, Roy H. (1999). *A Wampler Family History.* By the author.

Watring, Anna Miller and F. Edward Wright (2003). *Bucks County, Pennsylvania Church Records of the 17th and 18th Centuries, Volume 2 Quaker Records: Falls and Middletown Monthly Meetings.* Baltimore: Heritage.

Way of Plean, George, and Romilly Squire (1999). *Scottish Clan & Family Encyclopedia.* New York: Barnes & Noble.

Weis, Rene (1998). *The Yellow Cross: The Story of the Last Cathars.* New York: Penguin.

Wexler, Paul, (1996). *The Non-Jewish Origins of the Sephardic Jews.* Albany: State University of New York Press.

_____ (1993). *Ashkenazic Jews: A Slavo-Turkic People in Search of a Jewish Identity.* Columbus: Slavica.

Whitefield, Peter (2004). *Sir Francis Drake.* New York: New York University Press.

Whiznitzer, Arnold (1960). *Jews in Colonial Brazil.* New York: Columbia University Press.

Wiesenthal, Simon (1973). *Sails of Hope, the Secret Mission of Christopher Columbus.* New York: Macmillan.

Wiik, Kalevi (2008). "Where Did European Men Come From?" *Journal of Genetic Genealogy* 4:35–85.

Williamson, James Alexander (1969). *Sir John Hawkins, the Time and the Man.* Westport: Greenwood.

Wilson, James F. et al (2001). "Genetic Evidence for Different Male and Female Roles during Cultural Transitions in the British Isles." *PNAS* 98/9:5078–83.

Wilson, Charles Reagan, William Ferris, Ann J. Abadie and Mary L. Hart, eds.(1989). *Encyclopedia of Southern Culture.* Chapel Hill: University of North Carolina Press.

Woolley, Benjamin (2001). *The Queen's Conjuror: The Science and Magic of Dr. John Dee, Advisor to Queen Elizabeth I.* New York: Holt.

Wright, Dudley (2005). *Elias Ashmole: England's Masonic Pioneer.* Whitefish: Kessinger.

Wright, Philip (1976). *Jewish Tombstone Inscriptions.* Kingston: Privately printed.

Yates, Donald N. and Elizabeth Caldwell Hirschman (2010). "Toward a Genetic Profile of Melungeons in Southern Appalachia," *Appalachian Journal* 38:xx.

Yogev, Gedalia (1978). *Diamonds and Coral: Anglo Dutch Jews and Eighteenth-century Trade.* Leicester: Leicester University Press.

Zuckermann, Arthur (1972). *A Jewish Princedom in Feudal France, 760–900.* New York: Columbia University Press.

Index

Numbers in **_bold italics_** indicate pages with photographs.